DATA STRUCTURES

WITH

C++

William Ford
University of the Pacific

William Topp
University of the Pacific

Prentice Hall, Englewood Cliffs, New Jersey 07632

Library of Congress Cataloging-in-Publication Data

Ford, William
   Data structures with C++ / by William Ford/William Topp.
     p. cm.
   Includes bibliographical references and index.
   ISBN 0-02-420971-6 : $36.00
   1. C++ (Computer program language) 2. Data structures (Computer
science) I. Topp, William R., 1939– . II. Title.
QA76.73.C153F67 1996   94-10482
005.7′3—dc20   CIP

Editor-in-Chief: Marcia Horton
Acquisitions Editor: Alan Apt
Production Editor: Bayani Mendoza de Leon
Developmental Editors: Elizabeth Jones/Marcia Holman
Cover Designer: Precision Graphics
Production Coordinator: Spectrum Publisher Services
Buyer: Donna Sullivan
Editorial Assistant: Shirley McGuire

© 1996 by Prentice-Hall, Inc.
A Simon & Schuster Company
Englewood Cliffs, New Jersey 07632

The author and publisher of this book have used their best efforts in preparing this book. These efforts include the development, research, and testing of the theories and programs to determine their effectiveness. The author and publisher shall not be liable in any event for incidental or consequential damages in connection with, or arising out of, the furnishing, performance, or use of these programs.

All trademarks are the property of their respective owners.

Printed in the United States of America

10 9 8 7 6 5 4 3 2 1

ISBN 0-02-420971-6

Prentice-Hall International (UK) Limited, *London*
Prentice-Hall of Australia Pty, Limited, *Sydney*
Prentice-Hall Canada, Inc., *Toronto*
Prentice-Hall Hispanoamericana, S.A., *Mexico*
Prentice-Hall of India Private Limited, *New Delhi*
Prentice-Hall of Japan, Inc., *Tokyo*
Simon & Schuster Asia Pte. Ltd., *Singapore*
Editora Prentice-Hall do Brasil, Ltda, *Rio de Janeiro*

To

David Johnstone, Editor

*He shared a vision with us. Despite his tragic death
from an act of random violence, we kept alive the
vision in our work. We hope it is a fitting tribute.*

CONTENTS

CHAPTER 4   COLLECTION CLASSES   141

CHAPTER 5   STACKS AND QUEUES   184

CHAPTER 9   LINKED LISTS   383

CHAPTER 10   RECURSION   480

CHAPTER 13   ADVANCED NONLINEAR STRUCTURES   678

PREFACE

This book is designed to present the fundamentals of data structures from an object-oriented perspective. The study of data structures is core to a computer science curriculum. It provides a rich context for the study of problem-solving techniques and program design and utilizes powerful programming constructs and algorithms.

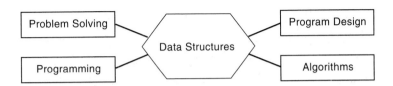

This book uses the versatile language C++ whose classes and object-oriented constructs are specifically designed to efficiently implement data structures. Although a number of object-oriented languages are available, C++ has developed a preeminence due to its origins in the popular C programming language and its use by many software vendors. We develop each data structure around the concept of an abstract data type (ADT) that defines both data organization and data handling operations. We are supported by the C++ language that provides a class type to represent an ADT and to efficiently use the structures in an object.

Design of the Book

Data Structures with C++ organizes the study of data structures around collection classes that include lists, trees, sets, graphs, and dictionaries. In the process, we cover the fundamental topics of data structures and develop object-oriented programming methodology. The structures and methodology are implemented in a series of complete programs and case studies. To evaluate the efficiency of algorithms, we give a simple and early introduction to Big-O notation.

Chapters 1 to 11 provide the traditional topics in a first course in data structures (CS 2). A formal treatment of inheritance and virtual functions is given in Chapter 12 and the topics are used to implement the advanced data structures in Chapters 13 and 14. Overall, the material in Chapters 12 to 14 defines topics traditionally covered in an advanced data structures/algorithms course (CS 7) and an advanced programming course. We include a careful development of templates and operator overloading to support generalized structures. We use these powerful C++ language constructs to simplify our use of the data structures.

A computer professional could use *Data Structures with C++* as a self-study guide to data structures, which would make it possible to understand most class libraries, research articles, and advanced trade publications.

Chapter Descriptions

Most of the book's chapters develop abstract data types and describe their implementation as a C++ class. The declaration of each class and its key methods also are included in the book. In many cases, the full definition is given, yet in others, the definition of selected class methods are given. The full implementation of the classes are included in a program supplement.

CHAPTER 1: INTRODUCTION

This chapter is an overview chapter that introduces abstract data types and object-oriented programming using C++. The concept of an ADT and the related attributes of data encapsulation and information hiding are developed. This chapter also introduces inheritance and polymorphism, which are formally covered in Chapter 12.

CHAPTER 2: BASIC DATA TYPES

Programming languages provide primitive numeric and character types that cover integer and floating point numbers, character data, and user-defined enumeration types. The primitive types combine to create array, record, string, and file structures. This chapter describes ADTs for language types using C++ as an example.

CHAPTER 3: ABSTRACT DATA TYPES AND CLASSES

This book as a whole provides a formal study of ADTs and their representation as C++ classes. Specifically, this chapter defines basic class concepts including data members, constructors, and method definitions.

CHAPTER 4: COLLECTION CLASSES

A collection is a storage class with data handling tools to add, delete, or update the items. The study of collection classes is the main focus of this book. Therefore, this chapter provides an example of the different collection types that are presented in the book. The chapter includes a simple early introduction to the Big-O notation, which measures the efficiency of an algorithm. The notation is used throughout the book to compare and contrast different algorithms. The chapter concludes with a study of the SeqList class that is a prototype of a general list structure.

CHAPTER 5: STACKS AND QUEUES

This chapter discusses stacks and queues, which are fundamental collection classes that maintain data in LIFO (last-in first-out) and FIFO (first-in first-out) order. It also develops the priority queue, a modified version of a queue in which the client always deletes the item of highest priority from the list. A case study uses priority queues to perform event-driven simulation.

CHAPTER 6: ABSTRACT OPERATORS

An abstract data type defines a set of methods to initialize and manage data. In this chapter, we extend language-defined operators (e.g., +, *, <<, etc.) to abstract data types. The process, called operator overloading, redefines standard operator symbols to implement operations in the ADT. A fully developed rational number class illustrates operator overloading and type conversion, as well as introducing friends to overload the standard C++ I/O operators.

CHAPTER 7: GENERIC DATA TYPES

C++ uses the template mechanism to provide for generic functions and classes that support different data types. Templates provide powerful generality to our data structures. This concept is illustrated with a template-based version of the Stack class and its application to infix expression evaluation.

CHAPTER 8: CLASSES AND DYNAMIC MEMORY

Dynamic data structures use memory allocated by the system at run time. They allow us to define structures without size constraints and enhance the usability of our classes. Their use, however, requires careful attention. We introduce the copy constructor, overloaded assignment operator, and destructor methods, which allow us to properly copy and assign dynamic data and then deallocate it when an object is deleted. The power of dynamic data is illustrated with the Array, String, and Set classes. These classes are used throughout the remainder of the book.

CHAPTER 9: LINKED LISTS

The use of lists to store and retrieve data is a continuing theme in the book because lists are fundamental to the design of most data applications. This chapter introduces linked lists, which allow for dynamic list handling. We use a twofold approach that first develops a basic node class and creates functions for adding or deleting items from the list. A more abstract approach creates a linked list class with a built-in traversal mechanism to scan the items in the list. The LinkedList class is used to implement the SeqList class and the Queue class. In each case, a linked list object is included by composition. The approach provides a powerful tool for developing data structures. This chapter also discusses circular and doubly linked lists that have interesting applications. The chapter features a printer queue case study as well.

CHAPTER 10: RECURSION

Recursion is an important problem-solving tool in both computer science and mathematics. We introduce recursion and illustrate its use in a variety of contexts. A series of applications uses recursion with mathematical formulas, combinatorics, maze traversal, and puzzles. The Fibonacci sequence is used to compare the efficiency of a recursive algorithm, an iterative algorithm, or direct calculations in computing a term of the sequence.

CHAPTER 11: TREES

Linked lists define a set of nodes that are sequentially accessed beginning at the head. The data structure is called a linear list. In many applications, objects exhibit a nonlinear order in which a member may have multiple successors. In Chapter 11, we introduce a basic nonlinear structure called a tree in which all data items emanate from a single source—the root. A tree is an ideal structure for describing a hierarchical structure such as a computer file system and a business reporting chart. In this chapter, we restrict our analysis to binary trees in which each node has, at most, two descendants. We develop the TreeNode class to implement these trees and present applications that include the classical preorder, inorder, and postorder scan algorithms. Binary trees find application as a list structure that efficiently stores large volumes of data. The structure, called a binary search tree, is implemented in the BinSTree class. The class is featured in a case study that develops a document concordance.

CHAPTER 12: INHERITANCE AND ABSTRACT CLASSES

Inheritance is a fundamental concept in object-oriented programming. This chapter discusses the main features of inheritance, carefully develops its implementation in C++, and introduces virtual functions as tools that utilize the power of inheritance. It also develops the concept of an abstract base class with pure virtual functions Virtual functions are fundamental to object-oriented programming and are used with subsequent topics in the book. This chapter includes the introduction of iterators that define a uniform and general traversal mechanism for the different lists in the book. It concludes with an example of inheritance and virtual functions to develop heterogenous arrays and linked lists.

CHAPTER 13: ADVANCED NONLINEAR STRUCTURES

This chapter continues the development of binary trees and introduces additional nonlinear structures. It describes array-based trees that model an array as a complete binary tree. An extensive study of heaps is provided, and the concept is used to implement the heap sort and priority queues. Although binary search trees are usually good structures with which to implement a list, degenerate cases can be inefficient. Data structures provide different height-balanced structures that ensure fast average search time. Using inheritance, a new search tree class called AVL trees is derived. The chapter concludes with an introduction to graphs that features a series of classic algorithms.

CHAPTER 14: ORGANIZING COLLECTIONS

This chapter looks at searching and sorting algorithms for general collections. In the process, the classical array-based selection, bubble, and insertion sort algorithms are developed. Our study includes the famous QuickSort algorithm. In this book, data that is stored in internal memory is emphasized. For larger sets, data can be stored on disk and external methods to search and sort the data can be used. We develop the BinFile class for direct file access, and use its methods to illustrate both the external index sequential search and the external merge sort algorithm. A section on associative arrays, or dictionaries, generalizes the concept of an array index.

Required Background

This book assumes the reader has completed a first course in programming and is fluent with basic C++. Chapter 2 defines the primitive data structures of C++ and illustrates their uses in several complete programs. This chapter can be used as a standard for defining the C++ prerequisites. For the interested reader, the authors provide a C++ tutorial that defines the primitive types of the language and the syntax for arrays, control structures, I/O, functions, and pointers. The tutorial includes a discussion of each topic along with examples, complete programs, and exercises.

Supplements

Complete source code listings for all classes and programs are available through an Internet ftp connection from the authors' institution, the University of the Pacific. The C++ code in the book has been tested and run using the latest Borland compiler. With very few exceptions, the programs also compile and run on a Macintosh system using Symantec C++ and on a Unix system using GNU C++.

For those having Internet connection, execute an ftp to "ftp.cs.uop.edu". Upon connecting to the system, your login name is "anonymous" and your password is your Internet mail address. The software is located in the directory "/pub/C++".

Readers may contact the authors directly to receive a copy of the tutorial. Order information is available by electronic mail—send to "billf@uop.edu"—or by the U.S. mail—write to Bill Topp, 456 S. Regent, Stockton, CA 95204.

The Instructor's Guide offers teaching tips for each chapter, answers to most written exercises, and sample tests. The guide features solutions to many of the programming exercises and is available from Prentice Hall.

Acknowledgments

The authors have been supported by friends, students, and colleagues throughout the preparation of *Data Structures with C++*. The University of the Pacific has generously provided resources and support to complete the project. Prentice Hall offered a dedicated team of professionals who handled the book design and production. We are especially grateful to editors Elizabeth Jones, Bill Zobrist, and Alan Apt, and to production editor Bayani de Leon. Production was jointly implemented by Spectrum Publisher Services and Prentice Hall. We were greatly assisted by Kelly Ricci and Kristin Miller at Spectrum.

Students have offered valuable criticism of the manuscript by giving us explicit feedback or unsolicited blank stares. Our reviewers offered guidance for early writing of the manuscript, providing detailed comments on both the content and the pedagogical approach. We took most of their recommendations into account. Special thanks go to Hamid R. Arabnia, University of Georgia; Rhoda A. Baggs, Florida Institute of Technology; Sandra L. Bartlett, University of Michigan–Ann Arbor; Richard T. Close, U.S. Coast Guard Academy; David Cook, U.S. Air Force Academy; Charles J. Dowling, Catonsville (Baltimore County) Community College; David J. Haglin; Mankato State University; Jim Murphy, California State University–Chico; and Herbert Schildt. Two colleagues, Ralph Ewton at the University of Texas–El Paso, and Douglas Smith at the University of the Pacific made extensive contributions. Their insights and support were invaluable to the authors and greatly improved the final design of the book.

William Ford
William Topp

C H A P T E R 1

INTRODUCTION

This book develops data structures and algorithms in the context of object-oriented programming using C++. We develop each data structure as an abstract type that defines both data organization and data handling operations. The structure, called an **abstract data type (ADT),** is an abstract model that describes an interface between a client (user) and the data. Using the C++ language, we develop a representation for each abstract structure. The C++ language provides a user-defined type called a **class** to represent an ADT and items of class type, called **objects,** to store and handle data in an application.

This chapter introduces the concept of an ADT and related attributes called data encapsulation and information hiding. Through a series of examples, we illustrate the design of an ADT and develop a format to define the data organization and operations.

The C++ class construct is fundamental to our study of data structures and is developed formally in Chapter 3. In this chapter, we start with an overview of a C++ class and illustrate its use in representing an ADT. Optional sections, marked with an asterisk(*), provide you with examples of C++ classes. This chapter gives an overview of object design, which includes object composition and inheritance. These concepts are the building blocks of object-oriented programming. The chapter includes an outline of program design that is used in larger applications and case studies in the book. Inheritance and polymorphism extend the power of object-oriented programming and make it possible to develop large programming systems based on class libraries. These topics are thoroughly developed in Chapter 12 and are used selectively to present advanced data structures.

This chapter previews the topics presented in the book. You will gain familiarity with key data structures and object-oriented concepts before they are formally developed.

1.1   Abstract Data Types

Data abstraction is a central concept in program design. The abstraction defines the domain and structure of the data, along with a collection of operations that access the data. The abstraction, called an abstract data type (ADT), creates a user-defined data type whose operations specify how a client may manipulate the data. The ADT is implementation independent and enables the programmer to focus on idealized models of the data and its operations.

EXAMPLE 1.1

1.   An accounting program for a small business maintains inventory information. Each item in the inventory is represented by a data record that includes the item's identification number, the current stock level, pricing information, and reordering information. A set of inventory handling operations updates the different information fields and initiates a reordering

of stock when inventory levels fall below a certain threshold. The data abstraction describes an item as a record containing a series of information fields and operations that would be used by a company manager for inventory maintenance. Operations might include changing the Stock on Hand value when units of the item are sold, changing the Unit Price when a new pricing policy is used, and initiating a reorder when the stock level falls below the reorder level.

Data

Identification	Stock on Hand	Unit Price	Reorder Level

Operations
UpdateStockLevel
AdjustUnitPrice
ReorderItem

2. A gaming program involves tossing a set of dice. In the design, the dice are described as an ADT whose data includes the number of dice that are tossed, the sum of the dice on the last toss, and a list that identifies the value of each die in the last toss. The operations include tossing the dice, returning the sum of the dice on a toss, and printing the value of each individual die in the list.

Data

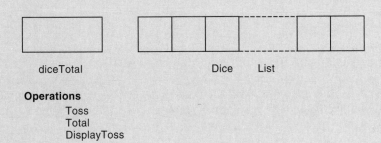

diceTotal   Dice   List

Operations
Toss
Total
DisplayToss

ADT FORMAT

We use a format to describe an ADT that includes a header with the name of the ADT, a description of the type of data, and a list of operations. For each operation we specify the **input** values that are provided by the client, **preconditions** that must apply to the data before the operation can be performed, and the **process** that is performed by the operation. After executing the operation, we specify the **output** values that are returned to the client and **postconditions** that indicate any change in the data. Most ADTs have an **initializer** operation that assigns initial values to the data. In the C++ language environment, the initializer is called a **constructor.** We use this term to simplify the transition from an ADT to its representation in C++.

ADT Format

ADT *ADT_Name* **is**

    Data
       Describe the structure of the data.

    Operations
       Constructor
          Initial values:　Data used to initialize an object.
          Process:　　　　Initialize the object.

       Operation$_1$
          Input:　　　　　Data from the client.
          Preconditions:　Necessary state of the system before executing the operation.
          Process:　　　　Actions performed with the data.
          Output:　　　　Data returned to the client.
          Postconditions:　State of the system after executing the operation.

       Operation$_2$
          . . .

       Operation$_n$
          . . .

  end ADT *ADT_Name*

EXAMPLE 1.2

1. The data for the abstract type Dice include a count *N* of the number of dice that make up a single toss, the dice total, and a list with *N* items that contains the individual die values on completion of a toss.

ADT *Dice* **is**

    Data
       The number of dice in each toss. The number is an integer value ≥ 1. An integer value containing the total of the dice on the last toss. If *N* dice are tossed, this value lies in the range *N* to 6*N*. A list containing the die values in a toss. Each member of the list is an integer value from 1 to 6.

Operations

Constructor

Initial values:	The number of dice to be tossed.
Process:	Initialize the data value specifying the number of dice in each toss.

Toss

Input:	None
Preconditions:	None
Process:	Toss the dice and compute the dice total.
Output:	None
Postconditions:	The total contains the sum of the dice on the toss, and the list identifies the value of each die in the toss.

DieTotal

Input:	None
Preconditions:	None
Process:	Retrieve the value of the data item specifying the total of the dice on the last toss.
Output:	Return the total of the dice from the last toss.
Postconditions:	None

DisplayToss

Input:	None
Preconditions:	None
Process:	Print the list of dice values for the last toss.
Output:	None
Postconditions:	None

end ADT *Dice*

2. A circle is defined as a set of points equally distant from a point called the center. For graphical display, an abstract data type for a circle includes both the radius and the center point. For measurement applications, an abstract data type requires only the radius. We design the Circle ADT for measurement and include operations to compute the area and circumference. The operations are defined without detailed reference to the mathematical formulas for the circumference and area. The ADT is used in the next section to illustrate the declaration of a C++ class and the use of objects in programming applications.

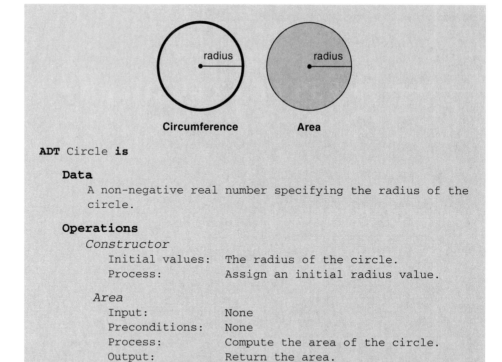

Circumference   **Area**

ADT Circle **is**

Data
A non-negative real number specifying the radius of the circle.

Operations
Constructor
Initial values: The radius of the circle.
Process: Assign an initial radius value.

Area
Input: None
Preconditions: None
Process: Compute the area of the circle.
Output: Return the area.
Postconditions: None

Circumference
Input: None
Preconditions: None
Process: Compute the circumference of the circle.
Output: Return the circumference.
Postconditions: None
end ADT Circle

1.2 C++ Classes and Abstract Types

The C++ language provides the user-defined **class** type to represent abstract data types. A class consists of **members** that include data values and operations for handling the data. The operations are also called **methods** because they define "methods" of accessing the data. A variable of the class type is called an **object.** A class contains two separate parts. The **public** part describes an interface that allows a client to manipulate objects of the class type. The public part represents the ADT and allows a client to use an object and its operations without knowledge of the internal details of an implementation. The **private** part contains the data and internal operations that assist in the implementation of the data abstraction. For

Class

```
private:
    Data members:    value₁      value₂

    Internal Operations


public:
    Constructor

    Operation₁
    Operation₂
```

instance, a class to represent the Circle ADT contains one private data member, the radius. The public members include the constructor and methods to compute the area and circumference.

Circle Class

```
private:
    radius


public:
    Constructor
    Area
    Circumference
```

ENCAPSULATION AND INFORMATION HIDING

The class **encapsulates** information by bundling the data items and methods and treating them as a single entity. The class structure hides implementation details and carefully restricts outside access to both the data and operations. This principle, known as **information hiding,** protects the integrity of the data.

A class uses its public and private portion to control access by clients in an application. Members in the private portion are used internally by the class methods and are isolated from their external environment. Data are generally defined in the private portion of the class to prevent unwanted access by a client. Public members interact with the external environment and may be used by clients.

For instance, in the Circle class, radius is a private data member that may be accessed only by the three methods. The constructor assigns a starting value to the radius. Each of the other methods uses the radius. For instance, area = π * radius^2. The methods are public members that may be called by all external program units.

MESSAGE PASSING

In an application, the public members of an object may be accessed by clients outside the object. The access is handled by **master control modules** (main program and subprograms) that oversee the interaction among objects. The control code directs an object to access its data by using one of its methods or operations. The process of directing the activities of objects is called **message passing.** A sender passes a message to a receiving object and asks the object to perform a task.

When appropriate, the sender includes information that is used by the receiver. This information is passed with the message as input data for the operation. After performing the task, the receiver may return information to the sender (output data) or pass messages to other objects requesting the execution of additional tasks. When the receiving object performs the operation, it may update some of its own internal data values. In this case, the object is said to undergo a **state change** and new postconditions occur.

1.3 Objects in C++ Applications*

The abstract data type gives a general description of the data and the operations on the data. A C++ class is normally given by first declaring the class without defining the member functions. This is known as the **class declaration** and is a concrete representation of an ADT. The actual definition of the methods is given in the **class implementation,** which is separate from the declaration.

The implementation of C++ classes and the use of objects are illustrated by the following complete program, which determines the cost of landscaping a pool. The program declares the Circle class and illustrates how objects are defined and used. A reading of the code illustrates the definition of public and private sections in a class and the use of C++ functions to define the operations. The main program is the client, who declares the objects and then uses their operations to perform the calculations. The main program is responsible for all message passing in the application.

APPLICATION: THE CIRCLE CLASS

Circle objects are used to describe a swimming pool and a surrounding walkway. With the circumference and area methods, we can compute the cost of concreting the walkway and surrounding the pool with a fence. The following conditions apply in our application.

Building code requires that a concrete walkway (the shaded area in the following figure) must surround a swimming pool and that the entire area must be enclosed by a fence. The current fencing costs are $3.50 per linear foot and concrete costs are $0.50 per square foot. The application assumes that the width of the walkway surrounding the pool is 3 feet and that the client specifies the radius of the circular pool. For output, the application must determine the cost of building a fence and a walkway while landscaping the pool.

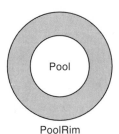

PoolRim

We declare a Circle object called Pool that describes the swimming area. A second object, PoolRim, is the Circle object that includes both the pool and the surrounding walkway. The constructor is called when an object is defined. For the Pool, the client provides the radius as a parameter and then uses this radius plus 3 feet to define the PoolRim object.

To invoke a class operation, give the name of the object followed by a period and the operation. For instance, Pool.Area() and PoolRim.Circumference() call the Circle operations for Pool.

The fencing is placed along the outside of the PoolRim. Call the circumference operation PoolRim.Circumference() to compute the fencing cost.

```
FenceCost = PoolRim.Circumference() * 3.50
```

The area of the concrete surface is determined by taking the outer PoolRim area and subtracting the Pool area.

```
ConcreteCost = (PoolRim.Area() - Pool.Area()) * 0.5
```

Program 1.1   Construction and Use of the Circle Class

Program 1.1 implements the pool application. We provide comments to assist in reading the C++ code. The declaration of the Circle class illustrates the representation of the Circle ADT and the use of the private and public directives to control access to the members.

The main program asks the client to enter the radius of the pool. This value is used to declare the Pool object. A second object, PoolRim, is declared to have an additional 3 feet for its radius to accommodate the walkway around the pool. The fencing and concrete costs are printed.

Outside the main module, the program defines the Circle class. The reader may note the use of the **const** qualifier for specifying that a member function does not change the data. The qualifier is used with the Circumference and Area methods in both their declaration and definition. The cost of construction materials for chainlink fence and concrete are given as constants.

```cpp
#include <iostream.h>

const float PI = 3.14152;
const float FencePrice = 3.50;
const float ConcretePrice = 0.50;

// declare Circle class with data and method declarations
class Circle
{
    private:
        // data member radius is a floating point number
        float   radius;

    public:
        // constructor
        Circle(float r);

        // measurement functions
        float Circumference(void) const;
        float Area(void) const;
};

// class implementation

// constructor initializes the radius data member
Circle::Circle(float r): radius(r)
{ }

// return circumference
float Circle::Circumference(void) const
{
    return 2 * PI * radius;
}

// return area
float Circle::Area(void) const
{
    return PI * radius * radius;
}

void main ()
{
    float radius;
    float FenceCost, ConcreteCost;

    // set fixed point output with 2 decimal places
    cout.setf(ios::fixed);
    cout.setf(ios::showpoint);
    cout.precision(2);
```

```
    // prompt for and input radius
    cout << "Enter the radius of the pool: ";
    cin >> radius;

    // declare the Circle objects
    Circle Pool(radius);
    Circle PoolRim(radius + 3);

    //  compute the cost of the fence and output its value
    FenceCost = PoolRim.Circumference() * FencePrice;
    cout << "Fencing Cost is $" << FenceCost << endl;

    //  compute the cost of the concrete and output its value
    ConcreteCost = (PoolRim.Area() - Pool.Area())*ConcretePrice;
    cout << "Concrete Cost is $" << ConcreteCost << endl;
}


/*
<Run of Program 1.1>

Enter the radius of the pool: 40
Fencing Cost is $945.60
Concrete Cost is $391.12
*/
```

Object Design   1.4

This book develops data structures with classes and objects. We start with classes that are defined by simple data members and operations. For more complex structures, the classes may contain data members that are themselves objects. The resulting classes, created by means of **composition,** have access to the member functions in the component objects. The use of object composition extends the concepts of data encapsulation and information hiding and provides code reuse. Object-oriented languages also allow a class to be derived by **inheritance** from other classes. This allows a designer to build new classes as refinements of other classes and to reuse code that was previously developed. Inheritance is a fundamental tool of C++ object-oriented programming. The topic is formally introduced in Chapter 12 and is used to enhance the design and implementation of more advanced data structures.

OBJECTS AND COMPOSITION

Geometric figures consist of sets of points that form lines, rectangles, and so forth. The basic building blocks of the figures are points that combine with a series of axioms to define geometric objects. In this section, we develop a point as a primitive geometric object and then describe lines and rectangles. We use these geometric figures to illustrate objects and composition.

A point is a location in a plane surface. We assume a point object is located on a grid with coordinates that measure a horizontal (*x*) and vertical (*y*) distance from a base point. For instance, point p(3,1) is 3 units to the right and 1 unit down from the base.

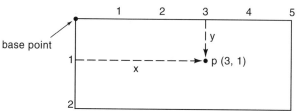

A line is composed of points, and two points determine a line. This latter fact is used to create a model for a line segment, which is defined by its endpoints *p1* and *p2* [Figure 1.1(A)].

A rectangle is a four-sided figure whose adjacent sides meet at right angles. For drawing purposes, a rectangle is determined by two points that mark the upper left-hand corner (ul) and lower right-hand corner (lr) of the box [Figure 1.1(B)].

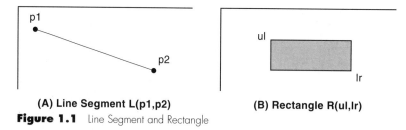

(A) Line Segment L(p1,p2)   **(B) Rectangle R(ul,lr)**

Figure 1.1 Line Segment and Rectangle

We use these facts to create Point, Line, and Rectangle classes. The data members in the Line and Rectangle classes are objects of Point type. Composition is an important tool in building classes with objects from other classes. Note that each class has a Draw method to display the figure on a drawing surface. The Point class also contains member functions to access the *x* and *y* coordinates of the point.

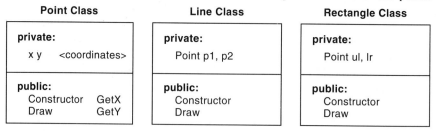

Point Class

private:
x y   <coordinates>

public:
Constructor   GetX
Draw   GetY

Line Class

private:
Point p1, p2

public:
Constructor
Draw

Rectangle Class

private:
Point ul, lr

public:
Constructor
Draw

EXAMPLE 1.3

Define a geometric object by giving the figure followed by the object name and the parameters to specify the object.

```
1. Point       p(1,3);              // declares the point (1,3)
2. Point       p1(4,2), p2(5,1);
   Line        l(p1,p2);            // line (4,2) to (5,1)
3. Point       p1(4,3), p2(6,4);
   Rectangle r(p1,p2);             // rectangle (4,3) to (6,4)
```
4. **The Draw method in each class sketches the figure on the drawing surface.**

```
   p.Draw();    l.Draw();    r.Draw();
```

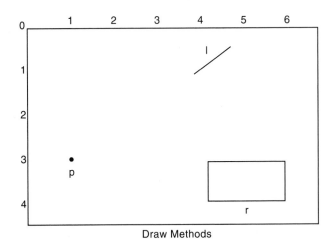

Draw Methods

C++ GEOMETRIC CLASSES*

The following are C++ declarations for the Point and Line classes. Note that the constructor for the Line class is passed the coordinates of the two points that determine the line. Each class has a member function Draw, which displays the figure on a drawing surface.

- -
Point CLASS SPECIFICATION

DECLARATION

```
class Point
{
   private:
      float x, y;              // horizontal and vertical positions

   public:
      Point (float h, float v); // assign h to x and v to y
      float GetX(void) const;   // return x (horizontal) coordinate
```

```
    float GetY(void) const;      // return y (vertical) coordinate
    void Draw(void) const;       // draw a dot at (x,y)
};
```

The Line Class includes two Point objects by composition. The points are initialized by the constructor.

Line CLASS SPECIFICATION

DECLARATION

```
class Line
{
    private:
        Point P1,P2;                 // two end points of the line

    public:
        Line (Point a, Point b); // assign a to p1 and b to p2
        void Draw(void) const;   // draw the line segment
};
```

OBJECTS AND INHERITANCE

Inheritance is an intuitive concept from which we can draw examples from everyday experience. Each of us inherits characteristics from our parents such as race, eye color, and blood type. We can think of a parent as a base from which we derive characteristics. The relationship is illustrated by two objects connected with an arrow pointing to the base object.

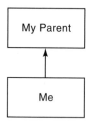

Zoology makes a formal study of animal inheritance. Figure 1.2 illustrates an animal hierarchy for mammals, dogs, and collies. A mammal is an animal that is warm blooded, has hair, and nourishes its young with milk. A dog is a mammal with canine teeth, is a meat eater, has a particular skeletal structure, and is a social animal. A collie is a dog with a pointed snout, a pattern of white and red coloring, and well-developed herding instincts.

In the hierarchy chain, a class inherits all of the characteristics of its predecessor class. For instance, a dog has all of the characteristics of a mammal plus additional characteristics which distinguish it from cats, elephants, and so forth. The bottom

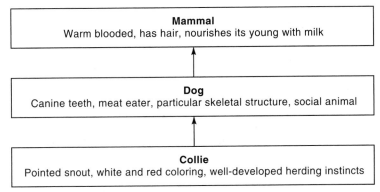

Figure 1.2   An Animal Inheritance Chain

to top ordering of the classes indicate that

A collie "is a" dog.   A dog "is a" mammal.

In the chain, "mammal" is termed the **base class** for "dog," and "dog" is called a **derived class.** Using the analogy of family inheritance, we refer to the base and derived classes as parent and child classes, respectively. In the case of an extended chain, a child inherits the characteristics of its parent and grandparent classes.

INHERITANCE IN PROGRAMMING

Object-oriented programming provides a mechanism by which a derived class is allowed to inherit the data and operations from a base class. The mechanism, called **class inheritance,** allows a derived class to use data and operations that have been previously defined in a base class. The derived class can add new operations or overwrite some of the base class operations as it sets up methods to handle its data. By analogy, a child may inherit a house or car from his or her parent. This child can then use the house or car. If appropriate, the child may modify the house to meet his or her special circumstances.

We illustrate class inheritance with a linear list, called **SeqList,** that stores information in sequential order. A list is an important and familiar data structure that is used to maintain inventory records, an appointment schedule, the type and number of groceries needed, and so forth. Inheritance occurs when we declare an ordered list that is a special type of sequential list. The ordered list uses all the basic list handling methods from the sequential list and provides its own insert operation so that items are stored in ascending order.

In a linear list containing N entries, the elements occupy a range of positions beginning with position 0 and ending with position $N - 1$. The first position is the

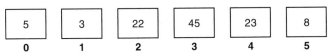

Figure 1.3   Unordered Linear List

Insert (10)

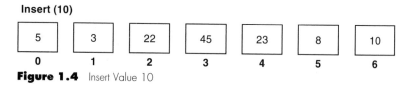

Figure 1.4 Insert Value 10

front and the last position is the rear of the list. Figure 1.3 depicts an unordered list of integers with six entries.

The basic SeqList operations include Insert, which adds a new item at the rear of the list (Figure 1.4), and Delete, which removes the first item in the list that matches the key. A second delete function, called DeleteFront, removes the first item in the list (Figure 1.5). The structure identifies the size of the list with ListSize and provides a Find operation that searches for an item in the list. For data management, the user may test whether the list is empty and may delete the list using the ClearList operation.

The class provides the method GetData that allows a client to read the data value at a particular position in the list. For instance, to find the maximum value in the list, we can start at position 0 and scan the list. The process terminates when we reach the end of the list whose position is known by using ListSize. At each location, update the maximum if the current value (GetData) is greater than the current maximum. For instance, at the second item compare 22 and the previous maximum, which is 3, and update the maximum to value 22. Ultimately, 23 is identified as the maximum element in the list.

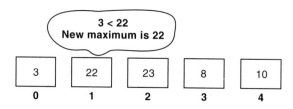

ADT SeqList **is**

  Data

    A non-negative integer specifying the number of items cur-
    rently in the list (size), and a list of data items.

  Operations

    Constructor
        Initial values: None
        Process: Set the size of the list to 0.

Delete (45)   **DeleteFront**

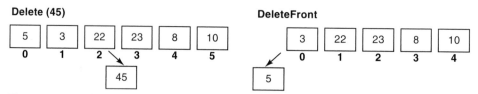

Figure 1.5 Delete Item 45 and DeleteFront

ListSize

Input:	None
Preconditions:	None
Process:	Read the size of the list.
Output:	The list size.
Postconditions:	None

ListEmpty

Input:	None
Preconditions:	None
Process:	Check the size of the list.
Output:	Return TRUE if the list is empty; otherwise return FALSE.
Postconditions:	None

ClearList

Input:	None
Preconditions:	None
Process:	Remove all elements from the list and set the list size to 0.
Output:	None
Postconditions:	The list is empty.

Find

Input:	An item to locate in the list.
Preconditions:	None
Process:	Scan the list for a match.
Output:	If the match fails, return FALSE; if the match occurs, return TRUE and return the data item from the list.
Postconditions:	None

Insert

Input:	Item to insert in the list.
Preconditions:	None
Process:	Add the item at the rear of the list.
Output:	None
Postconditions:	The list has a new item; its size increases by 1.

Delete

Input:	Value to delete from the list.
Preconditions:	None
Process:	Scan the list and remove the first occurrence of the item in the list. Take no action if the item is not in the list.
Output:	None
Postconditions:	If a match occurs, the list has one fewer items.

```
DeleteFront
    Input:              None
    Preconditions:      List must not be empty.
    Process:            Remove the first item from the list.
    Output:             Return the value of the item that is
                        removed.
    Postconditions:     The list has one fewer items.

GetData
    Input:              A position (pos) in the list.
    Preconditions:      An access error is generated if pos is
                        less than 0 or greater than size −1.
    Process:            Extract the value at location pos in
                        the list.
    Output:             The value of the item at position pos.
    Postconditions:     None
end ADT SeqList
```

ORDERED LISTS AND INHERITANCE

An ordered list is a special type of list that maintains the elements in ascending order. As an abstract data type, this special list obtains most of its operations from the SeqList class with the notable exception of Insert, which must add a new item at a position that maintains the ordering (Figure 1.6).

The operations ListSize, ListEmpty, ClearList, Find, and GetData are independent of any ordering of the elements. The Delete and DeleteFront operations remove an item but leave the remaining items in order. The following ADT reflects the similarity of operations between an ordered list and on SeqList.

```
ADT OrderedList is

    Data
        <same as the SeqList ADT>

    Operations
        Constructor     <executes the base class constructor>
        ListSize        <same as SeqList ADT>
        ListEmpty       <same as SeqList ADT>
        ClearList       <same as SeqList ADT>
        Find            <same as SeqList ADT>
        Delete          <same as SeqList ADT>
        DeleteFront     <same as SeqList ADT>
        GetData         <same as SeqList ADT>
```

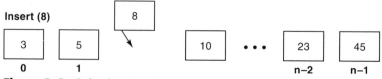

Figure 1.6 Ordered List: Insert 8

```
Insert
     Preconditions:     None
     Input:             Item to insert in the list.
     Process:           Add the new item at the position
                        that maintains order.
     Output:            None
     Postconditions:    The list has a new item and its
                        size increases by 1.
end ADT OrderedList
```

The OrderedList class is derived from the SeqList class. It inherits the operations from the base class and modifies the Insert operation to insert items in order.

SeqList Class

private:	
<implementation details>	

public:	
Constructor	Find
ListEmpty	Delete
ClearList	DeleteFront
ListSize	GetData

OrderedList Class

private:	

public:	
Constructor	
Insert	

SOFTWARE REUSABILITY

The object-oriented approach to data structures promotes the reuse of code that has already been developed and tested and that can be "plugged" into your application. We have already seen code reuse with composition. Inheritance is a very powerful tool for this purpose also. For instance, implementing the ordered list class requires us to write only the Insert and constructor methods. All other operations are given by code from the SeqList class. The reuse of code is a critical advantage in object-oriented design because it saves development time and promotes uniformity across applications and releases. For instance, an operating system upgrade adds new features. At the same time, the upgrade must permit existing applications to continue running. One approach is to define the original operating system as a base class. The upgraded system acts as a derived class with its new features and operations.

SEQLIST AND ORDEREDLIST CLASS SPECIFICATIONS*

A formal study of the SeqList class is given in Chapter 4. In this section, we give only the class specification so that you can relate the class and its methods with a very general ADT. We define the OrderedList class to illustrate inheritance. The type of data item in the list is represented by the generic name DataType.

- -

SeqList CLASS SPECIFICATION

DECLARATION

```
class SeqList
{
   private:
      // list storage array and number of current list elements
      DataType listitem[ARRAYSIZE];
      int size;

   public:
      // constructor
      SeqList(void);

      // list access methods
      int ListSize(void) const;
      int ListEmpty(void) const;
      int Find (DataType& item) const;
      DataType GetData (int pos) const;

      // list modification methods
      void Insert (const DataType& item);
      void Delete (const DataType& item);
      DataType DeleteFront (void);
      void ClearList (void);
};
```

DESCRIPTION

The ListSize, ListEmpty, Find, and GetData methods conclude with the word "const" after the function declaration. They are called constant functions because they do not alter the state of the list. The functions Insert, Delete have the word "const" as part of the parameter list. This C++ syntax passes a reference to the item but specifies that the value of the item is not altered.

C++ uses a simple syntax for declaring a derived class. In the header, the base class is specified after the colon (:). The following is a declaration for the OrderedList class. The specifics are discussed in Chapter 12, which provides a formal introduction to inheritance.

- -

OrderedList CLASS SPECIFICATION

DECLARATION

```
class OrderedList: public SeqList        // inherit the SeqList class
{
```

```
    public:
        OrderedList (void);                    // initialize base class to
                                               // create an empty list
        void Insert (const DataType& item);    // insert item in order
    };
```

DESCRIPTION

Insert overrides the base class method of the same name. It traverses the list inherited from the base class and inserts the item at the position that maintains ordering.

Applications with Class Inheritance   1.5

The concept of class inheritance has important applications in graphical user interface (GUI) programming and data base systems. The graphical applications focus on windows, menus, dialog boxes, and so forth. A basic window is a data structure with data and operations that are common to all types of windows. The operations include opening a window, creating or changing a window title, setting up scroll bars and drag regions, and so forth. GUI applications consist of dialog classes, menu classes, text window classes, and so forth that inherit the basic structure and operations from the window base class. For instance, the following class hierarchy includes a Dialog class and a TextEdit class that are derived from the Window class.

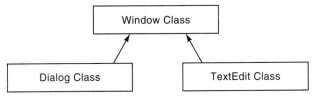

Figure 1.7 illustrates a GUI application with a dialog and text window.

The example of the window class illustrates single inheritance in which a derived class has exactly one base class. With **multiple inheritance,** however, the class is derived from two or more base classes. Some GUI applications use this feature. A word processing program combines an editor with a view manager to list text in a window. An editor reads a character stream and makes changes by inserting and deleting strings and embedding format information. The view manager is responsible for copying text to a screen using font and window information. A screen editor can be defined as a derived class that uses an editor class and a view class as base classes.

Multiple Inheritance

```
    ┌──────────────┐          ┌──────────────┐
    │  View Class  │          │ Editor Class │
    └──────────────┘          └──────────────┘
            ┌──────────────────────┐
            │  Screen Editor Class │
            └──────────────────────┘
```

```
                                        Find
        ⌀  ⊡  ◈  ⚄  ✓    Search for:    dataptr

  #ifndef HASH_TABLE_CLAS
  #define HASH_TABLE_CLAS
                            Replace with:
  #include "node.h"
  #include "link.h"
  #include "iterator.h"

  template <class K, clas
  class HashTable           ☐ Match Case         ☐ Multi-File Search
  {                         ☐ Entire Word
      private:              ☒ Wrap Around            Options...
          int bucketsize    ☐ Search Backwards
          LinkedList<D>
          int (*hf)(K ke    ☐ Grep        Patterns: ▼
          D *Find(Linked
  public:                   ---------------------------------------
          HashTable(int
          ~HashTable(voi      Cancel        Don't Find        Find
          D *Insert<K key
          D *Retrieve<K
          int InTable<K
          void Delete<K keyval);
          int TableEmpty(void);
          void ClearTable(void);
          int TableSize(void);

          friend class HashTableIterator<K,D>;
  }.
```

Figure 1.7 GUI Windows Application

1.6 Object-Oriented Program Design

Large software systems are becoming increasingly complex and require new design approaches. The traditional design uses a management model that assumes the existence of a top administrator who understands the system and delegates tasks to managers. This **top-down program design** views a system as a layered set of

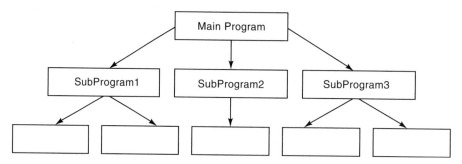

subprograms. At the top level, a main program controls the running of the system by making a sequence of calls to the subprograms that perform calculations and return information. The subprograms may further delegate tasks to other subprograms. Elements of top-down design are necessary for all systems. However, when the problem becomes too large, the approach can fail because its complexity overwhelms the ability of a single person to manage the hierarchy of subprograms. Also, simple design changes in subprograms near the top of the hierarchy can require expensive and time-consuming changes in the algorithms for subprograms that are lower in the chart.

Object-oriented programming uses a different model for system design. It views a large system as a set of objects (agents) that interact to carry out tasks. Each object has methods that manage its data.

The purpose of program design is to create a readable and maintainable architecture that can be extended as needs dictate. Well-organized systems are easier to understand, develop, and debug. All design philosophies attempt to master the complexity of a software system by means of the principle of divide and conquer. Top-down programming design treats a system as a layered set of functional modules. Object-oriented programming uses objects as the basis of design. There is no one way to design software and no rigid process that must be followed. Program design is a human activity that must include creative freedom and flexibility. In this book, we discuss a general approach that defines a **software development methodology.** The approach involves distinct phases in software development, including problem analysis and program definition, object and process design, coding, testing, and maintenance.

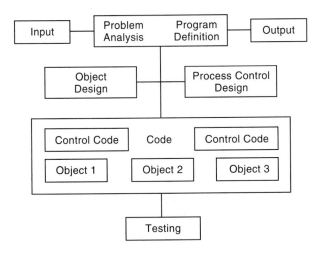

PROBLEM ANALYSIS/PROGRAM DEFINITION

Program development begins when a client identifies some problem that must be solved. The problem is often loosely defined without a clear understanding of exactly what data are available (input) and what new information should result (output). The programmer analyzes the problem with the client and determines what form the input and output should take and the algorithms that are involved in carrying out the calculations. This analysis is formalized in the design phase of the program.

DESIGN

Program design features a description of the objects that are the primary building blocks of the program. The design also describes the control modules that direct the interaction among the objects.

The object design phase identifies the objects that are going to be used in the program and writes a declaration for each class. A class is tested by using it with a small program that tests the class methods under controlled conditions. The fact that classes can be tested individually outside the realm of the large application is one of the powerful features of object-oriented design.

The process control design phase uses top-down design by creating a main program and subprograms to control the interaction among the objects. The main program and subprograms form the **design framework.**

The main control module corresponds to the main function in a C++ program and is responsible for the data flow of the program. With top-down programming design, the system is partitioned into a sequence of activities that are executed as independent subprograms. The main program and its subprograms are organized in a top-down hierarchy of modules called a **structure tree.** The main module is the root of the tree. Each module is enclosed in a rectangle, and each class that is used by a module is enclosed in an oval. We list each module by giving the function name, the input and output parameters and a brief description of its action.

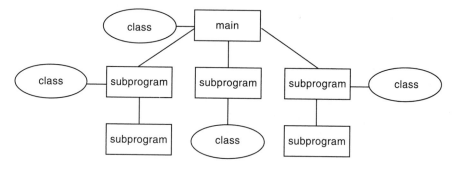

```
Function name
    Parameters passed:      <description of input parameters>
    Processing:             <description of function action>
    Parameters returned:    <list of return values>
```

CODING

The main program and subprograms that implement the program design framework are written in the coding phase.

TESTING

The implementation and testing of objects is done during the object design phase. This allows us to focus on the control module design. We can verify a program's coding by testing each object's interaction with the control modules in the design framework.

PROGRAM DESIGN ILLUSTRATION: A DICE GRAPH

The use of a graph to record the frequency of dice tosses illustrates the design and implementation of an object-oriented program. The following sections describe each phase in the life cycle of a program.

Problem Analysis   Assume an event is the tossing of two dice. For each toss, the sum lies in the range 2 to 12. Using repeated dice tosses, we determine the empirical probability that the sum is 2, 3, . . . , 11, or 12 and construct a graph that records the probability for each possible outcome.

Note: Empirical probability is determined by running a simulation over a large number of events and recording the outcomes. The ratio of number of occurrences to the number of events represents the empirical probability that an outcome will occur. For instance, if the tossing of dice is repeated 100,000 times and the sum 4 occurs 10,000 times, the empirical probability of tossing a 4 is 0.10.

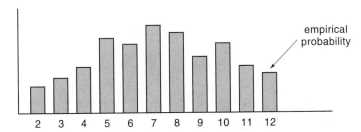

The problem must be clearly defined before useful problem-solving activities can occur. The process involves an understanding of the input and output and intermediate calculations. In the problem analysis phase, the client formulates a series of requirements for the system. These include monitoring input of data, specifying the computation and formulas that must be used, and describing the desired output.

Program Definition   The program asks the user to enter N, the number of tosses of the two dice. Since a dice toss has a random outcome, we use random numbers to simulate the N tosses. The program maintains a record of the number of occurrences for each possible sum S $(2 \le S \le 12)$. The empirical probability is determined by dividing the number of outcomes of S by N. For output, this fractional value is used to determine the height of a rectangle in our graph. The results are printed as a bar graph.

Object Design   The program uses the Line class to create the axes for the graph and the Rectangle class to plot the bars. These classes are introduced in Section 1.4 on Object Design. Tossing the dice is a method in the Dice class that handles two dice. The following is a declaration of the Dice class. Its implementation and testing is given in the program supplement along with the implementation and testing of the Line and Rectangle classes.

```
#include "random.h"
class Dice
{
    private:
        // member data
        int  diceTotal;        // sum of the two dice
        int  diceList[2];      // listing of the two dice faces
```

```
        // random number generator class used for dice toss
        RandomNumber rnd;

    public:
        // constructor
        Dice(void);

        // dice handling methods
        void Toss(void);
        int Total(void) const;
        void DisplayToss(void) const;
};
```

Process Control Design   For the dice graph, the main module calls three subprograms, which carry out the actions of the program. The function SimulateDie-toss uses methods from the Dice class to toss the dice *N* times. DrawAxes calls the Draw method in the Line class to draw the axes of the graph, and Plot draws the series of rectangles that creates the bar graph. The Plot function calls Max to determine the maximum number of occurrences of any one possible sum. This value allows us to compute the relative height of each rectangles in the bar graph. The structure tree for the program is given in Figure 1.8. The following are descriptions for each control module in the structure tree.

main
    Parameters passed:
       None

    Processing:
       Prompt the user for the number of dice tosses in the simula-
       tion. Call the function SimulateDieToss to complete the
       tosses and record the number of times each sum occurs (2 ≤
       Total ≤ 12). Draw the axes by calling DrawAxes and create the
       bar graph by calling Plot.

    Parameters returned:
       None

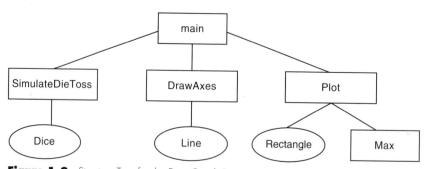

Figure 1.8   Structure Tree for the Dice Graph Program

SimulateDieToss
 Parameters passed:
  tossTotal   Array tossTotal holds the number of occur-
                 rences of each total in the range 2 to 12.
                 tossTotal[i] is the number of occurrences of
                 total i when tossing the dice tossCount times.
  tossCount   Number of tosses N in the simulation.

 Processing:
   Create a Dice object and use it to toss the dice the specified number of times, recording in array tossTotal the number
   of times the sum 2 occurs, the number of times the sum 3 occurs, . . . , the number of times the sum 12 occurs.

 Parameters returned:
   The array tossTotal with the number of times each sum occurred.

DrawAxes
 Parameters passed:
   None

 Processing:
   Create two Line objects, one for the vertical axis (y-axis)
   and one for the horizontal axis (x-axis). The y-axis is the
   line from (1.0,3.25) to (1.0,0.25). The x-axis is the line
   from (0.75,3.0) to (7.0,3.0). The vertical span of the graph
   is 2.75.

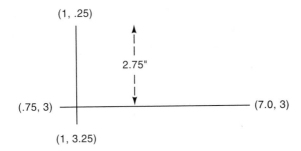

 Parameter returned:
   None

Max
 Parameter passed:
   a   Array containing long data values.
   n   The number of data values in a.

 Processing:
   Find the maximum value of the items in the array a.

Parameter returned:
   The maximum value in the array.

Plot
   Parameter passed:
      tossTotal   Array containing the number of occurrences for
                       each sum; computed in SimulateDieToss.

   Processing:
      Find the maximum sum (maxTotal) in the array tossTotal for
      the index range 2-12. Then every item in the array generates
      a relative portion (tossTotal[i]/maxTotal) of the vertical
      span of the graph. Separate the 6-inch x-axis span from
      (1.0,3.0) to (7.0,3.0) into 23 equal segments and plot the
      corresponding rectangles whose heights are float
      (tossTotal[i])/maxTotal * 2.75, $2 \leq i \leq 12$.

   Parameters returned:
      None

Coding*   The coding of the control modules completes the program. For instance,
the control modules for the dice graph are given by the following program.

Program 1.2   Dice Toss Graph

The main program asks the user to enter the number of tosses for the simulation.
Our run tests the case of 500,000 tosses. At the end of the run, the system waits
for a keystroke or mouse click before terminating. The Line and Rectangle classes
are contained in the file "figures.h" and the Dice class is contained in the file
"dice.h". The primitive draw routines are found in "graphlib.h".

```cpp
#include <iostream.h>

#include "figures.h"
#include "dice.h"
#include "graphlib.h"

// toss two dice tossCount times. record number of twos in
// tossTotal[2], number of threes in tossTotal[3], and so forth
void SimulateDieToss(long tossTotal[], long tossCount)
{
    long tossEvent;
    int i;
    Dice D;
```

```
    // clear each element of sumcount
    for(i=2;i <= 12;i++)
        tossTotal[i] = 0;

    // toss the dice tossCount times
    for(tossEvent=1;tossEvent <= tossCount;tossEvent++)
    {
        D.Toss();                    // toss the dice
        tossTotal[D.Total()]++;   // Increment count for dice total
    }
}


// find maximum value in the n element array a
long Max(long a[], int n)
{
    long lmax = a[0];              // locally holds the maximum
    int i;

    for (i=1;i < n;i++)
        if (a[i] > lmax)
            lmax = a[i];
    return lmax;
}


// draw the two axes
void DrawAxes(void)
{
    const float vertspan = 3.0;

    Line VerticalAxis(Point(1.0,vertspan+0.25),Point(1.0,0.25));
    VerticalAxis.Draw();

    Line HorizontalAxis(Point(0.75,vertspan),
                        Point(7.0,vert-span));
    HorizontalAxis.Draw();
}


// draw the bar graph
void Plot(long tossTotal[])
{
    const float vertspan = 3.0, scaleHeight = 2.75;
    float x, rectHeight, dx;
    long maxTotal;
    int i;

    // find the maximum value in tossTotal. Only look at index
    // range 2-12.
    maxTotal = Max(&tossTotal[2],11);
```

```
    // now generate the rectangles
    dx = 6.0/23.0;
    x = 1.0 + dx;

    //  loop 11 times. in the loop,
    //      determine height of bar to draw at current position.
    //      create the Rectangle object of correct position,
    //      height and width. draw the bar and move to position
    //      of next bar.
    for(i=2;i<= 12;i++)
    {
        rectHeight = (float(tossTotal[i])/maxTotal)*scaleHeight;
        Rectangle CurrRect(Point(x,vertspan-rectHeight),
                           Point(x+dx,vertspan));
        CurrRect.Draw();
        x += 2.0*dx;
    }
}


void main(void)
{
    long numTosses;
    long tossTotal[13];

    // prompt for the number of dice tosses in the simulation
    cout << "Enter the number of tosses: ";
    cin >> numTosses;

    SimulateDieToss(tossTotal, numTosses);   // toss the dice

    InitGraphics();            // initialize the graphics system

    DrawAxes();                // draw the axes
    Plot(tossTotal);           // plot the graph
    ViewPause();               // wait for key stroke or mouse click

    ShutdownGraphics();        // close down the graphics system
}

/*
<Run of Program 1.2>

Enter the number of tosses: 500000
*/
```

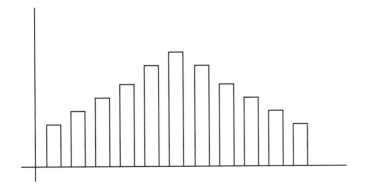

Program Testing and Maintenance 1.7

The use of object-oriented programming produces systems that allow for independent testing of the objects and the reuse of previously written classes. These advantages reduce the risk of error in building complex software systems because they are designed to evolve incrementally from smaller systems in which we have confidence. Testing is performed throughout the development of the software system.

OBJECT TESTING

A class type is a self-contained data structure that can pass information to and from an external program component. We can test each class by developing a short program that calls each public method. The program supplement illustrates the testing of methods in the Dice class.

CONTROL MODULE TESTING

The program must be thoroughly tested by running it on carefully selected test data. Before beginning this task, the correctness of the program can often be evaluated with a **structured walk-through** in which the programmer shows the complete design and implementation to another programmer and explains exactly what happens, starting with the object design and continuing through the design of the control modules. The process often uncovers conceptual erorrs, clarifies the logic of the program, and suggests tests that can be carried out.

Modern compilers support a **source-level debugger** that allows individual instructions to be traced and stops at selected breakpoints. During this controlled execution, the values of variables can be displayed, allowing for comparison of "program snapshots" before and after an error occurs.

The ultimate test of a program's correctness is its execution with sets of carefully selected data. By running tests, the programmer gains confidence in the correctness of the program. The programmer should also use invalid input to test the code's

robustness, which is a measure of the program's ability to identify invalid data and return error messages.

Test data are chosen by means of different approaches. One technique is the "hope and pray" approach in which the programmer runs the program several times with simple data and, if it works, he or she continues. A more reasonable approach selects a series of input data that tests the different algorithms in the program. The input should include simple data, typical data, extreme data that test special cases in the program, and invalid data that check the ability of the program to respond to input errors.

A fully structured test looks at the logical structure of the program. This approach assumes that a program is not thoroughly tested if some part of the code has not been executed. This exhaustive testing requires the programmer to select data to test the different algorithms in the program: each conditional statement, each loop construct, each function call, and so forth. Some compilers provide profilers that indicate the number of times functions within the program are called.

PROGRAM MAINTENANCE AND DOCUMENTATION

To meet additional demands, computer programs frequently need updates. Object-oriented programming simplifies program maintenance. Class inheritance allows for the reuse of existing software. These tools are effective only when supported by good program documentation that describes the classes and control modules to help users understand the program and its proper execution. Large programs are typically supported by a user's manual that includes information on installing the software and one or more tutorials to illustrate the central features of the product.

Object specifications and control module structure charts are excellent tools for program documentation. Within the program source code, comments describe the action of individual functions and classes. Comments also belong in places where the logic of an algorithm is particularly subtle.

1.8 The C++ Programming Language

This book introduces the reader to data structures using the object-oriented programming language C++. Although a number of object-oriented languages are available, C++ has developed a preeminence due to its origins in the popular C programming language and the quality of the compilers.

The C programming language was developed in the early 1970s as a structured language for systems programming. It contained facilities to call low-level system routines and implement high-level constructs. Over the years, fast and efficient C compilers have become available on most computer platforms. All but a small portion of the Unix operating system is written in C, and C is the primary language for programming in the Unix environment. The C++ programming language was developed at Bell Laboratories by Bjarne Stroustrup as an extension to C. The use of C meant that C++ did not have to be developed from scratch and this relation to C gave the new language a vast audience of quality programmers. C++ was originally called "C with Classes" and was made available to users in the early 1980s. Translators were written to convert the C with Classes source code to C source code before calling the C compiler to create the machine code.

The name C++ was coined by Rick Mascitti in 1983. He used the C increment operator "++" to reflect both the language's origins in C and its extensions to C. Groups have questioned whether C++ should retain compatibility with C, particularly as C++ develops powerful new constructs and facilities not present in C. As a practical matter, the language will probably continue to be an extension of C. The amount of existing C software and the number of C library functions will force developers of C++ to retain the strong tie to the C language. The definition of C++ continues to ensure that common C and C++ constructs have the same meaning in both languages.

The ideas for many of the constructs in C++ evolved in the 1970s from Simula 67 and Algol 68. These languages introduced strong type checking, class concepts, and modularity. The Department of Defense promoted the design of Ada, which codified many of the key advances in compiler construction. Ada inspired the use of generics to permit generalized class instantiations. C++ uses a similar template construct and also shares exception handling mechanisms with Ada.

The popularity of C++ and its migration to many platforms made the imposition of standards necessary. AT&T is active in the evolution of the language. A conscious effort is being made to tie C++ compiler writers to both the original language designers and the exploding population of users. AT&T has followed the course of its success with Unix and works cooperatively with users to coordinate the development of ANSI C++ standards and the publishing of the definitive C++ reference manual. It is expected that the ANSI (American National Standards Institute) standard for C++ will be part of the ISO (international) standardization effort.

Abstract Base Classes and Polymorphism*   1.9

Class inheritance combines with **abstract base classes** to create an important data structure tool. These abstract base classes specify the public interface of a class with its client independent of the internal implementation of a class's data and operations. The public interface of a class defines the methods of access to the data. A client wants the public interface to remain constant despite changes in the internal implementation. Object-oriented languages address this problem by using an abstract base class that declares the names and parameters for each of the public methods. The abstract base class provides limited implementation details and focuses on declaration of public methods. The declaration forces an implementation in a derived class. A C++ abstract base class declares some methods as **pure virtual functions.** The following declaration defines the abstract base class List that specifies list operations. The word "virtual" and the assignment of zero to the operation specifies a pure virtual function.

```
template <class T>
class List
{
    protected:
        // number of elements in the list. updated by derived class
        int size;
    public:
        // constructor
        List(void);

        // list access methods
        virtual int ListSize(void) const;
        virtual int ListEmpty(void) const;
        virtual int Find(T& item) = 0;

        // list modification methods
        virtual void Insert(const T& item) = 0;
        virtual void Delete(const T& item) = 0;
        virtual void ClearList(void) = 0;
};
```

This abstract base class is intended to describe very general lists. It is used as a base for a series of collection classes (list structures) in the later chapters. Using the abstract class as a base requires that the collections implement the general methods of the List class. To illustrate this process, the SeqList class is repeated in Chapter 12, where it is derived from List.

POLYMORPHISM AND DYNAMIC BINDING

The concept of inheritance is supported in C++ by a range of powerful constructs. We have already seen the use of pure virtual functions in an abstract base class. The general concept of virtual functions supports inheritance by allowing two or more objects in an inheritance hierarchy to have operations with the same declaration that perform distinct tasks. This object-oriented property, called **polymorphism,** allows objects from a variety of classes to respond to the same message. The receiver of the message is determined dynamically at runtime. For instance, a system administrator may use polymorphism to handle file backups in a multisystem environment. Assume the administrator has a 1/2-in. tape subsystem and a compact 1/4-in. tape unit. The classes HalfTape and QuarterTape are derived from a common Tape class and manage the respective drives. The tape class has a virtual Backup operation that contains actions common to all tape drives. The derived classes have a (virtual) Backup operation that uses specific internal information about the tape drives. When the administrator orders a system backup, each drive takes the Backup message and executes the specific operation that is defined for its hardware. An object of type HalfTape executes a backup to a 1/2-in. drive and an object of type QuarterTape executes a backup to a 1/4-in. drive.

The concept of polymorphism is fundamental to object-oriented programming. Professionals often refer to object-oriented programming as "inheritance with run-time polymorphism." C++ supports this construct using **dynamic binding** and **virtual member functions.** These concepts are discussed in Chapter 12. For now, we focus on the concepts without giving technical information on language implementation.

Dynamic binding allows many different objects in a system to respond to the same message. Each object responds to the message in a manner specific to its type. Consider the actions of a professional painter as he or she works on different kinds of houses. Certain common tasks must be done when painting a house. Assume these are described in the class House. Besides the common tasks, special techniques are required for different types of houses. Painting a wood frame house is different from painting a stucco house or a vinyl-sided house and so forth. In the context of object-oriented programming, the special painting tasks for each different house are given in a derived class that inherits the base class House. Assume that each derived class has a Paint operation. The House class has a Paint operation

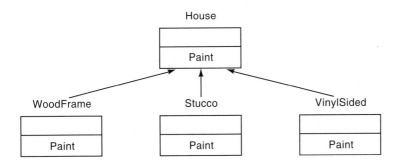

that is given as a virtual function. Suppose BigWoody is an object of type WoodFrame. We can direct BigWoody to paint the house by explicitly calling the Paint operation. This is called **static binding.**

```
BigWoody.Paint();              // static binding
```

However, assume that a paint contractor has a list of addresses for houses that need to be painted and that he broadcasts a message to his crew to go through the list and paint the houses. In this case each message is not bound to a particular house but rather to the address of a house object in the list. The crew goes to the house and selects the correct Paint operation only dynamically after it sees the type of house. This process is known as **dynamic binding.**

```
(House at address 414) .Paint();   // dynamic binding
```

The process calls the Paint operation corresponding to the house at the given address. If the house at address 414 is a wood frame house, the operation Paint() from the class WoodFrame is executed.

When using inheritance structures in C++, operations that are dynamically bound to their object are declared as **virtual member functions.** Code is generated to create a table specifying the locations of an object's virtual functions. A link is established between an object and this table. At runtime, when the location of an object is referenced, the system uses this location to gain access to the table and execute the correct function.

The concept of polymorphism is fundamental to object-oriented programming. We use it with more advanced data structures.

Written Exercises

1.1   Distinguish between encapsulation and information hiding for objects.

1.2   (a)   Design an ADT for a cylinder. Data include the radius and height of the cylinder. The operations are the constructor, area, and volume.

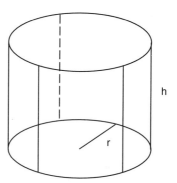

(b)   Design an ADT for a television set. The data are the settings for the volume control and the channel. The operations include turning the set On and Off, adjusting the volume, and changing the channel.

(c)   Design an ADT for a bowling ball. The data are its radius and its weight in pounds. Operations return the radius and weight of the ball.

(d)   Design the ADT for Example 1.1, part 2.

1.3 A solid is formed by drilling a circular hole of radius *rh* through the center of a cylinder of radius *r* and height *h*.

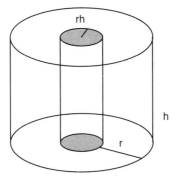

(a) Use the cylinder ADT developed in Exercise 1.2(a) to find the volume of the solid.

(b) Use the circle ADT developed in the text and the cylinder ADT to compute the area of the solid. The area must include the lateral surface area inside the hole.

1.4 Describe several messages that can be passed to the television set ADT of Exercise 1.2(b). What does the receiver do in each case?

1.5 Develop a class Cylinder that implements the ADT of Exercise 1.2(a).

1.6 Draw an inheritance chain involving the following terms: vehicle, automobile, truck, convertible, Ford, and semitractor trailer.

1.7 What is the design framework of a software system?

1.8 Give three reasons for the growing popularity of C++.

1.9 What is the relationship between C and C++?

1.10 List some C++ compilers in common use. To which do you have access? For each compiler, indicate whether it provides an integrated development environment (IDE) in which the system provides the editor, compiler, linker, debugger, and runtime system. The alternative is a command-line compiler.

1.11 (a) Explain what is meant by polymorphism.

(b) A graphical system encapsulates window operations in a base called TWindow. Derived classes implement main program windows, dialogs, and controls. Each class has a method SetupWindow that initializes various components of the window. Should polymorphism be used in the declaration of SetupWindow in the base class?

C H A P T E R 2

BASIC DATA TYPES

This chapter introduces a series of basic data types that include numbers, characters, user-defined enumerated types, and pointers. These types are native to most programming languages. Each basic data type includes data and operations, the components of an abstract data type (ADT). In this chapter, we provide ADTs for integer, character, real number, enumerated, and pointer types. Programming languages implement ADTs on a computer by using different representations for data, including binary numbers and the ASCII character set. In this text, the C++ language is used to illustrate the implementation of ADTs.

The number, character, and pointer types describe simple data because objects of these types cannot be divided into simpler parts. In contrast, structured data types have components that are built from simple types with rules to define relationships among the components. The structured types include arrays, strings, records, files, lists, stacks, queues, trees, graphs, and tables, which define the main topics of this book. Most programming languages provide language constructs or library functions to handle arrays, strings, records, and file structures. As such, we identify these as *built-in* structured data types. We provide abstract data types for these built-in structures and discuss their C++ implementations.

We present a series of applications for the built-in structured types that introduce the important sequential search and exchange sort algorithms. An application illustrates the implementation of the string type using the C++ string library. C++ uses an inheritance hierarchy to implement files. An application illustrates the handling of three different types of files.

Integer Types 2.1

Integers are positive or negative whole numbers that consist of a sign and a sequence of digits. Integers are referred to as *signed* numbers. For instance, the following are specific integer values called *integer constants:*

$$+35 \quad -278 \quad 19 \text{ (sign is } +) \quad -28976510$$

You are familiar with elementary arithmetic in which you define a series of operators that result in new integer values. Operators that take either a single operand (unary operator) or two operands (binary operators) create integer expressions:

(Unary +) $+35 = 35$	(Subtraction $-$) $73 - 50 = 23$
(Addition +) $4 + 6 = 10$	(Multiplication *) $-3 * 7 = -21$

Integer expressions can be used with arithmetic relational operators to produce a result that is True or False.

(Relational less than)	$5 < 7$	(True)
(Relational greater than or equal to)	$10 >= 18$	(False)

Theoretically, integers have no size limit, a fact that is implied in the definition of the ADT.

The ADTs we provide for the primitive types assume that the reader is familiar with the preconditions, input, and postconditions for each operation. For instance, a complete specification of integer division is:

```
Integer Division
    Input:              Two integer values u and v.
    Preconditions:      The denominator v cannot be 0.
    Process:            Divide v into u using integer division.
    Output:             Value of the quotient.
    Postconditions:     An error condition exists if v = 0.
```

In our specification, we use the C++ operator notation in place of generic operation names and only describe the process.

```
ADT Integer is

    Data
        Signed whole number N.
    Operations
        Assume that u and v are each integer expressions, and N is
        an integer variable.

        Assignment
            =       N = u       Assigns value of expression u to variable
                                N.

        Binary Arithmetic Operators
            +       u + v       Add two integer values.
            -       u - v       Subtract two integer values.
            *       u * v       Multiply two integer values.
            /       u / v       Compute the quotient using integer
                                division.
            %       u % v       Compute the remainder using integer
                                division.

        Unary Arithmetic Operators
            -       -u          Change sign (unary minus).
            +       +u          +u same as u (unary plus).

        Relational Operators
            (The relational expression is TRUE under the given con-
            dition.)
            ==      u == v      Result is True if u is equal to v.
            !=      u != v      Result is True if u is not equal to v.
            <       u < v       Result is True if u is less than v.
            <=      u <= v      Result is True if u is less than or equal
                                to v.
```

```
    >        u > v      Result is True if u is greater than v.
    >=       u >= v     Result is True if u is greater than or
                        equal to v.
```
end ADT Integer

EXAMPLE 2.1
───────

```
3 + 5              (expression has value 8)
val = 25 / 20      (val = 1)
rem = 25 % 20      (rem = 5)
```

COMPUTER STORAGE OF INTEGERS

Implementation of integers is provided by programming language type declarations and computer hardware. Computer systems store integers in fixed-size blocks of memory. The resulting domain of values lies in a finite range. The size of the storage block and the range of values are implementation dependent. To promote some standardization, programming languages supply primitive built-in data types for short and long integers. When very large integer values are required, an application must supply a library of subprograms to carry out the operations. A library of integer operations can extend the implementation of integers to any size although the routines often seriously degrade the runtime efficiency of an application.

In a computer, integers are stored as **binary numbers,** which consist of different sequences of the digits 0 and 1. The representation is modeled on the base 10 or decimal system, which uses digits 0, 1, 2, . . . , 9. A decimal number is stored as a set of digits d_0, d_1, d_2, etc., representing powers of ten. For instance, the k-digit number

$$N_{10} = d_{k-1}\ d_{k-2}\ \ldots\ d_i\ \ldots\ d_1\ d_0, \qquad \text{for } 0 \le d_i \le 9$$

represents

$$N_{10} = d_{k-1}(10^{k-1}) + d_{k-2}(10^{k-2}) + \cdots + d_i(10^i) + \cdots + d_1(10^1) + d_0(10^0)$$

The subscript 10 indicates that N is written as a decimal number. For instance, the four-digit decimal integer 2589 represents

$$2589_{10} = 2(10^3) + 5(10^2) + 8(10^1) + 9(10^0)$$
$$= 2(1000) + 5(100) + 8(10) + 9$$

Binary integers use digits 0 and 1 and powers of 2 ($2^0 = 1$, $2^1 = 2$, $2^2 = 4$, $2^3 = 8$, $2^4 = 16$, etc.). For instance, 13_{10} has the binary representation

$$13_{10} = 1(2^3) + 1(2^2) + 0(2^1) + 1(2^0) = 1101_2$$

A binary digit is called a **bit,** an abbreviation that includes "bi" from binary and "t" from digit. In general, a k-digit or k-bit binary number has the representation

$$N_2 = b_{k-1}b_{k-2} \ldots b_i \ldots b_1b_0$$
$$= b_{k-1}(2^{k-1}) + b_{k-2}(2^{k-2}) + \cdots + b_i(2^i) + \cdots + b_1(2^1) + d_0(2^0), \quad 0 \le b_i \le 1$$

The following 6-bit number gives the binary representation of 42. The decimal value of a binary number is computed by adding the terms in the sum:

$$101010_2 = 1(2^5) + 0(2^4) + 1(2^3) + 0(2^2) + 1(2^1) + 0(2^0) = 42_{10}$$

EXAMPLE 2.2
***

Compute the decimal value of a binary number:

1. $110101_2 = 1(2^5) + 1(2^4) + 0(2^3) + 1(2^2) + 0(2^1) + 1(2^0) = 53_{10}$
2. $10000110_2 = 1(2^7) + 1(2^2) + 1(2^1) = 134_{10}$

The conversion of a decimal number to its binary equivalent can be done by finding the largest power of 2 that is less than or equal to the number. The progression of powers of 2 gives the values 1, 2, 4, 8, 16, 32, 64, etc. This gives the leading digit in the binary representation. Fill in the remaining powers of 2 down through 0. For instance, consider the value 35. The largest power of 2 less than 35 is $32 = 2^5$, which implies that 35 is a 6-digit binary number:

$$35_{10} = 1(32) + 0(16) + 0(8) + 0(4) + 1(2) + 1 = 100011_2$$

Pure binary numbers are simply a sum of powers of 2. They have no sign associated with them and are referred to as **unsigned numbers.** The numbers represent positive integers. Negative integers use either twos-complement or signed-magnitude representation. In either format, a special bit called the **sign bit** indicates the sign of the number.

DATA IN MEMORY

Numbers are stored in memory as fixed-length sequences of binary digits. Common lengths include 8, 16, and 32 bits. A sequence of bits is measured in 8-bit units called a **byte.**

Number 35 as a Byte

Table 2.1 gives the range of unsigned and signed numbers for these common sizes.

TABLE 2.1
Number
Ranges and
Bit Sizes

Size	Unsigned Number Range	Signed Number Range
8 (1 byte)	0 to 255 = $2^8 - 1$	$-2^7 = -128$ to $127 = 2^7 - 1$
16 (2 bytes)	0 to 65,535 = $2^{16} - 1$	$-2^{15} = -32768$ to $32767 = 2^{15} - 1$
32 (4 bytes)	0 to 4,294,967,295 = $2^{32} - 1$	-2^{31} to $2^{31} - 1$

Computer memory is a sequence of bytes referenced by addresses 0, 1, 2, 3, and so forth. In memory, the **address** of the integer is the location of the first byte of the sequence. Figure 2.1 illustrates a view of memory with the number $87_{10} = 1010111_2$ stored in one byte at address 3, and the number $500_{10} = 0000000111110100_2$ at memory address 4.

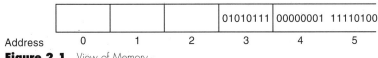

Address   0   1   2   3   4   5

Figure 2.1   View of Memory

C++ REPRESENTATION OF INTEGERS

The integer types in C++ are **int, short int,** and **long int**. The short int (short) type provides 16-bit (2-byte) integer values in the range -32768 to 32767. The long int (long) type provides the widest range of integer values and on most systems is implemented with 32 bits (4 bytes), and so its range is -2^{31} to $2^{31} - 1$.

The general int type identifies integers whose bit sizes are machine and compiler dependent. Typically, compilers use 16-bit or 32-bit integers. In some cases, the user is allowed to select the integer size as an option. The integer data types specify a domain of data values and a set of arithmetic and relational operators. Each data type gives an implementation of the integer ADT with the restriction that integer values are in a finite range.

Character Types   2.2

Character data include alphanumeric items that define uppercase and lowercase letters, digits, punctuation marks, and special symbols. The computer industry uses different representations of characters for applications. The 128-element ASCII character set has the widest application for word processing, text input and output, and data communication. We use the ASCII set for our character ADT. Like integers, the ASCII characters include an order relation that defines a series of relational operators. For alphabetic characters, the letters follow dictionary ordering. In this relation, all uppercase letters are less than lowercase letters:

T < W,   b < d,   T < b

ADT Character *is*

   Data
      ASCII character set

   Operations
      Assignment
         A character value can be assigned to a character
         variable.

      Relational
         The six standard relational operators apply to characters
         using the ASCII dictionary order relation.
end ADT Character

ASCII CHARACTERS

Most computer systems use the **ASCII** standard coding scheme for character representation. ASCII characters are stored as a 7-bit integer code in an 8-bit number. The $2^7 = 128$ different codes are divided into 95 printable characters and 33 control characters. A control character is used in data communications and causes a device to perform a control function, such as moving the monitor cursor down one line.

Table 2.2 shows the printable ASCII character set. The blank character is represented by ◆. The decimal code for each character is given with the tens digit along the rows and the ones digit along the columns. For instance, the character 'T' has ASCII value 84_{10} and is stored in binary as 01010100_2.

Within the ASCII character set, decimal digits, and alphabetic characters fall within well-defined ranges (Table 2.3). This facilitates conversion between uppercase and lowercase letters and from an ASCII digit ('0' ... '9') to the corresponding number (0 ... 9).

TABLE 2.2
Printable ASCII
Character Set

					Right Digit					
Left Digit	0	1	2	3	4	5	6	7	8	9
3			◆	!	"	#	$	%	&	'
4	(	)	*	+	,	−	.	/	0	1
5	2	3	4	5	6	7	8	9	:	;
6	<	=	>	?	@	A	B	C	D	E
7	F	G	H	I	J	K	L	M	N	O
8	P	Q	R	S	T	U	V	W	X	Y
9	Z	[	\	]	^	_	`	a	b	c
10	d	e	f	g	h	i	j	k	l	m
11	n	o	p	q	r	s	t	u	v	w
12	x	y	z	{	|	}	~			

The codes 00–31 and 127 are control characters, which are nonprintable.

ASCII Characters	Decimal	Binary
Blank space	32	00100000
Decimal digits	48–57	00110000–00111001
Uppercase letters	65–90	01000001–01011010
Lowercase letters	97–122	01100001–01111010

EXAMPLE 2.3

1. The ASCII value for digit '0' is 48. The digits are ordered in the range 48 to 57:

   ASCII digit: '3' is 51 (48 + 3)

   The corresponding numerical digit is obtained by subtracting '0' (ASCII 48):

   Numeric digit: 3 = '3' − '0' = 51 − 48

2. To convert a character from upper- to lowercase, add 32 to the ASCII value of the character:

   ASCII ('A') = 65 ASCII ('a') = 65 + 32 = 97

In C++, the primitive type **char** is used to store a character. The ASCII codes lie in the range 0 to 127; however, system-dependent extended characters are often defined to use the remaining values of the range. As an integer type, the value is the code for the character.

Real Data Types   2.3

The integer types, which are referred to as **discrete types,** represent data values that can be counted, e.g., −2, −1, 0, 1, 2, 3, and so forth. Many applications require numbers that have fractional values. These values, called **real numbers,** can be represented in **fixed-point** format with a whole and a fractional part:

   9.6789   −6.345   +18.23

Real numbers can also be written as floating point numbers in **scientific notation.** This format represents the numbers as a series of digits called the **mantissa** and an **exponent,** which represents a power of 10. For instance, 6.02e23 has a mantissa of 6.02 and an exponent of 23. A fixed-point number is just a special case of a floating-point number with an exponent of 0. As with integers and characters, real numbers constitute an abstract data type. The standard arithmetic and relational operations apply with real division used in place of integer division.

ADT Real *is*

   Data
      Numbers described with fixed-point or floating-point format.

   Operations
     Assignment
       A real expression can be assigned to a real variable.

     Arithmetic Operators
       The standard binary and unary arithmetic operations apply with real division used in place of integer division. No remaindering operator is available

     Relational
       The six standard relational operators apply to real numbers.
end ADT Real

REAL NUMBER REPRESENTATIONS

Like integers, the domain of a real number has no limit. The values of real numbers are unbounded in both the negative and positive directions, and the fractional part maps the real numbers onto the continuum of points on a number line. Real numbers are implemented in a finite storage block that bounds the range of values and forms discrete points on the number line.

Over the years, computer researchers have used a variety of formats to store floating-point numbers. The IEEE (Institute of Electrical and Electronics Engineers) format is a widely used standard. You are familiar with real numbers that use a fixed-point format. Such a number is partitioned into a whole number part and a fractional part whose digits are multiplied by 1/10, 1/100, 1/1000, and so forth. A decimal point separates the parts:

$$25.638 = 2\,(10^1) + 5(10^0) + 6(10^{-1}) + 3(10^{-2}) + 8(10^{-3})$$

As with whole numbers, there are corresponding binary representations for fixed-point real numbers. These numbers contain a whole number part, a binary fraction part, and a binary point, with the fractional digits corresponding to 1/2, 1/4, 1/8, and so forth. The general form of such a representation is

$$N = b_{n...}\, b_0 \,.\, b_{-1}b_{-2} \cdots = b_n2^n + \cdots + b_02^0 + b_{-1}2^{-1} + b_{-2}2^{-2} + \cdots$$

For instance,

$$1011.1101_2 = 1(2^3) + 1(2^1) + 1(2^0) + 1(2^{-1}) + 1(2^{-2}) + 1(2^{-4})$$
$$= 8 + 2 + 1 + 0.5 + 0.25 + 0.0625$$
$$= 11.8125_{10}$$

The conversion between decimal and binary floating-point numbers uses algorithms similar to those developed for whole numbers. Conversion to decimal numbers is accomplished by adding the products of the digits and the powers of 10. The reverse process is more complex, since the decimal number may require an infinite binary representation to create the equivalent floating-point number. On a computer, the number of digits is limited because only fixed-length floating-point numbers are used.

EXAMPLE 2.4

Convert a binary fixed-point number to a decimal number:

1. $0.01101_2 = 1/4 + 1/8 + 1/32$
    $\qquad\quad = 0.25 + 0.125 + 0.03125 = 0.40625_{10}$

Convert the decimal number to a binary floating-point number.

2. $4.3125_{10} = 4 + 0.25 + 0.0625 = 100.0101_2$

3. The decimal number 0.15 does not have an equivalent fixed-length binary fraction. The conversion from a decimal to a binary fraction requires an infinite binary expansion. Because computer storage is restricted to fixed-length numbers, the tail of the infinite expansion is chopped and the partial sum is an approximation to the decimal value:

    $$0.15_{10} = 1/8 + 1/64 + 1/128 + 1/1024 + \cdots = 0.0010011001\ldots_2$$

Most computers store real numbers in binary form using scientific notation, with a sign, mantissa, and exponent:

$$N = \pm D_nD_{n-1}\ldots D_1D_0 \,.\, d_1d_2 \ldots d_n \times 2^e$$

C++ supports three real data types, **float, double,** and **long double**. The type **long double** is available for calculations requiring high precision and is not used in this book. Often the float type is implemented using IEEE 32-bit floating-point format, whereas the 64-bit format is used for the double type.

2.4 Enumerated Types

The ASCII character set uses an integer representation of character data. A similar integer representation may be used to describe programmer-defined data sets. For example, the following is the list of months whose length is 30 days:

April, June, September, November

The set of months forms an **enumerated data type.** For each type, the ordering of the items is determined by the way the items are listed. For instance,

Hair Color

black	// first value
blond	// second value
brunette	// third value
red	// fourth value

black	blond	brunette	red

The type supports an assignment operation and the standard relational operators. For example,

| black < red | // black occurs before red |
| brunette >= blond | // brunette occurs after blond |

An enumerated type has data and operators and hence is an ADT.

ADT Enumerated *is*

   Data
      User-defined list of N distinct items.

   Operations
     Assignment
       A variable of enumerated type can be assigned any of the items in the list.

     Relational
       The six relational operators use the order relation determined by the way in which the items are listed.
end ADT Enumerated

IMPLEMENTING C++ ENUMERATED TYPES

C++ has an enumerated type that defines distinct integer values referenced by named constants.

EXAMPLE 2.5

1. The type Boolean can be declared an enumerated type. The value of the constant False is 0, and the value of True is 1. The variable Done is defined as Boolean with initial value False.

   ```
   enum Boolean {False, True};
   Boolean Done = False;
   ```

2. The months of the year are declared as an enumerated type. By default, the initial value Jan is 0. However, the integer sequence can begin at another value by assigning that value to the first item. In this case, Jan is 1 and the months correspond to the sequence 1, 2, . . . , 12.

   ```
   enum Month {Jan=1,Feb,Mar,Apr,May,Jun,Jul,Aug,
               Sep,Oct,Nov,Dec};
   Month Mon = Dec;
   ```

Pointers 2.5

The pointer data type is fundamental in any programming language. A **pointer** is an unsigned integer that represents a memory address. The pointer also serves as a reference to the data at the address. At the pointer address, the type of the data is called the **base type** and is used in defining the pointer. For instance, we describe a pointer to a character, a pointer to an integer, and so forth. For instance, pointer P has value 5000 in each of the cases of Figure 2.2. However, in (a) the pointer references a character and in (b) the pointer references a short integer.

A pointer allows efficient access to items in a list and is fundamental to the development of dynamic data structures such as linked lists, trees, and graphs.

POINTER ADT

As a number, a pointer makes use of certain arithmetic and relational operators. The arithmetic operations require special attention. A pointer can be incremented

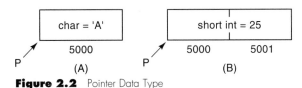

Figure 2.2 Pointer Data Type

or decremented by an integer value to reference new data in memory. Adding 1 updates the pointer to reference the next item of that type in memory. For instance, if p points at a char object, p + 1 points to the next byte in memory. Adding k > 0 moves the pointer k data positions to the right. For instance, if p points at a double, p + k references the double:

N = sizeof(double) * k bytes to the right of p.

Data Type	Current Address	New Address
char	p = 5000	p + 1 = 5001
int (2 bytes)	p = 5000	p + 3 = 5000 + 3 * 2 = 5006
double (4 bytes)	p = 5000	p − 6 = 5000 − 6 * 4 = 4976

A pointer makes use of the address operator "&" that returns the address in memory of a data item. Conversely, the operator "*" references the data associated with the pointer value. Pointers are ordered by comparing their unsigned integer values.

Dynamic memory is new memory allocated during the execution of a program. Dynamic memory differs from **static memory** whose existence is determined prior to beginning program execution. Dynamic memory is discussed in Chapter 8. The operator **new** accepts a type T, allocates memory dynamically for an item of type T, and returns a pointer to the memory it allocated. The operator **delete** takes a pointer as a parameter and destroys the dynamic memory previously allocated at that address.

ADT Pointer *is*

Data
The set of unsigned integers that represents a memory address for a data item of the base type T.

Operations
Assume that u and v are pointer expressions, i is an integer
expression, ptr is a pointer variable, and var is a variable
of type T.

Address
    &   ptr = &var   Assigns the address of var to ptr.

Assignment
    =   ptr = u   Assigns pointer value u to ptr.

Dereference
    *   var = *ptr   Assigns the item of type T refer-
                                enced by ptr to the variable var.

Dynamic Memory Allocation and Deallocation

new	ptr = new T	Creates dynamic memory for an item of type T and assigns its address to ptr.
delete	delete ptr	Destroys the dynamic memory allocated at address ptr.

Arithmetic

+	u + i	Points to the item located i data items to the right of the item referenced by u.
-	u - i	Points to the item located i data items to the left of the item referenced by u.
-	u - v	Returns the number of elements of the base type that lie between the two pointers.

Relational

The six standard relational operators apply to pointers by comparing their unsigned integer values.

end ADT Pointer

POINTER VALUES

A pointer value is a memory address that uses 16, 32, or more bits, depending on the machine architecture. As an example, PC is a pointer to a char (1 byte), and PX is a pointer to a short int (2 bytes).

```
char str[] = "ABCDEFG";
char *PC = str;          // PC points to string str


short X = 33;
short *PX = &X;          // PX points to short X
```

The following statements illustrate fundamental pointer operations.

```
cout << *PC << endl;      // print 'A'
PC+= 4;                   // move PC right 4 characters
cout << *PC << endl;      // print 'E'
PC--;                     // move PC left 1 character
cout << *PC << endl;      // print 'D'
cout << *PX + 3 << endl;  // print 36 = 33 + 3
```

The new and delete pointer operations are discussed in Chapter 8.

2.6 The Array Type

An array is an example of a data collection. A one-dimensional array is a finite, sequential list of elements of the same data type (**homogeneous array**). The sequence identifies the first element, the second element, the third element, and so forth. Associated with each element is an integer **index** that identifies the position of the element in the list. An array has an index operator that allows for **direct access** to the elements in the list when storing or retrieving an item.

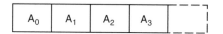

ADT Array *is*

Data

A collection of N items of the same data type; indices are chosen from the range of integers 0 to N - 1, which identify the position of an item in the list and allow direct access to the elements. Index 0 references the first item in the list, index 1 references the second item, and so forth.

Operations

Indexing []

Input:	Index
Preconditions:	Index is in the range 0 to N - 1.
Process:	On the right-hand side of an assignment statement, the index operator retrieves data from the item; on the left-hand side of an assignment statement, the index operator returns the address of the array element that stores the right-hand side of the expression.
Output:	If the indexing operation is on the right-hand side of an assignment statement, the operation retrieves data from the array and returns the data to the client.
Postconditions:	If the indexing operation is on the left-hand side, the corresponding array item is changed.

end ADT Array

THE BUILT-IN C++ ARRAY TYPE

As part of its basic syntax, C++ provides a built-in static array type that defines a list of items of the same type. The declaration explicitly gives the constant size *N* of the array and specifies that the indices are in the range 0 to *N* − 1. The declaration in Example 2.6 defines a static C++ array. Using pointers, we create dynamic arrays in Chapter 8.

EXAMPLE 2.6

1. Declare two arrays of type double. Array X has 50 items and array Y has 200 items:

```
double X[50], Y[200];
```

2. Declare the long array A with a size defined by the constant integer ArraySize = 10.

```
const  int ArraySize = 10;
long   A[ArraySize];
```

The array index, in the range 0 to ArraySize − 1, is used to access individual array elements. An element at index i is represented by A[i].

Array indexing is actually done by using the C++ indexing operator ([]). It is a binary operator whose left operand is the array name and whose right operand is the position of the element in the array. Elements in an array can be accessed on either side of an assignment operator:

```
A[i] = x;    // assign (store) x as data for the array element
t = A[i];    // retrieve the data from A[i] and assign it to
                variable t
A[i] = A[i+1] = x;
             // assign x to A[i+1]. A second assignment stores
                the data from A[i+1] in A[i]
```

STORAGE OF ONE-DIMENSIONAL ARRAYS

A C++ one-dimensional array A is logically stored as a consecutive sequence of items in memory. Each item is of the same data type.

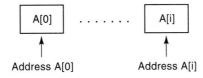

In C++, an array name is a constant and is considered to be the address of the first element of the array. Thus, in the declaration

```
Type A[ArraySize];
```

the array name A is a constant and is the location in memory of the first element A[0]. Elements A[1], A[2], and so forth follow consecutively. Assuming that sizeof(Type) = M, the entire array A occupies M * ArraySize bytes.

A[0]	A[1]	A[2]	A[3]	

The compiler sets up a table, called a **dope vector,** to maintain a record of the array characteristics. The table includes information on the size of each item, the starting address of the array, and the number of elements in the array:

Starting address:	A
Number of array elements:	ArraySize
Type size:	M = sizeof(Type)

The table is also used by the compiler to implement an **access function** that identifies the address of an item in memory. The function ArrayAccess uses the starting address of the array and the size the data type to map an index I to the address of A[I]:

```
Address A[I] = ArrayAccess(A, I, M)
```

ArrayAccess is given by

```
ArrayAccess(A, I, M) = A + I * M;
```

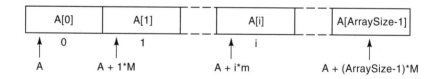

EXAMPLE 2.7
_____

Assume that a float is stored using 4 bytes (sizeof(float) = 4) and the array Height begins at memory location 20000.

```
float    Height[35];
```

Array element Height[18] is located at address

```
20000 + 18 * 4 = 20072
```

ARRAY BOUNDS

The array ADT assumes that indices are in the integer range 0 to N − 1 where N is the size of the array. C++ does the same. In reality, most C++ compilers do not generate code that tests whether an index is out of bounds during an array access. For instance, the following sequence would be accepted by most compilers:

```
int V = 20;
int A[20];    // size of array is 20; index range is 0 - 19
A[V] = 0;     // index V is greater than the upper limit
```

An array occupies memory within user data space. The array access function identifies the memory address for a particular element, and there is usually no checking to verify that the address is actually within the range of array elements. As a result, a C++ program may use indices that are out of range. The addresses for the elements that are out of range still may fall within the user data space. In the process, the program may overwrite other variables and cause unwanted runtime errors. Figure 2.3 provides a view of a program in memory.

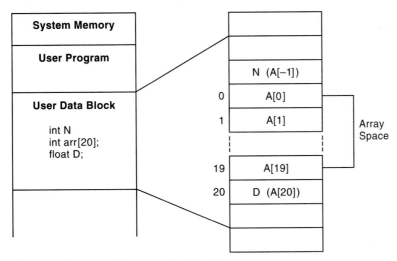

Figure 2.3 Array Allocation in User Data Space

Some compilers implement array index checking by generating runtime code to check that array indices are within bounds. Because this extra code slows execution, most programmers use array checking only during program development. Once the code is debugged, the option is turned off and the program is recompiled to more efficient code. Another approach to the problem is to develop a "safe array" that traps bad index references and prints an error message. Safe arrays are developed in Chapter 8.

TWO-DIMENSIONAL ARRAYS

A two-dimensional array, often called a matrix, is a structured data type that is created by nesting one-dimensional arrays. Items are accessed by row and column indices. For instance, the following is a 32-element matrix T with 4 rows and 8 columns. The value 10 is accessed by the (row,column) pair (1,2) and −3 is accessed by the pair (2,6).

Column

	0	1	2	3	4	5	6	7
0								
1			10					
2							−3	
3								

The concept of a two-dimensional array can be extended to cover general multidimensional arrays, in which elements are accessed by three or more indices. Two-dimensional arrays have applications in such diverse fields as data processing and the numerical solution of partial differential equations.

The C++ declaration of a two-dimensional array T defines the number of rows, the number of columns, and the data type of the elements:

```
<type> T [RowCount][ColumnCount];
```

The elements of T are referenced with the row and column indices:

```
T[i][j], 0 ≤ i ≤ RowCount-1, 0 ≤ j ≤ ColumnCount-1
```

For instance, matrix T is a 4 by 8 array of integers:

```
int T[4][8];
```

The value T[1][2] = 10 and T[2][6] = −3.

We can think of a two-dimensional array as a list of one-dimensional arrays. For instance, T[0] is row 0, which consists of ColumnCount individual elements. This concept is useful when a two-dimensional array is passed as a parameter. The notation int T[][8] indicates that T is list of 8-element arrays.

	0	1	2	3	4	5	6	7
T[0]								
T[1]			10					
T[2]							−3	
T[3]								

STORAGE OF TWO-DIMENSIONAL ARRAYS

A two-dimensional array can be initialized by assigning the items a row at a time. For instance, the array T specifies a 2 by 4 table:

```
int T[3][4] = {{20,5,-30,0},{-40,15,100,80}, {3, 0, 0 -1}};
```

	0	1	2	3
0	20	5	-30	0
Row 1	-40	15	100	80
2	3	0	0	-1

As an array, the items are stored in the order first row, second row, third row (Figure 2.4).

To access an element in memory, a compiler extends the dope vector to include information on the number of columns and the size of each row. The compiler uses a new access function, called MatrixAccess, to return the address of the element.

Starting address:	T
Number of rows:	RowCount
Number of columns:	ColumnCount
Type size:	M = sizeof(Type)
Row size:	RS = M * ColumnCount // size of an entire row

The **MatrixAccess** function takes a row and column index pair (I,J) and returns the address of the item from the element T[i][j]:

```
Address T[I][J] = MatrixAccess (T, I, J)
               = T + (I * RS) + (J * M)
```

The value (I * RS) gives the number of bytes required to store I rows of data. The value (J * M) gives the number of bytes to store the first J items in row I.

Array Stored by Rows

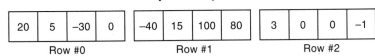

Figure 2.4 Storage of Matrix T

EXAMPLE 2.8

Let T be the 3 by 4 matrix of Figure 2.4. Assume the size of an integer is 2 and the matrix is stored at location 1000 in memory.

Starting address: 1000
Number of rows: 3
Number of columns: 4
Type size: 2 = sizeof(int)
Row size: 8 = 2 * 4 // size of entire row

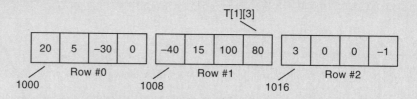

1. The addresses for the rows in storage are

    Row 0:   Address 1000
    Row 1:   Address 1000 + 1 * 8 = 1008 (row is 8 bytes)
    Row 2:   Address 1000 + 2 * 8 = 1016

2. The address of T[1][3] is

    ArrayAccess (T, 1, 3) = 1000 + (1 * 8) + (2 * 3)
                          = 1014

2.7 String Literals and Variables

An array is a structured data type that holds a homogeneous list of items. A special form of an array holds character data that identify names, words, sentences, and so forth. The structure, called a **string,** treats the characters as a single entity and provides operations to access character sequences within the string. A string is a critical data structure for most applications that use alphanumeric data. The structure is necessary to handle text processing with its editing operations, its search-and-replace algorithms, and so forth. For instance, a linguist may need information on the number of times a certain word occurs in a document or a programmer may use find/replace patterns to change source code in a document. Most languages declare string structures and provide built-in operators and library functions to handle strings.

To determine the length of a string, the structure can include a 0 at the end of a string (NULL-terminated string) or a separate length parameter. The following string representations contain the six-character string STRING.

NULL-terminated string (NULL character is 0)

S	T	R	I	N	G	NULL

Length count string

6		S	T	R	I	N	G

length

A series of operations process a string as a single block of characters. For instance, we can determine the length of a string, copy one string to another, join strings (concatenation), and process substrings with insertion, deletion, and pattern matching operations. Strings also have the comparison operation that allows for the ordering of strings. The operation uses ASCII ordering. For instance,

```
"Baker" is less than "Martin"    // B comes before M
"Smith" is less than "Smithson"

"Barber" comes before "barber"   // uppercase B precedes lowercase b

"123Stop" is less than "AAA"     // numbers precede letters
```

ADT String *is*

Data
   A string is a sequence of characters with an associated length. The string structure may have a NULL-terminating character or a separate length parameter.

Operations
   Length
      Input: None
      Preconditions: None
      Process: For a NULL-terminated string, count the
                          characters up to the NULL character;
                          for a length count string, retrieve the
                          length value.
      Postconditions: None
      Output: Return the string length.

Copy

Input:	Two strings STR1 and STR2. STR2 is the source and STR1 is the destination.
Preconditions:	None
Process:	Copy the characters from STR2 to STR1.
Postconditions:	A new string STR1 is created with length and data obtained from STR2.
Output:	Return access to STR1.

Concatenation

Input:	Two strings STR1 and STR2. Join STR2 onto the tail of STR1
Preconditions:	None
Process:	Find the end of STR1. Copy characters from STR2 onto the tail of STR1. Update information on the length of STR1.
Postconditions:	STR1 is modified.
Output:	Return access to STR1.

Compare

Input:	Two strings STR1 and STR2.
Preconditions:	None
Process:	Apply ASCII order to the strings
Postconditions:	None
Output:	Return a value as follows: STR1 less than STR2: return a negative value STR1 equal to STR2: return value 0 STR1 greater than STR2: return a positive value

Index

Input:	A string STR and a single character CH.
Preconditions:	None
Process:	Search STR for the input character CH.
Postconditions:	None
Output:	Return the address of the location containing the first occurrence of CH in STR or 0 if the character is not found.

RightIndex

Input:	A string STR and a single character CH.
Preconditions:	None
Process:	Search STR for the last occurrence of character CH.
Postconditions:	None
Output:	Return the address of the location containing the last occurrence of CH in STR or 0 if the character is not found.

Read

Input:	The file stream from which the characters are read and a string STR to hold the characters.
Preconditions:	None
Process:	Read a sequence of characters from the stream into the string STR.
Postconditions:	The string STR is assigned the characters read.
Output:	None

Write

Input:	A string that contains characters for output and a stream to which the characters are written
Preconditions:	None
Process:	Send the string of characters to the stream.
Postconditions:	None
Output:	The output stream is modified.

end ADT String

C++ STRINGS

Chapter 8 contains the specification and implementation of a compete C++ String class. The class contains an extended set of comparison operators and I/O operations. In this chapter, we use C++ NULL-terminated strings and the C++ string library to implement the ADT.

A **C++ string** is a NULL-terminated string with ASCII 0 designating the NULL character. The compiler identifies a **string literal** as a sequence of characters enclosed in double quotes. A **string variable** is a character array that contains a NULL-terminated sequence of characters. The following declaration creates a character array and assigns a string literal to the array:

```
char STR[9] = "A String";
```

The string "A String" is stored in memory as a nine-element character array:

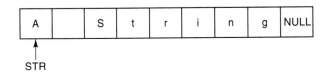

C++ provides a range of text I/O operators for the streams cin (keyboard), cout (screen), cerr (screen), and user-defined file streams.

TABLE 2.4
C++ String Functions and Examples

```
char s1[20] = "dir/bin/appl", s2[20] = "file.asm", s3[20];
char *p;
int result;
1. Length        int strlen(char *s);
        cout << strlen(s1) << endl;            // Output is 12
        cout << strlen(s2) << endl;            // Outout is 8
2. Copy      char *strcpy(char *s1, *s2);
        strcpy(s3,s1);                         // s3 = "dir/bin/appl"
3. Concatenation  char *strcat(char *s1, *s2);
        strcat(s3,"/");
        strcat(s3,s2);                         // s3 = "dir/bin/appl/file.asm"
4. Compare      int strcmp(char *s1, *s2);
        result = strcmp("baker", "Baker");     // result > 0
        result = strcmp("12", "12");           // result = 0
        result = strcmp("Joe", "Joseph");      // result < 0
5. Index       char *strchr(char *s, int c);
        p = strchr(s2,'.');                    // p points at '.' after file
        if (p)
            strcpy(p,".cpp");                  // s2 = "file.cpp"
6. RightIndex   char *strrchr(char *s,int c);
        p = strrchr(s1,'/');                   // p points at '/' after bin
        if (p)
            *p = 0;                            // terminate string after bin
                                               // s2 = "dir/bin"
7. Read        StreamVariable >> s
8. Write       StreamVariable << s
        cin >> s1;                             // if input is "hello world"
        cout << s1;                            // s1 is "hello"
                                               // output is "hello"
```

The C++ string library <string.h> contains a flexible collection of string handling functions that directly implements most ADT operations. Table 2.4 lists the key C++ string functions.

APPLICATION: REVERSING NAMES

A string application program illustrates the use of the C++ string library functions. In the application, the functions strchr(), strcpy(), and strcat() combine to copy a name such as "John Doe" to "Doe, John" in the string Newname. The following statements implement the algorithm.

```
char Name[10] = "John Doe", Newname[30];
char *p;
```

Statement 1: `p = strchr(Name, ' ');`
Return a pointer p to the first blank in Name. The first letter of the last name begins at address p+1.

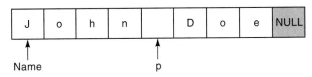

Statement 2: `*p = 0;  // replace the blank with a NULL character`

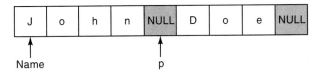

Statement 3: `strcpy(Newname,p+1);  // copy the last name to Newname`

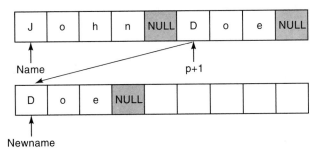

Statement 4: `strcat(Newname,", ");  // add ',' and blank to Newname`

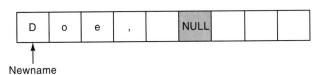

Statement 5: `strcat(Newname,Name); // concatenate the first name`

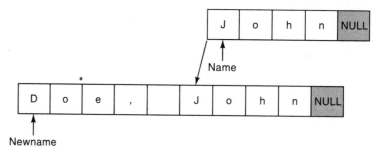

Program 2.1 Reverse a Name

The program uses statements 1 through 5 to reverse the name. The steps are coded in the function ReverseName. A loop tests the algorithm on three input strings. The reversed name is output in each case.

```
#include <iostream.h>
#include <string.h>

// reverse first and last name and separate them
// with a comma. copy result to newName.
void ReverseName(char *name, char *newName)
{
    char *p;

    // search for first blank in name; replace with NULL char
    p = strchr(name,' ');
    *p = 0;

    // copy last name to newName, append ", " and
    // concatenate first name
    strcpy(newName,p+1);
    strcat(newName,", ");
    strcat(newName,name);

    // replace the NULL char with the original blank
    *p = ' ';
}

void main(void)
{
    char name[32], newName[32];
    int  i;
```

```
    // read and process three names
    for (i = 0; i < 3; i++)
    {
        cin.getline (name,32,'\n');
        ReverseName(name,newName);
        cout << "Reversed name: " << newName << endl << endl;
    }
}


/*
<Run of Program 2.1>

Abraham Lincoln
Reversed Name: Lincoln, Abraham

Debbie Rogers
Reversed Name: Rogers, Debbie

Jim Brady
Reversed Name: Brady, Jim
*/
```

Records   2.8

A **record** is a structure that bundles items of different types into a single object. The items in the record are called **fields.** Like an array, a record has an access operator that allows for direct access to each field. For instance, Student is a record structure that describes information on a student attending school. The information includes name, local address, age, academic major, and grade-point average (GPA).

Name	Local Address	Age	Major	GPA
String	String	Integer	Enumeration Type	Real

The Name and Local Address fields contain string data, Age and GPA are numeric types, and Major is an enumeration type. Assuming that Tom is a student, we gain access to the individual fields by combining the record name and field using the access operator ".":

```
Tom.Name    Tom.Age    Tom.GPA    Tom.Major
```

A record allows for data of different types (**heterogeneous types**) in the structure. Unlike an array, a record describes a single value rather than a list of values.

ADT Record *is*

Data
> An item containing a set of fields of heterogeneous type.
> Each field has a name that allows for direct access to data
> in the field.

Operations
> *Access Operator* .

Preconditions:	None
Input:	Record name (recname) and field.
Process:	Access data in the field.
Output:	When retrieving data, return the field value to the client.
Postconditions:	When storing data, the record is changed.

end ADT Record

C++ STRUCTURES

C++ has a built-in struct type that represents a record. The structure is inherited from the language C and is retained for compatibility. C++ defines the struct type as a special case of a class in which all of the members are public. We use the struct type in this text only when dealing with a record structure.

EXAMPLE 2.9

```
struct Student
{
    int id;
    char name[30];
}


Student S = {555, "Davis, Samuel"};
cout << S.id << " " << S.name << endl;
```

2.9 Files

Most topics in this book focus on the design and implementation of **internal data structures,** which access information resident in memory. For applications, however, we often assume that data is available on an **external storage** device such as a disk. The device (physical file) stores information in a character stream and the operating system provides a series of operations to transfer data to and from memory. This allows us to input and output data that can be permanently stored on the external device. The stored data along with the transfer operations define a

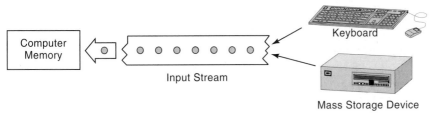

Figure 2.5 Input Data Stream

data structure, called a (logical) **file,** that has the important advantage of holding greater amounts of information than typically resides in memory.

Programming languages provide high-level file handling operations to free the programmer from having to use the low-level operating system calls. The file operations use a data **stream** that is logically connected to the file. The stream associates a data flow with the file. For input, the stream allows data to flow from the external device to memory (Figure 2.5). The same program can output information to a file using an output stream (Figure 2.6).

It is useful to define an ADT for a file. The data consists of a sequence of characters that represent text data or bytes that represent binary data. For text, the data are stored as a sequence of ASCII characters separated with newline characters. The ADT operations are given with great generality focusing on the primitive I/O operations. The input operation Read extracts a sequence of characters from the stream. The related output operation Write inserts a sequence of characters in the stream. The special operations Get and Put handle I/O for a single character.

A stream maintains a **file pointer** that identifies the current position in the stream. Input advances the file pointer to the next unread data item in the stream. Output locates the file pointer at the next output position. A seek operation allows us to position the file pointer. This operation assumes that we have access to all of the characters in the file and can move to a front, rear, or intermediate position. Typically, the seek operation is used for disk files.

A file is usually attached to a stream in one of three modes: read-only, write-only, and read-write. The modes read-only and write-only specify that the stream is used for input or output, respectively. The read-write mode allows for data flow in both directions.

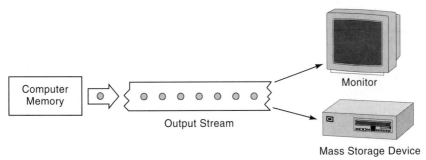

Figure 2.6 Output Data Stream

ADT File *is*

Data

An identification of the external file and the direction of
data flow. A sequence of characters that are read from or
written to the file.

Operations

Open

Input:	Name of the file and the direction of flow
Preconditions:	For input, the external file must exist.
Process:	Link a stream with the file.
Output:	A flag that indicates the operation is successful
Postconditions:	Data may flow between the external file and system memory through the stream.

Close

Input:	None
Preconditions:	None
Process:	Unlink the stream from the file.
Output:	None
Postconditions:	Data may no longer flow through the stream between the external file and system memory

Read

Input:	An array to hold blocks of data; a count N
Preconditions:	The stream must be open with read-only or read-write direction
Process:	Input N characters from the stream into the array. Stop on end-of-file
Output:	Return the number of characters that are read.
Postconditions:	The file pointer is moved forward N characters.

Write

Input:	An array; a count N
Preconditions:	The stream must be open with write-only or read-write direction
Process:	Output N characters from the array into the stream.
Output:	Return the number of characters that are written.
Postconditions:	The stream contains the output data, and the file pointer is advanced forward N characters.

Seek
    Input: Parameters to reset the file pointer.
    Preconditions: None
    Process: Reset the file pointer.
    Output: Return a flag that indicated whether
                         the seek is successful.
    Postconditions: A new file pointer is set.
end ADT File

C++ STREAM HIERARCHY

C++ provides for file handling with a stream I/O system that is implemented using a class hierarchy, as partially shown by Figure 2.7. A C++ stream is an object corresponding to a class in the hierarchy. Each stream identifies a file and the direction of the data flow.

    The root class in the hierarchy is **ios,** which contains data and operations for all the derived classes. The class contains flags that identify specific attributes of the stream and format methods that are in effect for input or output. For instance,

```
cout.setf(ios::fixed);
```

sets the display mode for real numbers to fixed format rather than scientific format.

    The **istream** and **ostream** clases provide basic input and output operations and are used as base classes for the remainder of the stream I/O hierarchy.

    The class **istream_withassign** is a variant of istream that allows object assignment. The predefined object **cin** is an object of this class. The predefined objects **cout** and **cerr** are objects of class type **ostream_withassign.** At runtime, these three streams are opened for input from the keyboard and output to the screen. Declarations are included in the file <iostream.h>.

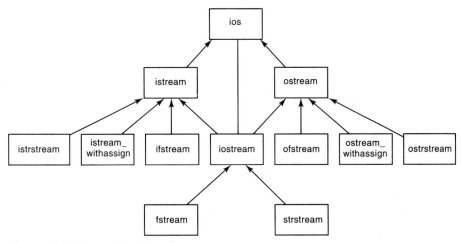

Figure 2.7 *Stream Class Hierarchy*

The **ifstream** class is an istream derivative used for disk file input; similarly, **ofstream** is used for disk file output. These classes are declared in the file <fstream.h>. Both classes contain the Open operation to attach a file to the stream and the Close operation to detach a stream from a file.

The two types of disk files are **text files** and **binary files.** A text file contains ASCII characters and is printable whereas a binary file contains pure binary data. For example, an editor uses text files and a spreadsheet program creates and uses binary files. An example of text file I/O is given in Program 2.2, and binary files are developed as a class in Chapter 14. The binary file class is used to implement external searching and sorting algorithms.

The class **fstream** allows the user to create and maintain files that require both read and write access. The class fstream is discussed in conjunction with applications in Chapter 14.

Array-based I/O is implemented by the classes **istrstream** and **ostrstream** and is declared in the file <strstream.h>. Here data are read from an array or written to an array instead of an external device. Text editors often use array-based I/O to perform complex formatting operations.

Program 2.2   File I/O

The program illustrates C++ streams, including text file and array-based I/O.

The program uses cout and cerr that are included in <iostream.h>. Text file input and array-based output use the files <fstream.h> and <strstream.h>, respectively. The program opens the file and reads each line containing variable/value pairs in the format Name Value. Using the array-based stream operation, the pair is written to array outputstr in the format

```
"name = value"
```

and then printed with a cout statement. For instance, the input lines

```
start 55
stop 8.5
```

are printed as the strings

```
start = 55    stop = 8.5
```

```
#include <iostream.h>
#include <fstream.h>
#include <strstream.h>
#include <stdlib.h>
#include <string.h>
```

```
void main(void)
{
    // input text file containing names and values
    ifstream fin;

    // read identifiers into name and write results to outputstr
    char name[30], outputstr[256];

    // declare an array-based output stream that uses outputstr
    ostrstream outs(outputstr, sizeof(outputstr));

    double value;

    // open 'names.dat' for input. make sure it exists.
    fin.open("names.dat", ios::in | ios::nocreate);
    if (!fin)
    {
        cerr << "Could not open 'names.dat'" << endl;
        exit(1);
    }

    // read a names and values. write to outs as 'name = value    '
    while(fin >> name)
    {
        fin >> value;
        outs << name << " = " << value << "    ";
    }
    // null-terminate the output string
    outs << ends;

    cout << outputstr << endl;
}

/*
<File "name.dat">

start    55
breakloop    225.39
stop    23

<Run of Program 2.2>

start = 55    breakloop = 225.39    stop = 23
*/
```

2.10 Array and Record Applications

Arrays and records are built-in data structures in most programming languages. This chapter introduces ADTs for these structures and discusses their C++ implementation. We use these structures to develop important algorithms throughout the book. An array is a fundamental data structure for lists. For many applications, we use search and sort utilities to find an item in an array-based list and to order the data. This section introduces the sequential search and the exchange sort that are simple to code and understand.

SEQUENTIAL SEARCH

A sequential search looks for an item in a list using a target value called the **key.** The algorithm begins at a user-supplied index, called start, and traverses the remaining items in the list, comparing each item with the key. The scan continues until the key is found or the list is exhausted. If the key is found, the function returns the index of the matched element in the list; otherwise, the value −1 is returned. The function SeqSearch requires four parameters, the list address, the starting index for the search, the number of elements, and the key. For instance, consider the following integer list contained in the array A:

```
A:        8   3   6   2   6
```

1. Key = 6, Start = 0, n = 5. Search the list from the beginning, returning the index of the first occurrence of element 6.

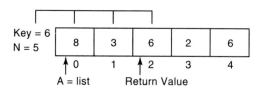

2. Key = 6, Start = 3, n = 2. Start at A[3] and search the list, returning a pointer to the first occurrence of element 6.

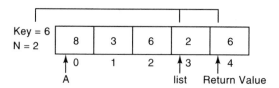

3. Key = 9, Start = 0, n = 5. Start at the first element and search the list for the number 9. Since it is not found, return the value −1.

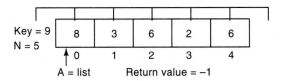

The sequential search algorithm applies to any array for which the operator "==" is defined for the item type. A fully general search algorithm requires templates and operator overloading. These topics are discussed in Chapters 6 and 7. The following function implements the sequential search for an integer array.

Sequential Search Function

```
int SeqSearch(int list[], int start, int n, int key)
{
        for(int i=start;i < n;i++)
                if (list [i] == key)
                        return i;
        }
        return -1;
}
```

Program 2.3 Repeated Search

This program tests the sequential search by counting the number of occurrences of a key in a list. The main program first inputs 10 integers into an array A and then prompts for a key.

The program makes repeated calls to SeqSearch using a different index start. Initially, we start at index 0, the beginning of the array. After each call to SeqSearch, the count of the number of occurrences is incremented if the key is found; otherwise the search terminates and the count is output. If the key is found, the return value identifies its position in the list. The next call to SeqSearch is made with start set to the element immediately to the right.

```
#include <iostream.h>

// search the n element integer array a for a match with key
// return a pointer to the data or NULL if key not found.
int SeqSearch(int list[], int start, int n, int key)
{
    for(int i=start;i < n;i++)
        if (list[i] == key)
            return i;          // return index of matching item
    return -1;                 // search failed. return −1
}

void main(void)
{
    int A[10];
    int key, count = 0, pos;

    // prompt for and enter a list of 10 integers
    cout << "Enter a list of 10 integers: ";
    for (pos=0; pos < 10; pos++)
        cin >> A[pos];

    cout << "Enter a key: ";
    cin >> key;

    // start search at first array element
    pos = 0;

    // move through list as long as key is found
    while ((pos = SeqSearch(A,pos,10,key)) != -1)
    {
        count++;
        // move to next integer after match
        pos++;
    }

    cout << key << " occurs " << count
         << (count != 1 ? " times" : " time")
         << " in the list." << endl;
}

/*
<Run of Program 2.3>

Enter a list of 10 integers: 5 2 9 8 1 5 8 7 5 3
Enter a key: 5
5 occurs 3 times in the list
*/
```

EXCHANGE SORT

The ordering of items in a list is important for many applications. For instance, an inventory list may sort records by their part numbers to allow quick access to an item, a dictionary maintains words in alphabetical order, and the registrar orders student records by social security number.

To create an ordered list, we introduce a sorting algorithm, called the **ExchangeSort** that orders the items in ascending order. The algorithm is illustrated with the list 8, 3, 6, 2 and produces the ordered list 2, 3, 6, 8.

Index 0: Consider the full list 8, 3, 6, 2. The item at index 0 is compared with each subsequent item in the list at index 1, 2, and 3. For each comparison, if the subsequent item is smaller than the element at index 0, the two entries are exchanged. After making all the comparisons, the smallest element is located at index 0.

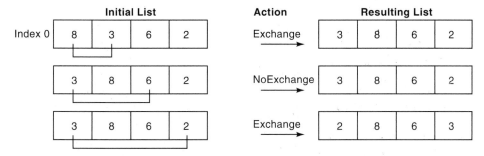

Index 1: With the smallest element already located at index 0, consider the sublist 8, 6, 3. Only the items from index 1 to the end of the list are considered. The item at index 1 is compared with the subsequent items at index 2 and 3. For each comparison, if the larger element is at index 1, the two entries are exchanged. After making the comparisons, the second smallest element in the list is stored at index 1.

Index 2: Consider the sublist 8, 6. The process continues for the two item sublist with indices 2 and 3. A single comparison, resulting in an exchange, is made between the items.

Index 2	Initial List				Action	Resulting List			
	2	3	8	6	Exchange	2	3	6	8

We are left with only the single item at index 3 and the list is sorted.

Final Sorted List

2	3	6	8

The C++ ExchangeSort function uses nested loops. Assume the list size is given by n. An outer loop increments index i through the range 0 to n − 2. For each index i, compare the subsequent items at indices j = i + 1, i + 2, ... n − 1. Make the comparison and then exchange (swap) elements if list[i] > list[j].

Program 2.4   Sorting a List

This program illustrates the sort algorithm. A list of 15 integers in the range of 0 to 99 fill a list. ExchangeSort orders the list, using the function Swap to exchange two array elements. The program prints the list before and after the sort.

```cpp
#include <iostream.h>

// interchange the values of the two integer variables x and y
void Swap(int & x, int & y)
{
    int temp = x;      // store original value of x

    x = y;             // replace x by y
    y = temp;          // assign y the original value of x
}

// sort the n element integer array a in ascending order.
void ExchangeSort(int a[], int n)
{
    int i, j;

    // implement n-1 passes. locate correct values in
    // a[0],...,a[n-2].
    for(i = 0; i < n-1; i++)
        // put minumum of a[i+1]...a[n-1] in a[i]
        for(j = i+1; j < n; j++)
            // exchange if a[i] > a[j]
            if (a[i] > a[j])
                Swap(a[i], a[j]);
}

// step through the list and print each value.
void PrintList(int a[], int n)
{
```

```
    for (int i = 0; i < n; i++)
        cout << a[i] << "   ";
    cout << endl;
}

void main(void)
{
    int list[15] = {38,58,13,15,51,27,10,19,
                    12,86,49,67,84,60,25};
    int i;

    cout << "Original List \n";
    PrintList(list,15);
    ExchangeSort(list,15);
    cout << endL <<"Sorted List" << endL;
    PrintList(list,15);
}

/*
<Run of Program 2.4>

Original List
38   58   13   15   51   27   10   19   12   86   49   67   84   60   25

Sorted List
10   12   13   15   19   25   27   38   49   51   58   60   67   84   86
*/
```

COUNTING C++ RESERVED WORDS

Section 2.8 discusses the record type that is implemented in C++ as a struct. As an illustration of records, a program computes the number of times the reserved words "else", "for", "if", "include", and "while" occur in a C++ program. The program uses string variables as well as an array of records.

The primary data structure of the program is the struct KeyWord whose fields consist of the string variable keyword and the integer count:

```
struct KeyWord
{
    char keyword[20];
    int  count;
};
```

A table for the five reserved words is created in the array KeyWordTable. Each item in the table is initialized by specifying the reserved word and an initial count of 0. For instance, the first array initializer {"else",0} causes the entry KeyWordTable[0] to contain the string "else" with a count of 0:

```
KeyWord KeyWordTable[] =
{
    {"else", 0},{"for", 0},{"if", 0},{"include", 0}, {"while", 0}
};
```

The program reads the individual words in a file with the function GetWord. A word is any sequence of characters that begins with a letter and continues with an optional number of letters or digits. For instance, when presented the line

```
"Expression: 3 + 5 = 8 (N1 + N2 = N3)"
```

GetWord extracts the words "Expression", "N1", "N2", and "N3" and discards the other symbols.

The function SeqSearch scans the table looking for a match on the keyword. When a match occurs, the function returns the index of the matching record, which can then have its count field incremented.

Program 2.5   Count Reserved Words

This program reads its own source code as input. A loop reads each word and calls SeqSearch to determine if the input matches a reserved word in KeyWordTable. If so, we increment the count field of the record. After completing the input, the number of occurrences of each keyword is printed.

The program illustrates an interesting statement that dynamically computes the number of elements in the array KeyWordTable, using the expression

```
sizeof(KeyWordTable)/sizeof(KeyWord)
```

This expression provides a machine-independent method of computing the number of elements in an array. If other keywords are added to the table, a subsequent compilation generates a new element count.

```
#include <iostream.h>
#include <fstream.h>
#include <string.h>       // must include if string functions used
#include <ctype.h>        // provides isalpha and isdigit
#include <stdlib.h>

// declare the word structure
struct KeyWord
{
        char keyword[20];
        int  count;
};
```

```
// declare and initialize the table of keywords
KeyWord KeyWordTable[] =
{
    {"else", 0}, {"for", 0},{"if", 0},{"include", 0},{"while", 0}
};


// a customized sequential search algorithm for keywords
int SeqSearch(KeyWord *tab, int n, char *word)
{
    int i;

    // scan list. compare word with keyword in current record
    for (i=0; i < n; i++, tab++)
        if (strcmp(word, tab->keyword) == 0)
            return i;            // return index if match
    return -1;                   // sorry, no match
}


// extract a word beginning with a letter and possibly
// other letters/digits
int GetWord (ifstream& fin, char w[])
{
    char c;
    int  i = 0;

    // skip non-alphabetic input
    while ( fin.get(c) && !isalpha(c))
        ;

    // return 0 (Failure) on end of file
    if (fin.eof())
        return 0;

    // record 1st letter of the word
    w[i++] = c;

    // collect letters and digits and NULL terminate string
    while (fin.get(c) && (isalpha(c) || isdigit(c)))
        w[i++] = c;
    w[i] = "\0";

    return  1;               // return 1 (Success)
}


void main(void)
{
    const int MAXWORD = 50;            // max size of any word
```

```
    // declare the table size and initialize its value
    const int NKEYWORDS = sizeof(KeyWordTable)/sizeof(KeyWord);

    int n;
    char word[MAXWORD], c;
    ifstream  fin;

    // open file with error checking
    fin.open("prg2_5.cpp",ios::in | ios::nocreate);
    if (!fin)
    {
        cerr << "Could not open file 'prg2_5.cpp'" << endl;
        exit (1);
    }


    // extract words until end of file
    while (GetWord(fin, word))
        // if a match in keyword table, increment count
        if ((n = SeqSearch(KeyWordTable, NKEYWORDS,word)) != -1)
            KeyWordTable[n].count++;

    // scan the keyword table and print record fields
    for (n = 0; n < NKEYWORDS; n++)
        if (KeyWordTable[n].count > 0)
        {
            cout << KeyWordTable[n].count;
            cout << "  " << KeyWordTable[n].keyword << endl;
        }
    fin.close();
}
/*
<Run of Program 2.5>

1  else
3  for
9  if
7  include
4  while
*/
```

Written Exercises

2.1 Compute the decimal value of each binary number:

    (a)   101   (b)   1110   (c)   110111   (d)   1111111

2.2 Write each decimal number in binary:

(a) 23   (b) 55   (c) 85   (d) 253

2.3 On modern computer systems, addresses are usually implemented at the hardware level as 16-bit or 32-bit binary values. It is natural to deal with addresses in binary rather than converting them to decimal. Since numbers of this size are cumbersome to write as a string of binary digits, base 16 or **hexadecimal** numbers are used. Such numbers, referred to as hex numbers, are an important representation for integers and permit an easy conversion to and from binary. Most system software deals with machine addresses in hex.

Hex numbers are constructed from a base of 16 with digits in the range 0–15 (decimal). The first 10 digits are inherited from the decimal numbers: 0, 1, 2, 3, . . . , 9. The digits from 10–15 are represented by A, B, C, D, E, and F. The powers of 16 are $16^0 = 1$ $16^1 = 16$ $16^2 = 256$ $16^3 = 4096$ and so on. In positional notation form, sample hex numbers are 17E, 48, and FFFF8000. The numbers are converted to decimal by expanding the powers of 16 just like the powers of 2 are expanded for binary numbers.

For instance, the hex number $2A3F_{16}$ is converted to decimal by expanding the powers of 16.

$$2A3F_{16} = 2(16^3) + A(16^2) + 3(16^1) + F(16^0)$$
$$= 2(4096) + 10(256) + 3(16) + 15(1)$$
$$= 8192 + 2560 + 48 + 15 = 10185_{10}$$

Convert each hexadecimal number to decimal.

(a) 1A   (b) 41F   (c) 10EC   (d) FF   (e) 10000

Convert each decimal number to hexadecimal.

(f) 23   (g) 87   (h) 115   (i) 255

2.4 The primary reason for introducing hex numbers is their natural correspondence with binary numbers. They permit compact representation of binary data and memory addresses. Hex digits have a 4-bit binary representation in the range 0–15. The following table lists the correspondence between binary and hex digits.

Hex and Binary Digits	Hex	Binary	Hex	Binary
	0	0000	8	1000
	1	0001	9	1001
	2	0010	A	1010
	3	0011	B	1011
	4	0100	C	1100
	5	0101	D	1101
	6	0110	E	1110
	7	0111	F	1111

To represent a binary number in hex, start at the right-hand end of the number and partition the bits into groups of four, adding leading 0s to the last group on the left, if necessary. Write each group of 4 bits as a hex digit. For example:

$$111100011101110_2 = 0111 \quad 1000 \quad 1110 \quad 1110 = 78EE_{16}$$

To convert from a hex number to a binary number, reverse the process and write each hex digit as 4 bits. Consider the following example:

$$A789_{16} = 1010 \quad 0111 \quad 1000 \quad 1001 = 1010011110001001_2$$

Convert from binary to hex.

(a)   1100   (b)   1010   0110   (c)   1111   0010
(d)   1011   1101   1110   0011

Convert from hex to binary.

(e) 0610_{16} (f) $AF20_{16}$

2.5   C++ enables the programmer to input and output numbers in hex. By placing the manipulator "hex" in the stream, the mode for input or output of numbers is hex. The mode stays in effect until it returns to decimal with the manipulator "dec". For instance:

```
cin >> hex >> t >> dec >> u; // t is read as hex; u as decimal
<input 100 256> t = 100₁₆ and u = 256₁₀
```

```
cout << hex << 100 << t << u; // output is 64  100  100
cout << dec << 100 << t << u; // output is 100 256  256
```

Consider the following declaration and executable statements:

```
int i, j, k;

cin >> i;
cin >> hex >> j >> dec;
cin >> k;
```

(a)   Assume <input> is 50   50   32. What is the output for the statement?

```
cout << hex << i << " " << j << " " << dec << k << endl;
```

(b)   Assume <input> is 32 32 64. What is the output for the statement?

```
cout << dec << i << " " << hex << j << " " << k << endl;
```

2.6   Write a complete specification for the operator % in the integer ADT. Do the same for the comparison operator !=.

2.7   The Boolean type defines data that have values of True or False. Some programming languages define a native type Boolean with a series of built-in functions to process the data. C++ associates a Boolean value with each numeric expression.

(a) Define a Boolean ADT that describes the domain of the data and its operations.

(b) Describe an implementation of the ADT using C++ language constructs.

2.8 (a) What ASCII character corresponds to the decimal number 78?

(b) What ASCII character corresponds to the binary number 1001011_2?

(c) What are the ASCII codes for the characters "*", "q", and a carriage return? Give your answers in decimal and binary.

2.9 What is printed by the following code fragment?

```
cout << char(86) << "  "<< int('q') <<"  "<<
       char(int("0") + 8) << endl;
```

2.10 Explain why the operator % (remainder) is not given in the ADT for real numbers.

2.11 Convert each fixed-point binary number to decimal:

(a) 110.110

(b) 1010.0101

(c) 1110.00001

(d) 11.111 ... 111 ... (*Hint:* Use the formula for the sum of a geometric series.)

2.12 Convert each fixed-point decimal number to binary:

(a) 2.25

(b) 1.125

(c) 1.0875

2.13 (a) In the ADT for real numbers, is there a smallest positive real number? Why or why not?

(b) When real numbers are implemented on a computer, is there a smallest positive real number? Why or why not?

2.14 The IEEE floating point format stores the sign of the number separately and stores the exponent and mantissa as unsigned numbers. A normalized form permits a unique representation for each floating point number.

Normalized form: The floating point number is adjusted to have a single nonzero digit to the left of the binary point.

$$N = \pm 1.d_1d_2 \ . \ . \ . \ d_{n-1} \times 2^e$$

The floating-point number 0.0 is stored with sign, exponent, and mantissa of 0.

As an example, two binary numbers are converted to a normalized form representation.

Binary Number	Normalized Form
1101.101×2^1	1.1011010×2^4
0.0011×2^6	1.1×2^3

Thirty-two-bit floating point numbers are stored in normalized form using internal IEEE format:

Sign   The left-most bit is used for the sign. A "+" has 0 sign bit, and a "-" has a 1 sign bit.

Exponent The exponent is stored in 8 bits. In order to ensure that all exponents are stored as positive (unsigned) numbers, the IEEE format specifies using "excess-127" notation for the exponent. The stored exponent, Exp_s, is created by adding 127 to the real exponent.

$$Exp_s = Exp + 127$$

True Exponent Range	Stored Exponent Range

$$-127 \leq Exp \leq 128 \quad 0 \leq Exps \leq 255$$

Mantissa Assuming that the number is stored in normalized form, the leading 1 digit is hidden. The fractional digits are stored in a 23-bit mantissa, given 24 bits of precision.

Sign	Exponent	Mantissa
1 bit	8 bits	23 bits

As an example, we compute the internal representation of -0.1875.

Normalized Form	$(-)\, 1.100 \times 2^{-3}$
Sign	1
Exponent	$Exp_s = -3 + 127 = 124 = 01111100_2$
Mantissa	$<1>\, 1000000 \ldots 0$

$$-0.1875 = 10111110010000000000000000000000$$

Record each number in 32-bit IEEE floating point notation.

(a) 7.5   (b) $-1/4$

What is the value of the following 32-bit IEEE formatted numbers in decimal form? Each number is given in hex.

(c) C1800000   (d) 41E90000

2.15 (a) List in calendar order the months of the year that have an "r" in their name. This is an enumerated type.

(b) Write a C++ implementation of the enumerated type.

(c) In the C++ implementation, which month corresponds to the integer 4? What is the position of October?

(d) Write the enum in alphabetical order. Do any months have the same position in both lists?

2.16 Add successor and predecessor operations to the ADT for enumerated types. Use complete specifications. The successor returns the next item in the list, and the predecessor returns the previous item. Be careful to define what happens at the extreme ends of the list.

2.17 Given the following declarations and statements, specify the contents of X, Y, and A after the statements execute:

```
int X=4, Y=7, *PX = &X, *PY;
double A[] = {2.3, 4.5, 8.9, 1.0, 5.5, 3.5}, *PA = A;
PY = &Y; (*PX)--; *PY += *PX; PY = PX;
*PY = 55; *PA += 3.0; PA++; *PA++ = 6.8;
PA += 2;
*++PA = 3.3;
```

2.18 (a) A is declared as

```
short A[5];
```

How many bytes are allocated for array A? If the address of the array is A = 6000, compute the addresses of A[3] and A[1].

(b) Assume the declaration

```
long A[] = {30, 500000, -100000, 5, 33};
```

If a long word is 4 bytes and the address of A is 2050,

- What is the contents at address 2066?
- Double the contents at address 2050 and address 2062. Write out the array A.
- What is the address of A[3]?

2.19 Assume A is an m × n array with row indices in the range of 0 to (m−1) and column indices in the range of 0 to (n−1). Generate an access function that computes the address of A[row][col] assuming that the elements are stored by columns.

2.20 A is declared as

```
short A[5][6];
```

(a) How many bytes are allocated for array A?
(b) If the address of the array is A = 1000, compute the addresses of A[3][2] and A[1][4].
(c) What array entry is located at address 1020? At address 1034?

2.21 (a) Declare a string NAME with the initial value of your first name.
(b) Consider the string variable declarations

```
char s1[50], s2[50];
```

and the input statements

```
cin >> S1 >> S2;
```

What is the value of S1 and S2 for input line "George flies!"?
What is the value of S1 and S2 on input of the following text (◇ is the blank character, and ¶ is end of line.)?:

```
Next¶
◇◇◇◇◇Word
```

2.22 Assume the following string declarations:

```
char S1[30] = "Stockton, CA", S2[30] = "March 5, 1994", *p;
char S3[30];
```

(a) What is the value of *p after executing each of the following statements?

```
p = strchr(S1, 't');
p = strrchr (S1, 't');
p = strrchr (S2, '6');
```

(b) What is the value in S3 after executing

```
strcpy (S3,S1);
strcat (S3,", ");
strcat (S3,S2);
```

(c) What is returned by the function call strcmp (S1,S2)?
(d) What is returned by the function call strcmp (&S1[5],"ton")?

2.23 The function

```
void strinsert(char *s, char *t, int i);
```

inserts string *t* into string *s* starting at index *i*. If *i* is greater than the length of *s*, the insert is not performed. Implement strinsert using the C++ library functions strlen, strcpy, and strcat. You will need to declare a temporary string variable to hold the original characters in *s* from index *i* to index strlen(s) −1. You may assume that this tail never exceeds 127 characters.

2.24 The function

```
void strdelete(char *s, int i, int n);
```

deletes a sequence of *n* characters from string *s* starting at index *i*. If *i* is greater than or equal to length of *s*, then no characters are deleted. If i + *n* is greater than or equal to the length of *s*, the end of the string is removed starting at index *i*. Implement strdelete using the C++ library functions strlen and strcpy.

2.25 An alternative to using NULL-terminated strings is to place the character count in the first element of the character array. This is called byte count format, and such strings are often called Pascal strings, since Pascal programming systems use this string format.

(a) Implement the function strcat assuming the strings are stored in byte count format.

(b) The functions PtoCStr and CtoPStr perform inplace conversion between the two string formats:

```
void PtoCStr(char *s); // convert s from Pascal to C++
void CtoPStr(char *s); // convert s from C++ to Pascal
```

Implement these two functions.

2.26 Add the assignment operator "=" to the record ADT using a complete specification. Carefully define what action takes place during assignment.

2.27 A complex number is of the form $x + iy$, where $i^2 = -1$. Complex numbers have vast applications in mathematics, physics, and engineering. They have an arithmetic governed by a series of rules including the following:

Let u = a + ib, v = c +id

$$u + v = (a + c) + i(b + d)$$
$$u - v = (a - c) + i(b - d)$$
$$u * v = (ac - bd) + i(ad + bc)$$
$$u / v = \frac{ac + bd}{c^2 + d^2} + i\left(\frac{bc - ad}{c^2 + d^2}\right)$$

Represent a complex number using the record structure:

```
struct Complex
{
   float real;
   float imag;
};
```

and implement the following functions that perform complex operations:

```
Complex cadd(Complex& x, Complex& y); // x + y
Complex csub(Complex& x, Complex& y); // x - y
Complex cmul(Complex& x, Complex& y); // x * y
Complex cdiv(Complex& x, Complex& y); // x / y
```

2.28 Add the operation FileSize to the ADT for streams. It must return the number of characters in the file. Carefully specify what preconditions must exist for this operation to make sense. (*Hint:* What about cin/cout?)

2.29 Carefully distinguish between a text and a binary file. Do you think it is possible to develop a program that takes a file name as input and determine whether it is a text or binary file?

Programming Exercises

2.1 Write a function

```
void BaseOut(unsigned int n, int b);
```

that outputs n in the base b, $2 \leq b \leq 10$. Print each number in the range $2 \leq n \leq 50$ in base 2, 4, 5, 8 and 9.

2.2 Write a function

```
void OctIn(unsigned int& n);
```

that reads a base 8 (octal) number and assigns it to n. Use OctIn in a main program that reads the following octal numbers and prints the decimal equivalents:

7, 177, 127, 7776, 177777

2.3 Write a program that declares three integer variables i, j, k. Input a value for i in decimal and values for j and k in hex. Print all three variables in both hex and decimal.

2.4 Examine the granularity of the real number representation on your computer by computing $1 + D$ for $D = 1/10, 1/100, 1/1000, \ldots, 1/10^n$ until $1 + D == 1.0$. If you have access to more than one machine architecture, try it on other machines.

2.5 Consider the enumerated type

```
enum DaysOfWeek {Sun,Mon,Tues,Wed,Thurs,Fri,Sat};
```

Write a function

```
void GetDay(DaysOfWeek& day);
```

that reads the name of a day from the keyboard as a string and assigns the corresponding enum value to day. Also write a function

```
void PutDay(DaysOfWeek day)
```

that writes the enum value to the screen. Develop a main program to test the two functions.

2.6 Input a series of words until end of file, converting each one to Pig-latin. If the word begins with a consonant, move the first character of the word to the last position and append "ay". If the word begins with a vowel, simply append "ay". for example,

Input: this is simple
Output: histay isay implesay

2.7 A string of text can be encrypted using a tabular mapping that associates each letter of the alphabet with a unique letter. For example, the mapping

```
abcdefghijklmnopqrstuvwxyz ==> ngzqtcobmuhelkpdawxfyivrsj
```

maps "encrypt" to "tkzwsdf".

Write a program that reads text until end of file and outputs the encrypted form.

2.8 Have your program create the tabular mapping that reverses the mapping used in Programming Exercise 2.7 Input an encrypted file and print its decrypted form.

2.9 Write a program that causes one or more array indices to go out of bounds. Make the situation bad enough so the program "crashes". Pretend that you do not know what the problem is. Use any debugger available to you and diagnose the cause of the behavior.

2.10 Modify the exchange sort so it sorts the list in descending order. Test the new algorithm by writing a main program similar to Program 2.4.

2.11 Consider the record declaration

```
struct Month
{
    char name[10];   // name of a month
    int monthnum;    // number of days in the month
};
```

(a) Write a function

```
void SortByName(Month months[], int n);
```

that sorts an array whose elements are of type month by comparing names (use C++ function strcmp). Also write a function

```
void SortByDays(Month months[], int n);
```

that sorts the list by comparing the number of days in a month. Write a main program that declares an array containing all the months of the year and sorts it using both functions. Print each sorted list.

(b) Note that sorting a list of months by number of days produces ties. When this happens a sorting method can use a **secondary key** to break ties. Write the function

```
void Sort2ByDays(Month months[], int n);
```

that sorts the list by first comparing the number of days and, if a tie occurs, breaks the tie by comparing names. Use the function in a main program to print out an ordered list of all the months in the year, ordered by number of days.

2.12 Write a program that reads a text file and prints a count of the number of occurrences of the punctuation marks (. , ! ?).

2.13 Using cin.getline, read a line beginning with a single character function name and followed by sequences of "x" with the characters "+" or "−" interspersed. A line may not end with "+" or "−". Form a string of the form

```
SingleCharFuncName(x)  = x**n ± x**m ± . . .
```

in an array using array-based output. If the exponent is 1, omit "**1". Write each string to a file "funcs.val". For example, the lines

```
F x x x + x x - x
G x x - x x x + x x x x
```

produce the file "funcs.val" having lines

```
F(x)  = x**3 + x**2 - x
G(x)  = x**2 - x**3 + x**4
```

2.14 Write a program that enters an N x N matrix A of integer values and prints the trace of the matrix. The trace is defined as the sum of the diagonal elements.

```
Trace (A)  = A[0, 0] + A[1, 1] + · · · + A[N − 1, N − 1]
```

2.15 This exercise uses the results of Written Exercise 2.27. Write a function f(z) that evaluates the complex polynomial function:

$$z^3 - 3z^2 + 4z - 2$$

Evaluate the polynomial for the following values of z:

```
z = 2 + 3i, -1 + i, 1 + i, 1 - i, 1 + 0i
```

Note the last three values are roots of f.

C H A P T E R 3

ABSTRACT DATA
TYPES AND CLASSES

Chapter 1 introduced abstract data types (ADTs) and their representation as C++ classes. The introductory material describes the structure of a class, which provides data encapsulation and information hiding. In this chapter, we provide an in-depth study of basic class concepts. We study the design and use of class constructors, implementation of class methods, and the use of classes with other data structures. To ensure that the reader has a good understanding of classes, we develop a wide range of examples and use them in complete programs. Appropriately chosen ADTs illustrate the relationship between the abstract structure and the class declaration.

3.1   The User Type CLASS

A **class** is a user-defined type with data items and functions (**methods**), called **members** of the class. A variable of the class type is called an **object.** A class creates different levels of access to its members by partitioning the declaration into private, protected, and public parts. A **private** part of an object can be accessed only by member functions in the class. A **public** part of an object can be accessed by external program units that have the object within their scope (Figure 3.1). **Protected** members are used with derived classes and are discussed in Chapter 12 on inheritance.

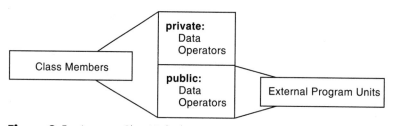

Figure 3.1   Access to Class Methods

CLASS DECLARATION

A class declaration begins with the **class head,** which consists of the reserved word **class** followed by the name of the class. The members are given in the **class body,** which is enclosed by braces and terminated with a semicolon. The reserved words **public** and **private** partition the members of the class, and these access specifiers are terminated by a colon. The data members are declared as C++ variables, and the methods are given as C++ function declarations. Here is the general form of a class declaration:

```
class <ClassName>
{
   private:
   // <Private data>
   // <Private method declarations>
   // . . . . . . . .
```

```
    public:
    // <Public data>
    // <Public method declarations>
    // . . . . . . . .
};
```

In general, it is a good idea to place the data members of a class in the private section. As a result, a data value is updated only by a member function. This avoids inadvertent changes to the data by the application code.

EXAMPLE 3.1
_____

THE RECTANGLE CLASS

For geometric measurement, a rectangle is determined by its length and width. These measurements allow us to compute the perimeter and area of the figure. The length and width data parameters and the operations combine to form an abstract data type for a rectangular figure. We leave the specification of the ADT as an exercise and design the C++ Rectangle class that implements the ADT. The class has a constructor and a set of methods—GetLength, PutLength, GetWidth, and PutWidth—that access the private data members. The following is a declaration of the Rectangle class:

```
class Rectangle
{
    private:
        // length and width of the rectangle object
        float length,width;
    public:
        // constructor
        Rectangle(float l = 0, float w = 0);
        // methods to retrieve and modify private data
        float GetLength(void) const;
        void  PutLength(float l);
        float GetWidth(void) const;
        void  PutWidth(float w);

        // compute and return rectangle measurements
        float Perimeter(void) const;
        float Area(void) const;
};
```

Note that the methods GetLength, GetWidth, Perimeter, and Area have the keyword **const** after the parameter list. This declares each to be a constant method. In the definition of a constant method, no class data item may be modified. In other words, executing a method declared as const does not change the state of the Rectangle object.

The private and public sections of the Rectangle class are clearly delineated. If the first access specifier is skipped, the initial members in a class are private by default. The members are private down to the first occurrence of a public or protected specification. C++ allows the programmer to interleave private, protected, and public sections, although this is not a recommended style.

CONSTRUCTOR

A function, called a class **constructor,** has the same name as the class. Like other C++ functions, a constructor can be passed parameters that are used to initialize one or more of the data members. In the Rectangle class, the constructor is given the name Rectangle and receives parameters l and w, which are used to initialize the length and width of an object, respectively. Note that the parameters have default values that indicate that the value 0 is used when parameter l or w is not explicitly passed.

Example 3.1 illustrates the **class declaration** since the methods are described only by function declarations. The C++ code to define the individual functions creates the **class implementation.**

OBJECT DECLARATION

A class declaration describes a new data type. The action of declaring an object of the class type creates an **instance** of the class. The declaration instantiates ("makes real") an object of the class type and automatically calls the constructor to initialize some or all data members. Parameters for the object are passed to the constructor by enclosing them in parentheses after the name of the object. Note that the constructor does not have a return type because it is called only during the creation of an object:

```
ClassName  object(<parameters>);  // parameter list may be empty
```

For instance, the following declarations create two objects of type Rectangle:

```
Rectangle room(12,10);
Rectangle t;                // use default parameters (0, 0)
```

Each object has the full range of data members and methods declared in the class. The public members are accessed by using the object name and the member name separated by a "." (period). For instance,

```
x = room.Area();          // assigns area = 12 * 10 = 120 to x
t.PutLength(20);          // assigns 20 as length of Rectangle
                         // obj. Currently the length is 0 since
                         // the default parameters are used.
cout << t.GetWidth();     // outputs the current width which is 0
                         // by default
```

In the declaration of object Room, the constructor initially sets length to 12 and width to 10. The client can change the dimensions by using the access methods PutLength and PutWidth:

```
room.PutLength(15);   // change length and width to 15 and 12
room.PutWidth(12);
```

A class declaration does not have to include a constructor. This action, which is not advised or used in the book, leaves an object with uninitialized data at the point of its declaration. For instance, the Rectangle class could avoid a constructor and have the client assign the length and width with public access methods. By including a constructor, we ensure that critical data is properly initialized. A constructor allows the object to initialize its own data members.

The Rectangle class contains data members of type float. In general, a class may contain items of any valid C++ type, even other classes. However, a class may not contain an object of its own type as a member.

CLASS IMPLEMENTATION

A definition must be provided for each method in the class declaration. The function definitions can be given inside the class body as inline code or can be written outside the class body. When placed outside the body, the class name, followed by a double colon, is prepended to the function name. The "::" symbol is called the **scope resolution operator** and indicates that the function belongs to the scope of the class. This allows all statements in the function definition to access the private members of the class. In the case of the Rectangle class, the identifier "Rectangle::" is prepended to the method names.

The following is the definition of GetLength() when it is written outside of the Rectangle class body:

```
float Rectangle::GetLength(void) const
{
    return length;    // access the private member length
}
```

Note that the const qualifier must also be used in the definition of a constant method.

A class member function may be written inside of the class body. In this situation, the code is expanded inline. There is no scope resolution operator since the code lies within the scope of the class body. The following is the inline definition of the GetLength operation:

```
class Rectangle
{
    private:
        float length;
        float width;

    public:
        . . .
        float GetLength(void) const    // code is given inline
        {
            return(length);
        }
        . . .
};
```

This book generally defines member functions outside of the class body in order to emphasize the distinction between the declaration and implementation of a class. Inline code is used sparingly in the book.

IMPLEMENTING A CONSTRUCTOR

The constructor can be defined inline or outside of the class body. For instance, the following code defines the Rectangle constructor:

```
Rectangle::Rectangle(float l, float w)
{
    length = l;
    width = w;
}
```

C++ provides special syntax to initialize data members. The **member initialization list** is a comma-separated list of class member data names, each followed by the initial value for the data enclosed in parentheses. The initial values are normally constructor parameters, which act to assign the parameter values to the corresponding data members in the list. The member initialization list is placed after the function header and separated from the parameter list by a colon:

```
ClassName::ClassName(parm list): data₁(parm₁),..., dataₙ(parmₙ)
```

For instance, the constructor parameters l and w can be assigned to the data members length and width:

```
Rectangle::Rectangle(float l, float w) : length(l), width(w)
{ }
```

BUILDING OBJECTS

One object can be used to initialize another in a declaration. For instance, the following statement is valid:

```
Rectangle square(10,10), yard = square, S;
```

The object square is created with a length and width of 10. The second object yard is created with initial data copied from object square. Object S has a default length and width of 0.

Objects can be freely assigned to one another. Unless the user creates a customized assignment operator, object assignment is done with a bitwise copy of data members. For instance, the assignment

```
S = yard;
```

copies all of the data from object yard into object S. In this case, the length and width of object yard is copied to the length and width in S.

An object can be created by referencing its constructor. For instance, the declaration Rectangle(10,5) creates a temporary object with the length = 10 and width = 5. In the following statement, the assignment operator copies data from the temporary object to rectangle S:

```
S = Rectangle(10,5);
```

EXAMPLE 3.2

1. The statements

    ```
    S = Rectangle(10,5);
    cout << S.Area() << endl;
    ```

    produce the output 50.
2. The statement

    ```
    cout << Rectangle(10,5).GetWidth() << endl;
    ```

    prints 5.

Program 3.1   Using the Rectangle Class

This program considers the relative cost of finishing the front of a garage. The user supplies the dimensions of the garage front, and the program supplies the various door sizes and door costs. The user notes that by choosing a larger door, less siding and molding material is required. Given the cost of lumber, a larger door may be cost effective.

Assume the molding goes around the perimeter of the front and the perimeter of the door opening. We prompt the user for the size of the garage front and then enter a loop allowing the selection of a door size. The loop terminates when the "Quit" option is exercised. For each door selection, the program determines the cost of finishing the garage front and outputs the value. We fix the cost of wood siding at $2 per square foot and the cost of molding at $0.50 per linear foot.

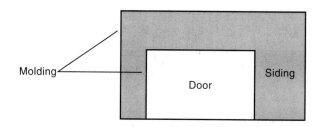

The length of the molding is the sum of the perimeters of the garage front and the door. The cost of the siding is the area of the garage front less the area of the door.

```cpp
#include <iostream.h>

class Rectangle
{
    private:
        // length and width of the rectangle object
        float length,width;
    public:
        // constructor
        Rectangle(float l = 0, float w = 0);

        // methods to retrieve and modify private data
        float GetLength(void) const;
        void  PutLength(float l);
        float GetWidth(void) const;
        void  PutWidth(float w);

        // compute and return rectangle measurements
        float Perimeter(void) const;
        float Area(void) const;
};
```

```cpp
// constructor. assign l to length and w to width
Rectangle::Rectangle (float l, float w) : length(l), width(w)
{}

// return the length of the rectangle
float Rectangle::GetLength (void) const
{
    return length;
}

// allow client to assign new value l to length of rectangle
void Rectangle::PutLength (float l)
{
    length = l;
}

// return the width of the rectangle
float Rectangle::GetWidth (void) const
{
    return width;
}

// allow client to assign new value w to width of rectangle
void Rectangle::PutWidth (float w)
{
    width = w;
}

// compute and return the perimeter of the rectangle
float Rectangle::Perimeter (void) const
{
    return 2.0 * (length + width);   // return rectangle perimeter
}

// compute and return the area of the rectangle
float Rectangle::Area (void) const   // return area of rectangle
{
    return length*width;
}

void main(void)
{
    // cost of siding and molding are constants
    const float sidingCost = 2.00, moldingCost = 0.50;

    // initially, selections are not complete
    int completedSelections = 0;
```

```cpp
// option from menu selected by user
char  doorOption;

// length/width and door cost
float glength, gwidth, doorCost;
// total cost includes door,siding,molding
float totalCost;

cout << "Enter the length and width of the garage: ";
cin >> glength >> gwidth;

// create garage object with user supplied dimensions.
// create door object with default dimensions.
Rectangle garage(glength,gwidth);
Rectangle door;


while (!completedSelections)
{
    cout << "Enter 1-4 or 'q' to quit" << endl << endl;
    cout << "Door 1 (12 by 8; $380)      "
         << "Door 2 (12 by 10; $420)" << endl;
    cout << "Door 3 (16 by 8; $450)      "
         << "Door 4 (16 by 10; $480)" << endl;
    cout << endl;

    cin >> doorOption;

    if (doorOption == 'q')
       completedSelections = 1;     // terminate loop
    else
    {
        switch (doorOption)
        {
            case '1': door.PutLength(12);    // 12x8 ($380)
                      door.PutWidth(8);
                      doorCost = 380;
                      break;

            case '2': door.PutLength(12);    // 12x10 ($420)
                      door.PutWidth(10);
                      doorCost = 420;
                      break;

            case '3': door.PutLength(16);    // 16x8 ($450)
                      door.PutWidth(8);
                      doorCost = 450;
                      break;
```

```
        case '4': door.PutLength(16);    // 16x10 ($480)
                  door.PutWidth(10);
                  doorCost = 480;
                  break;
      }
      totalCost = doorCost +
          moldingCost*(garage.Perimeter()+door.Perimeter())
          + sidingCost*(garage.Area()-door.Area());
      cout << "Total cost of door, siding, and molding: $"
          << totalCost << endl << endl;
    }
  }
}

/*
<Run of Program 3.1>

Enter the length and width of the garage: 20 12
Select the door by number or 'q' to quit

Door 1 (12 by 8; $380)     Door 2 (12 by 10; $420)
Door 3 (16 by 8; $450)     Door 4 (16 by 10; $480)

1
Total cost of door, siding, and molding is $720

Select the door by number or 'q' to quit

Door 1 (12 by 8; $380)     Door 2 (12 by 10; $420)
Door 3 (16 by 8; $450)     Door 4 (16 by 10; $480)

q
*/
```

Sample Classes   3.2

Two sample classes illustrate C++ class constructs. The Temperature class maintains records on high and low temperature values. As an application, an object could hold the high (boiling point) and low (freezing point) temperatures of water. The RandomNumber ADT defines a type for the creation of a sequence of integer or floating-point random numbers. In the C++ implementation, the constructor allows the client to seed the random number sequence or have the program seed the sequence with a system-dependent time function.

THE TEMPERATURE CLASS

The Temperature class holds information on high and low temperature values. A constructor assigns initial values to the two private data members highTemp and lowTemp, which are floating-point numbers. The UpdateTemp method takes a new data value and determines if one of the temperature values in the object should be updated. If the value marks a new low, then lowTemp is revised. Similarly, a new high would change highTemp. The class has two data access methods; GetHighTemp returns the high temperature and GetLowTemp returns the low temperature.

TEMPERATURE CLASS SPECIFICATION

DECLARATION

```
class Temperature
{
    private:
        float highTemp, lowTemp;        // private data members
    public:
        Temperature (float h, float l);
        void UpdateTemp (float temp);
        float GetHighTemp (void) const;
        float GetLowTemp (void) const;
};
```

DISCUSSION

The constructor must be passed the initial high and low temperature for the object. These values can be changed by the method UpdateTemp. The methods GetLowTemp and GetHighTemp are const functions since they do not alter any data members in the class. The class is in "temp.h".

EXAMPLE

```
// boiling/freezing point of water in Fahrenheit
Temperature fwater(212,32);
// boiling/freezing point of water in Celsius
Temperature cwater(100,0);

cout << "Water freezes at " << cwater.GetLowTemp << " C"
     << endl;
cout << "Water boils at " << fwater.GetHighTemp << " F" << endl;

Output:  Water freezes at 0 C
         Water boils at 212 F
```

TEMPERATURE CLASS IMPLEMENTATION

Each method in the class is written outside of the class body using the class scope operator. The constructor passes the initial high and low temperature readings, which are assigned the highTemp and lowTemp fields. These values can only be changed by the UpdateTemp method when a new high or low temperature is passed as a parameter. The access functions GetHighTemp and GetLowTemp return the high temperature and low temperature reading.

```
// constructor. assign data h to highTemp and 1 to lowTemp
Temperature::Temperature(float h, float l): highTemp(h)
                                  lowTemp (l)
{ }

// update current temperature readings if temp produces new high
// or low
void Temperature::UpdateTemp (float temp)
{
     if (temp > highTemp)
         highTemp = temp;
     else if (temp < lowTemp)
         lowTemp = temp;
}

// return the high
float Temperature::GetHighTemp (void) const
{
     return highTemp;
}

// return the low
float Temperature::GetLowTemp (void) const
{
   return lowTemp;
}
```

Program 3.2   Using the Temperature Class

```
#include <iostream.h>

#include "temp.h"    // "temp.h" contains
                         Temperature class

void main(void)
{
    // initialize the temperature object (high=70, low=50)
    Temperature today (70,50);
    float temp;

    cout << "Enter the noon temperature: ";
    cin >> temp;
```

```
                // update object to include noon temperature
                today.UpdateTemp(temp);
                cout << "At noon: High " << today.GetHighTemp();
                cout << "  Low " << today.GetLowTemp() << endl;

                cout << "Enter the evening temperature: ";
                cin >> temp;

                // update object to include evening temperatures
                today.UpdateTemp(temp);
                cout << "Today's High " << today.GetHighTemp();
                cout << "  Low " << today.GetLowTemp() << endl;
        }

        /*
        <Run of Program 3.2>

        Enter the noon temperature: 80
        At noon: High 80  Low 50
        Enter the evening temperature: 40
        Today's High 80  Low 40
        */
```

THE RANDOM NUMBER CLASS

Many applications require random data that represent chance events. Airplane simulation that tests a pilot's response to an unexpected change in the plane's behavior, card games that assume a dealer uses a shuffled deck, and market studies that assume variation in the arrival of customers are all examples of computer applications that rely on random data. A computer uses a **random number generator** that produces numbers in a fixed range in such a way that the numbers are uniformly distributed in the range. The generator uses a deterministic algorithm that begins with an initial data value called the **seed.** The algorithm manipulates the seed to generate a sequence of numbers. This process is deterministic since it takes an initial value and executes a fixed set of instructions. The outcome is uniquely determined by the data and instructions. As such, a computer does not produce truly random numbers, but produces sequences of **pseudorandom numbers** that are uniformly distributed in the range. Owing to the initial dependence on the seed, the generator produces the same sequence when the same seed is used. The ability to repeat a random sequence is used in simulation studies where the application wants to compare different strategies that respond to the same set of random conditions. For instance, a flight simulator uses the same sequence of random numbers to compare the effectiveness of two pilots responding to an airplane emergency. Each pilot is subject to the same set of events. However, a unique simulation is chosen if the seed is varied each time the simulator is run. This uniqueness is appropriate for a game that typically wants to provide a different sequence of events each time the game is played.

Most compilers provide library functions that implement a pseudorandom number generator. Unfortunately, the variation in this implementation across compilers is significant. To provide a random number generator that is portable from system to system, we create a class RandomNumber. The class contains a seed that must be initialized by the client. Corresponding to the initial seed value, the generator produces a pseudorandom sequence. The class allows automatic selection of the seed. This option is chosen when no seed is passed to the constructor and allows the client to create independent pseudorandom sequences.

- -
RANDOMNUMBER CLASS SPECIFICATION

DECLARATION

```
#include <time.h>

// used to generate a random number from the current seed
const unsigned long maxshort = 65536L;
const unsigned long multiplier = 1194211693L;
const unsigned long adder = 12345L;

class RandomNumber
{
    private:
      // private member containing current seed
      unsigned long randSeed;
    public:
      // constructor. default 0 gives automatic seeding
      RandomNumber(unsigned long s = 0);

      // generate random integer 0 <= value <= n-1
      unsigned short Random(unsigned long n);

      // generate random real number 0 <= value < 1.0
      double fRandom(void);
};
```

DESCRIPTION

The initial seed is an unsigned long value. The method Random accepts an unsigned long parameter $n \leq 65536$ and returns a 16-bit unsigned short value in the range $0, \ldots, n - 1$. Note that if the return value of Random is assigned to a signed integer variable, the value may be interpreted as negative unless $n \leq 2^{15} = 32768$. The function fRandom returns a floating-point number in the range $0 \leq \text{fRandom}() < 1.0$.

EXAMPLE

```
RandomNumber rnd;      // uses automatic seeding for the sequence
RandomNumber R(1);     // creates sequence with user seed of 1
```

```
cout << R.fRandom();   // prints real number in the range 0 to 1
// prints 5 random integers in range 0 to 99
for (int i = 0; i < 5; i++)
   cout << R.Random(100) << " ";       // <sample> 93 21 45 5 3
```

EXAMPLE 3.3
_____

CREATING RANDOM DATA

1. The value of a die face is in the range of 1–6 (six choices). To simulate
    the tossing of a die, use the function die.Random(6), which returns values
    in the range 0–5. Then add 1, which translates the random value to the
    correct range.

    ```
    RandomNumber Die;    // use automatic seeding
    dicevalue = die.Random(6) + 1;
    ```

2. The object FNum uses automatic seeding to create the random sequence:

    ```
    RandomNumber FNum;
    ```

    To compute a floating value in the range $50 \leq x < 75$, generate a random
    number in the range 0 to 25 by multiplying the result of fRandom by 25.
    This expands the range of random numbers from 1 unit ($0 \leq x < 1$) to 25
    units ($0 \leq x < 25$). Translate the low end of the new range by adding 50:

    ```
    value = FNum.fRandom()*25 + 50;   // multiply by 25; add 50
    ```

RANDOMNUMBER CLASS IMPLEMENTATION

To create pseudorandom numbers, we use a linear congruential algorithm. The
algorithm uses a large odd constant multiplier and a constant adder along with
the seed to iteratively create random numbers and update the value of the seed:

```
const unsigned long maxshort = 65536;
const unsigned long multiplier = 1194211693;
const unsigned long adder = 12345;
```

The random number sequence begins with an initial value for the long integer
randSeed. The setting of this initial value is called **seeding** the random number
generator and is provided by the constructor.

   The constructor enables the client to pass the seed or to use a system
dependent time function to create the seed. We assume a function time is declared
in the file <time.h>. When called with a parameter of 0, time returns an unsigned
long (32-bit) number specifying the number of seconds that have passed since

a base time. Base times in use include midnight January 1, 1970, and midnight January 1, 1904. In any case, it is a large unsigned long value:

```
// seed the generator
RandomNumber::RandomNumber (unsigned long s)
{
    if (s == 0)
        randSeed = time(0);   // seed using system time
    else
        randSeed = s;         // user supplies the seed
}
```

For each iteration, we use the constants to create a new unsigned long seed:

```
randSeed = multiplier * randSeed + adder;
```

The upper 16 bits of the 32-bit value randSeed are random ("mixed up well") by the multiplication and addition. Our algorithm creates a random number in the range 0 to 65535 by shifting randSeed 16 bits to the right. We map this number into the range 0 ... n−1 by taking the remainder upon division by n. The result is the value of Random(n).

```
// return random integer 0 <= value <= n-1 < 65536
unsigned short RandomNumber::Random (unsigned long n)
{
    randSeed = multiplier * randSeed + adder;
    return (unsigned short)((randSeed >> 16) % n);
}
```

For a floating-point number, we first call the integer method Random(maxshort), which returns the next random number in the range 0 to maxshort − 1. After dividing by double(maxshort), we create a real number in the interval $0 \leq \text{fRandom}() < 1.0$.

```
// return (value in range 0..65535) / 65536
double RandomNumber::fRandom (void)
{
    return Random(maxshort)/double(maxshort);
}
```

The declaration and implementation of RandomNumber is contained in the file "random.h".

Application: Frequency of Heads in Coin Tossing The RandomNumber class is used to simulate the repeated tossing of 10 coins. During the toss, some coins land as heads and the rest as tails. A toss of ten coins has a resulting head count in the range 0–10. Intuitively, you would assume that 0 heads or 10 heads in a toss of 10 coins is relatively unlikely. More likely, the landings would even out and the number of heads would be somewhere in the middle, say 4–6 heads. We will verify this intuition by making a large number (50,000) of repetitions of the toss. An array, head, maintains a count of the number of times the corresponding head count is 0, 1, . . . , 10.

> **head[i]** ($0 \leq i \leq 10$) is the number of times in the 50,000 repetitions that exactly i heads occur during the toss of 10 coins.

Program 3.3   Frequency Graph

The tossing of 10 coins constitutes an event. The method Random with a parameter of 2 creates a single toss of the coin by interpreting the return value of 0 as tails and the return value of 1 as heads. The function TossCoins declares a static RandomNumber object coinToss using automatic seeding. The object is static so each call to TossCoins uses the next value in a single random number sequence. The specified number of coins is tossed by accumulating 10 values produced by CoinToss.Random(2). The result that is returned increments the corresponding count in the array heads.

The program output is a frequency graph for the number of heads. A plot with the number of heads on the x-axis and the relative number of occurrences on the y-axis provides a pictorial representation of what is known as the *binomial distribution.* For each index i, the fraction of events that resulted in exactly i heads is

$$\texttt{heads[i]/float(NTOSSES)}$$

This fraction is used to place the symbol * at a relative location between column 1 and column 72 of the line. The resulting graph is an approximation to the binomial distribution.

```cpp
#include <iostream.h>
#include <iomanip.h>

#include "random.h"      // include random number generator

// toss numberCoins and return the total number of heads
int TossCoins(int numberCoins)
{
    // used for random toss of coins
    static RandomNumber coinToss;
    int i, tosses = 0;

    for (i=0;i < numberCoins;i++)
        // Random(2) = 1 indicates head
        tosses += coinToss.Random(2);
    return tosses;
}
```

```
void main(void)
{
    // number of coins per toss and number of tosses
    const int NCOINS = 10;
    const long NTOSSES = 50000;

    // heads[0]=number of 0 heads, heads[1] one head, etc.
    long i, heads[NCOINS + 1];

    int  j, position;

    // initialize the array tosses
    for (j=0;j <= NCOINS+1;j++)
        heads[j]  = 0;

    // toss coins 50,000 times and record results in array heads
    for (i=0;i < NTOSSES;i++)
        heads[TossCoins(NCOINS)]++;

    // Print out the frequency graph
    for (i=0; i < NCOINS+1;i++)
    {
        position = int(float(heads[i])/float(NTOSSES) * 72);
        cout << setw(6) << i << "   ";
        for (j = 0; j < position-1;j++)
            cout << " ";
        // '*' relative number of tosse resulting in i heads.
        cout << '*' << endl;                              }
    }

}

/*


<Run of Program 3.3>

      0   *
      1   *
      2     *
      3          *
      4              *
      5               *
      6              *
      7          *
      8     *
      9   *
     10   *
*/
```

3.3 Objects and Information Passing

An object is an instance of a data type and as such can be passed as a function parameter or returned as the value of a function. Like other C++ types, an object parameter can be passed by value or by reference. The concepts in this section are illustrated with examples from the Temperature class.

AN OBJECT AS A RETURN VALUE

Any class type can be the return type of a function. For instance, the function SetDailyTemp takes an array of numbers representing temperature readings. The function extracts the maximum and minimum readings from the list and returns a Temperature object with those extreme values.

```
Temperature SetDailyTemp (float reading[], int n)
{
    // create t with 1st reading as both high and low
    Temperature  t(reading[0], reading[0]);

    // update high or low if necessary
    for (int i = 1; i < n; i++)
        t.UpdateTemp(reading[i]);

    // return t with extreme temperatures for the day
    return t;
}
```

The array reading contains six temperature values. To determine the high and low temperatures, call SetDailyTemp and assign the result to the object today. Use the methods GetHighTemp and GetLowTemp to print the temperatures.

```
float reading[6] = {40, 90, 80, 60, 20, 50};

Temperature today = SetDailyTemp(reading,6);

  cout << "Today's high and low temperatures are "
      << today.GetHighTemp() << " and "
      << today.GetLowTemp() << endl;
```

AN OBJECT AS A FUNCTION PARAMETER

Objects can be passed as function parameters by value or by reference. The following temperature examples illustrate the syntax.

The function TemperatureRange uses a **call by value** Temperature parameter T and returns the difference between the high and low temperatures. When executing the function, the calling unit copies a Temperature object (actual parameter) to T.

```
float TemperatureRange(Temperature T)
{
   return T.GetHighTemp() - T.GetLowTemp();
}
```

The function Celsius uses a **call by reference** Temperature parameter T that is initially assumed to contain Fahrenheit values. The function creates a Temperature object whose high and low readings are converted to Celsius and assigns it to T.

```
void Celsius(Temperature& T)
{
   float hi, low;
   // c = 5/9 * (f - 32)
   hi  = float(5)/9 * (T.GetHighTemp()-32);

   low = float(5)/9 * (T.GetLowTemp()-32);

   T = Temperature(hi,low);
}
```

As an example, the object Water contains the boiling point (212° Fahrenheit) and freezing point (32° Fahrenheit) of water as its high and low temperature values. TemperatureRange illustrates that 180° is the Fahrenheit range for water. Using the Celsius function, convert the water temperatures to Celsius and call TemperatureRange to illustrate that 100° is the Celsius range.

```
Temperature Water(212,32);   // boil at 212F; freeze at 32F

cout << "The temperature range for water in Fahrenheit is "
     << TemperatureRange(Water) << endl;

Celsius(Water);              // convert Fahrenheit to Celsius
cout << "The temperature range for water in Celsius is "
     << TemperatureRange(Water) << endl;
```

Arrays of Objects   3.4

The element type of an array can include not only the built-in data types such as int or char but also user-defined class types. The resulting array of objects can be used to create lists, tables, and so forth. The use of object arrays, however, requires a warning. An array declaration calls the constructor for each object in the list. Compare the simple declaration of a single Rectangle object and an array of 100 Rectangle objects. In each declaration, the constructor is called to create the object, which sets the initial length and width. In the case of the array, the constructor is called for each of the 100 objects.

```
Rectangle pool(150,100);      // create a 150 x 100 pool

Rectangle room[100];          // The constructor is called for
                              // room[0]..room[99]
```

The declaration of the pool object passes initial values to the constructor. The room objects do have initial values because the Rectangle constructor assigns the default value of 0 to the length and width of an object:

```
Rectangle (float l=0, float w=0);    // default parameters
```

After declaring the array, the length and width of each object room[i] have values of 0:

```
cout << room[25].GetLength()      // output 0;
cout << room[25].GetWidth()       // output 0;

room[25].PutLength(10)            // set length of room[25] to 10
room[25].PutWidth(5)              // set width of room[25] to 5
```

The declaration of an array of Rectangle objects raises an important issue about arrays and classes. If the Rectangle class constructor did not have default parameters, the declaration of the room array would cause an error because each constructor would require parameters. The declaration would require an array initializer list that handles each element in the array. For example, to declare the 100-element room array and set the length and width parameters to 0, an initializer list of 100 Rectangle objects would be required. In reality, this is not practical.

```
Rectangle room[100] = {Rectangle(0,0), . . . , Rectangle(0,0)};
```

To declare an array of objects, we provide a constructor with default values or we provide a constructor that simply has no parameters.

THE DEFAULT CONSTRUCTOR

A **default constructor** is one that requires no parameters. This occurs when the constructor does not have any parameters or when every parameter has a default value. In this chapter, the Rectangle class contains a default constructor, whereas the Temperature class requires parameters when declaring an object.

- -

RECTANGLE CLASS

CONSTRUCTOR

```
Rectangle(float l = 0, float w = 0);
```

The constructor contains parameters l and w with a default value of 0. When creating a Rectangle array, the default values are assigned to each object.

```
Rectangle R[25];          // each item has value Rectangle(0,0)
```

TEMPERATURE CLASS

CONSTRUCTOR

```
Temperature(float h, float l);
```

The Temperature class does not contain a default constructor. Rather the object must be given an initial value for the high and low temperature. The declaration of objects today and week are invalid!

```
Temperature today;      // invalid; missing parameters
Temperature week[7];    // Temperature has no default constructor
```

Multiple Constructors 3.5

We have developed both default and nondefault constructors in our classes. Our discussion to this point may lead you to assume that these are mutually exclusive since all of our classes have had a single constructor. C++ recognizes our need for a variety of ways to initialize an object and allows us to define multiple constructors within the same class. The compiler uses function overloading to select the correct form of the constructor when we create an object. The concept of function overloading and its rules is discussed in Chapter 6. Multiple constructors add great flexibility to a class. A special kind of multiple constructor, called a **copy constructor,** is used with most classes that contain dynamic data members. The copy constructor is discussed in Chapter 8.

The Date class illustrates the use of multiple constructors. The class has three data members that designate the month, day, and year of a date.

month $1 \leq m \leq 12$	day $1 \leq d \leq 31$	year $1900 \leq y \leq 1999$

One constructor has three parameters corresponding to the three data members. The action of the constructor is to initialize the variables. A second constructor allows the client to declare a date as a string in the form "mm/dd/yy". It reads the string and converts the character pairs "mm" to month, "dd" to day, and "yy" to year. For each constructor, we assume that the parameter specifying the year is a two-digit value in the range 00–99. The actual year is stored by adding 1900 to the input value:

```
year = 1900 + yy
```

The Date class has an output method that prints the full date with month name, day, and year value. For instance, the first day in the twentieth century was

```
January 1, 1900
```

- -
DATE CLASS SPECIFICATION

DECLARATION

```
#include <string.h>
#include <strstream.h>

class Date
{
    private:
        // private members that specify the date
        int month, day, year;
    public:
        // constructors. default date is January 1, 1900
        Date (int m = 1, int d = 1, int y = 0);
        Date (char *dstr);

        // output the date in the format "month day, year"
        void PrintDate (void);
};
```

DESCRIPTION

The two constructors build a Date object but differ in their parameters. The compiler selects the constructor during the creation of a Date object. For instance, the following are demonstration objects.

EXAMPLE

```
Date day1(6,6,44);        // June 6, 1944
Date day2;                // default to January 1, 1900
Date day3("12/31/99");    // December 31, 1999
```

- -
DATE CLASS IMPLEMENTATION

The heart of the Date class is its two constructors, which define a date by passing the month, day, and year values or the string "mm/dd/yy".

The first constructor has three parameters with default values corresponding to January 1, 1900. With the default values, the constructor qualifies as a default constructor:

```
// constructor. month, day, year given as integers mm dd yy
Date::Date (int m, int d, int y) : month(m), day(d)
{
    year = 1900 + y;   // y is a year in the 20th century
}
```

An alternative form of the constructor takes a string parameter. The string has the form "mm/dd/yy". To convert the data pairs, we use array-based input, which converts the character pairs "mm" to an integer month, and so forth. Copy the parameter string to the array inputBuffer and then read the characters in this order:

month - ch - day - ch - year

The input of ch extracts the two separators "/" from the input string.

```
//constructor. month, day, year given as string "mm/dd/yy"
Date::Date (char *dstr)
{
    char inputBuffer[16];
    char ch;

    // copy to inputBuffer. declare array based input stream
    strcpy(inputBuffer,dstr);
    istrstream input(inputBuffer, sizeof(inputBuffer));

    // read from input stream. use ch to read the '/' characters
    input >> month >> ch >> day >> ch >> year;
    year += 1900;
}
```

For output, the Print method gives the full date text including the name of the month, the day, and the year. The array months contains an empty string (index 0) and the 12 names for the calendar months. The month value is used as an index into the array for the printing of the month name.

```
// print date with full month name.
void Date::PrintDate (void)
{
    // allocate static array of month names.
    static char *Months[] = {"","January","February",
                             "March","April", "May",
                             "June","July","August",
                             "September","October",
                             "November","December"};

    cout << Months[month] << "" << day << ", "<< year;
}
```

Program 3.4   Twentieth Century Date

The test program uses the constructors to set up demonstration objects. The resulting dates are printed. The Date class is contained in the file "date.h".

```
#include <iostream.h>

#include "date.h"                    // include the Date class

void main (void)
{
    // Date objects with integer, default and string parameters
    Date day1(6,6,44);               // June 6, 1944
    Date day2;                       // January 1, 1900
    Date day3("12/31/99");           // December 31, 1999


    cout << "D-Day in World War II - ";
    day1.PrintDate();
    cout << endl;
    cout << "The first day in the 20th century - ";
    day2.PrintDate();
    cout << endl;
    cout << "The last day in the 20th century - ";
    day3.PrintDate();
    cout << endl;
}

/*
<Run of Program 3.4>

D-Day in World War II - June 6, 1944
The first day in the 20th century - January 1, 1900
The last day in the 20th century - December 31, 1999
*/
```

3.6 Case Study: Triangular Matrices

A two-dimensional array, often called a **matrix,** provides an important data structure in mathematics. In this section, we explore **square matrices** (matrices with the same number of rows and columns) whose data items are real numbers. We develop the class TriMat, which defines **upper triangular matrices** in which all entries below the diagonal have the value 0.

$$
\mathbf{A} = \begin{bmatrix}
A_{00} & A_{01} & \cdots & & \cdots & A_{0\,n-1} \\
0 & A_{11} & A_{12} & \cdots & & A_{1\,n-1} \\
0 & 0 & A_{22} & \cdots & & A_{2\,n-1} \\
0 & \vdots & \vdots & \vdots & & \vdots \\
0 & \cdots & \cdots & A_{n-2\,n-2} & & A_{n-2\,n-1} \\
0 & 0 & \cdots & 0 & & A_{n-1\,n-1}
\end{bmatrix}
$$

In mathematical terms, $A_{i,j} = 0$, for $j < i$. The upper triangle is defined by the elements $A_{i,j}$, for $j \geq i$. These matrices have important algebraic properties and are used to solve systems of equations. The implementation of upper triangular matrix operations in the class TriMat shows how to store a triangular matrix efficiently as a one-dimensional array.

UPPER TRIANGULAR MATRIX PROPERTIES

While there are n^2 entries in the matrix, approximately half of the entries are 0 and do not need to be stored explicitly. To be specific, if we subtract the n diagonal elements from the total of n^2 entries, half of the remaining entries are 0. For instance, with $n = 25$, there are 300 entries with value 0:

$$(n^2 - n)/2 = (25^2 - 25)/2 = (625 - 25)/2 = 300$$

The following are a set of operations for triangular matrices. We define addition, subtraction, and multiplication of matrices as well as the determinant, which has important application for the solution of equations.

The sum or difference of two triangular matrices **A** and **B** results from adding or subtracting corresponding elements from the matrices. The resulting matrix is triangular.

Addition   **C = A + B**

where C is a triangular matrix with entries $C_{i,j}$ whose value is the sum $A_{i,j} + B_{i,j}$.

Subtraction   **C = A − B**

where C is a triangular matrix with entries $C_{i,j}$ whose value is the sum $A_{i,j} - B_{i,j}$.

$$C = \begin{bmatrix} 1 & 3 & 2 \\ 0 & 4 & 7 \\ 0 & 0 & 5 \end{bmatrix} + \begin{bmatrix} 2 & 1 & 9 \\ 0 & 8 & 2 \\ 0 & 0 & 1 \end{bmatrix} = \begin{bmatrix} 3 & 4 & 11 \\ 0 & 12 & 9 \\ 0 & 0 & 6 \end{bmatrix}$$

Multiplication   **C = A * B**

The product matrix **C** is a triangular matrix with entries $C_{i,j}$ whose value is computed from the entries in row i of **A** and column j of **B**:

$$C_{i,j} = (A_{i,0} * B_{0,j}) + (A_{i,1} * B_{1,j}) + (A_{i,2} * B_{2,j}) + \cdots + (A_{i,n-1} * B_{n-1,j})$$

For instance, if

$$A = \begin{bmatrix} 1 & 1 & 0 \\ 0 & 2 & 1 \\ 0 & 0 & 2 \end{bmatrix}, \quad B = \begin{bmatrix} 3 & -2 & 4 \\ 0 & 4 & 1 \\ 0 & 0 & 3 \end{bmatrix}$$

$C_{0,2}$ is the sum of the products of entries from row 0 of **A** and column 2 of **B**.

$$
\begin{bmatrix} 1 & 1 & 0 \\ & & \end{bmatrix} * \begin{bmatrix} 4 \\ 1 \\ 3 \end{bmatrix} = \begin{bmatrix} 5 \\ & \\ & \end{bmatrix}
$$

$$1 * 4 + 1 * 1 + 0 * 3 = 5$$

The product of **A** and **B** is

$$
\underset{\mathbf{A}}{\begin{bmatrix} 1 & 1 & 0 \\ 0 & 2 & 1 \\ 0 & 0 & 2 \end{bmatrix}} * \underset{\mathbf{B}}{\begin{bmatrix} 3 & -2 & 4 \\ 0 & 4 & 1 \\ 0 & 0 & 3 \end{bmatrix}} = \underset{\mathbf{C}}{\begin{bmatrix} 3 & 2 & 5 \\ 0 & 8 & 5 \\ 0 & 0 & 6 \end{bmatrix}}
$$

For a general square matrix, the determinant is a complex quantity to compute; however, it is simple to compute the determinant of a triangular matrix. Just form the product of the elements on the diagonal.

$$
\det(\mathbf{A}) = \begin{vmatrix} A_{00} & A_{01} & \cdots & \cdots & A_{0\,n-1} \\ 0 & A_{11} & A_{12} & \cdots & A_{1\,n-1} \\ 0 & 0 & A_{22} & \cdots & A_{2\,n-1} \\ 0 & \vdots & \vdots & \vdots & \vdots \\ 0 & \cdots & \cdots & A_{n-2\,n-2} & A_{n-2\,n-1} \\ 0 & 0 & \cdots & 0 & A_{n-1\,n-1} \end{vmatrix} = A_{00}A_{11} \ldots A_{n-1\,n-1}
$$

Storage of a Triangular Matrix   The standard array definition requires the allocation of a full n^2 memory locations in spite of the predictable zeros stored below the diagonal. To eliminate this space, we store entries from a triangular matrix in a one-dimensional array M. All entries below the main diagonal are not stored. Table 3.1 illustrates the number of entries that are stored in each row.

TABLE 3.1
Triangular
Matrix Storage
by Row

Row	Number Stored	Entries
0	n	$(A_{0,0} \ldots A_{0,n-1})$
1	n−1	$(A_{1,1} \ldots A_{1,n-1})$
2	n−2	$(A_{2,2} \ldots A_{2,n-1})$
. . .	. . .	. . . . .
n−2	2	$(A_{n-2,n-2} \ldots A_{n-2,n-1})$
n−1	1	$(A_{n-1,n-1})$

The storage algorithm requires an access function that must identify the location in array M that stores entry $A_{i,j}$. For $j < i$, the entry $A_{i,j}$ is 0 and is not stored in M. For $j \geq i$, the access function uses information on the number of stored entries in each row up to row i. This information can be computed for each row i and stored in an array (rowTable) for general use by the access function.

```
Row    RowTable                        Observation
0      rowTable[0] = 0                 0 entries before row 0
1      rowTable[1] = n                 n entries before row 1 (from
                                         row 0)
2      rowTable[2] = n + n-1           n + n-1 entries before row 2
3      rowTable[3] = n + n-1 + n-2     entries before row 3
. . . . . . .
n-1    rowTable[n-1] = n + n-1 + . . . + 2
```

EXAMPLE 3.4

Consider the 3×3 matrix **X**

$$A = \begin{bmatrix} 1 & 1 & 0 \\ 0 & 2 & 1 \\ 0 & 0 & 2 \end{bmatrix}$$

```
Row    RowTable            Observation
0      rowTable[0] = 0     0 stored entries before row 0
1      rowTable[1] = 3     3 entries from row 0 (1 1 0)
2      rowTable[2] = 5     5 entries from rows 0 and 1 (1 1 0
                             2 1)
```

Row Table

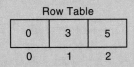

The entries from the triangular matrix are stored by row in array M.

Array M

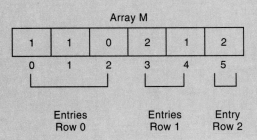

Assuming that entries from the triangular matrix are stored by row in array M, the access function for $A_{i,j}$ uses the following parameters:

Indices i and j,
Array rowTable

The algorithm to access $A_{i,j}$ is as follows:

1. If $j < i$, then $A_{i,j} = 0$ and the entry is not stored.
2. If $j \geq i$, then get the value rowTable[i], which is the number of entries that are stored in array M for the entries up to row i. In row i, the first i entries are zero and not stored in M. The entry $A_{i,j}$ is located in $M[\text{rowTable}[i] + (j - i)]$.

EXAMPLE 3.5

Consider the triangular matrix X[3][3] of Example 3.4:

1. $X_{0,2} = M[\text{rowTable}[0] + (2 - 0)]$
    $= M[0 + 2]$
    $= M[2] = 0$
2. $X_{1,0}$ not stored
3. $X_{1,2} = M[\text{rowTable}[1] + (2 - 1)]$
    $= M[3 + 1]$
    $= M[4] = 1$

The TriMat Class   The TriMat class implements a number of triangular matrix operations. Triangular matrix subtraction and multiplication are left to the end-of-chapter exercises. Given the restriction that we must use only static arrays, our class restricts row and column size to a maximum of 25. There are $300 = (25^2 - 25)/2$ zero entries, so the array M has 325 elements.

TRIMAT CLASS SPECIFICATION

DECLARATION

```
#include <iostream.h>
#include <stdlib.h>


// maximum number of upper triangular entries and rows
const int ELEMENTLIMIT = 325;
const int ROWLIMIT = 25;
```

```
class TriMat
{
    private:
      // private data members
        int rowTable[ROWLIMIT];   // starting index of rows in M
        int n;                    // row/column size
        double M[ELEMENTLIMIT];   // stores upper elements

    public:
      // constructor. no default parameters
        TriMat(int matsize);

        // matrix element access methods
        void PutElement (double item, int i, int j);
        double GetElement(int i,int j) const;

        // matrix arithmetic operations
        TriMat AddMat(const TriMat& A) const;
        double DetMat(void) const;

        // matrix I/O operations
        void ReadMat(void);
        void WriteMat(void) const;

        // get matrix dimension
        int GetDimension(void) const;
};
```

DESCRIPTION

The class constructor is passed the row and column size of the matrix. The methods PutElement and GetElement store and retrieve the upper-triangular matrix elements. GetElement returns a 0 for all lower-triangular elements. AddMat returns the sum of matrix A with the current object. The method does not change the value of the current matrix. The I/O operations ReadMat and WriteMat employ the full $n \times n$ matrix of elements. For ReadMat, only the upper-triangular elements are stored.

EXAMPLE

```
#include "trimat.h"          // include TriMat class

TriMat  A(10), B(10), C(10); // 10 x 10 triangular matrices
A.ReadMat();                 // enter matrices A and B
B.ReadMat();
C = A.AddMat(B);             // compute C = A + B
C.WriteMat();                // print the sum C
```

TRIMAT CLASS IMPLEMENTATION

The constructor initializes the private data member n with the parameter matsize. This identifies the row and column size of the matrix. The same parameter is used to initialize rowTable, which is used to access the matrix items. If matsize exceeds ROWLIMIT, an error message is output and the program terminates.

```
// initialize n and rowTable
TriMat::TriMat(int matsize)
{
    int storedElements = 0; // accumulates the stored entries

    // terminate program if matsize exceeds ROWLIMIT
    if (matsize > ROWLIMIT)
    {
        cerr << "The matrix cannot exceed size" << ROWLIMIT
                "x" << ROWLIMIT << endl;
        exit(1);
    }

    n = matsize;

    // set up the table
    for(int i = 0; i < n; i++)
    {
        rowTable[i] = storedElements;
        storedElements += n - i;
    }
}
```

Matrix Access Methods The key to triangular matrices is our ability to store the nonzero elements efficiently in a linear array. To obtain this efficiency and still use the usual two-dimensional indices i and j to access an element, we need the functions PutElement and GetElement to store and retrieve the matrix elements in the array.

The utility GetDimension gives the client access to the size of the matrix. This information can be used to ensure that the access methods are given parameters that correspond to a valid row and column:

```
// return the matrix dimension n
int TriMat::GetDimension(void) const
{
    return n;
}
```

The method PutElement looks at the indices i and j. If $j \geq i$, we store the data value in M using the matrix access function for triangular matrices: If i or j is not in the range $0 \ldots (n - 1)$, the program terminates:

```
// stores matrix item [i,j] in the array M
void TriMat::PutElement (double item, int i, int j)
{
    // terminate program if element indices are out of range
    if ((i < 0 || i>= n) || (j < 0 || j >= n))
    {
        cerr << "PutElement: index out of range 0 to "
            << n-1 << endl;
        exit (1);
    }
    // all elements below the diagonal are ignored
    if (j >= i)
            M[rowTable[i] + j-i] = item;
}
```

To retrieve an item, the method GetElement looks at the indices i and j. If i or j is not in the range 0 . . (n − 1), the program terminates. If j < i, the item is in the lower triangular matrix with value 0. GetElement simply returns the unstored value 0. Otherwise j ≥ i and the access method can retrieve the item from array M:

```
// retrieve matrix element {i, j} from array M
double TriMat::GetElement(int i,int j) const
{
    // terminate program if element indices are out of range
    if ((i < 0 || i >= n) || (j < 0 || j >= n))
    {
        cerr << "PutElement: index out of range 0 to "
            << n-1 << endl;
        exit (1);
    }
    if (j >= i)
        // retrieve entry if above diagonal
        return M[rowTable[i] + j-i];
    else
        // entry is 0 if below diagonal
        return 0;
}
```

Input/Output for TriMat Objects   Traditionally, matrix input assumes that data are entered a row at a time with a full set of row and column values. In a TriMat object, the lower triangular matrix is 0 and the values are not stored in the array. Nevertheless, the user is directed to input these 0 values in keeping with ordinary matrix input.

```
// reads matrix elements row by row. client must enter
// all n x n elements
void TriMat::ReadMat(void)
{
```

```
        double item;
        int i, j;

        for (i = 0; i < n; i++)          // scan rows
            for (j = 0; j < n; j++)      // for each row scan columns
            {
                cin >> item;             // Read matrix element [i,j]
                PutElement(item,i,j);    // store the element
            }
}

// writes matrix elements row by row
void TriMat::WriteMat(void) const
{
    int i,j;

    // fixed-point output, 3 decimal places, include trailing 0s
    cout.setf(ios::fixed);
    cout.precision(3);
    cout.setf(ios::showpoint);

    for (i = 0; i < n; i++)
    {
        for (j = 0; j < n; j++)
            cout << setw(7) << GetElement(i,j);
        cout << endl;
    }
}
```

Matrix Operations   The TriMat class computes the sum of two matrices and the determinant of a matrix. The AddMat method takes a single parameter, which is the right-hand operand in a sum. The current object corresponds to the left-hand operand. For instance, the sum of triangular matrices X and Y uses the AddMat method from object X. Assume the sum is stored in object Z. To compute

Z = X + Y

use the statement

```
Z = X.AddMat(Y);
```

The algorithm for adding two TriMat objects returns a new matrix B with entries $B_{i,j} = \text{CurrentObject}_{i,j} + A_{i,j}$:

```
// returns sum of A and current object. current obj not changed.
TriMat TriMat::AddMat (const TriMat& A) const
{
```

```
    int i, j;
    double itemCurrent, itemA;
    TriMat B(A.n);    // B will be the sum.

    for (i = 0; i < n; i++)      // cycle through the rows
    {
        for (j = i; j < n; j++) // skip entries below diagonal
        {
            itemCurrent = GetElement(i,j);
            itemA = A.GetElement(i,j);
            B.PutElement (itemCurrent + itemA, i, j);
        }
    }
    return B;
}
```

The method DetMat returns the determinant of the current object. The return value is a real number that is the product of the elements on the diagonal. See the software supplement for the implementation.

Program 3.5   TriMat Operations

A test program illustrates the TriMat class with its I/O operations and also the operations of matrix addition and determinant. Strings provide descriptive phrases for each section of the program.

```
#include <iostream.h>
#include <iomanip.h>

#include "trimat.h"          // include the TriMat class

void main(void)
{
    int  n;

    // create a uniform matrix size
    cout << "What is the matrix size? ";
    cin >> n;

    // declare three n x n matrices
    TriMat A(n), B(n), C(n);

    // read matrices A and B
    cout << "Enter a " << n << " x " << n
         << " triangular matrix" << endl;
    A.ReadMat();
    cout << endl;
```

```
        cout << "Enter a " << n << " x " << n
             << " triangular matrix" << endl;
        B.ReadMat();
        cout << endl;

        // execute operations and print the result
        cout << "The sum  A + B" << endl;
        C = A.AddMat(B);
        C.WriteMat();
        cout << endl;
        cout << "The determinant of A+B is " << C.DetMat() << endl;

}

/*
<Run of Program 3.5>

What is the matrix size? 4
Enter a 4 by 4 triangular matrix:
1 2 -4 5
0 2 4 1
0 0 3 7
0 0 0 5

Enter a 4 by 4 triangular matrix:
1 4 6 7
0 2 6 12
0 0 3 1
0 0 0 2

The sum  A + B
   2.000   6.000   2.000 12.000
   0.000   4.000 10.000 13.000
   0.000   0.000   6.000   8.000
   0.000   0.000   0.000   7.000

The determinant of A+B is 336.000
*/
```

Written Exercises

3.1 Give an ADT Coins for a set of n coins. The data include the number of coins, the total number of heads on the last toss, and a list of the coin faces on the last toss. Operations are to include initialization, tossing the coins, returning the total number of heads, and printing the faces of the coins on the last toss.

3.2 (a) Develop an ADT for a box. Include initialization and operations that return the lengths of the sides and compute the area and volume.

(b)   Write a class Box that implements the ADT.

(c)   A box girth is the perimeter of the rectangle formed by two sides. A box has three possible girth values. A mailing length is determined by a girth plus the distance of the third side. A package qualifies for mailing if any of its mailing lengths is less than 100. Write a code segment to determine if object B qualifies for mailing.

3.3   Determine all syntax errors in the class declarations.

(a)
```
class X
{
    private    int t;
    private    int q;
    public
        int X (int a, int b);
        {
            t = a; q = b;
        }

        void printX(void);
}
```

(b)
```
class Y
{
    private:
        int p;
        int q;
    public
        Y (int n, int m)  : n(p) q(m);
        {
        }
};
```

3.4   (a)   Declare the specification for a class X, which has the following:

Private members: Integer variables a, b, c
Public members: Constructor that assigns values to a, b, c. Default values are to be 1. A function F, which returns the maximum of a, b, c.

(b)   Write the constructor for class X in part (a).

(c)   Write the public function F by placing its definition outside the class.

3.5   Assume the following declaration:

```
class Student
{
    private:
        int studentid;
        int gradepts, units;
        float gpa;
        float ComputeGPA(void);
```

```
    public:
        Student(int studid; int studgradepts, int studunits);
        void ReadGradeInfo(void);
        void PrintGradeInfo(void);
        void UpdateGradeInfo(int newunits, int newgradepts);
};
```

The class maintains the grade record for a student. The variables gradepts and units are used by ComputeGPA to assign the student's grade point average to variable gpa. Use the formula

```
gpa = gradepts/units
```

Write the code for the member functions. The constructor and ComputeGPA must be done in-line.

3.6   An ADT Calendar contains the data items year and the logical data value leapyr. Its operations are as follows:

Constructor	Initialize year and leapyr.
NumDays(mm,dd)	Return the number of days from the first of the year to the given month mm and day dd.
Leapyear(void)	Indicates whether the year is a leap year.
PrintDate(ndays)	Prints the date ndays into the year in the format mm/dd/yy.

(a)   Formally write the ADT.
(b)   Implement the ADT Calendar as a class.

3.7   Design a declaration for a class that has the following data members. Declare operations appropriate for an object of that type.

(a)   Student name, major, proposed year of graduation, gpa
(b)   State, capitol, population, area, governor
(c)   A cylinder. Allow modification of both radius and height and include computation of the surface area and volume.

3.8   The following is a declaration for a class that represents a deck of cards.

```
class CardDeck
{
    private:
        // a deck of cards is implemented as an array of
        // integers from 0 to 51.
        int cards[52];
        int currentCard;
    public:
        // constructor. shuffle the deck
        CardDeck(void);

        // shuffle the deck
        void Shuffle(void);
```

```
// return the next card in the deck. HINT: you must
// establish a current location in the deck.
int GetCard(void);

// clubs 0-12, diamonds 13-25, hearts 26-38,
// spades 39-51. In each range, the first card
// is the ace and the last three cards are jack,
// queen, king. write card c as suit, card value
void PrintCard(int c);
};
```

(a) Implement the methods. HINT: To shuffle the cards, use a loop to scan the cards in the range 0..51. For card i, select a random number in the range from i to 51 and exchange the card at that random index with the card at index i.

(b) Write the function

```
void DealHand(CardDeck& d, int n);
```

that deals n cards from d, sorts them and prints their face value.

3.9 Using the Temperature class from Section 3.2, write a function

```
Temperature Average(Temperature a[], int n);
```

that returns the Temperature object containing the average low and high temperatures of n readings.

3.10 Use the Date class of Section 3.5.

(a) Modify the Date class to include the method IncrementDate. It takes a positive number of days in the range 0 to 365, adds it to the current date and returns an object having the new date.

(b) Allow the parameter for IncrementDate to be negative.

3.11 Illustrate the use of the random number class to simulate the following:

(a) One-fifth of automobiles in a state fail to meet smog emission standards. Use fRandom to determine if a randomly selected car meets the standards.

(b) The weight of an individual in a population ranges between 140 and 230 pounds. Use Random to select the weight of a person in this population.

3.12 Consider a class Event that is passed an initial value for the lower and upper bound of the time for an event. The bounds default to 0 and 1. The operations are:

Constructor   Initialize the data bounds. If the lower bound exceeds the upper bound, print an error message and exit the program.

GetEvent   Get a random event in the range lower bound to upper bound.

(a) Implement the class using inline code.

(b) Implement the class by defining the member functions outside the class declaration.

(c)   An application requires an array of five Event objects where each event occurs in the range 10 to 20? How will you initialize the array? Is the problem simpler if the range for each object is 0 to 1?

3.13   Write a function DateInterval that accepts two Calendar class objects of Written Exercise 3.6 and returns the number of days between the two dates.

3.14*   Matrices can be used to solve a system of simultaneous equations in n unknowns. We illustrate the algorithm for a system with three unknowns.

The entries $A_{i,j}$ are coefficients of the unknowns X_0, X_1, and X_2 in the system of equations. The right-hand side for the equations are given by the entries C_j.

$$
\begin{aligned}
A_{0,0}\, X_0 + A_{0,1} * X_1 + A_{0,2}\, X_2 &= C_0 \\
A_{1,0}\, X_0 + A_{1,1} * X_1 + A_{1,2}\, X_2 &= C_1 \\
A_{2,0}\, X_0 + A_{2,1} * X_1 + A_{2,2}\, X_2 &= C_2
\end{aligned}
$$

The equations can be described with the matrix equation

$$
\begin{bmatrix} A_{00} & A_{01} & A_{02} \\ A_{10} & A_{11} & A_{12} \\ A_{20} & A_{21} & A_{22} \end{bmatrix} * \begin{bmatrix} X_0 \\ X_1 \\ X_2 \end{bmatrix} = \begin{bmatrix} C_0 \\ C_1 \\ C_2 \end{bmatrix}
$$

where the matrix is called the **coefficient matrix.** For example, the system of equations

$$
\begin{aligned}
1X_0 + 1X_1 + 0X_2 &= 4 \\
-3X_0 - 1X_1 + 1X_2 &= -11 \\
2X_0 + 2X_1 + 2X_2 &= 14
\end{aligned}
$$

corresponds to the matrix equation

$$
\begin{bmatrix} 1 & 1 & 0 \\ -3 & -1 & 1 \\ 2 & 2 & 2 \end{bmatrix} * \begin{bmatrix} X_0 \\ X_1 \\ X_2 \end{bmatrix} = \begin{bmatrix} 4 \\ -11 \\ 14 \end{bmatrix}
$$

A mathematical theorem states that the equations can be reduced to a series of equivalent equations whose matrix of coefficients is triangular. In our example:

1.   Eliminate the term $A_{10} = -3$.

     Multiply the terms in row 0 by the constant 3, and add the terms in row 0 to those in row 1.

$$
\begin{bmatrix} 1 & 1 & 0 \\ 0 & 2 & 1 \\ 2 & 2 & 2 \end{bmatrix} * \begin{bmatrix} X_0 \\ X_1 \\ X_2 \end{bmatrix} = \begin{bmatrix} 4 \\ 1 \\ 14 \end{bmatrix}
$$

2. Eliminate the term $A_{20} = 2$.

   Multiply terms in row 0 by constant -2, and add terms in row 0 to those in row 2. The process also eliminates the term A_{21}.

$$
\begin{bmatrix} 1 & 1 & 0 \\ 0 & 2 & 1 \\ 0 & 0 & 2 \end{bmatrix} * \begin{bmatrix} X_0 \\ X_1 \\ X_2 \end{bmatrix} = \begin{bmatrix} 4 \\ 1 \\ 6 \end{bmatrix}
$$

The matrix equation for the new system has a triangular coefficient matrix.

(a) Reduce the algebraic system to an equation involving a triangular matrix.

$$
\begin{bmatrix} 1 & 2 & 3 \\ 3 & -1 & 1 \\ 2 & 4 & 2 \end{bmatrix} * \begin{bmatrix} X_0 \\ X_1 \\ X_2 \end{bmatrix} = \begin{bmatrix} 5 \\ 1 \\ 10 \end{bmatrix}
$$

(b) Find the determinant of the coefficient matrix.

Programming Exercises

3.1 Many program applications make use of an accumulator that is repeatedly updated. As a simple example of an abstract data type, assume that the Accumulator is a data type that is updated by an add operation and output using a print operation.

```
ADT Accumulator is
    Data
        A real value to serving as a total
    Operations

        Initialize
            Input:              Real value N.
            Preconditions:      None
            Process:            Assign N as the value of the
                                total.
            Postconditions:     The total is initialized.
            Output:             None

        Add
            Input:              A real number N.
            Preconditions:      None
            Process:            Add N to the total.
            Postconditions:     The total is updated.
            Output:             None
```

```
        Print
            Input:              None
            Preconditions:      None
            Process:            Read the total.
            Postconditions:     None
            Output:             Print the total.
    end ADT Accumulator
```

A banking application reads an initial balance and a sequence of transactions. A negative transaction identifies a debit and a positive transaction identifies a credit. Three objects of type Accumulator are used. The Balance object is defined with the starting balance as the constructor parameter. Objects Debits and Credits have initial value 0 and are used to maintain a running total of debit and credit transactions. The Add operator updates the sum in the objects.

Read in a sequence of transactions, terminating on a transaction of 0.00. Print the final values of the balance, debits, and credits.

3.2 Write a main program that uses the class implemented in Written Exercise 3.5 with the following data:

Student ID	Grade Points	Units
1047	120	40
3050	75	20
0020	100	75

(a) Print the information for each student.

(b) The last student (ID 0020) has additional records from summer school. Update the record with the following new data: grade points 40 with 10 units. Print the new data for this student.

3.3 Extend the Circle class of Section 1.3 to compute the area of a sector. The area of a sector is determined by the formula $(\theta/360) * \pi r^2$.

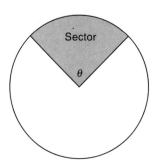

Use the class to solve the following problem:

A circular playground is defined as an object with radius 100 feet. The program determines the cost of fencing the circumference of the playground. Fencing is $2.40 per foot. The surface area of the playground is mostly grass. One sector, measured with a 30° angle is not lawn. The program determines the cost of rolling lawn at $4.00 per 2 × 8 strip (16 ft^2).

```
Fencing
  Cost = Circumference * 2.40
Lawn
  Lawn_Area = Area - Sector_Area
  Number_Rolls = Lawn_Area / 16
  Cost = Number_Rolls * 4.00.
```

3.4 Write a class that contains the sex indicator (M or F), age, and ID number in the range 0 to 1000. The operations include Read, Print, and functions GetId/GetAge/ GetGender, which return the id, age, and sex of the person stored in the object.

Write an application program that defines objects YoungWomen and OldMen. The program enters information on a sequence of individuals using the Read operation and assigns data on the youngest woman in YoungWomen and the oldest man in OldMen. The input terminates with ID number 0. Using Print, output data from these objects.

3.5 Implement a class Geometry whose private data contains two (2) data items V1 and V2 of type double and a variable figuretype of type Figure.

The class should contain two constructors, which take 1 or 2 parameters respectively, a method Border that returns the perimeter of the object, a method Area that returns the area and the method Diagonal that computes the diagonal.

```
Enum Figure {Circle, Rectangle}
class Geometry
{
   private:
      double V1, V2;
      Figure figuretype;
   public:
      Geometry(double radius);        // for a circle
      Geometry(double 1, double w);   // for a rectangle

      double Border(void) const;
      double Area(void) const;
      double Diagonal(void) const;
}
```

(a) Implement the class Geometry using external functions. The constructor for a circle will have one parameter and hence should assign Circle to figuretype and the other constructor should assign Rectangle to figuretype. The measurement methods will have to look at the figuretype before computing the return value.

(b)   The user enters an inside radius which is then used to create the small circle. Use this information to declare a circumscribed rectangle and a circumscribed outside circle. Print the border, area, and diagonal of each object.

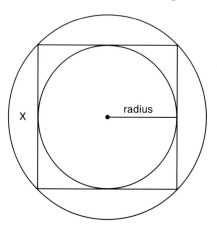

Compute the area of the outer band between the two circles (area outside of the small circle and inside the large circle).

Compute the perimeter of the small region marked with an X.

3.6   The class Ref counts the number of positive (>0) and negative (<0) numbers "submitted" to it. The constructor has no parameters, and initializes the data items positiveCount and negativeCount to 0.

```
class Ref
{
    private:
        int positiveCount;
        int negativeCount;
    public:
        Ref(void);
        void Count(int x);
        void Write(void) const;
};
```

An object of type Ref is passed to a function that uses it to record the number of positive and negative numbers in an input sequence of five integers. Two versions of the function illustrate the distinction between passing objects by value and by reference. The first version passes an object by value.

```
void PassByValue(Ref V)
{
    int num;
```

```
        for (int i = 0;i < 5;i++)
        {
            cin >> num;
            if (num != 0)
                v.Count (num);
        }
    }
```

A second version of the function passes the parameter by reference.

```
    void PassByReference (Ref & V)
    {
        int num;

        . . .

    }
```

Implement Ref and create a main program that calls each function and uses the method Write to print the results. In each instance, the data are 1, 2, 3, −1, and −7. Explain carefully why PassByValue fails to work correctly and PassByReference succeeds.

3.7 Consider the following class declaration:

```
    class Grade
    {
        private:
            char name[30];
            float score;
        public:
            Grade(char student[], float score);
            Grade(void);
            int Compare(char s[]);
            void Read(void);
            void Write(void);
    };
```

Write a main program by following parts (a) to (e).

(a) Write the implementation for the member functions. Use the string function strcpy to assign the name in the first constructor. Note that the second constructor is the default constructor. It should set name to the NULL string and score to 0.0. Compare returns 1 if s is equal to name and 0 otherwise. Use strcmp.

(b) In the main program, declare an array Students of five objects with an initial value of

```
    {Grade("John",78.3),  Grade("Sally",86.5),
       Grade("Bob",58.9), Grade("Donna",98.3)};
```

(c) The fifth object, Students[4], is to be input using member function Read().

(d) Write a function

```
int Search(Grade Arr[], int n, char keyname[]);
```

that searches the n element array Arr and returns the index of the object whose name matches keyname. Return −1 if keyname is not found in Arr.

(e) Call Search three times with different names to verify that it works correctly.

3.8 Use the class CardDeck developed in Written Exercise 3.8 to play the following card game called Hi-Low. Deal five cards. For each card, ask the player whether a randomly drawn card from the remaining cards in the deck will be higher or lower than the given card. An ace is the highest card in any suit, and the suits are ordered from clubs up to spades. Print the number of successful guesses.

3.9 For the following, use the Calendar class developed in Written Exercise 3.6. Write a function

```
int DayInterval(Calendar C, int mm1, int dd1, int mm2, int dd2);
```

that returns the number of days between the two dates. Write a main program that does the following:

1. Prints whether the current year is a leap year.
2. Uses NumDays to determine the number of days from the beginning of the year until Christmas.
3. Passes the result of (2) to PrintDate and verifies the correct date is printed.
4. Includes a computation of the number of days from today until Christmas.
5. Computes the number of the number of days between February 1 and March 1.

3.10 Extend the Dice class of Chapter 1 to toss n dice, $n \le 20$. If the number of dice is not supplied to the constructor, it should default to 2. Use the Dice class to solve the following problem:

Declare an array of 30 Dice objects. Initialize each element to toss five (5) dice. You will need to use the default constructor in the declaration and then loop to initialize each element for 5 dice.

Execute Toss for each element.

Scan the list and determine how many times a 5 or a 12 was thrown.

Indicate how many times a total was repeated on the next toss. For instance, 8 8 8 counts as two repeats.

Scan the list and find the largest total, displaying the die faces.

Sort the list by die count and print the totals.

3.11 Declare the enum

```
enum unit {metric, English};
```

The Height class contains the following private data members:

```
char name[20];
unit measureType;
float h; // height in measureType units (ft. or cm.)
```

The operations include

```
// constructor:parameters name, height, measurement type
Height(char nm[], float ht, unit m);
PrintHeight(void);   // prints height in appropriate unit
// input name, measurement type, and height
ReadHeight(void);
float GetHeight(void);   // return height
void Convert(unit m);    // convert h to measurement m
```

(a) Implement the class. There are 2.54 centimeters per inch.
(b) Write a function that scans a list and converts all the items to a unit of measurement that is given as a parameter. Assume that the objects are expressed in the other unit of measurement.
(c) Write a function that sorts an array of Height objects. It is assumed that each object uses the same unit of measurement.
(d) Write a function that scans an array and returns an object representing the tallest person. Assume all objects use the same unit of measurement.
(e) Write a program to test the class by creating a list of five items of type Height. Initialize the first three in the declaration and read the last two. Use the functions developed in parts (b), (c), and (d).

3.12 A bank with only one teller has noted that customer transactions fall in the range of 5 to 10 minutes. A line of 10 customers has formed at opening time. Use the class Event developed in Written Exercise 3.12 to compute the time it will take for the teller to service the 10 customers.

3.13 An ellipse or oval is determined by a circumscribing rectangle whose dimensions are $2a$ by $2b$.

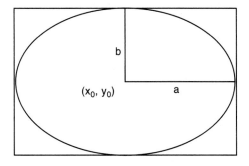

The constants *a* and *b* are called the semiaxes of the ellipse. An ellipse whose semiaxes are of the same length is a circle. The mathematical equation of an ellipse is

$$(x - x_0)^2/a^2 + (y - y_0)^2/b^2 = 1$$

and its area is πab. Develop a class Ellipse whose member functions consist of the constructor and an area method. Use Ellipse and the class Rectangle to solve the following problem:

An oval swimming pool whose semiaxes are of lengths 30 and 40 is to be built inside an 80 × 60 rectangular area. The cost of the pool is $25,000. Cement is to cover the area outside the pool, and its cost is $.50/ft². Compute the total cost of the construction.

3.14 The data for a baseball player includes the player's number, times at bat, hits, and batting average (NumberHits/NumberAtBats). This information is stored as data members in the private section of the class Baseball. All constructor parameters have defaults. The default uniform number is −1 and those for number of bats and hits are 0. When a default for the uniform number is accepted, it is assumed that the player's uniform number, number of hits, and number of at bats is to read using ReadPlayer. When the uniform number is known, ReadPlayer inputs the number of hits and at bats. The method GetBatAve returns the batting average. The private method ComputeBatAve() is used as a utility operation by the constructor and ReadPlayer to set the member variable containing the batting average. The method WritePlayer outputs all the information about the player in the format

```
Player <UniformNo> Average <BattingAvg>
```

The batting average is output as a three-digit integer. For instance, if the number of hits is 30 and the number of bats is 100, the batting average is output by WritePlayer as 300.

Baseball Class Declaration

```
class Baseball
{
    private:
        int playerno;
        int atbats;
        int hits;
        float batave;
        // ComputeBatAve is given with inline code.
        float ComputeBatAve (void) const // private method
        {
            if (playerno == -1 || atbats == 0)
                return(0);
            else
                return(float(hits)/atbats);
        }
```

```
    public:
        Baseball (int n = -1, int ab = 0, int h = 0);
        void ReadPlayer(void);
        void WritePlayer(void) const;
        float GetBatAve(void) const;
};
```

Implement the Baseball class and use it in a main program as follows:

1. Declare four objects:

Catcher	Uniform number 10, 100 at bats, 30 hits
Shortstop	Only uniform number 44 available
Centerfielder	No information available
Maxobject	No information available

2. Read the necessary information for the shortstop and centerfielder objects.
3. Write out all information for catcher, shortstop, and centerfielder.
4. Using the operation GetBatAve and object assignment, assign the player with the highest average to maxobject and print the information.

3.15   Add triangular matrix subtraction and multiplication to the class TriMat and test them in a program similar to Program 3.5.

3.16   When solving a general $n \times n$ system of algebraic equations, a series of operations reduces the problem to solving a triangular matrix equation. A triangular matrix equation has a unique solution, provided the determinant of the coefficient matrix is nonzero. The set of algebraic equations is obtained by multiplying each row in the coefficient matrix by the column array of unknowns. By solving the equations in the order $n - 1$ down to 0, we obtain a unique solution for the variables X_{n-1}, X_{n-2}, . . ., X_1, X_0. For example, the triangular system of equations discussed in Written Exercise 3.14 is solved by applying this technique.

Equation 0:	$1X_0 \quad + \; 1X_1 \quad + \; 0X_2 \quad = \; 4$
Equation 1:	$\qquad\qquad 2X_1 \quad + \; 1X_2 \quad = \; 1$
Equation 2:	$\qquad\qquad\qquad\qquad 2X_2 \quad = \; 6$
Solve for X_2:	In equation 2, $X_2 \; = \; 6/2 \; = \; 3$
Solve for X_1:	In equation 1, substitute 3 for X_2; solve the equation for the unknown X_1.

$$2X_1 + 3 = 1$$
$$X_1 = -1$$

Solve for X_0:   In equation 0, substitute -1 for X_1 and 3 for X_2; solve the equation for the unknown X_0.

$$X_0 \; - \; 1 = 4$$
$$X_0 \; = \; 5$$

The final solution is $X_0 = 5$, $X_1 = -1$, $X_2 = 3$.

Put these ideas together and develop the function

```
void SolveEqn(const TriMat& A, double X[], double C[]);
```

It determines the unique solution, if it exists, to the general triangular matrix equation

$$
\begin{bmatrix}
A_{00} & A_{01} & \cdot & \cdots & A_{0\,n-1} \\
0 & A_{11} & A_{12} & \cdots & A_{1\,n-1} \\
0 & 0 & A_{22} & \cdots & A_{2\,n-1} \\
0 & \vdots & \vdots & \vdots & \vdots \\
0 & \cdots & \cdots & A_{n-2\,n-2} & A_{n-2\,n-1} \\
0 & 0 & \cdots & 0 & A_{n-1\,n-1}
\end{bmatrix}
*
\begin{bmatrix}
X_0 \\ X_1 \\ X_2 \\ \vdots \\ X_{n-2} \\ X_{n-1}
\end{bmatrix}
=
\begin{bmatrix}
C_0 \\ C_1 \\ C_2 \\ \vdots \\ C_{n-2} \\ C_{n-1}
\end{bmatrix}
$$

(a)   Use SolveEqn in a program to solve the sample system of equations.

$$
\begin{bmatrix}
1 & 1 & 0 \\
0 & 2 & 1 \\
0 & 0 & 2
\end{bmatrix}
*
\begin{bmatrix}
X_0 \\ X_1 \\ X_2
\end{bmatrix}
=
\begin{bmatrix}
4 \\ 1 \\ 6
\end{bmatrix}
$$

(b)   Solve the system of equations in Written Exercise 3.14(a).

C H A P T E R 4

COLLECTION
CLASSES

Chapter 2 introduces the basic data types that are directly supported by a programming language. The types include primitive number and character data as well as the array, string, and record types. These structured data types are examples of **collections** that store data and provide access operations that add, delete, or update the data items. The study of collection types is the main focus of this book.

Collections are classified into two main categories: linear and nonlinear. Figure 4.1 uses methods of data access to further partition the categories and list the data structures that are presented in this book. This chapter gives a brief summary of each collection in the chart by describing its data, its operations, and some of its practical uses.

A **linear** collection contains lists of elements that are ordered by position (Figure 4.2). There is a first element, a second element, and so forth. An array with the index reflecting the order of the elements is a primary example of a linear collection.

A **nonlinear** collection identifies elements without positional order. For instance, the chain of command of workers in a plant or a set of pool balls in a rack are nonlinear collections (Figure 4.3).

This chapter also includes a study of algorithm efficiency. We describe the factors that determine efficiency and introduce Big-O notation as its measure. The measure is used throughout the book to compare and contrast different algorithms.

The SeqList class from Chapter 1 is a fundamental collection type. In this chapter we provide an array-based implementation of the class. The class is revisited in Chapter 9 when we define a linked list implementation. In Chapter 12, SeqList is used with inheritance to create an ordered list.

When C++ implements collections as classes, the compiler requires the function parameters to have specific data types and does strong type checking to verify consistency. To implement our collection types with full generality, we introduce C++ **template** classes in Chapter 7. Template classes are written using a generic name, such as T, for the data type handled by the collection. When an object is declared, the actual type for T is provided as a parameter. Templates are a powerful C++ tool for allowing generic declaration of classes. For instance, assume that a collection class has a 10-element array of items. The first declaration defines an

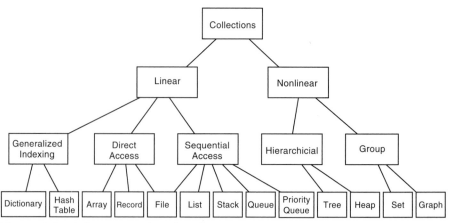

Figure 4.1   Collection Hierarchy and Roadmap

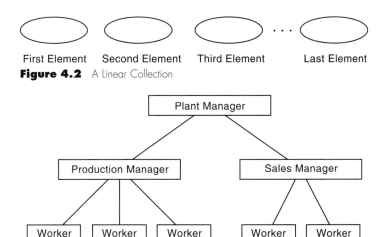

Figure 4.2 A Linear Collection

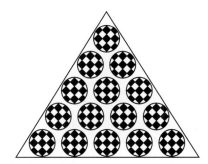

Figure 4.3 Nonlinear Collections

array of integers. The template version does not assume a specific type but allows the class to use the generic name T for the array element type. The actual type is supplied during the declaration of the object.

Declaration 1

```
class Collection
{
    . . . .
    int    A[10];      // array of integers is a data member
}

Collection object;    // A is an array of integers
```

Declaration 2

```
template <class T>
class Collection
{
```

```
    . . . .
    T A[10];                // generic declaration of the array;
                            // specify T when declaring the object
}


Collection<int> object;     // A is an array of integers
Collection<char> object;    // A is an array of characters
```

4.1 Describing Linear Collections

The method of accessing elements distinguishes the linear collections shown in Figure 4.1. With **direct access,** we can select an item directly without first accessing the preceding elements in the list. For instance, characters in a string can be directly accessed. The third letter in the word LIMEAR is misspelled. There is nothing wrong with the first two letters. We can correct the third letter without first having to access the first two letters. Some linear collections, however, called **sequential lists,** do not allow direct access. You access an element by starting at the front of the list and moving down the elements to the designated item. For instance, in baseball, the batter safely arrives at third base only after touching both first and second base.

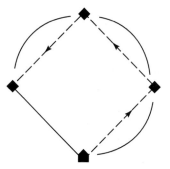

A parking garage offers a comparison between lists with direct access capability and sequential lists. The following diagram describes a parking garage that has a free lane running adjacent to the cars. The attendant can retrieve car 3 by getting directly into the car and using the free lane.

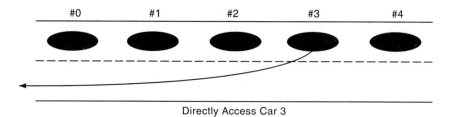

Directly Access Car 3

The next diagram illustrates a sequential parking garage in which all cars are parked in a single lane. The attendant can only access a car sequentially. To fetch car 3, the attendant must move cars 0 to 2 in that order.

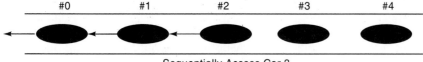

Sequentially Access Car 3

DIRECT ACCESS COLLECTIONS

An **array** is a collection of items having the same data type that are directly accessed by an integer index.

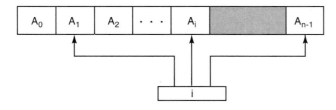

Array Collection

Data
    A collection of objects of the same (homogeneous) type.

Operations
    The data at each location in the array are directly accessed
    through an integer index.

A **static array** contains a fixed number of elements and is allocated a compilation time. A **dynamic array** is created using techniques of dynamic memory management and can be resized.

An array is a data structure that can be used to store a list. In the case of a sequential list, an array allows for the efficient addition of elements at the rear of the list. The structure is less efficient when deleting an element since we must often shift elements. The same shifting occurs when the array stores an ordered list and new items must be inserted.

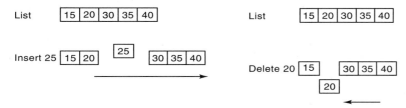

Chapter 8 introduces an Array class that extends the concept of a simple array. The class provides a new index operator that first tests that the index is in range before storing or retrieving data. The class, which implements *safe arrays,* allows the client to allocate the array dynamically at run time.

A **character string** is an array of characters with associated operations that determine the length of the string, concatenate two strings, delete a substring, and so forth. A general String class having an extended set of string operations is developed in Chapter 8.

String Collection

Data
> A collection of characters with a known length.

Operations
> There are operations to determine the string length, to copy or concatenate one string to another, to compare two strings, to perform pattern matching, and to perform input/output of strings.

A **record** is the basic collection structure for holding data that may consist of different types. For many applications, different data items are associated with a single object. For instance, an airline ticket includes data on flight number, seat number, passenger name, cost, ticketing agent, and so forth. A single ticket object is a set of fields of different types. The record collection bundles the fields while maintaining direct access to the data in the individual fields.

Record Collection

Data
> An item with a collection of fields of perhaps different types.

Operations
> The dot operator allows for direct access of the data in the field.

SEQUENTIAL ACCESS COLLECTIONS

A more general collection is a list that stores elements in sequential order. The structure, called a **linear list,** holds an arbitrary number of items. The size of the list is modified by adding or deleting an item from the list, and the items in the list are referenced by their position. The first element occurs at the head or front of the list, and the last element occurs at the rear of the list. Each element except the last has a unique successor.

List Collection

Data
An arbitrary collection of objects of the same (homogeneous) type.

Operations
We must traverse the list to reference the individual items. From a starting point, proceed from element to element until arriving at the desired location. Insertions and deletions alter the size of the list.

A linear list collection can have any number of items, and assumes that the collection will expand or contract as new items are added to the list or resident items are deleted. This list structure is limiting when one wants to access arbitrary elements, since there is no direct access. Access to list elements requires a traversal of elements from a starting point in the list. Depending on the implementation technique used, we are able to move in one of two ways: from left to right, or in both directions. In this chapter, we develop a class that implements a sequential list using an array. The resulting list is limited by the size of the array. A more powerful implementation in Chapter 9 removes any size limitation by using linked lists and dynamic structures.

A shopping list provides an example of a sequential list. The customer initially creates the list by writing down the names of the items. While shopping, the customer deletes the names from the list as the items are found or are no longer desired.

An **ordered linear list** is a linear list whose data values are in order with respect to one another. For instance, the list

3, 5, 6, 12, 18, 33

is in numerical order but the list

1, 6, 2, 5, 8

is not. The binary search, discussed in this chapter, is an algorithm that uses an ordered list.

Stacks and queues are special versions of a linear list with restricted access to data items. In a **stack,** items are added and deleted at only one end of the list called the *top.* A rack to hold the serving trays at a buffet dinner is a familiar example. The operation of removing an item from a list is called **popping** the stack. The addition of an item to the list is referred to as **pushing** an item on the stack.

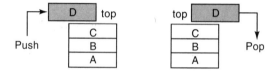

When an item is added, all other elements currently on the stack are "pushed lower" to make room for the new item at the top. As the items are removed ("popped") from the stack, they come off in the reverse order. The last item pushed on the stack is the first one off the stack. This type of storage of elements is referred to as *last-in/first-out* (LIFO) order.

Stack Collection

Data

A list of items that can be accessed only at the top of the list.

Operations

The list supports push and pop operations. A push adds a new item to the top of the list, and a pop removes an item from the top of the list.

We introduce stacks in a range of applications that include expression evaluation, recursion, and tree traversal. In these cases, we scan items and then access them in the LIFO order. Compilers pass parameters to functions using the stack and also use the stack for local variable storage.

A **queue** is a list with access only at the front and rear of the list. Items are inserted at the rear of the queue and deleted from the front. By using both ends of the list, items leave the queue in the same order as their arrival. The storage of elements occurs in a first-in/first-out (FIFO) order.

Queue Collection

Data

A list of items with access at the front and rear of the list.

Operations

Add an item at the rear of the list and remove an item from the front of the list.

A queue is a useful collection for maintaining waiting lists. A model for the queue is a bank or grocery store customer service line. Queues find computer applications in simulation studies and print job scheduling within an operating system.

For some applications, we modify the queue structure by prioritizing the items. When removing an object from the list, an item of highest priority is selected. This collection, called a **priority queue,** has insert and delete operations. Where data are inserted in the priority queue is incidental. The important fact is that the delete operation selects the item of highest priority. A hospital emergency ward uses a priority queue. Patients are served in order of arrival unless they have an immediate life-threatening condition, which gives them a higher priority and first access to the emergency services.

Priority Queue Collection

Data

A list of items such that each item has a priority.

Operations

Add an item to the list. Removing an item extracts the element of highest priority.

Priority queues are used for job scheduling within an operating system. Jobs of the highest priority must run first. Priority queues are also used in event-driven simulation. For instance, a case study in Chapter 5 performs a simulation of customer flow in and out of a bank. Each type of event, an arrival or a departure, is inserted into a priority queue. The event with the earliest time is removed and serviced first.

In a computer system, a **file** is an external collection that has an associated data structure called a *stream*. We equate a file with its stream and focus on the flow of data. Direct access is available for a disk file but tape files are sequential. The read operation deletes data from an input stream, and the write operation adds new data to the end of an output stream. A file is often used for the storage of large amounts of data. For instance, during the compilation of a program, the large tables that are generated are often stored in temporary files.

File Collection

Data

A sequence of bytes associated with an external device. Data flows through a stream to and from the device.

Operations

Open the file, read data from the file, write data to the file, seek a specified point in the file (direct access), and close the file.

GENERALIZED INDEXING

An array is a classical collection that allows for direct access of each item using an integer index. For many applications, we associate with a data record a key that is used to access the record. When calling a bank or insurance company to get information, we give our account number, which becomes the key to retrieve the record of our account. A collection called a **hash table** stores data associated with a key. The key is transformed into an integer index that is used to retrieve the data. In one frequently used hash table method, the integer value is an index into an array of collections. After transforming the key into an index, the associated collection is searched. The key need not be an integer. For instance, a data record may consist of a name, job classification, number of years with a company, salary, and so forth.

"Wilson, Sandra R."
3
15
42500

In this case, the string specifying the name is the key.

A real-world dictionary is a collection of words and their definitions. You look up a word by using the word as a key. In data structures, a collection called a **dictionary** consists of a set of key-value pairs called **associations.**

Association

For instance, the key may be a word and the value a string specifying the definition of the word. The value in an association is directly accessed using the key as an index. As a result, a dictionary is similar to an array, except that indices do not have to be integer values. For instance, if Dict is a dictionary collection, look up the definition of "dog" by referencing Dict["dog"]. Dictionaries are often called **associative arrays** because they associate a general index with a data value.

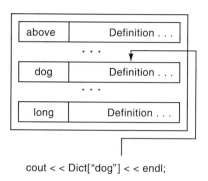

cout << Dict["dog"] << endl;

Describing Nonlinear Collections   **4.2**

Figure 4.1 indicates that nonlinear collections are partitioned into hierarchical and group structures. A **hierarchical collection** is an accumulation of items that are partitioned by levels. Items at a given level may have several successors at the next level. We introduce a specific hierarchical collection, called a **tree,** in which all data items emanate from a single source called the *root.* The elements in the tree are called *nodes,* each of which points to descendent nodes called *children.* Each item, except for the root, has a unique predecessor. Paths down the tree begin at the root and progress down the levels from parent to child.

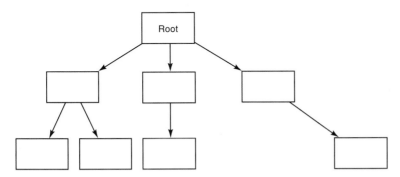

A tree is an ideal structure for describing a file system with directories and subdirectories. A model for a tree is a business organization chart that defines a chain of command starting with the boss (CEO, president) and moving to vice presidents, supervisors, and so forth.

In this book, we consider a special form of a tree in which each node has at most two descendants. The structure, a **binary tree,** has important applications in evaluating arithmetic expressions and in compiler theory. With additional ordering, the tree becomes a **binary search tree,** which efficiently stores large volumes of data. Binary search trees provide rapid access to elements by positioning nodes so the data can be located by moving down a short path from the root node. Figure 4.4 illustrates a tree with 16 nodes. The longest path from the root to a node involves

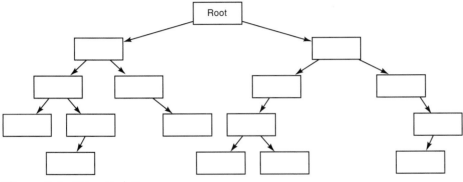

Figure 4.4   Sixteen-Node Tree

four branches. Assuming that the tree is relatively full of nodes, the ratio of nodes to path length improves significantly as we increase the size of the tree. As an example, if a binary search tree has $2^{20} - 1 = 1,048,575$ nodes that are placed on a minimum number of levels, a data item can be located by visiting no more than 20 nodes. A special type of binary search tree, an AVL tree, guarantees uniform distribution of nodes and guarantees very rapid search times.

Tree Collection

Data

A hierarchical collection of nodes that eminate from a root. Each node points to children nodes that are themselves roots of subtrees.

Operations

A tree structure allows for the addition and deletion of nodes. Even though a tree is a nonlinear structure, tree traversal algorithms allow us to visit the individual nodes and search for a key.

A **heap** is a special version of a tree in which the smallest element always occupies the root node. The delete operation removes the root node, and both the insert and delete operations cause the tree to reorganize so that the smallest element again occupies the root of the tree. A heap uses very efficient reorganization algorithms by scanning only short paths from the root down to the end of the tree. A heap can be used to order a list of elements. Rather than using slower sorting algorithms, we order them by repeatedly deleting the root node from a heap. This gives rise to the extremely fast *heapsort*. Also, a priority queue is most often implemented using a heap.

GROUP COLLECTIONS

A **group** represents those nonlinear collections that contain items without any ordering. A set of unique items is an example of a group. Operations on the set collection include union and intersection. Other set operations test for membership and the subset relation. In Chapter 8, we introduce the Set class with operator overloading to implement set operations.

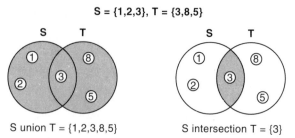

S = {1,2,3}, T = {3,8,5}

S union T = {1,2,3,8,5}   S intersection T = {3}

4.4 develops the running time for the sequential and binary search. Each algorithm has a worst and a best case complexity that are different. The best case for an algorithm is often not important since the circumstances are exceptional and not useful for deciding on the choice of an algorithm. The worst case can be important since those circumstances would most negatively affect your application. A client may not tolerate the worst case and may prefer you choose an algorithm that has a narrower range of efficiency. In general, it is mathematically more difficult to determine the average performance of an algorithm. We will use only very simple measures of expected values and leave the mathematical details to a course on complexity theory.

COMMON ORDERS OF MAGNITUDE

A small set of different orders defines the complexity of most data structure algorithms. We define the different orders and describe algorithms that result in these magnitudes.

If an algorithm is $O(1)$, its complexity is independent of the number of data items in the collection. The algorithm runs in **constant time.** For instance, assigning an element at the end of an array list is $O(1)$ provided you maintain an index that identifies the rear of list. The storing of the element involves a simple assignment statement.

Direct Insert at Rear

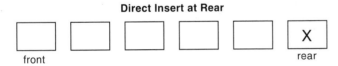

An $O(n)$ algorithm is said to be **linear.** The complexity of the algorithm is proportional to the size of the list. For instance, the insertion of an element at the rear of an n element list would be linear if we do not maintain a reference to the rear. Assuming that we can scan from item to item, the algorithm requires that we test n items before identifying the rear. The order of this process is $O(n)$. Finding the maximum of the elements in an n element array is $O(n)$ because each of the n elements must be checked.

Sequential Insert at Rear

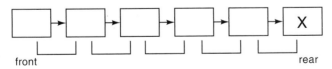

A variety of algorithms have complexity involving $\log_2 n$ and are termed **logarithmic.** This complexity occurs when the algorithm repeatedly subdivides the data into sublists that are 1/2, 1/4, 1/8, and so forth of the original list size. Logarithmic orders occur with binary trees. The binary search developed in Section 4.4 has an

TABLE 4.2
Various Orders
of Magnitude

n	$log_2 n$	$n \, log_2 n$	n^2	n^3	2^n
2	1	2	4	8	4
4	2	8	16	64	16
8	3	24	64	512	256
16	4	64	256	4096	65536
32	5	160	1024	32768	4294967296
128	7	896	16384	2097152	3.4×10^{38}
1024	10	10240	1048576	1073741824	1.8×10^{308}
65536	16	1048576	4294967296	2.8×10^{14}	Forget it!

average and worst case complexity of $O(log_2 n)$. Chapters 13 and 14 develop tree sorting algorithms and the quick sort of order $O(n \, log_2 n)$.

Algorithms with a complexity of $O(n^2)$ are **quadratic.** Most simple sorting algorithms such as the exchange sort are $O(n^2)$. Quadratic algorithms are practical only for relatively small values of n. Whenever n doubles, the running time of the algorithm increases by a factor of 4. An algorithm exhibits **cubic** time if its complexity is $O(n^3)$, and such algorithms are very slow. Whenever n doubles, the running time of the algorithm increases eightfold. Warshall's algorithm dealing with graphs is an $O(n^3)$ algorithm.

An algorithm with a complexity of $O(2^n)$ has **exponential complexity.** Such algorithms run so slowly that they are not useful unless n is small. This type of complexity is often associated with problems that require repeated searching of a decision tree.

Table 4.2 gives the linear, quadratic, cubic, exponential, and logarithmic orders of magnitude for selected values of n. Certainly the table tells you to avoid cubic and exponential algorithms unless n is small.

4.4 The Sequential and Binary Search

We now introduce the sequential search for the purpose of locating a value in a list. Assuming we search an integer list limits the use of the algorithm. In fact, we can search an array of any type as long as the operator "==" is defined. We must modify the sequential search to reference the generic type DataType, which is an alias for an actual type. We create this alias by using the typedef keyword. For instance,

```
typedef int DataType;      // DataType is int
```

or

```
typedef double DataType:   // DataType is double
```

If we assume that the programmer has defined DataType, the code for the general sequential search algorithm is

```
// search the n element array a for a match with key
// using the sequential search. return the index of the
// matching array element or −1 if a match does not occur
int SeqSearch(DataType list[], int n, DataType key)
{
   for(int i=0;i < n;i++)
     if (list[i] == key)
        return i;            // return index of the matching item
   return −1;               // search failed. return −1
}
```

The complexity of the sequential search distinguishes best and worst case behavior. The best case finds a match at the first element in the list and has running time $O(1)$. The worst case occurs when the item is not in the list or is found at the rear of the list. This requires searching all n terms, which has a complexity of $O(n)$. The average case requires a small amount of probabilistic reasoning. For a random list, a match is equally likely to occur at any position. After executing a large number of searches, the average position for a match is the midpoint $n/2$. The midpoint occurs after $n/2$ comparisons, which defines the expected cost of the search. For this reason, we say the average performance of the sequential search is $O(n)$.

BINARY SEARCH

The sequential search applies to any list. If the list is ordered, an algorithm, called the **binary search,** provides an improved search technique. Your experience in looking up a number in a large phone directory is a model for the algorithm. Given the name, you open the book near the front, middle, or end depending on the first letter in the last name. You might be lucky and land on the right page. Otherwise, you move to an earlier or later page in the phone book depending on the relative location of the person's name in the alphabet. For instance, if the person's name begins with "R" and you are in the "T's," you move to an earlier page. The process continues until you get a match or discover that the name is not in the book. A related idea applies to searching an ordered list. We go to the middle of the list and look for a quick match of our key with the midpoint value. If we fail to find a match, we look at the relative size of the key and the midpoint value and then move to the lower or upper half of the list. In general, if we know how the data are ordered, we can use that information to shorten the search time.

The following steps describe the algorithm. Assume that the list is stored as an array. The indices at the ends of the list are low = 0 and high = $n − 1$ where n is the number of elements in the array.

1. Compute the index of the array's midpoint:

```
mid = (low+high)/2.
```

2. Compare the value at this midpoint with the key.

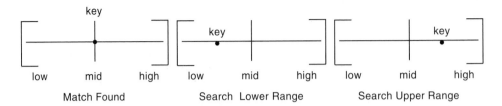

Match Found   Search Lower Range   Search Upper Range

If a match occurs, return the index mid to locate the key.

```
if (A[mid] == key)
    return(mid);
```

If A[mid] < key, a match must lie in the index range mid+1 . . . high, the right half of the original list. This is true because the list is ordered. The new boundaries are low=mid+1 and high.

If key < A[mid], a match must lie in the index range low . . . mid−1, the left half of the list. The new boundaries are low and high = mid−1.

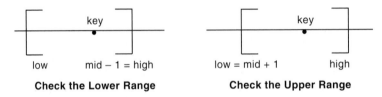

Check the Lower Range   **Check the Upper Range**

The algorithm refines the location of a match by halving the length of the interval in which key can exist and then executing the same search algorithm on the smaller sublist. Eventually, if the key is not in the list, low will exceed high and the algorithm returns the failure indicator of −1 (match not found).

EXAMPLE 4.2
―――――――

Consider the integer array A. The example gives a snapshot of the algorithm for the selected key = 33.

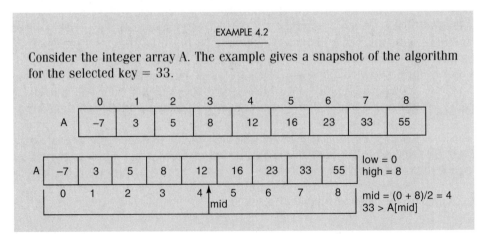

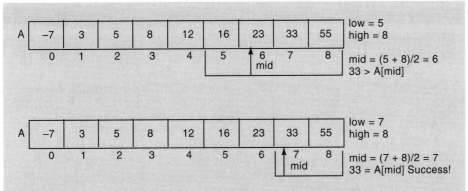

Note that the algorithm requires three (3) comparisons. If the list were searched linearly, it would take eight (8) comparisons.

BINARY SEARCH IMPLEMENTATION

The function uses the generic type DataType, which must support both the equality ('==') and the less than ('<') operators. Initially, low is 0 and high is $n - 1$, where n is the number of elements in the array. The function returns the index of the matching array element or -1 when a failure is identified (low > high).

```
// search a sorted array a for a match with key
// using the binary search. return the index of the
// matching array element or −1 if a match does not occur
int BinSearch(DataType list[], int low, int high, DataType key)
{
    int mid;
    DataType midvalue;

    while (low <= high)
    {
        mid = (low+high)/2;    // mid index in the sublist
        midvalue = list[mid];  // value at the mid index
        if (key == midvalue)
            return mid;        // have a match. return its location
        else if (key < midvalue)
            high = mid−1;      // go to lower sublist
        else
            low = mid+1;       // go to upper sublist
    }
    return −1;                 // did not find the item
}
```

The implementation of the sequential and binary searches is stored in the file "dsearch.h". Since the function depends on DataType, the definition of DataType must be provided before including the file.

Program 4.1 Comparison of Sequential and Binary Search

The program compares the computing time of the sequential and binary searches. An array A is filled with 1000 random integers in the range 0 .. 1999 and then sorted. A second array B is given 500 random integers in the same range. The elements in B are used as keys for the search algorithms. The timing function TickCount is defined in the file "ticks.h" and returns the number of 1/60*th* seconds since system startup. We measure the time it takes to complete the 500 searches using each algorithm. Output includes the time in seconds and the number of matches.

```cpp
#include <iostream.h>

typedef int DataType;          // integer data

#include "dsearch.h"
#include "random.h"
#include "ticks.h"

// sort the n element integer array in ascending order
void ExchangeSort(int a[], int n)
{
    int i, j, temp;

    // with n-1 passes, place correct values in a[0] ..a[n-2]
    for (i = 0; i < n-1; i++)
        // put minimum of a[i] ...a[n-1] in a[i]
        for (j = i+1; j < n; j++)
            // if a[j] < a[i], exchange them
            if (a[j] < a[i])
            {
                temp = a[i];
                a[i] = a[j];
                a[j] = temp;
            }
}

void main(void)
{
    // A holds list to search, B holds the keys
    int A[1000], B[500];
    int i, matchCount;
```

```
    // used for timing data
    long tcount;


    RandomNumber rnd;


    // create array A with 1000 random values between 0..1999
    for (i = 0; i < 1000; i++)
        A[i] = rnd.Random(2000);
    ExchangeSort(A,1000);


    // generate 500 random keys in the same range
    for (i = 0; i < 500; i++)
        B[i] = rnd.Random(2000);


    cout << "Timing the Sequential Search" << endl;
    tcount = TickCount();          // starting time
    matchCount = 0;
    for (i = 0; i < 500; i++)
        if (SeqSearch(A,1000, B[i]) != -1)
            matchCount++;
    tcount = TickCount() - tcount;  // number of 1/60 th secs.
    cout << "Sequential Search takes " << tcount/60.0
         << " seconds for " << matchCount << " matches." << endl;


    cout << "Timing the Binary Search" << endl;
    tcount = TickCount();          // starting time
    matchCount = 0;
    for (i = 0; i < 500; i++)
        if (BinSearch(A,0,999,B[i]) != -1)
            matchCount++;
    tcount = TickCount() - tcount;  // number of 1/60 th secs.
    cout << "Binary Search takes " << tcount/60.0
         << " seconds for " << matchCount << " matches." << endl;


}


/*
<Run of Program 4.1>


Timing the Sequential Search
Sequential Search takes 0.816667 seconds for 181 matches.
Timing the Binary Search
Binary Search takes 0.016667 seconds for 181 matches.
*/
```

Informal Analysis for the Binary Search   The best case outcome occurs when a match is found at the midpoint of the list. This has complexity $O(1)$ since only one equality comparison test is required. The complexity of the worst case is $O(\log_2 n)$, which occurs when the item is not in the list or the item is found on the last comparison. We can intuitively derive this complexity. The worst case occurs when we must continue to shrink the sublist to a length of 1. Each iteration that fails to match shrinks the length of the sublist by a factor of 2. The size of the sublists are

$$n \quad n/2 \quad n/4 \quad n/8 \quad \ldots \quad 1$$

The splitting of sublists requires m iterations, where m is approximately $\log_2 n$ (see the detailed analysis). For the worst case, we have an initial comparison with the midpoint of the list and then a series of $\log_2 n$ iterations. Each iteration requires one comparison operation:

```
Total Comparisons ≈ 1 + log₂n
```

As a result, the worst case for the binary search is $O(\log_2 n)$. This result is empirically verified by Program 4.1. The ratio of the running times for the sequential and binary searches is 49.0. The theoretical ratio of the expected running times is approximately $500/(\log_2 1000) = 50.2$.

Formal Analysis of the Binary Search   The first iteration of the loop deals with the entire list. Each subsequent iteration halves the size of the sublist. Thus, the list sizes for the algorithm are

$$n \quad n/2^1 \quad n/2^2 \quad n/2^3 \quad n/2^4 \quad \ldots \quad n/2^m$$

Eventually there will be an integer m such that

$$n/2^m < 2 \quad \text{or} \quad n < 2^{m+1}$$

Since m is the first integer for which $n/2^m < 2$, it must be true that

$$n/2^{m-1} \geq 2 \quad \text{or} \quad 2^m \leq n$$

It therefore follows that

$$2^m \leq n < 2^{m+1}$$

Take the log of each term and let $\log_2 n =$ the real number x:

$$m \leq \log_2 n = x < m + 1$$

The value m is the greatest integer that is $\leq x$ and is given by int(x). For instance, if $n = 50$, $\log_2 50 = 5.644$. Hence,

$$m = \text{int}(5.644) = 5$$

It can be shown that the average case is also $O(\log_2 n)$.

The Basic Sequential List Class   4.5

Shopping items, a bus schedule, a telephone directory, tax tables, and inventory records are examples of lists. In each case, the objects include a sequence of items. Many applications involve maintaining a list. For example, a business inventory maintains supply and reordering information, a personnel office creates payroll information for the list of company employees, keywords for a compiler are stored in a list of reserved words, and so forth.

Chapter 1 introduced the ADT for a basic sequential list. The basic list operations include inserting a new item at the rear of the list, deleting an item, accessing an item in the list by position, and clearing the list. We also have operations to test whether the list is empty or whether an item is in the list. As a real-world example of such a list, consider taking a grocery list to the store (Figure 4.6). While walking through the store, additional items come to mind, and you add them at the end of the list. When an item is located, you delete it from the list. A list with these simple operations can be used to solve significant problems. An application describes a video store that maintains a list of available movies and a list of customer rentals. When a film is rented, it moves off the inventory list and onto the rental list. A return of a film reverses the process.

The list ADT describes **homogeneous lists** in which each element has the same data type, called DataType. In the definition of the ADT, there is no mention of how

Original list   Add Tuna   Delete Bread

Delete Potatoes   Add Milk

Figure 4.6   Shopping List

the elements are stored. An array can be used, or the elements can be stored in a linked list using dynamic memory allocation. The implementations of the Insert, Delete, and Find operations depend on the technique used to store the list elements.

Chapter 1 provided only a sketch of the class specification. In this section, we develop an implementation of the SeqList class that stores the elements in an array. In Chapter 9, we design a new implementation of the class using linked lists and derive the class from the abstract base class List in Chapter 12. Classes of similar structure are developed for binary search trees, hash tables, and dictionaries in Chapters 11, 13, and 14.

SeqList CLASS SPECIFICATION

DECLARATION

```
#include <iostream.h>
#include <stdlib.h>

const int MaxListSize = 50;

class SeqList
{
    private:
        // list storage array and number of current list elements
        DataType listitem[MaxListSize];
        int size;

    public:
        // constructor
        SeqList(void);

        // list access methods
        int ListSize(void) const;
        int ListEmpty(void) const;
        int Find (DataType& item) const;
        DataType GetData(int pos) const;

        // list modification methods
        void Insert(const DataType& item);
        void Delete(const DataType& item);
        DataType DeleteFront(void);
        void ClearList(void);
};
```

DESCRIPTION

The declaration and implementation is found in the file "aseqlist.h". The name DataType is used to represent a general data type. Before including the class from the file, use typedef to equate the name DataType with a specific type. The variable size maintains the current size of the list. Initially size is set to 0. Since a static array is used to implement the list, the constant MaxListSize is the upper bound for the size of the list. An attempt to insert more than MaxListSize elements into the list causes an error message and program termination.

EXAMPLE

```
typedef int DataType;      // SeqList class stores integer data
#include "aseqlist.h"

void PrintList(const SeqList & L)      // print the list
{
    int i, length = L.ListSize();

    for (i = 0; i < length; i++)
        cout << L.GetData(i) << " ";    // output item at position i
    cout << endl;
}

SeqList L;                              // SeqListL

L.Insert(10);                          // put value 10 at the rear of the list
L.Delete(25);                          // delete value 25 from the list
PrintList (L);                         // print the modified list

if (L.Find(5))                         // determine if 5 is in the list
    cout << "Have 5 in list" << endl;

while (!L.ListEmpty())
    cout << L.DeleteFront() << endl;   // print and clear list
```

- -

SeqList CLASS IMPLEMENTATION.

This implementation of the SeqList class uses array listitem to store the data. The collection allocates storage for MaxListSize number of items of type Data-Type. The number of elements in the list is maintained in the data member size. The files "iostream.h" and "stdlib.h" are included to provide an error message and to terminate the program if Insert would cause size to exceed MaxListSize.

The private data member size maintains the length of the list for the Insert and Delete operations. The value of size is the focus for the constructor and the methods ListSize, ListEmpty, and ClearList. We include only the constructor that sets size to 0. See the software supplement for the definition of the other methods.

```
    // constructor. set size to 0
    SeqList::SeqList (void) : size(0)
    {}
```

LIST MODIFICATION METHODS

Insert adds a new element at the rear of the list and increases the length by 1. If insertion of an item will exceed the size of array listitem, the method prints an error message and terminates the program. The restriction on the size of the list is lifted in Chapter 9 when the class is implemented using a linked list.

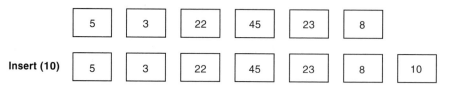

The parameter item is passed as a reference to a constant. If the size of DataType is large, the use of a reference parameter avoids the inefficient data copying that is required in a call by value parameter. The keyword const assures that the actual parameter cannot be modified. This same type of parameter passing is used by the method Delete.

Insert

```
// insert item at rear of list. terminate the program
// if the list size would exceed MaxListSize.
void SeqList::Insert(const DataType& item)
{
    // will an insertion exceed maximum list size allowed?
    if (size+1 > MaxListSize)
    {
        cerr <<"Maximum list size exceeded" << endl;
        exit(1);
    }

    // index of rear is current value of size
    listitem[size] = item;
    size++;                      // increment list size
}
```

The Delete method searches for the first occurrence in the list of the data value item. The function requires the relational equals operator "==" to be defined for DataType. In some cases, this may require that the user provide a special function that redefines the operator "==" for DataType. The topic is formally introduced in Chapter 6. If item is not found at index i, the operation quietly concludes without changing the list. If item is found, it is removed from the list by shifting all elements with indices $i + 1$ to the end of the list left one position.

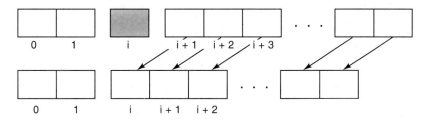

For instance, deleting 45 from the list causes the tail elements 23 and 8 to shift to the left. The length of the list goes from 6 to 5. Deleting 30 leaves the list unchanged.

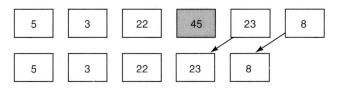

Delete

```
//search for item in the list and delete it if found
void SeqList::Delete(const DataType& item)
{
    int i = 0;

    // search for item
    while (i < size && !(item == listitem[i]))
        i++;

    if (i < size)              // successful if i < size
    {
        // shift the tail of the list to the left one position
        while (i < size-1)
        {
            listitem[i] = listitem[i+1];
            i++;
        }
        size--;                // decrement size
    }
}
```

List Access Methods   The GetData method returns the data value at position pos in the list. If pos does not lie the range 0 to size-1, an error message is printed and the program is terminated.

```
// return the value at position pos in the list. if pos is not a
// valid list position, terminate program with error message.
DataType SeqList::GetData(int pos) const
{
```

```
    // terminate program if pos out of range
    if (pos < 0 || pos >= size)
    {
        cerr << "pos is out of range!" << endl;
        exit(1);
    }
    return listitem[pos];
}
```

The access method Find takes a parameter that serves as the key and sequentially scans the list looking for a match. If the list is empty or no match is found, Find returns 0 (False). If the item is located in the list at index i, Find assigns the data record in listitem[i] to the matching list item and returns 1 (True).

On a match, the process of assigning the data value of the list item to the parameter is critical in applications involving data records. For instance, assume DataType is a struct with a key field and a value field and that the "==" operator tests only the key field. On input, the parameter item may define only the key field. On output, item is assigned both the key and value fields.

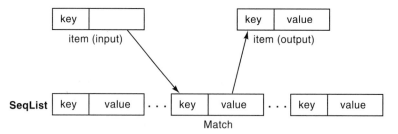

Find

```
// Use item as key and search the list. return True if item
// is in the list and False otherwise. If found,
// assign the list element to the reference parameter item
int SeqList::Find(DataType& item) const
{
    int i = 0;

    if (ListEmpty())
        return 0;                       // return False when list empty
    while (i < size && ! (item == listitem[i]))
        i++;
    if (i < size)
    {
        item = listitem[i];     // assign list element to item
        return 1;               // return True
    }
    else
        return 0;               // return False
}
```

The SeqList class does not provide a method to change the value of an item directly. To make such a change, we must first find the item and retrieve the data record, delete the item, modify the record, and reinsert the new data into the list. Of course, this changes the position because the new item goes at the rear of the list.

EXAMPLE 4.3

The record InventoryItem maintains a part number and the number of parts in stock. The relational equals operator compares two InventoryItem records by comparing the partNumber fields. SeqList object L is searched to locate a record with partNumber 5. If one is found, the record is updated by incrementing the count field.

```
struct InventoryItem
{
    int partNumber;
    int count;
}

int operator== (InventoryItem x, InventoryItem y)
{
    return x.partNumber == y.partNumber;
}

typedef InventoryItem DataType;
#include "aseqlist.h"
    . . .
SeqList L;
InventoryItem item;
    . . .
item.partNumber = 5;
if(L.Find(item))
{
    L.Delete(item);
    item.count++;
    L.Insert(item);
}
```

Since an element is always inserted at the rear of the list, the complexity (running time) of Insert is independent of n and is $O(1)$. Find performs a sequential search, so its average running time is $O(n)$. Over many trials, Delete must probe an average of $n/2$ list elements and must move an average of $n/2$ elements. This means that the average running time for Delete is $O(n)$. The worst case complexity for both Find and Delete is also $O(n)$.

Application   SeqList objects are used to maintain the list of available films and the list of rented films at a video store. Each item in a list is a record that consists of the film name and, for rentals, the customer name.

```
//record structure to store film and customer data
struct FilmData
{
    char filmName[32];
    char customerName[32];
}
```

Since the Find method in the SeqList class requires definition of the comparison operator "==", we overload the operator for the FilmData struct. The operator tests the file name using the C++ string function strcmp.

```
// overload "==" by comparing film names
int operator == (const FilmData &A, const FilmData *B)
{
    return strcmp(A.filmName, B.filmName);
}
```

To use FilmData with the SeqList class, include the declaration

```
typedef FilmData DataType;
```

The definition of the FilmData "==" operator and DataType is located in the file "video.h."

The video store maintains an inventory list of films. For simplicity, we assume that the store has only one copy of each film. A new video is simply added to the list using Insert. To check out a film, Find is used to search the inventory list. If the film is located, it is deleted from the inventory list and inserted into the list of rented films.

Program 4.2   The Video Store

A main program emulates video store transactions. Initially the entire inventory of films is read from the file "films" and stored in a list called inventoryList. We view a short span of store activities and look at four customer rental requests. In each case we input the customer name and film request and determine whether the film is currently available. If so, we remove it from the inventory list and add the customer to the list of renters. The customer is notified if the film is not available.

```
#include <iostream.h>
#include <fstream.h>

#include <stdlib.h>
#include <string.h>

include "video.h"            // video store data declarations
#include "aseqlist.h"         // include the SeqList class

// reads film inventory from disk
void SetupInventoryList(SeqList &inventoryList)
{
    ifstream filmFile;
    FilmData fd;

    // open the file with error checking
    filmFile.open("Films", ios::in | ios::nocreate);
    if (!filmFile)
    {
      cerr << "File 'films' not found!" << endl;
      exit(1);
     }

    // read lines until EOF; insert film names in inventory list
    while(filmFile.getline(fd.filmName,32,'\n'))
        inventoryList.Insert(fd);
}


// cycle through inventory list and print film names
void PrintInventoryList(const SeqList &inventoryList)
{
    int i;
    FilmData fd;

    for (i = 0; i < inventoryList.ListSize(); i++)
    {
        fd = inventoryList.GetData(i); // get film record
        cout << fd.filmName <<endl;    // print film name
    }
}


// cycle through customer list. print customer and film names
void PrintCustomerList(const SeqList &customerList)
{
    int i;
    FilmData fd;
```

```
        for (i = 0; i < customerList.ListSize(); i++)
        {
            fd = customerList.GetData(i);    // get customer record
            cout << fd.customerName << " (" << fd.filmName
            << ")" << endl;
        }
}

void main(void)
{
    // the two data bases
    SeqList inventoryList, customerList;
    int i;

    // film inventory file
    FilmData   fdata;

    char customer[20];

    SetupInventoryList(inventoryList);   // read inventory file

  // process 4 customers, asking for name and film desired. if
  // the film is available, insert film record into customer
  // list and delete it from inventory list; otherwise,
  // indicate it is not available.
  for (i = 0; i < 4; i++)
  {
        // get customer name and film request
        cout << "Customer Name: ";
        cin.getline(customer,32,'\n');
        cout << "Film Request: ";
        cin.getline(fdata.filmName,32,'\n');
        // check if film available if so, create customer record

        if (inventoryList.Find(fdata))
        {
          strcpy(fdata.customerName, customer);
          // insert in customer list
          customerList.Insert(fdata);
          // delete from inventory list
          inventoryList.Delete(fdata);
        }
        else
            cout << "Sorry! " << fdata.filmName
                    << " is not available." << endl;
    }
    cout << endl;
```

```
      // print the final customer and inventory lists.
      cout << "Customers Renting Films " << endl;
      PrintCustomerList(customerList);
      cout << endl;
      cout << "Films Remaining in Inventory:" << endl;
      PrintInventoryList(inventoryList);
}

/*
<Input file "Films">

War of the Worlds
Casablanca
Dirty Harry
Animal House
The Ten Commandments
Beauty and the Beast
Schindler's List
Sound of Music
La Strata
Star Wars

<Run of Program 4.2>

Customer Name: Don Baker
Film Request: Animal House
Customer Name: Teri Molton
Film Request: Beauty and the Beast
Customer Name: Derrick Lopez
Film Request: La Strata
Customer Name: Hillary Dean
Film Request: Animal House
Sorry! Animal House is not available.

Customers Renting Films
Don Baker (Animal House)
Teri Molton (Beauty and the Beast)
Derrick Lopez (La Strata)

Films Remaining in Inventory:
War of the Worlds
Casablanca
Dirty Harry
The Ten Commandments
Schindler's List
Sound of Music
Star Wars
*/
```

Written Exercises

4.1 Explain the difference between a linear and a nonlinear data structure. Give an example of each.

4.2 State which data structure is appropriate for the following situations:

(a) Store the absolute value of the number in element 5 of an integer list.

(b) Step through an alphabetized student list and print the grades.

(c) When an arithmetic operator is found, the two previous numbers are deleted from the collection.

(d) In the simulation study, each event is inserted into the collection and deleted in the order of its insertion.

(e) When a queen on a chess board can move to a position, that position is inserted into the collection.

(f) One field of the data structure is an integer, another is a real value, and the last field is a string.

(g) Permanently save the output of the program in order to examine it later.

(h) If the key is less than the current value in the list, examine descendants of the current value.

(i) The minimum value always filters up to the top of the list.

(j) A string is used as a key to locate a data record scattered somewhere in the collection.

(k) The word is used as an index to locate its definition in the collection.

(l) On holidays, a telephone network is overloaded. Determine an alternative set of paths to best route the calls.

4.3 The following are worst case measures of complexity for three algorithms that solve the same problem.

Algorithm 1	Algorithm 2	Algorithm 3
$O(n^2)$	$O(n \log_2 n)$	$O(2^n)$

Which method is preferable and why?

4.4 Perform a Big-O analysis for each of the following functions:

(a) $n + 5$

(b) $n^2 + 6n + 7$

(c) $\sqrt{n + 3}$

(d) $\dfrac{n^3 + n^2 - 1}{n + 1}$

4.5 (a) For what value of $n > 1$ does 2^n become larger than n^3?

(b) Show that $2^n + n^3$ is $O(2^n)$.

(c) Give a Big-O estimate for $\dfrac{n^2 + 5}{n + 3} + 6 \log_2 n$?

4.6 A list of integers is maintained in an array. What is the complexity of printing the first and last element in the array?

4.7 Explain why an algorithm of complexity $O(\log_2 n)$ is also $O(n)$.

4.8 Each loop is the primary component to an algorithm. Use Big-O notation to express the worst case computing time for each of the following loops as a function of n:

(a) ```
for (dotprd=0.0,i=0;i < n;i++)
     dotprd += a[i] * b[i];
```
(b)  ```
for(i=0;i < n;i++)
     if (a[i] == k)
          return 1;
return 0;
```
(c) ```
for (i=0;i < n;i++)
     for (j=0;j < n;j++)
          b[i][j] *= c;
```
(d)  ```
for (i=0;i < n;i++)
     for(j=0;j < n;j++)
     {
          entry = 0.0;
          for (k=0;k < n;k++)
               entry += a[i][k] * b[k][j];
          c[i,j] = entry;
     }
```

4.9 The following n element collections are used to store data. What is the computational complexity to find the minimum value in a

(a) stack?
(b) priority queue?
(c) binary search tree?
(d) sequential list in ascending order?
(e) list with direct access capability with items in descending order?

4.10 The sequence of Fibonacci numbers is

$$1, 1, 2, 3, 5, 8, 13, 21, 34, 55, 89, \ldots$$

The first two numbers are 1, and each succeeding Fibonacci number is the sum of the two preceding ones. The sequence is described by the recurrence relation

$$f_1 = 1, \quad f_2 = 1, \quad f_n = f_{n-2} + f_{n-1}, \quad \text{for } n \geq 3$$

The following function computes the n'th Fibonacci number. What is its complexity?

```
long Fibonacci(int n)
{
    long fnm2=1, fnm1=1, fn;
    int i;

    if (n <= 2)
        return 1;
```

```
        for (i=3;i <= n;i++)
        {
            fn = fnm2 + fnm1;
            fnm2 = fnm1;
            fnm1 = fn;
        }
        return fn;
}
```

In Chapter 10, a recursive function is written to compute the n'th Fibonacci number. This method exhibits exponential complexity. Clearly, the recursive solution is not acceptable!

4.11 (a) The sequential search is used with a list of 50,000 items.
- What is the least number of comparisons the search will take?
- What is the maximum number of comparisons required?
- What is the expected number of comparisons?

(b) The binary search is used with a list of 50,000 items.
- What is the least number of comparisons the search will take?
- What is the maximum number of comparisons required?

4.12 Assume a SeqList object L consists of items

34   11   22   16   40

(a) Give the items in the list after each of the following instructions.

```
n = L.DeleteFront();
L.Insert(n);
if (L.Find(L.GetData(0)*2)
    L.Delete(16);
```

(b) Using object L, give output for the following sequence of instructions.

```
for (int i = 0; i < 5; i++)
{
    L.Insert(L.DeleteFront());
    cout << L.GetData(i) << "   ";
}
```

4.13 Write a function to implement the specified task.

(a) Concatenate SeqList object L on the tail of object K.

```
void Concatenate(SeqList& K, SeqList& L);
```

(b) Reverse the order of the elements in SeqList object L.

```
void Reverse (SeqList& L);
```

4.14 The function Ques takes a SeqList object L whose elements are all positive integers. What is the action of the function with the list

{1, 3, 7, 2, 15, 0, 12} ?

Why must L be passed by reference?

```
typedef int Datatype;
#include "aseqlist.h"

int M(const SeqList &L)
{
    int i, mval, length = L.ListSize();

    if (length == 0)
    {
        cerr << "The list is empty" << endl;
        return -1;
    }

    mval = L.GetData(0);
    for (i = 1; i < length; i++)
        if (L.GetData(i) > mval)
            mval = L.GetData(i);
    return mval;
}

void Ques(SeqList &L)
{
    int mval = M(L);

    L.Delete(mval);
}
```

4.15 Explain why data movement is necessary when implementing the Delete method in the array-based SeqList class.

Programming Exercises

4.1 Use the SeqList class with DataType int to create the utility function InsertMax:

```
void InsertMax(SeqList& L, int elt);
```

InsertMax puts elt into list L only if it is larger than all existing elements in the list. Write a main program that reads 10 integers and calls InsertMax for each. Print the list.

4.2 Declare a record

```
struct Person
{
    char name[20];
    int age;
    char gender;
};
```

and invoke the SeqList class as follows:

```
#include <string.h>

// needed for SeqList class method Find
int operator== (Person x, Person y)
{
    return strcmp(x.name, y.name) == 0;
}


typedef Person DataType;
#include "aseqlist.h"
```

(a) Write a function

```
    void PrintByGender(const SeqList& L, char sex);
```

which traverses the list L and prints all of the records having the given gender.

(b) Write a function

```
    int InList (const SeqList&, char *nm, Person& p);
```

which determines whether a record with name field nm exists in list L. Do this by creating a Person object with name field nm and using the method Find. It is not necessary to initialize the age and gender fields of the record. The comparison of two records is done by comparing the name fields. If a match occurs, assign the record to parameter p and return a 1; otherwise, return a 0. The parameter p is not to be modified unless a match is found.

(c) Write a main program to test the functions.

4.3 Write a program that prompts the user for an integer n, generates an array of n random integers in the range 0 ... 999 and sorts the list using the exchange sort. Time the execution of the sort using the function TickCount defined in the file "ticks.h". Run the program using n = 50, 500, 1000, and 10000. This provides experimental evidence that the exchange sort is $O(n^2)$.

Note: Since a local array of 1000 or 10000 elements may exceed system heap capacity, allocate a dynamic array with the following syntax to store the elements. You can use standard array notation "a[i]" with the dynamic structure.

```
int  *a;           // defines a pointer
...
a = new int[n];    // n is the count 50, 500, 1000, or 10000
```

Write a program that prompts the user for an integer n, generates an array of n random integers in the range 0 . . . 999 and sorts the list using the exchange sort. Time the execution of the sort. Run the program using n = 50, 500, 1000, and 10000. This provides experimental evidence that the exchange sort is $O(n^2)$.

4.4 This exercise extends the video store application of Program 4.2 to include return of films. Ask a customer whether a video is to be rented or returned. If the film is returned, delete it from the list of rented films and insert it into the inventory list.

4.5 A testing situation provides an example of a SeqList structure. Students turn in tests face down on the teacher's desk (insertion at the rear of the list). Suppose an anxious student discovers the correct answer to a question and wants to check how he or she responded. The teacher must turn the pile over so the first test faces forward, scan through the tests until the student's test is located, and then delete the test from the list. After the student finishes checking the test, the teacher inserts it at the rear of the list.

Write a program that uses the SeqList class to model this situation. Associate a student with a test using the following record:

```
struct Test
{
    char name[30];
    int testNumber;
};
```

A loop in the main program directs processing by reading an integer:

1 = Turn in a test   2 = Let student look at a test
3 = Return a borrowed test   4 = Exit

Take action as follows:

Input 1: Prompt for the name and test number; insert the test into a list of submittedTests.
Input 2: Prompt for the name only, delete the test from submittedTests, and insert it in a list of borrowedTests.
Input 3: Prompt for the name, delete the record from borrowedTests, and insert it into submittedTests.
Input 4: The teacher is ready to leave, and all borrowed tests must be returned. Delete all items from borrowedTest, inserting them into submittedTests. Print the final list.

You must define the operator "==" in order to determine whether two Test records are equal. Do this using the function

```
#include <string.h>
int operator== (const Test& t1, Test& t2)
{
    return strcmp(t1.name, t2.name) == 0;
}
```

CHAPTER 5

STACKS AND QUEUES

In this chapter, we discuss in more detail the classical stack and queue, which are data structures that store and retrieve items from restricted portions of a list. We also discuss the priority queue, a modified version of a queue in which the item of highest priority is removed from the list. The stack, queue, and priority queue are implemented as C++ classes. Two case studies illustrate the main concepts of the chapter. We demonstrate the action of an RPN calculator with its operand stack. The performance of customers and tellers in a bank waiting line are featured in an event-driven simulation. The application uses a priority queue and introduces an important business management tool.

Stacks   5.1

A stack is one of the most frequently used and most important data structures. Applications of stacks are vast. For instance, syntax recognition in a compiler is stack based, as is expression evaluation. At a lower level, stacks are used to pass parameters to functions and to make the actual function call to and return from a function.

A **stack** is a list of items that are accessible at only one end of the list. Items are added or deleted from the list only at the **top** of the stack. Food trays in a dining hall or a pile of boxes are good models for a stack.

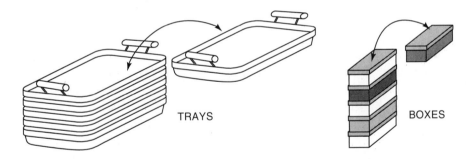

TRAYS   BOXES

A stack is designed to hold items that are naturally accessed from the top of a list. Suppose a skewer contains a series of cut vegetables that are prepared for a barbecue. In Figure 5.1, the order of vegetables on skewer 1 is onion, mushroom, green pepper, and onion. Before putting the skewer on the grill, a guest indicates that he cannot eat mushrooms and needs them removed. This request involves removing an onion (skewer 2), removing the mushroom (skewer 3), and then replacing the onion (skewer 4). A dislike of green peppers or onions would cause the cook more problems.

A stack structure features operations that add and delete items. A **Push** operation adds an item to the top of the stack. The operation of removing an element from the stack is said to **pop** the stack. Figure 5.2 illustrates a sequence of Push and Pop operations. The last item added to the stack is the first one removed. For this reason, a stack is said to have **LIFO** (last-in/first-out) ordering.

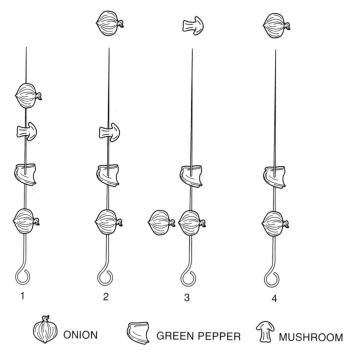

Figure 5.1 A Vegetable Stack

The abstract concept of a stack allows for an indefinitely large list. Logically, food trays could be stacked to the sky. In reality, food trays are stored in a rack and the vegetables are placed on a short skewer. When the rack or skewer is full, you cannot add (Push) another item on the stack. The stack has reached the maximum number of elements it can handle. The situation gives meaning to a "stack full" condition. At the other extreme, you cannot pick up a tray from an empty rack. A "stack empty" condition implies that you cannot remove (Pop) an element. A description of the ADT Stack involves only the stack empty condition. A stack full condition is relevant only when the implementation places an upper bound on the size of the list.

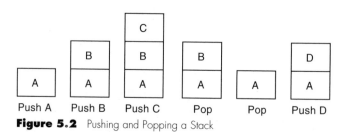

Figure 5.2 Pushing and Popping a Stack

ADT Stack is

Data

A list of items with a position
top that indicates the top of the stack.

Operations

Constructor

Initial values:	None
Process:	Initialize the top of the stack.

StackEmpty

Input:	None
Preconditions:	None
Process:	Check whether the stack is empty.
Output:	Return True if stack is empty and False otherwise.
Postconditions:	None

Pop

Input:	None
Preconditions:	Stack is not empty.
Process:	Remove the item from the top of the stack.
Output:	Return the element from the top of the stack.
Postconditions:	Element at the top of the stack is removed.

Push

Input:	An item for the stack.
Preconditions:	None
Process:	Store the item on the top of the stack.
Output:	None
Postconditions:	The stack has a new element at the top.

Peek

Input:	None
Preconditions:	Stack is not empty.
Process:	Retrieve the value of the item on the top of the stack.
Output:	Return the value of the item from the top of the stack.
Postconditions:	The stack is unchanged.

ClearStack

Input:	None
Preconditions:	None
Process:	Deletes all the items in the stack and resets the top of the stack.
Output:	None

Postconditions: The stack is reset to its initial conditions.

end ADT Stack

5.2 The Stack Class

The stack members include a list, an index or pointer to the top of the stack and the set of stack operations. We use an array to hold the stack elements. As a result, the stack size may not exceed the number of elements in the array and the stack full condition is relevant. In Chapter 9, we remove the restriction when we develop a Stack class with a linked list.

The declaration of a stack object includes the stack size that defines the maximum number of elements in the list. The size has a default value MaxStackSize = 50. The list (stacklist), the maximum number of elements in the stack (size) and the index (top) are private members. The operations are public.

Initially the stack is empty and top = −1. Items enter the array (Push) in

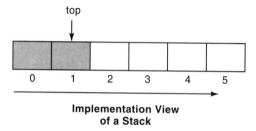

**Implementation View
of a Stack**

increasing order of the indices (top = 0, 1, 2) and come off the stack (Pop) in decreasing order of the indices (top = 2, 1, 0). For instance, the following is a stack of characters (DataType = char). After several Push/Pop operations, the index top = 2, and the element at the top of the stack is stacklist[top] = C.

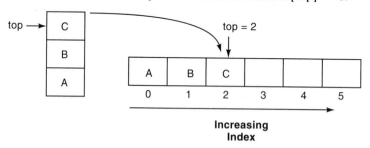

**Increasing
Index**

EXAMPLE 5.1

The following illustrates a five-element integer array with the sequence of operations Push 10; Push 25; Push 50; Pop; Pop. The index top is incremented by one on a Push and decremented by one on a Pop.

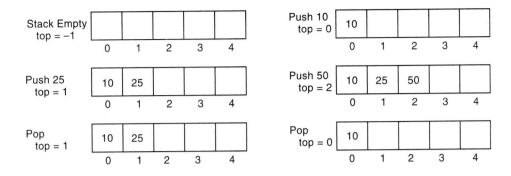

- -

STACK CLASS SPECIFICATION

DECLARATION

```
#include <iostream.h>
#include <stdlib.h>

const int MaxStackSize = 50;

class Stack
{
    private:
        // private data members. stack array, and top
        DataType stacklist[MaxStackSize];
        int top;
    public:
        // constructor; initialize the top
        Stack (void);

        // stack modification operations
        void Push (const DataType& item);
        DataType Pop (void);
        void ClearStack(void);

        // stack access
        DataType Peek(void) const;

        // stack test methods
        int StackEmpty(void) const;
        int StackFull(void) const;      // array implementation
};
```

DESCRIPTION

The data in the stack is of type DataType, which must be defined using typedef.

The user is responsible to check for a full stack before attempting to push an element on the stack and to check for an empty stack before a pop of the stack. If the preconditions for either push or pop are not satisfied, an error message is printed and the program terminates.

StackEmpty returns 1 (True) if the stack is empty and 0 (False) otherwise. Use StackEmpty to determine whether a Pop operation can be performed.

StackFull returns 1 (True) if the stack is full and 0 (False) otherwise. Use StackFull to determine whether a Push operation can be performed.

ClearStack makes the stack empty by setting top $= -1$. This method allows the stack to be used for another purpose.

EXAMPLE

The stack declaration and implementation is contained in the file "astack.h".

```
typedef int DataType;
#include "astack.h";          // includes the Stack class

Stack S;                      // declare a Stack object

S.Push(10);                   // insert 10 on the stack S
cout << S.Peek() << endl;     // print 10

// pop 10 from the stack and leave it empty
if (!S.StackEmpty())
    temp = S.Pop();
cout << temp << endl;

S.ClearStack();               // clear stack
```

STACK CLASS IMPLEMENTATION

The Stack constructor initializes the index top to have value -1, which is equivalent to a stack empty condition.

```
// initialize stack top
Stack::Stack (void) : top(-1)
{}
```

Stack Operations   The two primary stack operations insert (Push) and delete (Pop) an element from the stack. The class provides the Peek operation, which allows a client to retrieve the data from the item at the top of the stack without actually removing the item.

To Push an item on the stack, increment the index top by 1 and assign the new item to the array stacklist. An attempt to add an item to a full stack causes an error message and program termination.

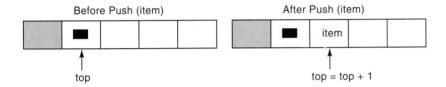

Before Push (item)   After Push (item)

top   top = top + 1

Push
```
// push item on the stack
void Stack::Push (const DataType& item)
{
    // if the stack is full, terminate the program
    if (top == MaxStackSize-1)
    {
        cerr << "Stack overflow!" << endl;
        exit(1);
    }

    // increment top and copy item to stacklist
    top++;
    stacklist[top] = item;
}
```

The Pop operation deletes an item from the stack by first copying the value from the top of the stack to a local variable temp and then decrementing top by 1. The variable temp becomes the return value. An attempt to delete an item from an empty stack causes an error message and the program terminates.

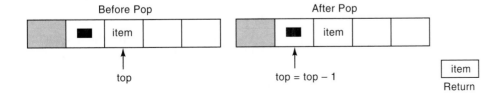

Before Pop   After Pop

top   top = top − 1

item
Return

Pop
```
// pop the stack and return the top element
DataType Stack::Pop (void)
{
    DataType temp;

    // if stack is empty, terminate the program
    if (top == -1)
    {
        cerr << "Attempt to pop an empty stack!" << endl;
        exit(1);
    }
```

```
    // record the top element
    temp = stacklist[top];

    // decrement top and return former top element
    top--;
    return temp;
}
```

The Peek operation essentially duplicates the definition of Pop with a single important exception. The index top is not decremented, leaving the stack intact.

Peek
```
// return the value at the top of the stack
DataType Stack::Peek (void) const
{
    // if the stack is empty, terminate the program
    if (top == -1)
    {
        cerr << "Attempt to peek at an empty stack!" << endl;
        exit(1);
    }
    return stacklist[top];
}
```

Stack Test Conditions   During execution, stack operations terminate the program when we attempt to access the stack incorrectly; for example, when we attempt to Peek into an empty stack. To protect the integrity of the stack, the class provides operations to test the status of the stack.

The function StackEmpty checks whether top is -1. If so, the stack is empty and 1 (True) is returned; otherwise, 0 (False) is returned.

```
// test for an empty stack
int Stack::StackEmpty(void) const
{
    // return the logical value top == -1
    return top == -1;
}
```

The function StackFull checks whether top is MaxStackSize-1. If so, the stack is full and 1 (True) is returned; otherwise, 0 (False) is returned.

```
// test for a full stack
int Stack::StackFull(void) const
{
```

```
    // test the position of top
    return top == MaxStackSize-1;
}
```

The ClearStack method resets the top of the stack to -1. This restores the initial condition determined by the constructor.

```
// clear all items from the stack
void Stack::ClearStack(void)
{
    top = -1;
}
```

The stack Push and Pop operations involve direct access to the top of the stack and do not depend on the number of elements in the list. Thus, both operations have computing time O(1).

Application: Palindromes   When DataType is Char, a character stack is maintained. The application identifies *palindromes,* which are strings that read the same forward and backward. Blanks are not included. For instance, "dad", "sees", and "madam im adam" are palindromes, but "good" is not a palindrome. Program 5.1 uses the Stack class to test for a palindrome.

Program 5.1   Palindromes

This program reads a line of text using cin.getline() and calls the function Deblank to strip all blanks from the text. The Deblank function copies the nonblank characters into a second string. The program tests to see if the deblanked string is a palindrome by scanning the string twice. On the first scan, each character is pushed onto a stack, producing a list containing the text in reverse order. During the second scan, each character is compared with an item that is popped from the stack. The scan terminates if two characters fail to match, in which case the text is not a palindrome. If the comparisons remain valid until the stack is empty, the text is a palindrome.

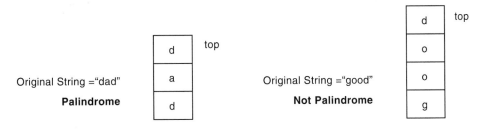

```
#include <iostream.h>

typedef char DataType;    // stack elements are characters

#include "astack.h"

// creates a new string with all blank characters removed
void Deblank(char *s, char *t)
{
    // loop through expression until NULL character is found
    while(*s != NULL)
    {
      // if character is a non-blank, copy to new string
      if (*s != ' ')
          *t++ = *s;
      s++;                    // move to next character
    }
    *t = NULL;              // append NULL to new string
}

void main()
{
    const int True = 1, False = 0;

    // stack S holds chars in reverse order
    Stack S;

    char palstring[80], deblankstring[80], c;
    int i = 0;
    int ispalindrome = True;   // assume string is a palindrome

    // read in the full-line string
    cin.getline(palstring,80,'\n');

    // remove blanks from string and put result in deblankstring
    Deblank(palstring,deblankstring);

    // push the chars of deblanked expression on the stack
    i = 0;
    while(deblankstring[i] != 0)
    {
        S.Push(deblankstring[i]);
        i++;
    }

    // now pop stack, comparing characters with original string
    i = 0;
    while (!S.StackEmpty())
    {
```

```
            c = S.Pop();     // get next character from stack
            // if chars don't match, break out of the loop
            if (c != deblankstring[i])
            {
                ispalindrome = False;    // not a palindrome
                break;
            }
            i++;
        }

    if (ispalindrome)
        cout << '\"' << palstring << '\"'
             << " is a palindrome << endl;
    else
        cout << '\"' << palstring << '\"'
             << " is not a palindrome << endl;
}

/*
<Run #1 of Program 5.1>

madam im adam
"madam im adam" is a palindrome

<Run #2 of Program 5.1>

a man a plan a canal panama
"a man a plan a canal panama" is a palindrome

<Run #3 of Program 5.1>
palindrome
"palindrome" is not a palindrome
*/
```

Application: Multibase Output Output statements from most programming languages print numbers in decimal as the default value. A stack can be used to print numbers in other bases. Binary (base 2) numbers are discussed in Chapter 2, and we assume that you can extend the principles to other bases.

EXAMPLE 5.2

The example converts decimal numbers to the designated base.

1. (Base 8) $28_{10} = 3 \cdot 8 + 4 = 34_8$
2. (Base 4) $72_{10} = 1 \cdot 64 + 0 \cdot 16 + 2 \cdot 4 + 0 = 1020_4$
3. (Base 2) $53_{10} = 1 \cdot 32 + 1 \cdot 16 + 0 \cdot 8 + 1 \cdot 4 + 0 \cdot 2 + 1 = 110101_2$

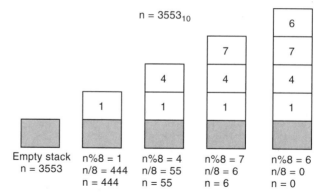

$n = 3553_{10}$

Empty stack	n%8 = 1	n%8 = 4	n%8 = 7	n%8 = 6
n = 3553	n/8 = 444	n/8 = 55	n/8 = 6	n/8 = 0
	n = 444	n = 55	n = 6	n = 0

Figure 5.3   Using a Stack to Print a Number in Octal

The problem of writing a number to the screen in a nondecimal base is solved using a stack. We describe the algorithm for a decimal number n that is printed as a base B number.

1. The right-most digit of n is $n \% B$. Push it on a stack S.
2. The remaining digits of n are given by n/B. Replace n by n/B.
3. Repeat steps 1–2 until $n = 0$ and there are no significant digits remaining.
4. The new representation of N as a base B number is now available on the stack. Pop and print characters from S until the stack is empty.

Figure 5.3 illustrates the conversion of $n = 3553_{10}$ to a base 8 number. The figure describes the growth of the stack while creating the four octal digits for n. Conclude the algorithm by popping and then printing each character from the stack. The output is 6741.

Program 5.2   Multibase Output

The program presents an output function that takes a non-negative long integer num and a base B in the range 2–9 and writes num to the screen as a base B number. The main program prompts the user for three non-negative integers and bases and then outputs them.

```
#include <iostream.h>

typedef int DataType;

#include "astack.h"
```

```
// print integer num in base B
void MultibaseOutput(long num, int B)
{
    // stack holds base B digits left to right
    Stack S;

    // extract base B digits right to left and push on stack S
    do
    {
        S.Push(num % B);      // convert to char and push on stack
        num /= B;             // remove right most digit
    } while (num != 0);       // continue til all digits computed

    while (!S.StackEmpty()) // flush the stack
        cout << S.Pop();
}

void main(void)
{
    long num;               // decimal number
    int  B;                 // base

    // read 3 positive numbers and the desired base 2 <= B <= 9
    for(int i=0;i < 3;i++)
    {
        cout << "Enter non-negative decimal number and base "
            <<"(2 <= B <= 9): ";
        cin >> num >> B;
        cout << num << " base " << B << " is ";
        MultibaseOutput(num, B);
        cout << endl;
    }
}

/*

<Run of Program 5.2>

Enter non-negative decimal number and base (2 <= B <= 9): 72 4
72 base 4 is 1020
Enter non-negative decimal number and base (2 <= B <= 9): 53 2
53 base 2 is 110101
Enter non-negative decimal number and base (2 <= B <= 9): 3553 8
3553 base 8 is 6741
*/
```

Expression Evaluation   5.3

Electronic calculators illustrate one of the primary uses for a stack. The user enters a mathematical expression with its numbers (operands) and operators and the calculator uses a single stack to compute numeric results. The calculator assumes the expression is entered in a specific numeric format. An expression such as

```
-8 + (4*12 + 5 ^ 2)/3
```

contains **binary operators** $(+, *, /, \hat{}\,)$, **operands** $(8, 4, 12, 5, 2, 3)$, and **parentheses** that create subexpressions. The first part of the expression includes the **unary operator** negation that acts on a single operand (e.g., -8). The other operators are termed binary because they require two operands. The operator $\hat{}$ (exponentiation) creates the expression $5^2 = 25$.

An expression is written in **infix** form if each binary operator is placed between its operands and each unary operator precedes its operand. For instance,

```
-2 + 3*5
```

is an infix expression. Infix is the most common format for writing expressions and is used in most programming languages and calculators. An infix expression is evaluated by an algorithm that uses two stacks of different data types, one to hold operands and the other to hold operators. Since our stack class in "astack.h" requires a single definition of "DataType", we cannot implement infix expression evaluation in this section. The topic is discussed in Chapter 7 where we develop templates and implement a template stack class. This class allows the use of two or more stack objects with different data types.

An alternative to infix is **postfix** where the operands come before the operator. The format is also called **RPN** or **Reverse Polish Notation.** For instance the infix expression "a + b" is written in postfix form as "a b +". With postfix format, we enter variables and numbers as they occur, and enter an operator at the point when its two operands are available. For instance, in the following expression, enter * immediately after its two operands b and c. Enter + when its operands a and (b * c) are available. Operator priority is explicit in postfix format. The operator * occurs before the +.

```
Infix:  a + b*c = a + (b * c)    Postfix:  a b c * +
```

Parentheses are not necessary with postfix format. The following is a series of infix expressions and their postfix equivalents.

Infix Expressions	Postfix Expressions
a*b + c	a b * c +
a*b*c*d*e*f	a b * c * d * e * f *
a + (b*c + d)/e	a b c * d + e / +
(b*b − 4*a*c)/(2*a)	b b * 4 a * c * − 2 a * /

POSTFIX EVALUATION

A postfix expression is evaluated by an algorithm that scans the expression from left to right and uses one stack. For this example, we assume that all operators are binary. We cover unary operators in the exercises.

An expression in postfix format contains only operands and operators. We read each term, and depending on its type, take the following actions. If the term is an operand, push its value on the stack. If the term is an operator <op>, pop the stack twice to retrieve the operands X and Y. Then, evaluate the expression using the operator <op> and push the result X <op> Y back on the stack. After reading each term in the expression, the top of the stack contains the result.

EXAMPLE 5.3

The infix expression 4 + 3*5 is written in postfix as 4 3 5 * +. Its evaluation requires five steps.

Steps 1–3: Read operands 4 3 5 and push each number on the stack.

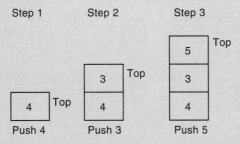

Step 4: Read operator * and evaluate the expression by popping the top two operands 5 and 3 and computing 3*5. The result 15 is pushed back onto the stack.

Step 5: Read operator + and evaluate the expression by popping the operands 15 and 4 and computing 4+15 = 19. The result 19 is pushed back onto the stack and becomes the final result for the expression.

| 19 | Top |

Step 5

APPLICATION: A POSTFIX CALCULATOR

We illustrate postfix expression evaluation by simulating the running of an RPN calculator that has operators +, −, *, /, and ^ (exponentiation). The machine accepts floating point data and evaluates expressions. The calculator data and operations are included in the Calculator class and a simple main program calls its methods.

The calculator class contains public member functions that input an expression and clear the calculator. A series of private member functions are used in evaluating the expression.

CALCULATOR CLASS SPECIFICATION

DECLARATION

```
enum Boolean {False, True};
typedef double DataType;        // calculator accepts real data
#include "astack.h"             // include Stack class


class Calculator
{
   private:
      // private members: calculator stack and operators
      Stack S;                  // holds operands

      void Enter(double num);
      Boolean GetTwoOperands(double& opnd1, double& opnd2);
      void Compute(char op);

   public:
      // constructor
      Calculator(void);

      // evaluate an expression and clear calculator
      void Run(void);
      void Clear(void);
};
```

DESCRIPTION

A default constructor creates an empty calculator stack. Since the machine is always running, the user must call Clear to clear the calculator stack and allow a subsequent run to evaluate a new expression.

The Run operation allows the input of an expression in RPN format. An input of "=" terminates the expression. Only the final value of the expression is displayed.

An error message "Missing operands" is printed when an operator does not have two operands. An attempt to divide by 0 also causes an error message. In either case, the calculator clears the stack and prepares for new input.

EXAMPLE

```
Calculator CALC;    // creates the calculator CALC


CALC.Run();
<Sample Run>
   4 3 * =
   12                  // result of expression 4 * 3 is displayed
```

- -
CALCULATOR CLASS IMPLEMENTATION

The calculator functions are performed by a series of methods that allow the client to input a number, perform a calculation, and print the result on the display. The definition of the class is placed in the file "calc.h".

The method **Enter** takes a floating-point argument and pushes it onto the stack.

```
// store data value on the stack
void Calculator::Enter(double num)
{
   S.Push(num);
}
```

The function **GetTwoOperands** is used by the method Compute to obtain the operands from the calculator stack and assign them to output parameters operand1 and operand2. The method does error checking and returns a value that indicates whether both operands exist.

```
// fetch operands from stack and assign value to parameters.
// print message and return False if two operands not present
Boolean Calculator::GetTwoOperands(double& opnd1, double& opnd2)
{
   if (S.StackEmpty())       // check for presence of operand
   {
      cerr << "Missing operand!" << endl;
      return False;
   }
   opnd1 = S.Pop();          // fetch right-hand operand
   if (S.StackEmpty())
   {
      cerr << "Missing operand!" << endl;
      return False;
   }
   opnd2 = S.Pop();          // fetch left-hand operand
   return True;
}
```

All internal calculations are under control of the **Compute** method that begins by calling GetTwoOperands to retrieve the top two stack values. If GetTwoOperands returns False, we have invalid operands and Compute clears the calculator stack. Otherwise, the Compute function executes the operation specified by the character parameter op ('+', '−', '*', '/', '^') and pushes the result on the stack. If division by 0 is attempted, an error message is printed, and the calculator stack is cleared. For exponentiation, we use the function

```
double pow(double x, double y);
```

that computes x^y. It is defined in the C++ library <math.h>.

```
//evaluate an operation
void Calculator::Compute(char op)
{
    Boolean result;
    double operand1, operand2;

    // fetch two operands and identify success or failure
    result = GetTwoOperands(operand1, operand2);

    // if success, evaluate the operator and push value on stack
    // otherwise, clear calculator stack. check for divide by 0.
    if (result == True)
        switch(op)
        {
            case '+':   S.Push(operand2+operand1);
                        break;

            case '-':   S.Push(operand2-operand1);
                        break;

            case '*':   S.Push(operand2*operand1);
                        break;

            case '/':   if (operand1 = 0.0)
                        {
                            cerr << "Divide by 0!" << endl;
                            S.ClearStack();
                        }
                        else
                            S.Push(operand2/operand1);
                        break;

            case '^':   S.Push(pow(operand2,operand1));
                        break;
        }
    else
        S.ClearStack();                     // error! clear calculator
}
```

The primary action of the calculator is implemented by the public **Run** method that implements postfix expression evaluation. A main loop in Run reads characters from the input stream and terminates when the character "=" is read. Whitespace characters are ignored. If a character is an operator ('+', '−', '*', '/', '^'), the corresponding operation is performed by calling the method Compute. If the character is not an operator, Run assumes that it is looking at the first character of an operand since the stream should only contain operators and operands. Run places the character back into the input stream so it can be subsequently read as part of a floating point operand.

```
// read chars and evaluate a postfix expression. stop on '='.
void Calculator::Run(void)
{
    char c;
    double newoperand;

    while(cin >> c, c != '=')         // read until '=' (Quit)
    {
        switch(c)
        {
            case '+':                 // check possible operators
            case '-':
            case '*':
            case '/':
            case '^':
                Compute(c);           // have operator; evaluate it
                break;

            default:
                // not operator; must be operand; put char back
                cin.putback(c);
                // read the operand and store it on the stack
                cin >> newoperand;
                Enter(newoperand);
                break;
        }
    }
    // answer stored on top of stack. print using Peek
    if (!S.StackEmpty())
        cout << S.Peek() << endl;
}


// clear operand stack
void Calculator::Clear(void)
{
    S.ClearStack();
}
```

Program 5.3   The Postfix Calculator

The object CALC is a calculator. A sample run calculates the length of the hypotenuse for the right triangle with sides 6, 8, and 10. Two other runs illustrate error handling.

```
    (√6²+8²) = 10     (RPN format: 6 6 * 8 8 * + .5 ^ =)

#include "calc.h"

void main(void)
{
    Calculator CALC;

    CALC.Run();
}

/*
<Run #1 of Program 5.3>

8 8 * 6 6 * + .5 ^ =
10

<Run #2 of Program 5.3>

3 4 + *
Missing operand!
3 4 + 8 * =
56

<Run #3 of Program 5.3>

1 0 / =
Divide by 0!
*/
```

5.4   Queues

A **queue** is a data structure that stores elements in a list and permits data access only at the two ends of the list (Figure 5.4). An element is inserted at the rear of

Figure 5.4   A Queue

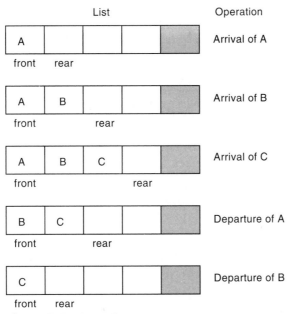

Figure 5.5 Queue Operations

the list and is deleted from the front of the list. Applications use a queue to store items in their order of occurrence.

Elements are removed from the queue in the same order in which they are stored and hence a queue provides **FIFO** (first-in/first-out) or **FCFS** (first-come/first-served) ordering. The orderly serving of store customers and the buffering of printer jobs in a print spooler are classic examples of queues.

A queue includes a list and specific references to the front and rear positions (Figure 5.5). These positions are used to insert and delete items in the queue. Like a stack, a queue stores items of generic type DataType. Like a stack, an abstract queue does not limit the number of entries. However, if an array is used to implement the list, a "queue full" condition can occur.

ADT Queue is

Data
    A list of items
    front: a position that references the first item in the queue
    rear: a position that references the last item in the queue
    count: the number of entries in the queue at any given time

Operations
    Constructor
        Initial Values: None
        Process: Initialize the front and rear of the queue.

QLength
Input:	None
Preconditions:	None
Process:	Determine the number of items in the queue.
Output:	Return the number of items in the queue.
Postconditions:	None

QEmpty
Input:	None
Preconditions:	None
Process:	Check whether the queue is empty.
Output:	Return 1 (True) if the queue is empty and 0 (False) otherwise. Note that this condition is equivalent to testing whether QLength is 0.
Postconditions:	None

QDelete
Input:	None
Preconditions:	Queue is not empty.
Process:	Remove an item from the front of the queue.
Output:	Return the item that is removed from the queue.
Postconditions:	An item is deleted from the queue.

QInsert
Input:	An item to store in the queue.
Preconditions:	None
Process:	Store an item at the rear of the queue.
Output:	None
Postconditions:	A new item is added to the queue.

QFront
Input:	None
Preconditions:	Queue is not empty.
Process:	Retrieve the value of the item at the front of the queue.
Output:	Return the value of the item at the front of the queue.
Postconditions:	None

ClearQueue
Input:	None
Preconditions:	None
Process:	Remove all items from the queue and restore initial conditions
Output:	None
Postconditions:	The queue is empty

end ADT Queue

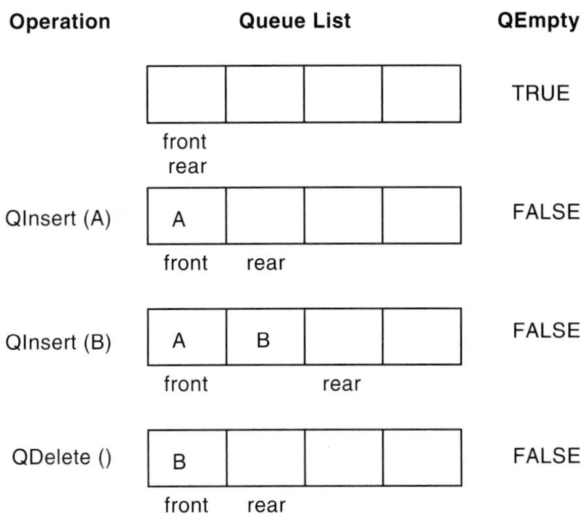

Operation	Queue List	QEmpty

Figure 5.6 Changes in a Four-Element Queue During Operations

EXAMPLE 5.4

Figure 5.6 represents changes in a four-element queue during a sequence of operations. In each case the value of the flag QEmpty is given.

Queues are used extensively in computer modeling, such as the simulation of teller lines in a bank. Multiuser operating systems maintain queues of programs waiting to execute and of jobs waiting to print.

The Queue Class 5.5

The Queue class implements the ADT by using an array to hold the list of items and by defining variables that maintain the front and rear positions. Since an array is used to implement the list, our class contains a method QFull to test whether the array is filled. This method will be eliminated when a linked list implementation of a queue is presented in Chapter 9.

QUEUE CLASS SPECIFICATION

DECLARATION

```
#include <iostream.h>
#include <stdlib.h>

const int MaxQSize = 50;
```

```
class Queue
{
    private:
       // queue array and its parameters
       int front, rear, count
       DataType qlist[MaxQSize];

    public:
       // constructor
       Queue (void);    // initialize data members

       // queue modification operations
       void QInsert(const DataType& item);
       DataType QDelete(void);
       void ClearQueue(void);

       // queue access
       DataType QFront(void) const;

       // queue test methods
       int QLength(void) const;
       int QEmpty(void) const;
       int QFull(void) const;
};
```

DESCRIPTION

The generic type DataType allows a queue to handle different data types. The Queue class contains a list (qlist) whose maximum size is determined by the constant MaxQSize.

The data member count records the number of elements in the queue. The value also determines whether the queue is full or empty.

QInsert takes an element item of type DataType and inserts it at the rear of the queue, and QDelete removes and returns the element at the front of the queue. The method QFront returns the value of the item at the front of the queue, which allows us to "peek" at the next element that will be deleted.

The programmer should test QEmpty before deleting an item and QFull before inserting a new member if there is a chance the queue is empty or full. If the preconditions for QInsert or QDelete are violated, the program prints an error message and terminates.

The queue declaration and implementation is contained in the file "aqueue.h".

EXAMPLE

```
typedef int DataType;

#include "aqueue.h"
```

```
Queue Q;                          // declare a queue

Q.QInsert(30);                    // insert 30 in the queue
Q.QInsert(70);                    // insert 70 in the queue
cout << Q.QLength() << endl;      // prints 2
cout << Q.QFront() << endl;       // prints 30
if (!Q.QEmpty())
    cout << Q.QDelete();          // prints the value 30
cout << Q.QFront() << endl;       // prints 70
Q.ClearQueue();                   // clear the queue
```

- -

QUEUE CLASS IMPLEMENTATION

The front of the queue is defined by the first customer in a line. The rear of the queue is the spot immediately beyond the end of the line. When the queue is full, customers must go to another checkout line. Figure 5.7 describes changes in the queue and illustrates some issues that affect our implementation. Assume the line is limited to four customers. In view 2, after customer A is served, customers B and C move forward. In view 3, customer B is served and C moves forward. In view 4, customers D, E, and F enter the line, filling up the queue, and Customer G must move to another line.

These views reflect the behavior of customers in a checkout line. Once a customer is served, the others in the queue move forward. From the perspective of a list, entries shift forward one position each time an item leaves the queue. The model does not provide for efficient computer implementation. Suppose the queue contains 1000 items. When an entry is deleted from the front, 999 items must move to the left.

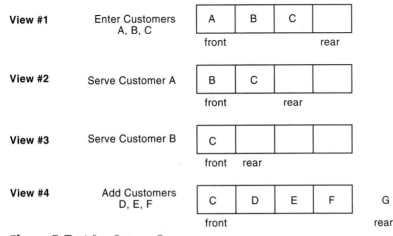

View #1	Enter Customers A, B, C
View #2	Serve Customer A
View #3	Serve Customer B
View #4	Add Customers D, E, F

Figure 5.7 A Four-Customer Queue

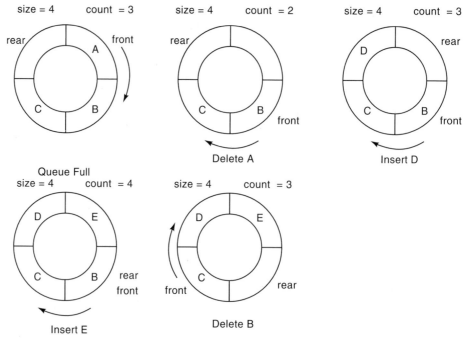

Figure 5.8   Circular Model of a Queue

Our queue implementation introduces a circular model. Rather than shifting items left when an element is deleted, the queue elements are logically arranged in a circle. The variable front is always the location of the first element of the queue, and it advances to the right around the circle as deletions occur. The variable rear is the location where the next insertion occurs. After an insertion, rear moves circularly to the right. A variable count maintains a record of the number of elements in the queue, and if count equals MaxQSize elements, the queue is full. Figure 5.8 illustrates the circular model.

Implement the circular motion using remaindering:

Move rear forward: rear = (rear+1) % MaxQSize;
Move front forward: front = (front+1) % MaxQSize;

EXAMPLE 5.5

Use the four-element integer array qlist (size = 4) to implement a circular queue. Initially count = 0 and indices front and rear have value 0. Figure 5.9 depicts a sequence of queue insertions and deletions.

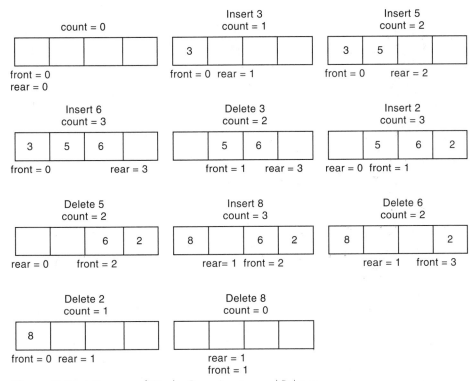

Figure 5.9 A Sequence of Circular Queue Insertions and Deletions

Queue Constructor   The Queue constructor initializes the data items front, rear, and count to 0. This establishes an empty queue.

```
// initialize queue front, rear, count
Queue::Queue (void) : front(0), rear(0), count(0)
{}
```

Queue Operations   A queue allows only a limited set of operations that add a new item (QInsert) or remove an item (QDelete). The class also provides QFront, which allows us to peek at the first element in the queue. For some applications, this "peek" operation allows us to determine whether an item should be removed from the list.

In this section, we develop the queue update operations that insert and delete items from the list. The other methods have models in the stack class and are found in the program supplement in the file "aqueue.h".

Before the insertion process begins, the index rear points at the next available position in the list. The new item is placed into this location and the queue count is increased by 1.

```
qlist[rear] = item;
count++;
```

After placing the element in the list, the rear index must be updated to point at the next location [Figure 5.10(A)]. Since we are using a circular queue model, the insert may occur at the end of the array (qlist[size−1]) with rear repositioned to the front of the list [Figure 5.10(B)].

The calculation is done using the remainder operator "%".

```
rear = (rear+1) % MaxQSize;
```

QInsert

```
// insert item into the queue
void Queue::QInsert (const DataType& item)
{
    // terminate if queue is full
    if (count == MaxQSize)
    {
        cerr << "Queue overflow!" << endl;
        exit(1);
    }
    // increment count, assign item to qlist and update rear
    count++;
    qlist[rear] = item;
    rear = (rear+1) % MaxQSize;
}
```

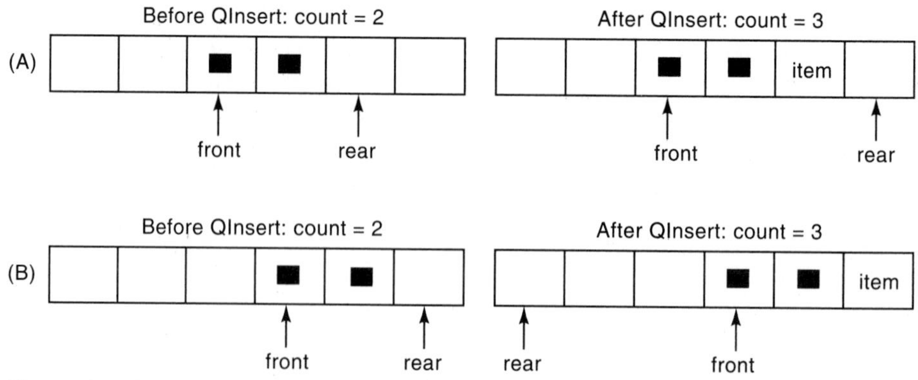

Figure 5.10 QInsert

The QDelete operation removes an item from the front of the queue, a position that is referenced by the index front. We start the deletion process by copying the value into a temporary variable and decrementing the queue count.

```
item = qlist[front];
count--;
```

In our circular model, front must be repositioned to the next element in the list by using the remainder operator "%" (Figure 5.11).

```
front = (front + 1) % MaxQSize;
```

The value from the temporary location becomes the return value.

QDelete
```
// delete element from the front of the queue and return its value
DataType Queue::QDelete(void)
{
    DataType temp;

    // if qlist is empty, terminate the program
    if (count == 0)
    {
        cerr << "Deleting from an empty queue!" << endl;
        exit(1);
    }

    // record value at the front of the queue
    temp = qlist[front];

    // decrement count, advance front and return former front
    count--;
    front = (front+1) % MaxQsize;
    return temp;
}
```

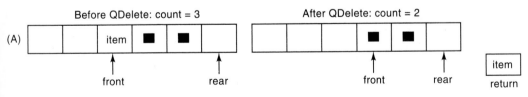

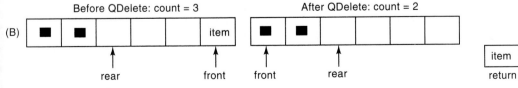

Figure 5.11   QDelete

The operations QInsert, QDelete, and QFront have efficiency $O(1)$ since each method directly accesses an item at either the front or rear of the list.

Program 5.4 Dance Partners

A square dance is held on Friday night. As men and women enter the dance hall, the men enter one line (queue) and the women another line. When dance time arrives, partners are selected by taking one man and one woman from the front of each line. If the two lines do not have the same number of people, the extras must wait for the next round.

The program obtains the men and women by reading the text file "dance.dat". Each entry of the file has the format

```
Sex  Name
```

where Sex is the single character "F" or "M". All the records are read from the file and the queues are formed. Partners are formed by deleting from each queue. This process stops when a queue becomes empty. If people are waiting, the program indicates how many and prints the name of the first person who will dance in the next round.

```cpp
#include <iostream.h>
#include <iomanip.h>
#include <fstream.h>

// record that declares a dancer
struct Person
{
    char   name[20];
    char   sex;                        // 'F' (female) 'M' (male)
};

// queue holds a list of Person objects
typedef Person DataType;

#include "aqueue.h"

void main(void)
{
    // two queues to separate male and female dancers
    Queue maleDancers(10), femaleDancers(10);

    Person p;
    char blankseparator;
    int i;
```

```
  // input file for the dancers;
  ifstream fin;


// open the file and check that the file exists
  fin.open("dance.dat");
  if (!fin)
  {
    cerr << "Unable to open file" << endl;
    exit (1);
  }



  // read input line that includes sex, name, and age
  while(fin.get(p.sex))              // terminate on eof
  {
      fin.get(blankseparator);      // clear blank
      fin.getline(p.name,20,'\n'); // read name
      // insert into correct queue
      if (p.sex == 'F')
          femaleDancers.QInsert(p);
      else
          maleDancers.QInsert(p);
  }



  // set a dancing pair by getting partners from two queues
  // quit when the male or female queue is empty
  cout << "The dancing partners are: " << endl << endl;
  while (!femaleDancers.QEmpty() && !maleDancers.QEmpty())
  {
      p = femaleDancers.QDelete();
      cout << p.name << "  ";      // announce the female dancer
      p = maleDancers.QDelete();
      cout << p.name << endl;      // announce the male dancer
  }
  cout << endl;



  // if either queue has unselected dancer(s), announce the
  // name of the first person in line
  if (!femaleDancers.QEmpty())
  {
      cout << "There are " << femaleDancers.QLength()
          << " women waiting for the next round." << endl;
      cout << femaleDancers.QFront().name
          << " will be the first to get a partner." << endl;
  }
```

```
        else if (!maleDancers.QEmpty())
        {
            cout << "There are " << maleDancers.QLength()
                    << " men waiting for the next round." << endl;
            cout << maleDancers.QFront().name
                    << " will be the first to get a partner." << endl;
        }
}

/*
<File "dance.dat">

M George Thompson
F Jane Andrews
F Sandra Williams
M Bill Brooks
M Bob Carlson
F Shirley Granley
F Louise Sanderson
M Dave Evans
M Harold Brown
F Roberta Edwards
M Dan Gromley
M John Gaston

<Run of Program 5.4>

The dancing partners are:

Jane Andrews   George Thompson
Sandra Williams  Bill Brooks
Shirley Granley  Bob Carlson
Louise Sanderson  Dave Evans
Roberta Edwards  Harold Brown

There are 2 men waiting for the next round.
Dan Gromley will be the first to get a partner.
*/
```

Application: Using a Queue to Sort Data In the early days of computing, a mechanical sorter was used to order a pile of punched cards. The following program simulates the action of the sorter. To explain the process, assume the cards contain two-digit numbers in the range 00–99 and the sorter contains ten bins that are marked 0–9. Two passes are made through the sorter to process first the 1's digit and then the 10's digit. Each card drops in the appropriate bin as it passes through the sort. This is called the **radix sort** and can be extended to sort numbers of any size.

Initial list: 91 46 85 15 92 35 31 22

In pass 1, distribute the cards by the 1's digit.

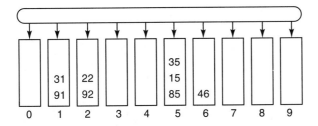

Collect the cards from the bins in the order 0 to 9.

List after pass 1:   91 31 92 22 85 15 35 46

In pass 2, distribute the cards by the 10's digit.

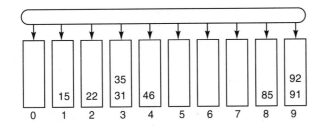

Collect the cards from the bins in the order 0 to 9.

List after pass 2: 15 22 31 35 46 85 91 92

The list is sorted after two passes. Intuitively, pass 1 ensures that all cards with smaller 1's digits precede cards with larger 1's digits. For instance, all the numbers ending in 1 precede the numbers ending in 2 and so forth. For pass 2, assume two cards have value $3s$ and $3t$ with $s < t$. They enter bin 3 in the order $3s$ followed by $3t$ (recall that all cards ending with s precede cards ending with t from pass 1). Since each bin is a queue, the cards leave bin 3 in FIFO ordering. After collecting the cards from pass 2, the cards are ordered.

Program 5.5 Radix Sort

This program performs a radix sort of two-digit numbers. A sequence of 50 random numbers is stored in a list represented by array L.

```
int L(50);   // holds 50 random integers
```

An array of queues simulate the 10 sorting bins:

```
Queue digitQueue[10];    // 10 queues of integers
```

Function Distribute is passed the array of numbers, an array of queues digitqueue, and the user-defined descriptor Ones or Tens to indicate whether the sort is by the 1's digit (pass 1) or the 10's digit (pass 2).

In pass 1, use L[i] % 10 to access the 1's digit and use this value to assign the number to the correct queue.

```
digitQueue[L[i] % 10].QInsert(L[i])
```

In pass 2, use L[i] / 10 to access the 10's digit and use this value to assign the number to the correct queue.

```
digitQueue[L[i] / 10].QInsert(L[i])
```

Function Collect scans the array of queues digitQueue in the order digit = 0 to 9 and extracts all items from each queue into a list L.

```
while (!digitQueue[digit].QEmpty())
    L[i++] = digitQueue[digit].QDelete();
```

Function Print writes out the numbers in the list. The numbers are printed 10 to a row with each number using five print positions.

```
#include <iostream.h>

#include "random.h"        // provides a random number generator

typedef int DataType;      // use queues of integers as the type

#include "aqueue.h"

// user type distinguishes ones and tens digit of a number
enum DigitKind {ones,tens};

// distribute the array of elements into one of 10 queues with
// indices 0-9. user-defined type DigitKind indicates whether the
// distribution uses the ones or tens digit of the number to
// place the element in the queue
void Distribute(int L[],Queue digitQueue[],int n,DigitKind kind)
{
    int i;
```

```
    // loop through the n element array
     for (i = 0; i < n; i++)
            if (kind == ones)
     // compute the ones digit and use as queue index
     digitQueue[L[i] % 10].QInsert(L[i]);
     else
     // compute the tens digit and use as queue index
        digitQueue[L[i] / 10].QInsert(L[i]);
}

// gather elements from the queues and copy back to array
void Collect(Queue digitQueue[], int L[])
{
    int i = 0, digit = 0;

    // scan the array of queues using indices 0, 1, 2,
    for (digit = 0; digit < 10; digit++)
        // collect items until queue  empty and copy them back
        while (!digitQueue[digit].QEmpty())
            L[i++] = digitQueue[digit].QDelete();
}

// scan the n element array and print each item.
// separate items into rows of 10
void PrintArray(int L[],int n)
{
    int i = 0;

    while(i < n)
    {
        cout.width(5);          // print width 5 spaces
        cout << L[i];           // print element
        if (++i % 10 == 0)      // set newline every 10 numbers
            cout << endl;
    }
    cout << endl;
}

void main(void)
{
    // 10 queues that act as bins to collect the numbers
    Queue digitQueue[10];

    // array of 50 integers
    int L[50];

    int i = 0;
    int item;
    RandomNumber rnd;           // provides random numbers
```

```
// initialize array with 50 random numbers in range 0 - 99
for (i = 0; i < 50; i++)
    L[i] = rnd.Random(100);

// distribute by ones digit into 10 bins; collect and print
Distribute(L, digitQueue, 50, ones);
Collect(digitQueue, L);
PrintArray(L,50);

// distribute by tens digit into 10 bins; collect and print
// sorted array
Distribute(L,digitQueue, 50, tens);
Collect(digitQueue,L);
PrintArray(L,50);
}

/*
<Run of Program 5.5>

    40   70   20   51   11   81   21   12   52   92
    62   72   82   82   62   72   52   83   63   23
     3   73   33   54   24   84   55   15   65   85
    25   16   46   86   36   67   17   27    7   97
    88   98   68   69   79   89   29   69   99   59

     3    7   11   12   15   16   17   20   21   23
    24   25   27   29   33   36   40   46   51   52
    52   54   55   59   62   62   63   65   67   68
    69   69   70   72   72   73   79   81   82   82
    83   84   85   86   88   89   92   97   98   99

*/
```

Each pass performs $O(n)$ operations consisting of division, queue insertion, and deletion operations. Since there are two passes, the complexity of the two-digit radix sort is $O(2n)$ and so is a linear algorithm. The radix sort can be extended to sort n numbers, each having m digits. In this case, the complexity is $O(mn)$, since the radix sort executes m passes, each involving $O(n)$ operations. This algorithm appears to be superior to the $O(n \log_2 n)$ sorting algorithms such as the heapsort and quicksort that we discuss in Chapters 13 and 14. However, the radix sort exhibits poorer space efficiency than these **in-place sorts.** In-place sorting algorithms sort the data in the original array and do not use temporary storage. The radix sort requires the use of 10 queues. Each queue has its own local storage for the front, rear, queue count, and the array. In addition, the radix sort is less efficient if the numbers contain many digits, since mn increases. Finally, it can be shown that the value of n for which the radix sort outperforms an $O(n \log_2 n)$ algorithm may be very large. For values of n encountered in practice, an $O(n \log_2 n)$ algorithm such as quicksort will outperform the radix sort.

Priority Queues   5.6

As discussed, a queue is a data structure that provides a FIFO ordering of elements. The queue removes the "oldest" item from the list. Applications often require a modified version of queue storage in which the item of highest priority is removed from the list. This structure, called a **priority queue,** has the operations PQInsert and PQDelete. PQInsert simply inserts a data element into the list, and the PQDelete operation removes the most important (highest priority) element from the list as measured by some external criterion that distinguishes the elements in the list. For instance, suppose a business provides a centralized secretarial pool to handle a variety of jobs for the staff. Company policy judges a job request by the president to be of highest priority followed by a request by the managers, then a request by the supervisors, and so forth. A person's rank in the company becomes a criterion that measures the relative importance of a job. Instead of handling jobs on a first-come/first-served basis (queue), the secretarial pool handles jobs in the order of their importance (priority queue).

Priority queues find applications in an operating system that records processes in a list and then executes them in the order of their priority. For instance, most operating systems give lower priority to a printer process than to other processes. Priority 0 is often defined as the "highest priority," with normal priority being a larger value such as 20. For instance, consider the following list of tasks and their priorities:

Task #1	Task #2	Task #3	Task #4	Task #5
20	0	40	30	10

Stored Order

The tasks execute in the order 2, 5, 1, 4, and 3.

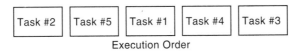

Execution Order

In most applications, elements in a priority queue are a **key-value pair** in which the key specifies the priority level. For instance, in an operating system, each task has a task descriptor and a priority level that serves as the key.

Priority Level	Task Descriptor

When deleting an item from a priority queue, there may be several elements in the list with the same priority level. In that case, we could require that these items be treated like a queue. This would have the effect of serving items of the same priority in the order of their arrival. In the following ADT, we make no assumption about the order of elements at the same priority level.

A priority queue describes a list with operations to add or delete elements from the list. A second series of operations measures the length of the list and indicates whether the list is empty.

ADT Priority Queue Is

Data
A list of items.

Operations

Constructor
Initial Values:	None
Process:	Initialize the number of list elements to zero.

PQLength
Input:	None
Preconditions:	None
Process:	Determine the number of elements in the list.
Output:	Return the number of elements in the list.
Postconditions:	None

PQEmpty
Input:	None
Preconditions:	None
Process:	Check whether the number of list elements is zero.
Output:	Return 1 (True) if there are no elements in the list and 0 (False) otherwise.
Postconditions:	None

PQInsert
Input:	An item to store in the list.
Preconditions:	None
Process:	Store the item in the list. This increases the length of the list by 1.
Output:	None
Postconditions:	A list has a new item and length.

PQDelete
Input:	None
Preconditions:	Priority queue is not empty.
Output:	None

Process:	Remove the element of highest priority from the list. This decreases the length of the list by one.
Output:	Return the item that is removed from the list.
Postconditions:	The element is deleted from the list which now has one less element.

ClearPQ

Input:	None
Preconditions:	None
Process:	Remove all items from the priority queue and restore initial conditions.
Output:	None
Postconditions:	The priority queue is empty.

end ADT Priority Queue

A PRIORITY QUEUE CLASS

In this book, we provide a variety of implementations for a priority queue. In each case, a list object is allocated to store the items. We use the count parameter and the list access methods to insert and delete items. In this chapter, we store items in an array whose elements are of generic type DataType. The storing of items in an array requires the class to provide PQFull method. In subsequent chapters, we use ordered lists and heaps to store the items in a priority queue.

- -

PQUEUE CLASS SPECIFICATION

DECLARATION

```
#include <iostream.h>
#include <stdlib.h>


// maximum size of the priority queue array
const int MaxPQSize = 50;


class PQuene
{
    private:
      // priority queue array and count
      int count;
      DataType pqlist[MaxPQSize];
```

```
    public:
        // constructor
        PQueue (void);

        // priority queue modification operations
        void PQInsert(const DataType& item);
        DataType PQDelete(void);
        void ClearPQ(void);

        // priority queue test methods
        int PQEmpty(void) const;
        int PQFull(void) const;
        int PQLength(void) const;
};
```

DESCRIPTION

The constant MaxPQSize determines the size of the array pqlist.

The PQInsert method simply inserts items into the list. The specification makes no assumptions about where the element is placed in the list.

The PQDelete method removes the element of highest priority from the list. We assume that the highest priority element is the one with the smallest value. The smallest value is determined by using the less than comparison operator "<" that must be defined for DataType.

EXAMPLE

```
typedef int DataType;                // "<" is defined for integers

PQueue PQ;

PQ.PQInsert(20);
PQ.PQInsert(10);
cout << PQ.PQLength() << endl;    // prints 2
N = PQ.PQDelete();                // extract N = 10
```

- -

PQUEUE CLASS IMPLEMENTATION

Priority Queue Operations　Like a queue, a priority queue has an operation to insert an item. The ADT makes no assumption about where an item is placed in the list, leaving the issue as an implementation detail in the PQInsert method. In our case, we first test if the list is full and terminate the program on this condition.

Otherwise, a new item is inserted at the rear of the list whose location is designated by pqlist[count].

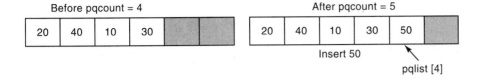

Before pqcount = 4

| 20 | 40 | 10 | 30 | | |

After pqcount = 5

| 20 | 40 | 10 | 30 | 50 | |

Insert 50

pqlist [4]

PQInsert
```
// insert item into the priority queue
void PQueue::PQInsert (const DataType& item)
{
    // if all elements of pqlist are used, terminate the program
    if (count == MaxPQSize)
    {
        cerr << "Priority queue overflow!" << endl;
        exit(1);
    }
    // place item at the rear of the list and increment count
    pqlist[count] = item;
    count++;
}
```

The PQDelete method requires that we must remove an element of highest priority from the list. The condition does not assume that we select the first element when two or more are available nor does the condition assume the elements maintain any order during the removal process. These are all implementation details. In our case, we first determine whether the list is empty and terminate the program if the condition is True. Otherwise, we scan for the minimum value, and delete it from the list by decrementing the length (count) and replacing the element with the last item in the list. The index of the last item is the new value of count.

In the following sample list, the minimum value is 10 at index 2. Delete the item by decrementing the length of the list by 1 and replacing the selected item with the last element in the list (pqlist[count]). Then delete 15, which is at the end of the list.

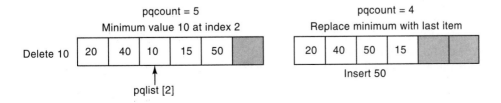

pqcount = 5
Minimum value 10 at index 2

Delete 10 | 20 | 40 | 10 | 15 | 50 | |

pqlist [2]

pqcount = 4
Replace minimum with last item

| 20 | 40 | 50 | 15 | | |

Insert 50

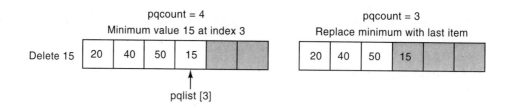

pqcount = 4
Minimum value 15 at index 3

pqcount = 3
Replace minimum with last item

Delete 15

pqlist [3]

PQDelete

```
// delete an element from the priority queue and return its value
DataType PQueue::PQDelete(void)
{
    DataType min;
    int i, minindex = 0;

    if (count > 0)
    {
      // find the minimum value and its index in pqlist
      min = pqlist[0];    // assume pqlist[0] is the minimum

      // visit remaining elements, updating minimum and index
      for (i = 1; i < count; i++)
         if (pqlist[i] < min)
         {
         // new minimum is pqlist[i], new minindex is i
            min = pqlist[i];
            minindex = i;
         }
      // move rear element to minindex and decrement count
      pqlist[minindex] = pqlist[count-1];
      count--;
    }
    // qlist is empty, terminate the program
    else
    {
       cerr << "Deleting from an empty pqueue!" << endl;
       exit(1);
    }
    // return minimum value
    return min;
}
```

The PQInsert operation has computing time $O(1)$ since it directly assigns an element to the end of the list. On the other hand, the operation PQDelete requires an initial scan of the list to identify the minimum value and its index. The operation has computing time $O(n)$, where n is the current length of the priority queue.

The data member count contains the number of elements in the list. This value is used in the implementation of PQLength, PQEmpty, and PQFull. The code for these methods is found on the program supplement in the file "apqueue.h".

Application: Company Support Services   The company staff is defined by the categories manager, supervisor, and worker. By creating an enum type with the different categories, we have a natural ordering, which gives each a priority level when requesting support services.

```
// employee priority level (manager = 0, etc)
enum Staff {Manager, Supervisor, Worker}; // Manager=0, etc
```

Company support services are supplied by a common secretarial pool. Each employee can make a job request by filling out a form that includes information on the category of employee requesting the service, an ID number for the job, and a time specifying how long the task will take. The information is stored in a record JobRequest. The job requests are entered into the priority queue with the priority measured by the category of the employee. This ordering is used to define the operation "<" for objects of type JobRequest.

```
// record defining a job request
struct JobRequest
{
    Staff staffPerson;
    int jobid;
    int jobTime;
};

// overload "<" to compare two JobRequest
int operator< (const JobRequest& a, const JobRequest& b)
{
    return a.staffPerson < b.staffPerson;
}
```

The file "job.dat" contains a list of job requests that are loaded into a priority queue. The application assumes the job requests have already been placed and are waiting to be processed. The items are extracted from the priority queue and executed. An array jobServicesUse holds the total amount of time spent servicing each of the different types of employees:

```
// time spent working for each category of employee
int jobServicesUse[3] = {0, 0, 0};
```

The print functions PrintJobInfo and PrintSupportSummary give information on each job and on the total number of minutes spent servicing each category of employee in the company:

```
// print a JobRequest record
void PrintJobInfo(JobRequest PR)
{
    switch (PR.staffPerson)
    {
        case Manager:    cout << "Manager        ";
                         break;
        case Supervisor: cout << "Supervisor     ";
                         break;
        case Worker:     cout << "Worker         ";
                         break;
    }
    cout << PR.jobid <<"      " << PR.jobTime << endl;
}


#include <iomanip.h>     // use manipulator setw
// print total job time allocated to each employee category
void PrintJobSummary(int jobServicesUse[])
{
    cout << "\nTotal Support Usage\n";
    cout << "   Manager     " << setw(3) <<
         << jobServicesUse[0] << endl;
    cout << "   Supervisor  " << setw(3) <<
         << jobServicesUse[1] << endl;
    cout << "   Worker      " << setw(3) <<
         << jobServicesUse[2] << endl;
```

Program 5.6 Job Services

Each job request is stored as a record in the file "job.dat". The record gives the
employee category ('M', 'S', 'W'), a job ID, and the job time. The records are read
until the end of file is reached, and each record is inserted into the priority
queue jobPool. On output, each job is extracted from the priority queue, and its
information is printed by PrintJobInfo. The program concludes by printing a
summary of the job services by calling PrintJobSummary. The JobRequest record
and associated functions are located in the file "job.h".

```
#include <iostream.h>
#include <fstream.h>


#include "job.h"              // defines JobRequest


// priority queue elements are of type JobRequest
typedef  JobRequest DataType;
```

```
#include "apqueue.h"        // include the PQueue class

void main()
{
    // handle up to 25 job requests
    PQueue jobPool;

    // job requests are read from fin
    ifstream fin;

    // time spent working for each category of employee
    int jobServicesUse[3] = {0, 0, 0};

    JobRequest PR;
    char ch;

    // open "job.dat" for input. exit program if open fails
    fin.open("job.dat", ios::in | ios::nocreate);
    if (!fin)
    {
        cerr << "Cannot open file 'job.dat'" << endl;
        exit(1);
    }

    // read the job file and insert each job into the priority
    // queue jobPool. each line starts with a charater that
    // identifies the type of staff person
    while (!fin. >> ch)
    {
        // assign staffPerson field
        switch(ch)
        {
            case 'M':    PR.staffPerson = Manager;
                         break;
            case 'S':    PR.staffPerson = Supervisor;
                         break;
            case 'W':    PR.staffPerson = Worker;
                         break;
            default:     break;
        }

        // read the integer jobid and jobTime files of PR
        fin >> PR.jobid;
        fin >> PR.jobTime;

        // insert PR into the priority queue
        jobPool.PQInsert(PR);
    }
```

```
        // delete jobs from priority queue and print information
        cout << "Category     Job ID     Job Time << endl";
        while (!jobPool.PQEmpty())
        {
            PR = jobPool.PQDelete();
            PrintJobInfo(PR);
            // accumulate job time for each category of employee
            jobServicesUse[int(PR.staffPerson)] += PR.jobTime;
        }

        PrintJobSummary(jobServicesUse);
}


/*
<Input file "job.dat">

M 300 20
W 301 30
M 302 40
S 303 10
S 304 40
M 305 70
W 306 20
W 307 20
M 308 60
S 309 30


<Run of Program 5.6>

Category      Job ID       Job Time
Manager         300          20
Manager         302          40
Manager         308          60
Manager         305          70
Supervisor      309          30
Supervisor      303          10
Supervisor      304          40
Worker          306          20
Worker          307          20
Worker          301          30

Total Job Usage
   Manager      190
   Supervisor    80
   Worker        70
*/
```

Case Study: Event-Driven Simulation   5.7

A simulation creates a model of a real-world situation so that we can better understand it. A simulation allows us to introduce a variety of conditions and observe their effects. For instance, a flight simulator challenges a pilot to respond to hostile conditions and measures the speed and appropriateness of the response. Marketing studies frequently use simulation to measure current business practices or to evaluate expansion. In this section, we illustrate a simulation that studies the arrival and departure patterns of bank customers as they pass through one of $n \geq 2$ teller lines. Our conclusion measures the efficiency of service by computing the average waiting time of each customer and the percentage of time each teller is busy. By using simulation, we can create different service patterns and evaluate them for cost and efficiency. The simulation approach carries out an **event-driven simulation** that defines objects to represent banking activities. We use probabilistic values that describe different expected arrival rates for customers and different expected service times for a teller to handle a customer. The simulation allows us to use a random number generator to mirror the arrival and departure of customers during a bank day.

The simulation also allows us to vary parameters and thus measure the relative effect on service if we change customer or teller behavior. For instance, suppose the marketing division estimates that a gift promotion would increase customer traffic by 20%. A simulation study would increase the expected arrival rate and measure the effect on teller performance. At some point, the bank would need additional tellers to maintain reasonable service and the added cost might nullify the benefit of the promotion. The simulation provides a bank manager with options to evaluate customer service. Should the average waiting time be too long, the manager can add a new teller. The simulation can be repeated again and again by simply changing conditions.

Simulation Design

As it runs, the simulation tracks separate customer arrivals and departures. For instance, assume the 50th customer arrives at the bank at 2:30 (arrival) with activities that require 12 minutes of teller time. Our simulation assumes each teller clearly posts his or her work schedule so that a new customer can identify who will be available and when service can begin.

— —

In our case, assume Teller 2 is idle, which allows the customer to immediately select that teller, go to the window, transact business, and leave at 2:42 (departure). This customer has 0 waiting time and Teller 2 has 12 additional minutes of work.

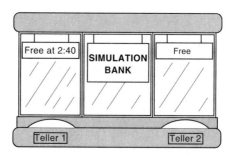

```
time(departure) = time(arrival) + servicetime
time(departure) = 2:30 + 0:12 = 2:42
```

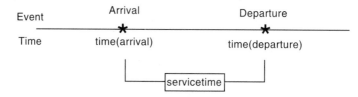

Consider different circumstances for the 50th customer. Assume the two tellers are busy and the customer must take up a position in line and wait for service. If Teller 1 is free at 2:40 and Teller 2 is free at 2:33, the new customer selects Teller 2. After waiting 3 minutes and using 12 minutes to transact business, the customer departs at 2:45, which is the next time Teller 2 is free.

```
time(departure) = time(arrival) + waittime + servicetime
time(departure) = 2:30 + 0:03 + 0:12 = 2:45
```

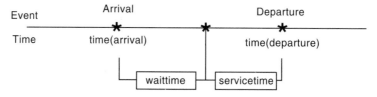

In our simulation, we have the customer select the teller, who then updates the "next time free" sign at the window to reflect the newly obligated service.

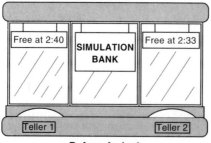

Before Arrival

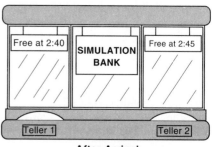

After Arrival

The key components of our bank simulation are customer events, which include both arrival and departure. During execution, real time is viewed as a sequence of random events that reflect the arrival, servicing, and departure of the customer. An event is declared as a C++ class with private data members that identify both the customer and teller as well as maintain information on the time the event occurs, the kind of event (arrival or departure), the length of service required by the customer, and the amount of time the customer is forced to wait before being served.

time	etype	customerID	tellerID	waittime	servicetime

When the customer enters the bank, we have an **arrival event.** For instance, if customer 50 arrives at 2:30, the corresponding record is

Arrival Event Data

2:30	Arrival	50	–	–	–
time	etype	customerID	tellerID	waittime	servicetime

The tellerID, waittime, and servicetime fields are not used for an arrival event. After arrival, these fields are determined and a departure event is generated.

After the customer checks on the availability of a teller, we can define a **departure** event that describes when the customer will leave. This object can be used to reconstruct the history of the customer in the bank system. For instance, the following is the departure event for a customer who arrives at 2:30, waits 3 minutes for teller 2, and leaves after 12 minutes of service:

Departure Event Data

2:45	Departure	50	2	3	12
time	etype	customerID	tellerID	waittime	servicetime

The data fields of an object describe all of the relevant information that pertains to the flow of a customer through the system. The class methods give us access to these data fields, which are used to gather information on the overall effectiveness of the service.

- -
EVENT CLASS SPECIFICATION

DECLARATION

```
#include <iostream.h>
#include "random.h"      // include random number generator

// specifies the two kinds of events
enum EventType {arrival, departure};
```

```
class Event
{
    private:
        // members that identify both customer and teller, as
        // well as maintain information on time of the event,
        // the event type, the length of service required by
        // the customer, and the amount of time customer is
        // forced to wait for service
        int time;
        EventType etype;
        int customerID; // customers are numbered 1, 2, 3, . . .
        int tellerID;   // tellers are numbered 1, 2, 3, . . .
        int waittime;
        int servicetime;
    public:
        // constructors
        Event(void);
        Event(int t, EventType et, int cn, int tn,
              int wt, int st);


        // methods to retrieve private data
        int GetTime(void) const;
        EventType GetEventType(void) const;
        int GetCustomerID(void) const;
        int GetTellerID(void) const;
        int GetWaitTime(void) const;
        int GetServiceTime(void) const;
};
```

DESCRIPTION

The default constructor allows an Event object to be declared and later initialized by assignment. The second constructor allows us to define each parameter when declaring the event. The remaining methods return the values of the data members.

EXAMPLE

The time is given in minutes from the start of the simulation run.

```
Event e; // declare an event using default constructor


// customer 3 departs at 120 minutes. After waiting 10 minutes,
// customer takes 5 minutes with teller 1 to transact business.

e = Event(120, departure,3,1,10,5);
cout << e.GetService();        // output service time 5
```

Simulation Information

During a simulation run, we accumulate information on each teller that indicates the total number of customers the teller served, the time the customers waited and the total amount of service provided by the teller during the day. We gather all of this information in a TellerStats record that also contains the field finishService, which represents the value of the sign hanging from the window.

TellerStats Record

finishService	totalCustomerCount	totalCustomerWait	totalService

```
// Structure for Teller Info
struct TellerStats
{
    int    finishService;      // when teller available
    int    totalCustomerCount; // total of customers serviced
    int    totalCustomerWait;  // total customer waiting time
    int    totalService;       // total time servicing customers
};
```

The simulation generates an arrival and departure event for each customer. All events are time-stamped and placed in a priority queue. The highest priority event in the priority queue is the event with the earliest time stamp. This list structure enables us to remove events so that we move in an increasing time sequence through the arrival and departure of customers.

The bank simulation uses a random number generator to determine the next arrival of a customer and the service time of the current customer. The generator assures that any outcome within a range of values is equally likely to occur. In the simulation, if the current arrival event occurs at T minutes, the next arrival occurs randomly in the range from T+arrivalLow to T+arrivalHigh minutes, and the amount of service demanded by a customer falls in the range serviceLow to serviceHigh minutes. For instance, assume that a customer arrives at 2 minutes and that the range within which the next customer arrives is arrivalLow = 4 to arrivalHigh = 12 minutes later. There is a 1/9 chance that any of the outcomes 6, 7, . . . , 14 minutes will occur.

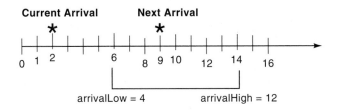

The sample outcome has a customer arriving at 2 minutes. We know there will be a subsequent event at 9 minutes that corresponds to the arrival of the next customer. We can create this event and place it in the priority queue for processing later in the simulation.

The data for a simulation and the methods that implement a simulation study are contained in the Simulation class. The data members include the length of the simulation (in minutes), the number of tellers, the number of the next customer, an array of TellerStats records that contain information on each of the tellers, and the priority queue that holds the event list. The class also contains the limits on the ranges for the next arrival and for service to the current customer.

--- --- --- --- --- --- --- --- --- --- --- --- --- --- --- --- --- --- ---

SIMULATION CLASS SPECIFICATION

DECLARATION

```
class Simulation
{
    private:
        // data used to run the simulation
        int simulationLength;          // simulation length
        int numTellers;                // number of tellers
        int nextCustomer;              // next customer ID
        int arrivalLow, arrivalHigh;   // next arrival range
        int serviceLow, serviceHigh;   // service range
        TellerStats tstat[11];         // max 10 tellers
        PQueue pq;                     // priority queue
        RandomNumber rnd;              // use for arrival
                                       // and service Times

        // private methods used by RunSimulation
        int NextArrivalTime(void);
        int GetServiceTime(void);
        int NextAvailableTeller(void);
    public:
        // constructor
        Simulation(void);

        void RunSimulation(void)           // execute study
        void PrintSimulationResults(void); // print stats
};
```

DESCRIPTION

The constructor initializes the TellerStats array and nextCustomer, which begins at 1. Index 0 in array tstat is not used. In this way, a teller number serves a direct index into array tstat.

The constructor prompts the client to input the data for the study. The data include the simulation length in minutes, the number of tellers, and the range of arrival and service times. The class provides for up to 10 tellers.

For each arrival event, we call the method NextArrivalTime to determine when a new customer will arrive at the bank. At the same time we call GetServiceTime to determine how long the current customer will occupy a teller and Next-AvailableTeller to determine which teller will service the customer.

The method RunSimulation executes the simulation study, and PrintSimulationResults outputs the final statistics.

Setting up the Simulation

The constructor initializes the simulation data and prompts the client for the simulation parameters.

```
Simulation::Simulation(void)
{
    int i;
    Event firstevent;


    // Initialize Teller Information Parameters
    for(i = 1; i <= 10; i++)
    {
        tstat[i].finishService = 0;
        tstat[i].totalService = 0;
        tstat[i].totalCustomerWait = 0;
        tstat[i].totalCustomerCount = 0;
    }
    nextCustomer = 1;


    // reads client input for the study
    cout << "Enter the simulation time in minutes: ";
    cin >> simulationLength;
    cout << "Enter the number of bank tellers: ";
    cin >> numTellers;
    cout << "Enter the range of arrival times in minutes: ";
    cin >> arrivalLow >> arrivalHigh;
    cout << "Enter the range of service times in minutes: ";
    cin >> serviceLow >> serviceHigh;


    // generate first arrival event
    // teller# waittime servicetime not used for arrival
    pq.PQInsert(Event(0,arrival,1,0,0,0));
}
```

Running the Simulation

The length of the simulation (simulationLength) is used to determine whether an arrival event should be generated for another customer. If the bank would be closed at the projected arrival time for a new customer (arrival time > simulationLength), no new customers are accepted, and the simulation study concludes by servicing the customers remaining in the bank. The nextCustomer data member is a counter that maintains a record of the number of customers in the study. Since our simulation gives the generic names Customer 1 and Customer 2 to the patrons of the bank, the nextCustomer value becomes the customer ID for the next arrival event.

The method NextArrivalTime returns the time interval until the arrival of the next customer. The method uses the random number generator and the parameters arrivalLow and arrivalHigh to generate a return value. The similar GetServiceTime method uses the parameters serviceLow and serviceHigh

```
// determine random time of next arrival
int Simulation::NextArrivalTime(void)
{
    return arrivalLow+rnd.Random(arrivalHigh-arrivalLow+1);
}

// determine random time for customer service
int Simulation::GetServiceTime(void)
{
    return serviceLow+rnd.Random(serviceHigh-serviceLow+1);
}
```

In the simulation, the arriving customer looks at the teller windows and reads the signs that indicate when each teller will be free. With this information, the customer selects the teller that will provide banking services. The data value finishService in each teller record represents the sign hanging at the window. The function NextAvailableTeller scans the array of tellers and returns the teller having the minimum finishService value. If all of the tellers are busy until after closing, the customer is assigned a random teller.

```
// return first available teller
int Simulation::NextAvailableTeller(void)
{
    // initially assume all tellers finish at closing time
    int minfinish = simulationLength;

    // assign random teller to customer who arrives
    // before closing but obtains service after closing
    int minfinishindex = rnd.Random(numTellers) + 1;

    // find teller who is free first
    for (int i = 1; i <= numTellers; i++)
        if (tstat[i].finishService < minfinish)
        {
```

```
newevent = Event(tstat[tellerID].finishService,
                departure, e.GetCustomerID(),tellerID,
                waittime,servicetime);
pq.PQInsert(newevent);
```

Departure

A departure event gives us access to the history of activities of the customer while in the bank. In a simulation study, this information can be printed. From the departure event, we must update the finishService field if the teller has no other customers. This occurs if the current value of finishService equals the departure time. In this case, set finishService to 0.

```
tellerID = e.GetTellerID();
// if nobody waiting for teller, mark teller free
if (e.GetTime() == tstat[tellerID].finishService)
    tstat[tellerID].finishService = 0;
```

Simulation Summary   To conclude a simulation, call PrintSimulationResults. It prints a summary of data about the customers and the individual tellers. The data are gathered from the TellerStats records that contain information on the number of customers each teller has served and the cumulative customer waiting time.

```
for (i = 1; i <= numTellers; i++)
  {
    cumCustomers += tstat[i].totalCustomerCount;
    cumWait += tstat[i].totalCustomerWait;
  }
```

The final summary gives the average waiting time of a customer and the percentage of time each teller is busy.

```
cout << endl;
cout << "******** Simulation Summary ********" << endl;
cout << "Simulation of " << simulationLength
     << "minutes" << endl;
cout << "  No. of Customers:   " << cumCustomers << endl;
cout << "  Average Customer Wait: ";

avgCustWait = float(cumWait)/cumCustomers + 0.5;
cout << avgCustWait << "minutes" << endl;
for(i=1;i <= numTellers;i++)
{
    cout << "    Teller #" << i << " % Working: ";
    // display percent rounded to nearest integer value
    tellerWork = float(tstat[i].totalService)/simulationLength;
    tellerWorkPercent = tellerWork * 100.0 + 0.5;
    cout << tellerWorkPercent << endl;
}
```

Sample Simulation   The main program defines a Simulation object S and then executes the event loop implemented by the RunSimulation. After the event loop concludes, PrintSimulationResults is called.

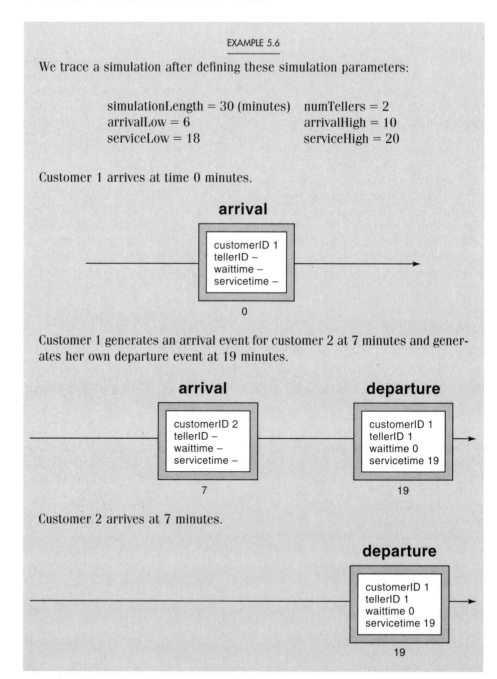

EXAMPLE 5.6

We trace a simulation after defining these simulation parameters:

simulationLength = 30 (minutes)   numTellers = 2
arrivalLow = 6   arrivalHigh = 10
serviceLow = 18   serviceHigh = 20

Customer 1 arrives at time 0 minutes.

arrival

customerID 1
tellerID –
waittime –
servicetime –

0

Customer 1 generates an arrival event for customer 2 at 7 minutes and generates her own departure event at 19 minutes.

arrival   **departure**

customerID 2   customerID 1
tellerID –   tellerID 1
waittime –   waittime 0
servicetime –   servicetime 19

7   19

Customer 2 arrives at 7 minutes.

departure

customerID 1
tellerID 1
waittime 0
servicetime 19

19

Customer 2 generates an arrival event for customer 3 at 16 minutes and generates his own departure event at 25 minutes.

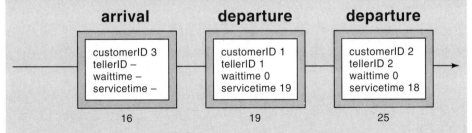

Customer 3 arrives at 16 minutes.

Customer 3 generates an arrival event that is past bank closing, which stops arrival event creation. Customer 3 must wait 3 minutes for teller 1 and generates her own departure event at 37 minutes.

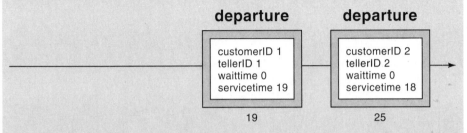

The departure events are deleted from the priority queue in this order: customer 1 at 19 minutes, customer 2 at 25 minutes, and customer 3 at 37 minutes.

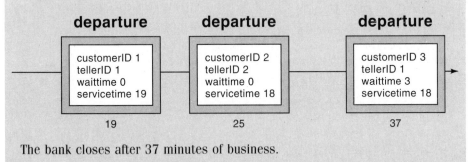

The bank closes after 37 minutes of business.

Program 5.7   Code and Execution

This program is run twice. The first run corresponds to the data in Example 5.6. The second run uses a simulation of 480 minutes (8 hours). The output method

PrintSimulationResults indicates the number of patrons, the average waiting time for each customer, and the amount of time each teller is busy. The implementation of the Event, TellerStats, and Simulation classes are contained in file "sim.h".

```
#include "sim.h"

void main(void)
{
    // declare an object S for our simulation
    Simulation S;

    // run the simulation
    S.RunSimulation();

    // print the results
    S.PrintSimulationResults();
}
/*
<Run #1 of Program 5.7>

Enter the simulation time in minutes: 30
Enter the number of bank tellers: 2
Enter the range of arrival times in minutes: 6 10
Enter the range of service times in minutes: 18 20
Time:  0   arrival of customer 1
Time:  7   arrival of customer 2
Time: 16   arrival of customer 3
Time: 19   departure of customer 1
        Teller 1  Wait 0  Service 19
Time: 25   departure of customer 2
        Teller 2  Wait 0  Service 18
Time: 37   departure of customer 3
        Teller 1  Wait 3  Service 18

******** Simulation Summary ********
Simulation of 37 minutes
    No. of Customers:   3
    Average Customer Wait: 1 minutes
    Teller #1  % Working: 100
    Teller #2  % Working: 49

<Run #2 of Program 5.7>

Enter the simulation time in minutes   480
Enter the number of bank tellers   4
Enter the range of arrival times in minutes   2 5
Enter the range of service times in minutes   6 20

<arrival and departure of 137 customers>
```

```
******** Simulation Summary ********
Simulation of 521 minutes
      No. of Customers:  137
      Average Customer Wait: 2 minutes
      Teller #1  % Working: 89
      Teller #2  % Working: 86
      Teller #3  % Working: 83
      Teller #4  % Working: 86
*/
```

Written Exercises

5.1 Circle all that apply. A STACK is a structure implementing

(a) first-in/last-out   (b) last-in/first-out   (c) first-come/first-serve
(d) first-in/first-out   (e) last-in/last-out

5.2 Give two applications for stacks in a computer program.

5.3 What is the output from the following sequence of stack operations? (DataType = int);

```
Stack S;
int x = 5, y = 3;

S.Push(8);
S.Push(9);
S.Push(y);
x = S.Pop();
S.Push(18);
x = S.Pop();
S.Push(22);
while (!S.StackEmpty())
{
    y = S.Pop();
    cout << y << endl;
}
cout << x << endl;
```

5.4 Write a function

```
void StackClear(Stack& S);
```

which clears a stack S. Why is it critical that S be passed by reference?

5.5 What is the action of the following function? (DataType = int):

```
void Ques5(Stack& S)
{
    int arr[64], n = 0, i;
    int elt;
```

```
      while (!S.StackEmpty())
        a[n++] = S.Pop();
      for(i=0;i < n;i++)
        S.Push(a[i]);
   }
```

5.6 What is the action of the following code segment?:

```
   Stack S1, S2, tmp;
   Datatype  x;
        . . .
   while (!S1.StackEmpty())
   {
      x = S1.Pop();
      tmp.Push(x);
   }

   while (!tmp.StackEmpty())
   {
      x = tmp.Pop();
      S1.Push(x);
      S2.Push(x);
   }
```

5.7 Write a function

```
   int StackSize(Stack S);
```

that uses stack operations to return the number of elements in the stack S.

5.8 What is the action of the following function Ques8? (DataType = int):

```
   void Ques8(Stack& S, int n)
   {
      Stack Q;
      int i;

      while(!S.StackEmpty())
      {
        i = S.Pop();
        if (i != n)
           Q.Push(i);
      }
      while(!Q.StackEmpty())
      {
        i = Q.Pop();
        S.Push(i);
      }
   }
```

5.9 If DataType is int, write a function

```
void SelectItem(Stack& S, int n);
```

that uses stack operations to find the first occurrence of item n on stack S and move it to the top of the stack. Maintain ordering for all other elements.

5.10 Convert the following infix expressions to postfix:

(a) a + b*c
(b) (a+b)/(d−e)
(c) $(b^2 − 4*a*c)/(2*a)$

5.11 Write the following expressions in infix form:

(a) a b + c *
(b) a b c + *
(c) a b c d e + + * * e f − *

5.12 Circle all that apply. A queue is a structure implementing

(a) first-in/last-out   (b) last-in/first-out   (c) first-come/first-serve
(d) first-in/first-out   (e) last-in/last-out

5.13 A queue is an applicable data structure for (circle all)

(a) expression evaluation
(b) operating system job scheduler
(c) simulation of waiting lines
(d) printing a list in reverse order

5.14 What is the output from the sequence of queue operations? (DataType = int):

```
Queue Q;
DataType x = 5, y = 3;

Q.QInsert(8);
Q.QInsert(9);
Q.QInsert(y);
x = Q.QDelete();
Q.QInsert(18);
x = Q.QDelete();
Q.QInsert(22);
while (!Q.QEmpty())
{
    y = Q.QDelete();
    cout << y << endl;
}
cout << x << endl;
```

5.15 What is the action of the following function? (DataType = int):

```
void Ques15(Queue& Q, int n = 50)
{
```

```
        Stack S;
        int elt;

        while (!Q.QEmpty())
        {
            elt = Q.QDelete();
            S.Push(elt);
        }
        while (!S.StackEmpty())
        {
            elt = S.Pop();
            Q.QInsert(elt);
        }
    }
```

Why is it critical that Q be passed by reference?

5.16 What is the action of the following code segment?

```
    (DataType = int)

    Queue Q1, Q2;
    int n = 0, x;
        . . .
    while (!Q1.QEmpty())
    {
        x = Q1.QDelete();
        Q2.QInsert(x);
        n++;
    }
    for (int i=0;i < n;i++)
    {
        x = Q2.QDelete();
        Q1.QInsert(x);
        Q2.QInsert(x);
    }
```

5.17 Assume the priority queue list contains integer values with the less than operator "<" defining the priority order. The current list contains the elements
By tracing the PQDelete and PQInsert methods in the PQueue class, describe the list after executing each of the following instructions:

45	15	50	25	65	30

(a) Item = pq.PQDelete()   Item =   List:
(b) pq.PQInsert(20)   List:
(c) Item = pq.PQDelete()   Item =   List:
(d) Item = pq.PQDelete()   Item =   List:

5.18   Rewrite the PQDelete routine to ensure a FIFO order of items at the same priority level.

Programming Exercises

5.1   Add the method

```
void QPrint(void);
```

that causes the queue to be printed, 8 elements to a line. Write a program that inputs 20 double values from the file "pq.dat" into a queue. Print the elements.

5.2   Read 10 integers into an array, pushing each onto a stack. Print the original list and then print the stack by popping the elements. Of course, the second printing lists the elements in reverse order.

5.3   A stack can be used to recognize certain types of patterns. Consider the pattern STRING1#STRING2 where neither string contains "#" and STRING2 must be the reverse of STRING1. For instance, the string 123&^a#a^&321 matches the pattern but the string a2qd#dq3a does not. Write a program that reads five strings and indicates whether each string matches the pattern.

5.4   In a second model of a stack, the stack grows in the direction of decreasing array indices. Initially the stack is empty and Top = 21. After pushing three characters on the stack, the index Top = 18, and the element at the top of the stack is LIST[TOP] = C.

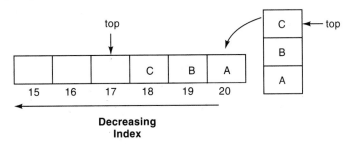

**Decreasing
Index**

In this model the index Top decreases on each Push operation and increases on each Pop operation. Write an implementation for the Stack class using this model. Test your work by running Program 5.1.

5.5   An array can be used to store two stacks, one growing up from the left end, the other growing down from the right end.

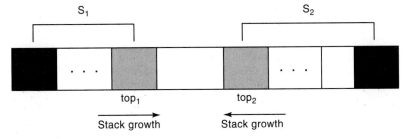

(a)   What is the condition for S_1 to be empty? When is S_2 empty?

(b)   What is the condition for S_1 to be full? When is S_2 full?

(c)   Implement the class DualStack whose declaration is given by

```
const int MaxDualStackSize = 100

class DualStack
{
    private:
        int top1, top2;
        DataType stackStorage[MaxDualStackSize];
    public:
        DualStack(void );
        // push elt on stack n
        void Push(DataType elt, int n);
        // pop from stack n
        DataType Pop(int n);
        // peek at stack n
        DataType Peek(int n);
        // is stack n empty?
        int StackEmpty(int n);
        // is stack n full?
        int StackFull(int n);
        // clear stack n
        void ClearStack(int n);
};
```

(d)   Write a main program that reads a sequence of 20 integers, pushing all of the even integers on one stack and the odd integers on the other. Print the contents of each stack.

5.6   Read a line of text, placing each nonblank character on both a queue and stack. Verify whether the text is a palindrome.

5.7   Extend the postfix calculator by adding the unary minus, represented by the symbol @. For example, enter the expression

```
7
@
12
+
    <Display> 5
```

5.8   This exercise extends the postfix calculator class to include evaluation of expressions with a variable. The new declaration is

```
class Calculator
{
```

```
    private:
        Stack S;
        struct component                    // NEW
        {
            short type;
            float value;
        };
        int expsize:                        // NEW
        component expComponent[50];  // NEW

        int  GetTwoOperands(double& operand1,
                            double& operand2);
        void Enter(double num);
        void Compute(char op);

    public:
        Calculator(void);
        void Run(void);
        void Clear(void);
        void Variable(void);            // NEW
        double Eval(double x);          // NEW
};
```

The operation Variable allows the user to enter a postfix expression that contains the variable x as well as numbers and operators. For instance, enter the expression

```
x x * 3 x * + 5 +
```

when you want to evaluate the infix expression $x^2 + 3x + 5$. As each component is read, make an entry in the array expComponent. The type field of each entry is set as follows: 1 = number, 2 = variable x, 3 = +, 4 = −, 5 = *, 6 = /. If type = 1, the number is stored in the value field. Increment expsize once for each new entry.

The member function Eval cycles through the expsize members of array expComponent and uses the stack to evaluate the expression. Whenever an element has a type field of 2, push the parameter x on the stack.

Write a main program that evaluates the expression

$$(x^2 + 1)/(x^4 + 8x^2 + 5x + 3)$$

for $x = 0, 10^1, 10^2, 10^3, \ldots, 10^8$.

5.9 Modify the simulation study in Program 5.7 to include the following information:

(a) Output the average time that a customer spends in the bank. Customer time is measured from arrival to departure.

(b) Currently all of the tellers remain at the bank until the last customer departs. This is costly if the tellers are kept after closing hours to handle a late arriving customer. Allow a teller to leave if the bank is closed and there is no customer waiting for service. Hint: add a field to the TellerStat record that specifies the total time the teller spends in the bank. Use this variable to compute the percentage of time the teller is busy.

5.10 Assume the bank creates a separate customer line for each teller. When a customer arrives, he or she selects the shortest line rather than considering the workload of the tellers. Modify the simulation program 5.7 to indicate the average waiting time of a customer and the amount of work done by each teller. Compare the results with the single line model of the study.

C H A P T E R 6

ABSTRACT
OPERATORS

An abstract data type defines a set of methods to initialize and manage data. With classes, the C++ language introduces powerful tools to implement an ADT. In this chapter, we extend language-defined operators (e.g., +, [], and so forth) to abstract data types. The process, called **operator overloading,** redefines standard operator symbols to implement operations for the abstract type. Operator overloading is one of the most exciting features of object-oriented programming. The concept allows us to use standard language operators with their precedence and associativity properties as class methods. For instance, assume a Matrix class defines addition and multiplication operations using AddMat and MultMat. With overloading, we can use the familiar infix operators "+" and "*". Assume that P, Q, R, S are objects of type Matrix:

Standard Class Methods	Overloaded Operators
`R = P.AddMat (Q);`	`R = P + Q`
`S = R.MultMat (Q.AddMat(P));`	`S = R * (Q+P)`

Relational expressions define an order between elements. We say that integer 3 is positive or that 10 is less than 15.

$$3 >= 0 \qquad 10 < 15$$

The concept of order applies to data structures other than numbers. In the Date class of Chapter 3, for example, two dates (objects) can be compared by chronology of the year.

```
Date(6,6,44) < (Date(12,25,80)      // D-Day occurred before
                                     // Christmas 1980
Date(4,1,99) == Date ("4/1/99")      // Two ways to create April
                                     // Fool's Day
Date(7,1,94) < Date("8/1/94")        // July occurs before August
```

C++ allows overloading of most of its native operators, including the stream operators. A programmer cannot create new operator symbols but must overload existing C++ operators.

The method PrintDate in the Date class takes an object D and outputs its fields in a standard format. The same method can be rewritten as an "<<" operator and used in the cout stream. For instance, the Date object D(12,31,99) defines the last day of the twentieth century. To create the output

```
The last day of the 20th century is December 31, 1999
```

we can use print method in Chapter 3 or overload the put operator.

```
PrintDate Method:
        cout << "The last day of the 20th century is ";
        D.PrintDate();

Overloaded "<<" Method:
        cout << "The last day of the 20th century is " << D;
```

Operator overloading is a topic that is introduced over several chapters. In this chapter we look at the arithmetic and relational operators and stream I/O. We develop a rational number class to illustrate the key concepts. You are familiar with "fractions" and have had years of experience in school working with the operations. The Rational class provides a good example of arithmetic and relational operations, type conversion between integer values and real numbers, and a simple definition for overloaded stream I/O.

Describing Operator Overloading   6.1

The term **operator overloading** implies that language operators such as +, !=, [], and = can be redefined for a class type. This class type gives us the ability to implement operations with abstract data types using familiar operator symbols. C++ provides a variety of techniques for defining operator overloading including client-defined external functions, class members, and friends. C++ requires that at least one argument of an overloaded operator must be an object or an object reference.

CLIENT-DEFINED EXTERNAL FUNCTIONS

In the SeqList class, the Find and Delete methods require that the relational equals operator "==" be defined for DataType. If the operator is not native to the type, the client must explicitly provide an overloaded version. The declaration uses the identifier "operator" and the symbol "==". Since the result of the operation is True or False, the return value is of type int:

```
int operator== (const DataType& a, const DataType& b);
```

For instance, suppose the list contains Employee records that consist of an ID field and other information including name, address, and so forth.

```
struct Employee
{
    int ID;
    . . .
}
```

ID	Name	Address	. . .

The relational equals operation compares the ID fields:

```
int operator == (const Employee& a, const Employee& b)
{
    return a.ID == b.ID;    // compare ID fields
}
```

An overloaded operator must have an argument of class type. Note that the following attempt to overload "==" for C++ strings will fail because no argument is an object or an object reference.

```
int operator== (char *s, char *t)    // invalid operator
{
    return strcmp(s,t) == 0;
}
```

Once the relational equals operator is declared, a client may use the Find or Delete functions of the SeqList class:

```
typedef Employee DataType;    // data type is Employee
#include "aseqlist.h"
    . . .
SeqList L;
Employee emp;                 // declare a SeqList object.
    . . .
emp.ID = 1000;                // look for employee with ID = 1000
if (L.Find(emp))
    L.Delete(emp);            // if found, remove the employee
```

To use the SeqList class, the client must have the technical knowledge to define the "==" operator as an external function. This is an additional but necessary requirement since the "==" operator is attached to the data type and not to the class.

CLASS MEMBERS

Arithmetic and relational operators have their origin in number systems. They allow the programmer to combine operands in expressions using infix notation. A class may have methods that combine objects in a similar fashion. In most cases, the methods can be written as overloaded member functions using standard C++ operators. When the left operand is an object, the operator can be executed as a method that is defined for that object. For instance, two-dimensional vectors provide operators that include addition, negation, and dot-product.

Vector Addition

Add two vectors $u = (u_1, u_2)$ and $v = (v_1, v_2)$ by forming the vector whose components are the sum of the components of each vector (see part (a) of Figure 6.1).

$$u + v = (u_1 + v_1, u_2 + v_2)$$

Vector Negation

Form the negative of vector $u = (u_1, u_2)$ by taking the negative of each component. The new vector has the same magnitude but opposite direction (see part (b) of Figure 6.1).

$$-(u_1, u_2) = (-u_1, -u_2)$$

Vector Multiplication (Dot Product)

The vector $u = (u_1, u_2)$ multiplied by the vector $u = (v_1, v_2)$ is the number obtained adding the products of corresponding components (see part (c) of Figure 6.1). The dot product represents the product of the magnitude of the vectors * cosine of the included angle.

$$v*w = u_1\,v_1 + u_2\,v_2 = \text{magnitude}(v)*\text{magnitude}(w)*\cos(\theta)$$

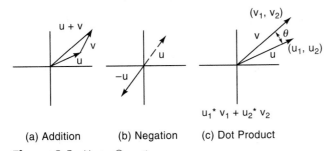

(a) Addition   (b) Negation   (c) Dot Product

Figure 6.1   Vector Operations

We declare the vector class Vec2d with its coordinates x and y as private data members. The class has a constructor, two binary operators (addition, dot product) and a unary (negation) operator as member functions, as well as friend functions that define the scalar product and stream output. The use of friends is discussed in the next section.

```
class Vec2d
{
    private:
        double x1,x2;                        // components

    public:
        // constructor with default values
        Vec2d(double h = 0.0, double v = 0.0);

        // member functions
        Vec2d operator- (void);              // negation
        Vec2d operator+ (const Vec2d& V);    // addition
        double operator* (const Vec2d& V);   // dot product
```

```
            // friend functions
            friend Vec2d operator* (const double c,const Vec2d& V);
            friend ostream& operator<< (ostream& os, const Vec2d& U);
   };
```

As member functions, the addition, negation, and dot-product operators assume that the current object is the left operand in an expression. Assume U and V are vectors.

Addition   The expression U + V uses the binary operator "+" associated with the object U. The method operator+ is called with parameter V.

```
   U.operator+ (V)   // returns the value Vec2d(x + V.x, y + V.y)
```

Negation   The expression −U uses the unary operator operator "−". The method operator− is executed for object U.

```
   U.operator- () // returns the value Vec2d(-x, -y)
```

Dot Product   Like addition, the expression U * V uses the binary operator "*" associated with the object U. The product is evaluated by the method for the current object U and the parameter V.

```
   U.operator* (V)   // returns the value x * V.x + y * V.y
```

For instance, with the objects

```
   Vec2d U(1,2), V(2,3);

   U + V = (1,2) + (2,3) = (3,5)
   -U = -(1,2) = (-1,-2)
   U * V = (1,2) * (2,3) = 8
```

Operator overloading requires that certain conditions be met.

1. Operators must obey the precedence, associativity, and number of operands dictated by the built-in definition of the operator. For example, '*' is a binary operator and must always have two parameters when it is overloaded.

2. All operators in C++ can be overloaded, with the exception of the following:

```
   , (comma operator)  sizeof  :: (class scope operator)
   ?: (conditional expression)
```

3. Overloaded operators cannot have default arguments; in other words, all operands for the operator must be present. For instance, this operator declaration is invalid.

```
double Vec2d::operator* (Vec2d V = Vec2d(1,1));
```

4. When an operator is overloaded as a member function, the object associated with the operator is always the left-most operand.

5. As member functions, the unary operators take no arguments, and binary operators take one argument.

FRIEND FUNCTIONS

Typically object-oriented programming requires that only member functions have access to the private data of a class. This provides data encapsulation and information hiding. This principle should extend to operator overloading whenever possible. In some situations, however, using overloading with a member function is impossible or too inconvenient. We need to use **friend functions** that are defined outside of the class but have access to the private data members. For instance, scalar multiplication is another form of vector multiplication, where each component of a vector is multiplied by a numeric value. The number (scalar) c multiplied by the vector $u = (u_1, u_1)$ is the vector whose components are formed by multiplying each component of u by c:

$$c*u = (cu_1, cu_2)$$

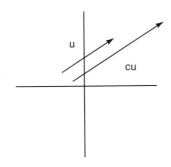

This is a natural operation to overload using the '*' operator.

However, operator overloading using a member function does not permit the placing of the scalar value C as the left-hand operand. The vector must be the left-hand operand.

We define '*' to be an operator outside of the class having parameters C and U. The operator has access to the private members x and y of the parameter U. This is done by defining the operator as a **friend** inside the class declaration.

A friend function is declared by preceding the function declaration in the class with the keyword friend.

```
friend Vec2d operator * (const double c,const Vec2d& U);
```

Since a friend function is external to a class, it does not lie within the scope of the class and is implemented as a standard function. Note that the keyword friend is not repeated in the function declaration.

```
Vec2d operator* (double c, Vec2d U)
{
    return Vec2d(c * U.x, c * U.y);
}
```

When using scalar multiplication, both arguments are passed to '*', and the scalar must be the left-hand parameter.

```
Vec2d Y(8,5), Z;
Z = 3.0 * Y;      // result Z is (24,15)
```

The use of friends and their access rights are described in the following list of rules.

1. A friend declaration is made by placing the function declaration inside the class preceded by the keyword *friend*. The acutal definition of a friend function is made outside the class block. The friend function is defined like any ordinary C++ function and is not a member of the class.

2. The keyword *friend* is used only within the function declaration in the class and not with the function definition.

3. A friend function has access to private members of the class.

4. A friend function gains access to members of the class only by being passed objects as parameters and using the dot notation to reference a member.

5. In order to overload a unary operator as a friend, pass the operand as a parameter. When overloading a binary operator as a friend, pass both operands as parameters. For instance,

```
friend Vec2d operator-(Vec2d X);            // unary negation
friend Vec2d operator+(Vec2d X, Vec2d Y); // binary addition
```

6.2 Rational Number System

The rational numbers are the set of quotients P/Q where P and Q are integers and $Q \neq 0$. The number P is called the *numerator* and the number Q is called the *denominator*.

2/3 −6/7 8/2 10/1 0/5 5/0 (invalid)

REPRESENTING RATIONAL NUMBERS

A rational number is a ratio between the numerator and denominator and hence represents one member of a collection of **equivalent numbers.** For instance,

```
2/3 = 10/15 = 50/75   // equivalent rational numbers
```

One member of a collection has a **reduced form** in which the numerator and denominator have no common divisor. The rational number in reduced form is the most representative value from the collection of equivalent numbers. For instance, 2/3 is the reduced form in the collection 2/3, 10/15, 50/75, and so forth. To create the reduced form of a number, we divide the numerator and denominator by their greatest common denominator (GCD). For instance,

```
10/15  = 2/3
   (GCD(10,15) = 5;  10/5 = 2    15/5 = 3)

24/21  = 8/7
   (GCD(24,21) = 3;  24/3 = 8    21/3 = 7)

5/9    = 5/9
   (GCD(5,9) = 1;    rational number already in reduced form)
```

In a rational number, both the numerator and denominator may be negative integers. In our storage of the two terms, we use a **standardized form** with a positive denominator.

```
2/-3 = -2/3    // -2/3 is standardized form
-2/-3 = 2/3    // 2/3 is standardized form
```

RATIONAL NUMBER ARITHMETIC

The reader is familiar with addition, subtraction, and comparison of fractions using common denominators and rules that describe how to multiply and divide these numbers. We give a few examples that suggest formal algorithms to implement the operations in the rational number class.

Addition/Subtraction   Add (subtract) two rational numbers by creating an equivalent fraction with a common denominator. Then, add(subtract) the numerators.

$$(+) \quad \frac{1}{3} + \frac{5}{8} = \frac{8*1}{3*8} + \frac{3*5}{3*8} = \frac{8*1+3*5}{3*8} = \frac{23}{24}$$

$$(-) \quad \frac{1}{3} - \frac{5}{8} = \frac{1*8}{3*8} - \frac{3*5}{3*8} = \frac{1*8-3*5}{3*8} = \frac{-7}{24}$$

Multiplication/Division   Multiply two rational numbers by multiplying the numerators and denominators. Perform division by inverting the second operand (exchanging numerator and denominator) and multiplying the terms.

$$(*) \quad \frac{1}{3} * \frac{5}{8} = \frac{1*5}{3*8} = \frac{5}{24}$$

$$(/) \quad \frac{1}{3} / \frac{5}{8} = \frac{1}{3} * \frac{8}{5} = \frac{8}{15}$$

Comparison   All relational operators use the same principle: Create equivalent fractions and compare the numerators.

$$(<) \quad \frac{1}{3} < \frac{5}{8} \text{ is equivalent to the relation } \frac{1*8}{3*8} < \frac{5*3}{8*3}$$

The relation is TRUE since $1*8 < 3*5$ ($8 < 15$)

EXAMPLE 6.1

This example illustrates rational number operations. Assume $U = 4/5$, $V = -3/8$, and $W = 20/25$.

1. $U + V = \dfrac{4}{5} + \left(-\dfrac{3}{8}\right) = \dfrac{32}{40} + \left(-\dfrac{15}{40}\right) = \dfrac{17}{40}$

    $\dfrac{U}{V} = \dfrac{4}{5} * \left(-\dfrac{3}{8}\right) = \dfrac{-12}{40}$

    $U > V$ since $\dfrac{32}{40} > -\dfrac{15}{40}$ $(32 > -15)$

2. $U == W$ since $\dfrac{4}{5} = \dfrac{100}{125}$, $\dfrac{20}{25} = \dfrac{100}{125}$

RATIONAL NUMBER CONVERSION

The set of rational numbers includes the integers as a subset. The representation of an integer as a rational number uses a denominator of 1. Hence,

(integer) 25 = 25/1 (rational)

A more complex conversion relates real and rational numbers. For instance, the real number 4.25 is 4 + 1/4, which corresponds to the rational number 17/4. The algorithm to convert a real number to a rational is given in Section 6.6. The reverse conversion from a rational number to a real number involves simple division of the numerator by the denominator. For instance,

3/4 = 0.75   // divide 3.0/4.0

The Rational Class   6.3

The ideas in Section 6.2 can be elegantly implemented in a class that uses numerator and denominator data members to describe a rational number and declares the basic arithmetic and relational operators as overload member functions. The stream input and output operators are implemented using friend overloading. Conversion between integer or real numbers and rational numbers and conversion between rational and real numbers makes creative use of constructor functions and C++ conversion operators.

RATIONAL CLASS SPECIFICATION

DECLARATION

```
#include <iostream.h>
#include <stdlib.h>

class Rational
{
   private:
       // defines a rational number as numerator/denominator
       long num, den;

       // private constructor used by arithmetic operators.
       // handles large numerators or denominators
       Rational (long num, long denom);

       // Rational utility functions
       void Standardize(void);
       long gcd(long m, long n) const;

   public:
       // constructors that handle conversion:
       // int->Rational, double->Rational
       Rational (int num=0, long denom=1);
       Rational (double x);

       // rational input/output
       friend istream& operator>> (istream& istr,
                                   Rational &x);
```

```
        friend ostream& operator<< (ostream& ostr,
                                     const Rational& x);

        // binary operators: add, subtract, multiply, divide
        Rational operator+ (Rational v) const;
        Rational operator- (Rational v) const;
        Rational operator* (Rational v) const;
        Rational operator/ (Rational v) const;

        // unary minus (change sign)
        Rational operator- (void) const;

        // relational operators
        int operator< (Rational v) const;
        int operator<= (Rational v) const;
        int operator== (Rational v) const;
        int operator!= (Rational v) const;
        int operator> (Rational v) const;
        int operator>= (Rational v) const;

        // conversion operator: Rational to double
        operator double(void) const;

        // utility methods
        int GetNumerator(void) const;
        int GetDenominator(void) const;
        void Reduce(void);
};
```

- -

DESCRIPTION

The private method Standardize converts a rational number to "standard form" with a positive denominator. The constructors use Standardize to assure the number is created in standard form. We also use the method when reading a number or when dividing two numbers, because these operations could result in a negative denominator. Addition and subtraction do not call Standardize because the two denominators are already non-negative. The private method gcd returns the greatest common divisor of the two integers m and n.

The public function Reduce converts a rational number object to its reduced form by calling gcd.

The two constructors for the class act as conversion operations from an integer (long int) and real number (double) to a Rational number. They are described in the section on type conversion operators.

For applications, we use the utility methods GetNumerator and GetDenominator to access the data members of a rational number.

The input operator "<<" is a friend function that reads a rational number in the form P/Q. For output, the number is given as P/Q. An attempt to input a rational number with zero denominator causes an error and program termination.

EXAMPLE

```
Rational A(-4,5), B, C;        // A is -4/5, B and C are 0/1
cin >> C;                      // with input -12/-18
                               // Standardize stores as 12/18
cout << C.GetNumerator();      // print the numerator 12
C.Reduce();                    // reduce C to the form 2/3
B = C + A;                     // B is 2/3 + (-4/5) = -2/15
cout << -B;                    // call negation; output 2/15
cout << float(A);             // converts to real number;
                               // output -.8

cout << .5 + Rational(3)       // converts .5 to the rational 1/2
                               // output the sum 1/2 + 3/1 = 7/2
```

Rational Operators as Member Functions 6.4

The Rational class declares arithmetic and relational operators as overloaded member functions. Each binary operator has a parameter that is the right-hand operand.

Assume *U, V,* and *W* are objects of type Rational in an addition expression:

Rational   *u, v, w*
w = u + v

The overloaded addition operator + is a member of object *u* (left-hand operand) and takes *v* as a parameter. The return value is an object of type Rational that is assigned to *w*. Technically,

w = u + v is evaluated as *w = u.+ (v)*

For the expression

v = −u

C++ executes the member negation operator "−" in object *u* (single operand). The return value is a Rational object that is assigned to *v*. Technically,

v = −u is evaluated as *v = u.−()*

IMPLEMENTING THE RATIONAL OPERATORS

The program supplement contains a complete listing of the Rational class. We implement addition and division, relational equals, and negation to illustrate member overloading. Assume the declarations

Rational u(a,b), v (c,d);

To add ("+") rational numbers, find a common denominator for the operands. The actual addition occurs by combining the numerators.

$$(+) \quad u + v = \frac{a}{b} + \frac{c}{d} = \frac{a*d}{b*d} + \frac{b*c}{b*d} = \frac{a*d+b*c}{b*d}$$

For the implementation, a and b are the data members num and den for the left-hand operand, which is the object associated with the "+" operator. The numbers c and d are the data members v.num and v.den of the right operand:

```
// Rational addition
Rational Rational::operator+ (Rational v) const
{
    return Rational(num*v.den + den*v.num, den*v.den);
}
```

Division ("/") occurs by inverting the right-hand operand and then multiplying the terms. The numbers a and b correspond to the data members of the left-hand operand. The numbers c and d refer to data members in object v, the right-hand operand. Since the result may have a negative denominator, the quotient is standardized.

$$(/) \quad \frac{u}{v} = \frac{a}{b} / \frac{c}{d} = \frac{a}{b} * \frac{d}{c} = \frac{a*d}{b*c}$$

```
// Rational division
Rational Rational::operator/ (Rational v) const
{
    Rational temp = Rational(num*v.den, den*v.num);
    // make sure denominator is positive
    temp.Standardize();
    return temp;
}
```

To evaluate a relational operator, compare the numerators when the rational numbers are placed over a common denominator. For relational equals "==", the return value is True when the numerators are equal. The following are logically equivalent ($\Leftrightarrow$) statements.

$$u == v \Leftrightarrow \frac{a}{b} == \frac{c}{d}$$
$$\Leftrightarrow \frac{a*d}{b*d} == \frac{b*c}{b*d}$$
$$\Leftrightarrow a*d == b*c$$

Test the condition $a * d == b * c$:

```
// relational "equal"
int Rational::operator == (Rational v) const
{
    return num*v.den == den*v.num;
}
```

The unary negation operator "−" works with the data members of the single operand that defines the operation. The calculation simply negates the numerator:

```
// Rational negation
Rational Rational::operator- (void) const
{
    return Rational(-num, den);
}
```

The Rational Stream Operators as Friends   6.5

The file <iostream.h> contains declarations for two classes named ostream and istream, which provide stream output and stream input, respectively. The I/O stream system provides definitions for the I/O stream operators ">>" and "<<" in the case of the primitive types char, int, short, long, float, double, and char*. For instance,

Input

```
istream & operator>> (short v);
istream & operator>> (double v);
```

Output

```
ostream & operator<< (short v);
ostream & operator<< (double v);
```

The user can overload the stream operators to implement I/O of a user-defined type. For instance, with the Date class, the operators "<<" and ">>" can provide stream I/O in the same manner used for the primitive types. For instance,

```
Date D;

cin >> D;        // <input> 10/5/75
cout << D;       // <output> October 5, 1975
```

If the operators for the Date class were to be overloaded as member functions, they would have to be explicitly declared in <iostream.h>. The class ostream would have to have an overloaded version of "<<" that accepts a Date parameter. This is clearly impractical and so we use friend overloading, which defines the operator outside the class but allows it access to private data members in the class.

The overloading of a stream operator uses a structured format, which we illustrate for a general class type CL.

```
class CL
{
    . . .
   public:
    . . .
       friend istream& operator>> (istream& istr, CL& Variable);
       friend ostream& operator<< (ostream& ostr, const CL& Value);
}
```

The parameter istr represents an input stream such as cin and ostr represents an output stream such as cout. Since the I/O process alters the state of a stream, the parameter must be passed by reference.

For input, the data item Variable is assigned a value from the stream, so it is passed by reference. The function returns a reference to an istream so that the operator can be used in a chain such as

```
cin >> m >> n;
```

In the case of output, Value is copied to the output stream. Since the data are not changed, Value is passed as a constant reference. This avoids the copying of a possibly large object by value. The function returns a reference to an ostream(output) so that the operator can be used in a chain such as

```
cout << m << n;
```

IMPLEMENTING RATIONAL STREAM OPERATORS

Input and output of Rational numbers is implemented by overloading the stream operators. With input, we read a number in the form P/Q where $Q \neq 0$. The program terminates if a 0 denominator is input.

```
// overload stream input operator. input in form P/Q
istream& operator >> (istream& istr, Rational& x)
{
    char c;                  // reads the separator '/'
```

```
    // as a friend, ">>" can access numerator/denominator of x
     istr >> x.num >> c >> x.den;
    // terminate if denominator is 0
     if (x.den == 0)
     {
         cerr << "A Zero denominator is invalid\n";
         exit(1);
     }
    // put x in standard form
     x.Standardize();
     return istr;
}
```

The overloaded stream output operator writes a rational number in the form P/Q.

```
    // overload stream output operator. output in form P/Q
    ostream& operator << (ostream& ostr, const Rational& x)
    {
        // as a friend, ">>" can access numerator/denominator of x
        ostr << x.num << '/' << x.den;
        return ostr;
    }
```

Converting Rational Numbers   6.6

The Rational class illustrates type conversion operators. A programmer can implement customized conversion operators analogous to the ones provided for standard types. Specifically, we focus on conversion between objects of a class type and a related C++ data type.

CONVERSION TO OBJECT TYPE

A class constructor can be used to build an object. As such, a constructor takes its input parameters and converts them to an object.

The Rational class has two constructors that serve as type conversion operators. The first constructor converts an integer to a rational number and the second constructor converts a floating-point number to a rational number.

When the constructor is called with a single integer parameter num, it converts the integer to the equivalent rational num/1. For instance, consider these declarations and statements:

```
Rational P(7), Q(3,5),R, S;  // explicit conversion of 7 to 7/1

  R = Rational(2);            // explicit conversion of 2 to 2/1
  S = 5;                      // build Rational(5)
                             // assign new object to S
```

The declarations of Q and R create the objects Q = 3/5 and R = 0/1. The assignment R = Rational(2) explicitly changes the value of R to 2/1. The assignment S = 5 causes type conversion. The compiler treats S = 5 as the statement S = Rational(5).

```cpp
// constructor. form the rational number num/den. If used with
// default value of den=1, converts an integer to a Rational
Rational::Rational(long p, long q): num(p), den(q)
{
    if (den == 0)
    {
        cerr << "A Zero denominator is invalid" << endl;
        exit(1);
    }
}
```

A second constructor converts a real number to a rational. For instance, the following statements create the rational numbers A = 3/2 and B = 16/5:

```cpp
Rational A = Rational(1.5), B;  // explicit conversion
B = 3.2;                        // convert 3.2 to Rational(16,5)
```

The conversion requires an algorithm that approximates an arbitrary floating-point number with the equivalent Rational. The algorithm involves shifting the decimal point in the floating-point number. Depending on the number of significant digits in the real number, the result may be only an approximation. After creating the rational number, we call the function Reduce, which stores the rational in a more readable reduced form.

```cpp
// constructor. approximate double x as a Rational number
Rational::Rational(double x)
{
    double val1, val2;

    // move decimal pt of x 8 pos to the right
    val1 = 100000000L*x;
    // move decimal pt of x 7 pos to the right
    val2 = 10000000L*x;
    // val1-val2 = 90,000,000 * x; by truncating
    // to a long, throw away the fractional part.
    // approx x by numerator/90,000,000
    num = long(val1-val2);
    den = 90000000L;
    // reduce to lowest terms
    Reduce ();
}
```

CONVERSION FROM OBJECT TYPE

The C++ language defines explicit conversions between primitive types. For instance, to print the ASCII code for a character c, we can write

```
cout << int(c) << endl;    // convert char to int
```

Implicit conversions are also defined between types. For instance, if I is a long integer and Y is a double, the statement

```
Y = I;                     // y = double (I)
```

converts I to a double and assigns the result to Y. A class may contain one or more member functions that convert an object to a value of another data type. In class CL, assume we wish to convert an object to the type named NewType. The operator NewType() takes an object and returns a value of type NewType. The target type, NewType, is often a standard type such as int or float. Since it is a unary operator, the conversion operator does not contain a parameter. Likewise, the conversion operator does not have a return type because it is implicit in the name NewType. The declaration takes the form:

```
class CL
{
    . . . .
    operator NewType(void);
};
```

The conversion operator is used as follows:

```
NewType a;
CL obj;

a = NewType(obj);      // explicit conversion
a = obj;               // implicit conversion
```

The Rational class contains an operator that converts an object to a double. The operator allows assignment of Rational data to floating-point variables. The converter takes the rational number p/q, divides the numerator by the denominator, and returns the result as a floating-point number. For instance

3/4 is 0.75   4/2 is 2.0

```
// convert Rational to double
Rational::operator double(void) const
{
    return double(num)/den;
}
```

EXAMPLE 6.2

Assume the declarations

```
Rational R(1,2), S(3,5)
double Y,Z;
```

1. The statement Y = doubie(R) makes explicit use of the converter. The result is Y = 0.5
2. The statement Z = S makes implicit conversion to a rational number. The result is Z = 0.6.

6.7 Using Rational Numbers

Before developing applications for rational numbers, we describe the algorithm to generate the reduced form of the fraction. The algorithm involves finding the greatest common divisor (gcd) of the numerator and denominator.

To create the reduced form of a rational number, Reduce uses the private member function gcd, which takes two positive integer parameters and returns the largest of their common divisors. The function gcd is implemented on the program supplement. For a nonzero rational number, Reduce divides the numerator and denominator by their gcd:

```cpp
// put the Rational object in lowest terms
void Rational::Reduce(void)
{
    int bigdivisor, tempnumerator;

    // tempnumerator is the absolute value of the numerator
    tempnumerator = (num < 0) ? -num : num;

    if (num == 0)
        den = 1;      // standardize to 0/1
    else
    {
        // find gcd of positive numbers
        // tempnumerator, denominator
        bigdivisor = gcd(tempnumerator, den);

        // if bigdivisor ==1, Rational in lowest terms.
        // otherwise, divide numerator and denominator by
        // their largest common divisor
```

```
        if (bigdivisor > 1) // don't divide if gcd is 1
        {
                num /= bigdivisor;
                den /= bigdivisor;
        }
    }
}
```

Program 6.1   Using the Rational Class

The program illustrates the main features of the Rational class. We illustrate various conversion techniques including integer to rational and rational to real number conversion. We also illustrate the addition, subtraction, multiplication, and division of rational numbers. The program ends by implicitly converting from a floating point number to a rational and back to a floating point number. The implementation of the Rational class is contained in the file "rational.h".

```
#include <iostream.h>

#include "rational.h"        // include the rational number class

// each operation is accompanied by output
void main(void)
{
    Rational r1(5), r2, r3;
    float    f;

    cout << "1. Rational value for integer 5 is " << r1 << endl;

    cout << "2. Enter a rational number: ";
    cin >> r1;
    f = float(r1);
    cout << "        Floating point equivalent is " << f << endl;

    cout << "3. Enter two rational numbers: ";
    cin >> r1 >> r2;
    cout << "        Results: " << r1+r2 << " (+)    "
        << r1-r2 << " (-)    " << r1*r2 << " (*)    "
        << r1/r2 << " (/)    " << endl;

    if (r1 < r2)
        cout << "        Relation (less than): " << r1 << " < "
            << r2 << endl;
    else if (r1 == r2)
        cout << "        Relation (equal to): " << r1 << " == "
            << r2 << endl;
```

```
        else
            cout << "        Relation (greater than): " << r1 << " > "
                << r2 << endl;

        cout << "4. Input a floating point number: ";
        cin >> f;
        r1 = f;
        cout << "      Convert to Rational " << r1 << endl;
        f = r1;
        cout << "      Reconvert to float " << f << endl;
    }


/*
<Run of Program 6.1>

1. Rational value for integer 5 is 5/1
2. Enter a rational number: -4/5
      Floating point equivalent is -0.8
3. Enter two rational numbers: 1/2 -2/3
      Results: -1/6 (+)    7/6 (-)    -2/6 (*)    -3/4 (/)
      Relation (greater than): 1/2 > -2/3
4. Input a floating point number: 4.25
      Convert to Rational 17/4
      Reconvert to float 4.25
*/
```

Application: Rational Number Utilities   The reader has had experience with fractions from early schooling. Remember the teacher's refrain to "give your answer as a mixed number." To illustrate an application of the Rational class, we describe a series of functions that do fraction calculations.

The function PrintMixedNumber writes a fraction as a mixed number:

Fraction	Mixed Number
10/4	2 1/2
−10/4	−2 1/2
200/4	50

In algebra, a fundamental task is to solve the general fraction equation

$$2/3X + 2 = 4/5$$

The process involves isolating the X term by moving 2 to the right-hand side of the equation:

$$2/3X = -6/5$$

The solution is obtained by dividing both sides of the equation by the rational number 2/3, the coefficient of X. We implement this process in the function SolveEquation.

```
X = -6/5 * 3/2 = -18/10 = -9/5 (reduced)
```

Program 6.2   Rational Number Utilities

The program uses the series of rational number utilities to carry out calculations.

```
PrintMixedNumber    // print a number as a mixed number
SolveEquation       // solve the general equation
```
$$// \frac{a}{b}X + \frac{c}{d} = \frac{e}{f}$$

The action of each operation is explicitly described in the output statement.

```cpp
#include <iostream.h>
#include <stdlib.h>

#include "rational.h"            // include the Rational class

// print a Rational number as a mixed number (+/-)N p/q
void PrintMixedNumber (Rational x)
{
    // whole part of the Rational number x
    int wholepart = int(x.GetNumerator() / x.GetDenominator());

    // stores the fractional part of the mixed number
    Rational fractionpart = x - Rational(wholepart);

    // if no fractional part, print integer
    if (fractionpart == Rational(0))
        cout << wholepart << "   ";
    else
    {
        // reduce fractional part
        fractionpart.Reduce();
        // print sign with the whole part
        if (wholepart < 0)
            fractionpart = -fractionpart;
        if (wholepart != 0)
            cout << wholepart << " " << fractionpart << "   ";
        else
            cout << fractionpart << "   ";
    }
}
```

```
// solve ax + b = c, where a, b, c are rational numbers
Rational SolveEquation(Rational a, Rational b, Rational c)
{
    // check to see if a is 0
    if (a == Rational (0))
    {
        cout << "Equation has no solution." << endl;
        // return Rational(0) if there is no solution.
        return Rational (0);
    }
    else
        return (c-b)/a;
}

void main(void)
{
    Rational r1, r2, r3, ans;

    cout << "Enter coefficients for"
        << "'a/b X + c/d = e/f': ";
    cin >> r1 >> r2 >> r3;

    cout << "Simplified equation: " << r1 << " X = "
        << (r3-r2) << endl;
    ans = SolveEquation(r1,r2,r3);
    ans.Reduce();
    cout << "X = " << ans << endl;

    cout << "Solution as a mixed number: ";
    PrintMixedNumber(ans);
    cout << endl;
}

/*
<Run #1 of Program 6.2>

Enter coefficients for 'a/b X + c/d = e/f': 2/3 2/1 4/5
Simplified equation is: 2/3 X = -6/5
X = -9/5
Solution as a mixed number: -1 4/5

<Run #2 of Program 6.2>

Enter coefficients for 'a/b X + c/d = e/f': 2/3 -7/8 -3/8
Simplified equation is: 2/3 X = 32/64
X = 3/4
Solution as a mixed number: 3/4
*/
```

Written Exercises

6.1 C++ allows two or more functions in a program to have the same name provided their argument lists are sufficiently different so that the compiler can resolve function calls. The compiler evaluates the parameters in the calling block and selects the correct function. This process is called **function overloading.** For instance, the C++ mathematics library <math.h> defines two versions of the function *sqr* that returns the square of its argument.

```
integer version: int sqr (long);        // select the integer version
float version:    double sqr(double);  // select the real
                                          number version
```

A series of rules defines valid operator overloading. They are as follows:

Rule #1: Functions require distinct parameter lists independent of return type and default values.

Rule #2: Enumerated types are distinct types for the purpose of overloading. The keyword typedef does not affect overloading.

Rule #3: If a parameter does not exactly match a formal parameter in a set of overloaded functions, a matching algorithm is applied to determine the "best matching" function. Conversion is performed if necessary. For instance, when passing a short variable to an overloaded function that has integer parameters, the compiler can create a match by converting the variable to an int. The compiler refuses to convert a parameter if the choice leads to an ambiguity.

For each of the following examples, indicate the rule that could apply. If the rule is violated, describe the error.

(a) Assume the following code segments are used to overload function f.

```
      <function 1>                    <function 2>
   int f(int x, int y)           double f(int x, int y)
   {                             {
      return x*y;                   return x * y;
   }                             }

          <function 3>
   int f(int x = 1, int y = 7)
   {
      return x + y + x*y;
   }
```

(b) The function max is overloaded with four distinct definitions.

```
      <function 1>                      <function 2>
   int max(int x, int y)         double max(double x, double y)
   {                             {
      return x > y ? x : y;         return x > y ? x : y;
   }                             }
```

```
        <function 3>                    <function 4>
int max(int x, int y, int z)   int max (void)
{                              {
    int lmax = x;                  int a, b;

    if (y > lmax)                  cin >> a >> b;
        lmax = y;                  return abs(a) > abs(b) ?
    if (z > lmax)                  a : b;
        lmax = z;              }
    return lmax;
}
```

(c) The three versions of the function read are designed to distinguish the input of integer and enumerated type data.

```
        <function 1>                    <function 2>
                                enum Boolean {FALSE,TRUE};
void read(int& x)               void read(Boolean& x)
{                              {
    cin >> x;                      char c;
}                                  cin >> c;
                                   x = (c == 'T') ? TRUE : FALSE;
                               }
```

```
        <function 3>
typedef int Logical;
const int TRUE = 1, FALSE = 0;

void read(Logical& x)
{
    char c;

    cin >> c;
    x = (c == 'T') ? TRUE : FALSE;
}
```

6.2 Use the max functions from Written Exercise 6.1(b) and assume the user inputs values $m = -29$ and $n = 8$. Indicate which function is called and what value is returned.

(a) `cin >> m >> n;` (b) `max();` (c) `max(m,-40,30);`
     `max(m,n);`

6.3 With the max functions from Written Exercise 6.1(b), what is the output from each of the statements?

```
int a = 5, b = 99, c = 153
int m, n;
double h1 = .01, h2 = .05;
long  t = 3000, u = 70000, v = -100000;
```

```
cout << "Maximum of a and b is " << max(a,b);
cout << "Maximum of a, b and c is " << max(a,b,c);
cout << "1.0 + max(h1,h2) = " << 1.0 + max(h1,h2);
cout << "Maximum of t, u and v is " << max(t,u,v);
```

6.4 Are the following functions distinct for the purpose of overloading? Why?

(a) `enum E1{one,two};`   (b) `type def double scientific;`
     `enum E2{three,four};`

```
int f(int x, E1 y);          double f(double x);
int f(int x, E2 y);          scientific f(scientific x);
```

6.5 Write overloaded versions of the function Swap that can take two int, float, and string (char *) parameters.

```
void Swap(int& a, int& b);
void Swap(float& x, float& y);
void Swap(char *s, char *t);
```

6.6 Explain the distinction between operator overloading using a member function and using a friend.

6.7 The class ModClass has a single integer data member dataval in the range 0 . . 6. The constructor takes any positive integer v and assigns to dataval the remainder upon division by 7.

dataval = v % 7

The addition operator adds two objects by summing their data members and finding the remainder after division by 7. For instance,

```
ModClass  a(10);    // dataval in a is 3;
ModClass  b(6);     // dataval in b is 6;
ModClass  c;        // c = a + b has value (3+6) % 7 = 2

class ModClass
{
   private:
      int dataval;
   public:
      ModClass(int v = 0);
      ModClass operator+ (const ModClass& x);
      int GetValue(void) const;
};
```

(a) Implement the class methods.
(b) Declare and implement the operator "*" as a friend of ModClass. The operator multiplies the value fields in two ModClass objects and finds the remainder after division by 7.

(c) Write a function

```
ModClass Inverse(ModValue& x);
```

that takes an object x with a non-zero value and returns a value y such that $x*y = 1$ (y is called the inverse of x). (HINT: Repeatedly multiply x by objects with values 1 to 6. One of these objects is the inverse.)

(d) Overload stream output for ModClass and add the method to the class.

(e) Replace GetValue by overloading the conversion operator int (). The operator converts a ModClass object to an integer by returning the dataval.

```
operator int (void);
```

(f) Write a function

```
void Solve(ModClass a, ModClass& x, ModClass b);
```

that solves the equation $ax = b$ for x by calling the method Inverse.

6.8 Add the full set of relational operators to the Date class of Chapter 3. Two dates are to be compared by chronology of the year. For example,

```
Date(5,5,77) > Date(10,24,73)
Date("12/25/44") <= Date(9,30,82)
Date(3,5,99) != Date(3,7,99)
```

6.9 A complex number is of the form $x + iy$, where $i^2 = -1$. Complex numbers have vast applications in mathematics, physics, and engineering. They have an arithmetic governed by a series of rules including the following:

Let $u = a + ib$, $v = c + id$
Magnitude $(u) = $ sqrt $(a^2 + b^2)$
Complex number corresponding to real number f is $f + i0$
Real Part of $u = a$
Imaginary Part of $u = b$
$u + v = (a + c) + i(b + d)$
$u - v = (a - c) + i(b - d)$
$u * v = (ac - bd) + i(ad + bc)$
$$u / v = \frac{ac + bd}{c^2 + d^2} + i\left(\frac{bc - ad}{c^2 + d^2}\right)$$
$-u = -a + i(-b)$

Implement the class Complex whose declaration is

```
class Complex
    {
        private:
            double real;
            double imag;
```

```
    public:
        Complex(double x = 0.0, double y = 0.0);

        // binary operators
        Complex operator+ (Complex x) const;
        Complex operator- (Complex x) const;
        Complex operator* (Complex x) const;
        Complex operator/ (Complex x) const;

        // Negation
        Complex operator- (void) const;

        // Stream I/O operator
        // output in format (real,imag)
        friend ostream& operator<< (ostream& ostr,const
                                            Complex& x);
    };
```

6.10 Add the methods GetReal and GetImag to the Complex class of Written Exercise 6.9.
They return the real and imaginary parts of a complex number. Use these methods
to write a function Distance that computes the distance between two complex numbers.

```
    double Distance (const Complex &a, const Complex &b);
```

6.11 (a)   Add a converter to the Rational class that returns a ModClass object.
(b)   Add a converter to the ModClass that returns a Rational object.

6.12 (a)   Implement the Vec2d class of Section 6.1.
(b)   Add a member function to the Vec2d class that provides scalar multiplication,
where the scalar operand is on the right. Implement the operator both as a
member function and as a friend.
Example:

Vec2d *v*(3,5);
cout << *v**2 << " " << 2*v << endl;
(6,10) (6,10)

6.13 A set is a collection of objects that is chosen from a group of objects called the
universal set. A set is written as a list separated by commas and enclosed in braces.

$$X = \{I_1, I_2, I_3, \ldots, I_m\}$$

In this problem, the set members are chosen from the integers in the range 0 to 499.
The class supports a series of binary operations for sets X and Y.

- Set Union ($\cup$) X $\cup$ Y is the set containing all elements in X and all elements in Y,
  without duplication.

- Set Intersection (∩) X ∩ Y is the set containing all elements that are in both X and Y.

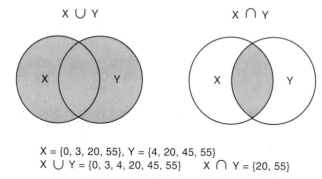

X ∪ Y   X ∩ Y

X = {0, 3, 20, 55}, Y = {4, 20, 45, 55}
X ∪ Y = {0, 3, 4, 20, 45, 55}   X ∩ Y = {20, 55}

- Set Membership (∈) n ∈ X is True if element n is a member of set X; otherwise, it is False.

  X = {0, 3, 20, 55} // 20 ∈ X is True, 35 ∈ X is False

SET CLASS SPECIFICATION

In this declaration, a set is a list of elements selected from the range of integers 0 ... SETSIZE−1, where SETSIZE is 500. The I/O, union, intersection, and element membership operations define set handling.

DECLARATION

```
const int SETSIZE = 500;
const int False = 0, True = 1;

class Set
{
   private:
      // members of the set
      int member[SETSIZE];

   public:
      // constructor. creates empty set
      Set(void);
      // constructor. creates set with initial
      // elements a[0], . . . , a[n-1]
      Set(int a[], int n);

      // operators union (+), intersection (*), membership (^)
      Set operator+ (Set x) const;            // set union
```

```
    Set operator* (Set x) const;              // set intersection
    friend int operator^ (int elt, Set x); // is elt in set x?


    // insert and delete methods
    void Insert (int n);    // add element n to the set
    void Delete (int n);    // delete element n from the set

    // Set stream output operator
    friend ostream& operator<< (ostream& istr, const Set& x);
};
```

DESCRIPTION

The first constructor simply creates an empty set. Elements are added to the set using Insert. The second constructor assigns the n integer values in the array a to the set. Each integer is checked to ensure it is in range.

An element n is in the set providing the corresponding array element is True.

```
n ∈ X if and only if member[n] is TRUE
```

For instance, the set X = {1, 4, 5, 7} corresponds to the array with entries member[1], member[4], member[5], member[7] are True and the other entries are False.

false	true	false	false	true	true	false	true	false	false	· · ·	false
0	1	2	3	4	5	6	7	8	9		499

The stream output operator should print sets with the elements separated by commas and contained in braces. For instance,

```
int setvals[] = {4,7,12};
Set S, T(setvals,3);

S.Insert(5);
cout << S << endl;
cout << T << endl;

<output>
{5}
{4,7,12}
```

(a) Implement the Set constructors.
(b) Implement the set member function in ('^'). It returns True if member[n] is True; otherwise, it returns False. Since the priority of the '^' operator is relatively low, an expression involving '^' should be parenthesized for safety. For instance,

```
Set A;
. . .
if ((0 ^ A) == 0)        // test for 0 in set A
```

(c)   S is the set {1,4,17,25} and T is the set {1,8,25,33,53,63}. Perform the following
operations:

    (i) S + T   (ii) S * T   (iii) 5 ^ S
    (iv) 4 ^ (S+T)   (v) 25 ^ (S*T)

(d)   Indicate the action of the following sequence of statements:

```
int a[] = {1,2,3,5};
int b[] = {2,3,7,9,25};
int n;
Set A(a,4), B(b,5), C;


C = A+B;  cout << C;
C = A*B;  cout << C;


cin >> n;   // input 55
A.Insert(n);
if (n^A)
cout << "Success" << endl;
```

(e)   Implement the remaining Set methods.

Programming Exercises

6.1   This program uses the result of Written Exercise 6.5. Write a program that takes
two integers and two floating-point numbers, prints their values, and then calls the
corresponding Swap function to reverse the values. The same program should input
two character strings, exchange their values using Swap, and print the resulting strings.

6.2   This program tests the class ModClass developed in Written Exercise 6.7. Write a
program to verify the distributive law for ModClass objects.

```
a*(b+c) = a*b + a*c
```

Define three objects a, b, and c that have constructor parameters 10, 20, and 30,
respectively. Your program should output the value of the expressions on each side
of the equation.

6.3 Use ModClass and the function Solve that are developed in Written Exercise 6.7. Form the array

```
ModClass a[] = {ModClass(4), ModClass(10), ModClass(50)};
```

The program must execute the loop

```
for(int i=0;i < 3;i++)
    cout << a[i] << " " << int(a[i]) << endl;
```

Use the function Solve to print the solution to the equation

```
ModClass(4) * x = ModClass(3)
```

6.4 This program uses the Date class operators from Written Exercise 6.8. Write a function

```
Date Min(const Date& x, const Date& y);
```

that returns the earlier of two dates. Define four objects D1 to D4 that correspond to

```
D1 is 6/6/44          D2 is New Year's day of the year 1999
D3 is Christmas, 1976 D4 is July 4, 1976
```

Test the function by comparing objects D1 and D2, D3 and D4.

6.5 Consider the following properties of two dimensional vectors:

(a) u*(v+w) = u*v + u*w (distributive property)
(b) Two vectors are perpendicular; their dot product is 0.
(c) c*v = v*c, where c is a real number.
Using the class Vec2d developed in Written Exercise 6.12, provide explicit examples that illustrate (a) and (c). The program should also read two real numbers x and y and verify that the vectors (x, y) and $(-y, x)$ are perpendicular.

6.6 This exercise uses the Complex number class that is developed in Written Exercise 6.9. The program must perform the following actions:

(a) Verify that $-i^2 = 1$.
(b) Write a function $f(z)$ that evaluates the complex polynomial function:

$$z^3 - 3z^2 + 4z - 2$$

Evaluate the polynomial for the following values of z:

$$z = 2+3i, \ -1+i, \ 1+i, \ 1-i, \ 1+0i$$

Note the last three values are roots of f.

6.7 Use the Rational number class and its conversion operators to make the following comparison of real and rational numbers. Declare the real number pi = 3.14159265 and the rational number approximation Rational(22,7) that is often used by young students. Write a program that makes the following two calculations and prints the results.

(a) Compute the difference between the two numbers as rational numbers. Rational(pi) − Rational(22,7)

(b) Compute the difference between the two numbers as real numbers. pi − float(Rational(22,7))

6.8 Chapter 8 develops an extensive string handling class using pointers and dynamic memory. This exercise develops a simple string class that stores data using an array. Consider the declaration

```
class String
{
    private:
        char str[256];
    public:
        String(char s[] = "");

        int Length(void) const;          // string length
        void CString(char s[]) const;    // copy string to C++
                                         // array s

        // *****Stream I/O *****
        friend ostream& operator<< (ostream& ostr,
                                        const String& s);

        // Read whitespace separated strings
        friend istream& operator>> (istream& istr,
                                        String& s);

        // ***** relational operator String == String  *****
        int operator== (String& s) const;

        // ***** string concatenation *****
        String operator+ (String& s) const;

};
```

Implement the class and test it by running the following program.

```
void main(void)
{
    String S1("It is a "), S2("beautiful day!"), S3;
    char s[30];
```

```
    if (S1 == String("It is a"))
       cout << "Equality test O.K." << endl;
    else
       cout << "Equality test failed." << endl;


    cout << "The length of S1 = " << S1.Length() << endl;

    cout << "Enter a string S3: ";
    cin >> S3;

    S3 = S1 + S2;
    cout << "The concatenation of S1 and S2 is "
         << S3 << endl;

    S3.CString(s);
    cout << "The C++ string stored in S3 is '"
         << s << "'" << endl;
}
```

6.9 This exercise tests your Set class of Written Exercise 6.13. Consider the sets

$$S = \{1,5,7,12,24,36,45,103,355,499\}$$
$$T = \{2,3,5,7,8,9,12,15,36,45,56,103,255,355,498\}$$
$$U = \{1,2,3,4,5, \ldots ,50\}$$

Create sets S, T, and U. Use Insert to initialize set U. Perform the following computations.

(1) Compute and print S+T.
(2) Compute and print S*T.
(3) Compute and print S*U.
(4) Delete 8, 36,103, and 498 from T and print the set.
(5) Generate a random number from 1 to 9, print it, and then verify whether it is in set T.

6.10 This exercise uses the Set class is used to simulate the probability of drawing five distinct random numbers in the range 0 to 4 in five consecutive draws. The mathematical probability is

$$1 \cdot 4/5 \cdot 3/5 \cdot 2/5 \cdot 1/5 = .0384$$

Write the function

```
int fillSet(void);
```

that performs the experiment of drawing the five numbers and inserting them into a set S. Make a test to see if 0 . . . 4 are in the set by looping five times and using the '^' operator. If all the integers are in the set, return a 1; otherwise, return 0.

Write a main program that calls fillSet 100000 times and records the number of instances when all five numbers are selected. Divide by 100000 to determine the simulated probability.

C H A P T E R   7

GENERIC DATA TYPES

The definitions of the SeqList, Stack, and Queue classes are designed for a generic type called DataType. Before using a class, the client equates a specific type with DataType by using the typedef directive. Unfortunately, this limits the client to a single type with any of the classes. An application could not use a stack of integers and a stack of records in the same program. The use of the generic DataType is too limiting. A better approach would link the data type with the object and not with the program. For instance,

```
SeqList<int>     A;      // List of integers
Stack<float>     B;      // Stack of real numbers
Queue<CL>        C;      // Queue of CL objects
```

C++ provides this capability with the **template** directive, which allows general type parameters for functions and classes. The use of templates with a collection class allows us to declare objects that store different data types. The use of templates with a function allows us to define generic parameters and make two or more function calls with runtime parameters of different types. Templates provide powerful generality to our data structures. We develop the topic in this chapter by first introducing template functions and then extending the concepts to template classes. For applications, we develop the sequential search as a template function and use templates to rewrite the Stack class. Multiple stacks are the primary data structure in the case study that describes infix expression evaluation.

7.1 Template Functions

Often an algorithm is designed to handle a range of data types. For instance, the sequential search algorithm takes a key and searches a list of items looking for a match. The algorithm assumes that the relational operator "==" is defined for data type. The same algorithm can be used to search a list of integers, characters, or objects. Up to this point in the book, we have found several applications for the sequential search. In each case, we have designed a specific version of the SeqSearch function for the type of items in the list. We have created multiple versions of the function to implement the same generic algorithm. We would like to write generic code that can be applied to different lists. With templates, C++ provides that ability. The following discussion introduces the main elements of syntax.

Template function declarations begin with a **template parameter list** of the form

```
template <class T₁, class T₂, . . . , class Tₙ>
```

The keyword **template** is followed by a nonempty parameter list of types that is enclosed in angle brackets. The types are preceded by the keyword *class*. An identifier T_i is a general name for a specific C++ data type that is passed as a parameter when the template function is used. The keyword "class" is present only to indicate that the name T_i represents a type. You can read class as "type". When the template is used, T_i can be a standard type, such as an int, or a user-defined type, such as a class. For instance, in the following template parameter lists, the names T and U refer to data types.

```
template <class T>             // T is a type
template <class T, class U>    // T and U are both types
```

After defining the template parameter list, the function follows the usual format and has access to all types in the list. For instance, the definition of SeqSearch as a template function is

```
// using key, search the n element arrray list for a match.
// if found return index at the match; otherwise return -1
template <class T>
int SeqSearch(T list[], int n, T key)
{
    for(int i=0;i < n;i++)
        if (list[i] == key)
            return i;    // return index of matching item
    return -1;           // search failed. return -1
}
```

When a program calls a template function, the compiler identifies the data types of the actual parameters and associates these types with items in the template parameter list. For instance, in calling the SeqSearch function, the compiler distinguishes between integer and real parameters.

```
int   A[10], Aindex;
float M[100], fkey = 4.5, Mindex;

Aindex = SeqSearch(A, 10, 25);      // search for int 25 in A
Mindex = SeqSearch(M, 100, fkey);   // search for fkey 4.5 in M
```

The compiler creates a separate instance of the SeqSearch function for each different runtime parameter list. In the first case, the template type T is int and SeqSearch scans a list of integers using the integer comparison operator "==". In the second case, the type parameter T is float, and the floating-point comparison operator "==" is used.

When a template-based function is called with a specific type, all operations must be defined for the type. If the function employs an operation that is not native to the type, the programmer must provide a user-defined version of the operation or must use a non-template version of the function. For instance, C++ does not define the comparison operator "==" for a struct or class. A generic version of the SeqSearch function cannot order class objects unless the operator is defined (overloaded) by the user.

As an example, consider the record type Student that includes both integer and floating point fields. The "==" operator is overloaded so that the SeqSearch function applies.

```
// student record containing an id and grade point average
struct Student
{
    int     studID;
    float   gpa;
};

// overload "==" by comparing student id
int operator == (Student a, Student b)
{
    return a.studID == b.studID;
}
```

The Student record declaration and the "==" operator are found in the file "student.h".

The C++ string type, char*, poses particular problems for the user. The "==" operator compares pointer values. It does not compare the actual strings character by character. Since char* is not a struct or class, we cannot define an overloaded "==" operator for the type. The user must use a non-template version of SeqSearch that applies to the C++ string type.

```
// search array of strings for match with string key
int SeqSearch(char *list[], int n, char *key)
{
    for(int i=0;i < n;i++)
        // compare using C++ string library function
        if (strcmp(list[i],key) == 0)
            return i;     // return index at match
    return -1;            // return -1 on failure
}
```

The main topics of this section are illustrated in a program on generic searching. The code for the template function SeqSearch and a specific version for C++ strings is contained in the file "utils.h".

Program 7.1   A Generic Search

The program illustrates the sequential search for three distinct data types.

- The array "list" is initialized with 10 integer values. We identify the index of data value 8 in the array.

- Operator overloading is used with the Student record type. The record {1550,0} is used as a key to search the list and identify the student ID. The return index provides access to the GPA 2.6.

- For the array of strings, the compiler uses the non-template SeqSearch function with data type "char *". The search looks for the string "two", which is found at index 2.

```cpp
#include <iostream.h>

// includes template based sequential search and a sequential
// search function specific to C++ strings
#include "utils.h"

// declaration of Student and "==" for Student
#include "student.h"

void main()
{
    // three different array types
    int     list[10] = {5, 9, 1, 3, 4, 8, 2, 0, 7, 6};
    Student studlist[3] = {{1000, 3.4}, {1555, 2.6},
                           {1625, 3.8}};
    char    *strlist[5] = {"zero", "one", "two", "three",
                           "four"};

    int     i, index;
    // this record is used as key to search array studlist
    Student studentKey = {1555, 0};

    if ((i = SeqSearch(list,10,8)) >= 0)
        cout << "Item 8 is found at index " << i << endl;
    else
        cout << "Item 8 is not found" << endl;
    index = SeqSearch(studlist, 3, studentKey);
    cout << "Student 1555 has gpa " << studlist[index].gpa
         << endl;

    cout << "String 'two' is at index "
         << SeqSearch(strlist,5,"two") << endl;
}

/*
<Run of Program 7.1>
Item 8 is found at index 5
Student 1555 has gpa 2.6
String 'two' is at index 2
*/
```

TEMPLATE-BASED SORT

The exchange sort provides an algorithm to order elements in a list using the comparison operator "<". The algorithm is implemented by a template-based function ExchangeSort that uses a single template parameter T. The operator "<" must be defined for the data type that corresponds to T, or an overloaded operator must be provided by the client.

```
// sort the n element a using the exchange sort algorithm
template <class T>
void ExchangeSort(T a[], int n)
{
    T temp;
    int i, j;

    // make n-1 passes
    for (i = 0; i < n-1; i++)
        // put smallest of a[i+1]. . .a[n-1] in a[i]
        for (j = i+1; j < n; j++)
            if (a[j] < a[i])
            {
                // swap a[i] and a[j]
                temp = a[i];
                a[i] = a[j];
                a[j] = temp;
            }
}
```

For convenience, the function ExchangeSort is stored in the file "utils.h".

7.2 Template Classes

We discuss the template-based Store class, which holds a data value that must be initialized before it is retrieved. In the process, we illustrate the main concepts of template-based classes.

DEFINING A TEMPLATE CLASS

For a **template class,** a template parameter list precedes the class declaration. The generic type names in the template definition are used to declare data items and member functions. The following is a declaration of the template class Store:

```
#include <iostream.h>
#include <stdlib.h>

template <class T>
class Store
{
```

```
    private:
      T item;              // item holds the data value
      int haveValue;       // flag set when item is initialized

    public:
      // constructor (default)
      Store(void);

      // data retrieval and storage operations
      T GetElement(void);
      void PutElement(const T& x);
  };
```

DECLARING TEMPLATE CLASS OBJECTS

Types are passed to the template class when creating an object. The declaration
binds the type with an instance of the class. For instance, the following declarations
create objects of type Store:

```
// data member in X has type int.
Store<int> X;



// creates an array of 10 Store objects with char data
Store<char> S[10];
```

DEFINING TEMPLATE CLASS METHODS

A template class method can be defined with in-line code or outside of the class
body. For an external definition, the method must be treated as a template function
with the template parameter list included in the function definition. All references
to the class as a data type must include the template types enclosed in angle
brackets. This applies to the class name in the class scope operator:

```
ClassName<T>::
```

For instance, the following code defines the function GetItem for Store:

```
// retrieve item if initialized
template <class T>
T Store<T>::GetElement(void)
{
    // terminate if client tries to access uninitialized data
    if (haveValue == 0)
    {
        cerr << "No item present!" << endl;
        exit(1);
```

```
    }
    return item;                    // returns item from storage
}
```

The method PutItem assumes that assignment is a valid operation for elements of type T:

```
// put item in storage
template <class T>
void Store<T>::PutElement(const T & x)
{
    haveValue++;                    // haveValue is TRUE
    item = x;                       // store x
}
```

The external definition of a constructor uses the class name with the class scope operator and as the name of the constructor method. As a class type, use the template parameter. For instance, the class type is Store<T>, whereas the name of the constructor is simply Store.

```
// declare that the data value is not initialized
template <class T>
Store<T>::Store(void): haveValue(0)
{ }
```

The declaration and implementation of Store is in the file "store.h".

Program 7.2   Using the Template Store Class

This program uses the template class Store for objects of type integer, for objects of record type Student, and for objects of type double. In the first two cases, a data value is assigned using PutElement and printed using GetElement. When the data type is double, an attempt is made to retrieve a data value that is not initialized, and the program terminates.

```
#include <iostream.h>

#include "store.h"
#include "student.h"

void main(void)
{
    Student graduate = {1000, 3.5};
    Store<int> A, B;
    Store<Student>  S;
    Store<double>   D;
```

```
    A.PutElement(3);
    B.PutElement(-7);
    cout << A.GetElement() << "   " << B.GetElement() << endl;

    S.PutElement(graduate);
    cout << "The student id is " << S.GetElement().studID
         << endl;

    // D is not initialized
    cout << "Retrieving object D  " << D.GetElement() << endl;
}

/*
<Run of Program 7.2>

3   -7
The student id is 1000
Retrieving object D  No item present!
*/
```

Template List Classes   7.3

We add flexibility to the collections in this book by using template classes. In this section, we redefine the Stack class with templates and use it for a case study in infix expression evaluation in Section 7.4. The template version of the class is included in the program supplement in the file "tstack.h".

The redefinition of the Stack class involves straightforward template mechanics. Begin the declaration by placing the template parameter list before the class declaration and replacing DataType by T.

- -
TEMPLATE STACK CLASS SPECIFICATION

DECLARATION

```
#include <iostream.h>
#include <stdlib.h>

const int MaxStackSize = 50;

template <class T>
class Stack
{
    private:
      // private data members. stack array and top
        T stacklist[MaxStackSize];
        int top;
```

```
    public:
      // constructor
        Stack (void);        // initialize top

        // stack modification operations
        void Push (const T& item);
        T Pop (void);
        void ClearStack(void);

        // stack access
        T Peek (void) const;

        // stack test methods
        int StackEmpty(void) const;
        int StackFull(void) const;
};
```

TEMPLATE-BASED STACK IMPLEMENTATION

We define each class method as an external template function. This requires the
template parameter list to be placed before each function and replacement of the
class type Stack with Stack<T>. In the actual function definition, we must replace
the generic type DataType with the template type T. The following listing gives a
new definition for the Push and Pop methods.

Push
```
    // push item on the stack
    template <class T>
    void Stack<T>::Push (const T& item)
    {
        // if all elements of stacklist used, terminate program
        if (top == MaxStacksize-1)
        {
            cerr << "Stack overflow!" << endl;
            exit(1);
        }
        // increment top and copy item to stacklist
        top++;
        stacklist[top] = item;
    }
```
Pop
```
    // pop the stack and return the top element
    template <class T>
    T Stack<T>::Pop (void)
    {
        T temp;
```

```
    // if stack is empty, terminate the program
    if (top == -1)
    {
        cerr << "Attempt to pop an empty stack!" << endl;
        exit(1);
    }


    // record the top element
    temp = stacklist[top];

    // decrement top and return former top element
    top--;
    return temp;
}
```

Infix Expression Evaluation   7.4

Chapter 5 illustrates the use of stacks in postfix or Reverse Polish Notation (RPN) expression evaluation. The topic of infix expression evaluation was deliberately skipped in the chapter since its implementation requires the use of two stacks, one for operands and one for operators. Because the data on the two stacks are of different types, infix evaluation makes effective use of templates. This section develops the infix expression evaluation algorithm and implements it with the template stack class.

You are familiar with expressions that combine arithmetic operations. For instance, the following expressions combine the unary operator −, the binary operators +, −, *, /, parentheses, and floating point operands:

```
8.5 + 2 * 3     -7 * (4/3 - 6.25) + 9
```

The expressions use infix notation with the binary operators positioned between the operands. A pair of parentheses creates a subexpression that is computed separately.

With high-level languages, there is an **order of precedence** and **associativity** among operators. The operator with the highest precedence is executed first. If more than one binary operator has the same precedence, the leftmost operator executes first in the case of left associativity (+, −, *, /) and the rightmost operator executes first in the case of right associativity (unary plus, unary minus).

Order of Precedence (Low to High)	Operator
1	+, −
2	*, /
3	unary plus, unary minus

EXAMPLE 7.1

1. $8.5 + 2 * 3 = 14.5$ // * executes before +
2. $(8.5 + 2) * 3 = 31.5$ // parentheses create a subexpression
3. $9 - -6 = 15$ // unary minus has highest priority;

Rank of an Expression   The algorithm to evaluate an infix expression uses the concept of **rank**, which assigns a value -1, 0, or 1 for each term in the expression:

Rank of a floating point operand is 1.
Rank of the unary operators $+$, $-$ is 0.
Rank of the binary operators $+$, $-$, $*$, $/$ is -1.
Rank of left parentheses is 0.

As we scan the terms in an expression, rank identifies misplaced operands or operators that would cause an invalid expression. For each term in the expression, we associate the **cumulative rank**, which is the sum of the rank of the individual terms from the first symbol through the given term. The cumulative rank is used to ensure that each binary operator has two surrounding operands and that no successive operands exist without an infix operator. For instance, in the simple expression

$2 + 3$

the successive rank values are

Scan 2:   cumulative rank = 1
Scan +:   cumulative rank = $1 + -1 = 0$
Scan 3:   cumulative rank = 1

Rule: For each term in an expression, the cumulative rank of the expression must be 0 or 1. The rank of the full expression must be 1.

EXAMPLE 7.2

The following are invalid expressions that are identified by the rank function.

Expression	Invalid Rank	Reason
1. 2.5 <u>4</u> + 3	Rank at 4 = 2	Too many consecutive operands
2. 2.5 + <u>*</u> 3	Rank at * = -1	Too many consecutive operators
3. 2.5 + 3 <u>−</u>	Final Rank = 0	Missing an operand

Infix Expression Algorithm   The infix expression algorithm uses an **operand stack** (stack of floating point values) to hold the operands and the results of intermediate calculations. A second stack, called the **operator stack,** holds the operators and left parentheses and allows us to implement precedence. While scanning the expression, the terms are pushed onto their respective stacks. An operand is pushed on the operand stack when it is encountered and is released (popped) when it is needed for an operation. An operator goes on the stack only when all operators of greater or equal precedence currently on the stack have been evaluated. The operator is released when it reaches its time for execution. This occurs when a subsequent operator is input with lower or equal precedence or at the end of the expression. Consider the expression

$$2 + 4 - 3 * 6$$

Input 2:   Push 2 on the operand stack.
Input +:   Push + on the operator stack.
Input 4:   Push 4 on the operand stack.

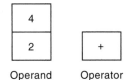

Operand   Operator

Input −:   The operator − has the same precedence as the operator + on the stack. First release the +, pop two operands and execute the addition operation. The result 2 + 4 = 6 is then pushed back onto the operand stack.
Push − on the operator stack.

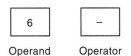

Operand   Operator

Input 3:   Push 3 on the operand stack.
*Input *:*   The operator * has higher precedence than the operator − on the stack. Push * on the operator stack.
Input 6:   Push 6 on the operand stack.

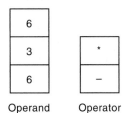

Operand   Operator

Done: Clear the operator stack. Pop * and execute the operation with operands 6 and 3 from the operand stack. Push the result 18 on the operand stack.

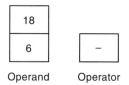

Operand   Operator

Pop the stack and execute the operation − with operands 18 and 3 from the operand stack. 6 − 18 = −12. This is the result.

Operator precedence is determined when the operator is first input and then again while it is on the stack. The initial value, called the **input precedence,** is used to compare the relative importance of the operator with those on the stack. Once an operator is pushed on the stack, it is given a new precedence, which is called the **stack precedence.** The distinction between input and stack precedence is used for parentheses and right associative operators. In these cases, the stack precedence is smaller than the input precedence. When a subsequent operator of the same priority and associativity is found, the input precedence now exceeds the stack precedence of the operator on the top of the stack. The first operator is not released and the new operator goes on the stack. The order of evaluation is then right to left.

Table 7.1 gives input and stack precedence and rank used for infix expression evaluation. The operators include parentheses and the binary operators +, −, *, and /. The binary operators are left associative and have equal input and stack precedence. Handling the right associative exponent operator is left as an exercise.

The expression evaluation algorithm is slightly more complex when parentheses are involved. When a left parenthesis is found, it represents the beginning of a subexpression and hence should be placed immediately on the stack. This is done by assigning "(" an input precedence that is greater than any of the operators. Once the left parenthesis is on the stack, it can be removed only when its matching right parenthesis is found and the subexpression is fully evaluated. While on the stack, the precedence of a left parenthesis must be less than all the operators so that it is not popped from the stack while computing the terms within the subexpression.

Algorithm   The algorithm is implemented with two stacks. The operand stack contains floating point numbers while the elements of the operator stack are objects of class type MathOperator.

TABLE 7.1
Input and Stack Precedence with Rank

| Symbol | Precedence | | Rank |
	Input Precedence	Stack Precedence	
+ − (binary)	1	1	−1
* /	2	2	−1
(	3	−1	0
)	0	0	0

```
// a class that handles operators on the operator stack
class MathOperator
{
   private:
     // an operator and its precedence
     char op;
     int inputprecedence;
     int stackprecedence;

   public:
     // constructor that initializes the object and a
     // default constructor that allows uninitialized data
     MathOperator(void);
     MathOperator(char ch);

     // member functions handling the operator on the stack
     int operator>= (MathOperator a) const;
     void Evaluate (Stack<float> &operandStack);
     char GetOp(void);
};
```

A MathOperator object stores the operator and the precedence values associated
with the operator. The non-default constructor sets both the inputprecedence and
stackprecedence of the operator.

```
// constructor that assigns operator and its precedences
MathOperator::MathOperator(char ch)
{
    op = ch;    // assign operator
    switch(op)
    {
        // '+' and '-' have input/stack precedence 1
        case '+':
        case '-':     inputprecedence = 1;
                      stackprecedence = 1;
                      break;

        // '*' and '/' have input/stack precedence 2
        case '*':
        case '/':     inputprecedence = 2;
                      stackprecedence = 2;
                      break;

        // '(' has input precedence 3, stack precedence -1
        case '(':     inputprecedence = 3;
                      stackprecedence = -1;
                      break;
```

```
                          // ')' has input/stack precedence 0
                       case ')':    inputprecedence = 0;
                                     stackprecedence = 0;
                                     break;
              }
       }
```

The MathOperator class overloads the C++ operator ">=", which is used to compare precedence values.

```
   // overload >= operator by comparing stackprecedence of
   // the current object with inputprecedence of a. used when
   // reading an operator to determine whether operators
   // on the stack should be evaluated before pushing the new
   // operator on the stack.
   int MathOperator::operator>= (MathOperator a) const
   {
       return stackprecedence >= a.inputprecedence;
   }
```

The class contains the member function Evaluate, which is responsible for executing the operations. The function pops two operands. After carrying out the operation, the result is pushed back on the operand stack.

```
   // evaluate operator for the current object. First pop two
   // operands from the operand stack, then execute operator and
   // push the result back onto the operand stack.
   void MathOperator::Evaluate (Stack<float> &operandStack)
   {
      float operand1 = operandStack.Pop(); // get left operand
      float operand2 = operandStack.Pop(); // get right operand

      // evaluate operator and push result back on the stack
      switch (op)                          // select operation
      {
          case '+':  operandStack.Push(operand2 + operand1);
                     break;

          case '-':  operandStack.Push(operand2 - operand1);
                     break;

          case '*':  operandStack.Push(operand2 * operand1);
                     break;

          case '/':  operandStack.Push(operand2 / operand1);
                     break;
      }
   }
```

The infix expression evaluation algorithm reads each term of the expression, pushes it on the corresponding stack, and updates the cumulative rank. The input terminates on end of expression or if the rank is out of the range. The following rules apply as terms are read.

Input an operand: Push the operand on the operand stack.

Input an operator: Pop all operators from the stack that have stack precedence greater than or equal to the input precedence of the current operator. Make the comparison by using the mathOperator method ">=". As operators come off the stack, execute the operator using the method Evaluate.

Input a right parenthesis ")": Pop and evaluate all operators on the stack that have stack precedence greater than or equal to the input precedence of ")", which is 0. Note that the stack precedence of "(" is −1, so the process stops when "(" is encountered. The effect is to evaluate all operators between the parentheses. If no "(" is found, the expression is invalid ("missing left parenthesis").

At the end of expression, flush the operator stack: The rank must be 1. If the rank is less than 1, an operand is missing. While clearing the stack, if a "(" is found, the expression is invalid ("missing right parenthesis"). As the operators are removed from the stack, the function Evaluate carries out each calculation. The final result of the expression is found by popping the operand stack.

Program 7.3   Evaluating an Infix Expression

The program illustrates the evaluation of an infix expression. We read each term of the expression, skipping all whitespace characters until "=" is found. During the process, error checking is performed with specific error messages printed. When the input is completed, the remaining terms of the expression are evaluated and the value of the expression is printed.

```
#include <iostream.h>
#include <stdlib.h>
#include <ctype.h>              // used for function 'isdigit'

#include "tstack.h"             // include template-based stack class
#include "mathop.h"             // defines the MathOperator class

// checks if character is an operator or parentheses
int isoperator(char ch)
{
    if (ch == '+' || ch == '-' || ch == '*' ||
        ch == '/' || ch == '(')
        return 1;
    else
        return 0;
}
```

```cpp
// checks if character is a whitespace character
int iswhitespace(char ch)
{
    if (ch == ' ' || ch == '\t' || ch == '\n')
        return 1;
    else
        return 0;
}

// error handling function
void Error(int n)
{
    // table gives the different error messages
    static char *errormsgs[] = {
                    "Operator expected",
                    "Operand expected",
                    "Missing left parenthesis",
                    "Missing right parenthesis",
                    "Invalid input"
                };

    // the parameter n is an error message index
    // print the message and terminate the program
    cerr << errormsgs[n] << endl;
    exit(1);
}

void main(void)
{
    // declaration of operator stack with MathOperator objects
    Stack<MathOperator> OperatorStack;

    // declaration of the operand stack.
    Stack<float> OperandStack;

    MathOperator opr1,opr2;
    int rank = 0;
    float number;
    char ch;

    // process the expression until '=' is read
    while (cin.get(ch) &&  ch != '=')
    {
        // ******** process a floating point operand ********
        if (isdigit(ch) || ch == '.')
        {
            // put back digit or '.' and read number
            cin.putback(ch);
            cin >> number;
```

```
        // rank of operand is 1, accumulated rank must be 1
        rank++;
        if (rank > 1)
            Error(OperatorExpected);
        // push the operand on the operand stack
        OperandStack.Push(number);
    }
// ********  process an operator  **********
else if (isoperator(ch))
{
        // rank of each operator other than '(' is -1.
        // accumulated rank should be 0
            if (ch != '(')  // rank of '(' is 0
                rank--;
            if (rank < 0)
                Error(OperandExpected);

        // build a MathOperator object holding current
        // operator. pop the operator stack and evaluate
        // as long as the operator on the top of the stack
        // has a precedence >= that of the current operator.
        // push the current operator on the operator stack
        opr1 = MathOperator(ch);
        while(!OperatorStack.StackEmpty() &&
             (opr2 = OperatorStack.Peek()) >= opr1)
        {
            opr2 = OperatorStack.Pop();
            opr2.Evaluate(OperandStack);
        }
        OperatorStack.Push(opr1);
}
// ********  process a right parenthesis  **********
else if (ch == rightparenthesis)
{
        // build a MathOperator object holding ')', which
        // has precedence lower than the stack precedence
        // of any operator except '('. pop the operator stack
        // and evaluate the subexpression until '(' surfaces
        // or the stack is empty. if the stack is empty, a
        // '(' is missing; otherwise, delete '('.
        opr1 = MathOperator(ch);
        while(!OperatorStack.StackEmpty() &&
             (opr2 = OperatorStack.Peek() >= opr1)
        {
            opr2 = OperatorStack.Pop();
            opr2.Evaluate(OperandStack);
        }
        if(OperatorStack.StackEmpty())
            Error(MissingLeftParenthesis);
```

```
                opr2 = OperatorStack.Pop(); // get rid of '('
          }
          // ********* have some invalid input  **********
          else if (!iswhitespace(ch))
              Error(InvalidInput);
      }

      // the rank of the complete expression must be 1
      if (rank != 1)
          Error(OperandExpected);


      // flush operator stack and complete expression evaluation.
      // if find left parenthesis, a right parenthesis is missing.
      while (!OperatorStack.StackEmpty())
      {
          opr1 = OperatorStack.Pop();
          if (opr1.GetOp() == leftparenthesis)
              Error(MissingRightParenthesis);
          opr1.Evaluate(OperandStack);
      }


      // value of expression is on top of operand stack
      cout << "The value is " << OperandStack.Pop() << endl;
}

/*
<Run of Program 7.3 #1>
2.5 + 6/3 * 4 - 3 =
The value is 7.5

<Run of Program 7.3 #2>
(2 + 3.25) * 4 =
The value is 21

<Run of Program 7.3 #3>
(4 + 3) - 7) =
missing left parenthesis
*/
```

Written Exercises

7.1 (a) Write code for the generic function Max that returns the larger of two values.

(b) Write an overloaded version of Max that works for C++ strings. Pass pointers to characters as parameters and return a pointer to the larger string.

7.2 Write a template class DataStore that has the following methods:

```
int Insert(T elt);
```
Insert elt into a private array dataElements having five elements of type T. The index of the next available location in dataElements is given by the data member loc, which is also the number of data values in dataElements. Return 0 if there is no more room left in dataElements.

```
int Find(T elt);
```
Search for element elt in dataElements and return its index if it is found and −1 if it is not.

```
int NumElts(void);
```
Return number of elements stored in dataElements.

```
T& GetData(int n);
```
Return the element at location n in dataElements. Generate an error message and exit if n < 0 or n > 4.

7.3 Write the function

```
template <class T>
int Max(T Arr[], int n);
```

that returns the index of the maximum value in the array.

7.4 Implement the function

```
template <class T>
int BinSearch(T A[], T key, int low, int high);
```

that executes the binary search for key in array A.

7.5 Write the function

```
template <class T>
void InsertOrder(T A[], int n, T elem);
```

that inserts elem into the array A so the list is maintained in ascending order. Note that when a position is located for elem, you must move all remaining elements to the right one position.

7.6 (a) Give a template-based declaration for the SeqList class.

(b) For the template class, implement the constructor and the methods DeleteFront and Insert.

(c) Before declaring a SeqList<T> object, what operators must be defined for the type T?

(d) Declare S as a Stack object in which the items of the stack are SeqList objects.

Programming Exercises

7.1 Test the functions Max from Written Exercise 7.1 by using them in a main program. Include in this main program two C++ strings.

7.2 Write a template function Copy with the declaration

```
template <class T>
void Copy(T A[], T B[], int n);
```

This function copies n elements from array B to A. Write a main program to test Copy. Include at least the following arrays:

```
(a)  int AInt[6], BInt[6] = {1,3,5,7,9,11};

(b)  struct Student
       {
           int field1;
           double field2;
       };

     Student AStudent[3];
     Student BStudent[3] = {{1,3.5},{3,0}, {5,5.5}};
```

7.3 This exercise uses the template class DataStore developed in Written Exercise 7.2. Write an overloaded "<<" operator that prints the data in a DataStore object using the method GetData. Let Person be a record:

```
struct Person
{
    char name[50];
    int age;
    int height;
};
```

Overload the operator "==" for Person so it compares the name fields.

Write a program that inserts data elements of type Person until a DataStore object is full. Include the following Person p in your input.

```
"John"
25
72
```

Search for p and then print the result of the search. Use "<<" to output the object.

7.4 Extend Program 7.3 to handle exponentiation, which is represented by the character "^". Exponentiation is right associative. For instance,

```
2 ^ 3 = 8                 // 2³ = 8
2 ^ 2 ^ 3 = 2 ^ (2 ^ 3) = 256.
```

To compute a^b, include the mathematics library <math.h> and use the function pow as follows:

a^b= pow(a,b)

7.5   The sequential search scans a list and looks for a match with the key. For each element, we have the twofold task of checking for a match and checking for the end of the list. A modified version of the search, called the **fast sequential search,** improves the algorithm by appending the key at the end of the list. The expanded list is then guaranteed to provide a match since there is at least one "key" element in the list.

The search process simply tests for a match and terminates when the key is located in the list.

(a)   Write the code for

```
template <class T>
int FastSeqSearch(T A[], int n, T key);
```

(b)   Rewrite Program 7.1 using the FastSeqSearch.

7.6   The mode is the value that occurs most frequently in a list. To gather this information for a list of arbitrary data types, define the DataInfo class that maintains two data fields, a value member, and a frequency member.

```
template <class T>
class DataInfo
{
   private:
      T data;          // the data value
      int frequency;   // occurrences of the data value

   public:
      // increment frequency
      void Increment(void);

      // relational operators. "==" and "<" must
      // be valid for type T

      // compare data values
      int operator== (const DataInfo<T>& w);
      // compare frequency counts
      int operator< (const DataInfo<T>& w);

      // stream operators. "<<" and ">>" must be valid
      for type T
      friend istream& operator>> (istream& is,
                                  DataInfo<T> &w);
      friend ostream& operator<< (ostream& os, const
                                  DataInfo<T>& w);
};
```

The class has an Increment method that increases the count by 1 and a stream output operator that outputs the object in the format "value:count". A record with an initial value and an initial count of 1 is created by executing the overloaded stream input operator ">>" that reads a data value from the input stream. The relational operators are added to facilitate searching a list of DataInfo objects for a particular data value and sorting a list in order of frequency.

(a)   Implement DataInfo in the file "datainfo.h".

(b)   Write a main program that prompts the user for the number of items that will be input into an integer list. Once this size is known, read the actual integer values and create the DataInfo<int> array dataList. Use the function SeqSearch to determine if an input value is in the array dataList. A return of −1 indicates that a new value has been read and hence a new entry must be stored in the dataList array. Otherwise, an entry in the array corresponds to the input value and its frequency must be updated. Conclude the program by calling ExchangeSort to sort dataList and then print each value and frequency.

7.7   Modify Programming Exercise 7.6 so that the DataInfo list is maintained in order and the binary search is used to determine if a value has already been encountered. Use the functions developed in Written Exercises 7.4 and 7.5. Of course, it is not necessary to perform a sort.

C H A P T E R 8

CLASSES AND
DYNAMIC MEMORY

Up to this point in the book we have used only **static data structures** to implement collection classes. The discussion has included static arrays to implement the SeqList, Stack, and Queue classes. The use of a static array presents problems since its size is fixed at compile time and cannot be resized during execution. Each class must allocate a reasonably large number of items to satisfy a range of client uses. For many applications, some memory is wasted. In some cases, the array size is not sufficient, and the user must have access to the source code of the program in order to increase the array size and recompile the program.

In this chapter we introduce **dynamic data structures,** which use memory obtained from the system during run time. We have some experience with memory allocation from our knowledge of program block structure. Compilers allocate global data and create automatic variables that are allocated upon entrance to a block and then deallocated upon exit from the block. For instance, the C++ compiler allocates global data, parameters, and local variables in the following code sequence:

```
int global = 8;  // variable in effect for the entire program
// allocate memory on system stack for parameters x and y
void subtask (int x, long *y)
{
    int z;        // allocate the local variable z
    ...           // upon exit, variable and parameters
                  // are deallocated
}
```

The type and size of each variable is known at compile time.

Compilers also provide the user with the ability to create dynamic data. An operator, **new,** allocates memory from a memory pool for use during program execution and a complementary **delete** operator returns the memory to the pool for subsequent allocation. Dynamic data structures find important uses in applications whose memory requirements are known only at run time. Their use is fundamental to the general study of collections and effectively removes the size limitation that occurs when we declare a static collection of data items. For instance, the Stack class restricts its maximum size to the default parameter MaxStackSize and asks the client to check the StackFull condition before adding (pushing) a new item. Dynamic memory enhances the usability of the Stack class because the class allocates sufficient memory to meet the needs of the application. Database applications often use temporary storage to hold tables and lists that are created by a user-supplied query. The memory can be allocated in response to the query and then deallocated after the response is made.

The use of dynamic memory has limitations and some dangers. An application may be designed to work with variable size data that are dynamically allocated. As the program runs, sufficient requests are made to eventually exhaust the supply of available memory and the client gets an "Out of Memory" message. In such a case, the application may be forced to terminate. This problem may occur when running an application with a graphical user interface. A program makes use of a series of windows to display data, to set up menus, and so forth. Even if the program is well structured, the user may have too many active graphical structures and eventually choke off the supply of available memory. When using dynamic storage, we must be aware that memory is a resource to be efficiently managed by the programmer. Memory that is dynamically allocated must be deallocated when no longer needed. The compiler follows this policy when allocating memory for parameters and local variables. The programmer must follow this policy using the delete operator.

C++ provides a series of methods for handling dynamic data. The **destructor** method deletes the dynamic memory allocated by the object when the object is destroyed. In addition, a class may have a **copy constructor** and an **overloaded assignment operator,** which are used for copying or assigning one object to another. These class methods are the focus of this chapter. To introduce the new methods, we use the simple DynamicClass for most of the examples.

Dynamic arrays allow us to allocate a block of memory at run time. For most applications, we know the needed size when creating the array. In special cases, however, we may need to extend the array and revise its size. To provide this capability, we develop the Array class that creates lists of arbitrary size and implements array bounds checking and list resizing. The class provides a powerful data structure and illustrates the use of a destructor, copy constructor, and overloaded assignment operator. Because we want an Array object to look like a standard C++ array, we overload the index operator "[]".

Strings are a fundamental data structure. In fact, some languages define a built-in string type. In this chapter, we develop a complete String class and use it to solve a problem in pattern matching. The string class is used throughout the remainder of the book.

Sets are the basis for a great deal of mathematical theory. In computer applications, sets are a powerful non-linear data structure that have application in fields such as textual analysis and spell checking and in the implementation of graphs and networks. A Set class that stores data of integral type is developed using the C++ bit operators. This approach provides excellent space and runtime efficiency. The Set class is used to implement the famous algorithm for finding prime numbers called the Sieve of Eratosthenes.

Pointers and Dynamic Data Structures 8.1

Pointers as a data structure are introduced in Chapter 2. In this section, we combine pointer variables with the C++ operators **new** and **delete** to allocate and deallocate dynamic memory.

THE MEMORY ALLOCATION OPERATOR NEW

C++ uses the operator new to allocate memory for data during program execution. Knowing the size of the data, the operator requests the system to supply sufficient memory to hold the data and returns a pointer to the newly allocated space. If sufficient memory is not available, the operator returns 0 (NULL).

The operator new requires a data type T as a parameter, and operator allocates memory for a variable of type T, returning the address of the newly created memory.

```
T  *p;        // declare p as a pointer to T
p = new T;    // p is the address of memory for data of type T
```

For instance, variables ptr1 and ptr2 point to data of type int and long, respectively.

```
int  *ptr1;      // size of int is 2
long *ptr2;      // size of long is 4
```

The operator new assigns the address of an int to ptr1 and the address of a long to ptr2.

```
ptr1 = new int;    // ptr1 points at an integer in memory
ptr2 = new long;   // ptr2 points at a long integer in memory
```

System Memory

Here, ptr1 contains the address of the 2-byte integer in memory. Similarly, ptr2 contains the address of the 4-byte long in memory. By default, the contents in memory have no initial value. If such a value is desired, it must be supplied as a parameter when the operator is used:

```
P = new T (value);
```

For instance, the operation

```
ptr2 = new long(100000);
```

allocates memory for the long integer and assigns it the value 100000.

DYNAMIC ARRAY ALLOCATION

The power of dynamic memory allocation is particularly evident when allocating an entire array. In an application, assume the size of the array is known at run time. The operator new can allocate memory for the array using the bracket notation ("[]"). Assume p points at data of type T. The statement

```
p = new T [n]; // allocate an array of n items of type T
```

assigns p to point at the first element of the array. An array allocated in this way cannot specify initial data.

EXAMPLE 8.1

The following statement allocates an array of 50 long integers provided sufficient memory is available. If p is NULL, the operator new fails to allocate the memory and the program terminates.

```
long *p;
p = new long [50]; // allocate an array of 50 long integers
if (p == NULL)
{
    cerr << "Memory allocation error! << endl;
    exit(1);         // terminate the program
}
```

THE MEMORY DEALLOCATION OPERATOR DELETE

Memory management is the responsibility of the programmer and C++ provides the operator **delete** to deallocate memory originally allocated by new. The syntax is simple and relies on the fact that the C++ runtime system retains information about each call of new. Assume P and Q point at dynamically allocated memory:

```
T *p, *q;        // p and q are pointers to type T

p = new T;       // points to a single item
q = new T[n];    // points to an array of n elements
```

The function delete uses a pointer to release the memory. In the case of array deallocation, delete combines with the "[]" operator.

```
delete p;        // deallocates the variable pointed to by p
delete [] q;     // deallocates the entire array pointed to by q
```

EXAMPLE 8.2

The delete operator deallocates the memory assigned to the dynamically created array p:

```
long *p;
p = new long [50]; // allocate an array of 50 long integers
delete [] p;       // deallocate the 50 long integers
```

8.2 Dynamically Allocated Objects

Like any variable, an object of a class type can be declared as a static variable or dynamically allocated using new. In each case, typically a constructor is called to initialize variables and dynamically allocate memory for one or more data members. The syntax follows the pattern for simple types and arrays. The operator new allocates memory for the object and initiates a call to a class constructor if one exists. Any parameters that are supplied are passed to the constructor.

To introduce dynamic allocation of objects, we use the template-based class DynamicClass that has a static data member and a dynamic data member. The following is the declaration of the class, whose methods are developed in this section and in section 8.3. The class is found in the file "dynamic.h", which is contained in the software supplement:

```
#include <iostream.h>
template <class T>
class DynamicClass
{
   private:
      // variable of type T and a pointer to data of type T
      T    member1;
      T    *member2;
   public:
      // constructors
      DynamicClass(const T& m1, const T& m2);
      DynamicClass(const DynamicClass<T>& obj);

      // destructor
      ~DynamicClass(void);

      // assignment operator
      DynamicClass<T>& operator= (const DynamicClass<T>& rhs);
};
```

The simple class with its two data members illustrates the essential action of member functions in handling dynamically allocated objects. This class is designed for demonstration purposes only and has no real usefulness.

The constructor for the class uses parameter m1 to initialize the static data member1. Action for member2 requires allocating memory for a variable of type T and giving it an initial value m2:

```
// constructor with parameters to initialize member data
template <class T>
DynamicClass<T>::DynamicClass(const T& m1, const T& m2)
{
```

```
        // parameter m1 initializes static member
        member1 = m1;
        // allocate dynamic memory and initialize it with value m2
        member2 = new T(m2);
        cout << "Constructor: " << member1 << '/'
             << *member2 << endl;
}
```

EXAMPLE 8.3

The following statements define a static variable staticObj and a pointer variable dynamicObj. The object staticObj has parameters 1 and 100 that initialize the data members:

```
// DynamicClass object
DynamicClass<int> staticObj(1,100);
```

The object to which dynamicObj points is created by the new operator. Parameters 2 and 200 are supplied as parameters to the constructor. When creating the object *dynamicObj, the class constructor initializes the data members to 2 and 200:

```
// pointer variable
DynamicClass<int> *dynamicObj;
// allocate an object
dynamicObj = new DynamicClass<int> (2,200);
```

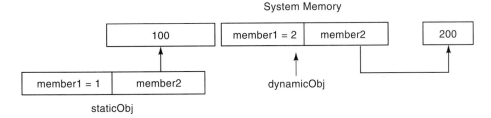

DEALLOCATING OBJECT DATA: THE DESTRUCTOR

Consider the function F that creates a DynamicClass object having integer data.

```
void DestroyDemo(int m1, int m2)
{
    DynamicClass<int> obj(m1,m2);
}
```

Upon return from DestroyDemo, obj is destroyed; however, the process does not deallocate the dynamic memory associated with the object. This situation is illustrated by Figure 8.1.

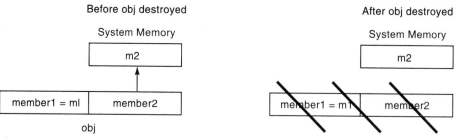

Figure 8.1 Need for a Destructor

For effective memory management, we need to deallocate the dynamic data within the object at the same time the object is being destroyed. We need to reverse the action of the constructor, which originally allocated the dynamic data. The language provides a member function, called the **destructor,** which is called by the compiler when an object is destroyed. For DynamicClass, the destructor has the declaration

```
~DynamicClass(void);
```

The character "~" represents "complement", so ~DynamicClass is the complement of a constructor. A destructor never has a parameter or a return type. For our sample class, the destructor is responsible to deallocate the dynamic data for member2:

```
// destructor. deallocates memory allocated by the constructor
template <class T>
DynamicClass<T>::~DynamicClass(void)
{
    cout << "Destructor: " << member1 << '/'
        << *member2 << endl;
    delete member2;
}
```

The destructor is called whenever an object is deleted. When a program terminates, all global objects or objects declared in the main program are destroyed. For local objects created within a block, the destructor is called when the program exits the block.

Program 8.1   The Destructor

This program illustrates the definition of a destructor and its use. The test program involves three objects. Obj_1 is a variable declared in the main program and Obj_2 references a dynamic object. The function DestroyDemo we have

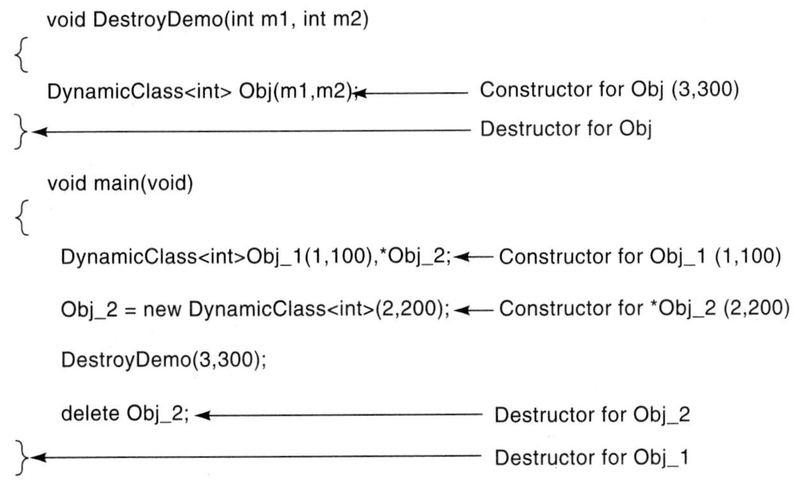

```
     void DestroyDemo(int m1, int m2)
 {
     DynamicClass<int> Obj(m1,m2);◄──────── Constructor for Obj (3,300)
 }◄──────────────────────────────────────── Destructor for Obj

     void main(void)
 {
      DynamicClass<int>Obj_1(1,100),*Obj_2;◄── Constructor for Obj_1 (1,100)

      Obj_2 = new DynamicClass<int>(2,200);◄── Constructor for *Obj_2 (2,200)

      DestroyDemo(3,300);

      delete Obj_2; ◄──────────────────────── Destructor for Obj_2
 }◄──────────────────────────────────────── Destructor for Obj_1
```

Figure 8.2 Initialization for DynamicClass A(3,5), B = A

discussed is included and declares a local object obj. Figure 8.2 marks the different occurrences of the constructor and destructor methods of the objects.

```
#include <iostream.h>

#include "dynamic.h"

void DestroyDemo(int m1, int m2)
{
   DynamicClass<int> obj(m1,m2);
}

void main(void)
{
   // create automatic object Obj_1 with member1=1, *member2=100
   DynamicClass<int> Obj_1(1,100);

   // declare a pointer to an object
   DynamicClass<int> *Obj_2;

   // allocate dynamic object pointed to by Obj_2 with
   // member1 = 2 and *member2 = 200
   Obj_2 = new DynamicClass<int>(2,200);

   // call function DestroyObject with parameters 3/300
   DestroyDemo(3,300);

   // explicitly delete Obj_2
   delete Obj_2;
```

```
        cout << "Ready to exit program." << endl;
}

/*
<Run of Program 8.1>

Constructor: 1/100
Constructor: 2/200
Constructor: 3/300
Destructor: 3/300
Destructor: 2/200
Ready to exit program.
Destructor: 1/100
*/
```

8.3 Assignment and Initialization

Assignment and initialization are basic operations that apply to any object. The assignment Y = X causes a bitwise copy of the data from object X to the data in object Y. Initialization creates a new object that is a copy of another object. The operations are illustrated with objects X and Y:

```
// creates DynamicClass objects X and Y
// data in Y is initialized by data in X
DynamicClass X(20,50), Y = X;

Y = X;                  // data in Y is over-written by data in X
```

Special consideration must be used with dynamic memory so that unintended errors are not created. We must create new methods that handle object assignment and initialization. In this section, we first discuss the potential problems and then create new class methods.

ASSIGNMENT ISSUES

The constructor for DynamicClass initializes member1 and allocates dynamic data pointed to by member2. For instance, in the declaration of objects A and B, we create two objects and two associated memory blocks that are allocated using the new operator.

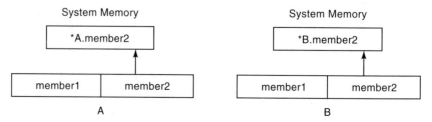

The assignment statement B = A causes the data in A to be copied to B.

```
member1 of B = member1 of A    // copies static data from A to B
member2 of B = member2 of A    // copies pointer from A to B
```

Since pointer value member2 in object B is assigned the pointer value member2 in object A, both pointers now reference the same location in memory, and the dynamic memory originally assigned to B is unreferenced. Assume the assignment statement occurs within a function F.

```
void F(void)
{
    DynamicClass<int> A(2,3), B(7,9);
        . . .
    B = A;                 // assign object A to object B
        . . .
}
```

Incorrect Assignment B = A

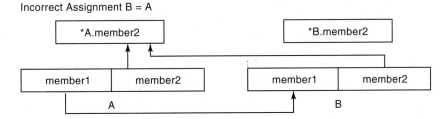

When returning from the function, all objects that are created within the block are destroyed by calling the class destructor, which deallocates the dynamic memory pointed to by member2. Assume object B is destroyed first. The destructor deallocates the variable *B.member2, which is the same data pointed to by member2 in A. When object A is destroyed, its destructor is called with the purpose of deallocating the variable *A.member2. This memory block was previously removed while destroying B and using the delete operation in the destructor for A is an error! In many cases, this is a fatal error.

The problem lies with the assignment statement B = A. The pointer member2 in A is copied into the pointer member2 in B. We really want the contents pointed to by member2 of A to be copied to the contents pointed to by member2 of B.

Correct Assignment B = A

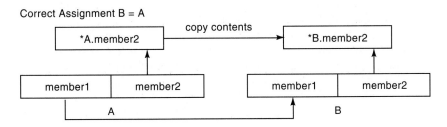

OVERLOADING THE ASSIGNMENT OPERATOR

In order to properly handle assignment of objects when dynamic data are involved, C++ allows for overloading of the assignment operator "=" as a member function. The syntax for the overloaded assignment operator in DynamicClass is

```
DynamicClass<T>& operator= (const DynamicClass<T>& rhs);
```

The binary operator is implemented as a member function with the parameter rhs representing the right-hand side operand. For instance,

```
B = A;      // implemented as B.=(A)
```

The overloaded operator "=" is executed for each assignment statement involving objects of type DynamicClass. Instead of the simple bitwise copy of data members from object A to B, the overloaded operator assumes the responsibility for explicitly assigning all data including private and public data members as well as the data pointed to by these members. The parameter rhs is passed by constant reference. In this way, we avoid copying what might be a large right-hand side object into the parameter but disallow any alteration of the object. Note also that whenever the name of a template class is used as a type, "<T>" must be appended to the name of the class.

For DynamicClass, the assignment operator must assign the data value member1 for object rhs to data value member1 of the current object. The assignment also copies the contents pointed to by member2 in rhs to the contents pointed to by member2 in the current object:

```
// overloaded assignment operator. returns a reference to the
// current object
template <class T>
DynamicClass<T>& DynamicClass<T>::operator=
                 (const DynamicClass<T>& rhs)
{
    // copy static data member from rhs to the current object
    member1 = rhs.member1;
    // contents of dynamic memory must be same as that of rhs
    *member2 = *rhs.member2;
    cout << "Assignment Operator: "<< member1 << '/'
         << *member2 << endl;
    return *this;
}
```

The reserved word **this** is used to return a reference to the current object and is discussed in the next section. The statements transferring data from object rhs to the current object guarantee correct execution of the assignment statement

```
B = A;
```

Because the operator "=" returns a reference to the current object, we can efficiently chain together two or more assignment statements. For instance

```
C = B = A;    // result (B = A) is assigned to C
```

THE THIS POINTER

Each C++ object has a pointer named **this,** which is automatically defined when the object is created. The identifier is a reserved word and can be used only inside a class member function. It is a pointer to the current object, and "*this" is the object itself. Within object A of type DynamicClass,

```
*this is the object A;
this->member1 is member1, the data value in A
this->member2 is member2, the pointer in A
```

For the assignment operator, the return value is a reference parameter. The expression "return *this" returns a reference to the current object.

INITIALIZATION ISSUES

Object initialization is an operation that creates a new object that is a copy of another object. Like assignment, when the object has dynamic data the operation requires a specific member function, called the **copy constructor.** We can anticipate the action of the copy constructor by looking at an example:

```
DynamicClass<int> A(3,5), B = A;   // initialize object B with A
```

The declaration creates object A whose initial data are member1 = 3 and *member2 = 5. The declaration of B creates an object with two data members that are then structured to store the same data values found in A. The initialization process should include copying data value 3 from A to member1 of B, allocating memory for data pointed to by member2 of B, and then copying value 5 from *A.member2 to the dynamically allocated data in B.

Initialization DynamicClass B = A;

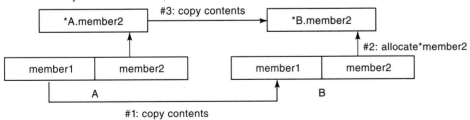

#1: copy contents

In addition to performing initialization when declaring objects, initialization also occurs when passing an object as a value parameter in a function and when an object is returned as the value of the function. For instance, assume function F has a value parameter X of type DynamicClass<int>.

```
DynamicClass<int> F(DynamicClass<int> X)      // value parameter
{
      DynamicClass<int> obj;
      . . . .
      return obj;
}
```

When a calling block uses object A as the actual parameter, the local object X is created by copying A:

```
DynamicClass<int> A(3,5), B(0,0);      // declare objects

B = F(A);                              // call F by copying A to X
```

When the return is made from F, a copy of obj is made, the destructors for the local objects X and obj are called, and the copy of obj is returned as the value of the function.

CREATING A COPY CONSTRUCTOR

In order to properly handle classes that allocate dynamic memory, C++ provides the copy constructor to allocate dynamic memory for the new object and initialize its data values. We illustrate the concept by developing a copy constructor for DynamicClass.

The copy constructor is a member function that is declared with the class name and a single parameter. Because it is a constructor, it does not have a return value:

```
DynamicClass(const DynamicClass<T>& X);    // copy constructor
```

The DynamicClass copy constructor copies the data in member1 from X to the current object. For the dynamic data, the copy constructor allocates memory pointed to by member2 and initializes it to the value *X.member2:

```
// copy constructor. initialize new object to have the
// same data as obj.
template <class T>
DynamicClass<T>::DynamicClass(const DynamicClass<T>& obj)
{
   // copy static data member from obj to current object
    member1 = obj.member1;
   // allocate dynamic memory and initialize it with
   // value *obj.member2.
    member2 = new T(*obj.member2);
    cout << "Copy Constructor: " << member1
         << '/' << *member2 << endl;
}
```

If a class has a copy constructor, it is used by the compiler whenever it needs to perform initialization. The copy constructor is used only when an object is created.

Despite their similarity, assignment and initialization are clearly different operations. Assignment is done when the object on the left-hand side already exists. In the case of initialization, a new object is created by copying data from an existing object. Furthermore, during the initialization process, the operator new must be used to allocate memory before copying the dynamic data.

The parameter in a copy constructor must be passed by reference. The consequence of failing to do so would be catastrophic if the compiler did not recognize the error. Assume you declare the copy constructor with a call by value parameter:

```
DynamicClass(DynamicClass<T> X);
```

The copy constructor is called whenever a function parameter is specified as call by value. In the copy constructor, assume object A is passed to the parameter X by value.

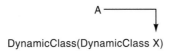

DynamicClass(DynamicClass X)

Since we pass A to X by value, the copy constructor must be called to handle the copying of A to X. This call in turn needs the copy constructor, and we have an infinite chain of copy constructor calls. Fortunately, this potential trouble is caught by the compiler, which specifies that the parameter must be passed by reference. In addition, the reference parameter X should be declared constant, since we certainly do not want to modify the object we are copying.

Program 8.2   Using DynamicClass

The program illustrates the action of the DynamicClass member functions by using integer data. Extensive comments facilitate understanding of the program.

```
#include <iostream.h>

#include "dynamic.h"

template <class T>
DynamicClass<int> Demo(DynamicClass<T> one,
                    DynamicClass<T>& two, T m)
{
    // calls the constructor (member1 = m, *member2 = m)
    DynamicClass<T> obj(m,m);
```

```
                // a copy of obj is made and returned as the
                // value of the function
                return obj;

            // the temporary objects T and one are destroyed upon
            // return from Demo.
        }

        void main ()
        {
                /*    A(3,5) calls the constructor (member1=3, *member2=5)


                      B = A calls copy constructor to initialize object B
                      from object A. (member1 = 3, *member2 = 5)


                      object C calls constructor (member1=0, *member2=0) */
                DynamicClass<int> A(3,5), B = A, C(0,0);

                /*    call function Demo. the copy constructor creates the
                      value parameter one (member1=3, *member2=5) by copying
                      object A. parameter two is passed by reference, so the
                      copy constructor is not called. upon return, a copy is
                      made of the local object obj. this copy is assigned to
                      object C */
                C =Demo(A,B,5);

            // all remaining objects are destroyed upon program exit.
        }

        /*
        <Run of Program 8.2>
        Constructor: 3/5
        Copy Constructor:   3/5
        Constructor: 0/0
        Copy Constructor:   3/5
        Constructor: 5/5
        Copy Constructor:   5/5
        Destructor: 5/5564
        Destructor: 3/5556
        Assignment Operator: 5/5
        Destructor: 5/5
        Destructor: 5/5
```

```
   Destructor: 3/5
   Destructor: 3/5
*/
```

A static array is a collection containing a fixed number of items that are referenced with an index operator. Static arrays are a fundamental data structure for implementing lists. Despite their importance, static arrays present problems. Their size is fixed at compile time and they cannot be resized during run time.

In response to limitations inherent in static arrays, we create a template-based Array class that contains a list of consecutive items of any data type and whose size can be revised during execution. The class contains methods that implement indexing and pointer type conversion. We overload the C++ **index operator "[]"** to allow indexed access to items in the list. Furthermore, we verify that every index corresponds to an element in the list. This property, called **array bounds checking,** generates an error message if the index is out of bounds. The resulting objects are called **safe arrays** because we trap invalid index references. So that an array object can be used with functions that take standard array parameters, we define a general **pointer conversion operator** T* that associates an Array object with an ordinary array whose elements are of type T.

THE ARRAY CLASS

The template-based Array class allocates a list of items of any data type.

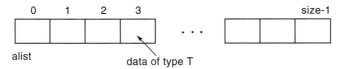

data of type T

ARRAY CLASS SPECIFICATION

DECLARATION

```
#include <iostream.h>
#include <stdlib.h>

enum ErrorType {invalidArraySize, memoryAllocationError,
                indexOutOfRange};

char *errorMsg[] =
{
```

```
        "Invalid array size", "Memory allocation error",
        "Invalid index: "
};

template <class T>
class Array
{
    private:
        // a dynamically allocated list containing size items
        T* alist;
        int size;

        // error handling method
        void Error(ErrorType errorCommitted,int badIndex = 0)const;

    public:
        // constructors and destructor
        Array(int sz = 50);
        Array(const Array<T>& X);
        ~Array(void);

        // assignment, indexing, and pointer conversion
        Array<T>& operator= (const Array<T>& rhs);
        T& operator[] (int i);
        operator T* (void) const;

        // size operations
        int ListSize(void) const;     // read the size
        void Resize(int sz);          // modify the size
};
```

DISCUSSION

The use of an overloaded index operator "[]" and a conversion operator allows an Array object to function like an ordinary language defined array. The assignment operator adds flexibility by implementing the assignment of one Array object to another. For language defined arrays, assignment is an invalid operation.

The Resize method allows us to change the size of the list. If the parameter sz is greater than the current size of the array (size), the old list is retained and additional locations are made available. If sz is less than the current size, we retain the first sz elements in the array and delete the rest.

Example:

```
    Array<int> A(20);         // array of 20 integers
    cout << A.Size();         // output current size of 20

    for(int i=0;i < 20;i++)   // array access using '[]'
        A[i] = i;
    A[25] = 50;               // an invalid index
    A.Resize(30);             // array size increased to 30;
```

```
A[25] = 50;                // now valid
ExchangeSort(A,30);        // conversion allows use of Array
                           // parameter
```

MEMORY ALLOCATION FOR THE ARRAY CLASS

We illustrate the constructor, destructor, and copy constructor, which perform necessary error checking.

The class constructor allocates a dynamic array whose elements are of type T. The initial array size is determined by the parameter sz, whose default value is 50:

```
// constructor
template <class T>
Array<T>::Array(int sz)
{
    // check for an invalid size parameter
    if (sz <= 0)
       Error(invalidArraySize);
    // assign the size and dynamically allocate memory
    size = sz;
    alist = new T[size];
    // make sure that system allocates the desired memory,
    if (alist == NULL)
       Error(memoryAllocationError);
}
```

The destructor deletes the memory allocated to the array alist:

```
// destructor
template <class T>
Array<T>::~Array(void)
{
    delete [] alist;
}
```

The copy constructor allows operations that are not available to language-defined arrays. The constructor allows us to initialize one array with another array X and pass an Array object by value to a function. Extract the size of object X, allocate that amount of dynamic memory, and copy the elements of X to the current object.

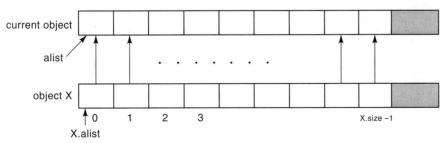

```
// copy constructor
template <class T>
Array<T>::Array(const Array<T>& X)
{
    // get size from object X and assign to current object
    int n = X.size;

    size = n;

    // allocate new memory for object and do error checking
    alist = new T[n];            // allocate dynamic memory
    if (alist == NULL)
        Error(memoryAllocationError);

    // copy array items from x to current object
    T* srcptr = X.alist;      // address at start of X.alist
    T* destptr = alist;       // address at start of alist
    while (n--)               // copy list
        *destptr++ = *srcptr++;
```

ARRAY BOUNDS CHECKING AND THE OVERLOADED [ ] OPERATOR

An array index is referenced using [] and appears in an expression of the form

```
P[n]
```

where P is a pointer to a type T and n is an integer expression. This is actually an operator in C++ called the **array indexing operator.** The operator has the two operands P and n and returns a reference to the data at location P + n.

The operator can be overloaded only as a member function and provides indexed access to an object's data.

We overload the index operator for the Array class. Assuming A is an Array object of integer type, we want to access the elements using the notation A[n]. For instance, the statement

```
A[0] = 5;
```

assigns the value 5 to the first item in the array (alist[0] = 5). The declaration of the member function [] takes the form

```
T& operator[] (int n);
```

where T is the type of data stored in the object and n is the index. The fact that the overloaded operator "[]" returns a reference parameter means that the indexing operator can occur on the left-hand side of an assignment statement.

```
value = A[n];     // assign alist[n] from A to value
A[n] = value;     // assigns value to alist[n]
```

For the Array class, the overloaded indexing operator provides safe array access by checking to see if the index n lies in the array index range 0 to size-1. If n is not in range, an error message is printed, and the program terminates. Otherwise, the operator returns alist[n].

```
// overloaded index operator
template <class T>
T& Array<T>::operator[] (int n)
{
        // do array bounds checking
        if ( n < 0 || n > size-1)
            Error(indexOutOfRange,n);
        // return the element from the private array list
        return alist[n];
}
```

CONVERTING AN OBJECT TO A POINTER

With pointer conversion, we allow the client to use an Array object as a run time parameter in any function that specifies an ordinary array. We do this by overloading the conversion operator T*(), which has the effect of converting an object to a pointer. In our case, we convert an Array object to the starting address of the array alist.

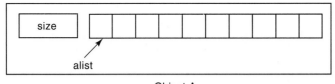

Object A

For instance, the functions ExchangeSort and SeqSearch take an array parameter. For object A of template type integer, the following function statements are valid:

```
// sort A with A.Size() items
ExchangeSort(A,A.Size());
// search for key in A
index = SeqSearch(A,A.Size(), int key);
```

In the function call, the object A is passed to the formal parameter T* Arr.

Declaration: ExchangeSort (T* arr, int n)

Call: ExchangeSort (A, A.Size());

The action causes the conversion operator to execute and assign the pointer alist to arr. The variable arr points to the array in object A:

```
// pointer conversion operator
template <class T>
Array<T>::operator T* (void) const
{
    // return address of the private array in the current object
    return alist;
}
```

Sizing Operators   The Array class provides a ListSize method that retrieves the current number of elements in the array. Of more dynamic effect is the Resize method that changes the number of array elements in the object. If the requested number of elements sz is identical to size, a simple return is executed; otherwise, new memory space is allocated. If we resize the list down (sz < size), the first sz number of elements are copied to the new array.

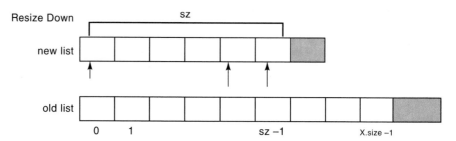

If we resize to a larger array, the old elements are copied to the new list and some unused space is made available. In each of the two cases, storage for the old array is deleted.

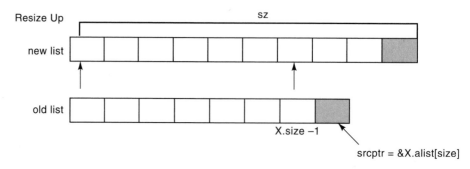

```
// resize operator
template <class T>
void Array<T>::Resize(int sz)
{
    // test new size parameter; terminate if size <= 0
    if (sz <= 0)
        Error(invalidArraySize);
    // nothing to do if size hasn't changed
    if (sz == size)
        return;

    // request new memory; verify system response
    T* newlist = new T[sz];
    if (newlist == NULL)
        Error(memoryAllocationError);

    // declare n with value sz (truncating list)
    // or otherwise declare n to be the current size
    int n = (sz <= size) ? sz : size;

    // copy n array items from old to new memory
    T* srcptr = alist;       // address at start of alist
    T* destptr = newlist;    // address at start of newlist
    while (n--)              // copy list
        *destptr++ = *srcptr++;

    // delete old list
    delete[] alist;

    // reset alist to point at newlist and update the size
    alist = newlist;
    size = sz;
}
```

USING THE ARRAY CLASS

The Array class implementation highlights most of the concepts of this chapter. A client can use the Array class in place of language defined arrays and take advantage of their safety and the flexibility provided by resizing.

Program 8.3   Resizing an Array

Let Array object A define a list of 10 integers in which we store the prime numbers:

```
Definition: A prime number is a positive integer >= 2 that is
            divisible only by itself and 1.
```

The program determines all prime numbers in the range 2 . . N where N is a user-supplied upper limit. Since we cannot predetermine the number of array locations that are needed, the program checks for a "list full" condition by comparing the current number of primes (primecount) with the array size. When the list is full, we resize the list and add 10 more elements. The program terminates by printing out the list of primes, 10 per line.

```cpp
#include <iostream.h>
#include <iomanip.h>

#include "array.h"

void main(void)
{
    // array holding primes begins with 10 elements
    Array<int>  A(10);

    // user supplies upperlimit which determines range of primes
    int    upperlimit, primecount = 0, i, j;

    cout << "Enter value >= 2 as upper limit for prime numbers:";
    cin >> upperlimit;

    A[primecount++] = 2;    // 2 is a prime
    for(i = 3; i < upperlimit; i++)
    {
        // if prime list is full, allocate 10 more elements
        if (primecount == A.ListSize())
            A.Resize(primecount + 10);

        // even numbers > 2 not prime. continue next iteration
        if (i % 2 == 0)
            continue;

        // check odd divisors 3,5,7,... up to i/2
        j = 3;
        while (j <= i/2 && i % j != 0)
            j += 2;

        // i prime if none of 3,5,7,... up to i/2 divides i
        if (j > i/2)
            A[primecount++] = i;
    }

    for (i = 0; i < primecount; i++)
    {
        cout << setw(5) << A[i];
```

```
        // output newline every 10 primes
        if ((i+1) % 10 == 0)
            cout << endl;
    }
    cout << endl;
}


/*
<Run of Program 8.3>

Enter a value >= 2 as the upper limit for prime numbers: 100
    2    3    5    7   11   13   17   19   23   29
   31   37   41   43   47   53   59   61   67   71
   73   79   83   89   97
*/
```

A String Class   8.5

Strings are a primary component in many non-numerical computing algorithms. They are used in areas such as pattern matching, compilation of programming languages, and data processing. As such, it is useful to have a string data type that encapsulates a variety of string handling operations and allows extensions. C++ string variables are null-terminated arrays of characters. Every C++ programming system supplies a library of functions in <string.h> to support string handling operations. In the hands of an experienced programmer, the functions are powerful tools to implement efficient string algorithms. However, for many applications, the functions are somewhat technical and clumsy to use.

Some languages, like BASIC, define operators to handle strings. For example, a BASIC string variable ends in $ and supports assignment with the "=" operator and string comparison with the "<" operator. The string type is part of the BASIC language definition:

```
NAME$ = "JOE"                              // assignment

IF $NAME < $STUDENTPRES THEN  . . .        // comparison
```

For some languages, compilers provide extensions that offer enhanced string handling capability. Most C++ programmers would like such an extension in order to have flexible access to strings.

This section develops a String class that defines a string type and provides a powerful set of string methods. Objects use dynamic memory to store variable-length strings and use operator overloading to create string expressions. The String class provides the user an alternative string type and yet allows full interaction with standard C++ strings, denoted by C++String. The String class is used in subsequent chapters of this book, and you will find its simplicity rewarding. To illustrate the use of the String class, consider the problem of comparing and assigning strings S and T. The following statements contrast the use of C++ library functions and the String class. We assign the smaller string to the variable first string.

C++ String Library Solution

```
if (strcmp(S,T) < 0)
    strcpy(firststring,S);
else
    strcpy(firststring,T);
```

String Class Solution

```
firststring = (S < T) ? S : T;
```

This section includes a complete listing of the String class declaration. We discuss the implementation of selected methods and provide a testing program. A complete listing of the String class is found in the file "strclass.h" in the program supplement. Section 8.6 introduces a pattern matching algorithm that makes extensive use of the String class.

- -

STRING CLASS SPECIFICATION

DECLARATION

```
#include <iostream.h>
#include <string.h>
#include <stdlib.h>

const int outOfMemory = 0, indexError = 1;

class String
{
    private:
        // pointer to the dynamically allocated string
        // length of the string includes the NULL character
        char *str;
        int  size;

        // error reporting function
        void Error(int errorType, int badIndex = 0) const;

    public:
        // constructors
        String(char *s = "");
        String(const String& s);

        // destructor
        ~String(void);
```

```
// assignment operators
// String=String, String=C++String
String& operator= (const String& s);
String& operator= (char *s);


// relational operators

// String==String, String==C++String, C++String==String
int operator== (const String& s) const;
int operator== (char *s) const;
friend int operator== (char *str, const String& s);


// String!=String, String!=C++String, C++String!=String
int operator!= (const String& s) const;
int operator!= (char *s) const;
friend int operator!= (char *str, const String& s);


// String<String, String<C++String, C++String<String
int operator< (const String& s) const;
int operator< (char *s) const;
friend int operator< (char *str, const String& s);


// String<=String, String<=C++String, C++ String<=String
int operator<= (const String& s) const;
int operator<= (char *s) const;
friend int operator<= (char *str, const String& s);


// String>String, String>C++String, C++String>String
int operator> (const String& s) const;
int operator> (char *s) const;
friend int operator> (char *str, const String& s);


// String>=String, String>=C++String, C++String>=String
int operator>= (const String& s) const;
int operator>= (char *s) const;
friend int operator>= (char *str, const String& s);


// String concatenation operators

// String+String, String+C++String, C++String+String
// String += String, String += C++String
String operator+ (const String& s) const;
String operator+ (char *s) const;
friend String operator+ (char *str,const String& s);
void operator+= (const String& s);
void operator+= (char *s);
```

```
        // String functions
        // begin at start, find c
        int Find(char c, int start) const;
        // find last occurrence of c
        int FindLast(char c) const;
        // extract a substring
        String Substr(int index,int count) const;
        // insert a String into String
        void Insert(const String& s, int index);
        // insert a C++String
        void Insert(char *s, int index);
        // delete a substring
        void Remove(int index, int count);

        // String indexing
        char& operator[] (int n);

        // convert String to C++String
        operator char* (void) const;

        // String I/O
        friend ostream& operator<< (ostream& ostr,
                                    const String& s);
        friend istream& operator>> (istream& istr,
                                    String& s);
        // read characters up to delimiter
        int ReadString(istream& is=cin,
                       char delimiter='\n');

        // additional methods
        Length(void) const;
        int IsEmpty(void) const;
        void Clear(void);
};
```

DESCRIPTION

String objects can interact with C++ strings (char *). This interaction is reflected when operators accept one parameter of each string type. For instance, three separate functions are provided for concatenating string variables using the "+" operator:

```
// String+String
String operator+ (const String& s);
// String+C++String
String operator+ (char *s);
// C++String+String
friend String operator+ (char *str,const String& s);
```

The String class has a destructor, copy constructor, and two overloaded assignment operators that allow the user to assign a String object or a C++ string to a new String object:

```
String S("Hello "), T = S, R;   // T = "Hello ", R is NULL
R = "World!";
```

The class implements a variety of string concatenation operators, including the operator "+=" for concatenating a string onto the current string:

```
R = T + "World!";   // R = "Hello World!"
R += " ";
R += S;             // R = "Hello World! Hello "
```

A series of relational operators uses ASCII ordering to compare two strings:

```
String U("Smith"), V("Smithsonian"), W("Thomas");

if (U >= V) . . .          // FALSE
if (W == "Thomas") . . .   // TRUE
if ("Tom" != W)      . . . // TRUE
```

A number of powerful and useful string operations are provided, including the ability to search for a particular character in a string, substring extraction, insertion of one string into another, and the deletion of a substring. Indexed access is provided for each character in the string, as if it were a simple character array.

```
int sindex;
String V ("Smithsonian");
// search for 's' beginning at index 0
sindex = V.Find('s',0);

R = V.Substr(sindex,3);    // R = "son"

V.Remove(sindex,6);        // V = "Smith"

R[0] = 'S';                // R = "Son"

R.Insert("ilvert",1);      // R = "Silverton"
```

The input operator ">>" uses whitespace to separate string input:

```
cin >> S >> T >> R;
<Input> Separate by blanks
   S = "Separate"   T = "by"   R = "blanks"
```

The ReadString method reads characters through the delimiter character, which is replaced by the NULL character:

```
R.ReadString(cin);
<Input> The fox leaped over the big brown dog<newline>
   R = "The fox leaped over the big brown dog"
```

Program 8.4   Using the String Class

This program illustrates selected methods in the String class. Each operation includes an output statement describing its action.

```cpp
#include <iostream.h>
#include "strclass.h"

#define TF(b)    ((b) ? "TRUE" : "FALSE")

void main(void)
{
    String s1("STRING "), s2("CLASS");
    String s3;
    int loc, i;
    char c, cstr[30];

    s3 = s1 + s2;
    cout << s1 << "concatenated with " << s2 << " = "
         << s3 << endl;
    cout << "Length of " << s2 << " = " << s2.Length() << endl;
    cout << "The first occurrence of 'S' in " << s2 << " = "
         << s2.Find('S',0) << endl;
    cout << "The last occurrence of 'S' in " << s2 << " is "
         << s2.FindLast('S') << endl;
    cout << "Insert 'OBJECT ' into s3 at position 7." << endl;
    s3.Insert("OBJECT ",7);
    cout << s3 << endl;

    s1 = "FILE1.S";
    for(i=0;i < s1.Length();i++)
    {
        c = s1[i];
        if (c >= 'A' && c <= 'Z')
        {
            c += 32;     // convert c to lower case
            s1[i] = c;
        }
    }
    cout << "The string 'FILE1.S' converted to lower case is ";
    cout << s1 << endl;

    cout << "Test relational operators with strings ";
    cout << "s1 = 'ABCDE'   s2 = 'BCF'" << endl;

    s1 = "ABCDE";
    s2 = "BCF";
```

```
       cout << "s1 < s2 is " << TF(s1 < s2) << endl;
       cout << "s1 == s2 is " << TF(s1 == s2) << endl;

       cout << "Use 'operator char* ()' to extract s1"
            << " to a C++ string: ";
       strcpy(cstr,s1);
       cout << cstr << endl;
}

/*
<Run of Program 8.4>

STRING concatenated with CLASS = STRING CLASS
Length of CLASS = 5
The first occurrence of 'S' in CLASS =  3
The last occurrence of 'S' in CLASS is 4
Insert 'OBJECT ' into s3 at position 7.
STRING OBJECT CLASS
The string 'FILE1.S' converted to lower case is file1.s
Test relational operators with strings s1 = 'ABCDE'   s2 = 'BCF'
s1 < s2 is TRUE
s1 == s2 is FALSE
Use 'operator char* ()' to extract s1 to a C++ string: ABCDE
*/
```

STRING CLASS IMPLEMENTATION

This section gives an overview of the String class implementation. The data members are a pointer variable str containing the address of a NULL-terminated string, and size, which holds the length of the string + 1, where the extra byte is used to store the NULL character. The value of size is thus the actual number of bytes of storage used for the string. If an operation modifies the size of the string, the old memory is deallocated and new memory is dynamically allocated to hold the modified string.

The str field in the String class is the address of a C++ string. The addition of the size field and, of course, access to the rich supply of member functions distinguish a String variable (object) from a C++ string variable.

Constructors and Destructor   The constructor creates a String object containing the C++String that is passed as a parameter. During the initialization process, it assigns the size, allocates dynamic memory and copies the C++String into the dynamically created data member str. By default, a NULL string is assigned. The copy constructor follows the same procedure but copies the string from an initial String object rather than a C++String. The destructor deletes the character array that holds the string.

```
// constructor. allocate memory and copy in a C++String
String::String(char *s)
{
```

```
   // length includes the NULL character
   size = strlen(s) + 1;

   // make room for string and NULL char and copy s.
   str = new char [size];
   // terminate program if memory is exhausted.
   if (str == NULL)
      Error(outOfMemory);
   strcpy(str,s);
}
```

Overloaded Assignment Operators   The assignment operator allows for the assignment of either a String object or a C++String to a String. For instance, assume the following declarations:

```
String  S("I am a String variable"), T;
// assigns a String to a String
T = S;
// assigns a C++String to a String
T = "I am a C++ String";
```

To assign a new String object s to the current object, compare the length of the two strings. If they differ, the operator deletes the current object's dynamic memory and reallocates s.size characters. It then copies s.str into the new memory.

```
// assignment operator. String to String
String& String::operator= (const String& s)
{
   // if sizes differ, delete current string and reallocate
   if (s.size != size)
   {
      delete [] str;
      str = new char [s.size];
      if(str == NULL)
         Error(outOfMemory);
      // assign size to be size of s
      size = s.size;
   }

   // copy s.str and return reference to current object
   strcpy(str,s.str);
   return *this;
}
```

Relational Operators   The String class provides a complete set of relational operators that compare strings in ASCII order. The operators compare two String objects or a String object with a C++String.

```
String S("Cat"), T("Dog");

// compare strings
if (S == T) . . .              // condition FALSE

if (T < "Tiger") . . .         // condition TRUE

if ("Aardvark" >= T) . . . // condition FALSE
```

The relational operator "==" tests for equality between a String object and the C++ string s. Note that the version of "==" that allows a C++ string variable to appear as the left operand must be overloaded as a friend function:

```
// C++String == String. a friend function
// since C++String on left
int operator== (char *str, const String& s)
{
    return strcmp(str,s.str) == 0;
}
```

String Operators   The class has a set of functions used to concatenate strings. Concatenation is done by overloading the "+" and "+=" operators. In the first case, concatenation returns a new string. The second case concatenates a string onto the current string. For instance, the string "Cool Water" is produced using three versions of the concatenation operator:

```
String S("Cool"), T("Water"), U, V;
U = S + T;             // concatenate two Strings
V = S + " Water";      // concatenate a String and a C++String
S += T;                // S is now "Cool Water"
```

The following code implements the "String + String" version of the concatenation operator. The function returns a String object that is the concatenation of the current String object and the String on the right. In the algorithm, we first create a String object temp, which holds size+s.size−1 characters including the NULL character. Note that when temp is declared, we first delete the NULL string created by the constructor. The method copies the characters from the current object to the new string and concatenates the characters from s. The string temp constitutes the return value.

```
// concatention: String + String
String String::operator+ (const String& s) const
{
    // build the new string with length len in temp
    String temp;
    int len;
```

```
    // delete the NULL string created when temp declared
    delete [] temp.str;

    // compute length of concatenated string and allocate
    // memory in temp
    len = size + s.size - 1;    // only one NULL terminator
    temp.str = new char [len];
    if (temp.str == NULL)
       Error(outOfMemory);

    // assign concatenated string size and build string
    temp.size = len;
    strcpy(temp.str,str);              // copy str to temp
    strcat(temp.str, s.str);           // concatenate s.str
    return temp;                       // return temp
}
```

String Functions   The method Substr returns a substring of the current string, which begins at position index and extends for count characters:

```
    String Substr(int index, int count);
```

Substr is used extensively in pattern matching algorithms. For instance,

```
    String S("Cool Water"), U;
    U = S.Substr(1,2);         // extracts 'oo' from Cool
```

If index exceeds the position of the last string character, the function returns the NULL string object. The number of characters in the string from index to the end of the string is (size−index−1). If count exceeds this value, use the tail of the string as the substring by assigning the value to count. To implement the method, allocate memory space for count+1 characters in an object temp. Copy count characters from position index in the string object to the newly created space in object temp and NULL terminate the string. Assign size for temp to be count+1 and return temp as the value of the function.

```
// return substring starting at index for count characters
String String::Substr(int index, int count) const
{
    // number of characters from index to end of string
    int charsLeft = size-index-1,i;

    // build substring in temp
    String temp;
    char *p, *q;
```

```
// return NULL string if index too large
if (index >= size-1)
    return temp;

// if count > remaining chars, use remaining chars
if (count > charsLeft)
    count = charsLeft;

// delete the NULL string created when temp declared
delete [] temp.str;

// allocate dynamic memory for the substring
temp.str = new char [count+1];
if (temp.str == NULL)
    Error(outOfMemory);

// copy count chars from str to temp.str
for(i=0,p=temp.str,q=&str[index];i < count;i++)
    *p++ = *q++;
// NULL terminate
*p = 0;

temp.size = count+1;
return temp;
}
```

Substr(3,3)

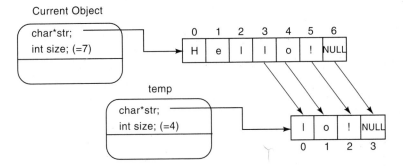

The member functions Find and FindLast search for the occurrence of a character in a string. They both return −1 if the character is not in the string. The method

```
int Find(char c, int start) const;
```

begins at position start and searches for the first occurrence of C. If the character is found, Find returns its position in the string. The method

```
int FindLast(char c) const;
```

searches for the last occurrence of c. If the character is found, FindLast returns its position in the string.

```
// return index of last occurrence of c in string
int String::FindLast(char c) const
{
    int ret;
    char *p;

    // use C++ library function strrchr. returns pointer to
    // the last occurrence of a character in the string
    p = strrchr(str,c);
    if (p != NULL)
        ret = int(p-str);   // compute index
    else
        ret = -1;               // return -1 on failure
    return ret;
}
```

String I/O   The string stream operators ">>" and "<<" are implemented by using the stream input and output operations for C++ strings. As a result, ">>" reads whitespace-separated words of text.

The method ReadString reads a line of text (up to 255 characters or a specified delimiter character) from a text file and incorporates it into a String. If no file parameter is passed, the input file defaults to cin. Input terminates on the delimiter, which is not retained in the string. A default value of newline ('\n') is used for the delimiter. ReadString returns the number of characters, which is −1 at end of file. For instance,

```
String S, T;

cin >> S;           // skips whitespace; reads next token
T.ReadSTring();     // reads up to end of line
cout << "The components are: " << S << " and " << T << endl;


<input>
Super! Grade A      // blank after! is part of T
<output>
The components are: Super! and Grade A
```

Use getline to read through the delimiter or up to 255 characters from the input stream istr into the character array tmp. If getline indicates end of file, return −1; otherwise, delete the existing dynamic array str and reallocate another of size = strlen(tmp) + 1. Copy tmp to the new array and return the number of characters read (size−1).

```
// read a line of text from stream istr
int String::ReadString (istream& istr, char delimiter)
{
    // read line into tmp
    char tmp[256];

    // if not eof, read line of up to 255 characters
    if (istr.getline(tmp, 256, delimiter))
    {
        // delete string and allocate memory for new one
        delete [] str;
        size = strlen(tmp) + 1;
        str = new char [size];
        if (str == NULL)
            Error(outOfMemory);

        // copy tmp. return number of chars read
        strcpy(str,tmp)
        return size-1;
    }
    else
        return -1;              // return -1 on end of file
}
```

8.6 Pattern Matching

A common pattern matching problem involves searching for one or more occurrences of a string in a text file. Most editors have a Search menu, which contains several pattern matching items such as Find, Replace, and Replace All.

```
┌─────────────────────────────────┐
│ Search                          │
├─────────────────────────────────┤
│  Find ...                       │
│  Find Again                     │
│                                 │
│  Replace                        │
│  Replace and Find Again         │
│  Replace All ...                │
│                                 │
│  Find in Next File              │
│                                 │
│  Go to Top                      │
│  Go to Bottom                   │
│  Go to Line # ...               │
└─────────────────────────────────┘
```

Find begins at the current location in the file and searches either forward or backward for the next occurrence of the pattern. Replace replaces the pattern matched with Find by another pattern. Replace All cycles through a file and replaces all occurrences of a pattern with a replacement pattern.

THE FIND PROCESS

Find is illustrated for a simple situation. Given string variables S and P, begin at a given position in S and look for pattern P. If it exists, return the index in S of the first character of the pattern. If P does not exist in S, return −1. For instance,

1. Given the string S = "aaacabc" and P = "abc", the pattern P is located beginning at position 4 in S.
2. If S = "Blue Bar ranch lies outside the city of the animals." and P = "the", then P appears twice in S at indices 28 and 40.
3. The pattern P = "aca" is not present in the string P = "acbaccacbcbcac".

Program 8.5 illustrates a pattern matching algorithm that makes use of the String class.

PATTERN MATCHING ALGORITHM

The algorithm is implemented by the function FindPat, which starts at position startindex of S and looks for the first occurrence of pattern P. We introduce the code first since our analysis of the algorithm makes specific reference to the variables in the function.

```
int FindPat(String S, String P, int startindex)
{
    // first and last character of the pattern and pattern length
    char    patStartChar, patEndChar;
    int     patLength;

    // index last char of the pattern
    int     patInc;

    // start at searchIndex and look for match of 1st char of
    // pattern. match found at index matchStart. check for match
    // at index matchEnd with last char of pattern.
    int     searchIndex, matchStart, matchEnd;

    // index of last character in S. matchEnd must be
    // less than or equal to this value
    int     lastStrIndex;
```

```
// if match at ends, copy interior substring to
// insidePattern
String insidePattern;

patStartChar = P[0];        // first character in the pattern
patLength = P.Length();     // length of the pattern
patInc = patLength-1;       // index last char in the pattern
patEndChar = P[patInc];     // last character in the pattern

// if pattern length > 2, extract all but the first and last
// characters of the pattern
if (patLength > 2)
    insidePattern = P.Substr(1,patLength-2);

lastStrIndex = S.Length()-1;    // index last char in S
// Start search from here to match 1st characters
searchIndex = startindex;

// look for match with 1st char of the pattern
matchStart = S.Find(patStartChar,searchIndex);
// index of last char of possible match
matchEnd = matchStart + patInc;

// repeatedly look for match at 1st char and then test
// the last char provided it is not
// past the end of the string.
while(matchStart != -1 && matchEnd <= lastStrIndex)
{
    // do 1st and last chars match?
    if (S[matchEnd]==patEndChar)
    {
        // if pattern one or two chars, we have a match
        if (patLength <= 2)
           return matchStart;

        // compare all but 1st and last characters
        if (S.Substr(matchStart+1,patLength-2) ==
                    insidePattern)
           return matchStart;
    }

        // pattern not found. continue search at next char
        searchIndex = matchStart+1;
        matchStart = S.Find(patStartChar,searchIndex);
        matchEnd = matchStart+patInc;
    }
    return -1;          // we did not find a match
}
```

The following steps outline the algorithm. References are made to the sample string •

```
S = b a d c a b c a b d a b c
```

and the pattern

```
P = a b c
```

1. The pattern is a block of text with a starting character patStartChar = P[0], length patLength = P.Length(), an increment patInc = patLength−1, which gives the index of the last character in the pattern and an ending character patEndChar = P[patInc]. As we will see in steps 3 and 4, the algorithm compares the first and last characters of a text block in S having patLength characters with the first and last characters in P. If the length of P (patLength) exceeds 2, we extract the substring of characters that does not include the first and last (P.Substr(1,patLength−2)) and assign this string to the variable insidePattern.

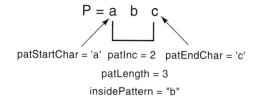

2. To mark the end of the string S, assign the index of the last character to lastStrIndex(S.Length()−1). The starting index (startIndex) can be 0 (search from the start of the string) or some positive value if you wish to start the search inside the string. Initialize searchIndex to have value startIndex. This variable serves as a launching point for an attempt to match the first character of the pattern.

3. Beginning at searchIndex, use the String method Find to search for a character in the string that matches patStartChar. Assign the index of the match to the variable matchStart. The variable matchEnd(matchStart + patInc) is the index of the last character of the string S that must match patEndChar. Terminate with failure if Find does not identify a match with patStartChar or matchEnd exceeds lastStrIndex.

4. Compare patEndChar with the last character of the text block in S (S[matchEnd] == patEndChar). If these characters do not match, we must proceed to step 5 and execute another series of comparisons. Comparing the last characters is an optimizing feature to keep us from needlessly testing for patterns that could not match. If the length of the pattern is 1 or 2 (patLength <= 2), we have a match and return index matchStart. Otherwise, compare the characters in the text block excluding the first and last(S.Substr(matchStart+1,patLength−2)) with the string insidePattern. If they match, return matchStart. In the sample,

matchStart = 1 and matchEnd = 3. The string block and the pattern match on
the ends. The strings insidePattern ="b" and S.Substr(2,1) = "d" do not match.

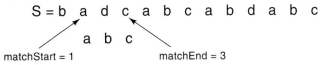

5. Repeat steps 3 and 4 but this time begin at index searchIndex = matchStart+1
   in the string. In the sample, the next match with the first character of P occurs
   at index 4.

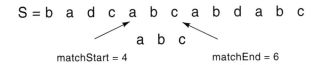

The last character of P and the last character of the text block match and so
do S.Substr(5,1) and insidePattern. Return the index 4(matchStart).

6. To find multiple occurrences of the pattern, call the function again with a starting
   index that is one greater than the last index returned by FindPat. For instance,
   continuing the search for "abc" produces the following results:

   • A possible match at index 7 fails.

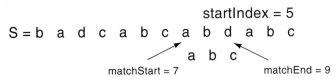

   • A possible match at index 10 succeeds. Return 10.

S = b a d c a b c a b d a b c
                                  a b c
          matchStart = 10   matchEnd =12

Program 8.5 Pattern Matching

The function FindPat implements the pattern matching algorithm just described.
It is located in the file "findpat.h".

This program reads a string object pattern and then begins reading the string
object linestr (a line of text) until the end of the file is reached. The function
FindPat is called to find the number of occurrences of the pattern in each line.
We then print the number of occurrences along with the line number.

```
#include <iostream.h>

#include "strclass.h"
#include "findpat.h"

void main()
{
    // define pattern string and string to search
    String pattern, lineStr;

    // search parameters
    int    lineno = 0, lenLineStr, startSearch, patIndex;

    // number of matches in current string
    int numberOfMatches;

    cout << "Enter the pattern to search for: ";
    pattern.ReadString();

    cout << "Enter a line or EOF: ";
    while(lineStr.ReadString() != -1)
    {
        // maintain line count and setup search parameters
        lineno++;
        lenLineStr = lineStr.Length();
        startSearch = 0;
        numberOfMatches = 0;

        // search for the pattern up to end of string
        while(startSearch <= lenLineStr-1 &&
        (patIndex = FindPat(lineStr,pattern,startSearch)) != -1)
        {
            numberOfMatches++;

            // continue search for next occurrence of pattern
            startSearch = patIndex+1;
        }
        cout << numberOfMatches << " matches on line "
            << lineno << endl;
        cout << "Enter a line or EOF: ";
    }
}

/*
<Run of Program 8.5>

Enter the pattern to search for: iss
Enter a line or EOF:
```

```
Alfred the snake hissed because he missed his Missy.
3 matches on line 1
Enter a line or EOF:
Mississippi
2 matches on line 2
Enter a line or EOF:
He blissfully walked down the sunny lane.
1 matches on line 3
Enter a line or EOF:
It is so.
0 matches on line 4
Enter a line or EOF:
*/
```

ANALYSIS OF THE PATTERN MATCHING ALGORITHM

Assume that the pattern has m characters and the string has n characters. If the first m characters of S match P, we find a match after m comparisons. The best case for the algorithm is thus $O(m)$. To determine a worst case estimate, assume that we do not execute the optimization feature where we compare the last characters. Furthermore, we assume that we always match the first characters but never the pattern. For instance, this is true if

```
P = "abc" and S = "aaaaaaaa" (m = 3, n = 8)
```

In this sample, the $m = 3$ characters of the pattern "abc" must be compared with text blocks in S a total of $n-m+1 = 6$ times. In the general case, we must compare m characters a total of $(n-m+1)$ times, for a total of $m(n-m+1)$ comparisons.

n − m+1 blocks, each requiring m comparisons

Since

```
m(n-m+1) ≤ m(n-m+m) = mn,
```

a worst case estimate for the algorithm is $O(mn)$.

Pattern matching is a very important topic in computer science and is extensively studied in the literature. For instance, the Knuth-Morris-Pratt pattern matching algorithm (Knuth, 1977) has computing time $O(m+n)$, which is superior to the simple algorithm we have presented.

8.7 Integral Sets

A set is a group of objects that is chosen from a collection called the **universal set.** A set is written as a list, separated by commas and enclosed in braces.

$$X = \{I_1, I_2, I_3, \ldots, I_m\}$$

- Set Union ($\cup$) $X \cup Y$ is the set containing all elements in X and all elements in Y, without duplication.
- Set Intersection ($\cap$) $X \cap Y$ is the set containing all elements that are in both X and Y.

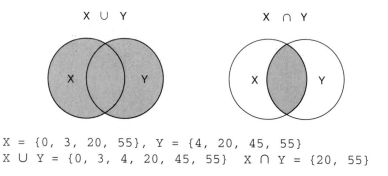

$$X = \{0, 3, 20, 55\}, \ Y = \{4, 20, 45, 55\}$$
$$X \cup Y = \{0, 3, 4, 20, 45, 55\} \quad X \cap Y = \{20, 55\}$$

- Set Membership ($\in$) $n \in X$ is TRUE if element n is a member of set X; otherwise, it is FALSE.

$$X = \{0, 3, 20, 55\} \ // \ 20 \in X \text{ is TRUE}, \ 35 \in X \text{ is FALSE}$$

SETS OF INTEGRAL TYPES

An **integral type** is any type whose members are represented by integer values. Types char, int of all sizes, and enumerations are called integral types. For instance, the ASCII character set corresponds to 8-bit integers in the range 0 to 127. While an application uses the traditional 'A', 'B', . . . representation of characters, their internal storage use integer codes 65, 66, and so forth. A programmer has the flexibility of using either representation.

```
char ch1 = 'A', ch2 = 97, ch3;

ch3 = ch1 + 4;                      // ch3 = 'E'
cout << ch2 << " " << int('A');    // print: a 65
```

In this section, we develop sets whose elements are of integral type. The universal set has a one-to-one correspondence with unsigned integers in the range 0 to setrange-1, where setrange is the number of elements in the set. Consider the following:

Set of digits = {0,1,2,3,4,5,6,7,8,9}
   corresponds to the range 0 . . . 9

Set of ASCII characters = {. . . , 'A', 'B', . . . , 'Z', . . .}
   corresponds to the range 0 . . . 127

enum Color (red, white, blue)
Set of Color
   corresponds to the range 0 . . . 2

We can implement a Set type by maintaining an array of 0 and 1 values. In the array, the value at location i is 1 (TRUE) if element i is in the set or 0 (FALSE) if it is not in the set. Written Exercise 6.13 discusses a method for implementing a set of integer values using a static array. This approach uses one integer value for each possible set member. We can allocate the array of integers dynamically.

```
// declare a set with elements in the range 0 to setrange-1
class Set
{
   private:
      int *member;          // pointer to the set array
      int setrange;
      . . .
   public:
      // constructor to allocate the set array
      Set(int n): setrange (n)
      {
         member = new int [setrange];
         . . .
      }
};
   . . .
Set S(20);                     // set of {0, . . . , 19}
n ∈ S ==> S.member[n] == 1 // entry is 1 if n in Set
```

The storage needed is dramatically reduced if we maintain the set using C++ bit handling operators. Furthermore, we can generalize the approach to handle any integral type by using templates.

C++ BIT HANDLING OPERATORS

The operators OR ("||"), AND ("&&"), and NOT ("!") are used in logical expressions to combine integral operands and return the result TRUE (1) or FALSE (0). The same operands can be evaluated with equivalent arithmetic operators that apply to their individual bits. The bit operators OR("|"), AND ("&"), NOT ("~"), and EOR ("^") are defined for individual bits and return values 0 and 1. Table 8.1 defines the operators. The operator EOR might not be familiar. The result is a 1 only if the two bits differ.

TABLE 8.1
Bit Operations

x	y	$\sim x$	$x \mid y$	$x \& y$	$x \wedge y$
0	0	1	0	0	0
0	1	1	1	0	1
1	0	0	1	0	1
1	1	0	1	1	0

The bit operations are applied to n-bit values by executing the operations on each bit. Assume

$$a = a_{n-1}a_{n-2} \ldots a_2a_1a_0 \quad b = b_{n-1}b_{n-2} \ldots b_2b_1b_0$$

The result c = a op b is given by

$$c = c_{n-1}c_{n-2} \ldots c_2c_1c_0 = a_{n-1}a_{n-2} \ldots a_2a_1a_0 \text{ op } b_{n-1}b_{n-2} \ldots b_2b_1b_0$$

where

$$c_i = a_i \text{ op } b_i, \ 0 \leq i \leq n-1 \text{ and op } = \text{ '}|\text{', '}\&\text{', '}\wedge\text{'}$$

The unary operator '~' inverts the bits of its operand.

EXAMPLE 8.4

The 8-bit numbers x = 11100011 and y = 01110110 are used with the operations a. x OR y, b. x AND y, and c. x EOR y.

a. x   11100011   b. x   11100011   c. x   11100011
   OR y <u>01110110</u>   AND y <u>01110110</u>   EOR y <u>01110110</u>
         11110111   01100010   10010101
d. ~x = 00011100

C++ also provides bit shifting operators that shift the bits in a number left ("<<") or right (">>"). The expression a << n multiples a by 2^n, and a >> n divides a by 2^n. Generally, using a bit operator speeds up any computation that involves multiplying or dividing an integer value by a power of 2.

The bit operators are typically used with unsigned integer operands. We will apply them only in this case.

EXAMPLE 8.5

Assume that the variables x, y, and z are defined as follows:

```
// each variable is 16 bits
unsigned short x = 10, y = 13, z;
```

Parts a–d illustrate bit operator calculations.

```
a.  z = x | y;           // z = 15
b.  z = x & y;           // z = 8
c.  z = ~0 << 2;         // z = 65532
d.  z = ~x & (y >> 2);   // z = 1
```

- -

SET CLASS SPECIFICATION

In the Set class, an object consists of a list of elements selected from an integral type whose range of values is 0. . . setrange−1. The integral type is identified by the template type name T. We assume that the int converter is defined for the type T and that an integer value can be explicitly converted to type T. For instance, let val be an element of type T and I be an integer variable:

```
T val;
int I ;
```

If I is the integer equivalent of the data item val, then

```
I = int(T) and val = T(I)
```

EXAMPLE 8.6

a. Char is an integral type.

```
char c = 'A';
int i;

i = int(c);     // i = 65
c = char(i);    // c = 'A'
```

b. An enumerated type is an integral type.

```
enum Days {Sun,Mon,Tues,Wed,Thurs,Fri,Sat};

Days day = Thurs;
int d;

d = int(day);   // d = 4
day = Days (d); // day = Thurs
```

REPRESENTING SET ELEMENTS

Using the C++ bit operators, individual bits in a word are used to efficiently implement a Set object. The range of set values (0 . . setrange−1) is stored in a dynamic array of 16-bit unsigned integers. The array, called member, links the integers in the range 0 . . . setsize−1 as a chain of bits. Each bit represents one set element, and an element is in the set if the bit is 1. The set element 0 is represented by the right-most bit of the first array element, and 15 is represented by the left-most bit of the first array element. We continue with the right-most bit of the second array element representing 16, and so forth. The storage scheme is illustrated by the following figure.

```
15 14 13 12 11 10 9 8 7 6 5 4 3 2 1 0    31 30 29 28 27 26 25 24 23 22 21 20 19 18 17 16
 1  0  0  0  0  0 1 0 0 0 1 0 0 0 0 1      0  0  0  1  0  0  0  0  0  0  0  0  0  0  1  0  ...
           member[0]                                     member[1]
```

In this case, the integral values 0, 5, 9, 15, 17, and 28 are in the set.

DECLARATION

```cpp
#include <iostream.h>
#include <stdlib.h>

enum ErrorType
{
    InvalidMember, ExpectRightBrace, MissingValue,
    MissingComma, InvalidChar, MissingLeftBrace,
    InvalidInputData, EndOfFile, OutOfMemory,
    InvalidMemberRef, SetsDifferentSize
};

template <class T>
class Set
{
    private:
        // max number of elements in the set
        int setrange;

        // number of bytes in bit array and the array pointer
        int arraysize;
        unsigned short *member;

        // fatal error utility function
        void Error(ErrorType n) const;

        // implement the mapping of set elements to bits
        // within 16-bit short integers
        int ArrayIndex(const T& elt) const;
        unsigned short BitMask(const T& elt) const;
```

```
    public:
        // constructor. create an empty set
        Set(int setrange);

        // copy constructor
        Set(const Set<T>& x);

        // destructor
        ~Set(void);

        // assignment operator
        Set<T>& operator= (const Set<T>& rhs);

        // element membership
        int IsMember(const T& elt);

        // set equality
        int operator== (const Set<T>& x) const;

        // set union
        Set operator+ (const Set<T>& x) const;
        // set intersection
        Set operator* (const Set<T>& x) const;

        // set insertion/deletion operations
        void Insert(const T& elt);
        void Delete(const T& elt);

        // Set stream I/O operators
        friend istream& operator>> (istream& istr,
                                    Set<T>& x);
        friend ostream& operator<< (ostream& ostr,
                                    const Set<T>& x);
};
```

DESCRIPTION

The template class Set implements a set of integral values. The type T may be any type for which i = int(v) and v = T(i) apply, where v and i are given by the declarations

```
    T v;
    int i;
```

The constructor creates an empty Set, and the arithmetic operators are used to define the set operations of union ("+"), intersection ("*"), and equality ("=="). The Insert and Delete methods as well as the assignment operator are used to update a Set.

The I/O operations enter and print sets with braces surrounding elements separated by commas.

Example:

```
// set of integers in range 0..24
Set<int> S(25);
// set of ASCII characters
Set<char> T(128), U(128);

cin >> S;            // input {4,7,12}
S.Insert(5);
cout << S << endl;   // output {4, 5, 7, 12}
cin >> T;            // input {a,e,i,o,u,y}
U = T;               // U = {a,e,i,o,u,y}
T.Delete('y');
cout << T << endl;   // output {a, e, i, o, u}

if (T*U == T)
    cout << T << " is a subset of " << U << endl;
```

The implementation of the Set class is contained in the file "set.h".

The Set class provides the client the ability to create sets of user-defined enumerated types and sets of standard integral types, such as int and char. If set I/O for enumerated types is desired, the stream operators must be overloaded.

EXAMPLE 8.7

Consider the enumerated type

```
enum Days {Sun,Mon,Tues,Wed,Thurs,Fri,Sat};
```

The program supplement contains the overloaded operator "<<" for this type. It is found along with a main program in the file "enumset.cpp".
The following declarations and statements illustrate the use of these tools.

```
// declare 4 objects that represent different sets of days
Set<Days> weekdays(7), weekend(7), week(7);

// array wd and we define lists of days in the week. the
// lists initialize the set objects weekdays and weekend
Days wd[] = {Mon,Tues,Wed,Thurs,Fri}, we[] = {Sat,Sun};
```

```
// insert array values into the sets
for(int i=0;i < 5;i++)
    weekdays.Insert(wd[i]);
for(i=0;i < 2;i++)
    weekend.Insert(we[i]);


// print the sets in bracket notation
cout << weekdays << endl;
cout << weekend << endl;


// form the union ('+') of the two sets and print it
week = weekdays + weekend;
cout << week << endl;


<Run>


{Mon, Tues, Wed, Thurs, Fri}
{Sun, Sat}
{Sun, Mon, Tues, Wed, Thurs, Fri, Sat}
```

THE SIEVE OF ERATOSTHENES

The Greek mathematician and philosopher Eratosthenes lived in the 3rd century B.C. He discovered an intriguing method of using sets to find all primes less than or equal to an integer value n. The algorithm begins by initializing a set to contain all the elements in the range 2 to n. Through repeated passes over the elements in the set, we shake elements free and they pass through the sieve. At the end, only prime numbers remain. The sieve starts with its smallest number $m=2$ that serves as a key value. We scan the set and remove all the higher multiples (factor > 1) $2*m$, $3*m$, ..., $k*m$ of the key that remain in the set. These multiples cannot be primes since they are divisible by m. The next larger number in the sieve is the key $m=3$, which is prime. As with the initial value 2, we remove all higher multiples of 3 starting at 6. Since 6, 12, 18, and so forth have already been removed as multiples of 2, this pass deletes 9, 15, 21, ... As the process continues, we move to the next larger number in the set, which is the prime number 5. Recall that 4 was removed as a multiple of 2. With 5, we pass over the elements and remove any higher multiple of 5 (25, 35, 55, ...). The process continues until we have scanned the set and removed multiples for each key value. The numbers that remain in the sieve are the prime numbers in the range 2 .. n.

EXAMPLE 8.8
___

This figure illustrates the sieve of Eratosthenes by finding all the prime numbers in the range 2 .. 25.

Sieve of Eratosthenes: n = 25

Delete multiples of 2

| 2 | 3 | 4 | 5 | 6 | 7 | 8 | 9 | 10 | 11 | 12 | 13 | 14 | 15 | 16 | 17 | 18 | 19 | 20 | 21 | 22 | 23 | 24 | 25 |

Delete multiples of 3

| 2 | 3 | 5 | 7 | 9 | 11 | 13 | 15 | 17 | 19 | 21 | 23 | 25 |

Delete multiples of 5

| 2 | 3 | 5 | 7 | 11 | 13 | 17 | 19 | 23 | 25 |

7,11,13,17,19,and 23 contain no multiples in the set

Primes {2,3,5,7,11,13,19,23}

The sieve works since it removes all numbers that are not primes. To verify this, assume that a composite (non-prime) number m remains in the sieve. Such a number can be written as

```
m = p*k,   p > 1
```

where p is a prime in the range from 2 to m−1. In the sieve algorithm, p would be a key value and m would be removed since it is a multiple of p.

___

Program 8.6   The Sieve of Eratosthenes
___

The function PrintPrimes implements the sieve. The algorithm uses an optimization feature by looking at key values m in the range $2 \leq m \leq \sqrt{n}$. This limited number of key values still removes all non-prime numbers from the set. To verify the fact, assume some composite number t = p * q remains. If both factors p and q were greater than $\sqrt{n}$,

```
t = p * q > √n * √n = n
```

and t is not in the set. Thus, one factor p must be $\leq \sqrt{n}$. This small factor would be a key value or a multiple of a key value and hence t would be removed as a multiple of a key. Rather than compute the square root of n, we test all numbers m such m*m $\leq$ n.

___

```
#include <iostream.h>
#include <iomanip.h>
```

```
#include "set.h"      // use the Set class

// compute and print all primes <= n using the
// Sieve of Eratosthenes
void PrintPrimes(int n)
{
   // set(sieve) must handle values 2..n
   Set<int> S(n+1);
   int m, k, count;

   // insert all values 2..n into the set
   for(m=2;m <= n;m++)
      S.Insert(m);

   // look at all numbers from 2 to sqrt(n)
   for(m=2;m*m <= n;m++)
      // if m in S, delete all multiples of m from set
      if(S.IsMember(m))
         for(k=2*m;k <= n;k += m)
            if (S.IsMember(k))
               S.Delete(k);

   // all elements remaining in S are prime.
   // print the primes 10 per line
   count = 1;
   for(m=2;m <= n;m++)
      if (S.IsMember(m))
      {
         cout << setw(3) << m << " ";
         if (count++ % 10 == 0)
            cout << endl;
      }
   cout << endl;
}

void main(void)
{
   int n;

   cout << "Enter n: ";
   cin >> n;
   cout << endl;

   PrintPrimes(n);
}

/*
<Run of Program 8.6>
```

```
Enter n: 100
    2     3     5     7    11    13    17    19    23    29
   31    37    41    43    47    53    59    61    67    71
   73    79    83    89    97
*/
```

SET CLASS IMPLEMENTATION

The private methods ArrayIndex and BitMask implement the storage scheme. ArrayIndex determines the array element to which a value elt belongs. Simply divide by 16, efficiently implementing the division by shifting four bits to the right.

```
// determine the index of the array element
// containing the bit representing elt
template <class T>
int Set<T>::ArrayIndex(const T& elt) const
{
    // convert elt to int and shift
    return int(elt) >> 4;
}
```

When the correct array index is located, BitMask returns an unsigned short value containing a 1 in the bit position representing elt. This **mask** can be used to set or clear the bit.

```
// create an unsigned short value with a 1
// in the bit position of elt
template <class T>
unsigned short Set<T>::BitMask(const T& elt) const
{
    // use & to find remainder after dividing by
    // 16. 0 stays in right-most bit, 15 goes on far left
     return 1 << (int(elt) & 15);
}
```

Error Handling   The class responds to a collection of error conditions by calling the private member function Error. An enum type ErrorType is used for convenient naming of the possible errors. The function is passed an ErrorType parameter that is used in a switch statement to identify the error and terminate the program. Error is implemented in the program supplement.

The Set Constructors   There are two constructors that create a set object, one that creates an empty set and a copy constructor. An empty set is built by determining the number of arraysize unsigned short array elements needed to represent the range of data values, allocating the array, and then filling it with 0 values.

```
// constructor. create an empty set
template <class T>
Set<T>::Set(int sz): setrange(sz)
{
    // number of unsigned shorts needed to hold set elements
    arraysize = (setrange+15) >> 4;

    // allocate the array
    member = new unsigned short [arraysize];
    if (member == NULL)
        Error(OutOfMemory);

    // create an empty set by setting all bits to 0
    for (int i = 0; i < arraysize; i++)
        member[i] = 0;
}
```

Set Operators   The binary operations of union and intersection are implemented
by overloading the C++ operators "+" and "*". For the union operator ("+"),
construct a set object tmp containing elements in the range 0 .. setrange − 1.
Assign its elements to be the bitwise OR of the array elements representing the
current set and set x. Return this new set as the value of the method. Note that we
invoke an error if the two sets do not have the same size.

```
// form and return the union of the current Set
// object and object x
template <class T>
Set<T> Set<T>::operator+ (const Set<T>& x) const
{
    // the sets must have the same range
    if (setrange != x.setrange)
        Error(SetsDifferentSize);

    // form the union in tmp
    Set<T> tmp(setrange);

    // each array element of tmp is the bitwise
    // OR of the current object and x
    for (int i = 0; i < arraysize; i++)
        tmp.member[i] = member[i] | x.member[i];

     // return the union
     return tmp;
}
```

Like union, the intersection operation ("*") creates a set object tmp, which is
the intersection. We create the new set by forming the bitwise AND of the array
elements in the current set and x. Return the new set as the value of the method.

The method IsMember determines set membership and returns TRUE if the bit corresponding to elt is 1 and FALSE otherwise.

```
// determine whether elt is in the set
template <class T>
int Set<T>::IsMember(const T& elt)
{
    // is int(elt) in range 0 to setrange-1 ?
    if (int(elt) < 0 || int(elt) >= setrange)
        Error(InvalidMemberRef);

    // return the bit corresponding to elt
     return member[ArrayIndex(elt)] & BitMask(elt);
}
```

Set Insertion and Deletion   Insertion is implemented by setting the bit corresponding to the parameter elt.

```
// insert elt into the set
template <class T>
void Set<T>::Insert(const T& elt)
{
    // is int(elt) in range 0 to setrange-1 ?
    if (int(elt) < 0 || int(elt) >= setrange)
        Error(InvalidMemberRef);

    // set bit corresponding to elt
    member[ArrayIndex(elt)] |= BitMask(elt);
}
```

Deletion turns off the bit corresponding to elt. The process uses the AND operator and a mask that contains all 1s except for the specific "elt" bit. The mask is created by using the complement operator "~".

```
// delete elt from the set
template <class T>
void Set<T>::Delete(const T& elt)
{
    // is int(elt) in range 0 to setrange-1 ?
    if (int(elt) < 0 || int(elt) >= setrange)
        Error(InvalidMemberRef);

    // clear the bit corresponding to elt. note
    // that ~BitMask(elt) has a 0 in the bit
    // we are interested in a 1 in all others
    member[ArrayIndex(elt)] &= ~BitMask(elt);
}
```

Set I/O   The stream operators ">>" and "<<" are overloaded to implement Set stream I/O. The Input operator ">>" reads set x in the format $\{i_0, i_1, \ldots, i_m\}$. The set elements are enclosed in brackets and are separated by commas. Each integral value i_n represents a member of the set. The output operator ("<<") writes set x in the format $\{i_0, i_1, \ldots, i_m\}$, where $i_0 < i_1 < \ldots < i_m$ are the elements in the set.

Input is the most difficult method to implement. It skips whitespace using the single character input function get, and then checks to see if the current character is "{". If not, the error method is called, which prints an error message and terminates the program. Once the leading brace is found, the method moves through the comma-separated list of integral values and adds each element to the set. Error checking is done to ensure that commas are correctly placed and that the set elements stay in the range 0 to setrange-1. Any amount of whitespace can be used to separate items in the list.

Written Exercises

8.1   Declare an array of 10 integers and a pointer to an int:

```
int a[10], *p;
```

Consider the following statements:

```
for(i=0;i < 2;i++)
{
    p = new int[5];
    for (j=0;j < 5;j++)
        a[5*i+j] = *p++ = i+j;
}
```

(a)   Give the output for the statements:

```
for(i=0;i < 10;i++)
    cout << a[i] << " ";
cout << endl;
```

(b)   Discuss whether the statement

```
p = p - 10;
```

resets p to the beginning of the initial dynamic list.

(c)   Assume that q is a pointer to the initial dynamic list. Does this code produce the same output as a?

```
for(i=0;i < 10;i++)
    cout << *(q+i) << " ";
cout << endl;
```

8.2 For each declaration, use the operator new to dynamically allocate the specified memory.

(a) `int* px;`

   Create an integer pointed to by px having value 5.

(b) ```
     long *a;
     int n;
     cin >> n;
     ```

   Create a dynamic array of n long integers pointed to by a.

(c)  ```
     struct DemoC
     {
         int one;
         long two;
         double three;
     }
     DemoC *p;
     ```

   Create a node pointed to by p. Then assign the fields to be {1, 500000,3.14}.

(d) ```
     struct DemoD
     {
         int one;
         long two;
         double three;
         char name[30];
     };
     DemoD *p;
     ```

   Dynamically create a node pointed to by p and assign the fields to be {3, 35, 1.78, "Bob C++").

(e)  Give statements that deallocate the memory for each part a–d.

**8.3** For the class DynamicInt, the constructor uses the new operator to dynamically allocate an integer and assign its address to data value pn. The public methods GetVal and SetVal store and fetch data from the dynamic memory.

```
class DynamicInt
{
   private:
      int *pn;
   public:
      // constructor and copy constructor
      DynamicInt(int n = 0);
      DynamicInt(const DynamicInt& x);
```
```

```
            // destructor
            ~DynamicInt(void);

            // assignment operator
            DynamicInt& operator= (const DynamicInt& x);

            // data handling methods
            int GetVal(void);        // get integer value
            void SetVal(int n);      // set integer value
            // conversion operator
            operator int(void);      // return integer value


            // stream input and output
            friend ostream& operator<< (ostream& ostr,const Dy-
                                        namicInt& x);
            friend istream& operator>> (istream& istr,
                                        DynamicInt& x);
    };
```

(a)   Write code to implement the constructor and destructor methods.
(b)   Write the methods that overload the assignment operator "=" and implement the copy constructor.
(c)   Implement GetVal, operator int, and SetVal.
(d)   Implement the stream I/O functions so they read and write the value of the *pn.

8.4   Use the declaration of DynamicInt from Written Exercise 8.3 for the following exercises.

(a)   ```DynamicInt *p;```

Give the declaration to allocate a single object whose initial data value is 50.

(b)   ```DynamicInt *p;```

Allocate an array p with three elements. What is the data value for each object in the array?

(c)   ```DynamicInt a[10];```

Indicate how you would declare an array of 10 objects of type DynamicInt and initialize each element to have value 100?

(d)   Give the delete statements that deallocate the dynamic memory used in a–c.

8.5   Write the DynamicInt class of Written Exercise 8.3 as the template class DynamicType.

```
        template <class T>
        class DynamicType
        {
           private:
               T *pt;
```

```
        public:
            // constructor and copy constructor
            DynamicType(T value);
            DynamicType(const DynamicType<T>& x);

            // destructor
            ~DynamicType(void);

            // assignment operator
            DynamicType<T>& operator= (const DynamicType<T>& x);

            // data handling methods
            T GetVal(void);          // retrieve value
            void SetVal(T value);   // set value
            // conversion operator
            operator T(void);        // return value

            // stream input and output
            friend ostream& operator<< (ostream& ostr, const
                                        DynamicType<T>& x);
            friend istream& operator>> (istream& istr,
                                        DynamicType<T>& x);
    };
```

8.6 This exercise uses the classes DynamicInt and DynamicType developed in Written Exercises 8.3 and 8.5. Declare the object:

```
    DynamicType< DynamicInt > D(DynamicInt(5));
```

What is the output from the following statements?

```
    cout << D << endl;
    cout << D.GetVal().GetVal() << endl;
    cout << int(D.GetVal()) << endl;
    cout << DynamicInt(D) << endl;
    cout << int(DynamicInt(D)) << endl;
```

8.7 Consider the class ReadFile declared as follows:

```
    class ReadFile
    {
        private:
            // character stream read from fin to dynamically
            // allocated array buffer with bufferSize characters
            ifstream fin;
            char *buffer;
            int bufferSize;
```

```
    public:
        // constructor is passed file name and buffer size
        ReadFile(char *name, int size);
        // print error message and return
        ReadFile(const ReadFile& f);
        // delete buffer and close fin
        ~ReadFile(void);
        // print error message and return
        void operator= (const ReadFile x);
        // read next line from file. return 0 if end of file
        int Read(void);
        // copy the current line to buf
        void CopyBuffer(char *buf);
        // print current line to cout
        void Printbuffer(void);
    };
```

(a) Implement the class.
(b) Write a function

```
    void LineNum(ReadFile& f);
```

that reads f and lists the corresponding file with line numbers.

8.8 The class DynamicType is developed in Written Exercise 8.5. Assuming the following declarations, answer each question.

```
    DynamicType<int> *p, Q;
    DynamicType<char> *c;
```

(a) Write a statement that allocates a DynamicType object with value 5 pointed to by p.
(b) Print the value 5 allocated in *p using three different methods.
(c) Is each statement valid? If so, what is its action?

```
    c = new DynamicType<char> [65];
    c = new DynamicType<char> (65);
```

(d) If the input is 35, what is the output?

```
    cin >> *p;
    Q = *p;
    cout << Q << endl;
```

(e) Using the value of Q from d, what is the output?

```
    DynamicType<int> R(Q);

    cout << Q << endl;
```

(f)   What is output?

```
Q = DynamicType<int> (68);
c = DynamicType<char> (char(int (Q)));

cout << c << char(c) << int(c) << endl;
```

(g)   Write statements that delete objects *p and *c. What happens if you execute?

```
delete Q;
```

8.9   (a)   If CL is a class, explain why you cannot declare its copy constructor as follows:

```
CL(const CL x);
```

(b)   Explain why in general you would not want to declare the assignment operator for CL as follows:

```
void operator= (const CL& x);
```

8.10   (a)   What is the meaning of the keyword this? Explain why it is valid only inside a member function.

(b)   Name a primary use for this.

8.11   The class Rational of Chapter 6 implements rational number arithmetic. The "+=" operator is to be added to the class. Explain why the following implementation is correct.

```
Rational& Rational::operator+= (const Rational& r)
{
    *this = *this + r;
    return *this;
}
```

8.12   The class ArrCL implements array bounds checking using an overloaded array indexing operator "[]" and pointer conversion. It contains an array of 50 elements and a length field. When creating an object of type ArrCL, the client can stipulate a maximum length for the list and pass this value as a parameter to the constructor.

```
const int ARRAYSIZE = 50;

template <class T>
class ArrCL
{
    private:
        T arr[ARRAYSIZE];
        int length;
    public:
        // constructor
        ArrCL(int n = ARRAYSIZE);
```

```
      // return size of list
      int ListSize(void) const;

      // index operator implementing a "safe array"
      T& operator[] (int n);

      // pointer conversion. return address arr.
      operator T* (void) const;
};
```

The size of the embedded list arr is bounded by ARRAYSIZE = 50. If the client attempts to reserve an array of greater size, the constructor sets the size to ARRAYSIZE and prints a warning message.

(a)   Write declarations that reserve a 20-integer array A, a 50-element char array B, and a 25-element float array C.

(b)   Is there a problem with this loop?

```
      ArrCL<long> A(30);

      for(int i=0;i <= 30;i++)
         A[i] = 0;
```

(c)   Explain why the output is 420   420

```
      int Sum1(const ArrCl<int>& A)
      {
         int s = 0;

         for(int i=0;i<A.ListSize();i++)
            s += A[i];
         return s;
      }
   int Sum2(int *A, int n)
   {
      int s = 0;

      for(int i=0;i < n;i++)
         s += *A++;
      return s;
   }
   . . .
   ArrCL<int> arr(20);

   for(int i=0;i < 20;i++)
      arr[i] = 2*(i+1);
   cout << Sum1(arr) << " " << Sum2(arr,20) << endl;
```

(d)   Implement the class.

8.13   Consider the declarations:

```
String A("Have a ", B("nice day!"), C(A), D=B;
```

  (a)   What is the value of C?
  (b)   What is the value of D?
  (c)   Give the value of D = A + B;
  (d)   Give the value of C += B?

8.14   Consider the strings:

```
String S("abc12xya52cba"), T;
```

  (a)   What is the value of S.FindLast('c')?
  (b)   What is the value of S[6]?
  (c)   What is the value of S[3]?
  (d)   What is the value of S[24]?
  (e)   What is the value of T = S.Substr(5,6)?
  (f)   What is the value of T after

```
T = S;
T.Insert("ABC",5);
```

8.15   Make the following declarations:

```
#define TF(b)   ((b) ? "TRUE" : "FALSE")

String s1("STRING "), s2("CLASS");
String s3;

int loc, i;
char c, cstr[30];
```

Determine the output of each statement sequence.

  (a)
```
s3 = s1 + s2;
cout << s1 << "concatenated with " << s2
     << " = " << s3 << endl;
```

  (b)
```
cout << "Length of " << s2 << " = "
     << s2.Length() << endl;
```

  (c)
```
cout << "The first occurrence of 'S' in " << s2
     << " = " << s2.Find('S',0) << endl;
cout << "The last occurrence of 'S' in " << s2
     << " = " << s2.FindLast('S') << endl;
```

  (d)
```
cout << "Insert 'OBJECT ' into s3 at position 7."
     << endl;
s3 = s1 + s2;
s3.Insert("OBJECT ",7);
cout << s3 << endl;
```

```
(e)   s1 = "FILE1.S";
      for(i=0;i < s1.Length();i++)
      {
         c = s1[i];
         if (c >= 'A' && c <= 'Z')
         {
            c += 32;
            s1[i] = c;
         }
      }
      cout << s1 << endl;

(f)   s1 = "ABCDE";
      s2 = "BCF";

      cout << "s1 < s2 = " << TF(s1 < s2) << endl;
      cout << "s1 == s2 = " << TF(s1 == s2) << endl;

(g)   s1 = "Testing pointer conversion operator.";
      strcpy(cstr,s1);
      cout << cstr << endl;
```

8.16 Assume that the variables x, y, and z are defined as follows:

```
      unsigned short x = 14, y = 11, z;
```

What value is assigned to z as a result of each statement?

```
(a)   z = x | y;
(b)   z = x & y;
(c)   z = ~0 << 4;
(d)   z = ~x & (y >> 1);
(e)   z = (1 << 3) & x;
```

8.17 This exercise presents four functions that perform bit handling operations. Match each function with one of the following descriptive phrases:

(a)   Determine the number of bits in an int for a particular machine.
(b)   Return the numerical value of the n bits beginning at bit position p.
(c)   Invert n bits beginning a bit position p. Bit position 0 is the left-most bit of the integer value.
(d)   Rotate the bits of an integer clockwise.

```
         unsigned int one(unsigned int n, int b)
         {
            int rightbit;
            int lshift = three() - 1;
            int mask = (unsigned int) ~0 >> 1;

            while (b--)
            {
```

```
            rightbit = n & 1;
            n = (n >> 1) & mask;
            rightbit = rightbit << lshift;
            n = n | rightbit;
        }
        return n;
}

unsigned int two(unsigned int x, int p, int n)
{
    unsigned int mask = (unsigned int) ~(~0 << n);

    return (x >> (p-n+1)) & mask;
}

int three(void)
{
    int i;
    unsigned int u = (unsigned int) ~0;

    for(i=1;u = u >>1;i++);
    return i;
}

unsigned int four(unsigned int x, int p, int n)
{
    unsigned int mask;
    mask = ~0
    return x ^ (~(mask >> n) >> p);
}
```

8.18   Add the operator difference ("−") to the Set class. The operator takes two set parameters, X and Y, and returns the set consisting of elements in X that are not in Y. Require that the two sets have the same number of elements.

X − Y

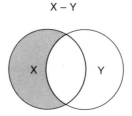

```
X = {0, 3, 7, 9}, Y = {4, 7, 8, 10, 15}
X - Y = {0, 3, 9}
```

```
template <class T>
Set<T> Set<T>::operator - (const Set<T> &x);
```

(HINT: Compute diff.member[i] = member[i] & ~x.member[i])

8.19 Add the complement operator (~) to the Set class. This unary operator returns a set that consists of all the values in the universal set that are not in X.

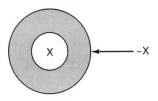

```
Set<int> X(10), Y(10);

for(int i=0;i < 10;i += 2)
    X.Insert(i);
Y = ~X; // X = {1,3,5,7,9}
```

8.20 (a) Use the complement operator to create the universal set as a Set object.
       (b) Implement the difference operator in Written Exercise 8.18 with the complement and intersection operators.

Programming Exercises

8.1 This exercise uses the DynamicInt class developed in Written Exercise 8.3.

(a) Overload the operator "<" for DynamicInt as an external function. It may not be a friend of the class.

(b) Write a function

```
DynamicInt *Initialize(int n);
```

that returns a pointer to an array of n dynamically allocated objects. Initialize the object values to be random integers in the range 1. .1000.

(c) The main program should read an integer n and use Initialize to create an array of DynamicInt objects. Use the template-based exchange sort of Chapter 7 to sort the list. Print the resulting list.

8.2 This program uses the ReadFile class of Written Exercise 8.7. Use the function LineNum to read a file and print it to the screen with line numbers.

8.3 This program uses the ReadFile class of Written Exercise 8.7.

(a) Write a function

```
void CapLine(ReadFile& f, char *capline);
```

that reads the next line from a file f, capitalizes it, and returns the line in capline.

(b) Use the function to read a file and print it in uppercase.

8.4 This exercise uses the ArrCL class in Written Exercise 8.12. Create a safe array with 10 integers and then ask the user to input 10 data items. After calling the template-based exchange sort in the file "arrsort.h", print the ordered list. Attempt to access A[10] to produce an error message and program termination.

8.5 This exercise modifies the template-based Stack class developed in Chapter 7 ("tstack.h"). Replace the static array data member stacklist by an Array object initially containing MaxStackSize elements. Eliminate the stack size parameter from the constructor and rewrite the Push method so the stack size grows as needed. Test your modifications by pushing the integer values 1 . . 100 on the stack and then deleting them, printing every 10*th* value.

8.6 Read a file using the stream method getline and store the strings in an Array object called a string pool. Insert a line into the pool by doing a Resize operation to add sufficient space to the pool, and place the starting index of the line in an array of string indices, resizing it if necessary. This array will identify the starting location of each successive string in the pool. Enter an integer N and print the last N lines of the file. If the file has fewer than N lines, print the entire file.

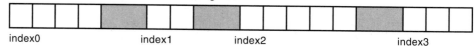

Array of String Indices

index0	index1	index2	index3

String Pool

index0   index1   index2   index3

8.7 Modify Program 8.3 by maintaining a list of all the prime numbers you have computed so far. For the next integer n in the sequence, test only the primes in your list rather than all the divisors from 3 to n/2. If none of the primes in the list divide n, then n is a new prime that can be added to the list. This fact is derived from the mathematical result that any number can be written as a product of its prime divisors.

8.8 (a) Write a function

```
void Replace(String& source, int pos,
             const String& repstr);
```

that replaces repstr.Length() characters of S starting at index pos. If fewer than repstr.Length() characters exist in the tail of S, insert all the characters of repstr.

(b) Write a function

```
void Center(String& S);
```

that calls Replace to print S centered within an 80-character line of "%" characters.

Write a main program which tests (a) and (b).

8.9 Read an integer n representing the number of lines of text in a document. Dynamically allocate space for n pointers to String objects. Read n String objects using ReadString.

The lines of text may contain the special symbols "#" and "&". For example:

Dear #

Your lucky gift is available at &. By going to & and identifying your name, the attendant will give you your prize. Thank you # for your interest in our contest.

Sincerely,
The String Man

Enter a string poundstr, which substitutes for all occurrences of "#" in your document. Enter a string ampstring, which substitutes for all occurrences of "&" in your document. Traverse your array of string pointers and perform the substitutions. Print the final document.

8.10   Write a program that initializes two 10-element integer arrays intA and intB and uses them to create sets A and B. The set difference operator "$-$" is defined in Written Exercise 8.18. The program should compute A$-$B and B$-$A and print the results. The program should also verify that

$$A+B = A-B + B-A + A*B$$

8.11   The function

```
template <class>T
Set <T> ExclusiveUnion(const Set<T>& X, const Set<T>& Y);
```

returns a set containing all the elements that are in either X or Y, but not both.

(a)   Use a graphical argument to show that ExclusiveUnion can be computed using either of the following formulas:

    1. $(X-Y) + (Y-X)$
    2. $X * {\sim}Y + {\sim}X * Y$

The operations of set difference ("$-$") and complement ("$\sim$") are defined in Written Exercises 8.18 and 8.19.

(b)   Implement ExclusiveUnion using 2. Test your work using the sets

$$X = \{1,3,4,5,7,8,12,20\}, \ Y = \{3,5,9,10,12,15,20,25\}$$

for which

```
ExclusiveUnion(X,Y) = {1,4,7,8,10,15,25}
```

8.12   Two queens on a chessboard are said to be attacking if either can move to the position of the other, that is, if they are in the same row, column, or diagonal. The accompanying figure shows an example of attacking and non-attacking queens.

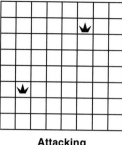

**Attacking
Queens**

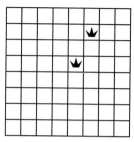

**Non-attacking
Queens**

Given the position of each queen, consider the problem of determining the set of all possible moves by each queen and of determining whether the queens are attacking.

Each position on the chessboard can be viewed using a row number and column number, each ranging from 0 to 7. A unique number between 0 and 63 can be assigned to each square of the board by associating each row/column pair (i, j) with the integer i*8+j. We can now view a chessboard as a set of 64 integers ranging from 0 to 63. Write the function

```
void ComputeQueenPositions(Set<int>& Board, int rowq,
                           int colq);
```

which takes the set Board, a queen's position (rowq,colq), and assigns all squares to which the queen can move to the set.

Write the function

```
void PrintQueenPositions(Set<int> Queen,int QRow,int QCol,
                         int QOtherRow,int QOtherCol);
```

A queen is at location (QRow, QCol), and Queen is a set of positions to which the queen can move. Another queen is at position (QOtherRow, QOtherCol). The function prints the board by placing the character "X" at each square to which the queen at position (QRow,QCol) can move and " " at the others. If one of the queens is at a square, print "Q".

Write the function

```
int AttackingQueens(int Q1Row,int Q1Col,
                    int Q2Row,int Q2Col);
```

which takes the position of the two queens and determines if they are attacking. This is done by determining if they share the same row, column, or diagonal.

Write a main program that reads the positions of the two queens and prints the set of possible locations to which each queen can move. A message then indicates whether the queens are attacking.

C H A P T E R 9

LINKED LISTS

We already have defined collection classes that use array-based implementations. The collections have included stacks, queues, and the more general SeqList class that maintains a sequential list of items. In this chapter, we develop linked lists that provide more flexible methods for adding and deleting items.

An array can be used with simple list storage applications. For instance, many commuter airlines sell nonreserved tickets that can be redeemed by customers as a boarding pass. As preflight tickets are purchased, the airline maintains a list of customers by adding their names to a list. Prior to flight, each customer registers with a flight attendant who removes the name from the ticket list and adds it to a list of on-board customers. With the lists, the airline can access the number of passengers on the plane and the number still outstanding.

Array-based lists are inadequate for applications that need more flexible list handling methods. Consider, for instance, a restaurant that allows reservations. The maitre d' would need to enter names in a list ordered by time and use several criteria to delete a name from the list. An immediate deletion occurs if the customer calls and cancels the reservation or if the customer arrives and is seated. Periodically, the maitre d' must scan the list and delete the names of customers who lose the reservation by not showing up within 15 minutes of the requested time.

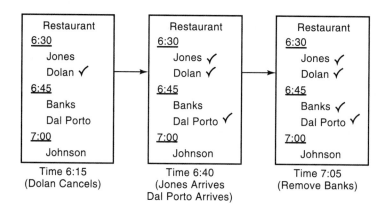

The array-based list cannot efficiently handle a restaurant reservation system. Names must be inserted at various locations in the list to account for different arrival times. This requires that names be shifted to the right. Deletions require that names be shifted to the left. The restaurant cannot predict the number of reservations and must allocate an exaggerated amount of memory to handle an extreme case. Once service begins, the reservation list is very dynamic with names moving quickly on and off the list. Arrays, with their contiguous storage, do not respond well to these dynamic changes. In the following discussion, we look at some of the problems with arrays and develop solutions that introduce dynamic linked lists.

An array is a fixed-length structure. Even a dynamic array has fixed size after a resize operation. For instance, A is dynamically created as a six-element array of integers:

A = new int [6];

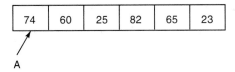

Once the array is full, we can add items only after resizing the list, a process that requires the copying of each element to new memory. Frequent resizing of large lists could significantly affect performance.

An array stores items in contiguous memory locations, which allows for direct access to an item but does not efficiently handle the addition and deletion of items unless these activities occur at the end of the array. For instance, assume you are deleting item 60 from the second position in the following list:

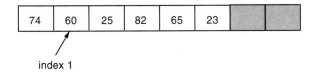

To maintain the contiguous order of elements in the list, we must shift four items to the left.

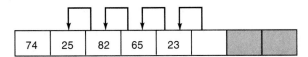

Suppose we add a new element 50 at index 2. Since an array stores elements in contiguous order, we must open a slot in the list by shifting three elements to the right one position:

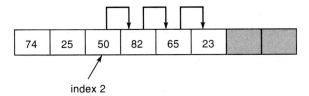

For an N-element list, insertion and deletion of an element at the rear of the list require computing time $O(1)$. For the general case, however, the expected number of shifts is N/2 with computing time $O(N)$.

DESCRIBING A LINKED LIST

The problem of efficient data management is critical to any implementation of a list. We need to develop a new structure that frees us from a contiguous data storage arrangement. We can use the model of links in a chain.

The length of the list can grow without limits by adding new links. Furthermore, new items can be inserted into the list by merely breaking a connection, adding a new link, and restoring the connection.

Before   After

Items are removed from the list by breaking two connections, removing a link, and then reconnecting the chain.

Before   After

In this chapter, we develop this structure, which is called a **linked list,** to implement a sequential list. Linked lists provide efficient list handling methods and overcome many of the limitations we noted with arrays.

CHAPTER OVERVIEW

The independent items in a linked list are called **nodes.** We develop a Node class that defines individual node objects and provides linked list handling methods. In particular, we implement node methods that insert and remove nodes after the current node. We develop algorithms that allow you to use the individual nodes and create a linked list, scan the nodes, and update their values.

We design a LinkedList class that encapsulates the primary node algorithms in a class structure. We use this class to implement the Queue and SeqList classes, thereby overcoming the limitation of array-based lists. We use the class to solve a variety of interesting problems including removing all duplicate data values from a list. The LinkedList class is used in the development of two case studies. The print spooler study uses the class to stimulate an operating system print manager. A second study discusses the construction of dynamic window lists.

The design of a list as a circular structure provides both conceptual and coding advantages. Doubly linked lists have applications when we need to search for elements in both directions. We define the CNode and DNode classes that implement the circular and doubly linked list structures.

The Node Class 9.1

A **node** consists of a data field and a pointer indicating the "next" item in the list. The pointer is the connecter that ties together the individual nodes of the list.

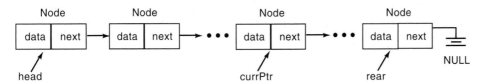

A linked list consists of a set of nodes whose first element, or **front,** is a node pointed to by **head.** The list chains nodes together from the front of the list to the end or the **rear** of the list. The rear is identified as the node whose pointer field has the value **NULL** = 0. We can think of a linked list as a freeway that has an "on-ramp" at the head and an "off-ramp" at NULL. List applications traverse the nodes by following each pointer to the next node. At any point in the scan, the current location is referenced by the pointer **currPtr.** In a case in which the list does not contain a node, the head pointer is NULL.

head ⎯⎯⎯

NULL

DECLARING A NODE TYPE

A node, with its data and pointer fields, is the building block for a linked list. The node structure has operations that initialize the data members and pointer methods to access the next node. Each node is equipped with operations to insert a new node after itself or to delete the following node.

The following figures illustrate basic node handling operations. At any given node p, we can implement the operation **InsertAfter,** which attaches a new node after the current one. The process begins by unlinking the connection to the successor node q, inserting newNode, and resetting the links.

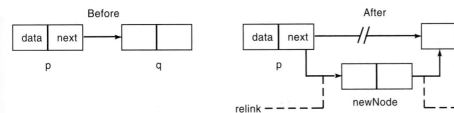

A similar process describes the operation **DeleteAfter,** which removes the node following the current node. We unlink p from its successor q and then relink it to the successor of q.

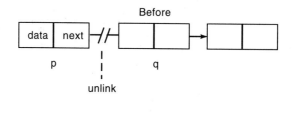

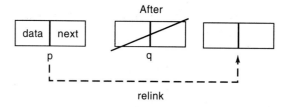

The node structure with the insert and delete operations describes an abstract data type. For each node, the operations pertain directly to its succeeding (next) node.

ADT *Node* **is**

Data
The data field is used to hold information. Except for initialization, the value is not used in any other operation. The field next is a pointer to the following node. If next is NULL, there is no next node.

Operations

Constructor
| Initial values: | A data value and a pointer to the next node. |
| Process: | Initialize the two fields. |

NextNode
Input:	None
Preconditions:	None
Process:	Retrieve the value of the field next.
Output:	Return the value of the next.
Postconditions:	None

InsertAfter
| Input: | A pointer to a new node. |
| Preconditions: | None |

Process:	Reset the value next to point at the new node and adjust the value of next in the new node to reference the successor of the current node.
Output:	None
Postconditions:	The node is now pointing to a new node.

DeleteAfter

Input:	None
Preconditions:	None
Process:	Unlink the next node and assign the value next to reference the successor of the next node.
Output:	A pointer to the deleted node.
Postconditions:	The node has a new value next.

end ADT *Node*

The Node ADT is described by a C++ template-based class.

- -

NODE CLASS SPECIFICATION

DECLARATION

```
template <class T>
class Node
{
   private:
      // next is the address of the following node
      Node<T> *next;
   public:
      // the data is public
      T data;

      // constructor
      Node (const T& item, Node<T>* ptrnext = NULL);

      // list modification methods
      void InsertAfter(Node<T> *p);
      Node<T> *DeleteAfter(void);

      // obtain the address of the next node
      Node<T> *NextNode(void) const;
};
```

DESCRIPTION

The value of the field next is a pointer to a Node. The Node class is a **self-referencing** structure in which a pointer member refers to objects of its own type.

We use Node objects for a variety of collection classes such as dictionaries and hash tables. We declare a public data field to provide convenient data access. This approach is less cumbersome to the client than using a pair of member functions such as GetData/SetData. The advantages become clearer when a reference to the data member must be available. This is a requirement when implementing more advanced classes such as dictionaries. The field next remains private and is accessed by the member function NextNode. It is changed only by the methods InsertAfter and DeleteAfter.

The constructor for the Node class initializes the public data field and the private pointer field. By default, the next value is set to NULL.

EXAMPLE

```
Node<int> t(10),          // create node t with data
                          // value = 10 and next = NULL
```

P = &t

```
Node<int> *u;
u = new Node<int>(20);    // allocates object at u
                          // value = 20 and next = NULL

Node<char> *p, *q, *r;
q = new Node<char>('B');  // q has data 'B'
p = new Node<char>('A',q); // declare node p with data 'A'
                          // next field points to q

r = new Node<char>('C');  // declare node r with data 'C'
q->InsertAfter(r);        // insert r at rear of the list
cout << p->data;          // print character 'A'
p = p->NextNode();        // move to the next node
cout << p->data;          // print character 'B'
cout << endl;
r = q->DeleteAfter();     // unlink rear; assign value to r
```

IMPLEMENTING THE NODE CLASS

The Node class contains both a public and a private data member. We have public data so that the client and collection classes can have direct access to its value. The field next is private, because access to this pointer field is handled by the member functions. We allow only the InsertAfter and DeleteAfter methods to change the value of this field. To make the field public would allow the user to break a link and destroy the linked list. The Node class contains the member function NextNode, which allows a client to traverse a linked list.

Constructor The constructor initializes both the data value and the pointer next. The class requires that the data members of each new node object be initialized. A parameter for the pointer field next may be passed to the constructor. In this case, the object is initially set to point at the node with the given address. If a parameter is not passed, the pointer field has the default value NULL.

```
// constructor. initialize data and pointer members
template <class T>
Node<T>::Node(const T& item, Node<T>* ptrnext):
            data(item), next(ptrnext)
{}
```

List Operations The method NextNode provides the client with access to the pointer field next. The method returns the value next and is used to traverse a list.

```
// return value of private member next
template <class T>
Node<T> *Node<T>::NextNode(void) const
{
    return next;
}
```

The functions InsertAfter and DeleteAfter are the primary list building operations. In each case, the process involves only pointer updates.

InsertAfter takes node p as a parameter and appends it as its next node. Initially, the current object points to a node whose address is q, the value in the field next. The algorithm changes two pointers. The pointer field of p is set to q, and the pointer field in the current object is given value p.

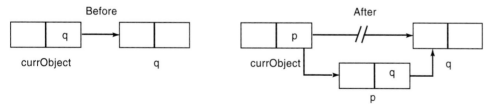

```
// insert a node p after the current one
template <class T>
void Node<T>::InsertAfter(Node<T> *p)
{
    // p points to successor of the current node
    // and current node points to p.
    p->next = next;
    next = p;
}
```

The order of the pointer assignments is critical. Assume the assignment statements are reversed.

```
next = p;          // Node following current object is lost!
p->next = next
```

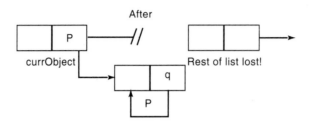

DeleteAfter removes the node that follows the current object and links its pointer field to the next node in the list. If there is no node after the current object (next == NULL), the function returns NULL. Otherwise, the function returns the address of the deleted node in case the programmer chooses to deallocate its memory. The DeleteAfter algorithm saves the address of the next node in tempPtr. The next field of tempPtr identifies the node in the list to which the current object must now point. The value tempPtr is returned. The process requires only one pointer assignment.

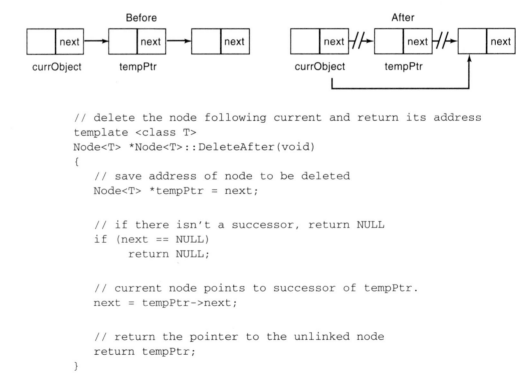

```
// delete the node following current and return its address
template <class T>
Node<T> *Node<T>::DeleteAfter(void)
{
    // save address of node to be deleted
    Node<T> *tempPtr = next;

    // if there isn't a successor, return NULL
    if (next == NULL)
        return NULL;

    // current node points to successor of tempPtr.
    next = tempPtr->next;

    // return the pointer to the unlinked node
    return tempPtr;
}
```

Building Linked Lists   9.2

We use the Node class to build linked lists. During this process we introduce the fundamental linked list algorithms used in most applications. The material in this section is important for your understanding of linked lists because here you learn how to create lists and access nodes. We implement our linked list algorithms as independent functions. Mastering this fundamental material wil help you when the techniques are used to create a general linked list class. For simplicity, our discussion assumes that list nodes hold integer data.

A linked list begins with a node pointer that references the start of the list. We call this pointer the **head** since it points to the beginning of the list. Initially, the value of head is NULL to indicate an empty list.

We can build the linked list in different ways. We begin by exploring the case where each new node is placed at the head of the list. Later, we consider the case where nodes are added at the rear of the list or at intermediate locations.

CREATING A NODE

We implement the creation of a node using the template-based function **GetNode,** which takes an initial data value and a pointer value and dynamically allocates a new node. If the memory allocation fails, the program terminates; otherwise, the function returns a pointer to the new node.

```
// allocate a node with data member item and pointer nextPtr
template <class T>
Node<T> *GetNode(const T& item, Node<T> *nextPtr = NULL)
{
   Node<T> *newNode;

   // allocate memory while passing item, NextPtr to
   // constructor. terminate program if allocation fails
   newNode = new Node<T>(item, nextPtr);
   if (newNode == NULL)
   {
       cerr << "Memory allocation failure!" << endl;
       exit(1);
   }
   return newNode;
}
```

INSERTING A NODE: INSERTFRONT

The operation of inserting a node at the front of a list requires us to reassign a value to the pointer head since the list has a new front. The problem of maintaining the head of the list is fundamental to list management. If you lose the head, you lose the list!

Before beginning the insertion, head identifies the front of the list. After the insertion, the new node will occupy the front of the list and the previous front of the list will occupy the second position. Hence, the pointer field of the new node is assigned the current value of head, and head is assigned the address of the new node. This assignment is performed by using GetNode to create the new node.

```
head = GetNode(item,head);
```

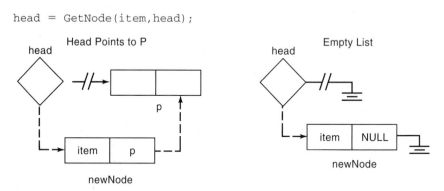

The function InsertFront takes the current head of the list, which is a pointer that defines the list, and also takes the new data value. It inserts the data value in a node at the front of the list. Since the head is going to be modified by the operation, head is passed as a reference parameter.

```
// insert item at the front of list
template <class T>
void InsertFront(Node<T>* & head, T item)
{
    // allocate new node so it points to original list head
    // update the list head
     head = GetNode(item,head);
}
```

This function and GetNode are found in the Node library file "nodelib.h".

TRAVERSING A LINKED LIST

The starting point of any traversal algorithm is the head pointer because it identifies the start of the list. As we move through the list, we use the pointer currPtr to reference our current location. Initially currPtr is set to the front of the list:

```
currPtr = head;
```

During the scan, we want to access the data field at the current location. Since data is a public member, we can retrieve the value or assign a new value.

```
currentDataValue = currPtr->data;
currPtr->data = newData;
```

For instance, a simple cout statement would be included in a traversal that prints the value of each node.

```
cout << currPtr->data;      // fetch the data value and print it
```

In the scan, we continuously move currPtr to the next node until we reach the end of the list. We use the function NextNode to determine the next node in the list.

```
currPtr = currPtr->NextNode();
```

The list traversal terminates when currPtr is NULL. For instance, the function PrintList prints the data value for each node. The head is passed as a parameter to define the list. A second parameter of user type AppendNewline indicates whether the output should be followed by two spaces or by a newline character. The function is contained in the file "nodelib.h".

```
enum AppendNewline {noNewline,addNewline};

// print a linked list
template <class T>
void PrintList(Node<T> *head, AppendNewline addnl)
{
    // currPtr chains through the list, starting at head
    Node<T> *currPtr = head;

    // print the current node's data until end of list
    while(currPtr != NULL)
      {
        // output newline if addl == addNewline
        if(addnl == addNewline)
            cout << currPtr->data << endl;
        else
            cout << currPtr->data << " ";

        // move to next node
        currPtr = currPtr->NextNode();
      }
}
```

Program 9.1   Matching a Key

The program generates 10 random numbers in the range 1 to 10 and inserts the values as nodes at the head of a linked list using InsertFront. We use Printlist to display the list.

The program contains code that counts the number of occurrences of a key in the list. The user is first prompted to enter the key. Then a traversal compares the key with the data field at each list node. The total number of occurrences is printed.

```cpp
#include <iostream.h>

#include "node.h"
#include "nodelib.h"
#include "random.h"

void main(void)
{
    // set list head to NULL
    Node<int> *head = NULL, *currPtr;

        int i, key, count = 0;
        RandomNumber rnd;

    // insert 10 random integers at front of list
    for (i=0;i < 10;i++)
        InsertFront(head, int (1+rnd.Random(10)));

    // print the original list
    cout << "List: ";
    PrintList(head,noNewline);
    cout << endl;

    // prompt user for an integer key
    cout << "Enter a key: ";
    cin >> key;

    // cycle through the list
    currPtr = head;
    while (currPtr != NULL)
      {
        // if data matches key, increment count
        if (currPtr->data == key)
            count++;

        // move to the next node of the list
        currPtr = currPtr->NextNode();
      }

      cout << "The data value " << key << " occurs " << count
           << " times in the list" << endl;
}
```

```
/*
<Run of Program 9.1>

List: 3  6  5  7  5  2  4  5  9  10
Enter a key: 5
The data value 5 occurs 3 times in the list
*/
```

INSERTING A NODE: INSERTREAR

Placing a node at the rear of a list requires an initial test to determine if the list is empty. If it is, create a new node with a NULL pointer field and assign its address to head. The operation is implemented by InsertFront. For a non-empty list, we must scan the nodes in the list to locate the rear node. We identify its position when the next field of the current object is NULL.

```
currPtr->NextNode() == NULL
```

The insertion is executed by first creating a new node (GetNode) and then inserting it after the current Node object (InsertAfter).

Since an insertion may change the value of the head pointer, head is passed as a reference parameter:

```
// find rear of the list and append item
template <class T>
void InsertRear(Node<T>* & head, const T& item)
{
   Node<T> *newNode, *currPtr = head;

   // if list is empty, insert item at the front
   if (currPtr == NULL)
       InsertFront(head,item);
   else
    {
       // find the node whose pointer is NULL
       while(currPtr->NextNode() != NULL)
          currPtr = currPtr->NextNode();
```

```
      // allocate node and insert at rear (after currPtr)
      newNode = GetNode(item);
      currPtr->InsertAfter(newNode);
   }
}
```

InsertRear is contained in the library file "nodelib.h".

Program 9.2   Word Jumble

This program randomly mixes the letters of a word to create a word jumble puzzle. The process scans each character in a string and randomly places it at either the front or the rear of a list. For each character, call random(2). If the return value is 0, call InsertFront; otherwise, call InsertRear. For instance, with input j-u-m-b-l-e and the sequence of random numbers 0 1 1 0 0 1, the resulting list is "lbjume". The program reads and jumbles four words.

```
#include <iostream.h>

#include "random.h"
#include "strclass.h"
#include "nodelib.h"

void main(void)
{

   // node list to hold jumbled characters
   Node<char> *jumbleword = NULL;

   // input string, random number object, counters
   String  s;
   RandomNumber rnd;
   int i, j;

   // input four strings
   for (i = 0; i < 4; i++)
   {
      cin >> s;
      // use Random(2) to determine if char moves to
      // front (value = 0) or rear (value = 1) of list
      for (j = 0; j < s.Length(); j++)
         if (rnd.Random(2))
            InsertRear(jumbleword, s[j]);
```

```
        else
            InsertFront(jumbleword, s[j]);

        // print the input string and its jumbled variation
        cout << "String/Jumble: " << s << "   ";
        PrintList(jumbleword);
        cout << endl << endl;
    }
 }

/*
<Run of Program 9.2>

pepper
String/Jumble: pepper    r  p  p  e  p  e

hawaii
String/Jumble: hawaii    i  i  h  a  w  a

jumble
String/Jumble: jumble    e  b  m  j  u  l

C++
String/Jumble: C++    +  C  +
*/
```

Deleting a Node   In this section, we have discussed algorithms to scan a list and to insert new nodes. A third list operation, deleting a node from a list, introduces a new set of issues. We often want to delete the first node in the list. The operation requires that we update the list head to point at the successor of the front node.

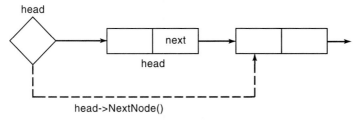

We design the function DeleteFront that is passed the head of the list as a reference parameter, unlinks the first node, and deallocates its memory.

```
// delete the first node of the list
template <class T>
void DeleteFront(Node<T>* & head)
{
```

```
    // save the address of node to be deleted
    Node<T> *p = head;

    // make sure list is not empty
    if (head != NULL)
    {
      // move head to second node and delete original
        head = head->NextNode();
        delete p;
    }
}
```

A general delete function searches the list and deletes the first node whose data value matches a key. Initialize prevPtr to NULL and currPtr to head. We then move currPtr down the list looking for a match and maintain prevPtr, so that it references the previous location of currPtr.

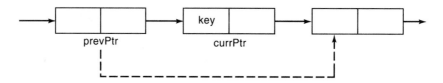

The pointers prevPtr and currPtr move down the list in tandem until currPtr becomes NULL or currPtr identifies a match (currPtr−>data == key).

```
while (currPtr != NULL && currPtr->data != key)
{
    // move prevPtr forward to currPtr
    prevPtr = currPtr;
    // move currPtr forward one node
    currPtr = currPtr->NextNode();
}
```

A match occurs if we exit the "while" statement with currPtr != NULL. We are then in a position to delete the current node. There are two possibilities. If prevPtr is NULL, delete the first node of the list. Otherwise, delete the node by executing DeleteAfter for the node prevPtr.

```
if (prevPtr == NULL)
      head = head->NextNode();
else
      prevPtr->DeleteAfter();
```

The Delete method quietly returns if the key is not found. Since a deletion at the front of the list forces an update of the head, we must pass the variable by reference.

```
// delete the first occurrence of key in the list
template <class T>
void Delete (Node<T>* & head, T key)
{
    // currPtr moves through list, trailed by prevPtr
    Node<T>  *currPtr = head, *prevPtr = NULL;

    // return if the list is empty
    if (currPtr == NULL)
        return;

    // cycle list until key is located or come to end
    while (currPtr != NULL && currPtr->data != key)
    {
        // advance currPtr so prevPtr trails it
        prevPtr = currPtr
        currPtr = currPtr->NextNode();
    }

    // if currPtr != NULL, key located at currPtr.
    if (currPtr != NULL)
    {
        // prevPtr == NULL means match at front node
        if (prevPtr == NULL)
            head = head->NextNode();
        else
            // match at 2nd or subsequent node
            prevPtr->DeleteAfter();

            // dispose of the node
            delete currPtr;
    }
}
```

APPLICATION: STUDENT GRADUATION LIST

The record StudentRecord gives the name and GPA of a candidate for graduation from a university. We set out to develop a list of students that will walk through the graduation ceremony. A list of candidates for graduation is read from the file "studrecs" and inserted at the front of the list. Since university policy does not approve for graduation a student with a GPA of less than 2.0, we scan the list and remove all candidates that do not meet the minimum GPA requirement. A second list, from file "noattend", represents students that choose not to attend the ceremonies. The list of names, given one per line, are used to delete additional names from the graduation list. The remaining items represent a list of qualified students that plan on participating in the graduation ceremonies.

```
struct StudentRecord
{
```

```
            String name;
            float gpa;
    };
```

We include with the class overloaded input and output operators to read and write student records. The overloaded "!=" operator allows the use of student data with the Delete function.

Program 9.3   Graduation List

The file "studrecs" is read and each record is inserted at the front of the linked list graduateList using the Node library function InsertFront. Pointers prevPtr and currPtr are used to scan the list and delete all students whose GPA is less than 2.0. After removing unqualified students, we read the names from file "noattend" and delete the students from the list. At the conclusion, we print the list of graduates attending the ceremonies.

```cpp
#include <iostream.h>
#include <fstream.h>
#include <stdlib.h>
#include <iomanip.h>

#include "node.h"
#include "nodelib.h"
#include "studinfo.h"

void main(void)
{
    Node<StudentRecord> *graduateList=NULL,
                        *currPtr, *prevPtr,
                        *deleteNodePtr;
    StudentRecord srec;
    ifstream fin;

    fin.open("studrecs",ios::in | ios::nocreate);
    if (!fin)
    {
        cerr << "Cannot open file studrecs." << endl;
        exit(1);
    }

    // print gpa with one decimal place
    cout.setf(ios::fixed);
    cout.precision(1);
    cout.setf(ios::showpoint);
```

```
while(fin >> srec)
    // insert srec at the head of the list
    InsertFront(graduateList,srec);

// remove students below 2.0
prevPtr = NULL;                     // prevPtr trails currPtr
currPtr = graduateList;             // currPtr at start of list
while (currPtr != NULL)             // traverse to end of list
{
    if (currPtr->data.gpa < 2.0) // does student graduate?
    {
        if (prevPtr == NULL)        // student at front of list?
        {
            graduateList = currPtr->NextNode();
            deletedNodePtr = currPtr;
            currPtr = graduateList;
        }
        else    // delete node inside the list
        {
            currPtr = currPtr->NextNode();
            deletedNodePtr = prevPtr->DeleteAfter();
        }
        delete deletedNodePtr;  // remove deleted node
    }
    else
    {
        // no deletion. move down the list
        prevPtr = currPtr;
        currPtr = currPtr->NextNode();
    }
}
fin.close();

fin.open("noattend",ios::in | ios::nocreate);
if (!fin)
{
    cerr << "Cannot open file noattend." << endl;
    exit(1);
}

// read from no attend file, delete from graduation list
while(srec.name.ReadString(fin) != -1)
    Delete(graduateList,srec);

// print the remaining students in graduation list
cout << "Students attending graduation:" << endl;
PrintList(graduateList,addNewline);
}
```

```
/*
<File "studrecs">
Julie Bailey
1.5
Harold Nelson
2.9
Thomas Frazer
3.5
Bailey Harnes
1.7
Sara Miller
3.9
Nancy Barnes
2.5
Rebecca Neeson
4.0
Shannon Johnson
3.8

<File "noattend">
Thomas Frazer
Sara Miller

<Run of Program 9.3>
Students attending graduation:
Shannon Johnson 3.8
Rebecca Neeson 4.0
Nancy Barnes 2.5
Harold Nelson 2.9
*/
```

CREATING AN ORDERED LIST

In many applications, we wish to maintain an ordered list of data with the nodes given in ascending or descending order. The insertion algorithm must first scan the list to identify the correct location at which to add the new node. The following discussion illustrates the process of creating a list in ascending order.

To enter data value X, we first scan the list and position currPtr at the first node whose data value is greater than X. The new node with value X should be inserted immediately to the left of currPtr. During the scan, prevPtr moves in tandem with currPtr and maintains a record of the previous position.

The following examples illustrate the algorithm. Assume list L initially contains the integers 60, 65, 74, and 82.

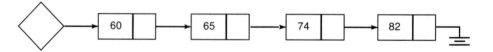

Insert 50 in the list: Because 60 is the first node in the list that is greater than 50, we insert 50 at the head of the list.

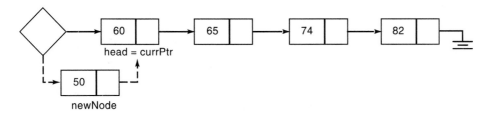

```
InsertFront(head,50);
```

Insert 70 in the list: 74 is the first node in the list greater than 70. Pointers prevPtr and currPtr designate nodes 65 and 74, respectively.

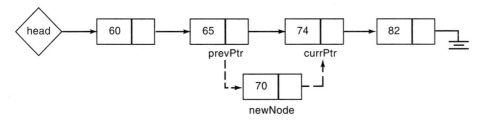

```
newNode = GetNode(70);
prevPtr->InsertAfter(newNode);
```

Insert 90 in the list: We scan the entire list and cannot find a node greater than 90 (currPtr == NULL). The new value is greater than or equal to all other values in the list, and hence the new node must be located at the rear of the list. When the scan terminates, insert the new node after prevPtr.

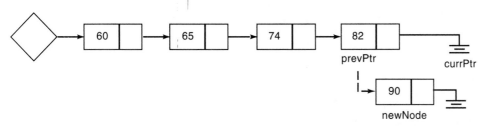

```
newNode = GetNode(90);
prevPtr->InsertAfter(newNode);
```

The following function implements the general in-order insertion algorithm. If the list has n elements, the worst case performance occurs when the new element is inserted at the end of the list. In this case, n comparisons must be executed, so the worst case is O(n). On the average, we expect to search half the list to find an insertion point. As a result, the average case is O(n). Of course, the best case is O(1).

```cpp
// insert item into the ordered list
template <class T>
void InsertOrder(Node<T>* & head, T item)
{
    // currPtr moves through list, trailed by prevPtr
    Node<T> *currPtr, *prevPtr, *newNode;

    // prevPtr == NULL signals match at front
    prevPtr = NULL;
    currPtr = head;

    // cycle through the list and find insertion point
    while (currPtr != NULL)
    {
        // found insertion point if item < current node data
        if (item < currPtr->data)
            break;

        // advance currPtr so prevPtr trails it
        prevPtr = currPtr;
        currPtr = currPtr->NextNode();
    }

    // make the insertion
    if (prevPtr == NULL)
        // if prevPtr == NULL, insert at front
        InsertFront(head,item);
    else
    {
        // insert new node after previous
        newNode = GetNode(item);
        prevPtr->InsertAfter(newNode);
    }
}
```

APPLICATION: SORTING WITH LINKED LISTS

InsertOrder can be used to sort a collection of items provided the comparison operator "<" is defined for the data type T. The function LinkSort takes an n-element array A and inserts the elements in an ordered linked list. The list is traversed and the ordered elements are copied back into the array. A call to the function ClearList deallocates memory associated with each node of the list. It traverses the list and, for each node, records its address, moves to the next node, and then deletes the original node. ClearList is a member of the library "nodelib.h".

```
// delete all the nodes in the linked list
template <class T>
void ClearList(Node<T> * &head)
{
    Node<T> *currPtr, *nextPtr;

    // chain through the list deleting nodes
    currPtr = head;
    while(currPtr != NULL)
    {
        // record address of next node. delete current node
        nextPtr = currPtr->NextNode();
        delete currPtr;

        // move current node forward
        currPtr = nextPtr;
    }

    // mark list as empty
    head = NULL;
}
```

Program 9.4 List Insertion Sort

This program takes a 10-element integer array A and sorts the list using the template function LinkSort. The resulting ordered array is printed using PrintArray.

```
#include <iostream.h>

#include "node.h"
#include "nodelib.h"

template <class T>
void LinkSort(T a[], int n)
{
    // set up the linked list ordlist to hold array items
    Node<T> *ordlist = NULL, *currPtr;
    int i;
```

```
    // insert the elements from the array to the list in order
    for (i=0;i < n;i++)
        InsertOrder(ordlist, a[i]);

    // scan the list and copy the data values back to the array
    currPtr = ordlist;
    i = 0;
    while(currPtr != NULL)
    {
        a[i++] = currPtr->data;
        currPtr = currPtr->NextNode();
    }

    // delete all the nodes created for the ordered list
    ClearList(ordlist);
}


// scan the array and print its elements
void PrintArray(int a[], int n)
{
    for(int i=0;i < n;i++)
        cout << a[i] << "  ";
}

void main(void)
{
    // sort these 10 integer values
    int A[10] = {82,65,74,95,60,28,5,3,33,55};

    LinkSort(A,10);                    // sort the array
    cout << "Sorted array:     ";
    PrintArray(A,10);                  // print the array
    cout << endl;
}


/*
<Run of Program 9.4>

Sorted array:     3  5  28  33  55  60  65  74  82  95
*/
```

An analysis of the runtime efficiency of the LinkSort algorithm must take into account the initial ordering of the array elements. The worst case running time occurs when the list is already in ascending order. Each element is inserted at the end of the list. The first insertion takes no comparisons, the second insertion takes one comparison, the third takes two comparisons, and so forth. The total number of comparisons is

$$0 + 1 + 2 + \ldots + (n - 1) = \frac{(n - 1) * n}{2}$$

which is $O(n^2)$. At the other extreme, a list that is sorted in descending order requires only $n - 1$ comparisons since each array element is inserted at the front of the list. The best case is therefore $O(n)$ and the worst case runtime efficiency is $O(n^2)$. Intuitively, the average case has n insertions with the ith entry requiring an expected $i/2$ comparisons. The total number of comparisons is $O(n^2)$. Unlike an in-place sort such as the ExchangeSort, LinkSort requires additional storage for all n data elements as well as storage for the pointers in the linked list. It also spends time copying elements to and from the linked list.

Designing a Linked List Class   9.3

A programmer can use the Node class along with the utility functions in "nodelib.h" to handle linked list applications. The approach forces the programmer to create each node and to perform directly the low-level list operations. A more structured approach defines a linked list class that organizes the basic list operations as member functions. In this section, we discuss the kind of data members and operations that should be included in a linked list class by using the knowledge gained in designing algorithms with the Node class. We also anticipate the fact that our linked list class will be used to implement other list collections, which include linked stacks, queues, and the SeqList class. In the next section we declare the LinkedList class and define its member functions.

LINKED LIST DATA MEMBERS

A linked list consists of a set of Node objects chained together from the front of the list to the rear of the list. The list has a starting node called the head that identifies the first node of the list. Since the head points at the front of the list, we will refer to it as front. The last node in the list has a pointer field with value NULL and is referenced with the pointer rear. We want the linked list class to maintain pointers to the front and rear of the list since this is useful in many applications and critical when implementing a linked queue.

A linked list provides sequential access to the data items and uses a pointer to specify the current traversal location in the list. Our linked list contains the pointer currPtr to reference this current location and a companion pointer, prevPtr, to reference the previous location. In addition, we maintain a variable called position, which describes the current location in terms of its place in the list. The front of the list has position 0 with the next item at position 1 and so forth. The number of elements in the linked list is maintained in the variable size. This allows us to identify an empty list or return a count of the number of elements in the list. In the following list, the current location is node 90, which is situated at position 3 in the list:

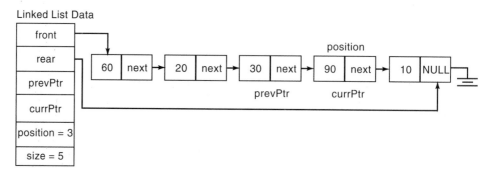

The address prevPtr is used to insert and delete a node at the current location using the Node methods InsertAfter and DeleteAfter. For instance, in the following linked list, we illustrate an insertion using the Node object referenced by prevPtr:

Insertion: prevPtr->InsertAfter(p)

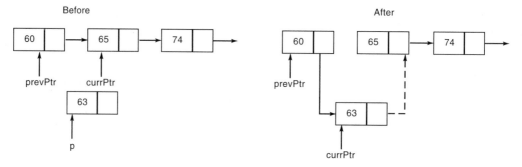

The node referenced by prevPtr is also used when deleting an item from the linked list:

Deletion: prevPtr->DeleteAfter(p)

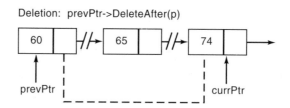

LINKED LIST OPERATIONS

The user must be able to move from element to element in the list. A simple method called Next advances the current location to the next node. At the current location, the operation Data returns a reference to the data field of the node. This gives us the ability to retrieve or modify the data field of a node without requiring the user to understand how the data are stored by the Node class. To illustrate the operations, assume L is a linked list of integers whose current location is at a node with data value 65. The following statements update the current node value to 67 and the value of the next node to 100:

```
LinkedList<int> L;
    . . .
if (L.Data() < 70)   // compare value of current node with 70
    L.Data() = 67;   // if less, assign a new data value of 67
L.Next();            // advance current location to next node
L.Data() = 100;      // inserts 100 into the new location
```

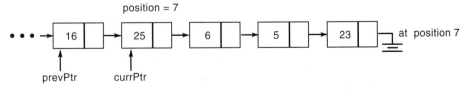

In applications, we sometimes need to set our current location at a specific place in the list. The method Reset does this. It takes a parameter pos and moves the current list location to that position. The default value of pos is 0, which sets the current location to the front of the list. From there, an application can scan the nodes using Next. The list scan terminates when the condition EndOfList is true. For instance, a simple loop prints the items in a list. Before scanning the list, we first test the ListEmpty condition:

```
L.Reset();                   // set currPtr at front of list
if (L.ListEmpty())           // test for empty list
    cout << "Empty list\n";
else
    while(!L.EndOfList())    // scan to end of list
    {
        cout << L.Data() << endl; // print the data value
        L.Next();                 // move to the next node
    }
```

The client has access to the current list position using the method CurrentPosition. If movement is made farther down the list, the method Reset can be used to restore the list to the original position. This capability is used in such problems as finding the maximum value in a list and positioning the list at that node for a subsequent deletion or insertion.

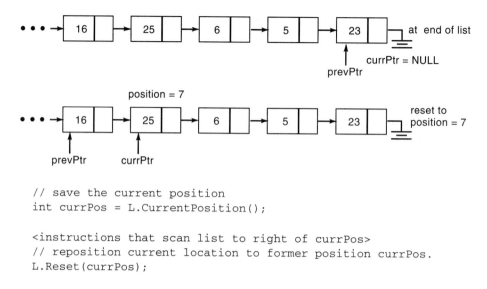

```
// save the current position
int currPos = L.CurrentPosition();

<instructions that scan list to right of currPos>
// reposition current location to former position currPos.
L.Reset(currPos);
```

The addition and deletion of nodes are basic operations in a linked list. The operations can occur at the front or rear of the list or at the current location.

Insert Operations   The insert operations create a new node with a new data field. The node is then placed in the list at the current location or immediately after the current location.

The InsertAfter operation places the new node after the current position and assigns currPtr to the new node. The operation serves the same purpose as the InsertAfter method in the Node class.

The InsertAt method places the new node at the current location. The new node is placed immediately before the current node. The current position is set to the new node. This operation is used when creating an ordered list.

Our linked list class provides the operations InsertFront and InsertRear to add new nodes at the front and rear of the list. The operations set the current position to the new node.

Delete Operations   The delete operations remove a node from the list. DeleteAt removes the node at the current position, and DeleteFront removes the first node in the list.

```
Example:     Linked List<int> L;

             L.InsertFront(100);     // List is 100
             L.InsertAfter(200);     // List is 100 200
             L.InsertAt(300);        // List is 100 300 200
             L.InsertRear(50);       // List is 100 300 200 50
             L.Reset(1);             // Set currPtr to 300
             L.DeleteAt();           // List is 100 200 50
```

```
        L.DeleteAt();              // List is 100 50
        L.DeleteAt();              // List is 100;
```

Other Methods   A linked list class creates dynamic data so it must have a copy constructor, a destructor, and an overloaded assignment operator. The user may explicitly clear a list with the operation ClearList.

The LinkedList Class   9.4

This section presents the class LinkedList as a simple but powerful toolbox for dynamic list handling. The focus is on the class specification and sample programs that illustrate its use. The class declaration and implementation is found in the file "link.h".

– –
LINKEDLIST CLASS SPECIFICATION

DECLARATION

```
    #include <iostream.h>
    #include <stdlib.h>

    #include "node.h"

    template <class T>
    class LinkedList
    {
       private:
           // pointers maintain access to front and rear of list
           Node<T> *front, *rear;

           // used for data retrieval, insertion and deletion
           Node<T> *prevPtr, *currPtr;

           // number of elements in the list
           int size;

           // position in the list; used by Reset
           int position;

           // private methods allocate and deallocate nodes
           Node<T> *GetNode(const T& item, Node<T>* ptrNext = NULL);
           void FreeNode(Node<T> *p);

           // copies list L to current list
           void CopyList(const LinkedList<T>& L);
```

```
public:
    // constructors
    LinkedList(void);
    LinkedList(const LinkedList<T>& L);

    // destructor
    ~LinkedList(void);

    // assignment operator
    LinkedList<T>& operator= (const LinkedList<T>& L);

    // methods to check list status
    int ListSize(void) const;
    int ListEmpty(void) const;

    // Traversal methods
    void Reset(int pos = 0);
    void Next (void);
    int EndOfList(void) const;
    int CurrentPosition(void) const;

    // Insertion methods
    void InsertFront(const T& item);
    void InsertRear(const T& item);
    void InsertAt(const T& item);
    void InsertAfter(const T& item);

    // Deletion methods
    T DeleteFront(void);
    void DeleteAt(void);

    // Data retrieval/modification
    T& Data(void);

    // method to clear the list
    void ClearList(void);
};
```

DISCUSSION

The class uses dynamic memory, and so a copy constructor, destructor, and overloaded assignment operator are provided. The private methods GetNode and FreeNode perform all memory allocation for the class. If a memory allocation fails, GetNode terminates the program.

The class maintains the size of the list that can be accessed using the methods ListSize and ListEmpty.

The private data members currPtr and prevPtr maintain a record of the current traversal location in the list. The insertion and deletion methods are responsible to update these data values after completing the operation. The Reset method explicitly sets the value of both currPtr and prevPtr.

The class contains flexible traversal methods. Reset takes a position parameter and sets the current location at that position. It has a default parameter of 0, so that when it is used with no argument, the method sets the current position to the front of the list. The method Next advances to the next node of the list, and EndOfList indicates whether the end of the list has been reached. For list L, a FOR loop creates a sequential scan of the list.

```
for (L.Reset(); !L.EndOfList(); L.Next())
    <visit the current location>
```

CurrentPosition returns the current location in the list traversal. To visit the current node later, save the return value and subsequently supply it as a parameter to Reset.

Insertions can occur at either end of the list using InsertFront and InsertRear. InsertAt inserts a new node at the current position in the list, and InsertAfter inserts the node after the current position. If the current location is at the end of the list (EndOfList == True), both InsertAt and InsertAfter place the new node at the rear of the list.

DeleteFront removes the first element from the list, and DeleteAt removes the node at the current list position. With either method, an attempt to delete from an empty list terminates the program.

The method Data is used to read or modify the data at the current position in the list. Since Data returns a reference to the data in a node, it can be used on the right- or left-hand side of an assignment statement.

```
// fetch data from the current location and increment its
// value by 5
L.Data() = L.Data() + 5;
```

ClearList removes all the nodes of the list and marks the list as empty.

EXAMPLE

```
LinkedList<int> L, K;   // declare integer lists L,K

// add 25 integers to the lists
for(i=0; i < 25; i++)
{
    cin >> num;
    L.InsertRear(num);   // nodes enter in order of input
    K.InsertFront(num);  // nodes in reverse order of input
}
```

```
// scan list L updating each node to its absolute value
for(L.Reset();!L.EndOfList();L.Next())
   // if data is negative store a new value
   if (L.Data() < 0)
      L.Data() = -L.Data();

K.InsertFront(100);          // store 100 at front of K
K.InsertAfter(200);          // insert 200 after 100
K.InsertAt(150);             // insert 150 between 100 and 200

// print list L
void PrintList(LinkedList<int>& L)
{
   // move to front of L and traverse list printing each item
   for(L.Reset(); !L.EndOfList(); L.Next())
      cout << L.Data() << "  ";
}
```

Before implementing the LinkedList class, we illustrate its main features in a series of examples. A concatenate function joins two lists by appending the second list on the tail of the first. A second example implements a linked list version of the selection sort. A classical version of the algorithm sorts an array in place. Our implementation makes extensive use of insertions and deletions with linked lists. We complete the section with an algorithm that removes duplicate nodes from a list.

Concatenating Two Lists

The function concatenates two lists by sequencing through the nodes in the second list and inserting each of its values at the rear of the first list. The function is used in a complete program "concat.cpp" in the program supplement.

The function ConcatLists scans the second list and extracts the data value from each node using the method Data. The value is then used to append a new node at the rear of the first list using the method InsertRear.

```
template <class T>
// concatenate L2 onto the end of L1
void ConcatLists(LinkedList<T>& L1, LinkedList<T>& L2)
{
   // reset both lists to the front
   L1.Reset();
   L2.Reset();

   // traverse L2. insert each data value at the rear of L1
   while (!L2.EndOfList())
   {
      L1.InsertRear(L2.Data());
      L2.Next();
   }
}
```

Sorting a List

We implement a linked list version of the selection sort by using two separate linked lists. The first list, L, contains the unsorted set of data. The second list, K, is created as a copy of list L with values in sorted order. The algorithm deletes the elements from list L in order from greatest to least and inserts them at the front of list K, which then becomes an ordered list.

The selection sort requires repeated scanning of a list. We use the function FindMax to scan the list and set the current position at the maximum element. After retrieving the data value from this position, we insert a new node with that value in the front of list K using InsertFront and then delete this maximum node in list L using DeleteAt.

Consider the following example:

List L contains elements 57, 40, 74, 20, 62

Step 1: Find the maximum value 74. Delete from L and add to K.

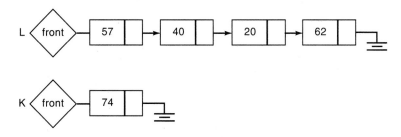

Step 2: Find the maximum value 62. Delete from L and add to K.

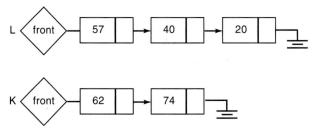

Program 9.5   List Selection Sort

The program creates a list L with 10 random numbers in the range 0 to 99. After printing the initial list with the function PrintList, we use the selection sort algorithm to transfer the elements from list L to list K. PrintList is called again to output the values from K, which contains the elements in ascending order.

```cpp
#include <iostream.h>

#include "link.h"          // include the linked list class
#include "random.h"

// position the list L at its maximum element
template <class T>
void FindMax(LinkedList<T> &L)
{
    if (L.ListEmpty())
    {
        cerr << "FindMax: list empty!" << endl;
        return;
    }

    // reset to start of the list
    L.Reset();

    // record first value at position 0 as current maximum
    T max = L.Data();
    int maxLoc = 0;

    // move to second data value and scan the list
    for (L.Next(); !L.EndOfList(); L.Next())
        if (L.Data() > max)
        {
            // new maximum. record its value and the list position
            max = L.Data();
            maxLoc = L.CurrentPosition();
        }

    // reset the list back to the maximum value
    L.Reset(maxLoc);
}

// print list L
template <class T>
void PrintList (LinkedList<T>& L)
{
    // move to front of list. traverse and print nodes
    for (L.Reset(); L.EndOfList(); L.Next())
        cout << L.Data() <<"  ";
}

void main(void)
{
```

```
// list L is placed in sorted order in list K
LinkedList<int> L, K;

RandomNumber rnd;
int i;

// L is a list of 10 random integers in range 0-99
for(i=0; i < 10; i++)
    L.InsertRear(rnd.Random(100));

cout << "Original list: ";
PrintList(L);
cout << endl;

// delete data from L until it is empty, inserting into K
while (!L.ListEmpty())
{
    // locate max of remaining elements.
    FindMax(L);

    // insert max at front of list K and delete it from L
    K.InsertFront(L.Data());
    L.DeleteAt();
}

cout << "Sorted list:   ";
PrintList(K);
cout << endl;
}

/*
<Run of Program 9.5>
Original list: 82  72  62  3  85  33  58  50  91  26
Sorted list:    3  26  33  50  58  62  72  82  85  91
*/
```

Removing Duplicates An algorithm to remove duplicates in a list provides an interesting application of the LinkedList class. After creating a list L, we begin a scan of its nodes. At each node, record the position of the node and its data value. This gives us a key to begin looking for duplicates in the remainder of the list and also gives us a position to return to after removing duplicates. From the current position, scan the tail of the list, removing all nodes whose data value matches the key. Then reset the traversal location back to the position of the original value and step forward one node to continue the process.

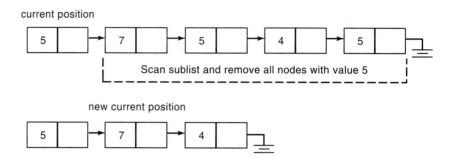

current position

Scan sublist and remove all nodes with value 5

new current position

Program 9.6 Removing Duplicates

This program uses the algorithm to remove duplicates. An initial list has 15 random values in the range 1–7. After printing the list, we call the function RemoveDuplicates, which deletes the duplicates from the list. The resulting list is then printed, using the function PrintList which is included in "link.h".

```cpp
#include <iostream.h>

#include "link.h"                       // include LinkedList class
#include "random.h"

void RemoveDuplicates(LinkedList<int>& L)
{
   // current list position and data value
   int currPos, currValue;

   // move to the front of the list
   L.Reset();

   // cycle through the list
   while(!L.EndOfList())
   {
      // record the current list data value and its position
      currValue = L.Data();
      currPos = L.CurrentPosition();

      // move one node to the right
      L.Next();

      // move forward until end of list, deleting
      // all occurrences of currValue
      while(!L.EndOfList())
         // if node deleted, current position is next node
         if (L.Data() == currValue)
```

```
                L.DeleteAt();
            else
                L.Next();                       // move to the next node

        // move to first node with value currValue; go forward
        L.Reset(currPos);
        L.Next();
    }
}

void main(void)
{
    LinkedList<int> L;
    int i;
    RandomNumber rnd;

    // insert 15 random integers in range 1-7 and print list
    for(i=0; i < 15; i++)
        L.InsertRear(1+rnd.Random(7));
    cout << "Original list: ";
    PrintList(L);
    cout << endl;

    // remove all the duplicate values and print new list
    RemoveDuplicates(L);
    cout << "Final list:    ";
    PrintList(L);
    cout << endl;
}

/*
<Run of Program 9.6>

Original list: 1  7  7  1  5  1  2  7  2  1  6  6  3  6  4
Final list:    1  7  5  2  6  3  4
*/
```

Implementing the LinkedList Class   9.5

The specification of the LinkedList class makes reference to the Node class. The implementation of the LinkedList class uses many of the techniques discussed in Section 9.1 with the Node class. For instance, the algorithms to insert and delete a node at the front of a linked list are used in the LinkedList class. The algorithms used by the functions in "nodelib.h" are the basis for our development of the LinkedList class. You must be aware, however, of the additional complexity to maintain the pointers front and rear that define access to the list, the pointers currPtr and prevPtr that maintain information on the current traversal location, and the integer values position, and size. The LinkedList methods are responsible for updating these data values whenever the state of the list is changed.

Private Data Members   The class restricts access to the data since this information is used only by the member functions. A linked list consists of a set of Node objects chained together from the front of the list to the rear of the list. We identify the front or head of the list as a data member. To facilitate insertions at the rear of the list, the class maintains a pointer rear to the last node of the list. This saves scanning the entire list to locate the rear. The variable size maintains a count of the number of nodes in the list. The value is used to determine whether the list is empty and to return the number of data values in the list. The variable position facilitates the repositioning of the current traversal location in the Reset methods.

A LinkedList object contains two pointers that identify the current location in the list(currPtr), and the previous location(prevPtr). The pointer currPtr references the current node of the list and is used by the Data method and by the insertion method InsertAfter. The pointer prevPtr is used for the DeleteAt and InsertAt methods that operate at the current location. When insertions and deletions are done, the class updates the front, rear, position, and size fields of the list object.

LinkedList Class Data

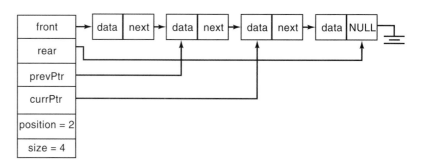

Memory Allocation Methods   The class performs all insertions and deletions for the client. The copy constructor and the insertion methods allocate nodes, whereas ClearList and the delete methods destroy nodes. The LinkedList class could use the operators new and delete directly in these methods. However, the functions GetNode and FreeNode provide a more structured access to memory management.

The method GetNode attempts to allocate dynamically a node with a given data value and pointer field. If the allocation is successful, it returns a pointer to the new node; otherwise, it prints an error message and terminates the program. The method FreeNode simply deletes the memory occupied by a node.

Constructors and Destructor   The constructor creates an empty list with all of the pointer values set to NULL. In this initial state, the size is set to 0 and the position value is set to -1.

```
// create empty list by setting pointers to NULL, size to 0
// and list position to -1
template <class T>
LinkedList<T>::LinkedList(void): front (NULL), rear(NULL),
       prevPtr(NULL),currPtr(NULL), size(0), position (-1)
{}
```

The copy constructor and the assignment operator copy a LinkedList object L. For this purpose, the class implements the method CopyList that traverses a list L and inserts each data value at the rear of the current list. The private function is called only when the current list is empty. It assigns the traversal parameters prevPtr, currPtr, and position to be in the same configuration as list L. In this way, the two lists have the same traversal state after an assignment or initialization.

```
// copy L to the current list, which is assumed to be empty
template <class T>
void LinkedList<T>::CopyList(const LinkedList<T>& L)
{
    Node<T> *p = L.front;        // use p to chain through L

    // insert each element in L at the rear of current object
    while (p != NULL)
    {
        InsertRear(p->data);
        p = p->NextNode();
    }

    // if list is empty return
    if (position = -1)
        return;

    // reset prevPtr and currPtr in the new list
    prevPtr = NULL;
    currPtr = front;
    for (int pos = 0; pos != position; pos++)
    {
        prevPtr = currPtr;
        currPtr = currPtr->NextNode();
    }
}
```

ClearList traverses the linked list and destroys all the nodes using the algorithm developed in Section 9.1. The destructor is implemented by simply calling ClearList.

```
template <class T>
void LinkedList<T>::ClearList(void)
```

```
{
    Node<T> *currPosition, *nextPosition;

    currPosition = front;
    while(currPosition != NULL)
    {
        // get address of next node and delete current node
        nextPosition = currPosition->NextNode();
        FreeNode(currPosition);
        currPosition = nextPosition;   // Move to next node
    }
    front = rear = NULL;
    prevPtr = currPtr = NULL;
    size = 0;
    position = -1;
}
```

List Traversal Methods   Reset sets the current traversal location to the position designated by the parameter pos. At the same time, the method updates the location of both currPtr and prevPtr. If pos is not in the range 0 . . . size − 1, an error message is printed and the program terminates. To set currPtr and prevPtr, the function distinguishes the case where pos is the head of the list and an interior position in the list.

pos == 0: Reset the current location to the front of the list by setting prevPtr to NULL and currPtr to front and position to 0.

pos! = 0: Since the case where pos == 0 has already been considered, we may assume the value of pos must be greater than 0 and the list traversal must be set to an interior position. To reposition currPtr, start at the second node of the list and move to location pos.

```
// reset the list position to pos
template <class T>
void LinkedList<T>::Reset(int pos)
{
    int startPos;

    // if the list is empty, return
    if (front == NULL)
        return;

    // if the position is invalid, terminate the program
    if (pos < 0 || pos > size-1)
    {
        cerr << "Reset: Invalid list position: " << pos
             << endl;
        return;
    }
```

```
        // move list traversal mechanism to node pos
        if(pos == 0)
        {
            // reset to front of the list
            prevPtr = NULL;
            currPtr = front;
            position = 0;
        }
        else
        // reset currPtr, prevPtr, and position
        {
            currPtr = front->NextNode();
            prevPtr = front;
            startPos = 1;
            // move right until position == pos
            for(position=startPos; position != pos; position++)
            {
                // move both traversal pointers forward
                prevPtr = currPtr;
                currPtr = currPtr->NextNode();
            }
        }
    }
}
```

For a sequential scan of the list, we move from element to element in the list by executing the method Next. The function moves prevPtr to the current node and moves currPtr forward one node. If we have traversed all of the nodes in the list, the variable position has value size and currPtr is set to NULL.

```
// move prevPtr and currPtr forward one node
template <class T>
void LinkedList<T>::Next(void)
{
    // if traversal has already reached the end of the list or
    // the list is empty, just return
    if (currPtr != NULL)
    {
        // advance the two pointers one node forward
        prevPtr = currPtr;
        currPtr = currPtr->NextNode();
        position++;
    }
}
```

Data Access   Use the method Data to access the data value in a list node. If the list is empty or the traversal has reached the end of the list, an error message is printed and the program terminates; otherwise, Data returns currPtr−>data.

```
// return a reference to the data value in the current node
template <class T>
T& LinkedList<T>::Data(void)
{
    // error if list is empty or traversal completed
    if (size == 0 || currPtr == NULL)
    {
        cerr << "Data: invalid reference!" << endl;
        exit(1);
    }
    return currPtr->data;
}
```

List Insertion Methods   The LinkedList class provides a series of operations to add a node at the front or rear of the list (InsertFront, InsertRear) or relative to the current position (InsertAt and InsertAfter). The insert methods are passed a data value that is used to initialize the data field of the new node.

InsertAt inserts a node with data value item at the current position in the list. The method uses GetNode to allocate a node with data value item having address newNode, increments the size of the list, and sets the current location to the new node. The algorithm must handle two cases. If the insertion takes place at the front of the list (prevPtr == NULL), update front to point at the new node. If the insertion take place inside the list, place the new node after prevPtr by executing the Node method InsertAfter. Special handling of the pointer rear must occur if the item is inserted into an empty list or at the rear of a non-empty list.

InsertAt (empty list)

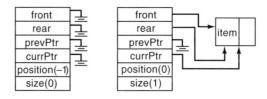

InsertAt (insertion at rear)

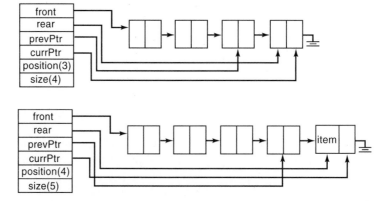

```
// Insert item at the current list position
template <class T>
void LinkedList<T>::InsertAt(const T& item)
{
    Node<T> *newNode;

    // two cases: inserting at the front or inside the list
    if (prevPtr == NULL)
    {
        // inserting at the front of the list. also places
        // node into an empty list
        newNode = GetNode(item,front);
        front = newNode;
    }
    else
    {
        // inserting inside the list. place node after prevPtr
        newNode = GetNode(item);
        prevPtr->InsertAfter(newNode);
    }

    // if prevPtr == rear, insert into an empty list or at the
    // rear of a non-empty list; update rear and position
    if (prevPtr == rear)
    {
        rear = newNode;
        position = size;
    }

    // update currPtr and increment the list size
    currPtr = newNode;
    size++;                 // increment list size
}
```

List Deletion Methods   Two delete operations remove a node from the front of the list (DeleteFront) or from the current position (DeleteAt).

DeleteAt removes the node at address currPtr. If currPtr is NULL, the list is empty or the client has already traversed the entire list. In this case, the function outputs an error message and terminates the program. Otherwise, the algorithm handles two cases. If the deletion removes the first node of the list (prevPtr == NULL), update the pointer front. If this is the last node of the list, front becomes NULL. The second case occurs when prevPtr ≠ NULL and the deleted node is positioned inside the list. Use the Node class method DelteAfter to unlink the node following prevPtr from the list.

Like the InsertAt method, we must pay special attention to the pointer rear. If the node we delete is at the rear (currPtr == rear), the new rear is now prevPtr, position is decremented, and currPtr is NULL. In all other cases, position remains the same. If we delete the last node in the list, the rear becomes NULL, and the value of position changes from 0 to -1. Call FreeNode to delete the node from memory and decrement the list size.

DeleteAt (list becomes empty)

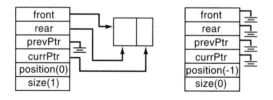

DeleteAt (currPtr is rear)

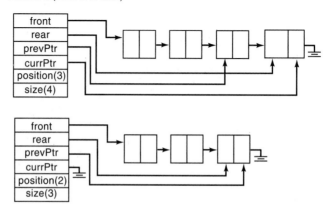

```
// Delete the node at the current list position
template <class T>
void LinkedList<T>::DeleteAt(void)
{
    Node<T> *p;

    // error if empty list or at end of list
    if (currPtr == NULL)
    {
        cerr << "Invalid deletion!" << endl;
        exit(1);
    }

    // deletion must occur at front node or inside the list
    if (prevPtr == NULL)
    {
        // save address of front and unlink it. if this
        // is the last node, front becomes NULL
        p = front;
        front = front->NextNode();
```

```
   }
   else
      // unlink interior node after prevPtr. save address
      p = prevPtr->DeleteAfter();

   // if rear is deleted, new rear is prevPtr and position
   // is decremented; otherwise, position is the same
   // if p was last node, rear = NULL and position = -1
   if (p == rear)
   {
      rear = prevPtr;
      position--;
   }

   // move currPtr past deleted node. if p is last node
   // in the list, currPtr becomes NULL
   currPtr = p->NextNode();

   // free the node and decrement the list size
   FreeNode(p);
   size--;
}

#endif  // LINKEDLIST_CLASS
```

Implementing Collections with Linked Lists   9.6

To this point in the book, we have used array-based implementations of the Stack, Queue, and SeqList classes. In each case, the list of items is stored in an array that is defined as private data member of the class. In this chapter we develop the LinkedList class that provides a powerful dynamic storage structure along with a variety of methods to add and delete items and update data values. By storing the items in a linked list object rather than an array, we have a new implementation strategy that enhances the power and efficiency of our basic list classes. By using the various methods in the LinkedList class, we have the tools to implement the stack, queue, and list operations in a simple and straightforward manner.

In this section, we develop new implementations for the Queue and SeqList classes using linked lists. For the SeqList class, we compare the efficiency of dynamic linked list storage to array-based storage. The Queue class is used in the next section where we develop a printer spooler simulation. A linked list implementation of the Stack class is left as an exercise.

LINKED QUEUES

A LinkedList object is a flexible storage structure for a list of items. The Queue class provides a straightforward implementation of a queue by using composition to include a LinkedList object. The object performs Queue operations by executing the equivalent LinkedList operations. For instance, a LinkedList object allows insertion of an item at the rear of the list (InsertRear) and the deletion of an item from the front of the list (DeleteFront). By repositioning the current pointer to the head of the list (Reset), we can define the QFront operation that extracts the data value from the front of the list. All other queue methods evaluate the state of the list, a task that is handled by the list operations ListEmpty and ListSize. The queue is cleared by simply calling the list method ClearList.

QUEUE CLASS SPECIFICATION (USING A LINKEDLIST OBJECT)

DECLARATION

```
#include "link.h"

template <class T>
class Queue
{
    private:
        // a linked list object to hold the queue items
        LinkedList<T> queueList;
    public:
        // constructor
        Queue(void);

        // queue modification methods
        void QInsert(const T& elt);
        T QDelete(void);

        // queue access
        T QFront(void) const;

        // queue test methods
        int QLength(void) const;
        int QEmpty(void) const;
        void QClear (void);
};
```

DESCRIPTION

The LinkedList object queueList holds the queue items. The object supplies the full range of linked list operations that are used to implement the public Queue methods.

The Queue class does not contain its own destructor, copy constructor, or assignment operator. These methods are not necessary, since they are implemented for the queueList object. The compiler implements assignment and initialization by executing the assignment operator or copy constructor for the object queueList. The destructor for queueList is automatically called when a Queue object is destroyed.

Since items are stored in a linked list, the queue size is not bounded by an implementation constant like MaxQueueSize.

EXAMPLE

```
Queue<int> Q1,Q2;      // declare two queues of integers values

Q1.QInsert(10);        // add 10 and then 50 to Q1

Q1.QInsert(50);

cout << Q1.QFront(); // print value 10 at front of queue


Q2 = Q1;               // use = operator for queueList

Q1.QClear();           // clear the queue and deallocate memory
```

The linked list implementation of the Queue class is found in the file "queue.h".

IMPLEMENTING QUEUE METHODS

To illustrate the implementation of Queue methods, we define the queue modification methods QInsert and QDelete as well as the access method QFront. Each makes direct calls to the equivalent LinkedList method.

The QInsert operation adds an item at the rear of the queue using the LinkedList operation InsertRear.

```
// LinkedList method InsertRear inserts item at rear
template <class T>
void Queue<T>::QInsert(const T& elt)
{
    queueList.InsertRear(elt);
}
```

QDelete first checks the status of the queue and terminates on an empty list. Otherwise, the operation of unlinking the first item from the queue, deleting the memory, and returning the data value is performed using the list operation DeleteFront.

```
// LinkedList method DeleteFront removes item from front
template <class T>
T Queue<T>::QDelete(void)
{
```

```
    // test for an empty queue and terminate if true
    if (queueList.ListEmpty())
    {
        cerr << "Calling QDelete for an empty queue!" << endl;
        exit(1);
    }
    return queueList.DeleteFront();
}
```

The QFront operation retrieves the data value from the first element of queueList. This requires positioning the current pointer to the head of the list and reading its data value. An attempt to call this function with an empty queue creates an error message and terminates the program.

```
// return the data value from the first item in the queue
template <class T>
T Queue<T>::QFront(void)
{
    // test for an empty queue and terminate if true
    if (queueList.ListEmpty())
    {
        cerr << "Calling QFront for an empty queue!" << endl;
        exit(1);
    }

    // reset to front of the queue and return data
    queueList.Reset();
    return queueList.Data();
}
```

LINKED SEQLIST CLASS

The SeqList class defines a restricted storage structure that allows items to be inserted only at the rear of the list and that deletes only the first item in the list or an item that matches a key. The client is permitted to access data in the list using the Find method or by using a position index to read the data value in a node. Like a linked queue, we can use a LinkedList object to hold the data when implementing the SeqList class. Furthermore, the object provides a powerful toolbox of operations to implement the class methods.

- -

SEQLIST CLASS SPECIFICATION

DECLARATION

```
#include "link.h"

template <class T>
class SeqList
{
```

```
    private:
        // linked list object
        LinkedList<T> llist;

    public:
        // constructor
        void SeqList(void);

        // list access method
        int ListSize(void) const;
        int ListEmpty(void) const;
        int Find (T& item);
        T GetData(int pos);

        // list modification methods
        void Insert(const T& item);
        void Delete(const T& item);
        T DeleteFront(void);
        void ClearList (void);
};
```

DESCRIPTION

The class methods are identical to those defined for the array-based version in "aseqlist.h". There is no need to define a destructor, copy constructor, and assignment operator. The compiler creates them by using the corresponding operations in the LinkedList class. The class is located in the file "seqlistl.h".

EXAMPLE

```
SeqList<int> chList;   // allocate a dynamic list of ints
chList.Insert(40);     // add 40 at end of the list
cout << chList.DeleteFront () << endl;   // print 40
```

IMPLEMENTING SEQLIST DATA ACCESS METHODS

The SeqList class permits the user to access data by a key using the Find method or to access data by position in the list. In the first case, we use the traversal mechanism of the LinkedList class to scan the list and search for the key.

```
// take item as the key and search the list. return True if item
// is in the list and False otherwise. if found,
// assign the list element to the reference parameter item
template <class T>
int SeqList<T>::Find (T& item)
{

    // search for the item in list. if found, set result to True
    for(llist.Reset();!llist.EndOfList();llist.Next())
        if (item == llist.Data())
        {
```

```
        result++;
        break;
    }

    // if result is True, update item and return True;
    // otherwise, return False
    if (result)
        item = llist.Data();
    return result;
}
```

GetData is used to access a data element by its position in the list. Use the LinkedList method Reset to establish the traversal mechanism at the required location in the list and execute the Data method to extract the data value.

```
// return the data value of item at position pos
template <class T>
T SeqList<T>::GetData(int pos)
{
    // check for a valid position
    if (pos < 0 || pos >= llist.ListSize())
    {
        cerr << "post is out of range!" << endl;
        exit(1);
    }

    // set current linked list position to pos and return data
    llist.Reset(pos);
    return llist.Data();
}
```

APPLICATION: COMPARING SEQLIST IMPLEMENTATIONS

The array-based version of the SeqList class requires significant overhead to delete an item since all of the elements at the tail of the list must shift to the left. With a linked list implementation, the same operations occur with simple unlinking of pointers. To illustrate the effect of using a linked list storage structure, we compare the array-based and the linked list versions of the SeqList class. After creating an initial list with 500 members, the test repeatedly deletes an item from the front of a list and then inserts an item at the rear of the list. The process is repeated 50,000 times and represents the worst case situation for an array-based SeqList object. We run two equivalent programs on the same computer system and compute the time in seconds to execute the 50,000 insertion/deletion operations.

Program 9.7a   (List Class—Array Implementation)

This test case uses the array-based SeqList class from the file "aseqlist.h". For the purposes of this program only, the constant ARRAYSIZE is modified to allow a list of 500 items. The task was completed in 55 seconds.

```
#include <iostream.h>

// use DataType = int to store integer values in the list
typedef int DataType;

// include the array-based SeqList class
#include "aseqlist.h"

void main(void)
{
    // a list with capacity 500 integers
    SeqList L;
    long  i;

    // initialize the list with values 0 .. 499
    for (i = 0; i < 500; i++)
       L.Insert(i);

    // exercise the delete/insert operations 50000 times
    cout << "Program begin!" << endl;
    for (i = 1; i <= 50000; i++)
    {
       L.DeleteFront();
       L.Insert(0);
    }
    cout << "Program done!" << endl;
}

<Run of Program 9.7a>

Program begin!
Program done!      // 55 seconds
```

Program 9.7b   (List Class—Linked List Implementation)

This program tests the linked list version of the SeqList class from file "seqlistl.h". The task completes execution in 4 seconds!

```
#include <iostream.h>

// include the linked list implementation of the SeqList
#include "seqlistl.h"

void main(void)
{
```

```
        // define an integer list
        SeqList<int> L;
        long  i;

        // initialize the list with values 0 .. 499
        for (i = 0; i < 500; i++)
           L.Insert(i);

        // exercise the delete/insert operations 50000 times
        cout << "Program begin!" << endl;
        for (i = 1; i <= 50000; i++)
        {
           L.Delete Front();
           L.Insert(0);
        }
        cout << "Program done!" << endl;
}


<Run of Program 9.7b>


Program begin!
Program done!    // 4 seconds
```

9.7 Case Study: A Print Spooler

Queues are used to implement print spoolers in an operating system. A print spooler accepts a print request and inserts the file to be printed into a queue. When the printer is available, the spooler deletes a job from the queue and prints the file. The action of a spooler enables printing to occur in the background while the users execute foreground processes.

Problem Analysis

The case study develops a Spooler class whose operations simulate a user adding new jobs to a print queue and checking on the status of jobs already in the queue. A print job is a structure that contains an integer job number, a file name, and a page count.

```
        struct PrintJob
        {
            int  number;
            char filename[20];
            int  pagesize;
        };
```

The simulation assumes the printer operates continuously at the rate of eight pages per minute.

The following time chart illustrates a user sending three jobs to the print spooler.

Job	Name	Number of Pages
45	Thesis	70
6	Letter	5
70	Notes	20

During a time period of 12 minutes, the user adds the three jobs and twice requests a listing of jobs in the queue. The units 4, 1, 5, and 2 represent time between user operations. The values 70, 38, 35, 20, and 4 indicate the number of pages remaining to print at the time of each user operation.

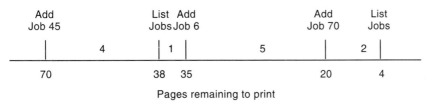

Figure 9.1 tracks the spooler operations from minute 0 through 12. At each event, the number of pages in the spooler, the total number of pages already printed, and the print queue is listed.

Program Design

The print spooler is a list that stores the PrintJob records. Since jobs are handled on a first-come/first-served basis, we treat the list as a queue with job requests inserted at the rear of the list and actual printing handled by removing the job requests from the front of the list. In our case study, we perform tasks that are not available in a formal queue collection. We scan the job requests in the list and print their status. On an update, we modify the page size of the current job without deleting it from the list. To have flexible access to the print jobs, we implement the spooler as a linked list.

The case study uses events to direct the simulation. An event can include adding a print job to the spooler, listing the jobs in the spooler, and checking whether a specific job remains to be printed. Randomly selected time blocks in the range of 1 to 5 minutes separate the events. To simulate the continuous printing of jobs in the background, the study uses the occurrence of an event to update the print queue. Information on the length of time between events is maintained so that we know how many pages have been printed. Assuming the intervening time from the last event is deltaTime, the number of pages that were printed is

```
pagesPrinted = deltaTime * 8
```

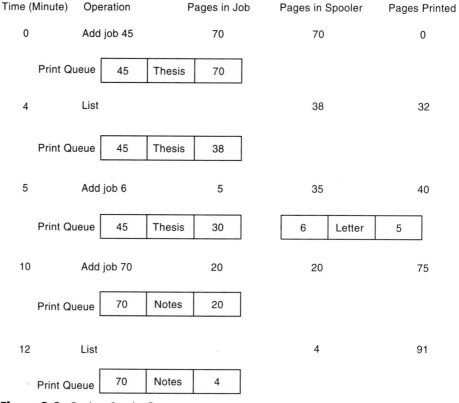

Time (Minute)	Operation	Pages in Job	Pages in Spooler	Pages Printed
0	Add job 45	70	70	0

Print Queue | 45 | Thesis | 70 |

| 4 | List | | 38 | 32 |

Print Queue | 45 | Thesis | 38 |

| 5 | Add job 6 | 5 | 35 | 40 |

Print Queue | 45 | Thesis | 30 | | 6 | Letter | 5 |

| 10 | Add job 70 | 20 | 20 | 75 |

Print Queue | 70 | Notes | 20 |

| 12 | List | | 4 | 91 |

Print Queue | 70 | Notes | 4 |

Figure 9.1 Tracking Spooler Operations

The storage of print jobs and spooler access functions are defined by the following Spooler class.

SPOOLER CLASS SPECIFICATION

DECLARATION

```
#include "random.h"          // simulate print times
#include "link.h"            // contains the LinkedList class

const int PRINTSPEED = 8;    // pages per minute

// the print spooler class
class Spooler
{
```

```
        private:
            // queue that holds print jobs and status
            LinkedList<PrintJob> jobList;

            // deltaTime holds a random value in the range 1 to 5
            // minutes to simulate elapsed time.
            int deltaTime;
            // Job info is updated by the UpdateSpooler method
            void UpdateSpooler(int time);
            RandomNumber rnd;

        public:
            // constructor
            Spooler(void);

            // add job to spooler
            void AddJob(PrintJob J);

            // spooler evaluation methods
            void ListJobs(void);
            int CheckJob(int jobno);
            int NumberOfJobs(void);
    };
```

DESCRIPTION

The private data member deltaTime simulates the number of minutes printing has occurred since the last spooler event. At the start of each event, the operation UpdateSpooler is called with deltaTime as its parameter. This function updates jobList to reflect the fact that printing has occurred in the background for deltaTime minutes. Each public method is responsible for assigning a new value to deltaTime. The value, created by the RandomNumber generator in the range 1 to 5, specifies the number of minutes before the next update event.

Print jobs are added to the spooler using the method AddJob. Two operations ListJobs and CheckJob provide information on the status of the spooler. At any time, the list of jobs in the spooler is printed by calling ListJobs. The method CheckJob accepts a job number and returns information on its status in the spooler. It returns the number of pages remaining to be printed or 0 if it has completed.

NumberOfJobs returns a count of the number of jobs remaining to be printed. The declaration of PrintJob, PRINTSPEED, and the spooler class is embedded in the file "spooler.h".

IMPLEMENTING THE SPOOLER UPDATE METHOD

The update process deletes all jobs whose cumulative page count is less than the pages printed. If the backlog of pages to print is less than or equal to the potential print total, then all of the jobs have finished and the queue is empty. Otherwise, one or more jobs may be deleted from the queue and some pages from the current job may be printed. The update leaves the current job partially complete.

```cpp
// spooler update. assumes time elapses during which pages
// are printed. method deletes completed jobs and updates
// the remaining pages for the current running job
void Spooler::UpdateSpooler(int time)
{
    PrintJob J;

    // number of pages that could print in the given time
    int printedpages = time*PRINTSPEED;

    // use value printedpages and scan list of jobs in queue.
    // update the printqueue for each job.
    jobList.Reset();
    while (!jobList.ListEmpty() && printedpages > 0)
    {
        // look at first job
        J = jobList.Data();

        // if pages printed greater than pages for job,
        // update printed pages count and delete job
        if (printedpages >= J.pagesize)
        {
            printedpages -= J.pagesize;
            jobList.DeleteFront();
        }
        // part of a job complete; update remaining pages
        else
        {
            J.pagesize -= printedpages;
            printedpages = 0;
            jobList.Data() = J;              // update info in node
        }
    }
}
```

SPOOLER EVALUATION METHODS

The spooler evaluation methods respond to a client's request for information on the jobs waiting to print and the status of a particular job. The methods ListJobs and CheckJob make a sequential scan of the spooler list. We illustrate the algorithm for ListJobs and refer the reader to the other methods in the file "spooler.h".

ListJobs begins at the head of the list (Reset) and continues from node to node (Next) up to the end of the list (EndOfList). The information for each PrintJob is output.

```
// update spooler and list all jobs currently in spooler
void Spooler::ListJobs(void)
{
    PrintJob J;

    // update the print queue
    UpdateSpooler(deltaTime);

    // generate the time until the next event
    deltaTime = 1 + rnd.Random(5);

    // check for empty spooler before scanning the list
    if (jobList.ListSize() == 0)
        cout << "Print queue is empty\n";
    else
    {
        // reset to beginning of list and use a
        // loop to scan the list of jobs. stop on end of list.
        // print information fields for each job
        for(jobList.Reset(); !jobList.EndOfList();
                                        jobList.Next())
        {
            J = jobList.Data();
            cout << "Job " << J.number << ": " << J.filename;
            cout << "    " << J.pagesize << " pages remaining"
                << endl;
        }
    }
}
```

Program 9.8   A Print Spooler

This main program defines a Spooler object spool and creates an interactive dialog with the user. With each iteration, the user is provided a menu of four choices. The choices 'A' (AddJob), 'L' (ListJob), and 'C' (CheckJob) update the print queue and execute a spooler operation. Choice 'Q' terminates the program. Choices 'L' and 'C' are not listed if the print queue is empty.

```
#include <iostream.h>
#include <ctype.h>

#include "spooler.h"

void main(void)
{
```

```cpp
// the print spooler object
Spooler spool;
int jnum, jobno = 0, rempages;
char response = 'C';
PrintJob J;

for (;;)
{
    // user choices. can check only if jobs present
    if (spool.NumberOfJobs() != 0)
        cout << "Add(A) List(L) Check(C) Quit(Q) ==> ";
    else
        cout << "Add(A) Quit(Q) ==> ";
    cin >> response;
    // convert response to uppercase
    respond = toupper(response);

    // action dictated by the response
    switch(response)
    {
        //   add a new job with next number used as id; read
        // file name and the number of pages.
        case 'A':
            J.number = jobno;
            jobno++;
            cout << "File name: ";
            cin >> J.filename;
            cout << "Number of pages: ";
            cin >> J.pagesize;
            spool.AddJob(J);
            break;

        // print info for each remaining printer job
        case 'L':
            spool.ListJobs();
            break;

        // input job id; scan list with this key. indicate if
        // job complete or number of remaining pages to print
        case 'C':
            cout << "Enter job number: ";
            cin >> jnum;
            rempages = spool.CheckJob(jnum);
            if (rempages > 0)
                cout << "Job is in the queue. " << rempages
                     << " pages remain to print" << endl;
            else
                cout << "Job has completed" << endl;
            break;
```

```
                    // exit the switch and test for input 'Q'
                    case 'Q':
                        break;

                    // indicate an invalid request and redraw the menu
                    default:
                        cout << "Invalid spooler command.\n";
                        break;
                }
            if (response == 'Q')
                break;
            cout << endl;
        }
}


/*
<Run of Program 9.8>

Add (A)    Quit (Q) ==> a
File name: notes
Number of pages: 75


Add (A)    List(L)    Check (C)    Quit (Q) ==> a
File name: paper
Number of pages: 25


Add (A)    List(L)    Check (C)    Quit (Q) ==> l
Job 0: notes    19 pages remaining
Job 1: paper    25 pages remaining


Add (A)    List(L)    Check (C)    Quit (Q) ==> c
Enter job number: 1
Job is in the queue. 20 pages remain to be printed


Add (A)    List(L)    Check (C)    Quit (Q) ==> l
Print queue is empty


Add (A)    Quit (Q) ==> q
*/
```

Circular Lists   9.8

A NULL-terminated linked list is a sequence of nodes that begins with a head node and ends with a NULL pointer field. In Section 9.1, we developed a library of functions to scan such a list and to insert and delete nodes. Each algorithm has increased complexity deriving from tests to determine if the list is empty or has additional code to update the head pointer. In this section, we develop an alternative model for a list called a **circular linked list,** which simplifies the design and coding of sequential list algorithms. Many professional programmers use the circular model to implement linked lists.

An empty circular list contains a node, which has an uninitialized data field. This node is called the **header** and initially points to itself. The role of the header is to point to the first "real" node in the list and hence the header is often referred to as a **sentinel** node. In the circular model of a linked list, an empty list actually contains one node, and the NULL pointer is never used. We illustrate the header by using angle lines for the side of the node.

Note that for a standard linked list and a circular linked list, the tests to determine if a list is empty are different.

```
Standard linked list:       head == NULL
Circular linked list:       header->next == header
```

As nodes are added to the list, the last node points to the header node. We can think of a circular linked list as being a bracelet with the header node serving as a clasp. The header ties together the real nodes in the list.

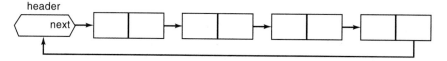

In Section 9.1, we described the Node class and used its methods to build linked lists. In this section, we declare the CNode class, which builds nodes for a circular list. The class provides a default constructor that allows an uninitialized data field. This constructor is used to create the header.

- -

CIRCULAR NODE CLASS SPECIFICATION

DECLARATION

```
template <class T>
class CNode
{
    private:
        // circular link to the next node
        CNode<T> *next;
```

```
public:
    // data is public
    T data;

    // constructors
    CNode(void);
    CNode (const T& item);

    // list modification methods
    void InsertAfter(CNode<T> *p);
    CNode<T> *DeleteAfter(void);

    // obtain the address of the next node
    CNode<T> *NextNode(void) const;
};
```

DESCRIPTION

The class is similar to the Node class in Section 9.1. In fact, all the class members have the same name and the same function. The details for the public members is given in the next section on the class implementation. The circular node class is contained in the file "cnode.h".

CIRCULAR NODE CLASS IMPLEMENTATION

The constructors initialize a node by having it point to itself, so each node can serve as a header for an empty list. Conveniently, "itself" is the pointer this and hence the assignment becomes

```
next = this;        // the next node is itself
```

For the default constructor, the data field is not initialized. A second constructor takes a parameter and uses it to initialize the data field.

Neither constructor requires a parameter specifying an initial value for the next field. All required alterations of the next field are accomplished by using the InsertAfter and DeleteAfter methods.

```
// constructor that creates an empty list and initializes data
template <class T>
CNode<T>::CNode(const T& item)
{
    // set node to point to itself and initialize data
    next = this;
    data = item;
}
```

Circular Node Operations   The Circular Node class provides the NextNode method, which is used to traverse a list. Like the Node class method, NextNode returns the pointer value next.

InsertAfter adds node p immediately after the current object. No special algorithm is required to load a node at the front of a list since we merely execute InsertAfter(header). The presence of a sentinel or header node eliminates the technical special case of the head that haunts list processing.

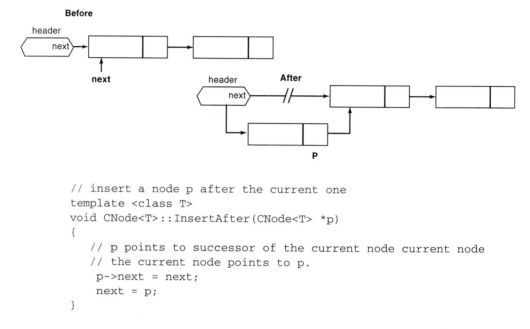

```
// insert a node p after the current one
template <class T>
void CNode<T>::InsertAfter(CNode<T> *p)
{
    // p points to successor of the current node current node
    // the current node points to p.
    p->next = next;
    next = p;
}
```

The removal of a node from the list is handled by the DeleteAfter method. DeleteAfter removes the node immediately following the current node and then returns a pointer to the deleted node. If next == this, there are no other nodes in the list, and a node should not delete itself. In this case, the operation returns the value NULL.

```
// delete the node following current and return its address
template <class T>
CNode<T> *CNode<T>::DeleteAfter(void)
{
    // save address of node to be deleted
    CNode<T> *tempPtr = next;

    // if next is the address of current object (this), we are
    // pointing to ourself. we don't delete ourself! return NULL
    if (next == this)
        return NULL;

    // current node points to successor of tempPtr.
    next = tempPtr->next;
```

```
        // return the pointer to the unlinked node
        return tempPtr;
}
```

APPLICATION: SOLVING THE JOSEPHUS PROBLEM

The Josephus problem presents an interesting application that provides an elegant circular linked list solution. The following is a version of the problem.

> A travel agent selects n customers to compete in a contest for a free world cruise. The agent places the customers in a circle and then draws a number m (m ≤ n) from a hat. The game is played by having the agent rotate clockwise about the circle and stop at every mth contestant. This person is removed from the game and the process continues with the agent eliminating every m'th person until only one remains. That survivor wins the world cruise.

For example, if n = 8 and m = 3, then people are eliminated in the order 3, 6, 1, 5, 2, 8, 4, and person 7 wins the cruise.

Program 9.9   The Josephus Problem

This program emulates the world cruise contest. The function Createlist builds the circular list 1, 2, . . . , n using the CNode method InsertAfter.

The selection process is handled by the function Josephus that takes the header for the circular list and the random number m. It executes n − 1 iterations, each time counting m successive items in the list and deleting the m'th item. As we continue to circle the list, we print the number of each person that is eliminated. At the conclusion of the loop, one item remains.

The main program prompts for the number of contestants n and uses CreateList to build the circular list. A random number m in the range 1 . . . n is generated, and Josephus is called to determine the order of contestant elimination and the winner of the world cruise.

```
#include <iostream.h>

#include "cnode.h"
#include "random.h"

// create integer circular linked list with given header node
void CreateList(CNode<int> *header, int n)
{
    // begin inserting after the header
    CNode<int> *currPtr = header, *newNodePtr;
    int i;
```

```cpp
    // build the n element circular list
    for(i=1;i <= n;i++)
    {
        // allocate node with data value i
        newNodePtr = new CNode<int>(i);

        // insert at end of the list and advance currPtr to end
        currPtr->InsertAfter(newNodePtr);
        currPtr = newNodePtr;
    }
}

// given an n item circular list, solve the Josephus problem
// by deleting every m'th person until only one remains.
void Josephus(CNode<int> *list, int n, int m)
{
    //prevPtr trails currPtr around the list.
    CNode<int> *prevPtr = list, *currPtr = list->NextNode();

    CNode<int> *deletedNodePtr;

    // delete all but one person from the list
    for(int i=0;i < n-1;i++)
    {
        // counting current person at currPtr, visit m persons.
        // we must advance m-1 times.
        for(int j=0;j < m-1;j++)
        {
            // advance the pointers
            prevPtr = currPtr;
            currPtr = currPtr->NextNode();

            // if currPtr at the header, move pointers again
            if (currPtr == list)
            {
                prevPtr = list;
                currPtr = currPtr->NextNode();
            }
        }

        cout << "Delete person " << currPtr->data << endl;

        // record node to delete and advance currPtr
        deletedNodePtr = currPtr;
        currPtr = currPtr->NextNode();

        // delete node from the list
        prevPtr->DeleteAfter();
        delete deletedNodePtr;
```

```
        // if currPtr at the header, move pointers again
        if (currPtr == list)
        {
            prevPtr = list;
            currPtr = currPtr->NextNode();
        }
    }

    cout << endl << "Person " << currPtr->data
        << " wins the cruise." << endl;

    // delete the one remaining node
    deletedNodePtr = list->DeleteAfter();
    delete deletedNodePtr;
}

void main(void)
{
    // the list of persons
    CNode<int> list;

    // n is number of persons, m is rotation selector
    int n, m;
    // use to generate random value 1 <= m <= n
    RandomNumber rnd;

    cout << "Enter the number of contestants? ";
    cin >> n;

    // create circular list with persons 1, 2, ... n
    CreateList(&list,n);

    m = 1+rnd.Random(n);
    cout << "Generated the random number " << m << endl;

    // solve the Josephus problem and print the cruise winner
    Josephus(&list,n,m);
}

/*
<Run of Program 9.9>

Enter the number of contestants? 10
Generated the random number 5
Delete person 5
Delete person 10
Delete person 6
Delete person 2
Delete person 9
```

```
Delete person 8
Delete person 1
Delete person 4
Delete person 7


Person 3 wins the cruise.
*/
```

9.9   Doubly Linked Lists

The scanning of either a NULL-terminated or circular linked list occurs from left to right. The circular list is more flexible, allowing a scan to begin at any location in the list and continue around to the starting position. These lists have limitations since they do not allow the user to retrace steps and scan backward in the list. They inefficiently handle the simple task of deleting a node p since we must traverse the list and find the pointer to the node preceding p.

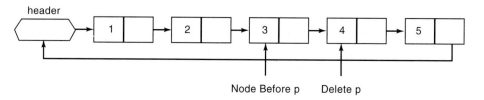

With some applications, the user wants to access a list in reverse order. For instance, a baseball manager maintains a list of players ordered by batting average from lowest to highest. To measure the hitting proficiency of the players for the batting title, the list must be traversed in reverse. This can be done using a stack but the algorithm is not very convenient.

In cases where we need to access nodes in either direction, a **doubly linked list** is helpful. A node in a doubly linked list contains two pointers and the data field.

Doubly linked nodes extend a circular list to create a powerful and flexible list handling structure.

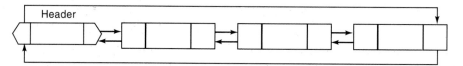

There is an insert and delete operation in each direction. The following picture illustrates the problem of inserting a node p to the right of the current node. Four new links must be assigned.

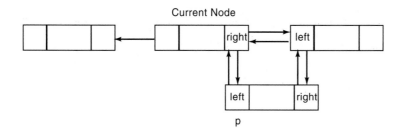

With a doubly linked list, a node can remove itself from the list by changing two pointers. The following highlights the changes.

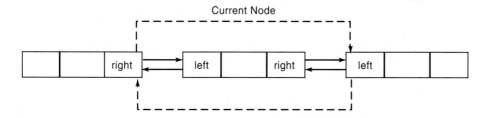

The class DNode is a node handling class for circular doubly linked lists. The class declaration and member functions are contained in the file "dnode.h".

- -
DNODE CLASS SPECIFICATION

DECLARATION

```
template <class T>
class DNode
{
    private:
      // circular links to the left and right
        DNode<T> *left;
        DNode<T> *right;
    public:
      // data is public
      T data;

      // constructors
      DNode(void);
      DNode (const T& item);
```

```
                // list modification methods
                void InsertRight(DNode<T> *p);
                void InsertLeft(DNode<T> *p);
                DNode<T> *DeleteNode(void);

                // obtain address of the next node to the left or right
                DNode<T> *NextNodeRight(void) const;
                CNode<T> *NextNodeLeft(void) const;
        };
```

DESCRIPTION

The data members are similar to the singly linked CNode class except that two "next" pointers are used. There are two insert operations, one for each direction, and the delete operation, which removes the current node from the list. The value of a private pointer is returned using the functions NextNodeRight and NextNodeLeft.

EXAMPLE

```
    // a doubly linked list with header = dlist
    DNode<int> dlist;

    // scan the list, printing node values until we return to
    // the header node
    DNode<int> *p = &dlist;       // initialize a pointer
    p = p->NextNodeRight();       // set p to first node in list

    while (p != &dlist)
    {
       cout << p->data <<" ";     // print the data value
       p = p->NextNodeRight();    // set p to next node in list
    }

    DNode<int>   *newNode1(10);   // allocate nodes with values
    DNode<int>   *newNode2(20);   // 10 and 20
    DNode<int>   *p = &dlist;     // p points at header node
    p->InsertRight(newNode1);     // insert at front of list
    p->InsertLeft(newNode2);      // insert at rear of list
```

APPLICATION: DOUBLY LINKED LIST SORT

The InsertOrder function is used in Program 9.4 to create a sorted list. The algorithm starts at the head node and scans the list, looking for the insertion point. With a doubly linked list, we can optimize the process by maintaining the pointer currPtr that identifies the last node that was placed in the list. To insert a new item, we compare its value with the data at the current location. If the new item is smaller, use the left pointers to scan down the list. If the new item is larger, use the right pointers to scan up the list. For instance, assume we have just stored 40 in list "dlist".

dlist: 10 25 30 40 50 55 60 75 90

To add node 70, scan up the list and insert 70 to the right of 60. To add node 35, scan down the list and insert 35 to the left of 40.

Program 9.10 Sorting with Doubly Linked Lists

DLinkSort uses a doubly linked list to sort an n-element array by creating an ordered list and then copying the elements back to the array. The function InsertHigher adds a new node to the right of the current list position. The symmetric function InsertLower adds a new node to the left of the current position.

Insert item 1
    call InsertRight with the header and store a[0]

Insert items 2 − 10
    if item < currPtr->data, call InsertLower
    if item > currPtr->data, call InsertHigher

In this program a list of 10 integers is sorted using DLinkSort. The sorted list is output using PrintArray.

```
#include <iostream.h>

#include "dnode.h"

template <class T>
void InsertLower(DNode<T> *dheader, DNode<T>* &currPtr, T item)
{
    DNode<T> *newNode= new DNode<T>(item), *p;

    // look for the insertion point
    p = currPtr;
    while (p != dheader && item < p->data)
        p = p->NextNodeLeft();

    // insert the item
    p->InsertRight(newNode);

    // reset currPtr to the new node
    currPtr = newNode;
}
```

```cpp
template <class T>
void InsertHigher(DNode<T>* dheader, DNode<T>* & currPtr,
                T item)
{
    DNode<T> *newNode= new DNode<T>(item), *p;

    // look for the insertion point
    p = currPtr;
    while (p != dheader && p->data < item)
        p = p->NextNodeRight();

    // insert the item
    p->InsertLeft(newNode);

    // reset currPtr to the new node
    currPtr = newNode;
}

template <class T>
void DLinkSort(T a[], int n)
{
    // set up the doubly linked list to hold array items
    DNode<T> dheader, *currPtr;
    int i;

    // insert the first element in dlist
    DNode<T>  *newNode = new DNode<T>(a[0]);
    dheader.InsertRight(newNode);
    currPtr = newNode;

    // insert the remaining elements in dlist
    for (i=1;i < n;i++)
        if (a[i] < currPtr->data)
            InsertLower(&dheader,currPtr,a[i]);
        else
            InsertHigher(&dheader,currPtr,a[i]);

    // scan the list and copy the data values back to the array
    currPtr = dheader.NextNodeRight();
    i = 0;
    while(currPtr != &dheader)
    {
        a[i++] = currPtr->data;
        currPtr = currPtr->NextNodeRight();
    }

    // delete all nodes in the list
    while(dheader.NextNodeRight() != &dheader)
    {
```

```
                currPtr = (dheader.NextNodeRight())->DeleteNode();
                delete currPtr;
        }
}

// scan the array and print its elements
void PrintArray(int a[], int n)
{
    for(int i=0;i < n;i++)
        cout << a[i] << "  ";
}

void main(void)
{
    // initialized array with 10 integer values
    int A[10] = {82,65,74,95,60,28,5,3,33,55};

    DLinkSort(A,10);                    // sort the array
    cout << "Sorted array:     ";
    PrintArray(A,10);                   // print the array
    cout << endl;
}

/*
<Run of Program 9.10>

Sorted array:    3  5  28  33  55  60  65  74  82  95
*/
```

DNODE CLASS IMPLEMENTATION

A constructor creates an empty list by assigning the node address this to both left and right. If a parameter item is passed to the constructor, the node's data member is initialized to item.

```
// constructor that creates an empty list and initializes data
template <class T>
DNode<T>::DNode(const T& item)
{
    // set node to point to itself and initialize data
    left = right = this;
    data = item;
}
```

List Operations   To insert node p to the right of the current node, four pointers must be assigned. Figure 9.2 shows the correspondence between the C++ statements and the new links. Note that the assignments cannot be done in arbitrary order. For instance, if (4) is done first, the link to the node following the current

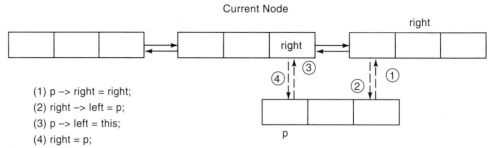

(1) p –> right = right;
(2) right –> left = p;
(3) p –> left = this;
(4) right = p;

Figure 9.2 Inserting a Node to the Right in a Circular Doubly Linked List

node is lost. The reader should verify that the algorithm works correctly in the case of insertion into an empty list.

```
// insert a node p to the right of current node
template <class T>
void DNode<T>::InsertRight(DNode<T> *p)
{
    // link p to its successor on the right
    p->right = right;
    right->left = p;

    // link p to the current node on its left
    p->left = this;
    right = p;
}
```

The InsertLeft method exchanges right with left in the algorithm for InsertRight.

```
// insert a node p to the left of current node
template <class T>
void DNode<T>::InsertLeft(DNode<T> *p)
{
    // link p to its successor on the left
    p->left = left;
    left->right = p;

    // link p to the current node on its right
    p->right = this;
    left = p;
}
```

To delete the current node, two pointers must be changed, as depicted in Figure 9.3. The reader should verify that the algorithm words correctly in the case where the last node of a list is deleted. The method returns a pointer to the deleted node.

```
// unlink the current node from the list and return its address
template <class T>
```

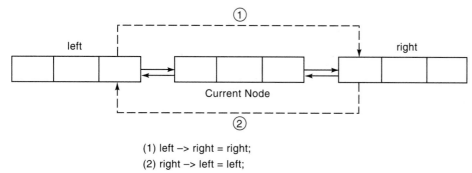

(1) left –> right = right;

(2) right –> left = left;

Figure 9.3   Deleting a Node in a Circular Doubly Linked List

```
DNode<T> *DNode<T>::DeleteNode(void)
{
   // node on the left is linked to right node
   left->right = right;

   // node on the right is linked to left node
   right->left = left;

   // return the address of the current node
   return this;
}
```

Case Study: Window Management   9.10

A graphical user interface (GUI) maintains multiple windows on the screen. They are organized in layers with the front window considered to be the **active window.** Some application programs maintain a list of currently open windows. The list is available from the menu and allows the user to select a title and make it the front or active window. This can be particularly helpful when a rear window is blocked from view. For instance, Figure 9.4 illustrates three windows where (at left) "Window_0" is the active window. The selection of "Window_1" from the menu list activates that window and makes it the front window.

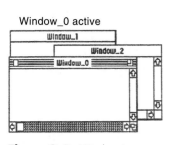

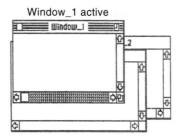

Figure 9.4   Window Lists

Each window on the screen is associated with a file. A window is created when the corresponding file is opened and the window is destroyed when the file is closed. We use a linked list to hold our window list. For each file operation, we associate a corresponding operation on the window list. The file operations New creates a front window, which is added at the front of the list. The file operations such as Close and Save As apply to the active window at the front of the list. A general operation such as Close All can be implemented by deleting each window from the list and closing both the window and corresponding file.

This case study maintains a list of windows for a GUI application. The application supports the following file and list operations.

New: Inserts a window with name "Untitled".
Close: Deletes the front window.
Close All: Closes all windows by clearing the list.
Save As: Saves the contents of the window under a different file name and updates the title in window entry.
Quit: Terminates the application.
Menu Display: The window menu displays the number and name of each window in the order of its layering. The user may enter the number and activate the window, moving it to the front of the window list.

THE WINDOW LIST

At any time, a maximum of 10 open windows is allowed. Each open window has a corresponding number in the range 0 to 9. When a window is closed, the number becomes available for the New operation that creates a new open window. Handling the individual windows and changing the current active window is the responsibility of the Close, Close All, Save As, and Activate methods. Each window is represented by a window object that specifies the name of the window and its number (index) in the list of available windows.

A window object is described by the Window class that contains a windowTitle and a windowNumber field. The class contains member functions to change the window title, to get the window number, and output the information in the format Title[window number]. An overloaded relational equals operator ("==") compares two Window records by window number.

- -

WINDOW CLASS SPECIFICATION

DECLARATION

```
// class that contains information for an individual window
class Window
{
    private:
        // window data includes its title and its index in
```

```
                // the table of available windows
                String windowTitle;
                int windowNumber;

        public:
                // constructors
                Window(void);
                Window(const String& title, int wnum);

                // data access methods
                void ChangeTitle(const String& title);
                int GetWindowNumber(void);

                // overloaded operators
                int operator== (const Window& w);
                friend ostream& operator<< (ostream& ostr,
                                            const Window& w);
    };
```

The complete implementation of the Window class is given in "windlist.h". The window list and the operations to create, save, close, and activate window objects are defined by the WindowList class.

- -

WINDOWLIST CLASS SPECIFICATION

DECLARATION

```
    #include "link.h"       // use LinkedList class

    // linked list storage structure that holds Window objects
    class WindowList
    {
        private:
            // list of active windows
            LinkedList<Window> windList;

            // list of available windows and number of open windows
            int windAvail[10];
            int windCount;

            // functions to get and free windows
            int GetWindowNumber(void);
            int FindAndDelete(Window& wind);

            // print list of open windows
            void PrintWindowList(void);
```

```
        public:
            // constructor
            WindowList(void);

            // window menu methods
            void New(void);
            void Close(void);                      // close front window
            void CloseAll(void);                   // close all windows
            void SaveAs(const String& name);       // change name
            void Activate(int windowum);           // activate windownum

            // simulate a menu manager
            void SelectItem(int& item, String& name);
    };
```

DESCRIPTION

The constructor assigns initial window data. It sets the window count to zero and marks each window in the range 0–9 available. New gets a window from the list of available windows and assigns the index as the window number. The window is given the generic title "Untitled". The new window is inserted at the front of the open window list.

The WindowList class supports the additional operations, Close, Close All, Save As, and Activate. These operations implement the corresponding menu options.

The operation SelectItem implements the menu. The user may type either an alphabetic character N (New), C (Close), A (CloseAll), S (SaveAs), Q (Quit) or a digit 0, 1, ... The method returns the input selection and an interally generated item number that indicates the operation. The following table relates the item number and the selection.

Item Number	Name	Character Code to Select
1	New	n (N)
2	Close	c (C)
3	Close All	a (A)
4	Save As	s (S)
5	Quit	q (Q)
6	WindowName[i_0]	i_0
7	WindowName[i_1]	i_1
	. . .	
15	WindowName[i_9]	i_9

Menu items 2–4 are printed only if there is at least one window open. The printing of the window names and numbers is controlled by the private method PrintWindowList. The items from 6 on correspond to the list of currently open windows. Item 6 is the front window with window number i_0; item 7 is the second window with number i₁, and so forth. A window is brought to the front of the list by typing its window number. New windows are given the smallest available window number in the range 0–9. For instance, if window numbers 0, 1, 3, and 5 are in use and 0 is closed, the next new window is created with window number 0. The function GetWindowNumber executes the algorithm for allocating window numbers.

EXAMPLE

The following table gives a sequence of window commands. After completing an operation, we give the window list with the first entry being the active window. For the SaveAs command, followup input is included in parentheses.

Selection	Item Number	Action	Window List
N	1	new window	Untitled[0]
N	1	new window	Untitled[1] Untitled[0]
S (One)	4	save as "one"	One[1] Untitled[0]
0	7	activate 0	Untitled[0] One[1]
N	1	new window	Untitled[2] Untitled[0] One[1]
C	2	close	Untitled[0] One[1]
C	2	close	One[1]
N	1	new window	Untitled[0] One[1]
A	3	close all	<empty>
Q	5	quit	terminate application

WINDOWLIST CLASS IMPLEMENTATION

A complete listing of the WindowList methods is contained in "windlist.h". We describe the code for several of the functions to illustrate the use of a linked list in maintaining the list of open windows and executing menu options. The function GetWindowNumber traverses the array windAvail searching for an available window number. It returns the first one found. As a result, all new windows receive the lowest possible window number.

```
// get first free window from available window list
int WindowList::GetWindowNumber(void)
{
    for(int i=0;i < 10;i++)
      // if it is available, select it.
      // set the window to be unavailable.
        if (windAvail[i])
        {
            windAvail[i] = 0;
            break;
        }
    return i;          // return window index
}
```

The private PrintWindowList function scans the window list and prints the title and number for each window. The method implements a simple sequential scan of the list starting at the first window (Reset) and moving from window to window (Next) until reaching the end of the list (EndOfList). The "<<" operator from the Window class prints the window data in the format Title[#].

```
// print window information for all active windows
void WindowList::PrintWindowList(void)
{
    for(windList.Reset(); !windList.EndOfList();
        windList.Next())
            cout << windList.Data();
}
```

Window List Operations   To create a window, the method New assigns a Window object win to have the title "Untitled". By calling GetWindowNumber, the function assigns a window number to the object, inserts it in the window list, and increments the window count.

```
// get a new window and give it the name 'untitled'
void WindowList::New(void)
{
    // check if a window is available. if not, quietly return
    if (windCount == 10)
    {
        cerr << "No more windows available until one is"
            << "closed" << endl;
        return;
    }

    // get a new 'Untitled' window by calling GetWindowNumber
    Window win("Untitled", GetWindowNumber());

    // make it active by inserting it in the front of the list
    windList.InsertFront(win);
    windCount++;
}
```

To activate a window that is layered behind other windows, we must first find the window using its number as a key and then delete that entry from the list. By reinserting the window at the front of the list, it becomes active. We call the private method FindAndDelete, which scans the list looking for a match with the window number. When the window is located, the method unlinks it from the list and returns the window data. This information is then used to create a new window, which is inserted at the front of the list.

```
// find object with matching window number in windList
// delete it and return its value in wind
```

```
int WindowList::FindAndDelete(Window& wind)
{
    int retval;

    // cycle through the list search for wind
    for (windList.Reset();!windList.EndOfList();windList.Next())
        // window "==" operator compares window numbers
        // break loop if have a match
        if(wind == windList.Data())
            break;
    // have window numbers matched?
    if(!windList.EndOfList())
    {
        // assign wind, delete record and return 1 (success)
        wind = windList.Data();
        windList.DeleteAt();
        retval = 1;
    }
    else
        retval = 0;          // return 0 (failure)
    return retval;
}
// bring windownum to the front
void WindowList::Activate(int windownum)
{
    Window win("Dummy Name", windownum);

    if (FindAndDelete(win))
        windList.InsertFront(win);
    else
        cerr << "Incorrect window number." endl;
}
```

Program 9.11   *Maintaining a Window List*

This main program defines a WindowList object windops that contains the list
of open windows. An event loop calls the function SelectItem and responds to
the item number it returns. The loop continues until the user selects "Q" (Quit).

```
#include <iostream.h>

// include the Window class and WindowList class
#include "windlist.h"

// used to clear the input buffer to end of line
void ClearEOL(void)
```

```
{
    char c;

    do
        cin.get(c);
    while (c != '\n');
}

void main(void)
{
    // list of available windows for the program
    WindowList windops;

    // window tiles
    String wtitle, itemText;

    int done = 0, item;

    // run the simulation until user types 'q'
    while(!done)
    {
        // print the menu options and get a user selection.
        windops.SelectItem(item,itemText);

        // if the user selects a number, activate that window
        if (item >= 6)
            windops.Activate(itemText[0] - '0');

        // otherwise select from the options 0-5
        // call the method to process the request
        else
            switch(item)
            {
                case 0:     break;
                case 1:     windops.New();
                            break;
                case 2:     windops.Close();
                            break;
                case 3:     windops.CloseAll();
                            break;
                case 4:     cout << "New Window Title: ";
                            ClearEOL();
                            wtitle.ReadString();
                            windops.SaveAs(wtitle);
                            break;
                case 5:     done = 1;
                            break;
            }
    }
}
```

```
/*
<Run of Program 9.11>

New   Quit: n
New   Close   Close All   Save As   Quit   Untitled[0]: n
New   Close   Close All   Save As   Quit   Untitled[1]   Untitled[0]: s
New Window Title: one
New   Close   Close All   Save As   Quit   one[1]   Untitled[0]: 0
New   Close   Close All   Save As   Quit   Untitled[0]   one[1]: s
New Window Title: two
New   Close   Close All   Save As   Quit   two[0]   one[1]: n
New   Close   Close All   Save As   Quit   Untitled[2] two[0] one[1]: s
New Window Title: three
New   Close   Close All   Save As   Quit   three[2]   two[0]   one[1]: 0
New   Close   Close All   Save As   Quit   two[0]   three[2]   one[1]: c
New   Close   Close All   Save As   Quit   three[2]   one[1]: a
New   Quit: q
*/
```

Written Exercises

9.1 Assume the following sequence of statements are executed:

```
Node<int> *p1, *p2;

p1 = new Node<int>(2);
p2 = new Node<int>(3);
```

What is printed by each program segment?

(a) `cout << p1->data << " " << p2->data << endl;`

(b) `p1->data = 5;`
     `p1->InsertAfter(p2);`
     `cout << p1->data << " " << p1->NextNode()->data << endl;`

(c) `p1->data = 7;`
     `p2->data = 9;`
     `p2 = p1;`
     `cout << p1->data << " " << p2->data << endl;`

(d) `p1->data = 8;`
     `p2->data = 15;`
     `p2->InsertAfter(p1);`
     `cout << p1->data << " " << p2->NextNode()->data << endl;`

(e) `p1->data = 77;`
     `p2->data = 17;`
     `p1->InsertAfter(p2);`
     `p2->InsertAfter(p1);`
     `cout << p1->data << " " << p2->NextNode()->data << endl;`

9.2 You are given the following linked list of Node objects and pointers P1, P2, P3, and P4. For each code segment, draw a similar figure indicating how the list changes.

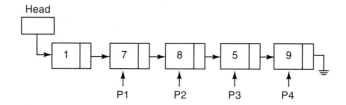

(a) `P2 = P1->NextNode();`
(b) `head = P1->NextNode();`
(c) `P3->data = P1->data;`
(d) `P3->data = P1->NextNode()->data;`
(e) `P2 = P1->DeleteAfter();`
`delete P2;`
(f) `P2->InsertAfter(new Node<int>(3));`
(g) `P1->NextNode()->NextNode()->NextNode()->data = P1->data;`
(h) `Node<int> *P = P1;`

```
while(P != NULL)
{
    P->data *= 3;
    P = P->NextNode();
}
```

(i) `Node<int> *P = P1;`

```
while(P->NextNode() != NULL)
{
    P->data *= 3;
    P = P->NextNode();
}
```

9.3 Write a code segment that creates the linked list with data values 1..20.

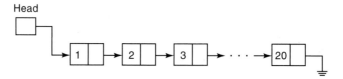

9.4 List the contents of the linked list after each of the following statements. For the "cout" statement, give the output.

```
Node<char> *head, *p, *q;

head = new Node<char>('B');
head = new Node<char>('A',head);
q = new Node<char>('C');
p = head;
p = p->NextNode();
p->InsertAfter(q);
cout << p->data << " " << p->NextNode()->data << endl;
```

```
q = p->DeleteAfter();
delete q;
q = head;
head = head->NextNode();
delete q;
```

9.5   Write the function

```
template <class T>
Node<T> *Copy(Node<T> *p);
```

that creates a linked list that is a copy of the list beginning with node p.

9.6   Assume you are writing a Node class method and thus are able to alter the next data member. Describe the effect of the statements. Since the code occurs in a method, you have access to the pointers "next" and "this".

```
Node<T> *p;
```

(a)   `p = next;`
       `p->next = next;`
(b)   `p = this;`
       `next->next = p;`
(c)   `next = next->next;`
(d)   `p = this;`
       `next->next = p->next;`

9.7   Instead of maintaining a pointer to the head of a linked list of Node objects, we can maintain a header node. Its data value is not considered part of the list, and its next data member points to the first data node in the linked list. The header is called a sentinel node and avoids the case of an empty list.

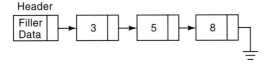

Assume a linked list of integers is maintained using the header node

```
Node<int> header(0);
```

(a)   Write a code sequence to insert a node p at the front of the list.
(b)   Write a code sequence to delete a node from the front of the list.

9.8   This exercise assumes that linked lists are created and maintained using the Node class. Two ordered lists L1 and L2 can be merged into a third list L3 by carefully traversing the two ordered lists and inserting nodes into the third list. At any point, you consider one value from L1 and one from L2, inserting the lesser value at the rear of L3. When a value is inserted, move forward in its list. For instance, consider the following sequence of insertions. The current elements under consideration in L1 and L2 are circled.

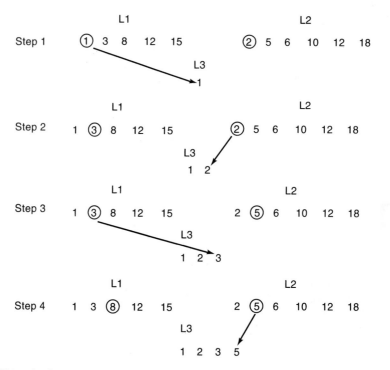

Write the function

```
void MergeLists(Node<T> *L1, Node<T>* L2, Node<T>* &L3);
```

to merge L1 and L2 into L3.

9.9 What is the action of this code sequence?

```
while(currPtr != NULL)
{
   currPtr->data += 7;
   currPtr = currPtr->NextNode();
}
```

9.10 Describe the action of function F.

```
template <class T>
void F(Node<T>* &head)
{
   Node<T> *p, *q;

   if (head != NULL&& head->NextNode()!=NULL)
   {
      q = head;
      head = p = head->NextNode();
```

```
        while(p->NextNode() != NULL)
            p = p->NextNode();
        p->InsertAfter(q);
    }
}
```

9.11 Write a function

```
template <class T>
int CountKey(const Node<T> *head, T key);
```

that counts the number of times key occurs in a list.

9.12 Write the function

```
template <class T>
void DeleteKey(Node<T>* &head, T key);
```

that deletes all occurrences of key from a list.

9.13 Modify the function InsertOrder in Section 9.2 so that data values are added at the beginning of a sequence of duplicates.

9.14 For each of a–d, what is the list that results from the given sequence of instructions.

```
LinkedList<int> L;
int i, val;
```

(a) ```
     for(i=1;i <= 5;i++)
         L.InsertFront (2*i);
     ```
(b)  ```
     for(i=1;i <= 5;i++)
         L.InsertAfter(2*i);
     ```
(c) ```
     for(i=1;i <= 5;i++)
         L.InsertAt(2*i);
     ```
(d)  ```
     for(i=1;i <= 5;i++)
     {
         L.InsertAt(i);
         L.Next();
         L.InsertAt(2*i)
         val = L.DeleteFront();
     }
     ```
(e) Using InsertFront, write a for statement that creates the list

```
50,40,30,20,10
```

(f) Repeat e using InsertRear, InsertAt, and InsertAfter.

9.15 Assume the declarations

```
LinkedList<int> L;
int i, val;
```

Assume linked list L contains the values 10, 20, 30, . . . , 100. What are the data values in the list after executing each of the following?

(a)
```
L.Reset();
for(i=1;i <= 5;i++)
    L.DeleteAt();
```

(b)
```
L.Reset();
for(i=1;i <= 5;i++)
{
    L.DeleteAt();
    L.Next();
}
```

(c)
```
L.Reset();
for(i=1;i <= 3;i++)
{
    val = L.DeleteFront();
    L.Next();
    L.InsertAt(val);
}
```

9.16 Write a function

```
template <class T>
void Split(const LinkedList<T>& L, LinkedList<T>& L1,
           LinkedList<T>& L2);
```

that takes a list L and creates two new lists L1 and L2. L1 contains the first, third, fifth, and successive odd-numbered nodes. L2 contains the even-numbered nodes.

9.17 Assume L is a list of integers. Write a function

```
void OddEven(const LinkedList<int>& L,LinkedList<int>&
             L1,LinkedList<int>& L2);
```

that takes a linked list L and creates two new lists L1 and L2. L1 contains the nodes of L whose data value are an odd number. L2 contains the nodes whose data values are even numbers. Use an iterator.

9.18 Write a List class method

```
int operator+ (const List<T>& L);
```

that concatenates list L onto the end of the current list. Return 1 if the operator is successful or 0 if memory for the new nodes could not be allocated. Do not allow an attempt to concatenate a list onto itself. In this case, return 0.

9.19 Write a function

```
template <class T>
void DeleteRear(LinkedList<T>& L);
```

that deletes the rear of list L.

9.20 Draw a picture of the linked stack

```
Stack<int> L;
```

of integer data after the series of operations

```
Push(1), Push(2), Pop, Push(5), Push(7), Pop, Pop.
```

9.21 Implement the Stack class by including a LinkedList object using composition. Model your solution after the Queue class of Section 9.6.

9.22 Implement the Stack class by maintaining a linked list of Node objects.

9.23 What is the action of this function?

```
template <class T>
void ActionS(LinkedList<T>& L)
{
    Stack<T> S;

    for(L.Reset();!L.EndOfList();L.Next())
        S.Push(L.Data());
    L.Reset();
    while(!S.StackEmpty())
    {
        L.Data() = S.Pop();
        L.Next();
    }
}
```

9.24 Draw a picture of the linked queue

```
Queue<int> Q;
```

of integer data after the series of operations

```
QInsert(1), QInsert(2), QDelete, QInsert(5), QInsert(7),
QDelete, QInsert(9).
```

Make sure to include pointer rear in the picture.

9.25 What is the action of this function?

```
template <class T>
void ActionQ(LinkedList<T>& L, Queue<T>& Q)
{
    Q.QClear();
    for(L.Reset();!L.EndOfList();L.Next())
        Q.Q.Insert(L.Data());
}
```

9.26 Modify the Queue class in Section 9.6 so it contains member functions

```
T PeekFront(void);
T PeakRear(void);
```

that return the data values at the front and rear of the queue, respectively.

9.27 The Queue class does not have an explicit assignment operator. Explain why two Queue objects Obj1 and Obj2 can appear in the statement

```
Obj2 = Obj1;
```

9.28 Implement the function Replace that looks for a data value in a circular linked list.

```
template <class T>
CNode<T> *Replace(CNode<T> *header, CNode<T> *start, T elem,
                  T newelem);
```

Beginning at node start, scan the list looking for elem. If elem is found in the list, replace it with the new data value newelem and return the pointer to the matching node; otherwise, return NULL. *Note:* Your scan may pass through the header.

9.29 Implement the function

```
template <class T>
void InsertOrder(CNode<T> *header, CNode<T> *elem);
```

that inserts node elem into a circular list so the data are in order.

9.30 Consider the structure

```
template <class T>
struct CList
{
    CNode<T> header;
    CNode<T> *rear;
};
```

It defines a circular linked list with a rear pointer.

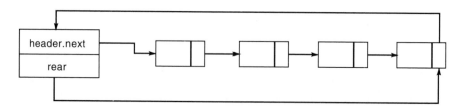

Develop functions

```
// Insert node p at the front of list L
template <class T>
void InsertFront(CList<T>& L, CNode<T> *p);

// Insert node p at the rear of list L
template <class T>
void InsertRear(CList<T>& L, CNode<T> *p);

// delete the first node of list L
template <class T>
CNode<T> *DeleteFront(CList<T>& L);
```

Be sure to correctly maintain rear so at all times it points at the last node of the list.

9.31 (a) Write a function

```
template <class T>
void Concat(CNode<T>& s, CNode<T>& t);
```

that concatenates the circular list with header t onto the end of the circular list with header s.

(b) Write a function

```
template <class T>
int Length(CNode<T>& s);
```

that determines the number of elements in a circular list with header s.

(c) Write a function

```
template <class T>
CNode<T> *Index(CNode<T>& s, T elem);
```

that returns a pointer to the first node in the circular list with header s containing data value elem. Return the header if elem is not found.

(d) Write a function

```
template <class T>
void Remove(CNode<T>& s, T elem);
```

that removes all nodes from list s that contain data value elem.

9.32 Write member functions

```
DNode<T> *DeleteNodeRight(void);
DNode<T> *DeleteNodeLeft(void);
```

for the doubly linked node class. DeleteNodeRight deletes the node to the right of the current node and DeleteNodeLeft deletes the node to the left.

Programming Exercises

9.1 This exercise extends the node utility functions in the file "nodelib.h". Write functions whose declarations are

```
// delete the rear node in the list;
// return a pointer to the
// deleted node
template <class T>
Node<T> *DeleteRear(Node<T> * & head);


// Delete all occurrences of a key in the list
template <class T>
void DeleteKey(Node<T> * & head, const T& key);
```

Write a program to test the functions.

- Input 10 integers and store them in a list using InsertFront. Use PrintList to output the list.

- Enter an integer that serves as a key. Use DeleteKey to remove all occurrences of the key from the list. Print the resulting list.

- Clear all of the nodes from the list using DeleteRear. For each deletion, output the data value.

9.2 Use the Node class for this exercise. The data field for the exercise is the struct IntEntry.

```
struct IntEntry
{
    int  value;    // integer number
    int  count;    // occurrences of value
};
```

Input 10 integers and create an ordered list of IntEntry nodes that use the count field to specify duplicates in the list. Print the resulting node information that should include the distinct integer values and the number of occurrences of each integer in the list. You should modify InsertOrder to update a node's data value when a duplicate is found.

Enter a key and delete all nodes whose data value is greater than the key. Print the resulting list.

9.3 Use the Node class for this exercise. The data represent an employee with a name, idnumber, and hourly salary.

```
struct Employee
{
    char   name[20];
    int    idnumber;
    float  hourlypay;
};
```

Overload "<<" and ">>" to perform I/O for an employee and use PrintList to print the list. Enter the following data records and store them in a linked list.

```
40  9.50  Dennis Williams
10  6.00  Harold Barry
25  8.75  Steve Walker
```

Implement the following update operations that modify the list:

(a) Read an idnumber and search for the employee's record in the list. If it is found, increase the employee's hourly payrate by $3.00. Print the resulting list. (You must overload "==".)

(b) Scan the list and delete all employees that make more than $9.00 per hour. Print the resulting list.

9.4. Two lists L = {L$_0$, L$_1$, . . . , L$_i$} and M = {M$_0$, M$_1$, . . . , M$_j$} can be merged pairwise to produce the list {L$_0$, M$_0$, L$_1$, M$_1$, . . . L$_i$ M$_i$ . . . M$_j$}, j ≥ i. Write a program using the Node class that generates a lists L with i numbers (i ≤ i ≤ 10) and a list M with j numbers (1 ≤ j ≤ 20). The entries in list L are random numbers in the range 0 to 99 and the entries in M are random numbers in the range 100 to 199. The program prints the initial lists L and M, merges them into a new list N, and prints the resulting list.

9.5. Repeat Programming Exercise 9.4 using two LinkedList objects L and M.

9.6 Using the Node class, write a program that enters 5 integers into a linked list using the following algorithm:

For each input N, insert N at the front of the list. Scan the remainder of the list, deleting all nodes which are less than N.

Run the program three times using the following input. Print the resulting list.

```
1,2,3,4,5
5,4,3,2,1
3,5,1,2,4
```

9.7 The LinkedList class contains both a copy constructor and an overloaded assignment operator. Write a test program that evaluates the correctness of the two methods.

9.8 Use the String class of Chapter 8 to read whitespace-separated tokens of text. Input a line that may include strings that begin with '−'. For instance,

```
// t and includelist are options
run -t -includelist linkdemo
```

In this example, the strings include options (tokens beginning with '−') and non-tokens. Using the LinkedList class, store the non-option tokens on a linked list tokenlist and the option tokens on a linked list optionlist. Each token is inserted at the rear of its list. Print the tokens from each list.

9.9 A positive integer n (n > 1) can be written uniquely as a product of primes. This is called the *prime factorization* of the number. For instance

$$12 = 2 * 2 * 3 \qquad 18 = 2 * 3 * 3 \qquad 11 = 11$$

The function LoadPrimes uses the IntEntry record structure of Programming Exercise 902 to create a linked list that identifies the different primes and the number of occurrences of the primes in the factorization of a number. For instance, with 18, the prime 2 occurs 1 time and the prime 3 occurs 2 times.

```
void LoadPrimes(LinkedList<IntEntry> &L, int n)
{
    int i = 2;
    int nc =0;   // count of the repeats of the curr prime

    do
    {
        if (n % i == 0)
        {
            nc++;
            n = n/i;
        }
        else
        {
            if (nc > 0)
                <load i and nc as a node at rear of the list>
            nc = 0;
            i++;
        }
    }
    while (n > 1);
}
```

Write a program that enters two integers M and N and uses the function LoadPrimes to create a linked list of the primes. Scan the list and print the prime factorization of each number.

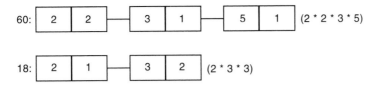

60: | 2 | 2 |—| 3 | 1 |—| 5 | 1 | (2 * 2 * 3 * 5)

18: | 2 | 1 |—| 3 | 2 | (2 * 3 * 3)

Create a new list that consists of all the primes that are common to both the M and N lists. As you identify each such prime, take the minimum count in the two nodes and use that as the count in the node for the new list. For instance, 2 is a prime factor of 60 and 2 is a prime factor of 18.

```
18 = 2 * 3 * 3        // 2 has count 1
60 = 2 * 2 * 3 * 5    // 2 has count 2
```

In the new list, 2 is a value with count 1 (minimum of 1,2). The resulting number is the greatest common devisor of M and N, GCD(M,N).

9.10 An n*th* degree polynomial is expression of the form

$$f(x) = a_n x^n + a_{n-1} x^{n-1} + \ldots + a_2 x^2 + a_1 x^1 + a_0 x^0$$

where terms a_i are called coefficients. Use the LinkedList class for this exercise with the data record Term that contains the coefficient and power of x for each term.

```
struct Term
{
    double coeff;
    int power;
};
```

In the program, enter a polynomial as a series of coefficient and power pairs. Terminate on input of coefficient 0. Store each coefficient/power in a linked list ordered by the power.

(a) Write each term of the resulting polynomial in the form

```
a_i * x^i
```

(b) Enter 3 values of x and call a function

```
double poly(LinkedList<Term>& f);
```

that evaluates the polynomial at x and outputs the result.

9.11 This exercise uses the functions developed in Written Exercises 9.12 and 9.13. Read in an ordered list of 10 integer values and print the list. Prompt the user for a data value and, using CountKey, determine how many times the value occurs in the list. Use DeleteKey to delete all occurrences of the value from the list. Print the new list.

9.12 Test the function MergeLists in Written Exercise 9.8 using integer data. Include the lists L1 = {1,3,4,6,7,10,12,15}, and L2 = {3,5,6,8,11,12,14,18,22,33,55} in your tests.

9.13 Use the CNode class to develop an implementation of the Queue class. Declare a header node in the private section of the class and perform insertions and deletions as follows:

QInsert: InsertAfter the current node and move to the new node.
QDelete: DeleteAfter the header node. Be careful not to delete from an empty queue.

Empty Queue

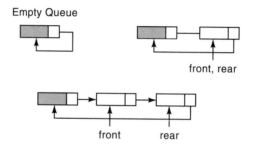

front, rear

front   rear

Test your implementation by inserting the integer values 1, 2, . . . , 10 into a queue. Empty the queue and print the values.

9.14 We can implement a Set class with elements of type T by storing unique data elements in a linked list. Implement the two functions

```
template <class T>
LinkedList<T> Union(LinkedList<T>& x, LinkedList<T>& y);

template <class T>
LinkedList<T> Intersection(LinkedList<T>& x, LinkedList<T>& y);
```

Union returns a linked list representing the set of all the elements that are found in at least one of x or y. Intersection returns a linked list representing the set of all elements in both x and y. Let A be the set of integers {1, 2, 5, 8, 12, 33, 55} and B the set {2, 8, 10, 12, 33, 88, 99}. Use the two functions to compute and print

A ∪ B = {1, 2, 5, 8, 10, 12, 33, 55, 88, 99}

and

A ∩ B = {2, 8, 12, 33}

9.15 Start with an empty circular doubly linked list of integers. Enter 10 integers, inserting the positive numbers immediately to the right of the header and the negative numbers to the left. Print the list. Split the list into two singly linked lists containing the positive and negative numbers respectively. Print out each list.

9.16 This exercise modifies the Window class of Section 9.10. Add the method SaveAll. It must traverse the window list from front to back and print the title of each window and the message "Saving <window title>". If a window is currently Untitled, prompt for a window title.

C H A P T E R 10

RECURSION

Recursion is an important problem-solving tool in computer science and mathematics. It is used in programming languages to define language syntax and in data structures to develop searching and sorting algorithms for list and tree structures. Mathematicians apply recursion in the field of combinatorics, which considers a rich variety of counting and probability problems. Recursion is an important topic with theoretical and practical application in the general study of algorithms, operations research models, game theory, and the study of graphs.

In this chapter, we give a general introduction to recursion and illustrate its use in a variety of applications. In subsequent chapters, we apply recursion to the study of trees and sorting.

The Concept of Recursion   10.1

Most people do not naturally think recursively. For instance, if you are asked to define the power function x^n, where x is a real number and n is a non-negative integer, a typical response would use repeated multiplication of x:

$$x^n = \underbrace{x * x * x * \ldots * x * x}_{n \ x's}$$

For instance, the following are various values for powers of 2.

```
2⁰ = 1                      // special definition
2¹ = 2
2² = 2 * 2 = 4
2³ = 2 * 2 * 2 = 8
2⁴ = 2 * 2 * 2 * 2 = 16
```

The function $S(n)$ computes the sum of the first n positive integers, a problem that is solved using repeated addition.

$$S(n) = \sum_1^n i = 1 + 2 + 3 + \ldots + n - 1 + n$$

For instance, with $S(10)$ we sum the first 10 integers to arrive at the answer 55:

$$S(10) = \sum_1^{10} i = 1 + 2 + 3 + \ldots + 9 + 10 = 55$$

If we wanted to apply the same algorithm to compute $S(11)$, the process would repeat all the additions. A more practical approach would be to use the previous result for $S(10)$ and then add 11 to get the answer $S(11) = 66$:

$$S(11) = \sum_1^{11} i = S(10) + 11 = 55 + 11 = 66$$

This approach uses a previous calculation with a smaller value to arrive at the answer. We call it a recursive process.

Let's go back to the power function and develop it as a recursive process. When evaluating the successive powers of 2, we note that the previous value can be used to compute the next value. For instance,

$$2^3 = 2 * 2^2 = 2 * 4 = 8$$
$$2^4 = 2 * 2^3 = 2 * 8 = 16$$

Once we have a value for the initial power of 2 ($2^0 = 1$), the successive powers of 2 are just twice the previous value. The process of using a smaller power to compute another leads to a recursive definition of the power function. For a real number x, the value x^n is given by

$$x^n = \begin{cases} 1, & n = 0 \\ x * x^{(n-1)}, & n > 0 \end{cases}$$

A similar recursive definition describes the function $S(n)$, which gives the sum of the first n integers. For the simple case $S(1)$, the sum is 1. We can evaluate the general sum $S(n)$ by using $S(n-1)$, which gives the cumulative total through $n-1$:

$$S(n) = \begin{cases} 1, & n = 1 \\ n + S(n - 1), & n > 1 \end{cases}$$

Recursion occurs when you solve a problem by partitioning it into smaller subproblems that are solved by using the same algorithm. The partitioning process terminates when we reach simpler subproblems that can be solved. We call these problems stopping conditions. Recursion employs a divide-and-conquer design.

An algorithm is defined recursively if its definition consists of

1. One or more stopping conditions which can be evaluated for certain parameters
2. A recursive step in which a current value in the algorithm can be defined in terms of a previous value. Eventually, the recursive step must lead to stopping conditions.

For instance, the recursive definition of the power function has a single stopping condition for the case when $n = 0$ ($x^0 = 1$). The recursive step describes the general case

$$x^n = x * x^{(n-1)}, n > 0$$

RECURSIVE DEFINITIONS

Programming languages use a variety of recursive methods to define syntax. Most readers are familiar with railroad diagrams. The following diagram describes an *identifier* that consists of an initial letter followed by an optional string of letters or digits. For instance, class, float, and var4 are valid identifiers that might occur in a C++ program while X++ and 2team are not identifiers.

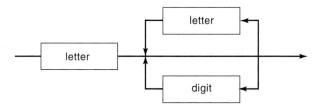

With the diagram, you enter on the left and move along the railroad track until you exit on the right. The arrows indicate valid directions of travel on the track. During your movement in the diagram, include any symbol that is contained in a rectangular region. For instance, the simplest passage in the diagram has you enter on the left, pass through a letter symbol and continue along the path to the exit point. This corresponds to a single letter identifier like A, n, t, and so forth. For each of the following identifiers, we describe the path within the diagram.

Identifier	Path
A	Enter "letter (A)", exit diagram
XY3	Enter "letter(X)", loop through "letter (Y)", cycle through "Digit (3)", exit diagram
7A	Invalid identifier; no path exits

While railroad diagrams are effective for describing some languages, the syntax of virtually all programming languages is described with recursive notation, known as **Bakus-Naur Form (BNF).** The form was developed to define Algol 60 and consists of production rules that define how a nonterminal symbol can be replaced by a string of other nonterminal or terminal symbols. The production rules use the "|" symbol to separate alternative replacement strings. The nonterminal symbols are enclosed in angle brackets "<>" and represent language constructs such as identifiers and expressions. The terminal symbols define the actual tokens in the language. For instance, the BNF definition of an identifier is given by the following production rules. The symbol identifier is a nonterminal located on the left-hand side of the "::=" operator.

```
<identifier> ::= <letter> | <identifier> <letter> |
                 <identifier> <digit>
<letter> ::= a|b|c|d|e|f|g|h|i|j|k|l|m|n|o|p|q|r|s|t|u|v|w|x|y|z
<digit> ::= 0|1|2|3|4|5|6|7|8|9
```

The production rules specify that an identifer is a letter or a letter followed by a sequence of letters or digits. Note that an identifier is defined in terms of itself, so its definition is recursive.

Interpreting recursive definitions is a natural application for recursive functions. For instance, some compilers use the BNF definition of language syntax and recursive descent parsing algorithms to translate a program into machine code. The different production rules are coded as functions, which may end up calling themselves or other production rules. The process can involve **indirect recursion** when, for instance, a rule P calls rule Q, which ends up calling rule P.

EXAMPLE 10.1

Simplified arithmetic expressions allowing only the binary operators +, −, *, and / have the following BNF formulation:

```
<expression> ::= <term> + term> | <term> - <term> | <term>
<term> ::= <factor>*<factor> | <factor>/<factor> | <factor>
<factor> ::= (<expression>} | <letter> | <digit>
```

For instance, the following are expressions

```
A + 5,  B*C + D,  2*(3+4+5),  (A+B*C)/D
```

These rules involve indirect recursion. For example, an expression may be a term, which may be a factor, which may be a parenthesized expression. As such, an expression is defined indirectly in terms of itself.

RECURSIVE PROBLEMS

The power of recursion provides very simple and elegant solutions to a range of problems. We give an overview of problems and problem-solving techniques that take advantage of recursion.

The Tower of Hanoi   Puzzle fans have long been fascinated with the Tower of Hanoi problem.

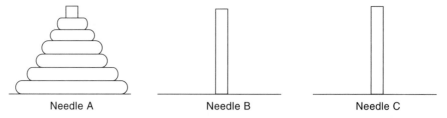

Needle A   Needle B   Needle C

Legend has it that priests in the Temple of Brahma have a brass platform with three diamond needles. On a single needle A are stacked 64 golden disks, each one slightly

smaller than the one under it. The world ends when the priests move the disks from
needle A to needle C. The task has very specific conditions, however. The disks can
be moved only one at a time from needle to needle and at no time can a larger disk
be placed on top of a smaller disk. The priests are certainly still working since the
problem involves $2^{64} - 1$ moves. At one move per second, the task requires more
than 500 billion years.

A puzzle solver is challenged by the Tower of Hanoi. A computer scientist sees
a quick recursive solution. We illustrate the problem with needles that hold six
disks. We begin by focusing on moving the top five disks to needle B and then moving
the largest disk to needle C.

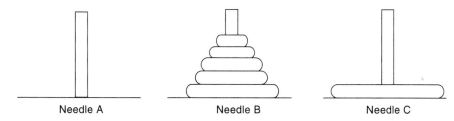

| Needle A | Needle B | Needle C |

We are then left with the simpler problem of moving only five disks from needle B
to needle C. Using the same algorithm, we focus on the top four disks and move
them off the pile. We then move the largest disk from needle B to needle C and
leave an even smaller pile of four disks. The process continues until we are left
with only one disk that is finally moved to needle C.

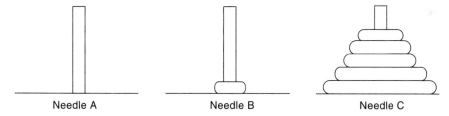

| Needle A | Needle B | Needle C |

Clearly this solution is recursive. It splits the problem into a sequence of smaller
problems of the same type. The simple task of moving one disk is the stopping condition.

The Maze   Everyone is familiar with the challenge of migrating through a maze
with the possibility of endless choices that lead to dead ends and ultimate entrap-
ment. Psychology researchers use a maze and a piece of cheese as bait to study
learning patterns in rats. We suggest that the failure of the animal to capture the
cheese is caused by its inability to think recursively. Consider Figure 10.1 and a
strategy that will guarantee safe passage to the "End". We introduce an important
problem-solving tool called backtracking.

A maze is a connected set of intersections. Each intersection has three associated
values that represent left, straight, and right. If a value is 1, a move can be made
in that direction. A value of 0 indicates that movement in that direction is blocked.

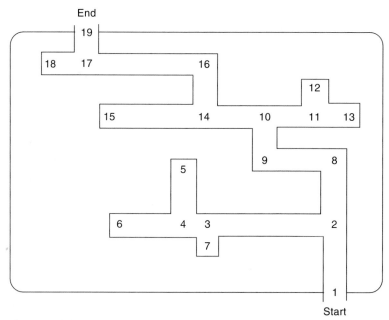

Figure 10.1 Traversing a Maze

A set of three 0 values represents a dead end or cul-du-sac in the maze. We successfully migrate through the maze when we arrive at "End". The process involves a series of recursive steps. At each intersection, we explore our options. If possible, we first attempt to go left. When we arrive at the next intersection we again consider our options and attempt to go left. If the choice of left leads to a cul-du-sac, we backtrack and make a second choice to go straight if that is available. If that choice leads to a cul-du-sac, we backtrack and go right. If all of our choices from the intersection lead to a dead end, we step back to the previous intersection and make a new selection. This rather tedious and conservative strategy won't set records for efficiency but will guarantee that we ultimately find a path out of the maze. We look at the first 10 choices in our maze.

Intersection	Choice	Resulting Intersection
At 1:	go straight	2
At 2:	go left	3
At 3:	go left	7
At 7:	at cul-du-sac; backtrack to 3	3
At 3:	go straight	4
At 4:	go straight	6
At 6:	at cul-du-sac; backtrack to 4	4
At 4:	go right	5
At 5:	at cul-du-sac; backtrack to 4, 3, 2	2
At 2:	go straight	8
	...	

Combinatorics   Recursion finds a variety of applications in combinatorics, which is the branch of mathematics concerned with the counting of objects. For instance, assume we toss three dice and record their total. A combinatoric question asks for the number of different ways we can get a total of 8. The recursive approach attempts to reduce the problem to progressively simpler problems and to use those results to solve the more complex problem. In our case, we consider three dice to be the complex problem and focus on the simpler case of tossing two dice. We assume we can take two dice and any total N in the range 2 to 12 and determine all different ways of tossing two dice that total N. In the case of three dice totaling 8, we toss the first die, and record the value in a table along with the value N that represents the remaining total that must be obtained by the next two dice. For instance, if the first die is a 3, then the final two dice must total 5. Using our "two dice" skills, we determine that there are four possible ways of tossing two dice and getting a 5. By combining these outcomes with the 3 on the first die, we have found at least four ways to get an 8 with three dice.

The following table lists all 15 ways of getting an 8 with three dice. Since the number of tosses is small, we can list all the choices without using the power of recursion. We will look at similar cases that would be impractical to solve with a table.

Dice 1	N	Different Two-Dice Outcomes	Number
1	7		0
2	6	(3,3) (4,2) (2,4) (5,1) (1,5)	5
3	5	(4,1) (3,2) (1,4) (2,3)	4
4	4	(3,1) (2,2) (1,3)	3
5	3	(2,1) (1,2)	2
6	2	(1,1)	1
			15

To compute the odds of getting an 8 with three dice, we need to divide 15 by the total number of different outcomes that could occur when tossing 3 dice. The number is $6^3 = 216$, and the odds of tossing an 8 are 15/216 or 7%.

Expression Trees   Our study of stacks introduces the infix and postfix (RPN) formats for writing arithmetic expressions. The formats can be compared by storing the operators and operands as nodes in a binary tree. The operands are placed as leaf nodes at the end of a branch. The precedence of an operator is reflected by its level in the tree. The operators at greater depth in the tree must be evaluated before operators at lesser depth. For instance, the expression

```
a * b + c/d
```

has the corresponding seven-node expression tree:

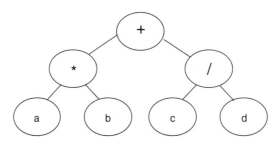

As with the maze, we can develop recursive scanning methods that make choices at each node in the tree. For example, assume we follow these rules:

Go to the left node if possible.
Write out the value in the node.
Go to the right node if possible.

Since we write out the value of the node between scan directives, we call this an **inorder scan.** A scan of the expression tree results in our visiting the following sequence of nodes. Stopping conditions occur when we cannot go to the left or to the right.

Action	Resulting Node	Output
Start at root	+	
Go left	*	
Go left	a	
(no left branch from a)		
Write out value		a
(no right branch from a)		
(backup to node *; go left is complete)		
Write out value		a *
Go right	b	
(no left branch from b)		
Write out value		a * b
(no right branch from b)		
(backup to node +; go left is complete)		
Write out value		a * b +
Go right	/	
Go left	c	
(no left branch from c)		
Write out value		a * b + c
(no right branch from c)		
(backup to node /; go left is complete)		
Write out value		a * b + c/

Action	Resulting Node	Output
Go right	d	
(no left branch from d)		
Write out value		a * b + c/d
(no right branch from d)		

After all right branches have been visited, the scan terminates and we have the infix format for the expression.

A different recursive scanning order is defined by the following rules. Since the writing of the value of the node occurs after both scan directives, we call this **postorder scan.**

Go to the left node if possible.
Go to the right node if possible.
Write out the value in the node.

Without giving all of the details, the nodes are written in the order:

```
a  b  *  c  d  /  +
```

which is the postfix or RPN form of the expression.

Recursion is a powerful tool for defining and scanning trees. We will use a variety of recursive algorithms in Chapter 11. In Chapter 13 we develop iterative equivalents of these algorithms in order to design tree iterators.

Designing Recursive Functions   10.2

The structure of a recursive function is illustrated by the problem of computing the factorial of a non-negative integer. We highlight this structure by developing both the iterative and recursive definition of the function.

The factorial of a non-negative integer, Factorial(n), is defined as the product of all positive integers less than or equal to N. The value, denoted by $N!$, is given by

$$N! = N * (N-1) * (N-2) * ... * 2 * 1$$

For instance,

```
Factorial (4) = 4! = 4 * 3 * 2 * 1 = 24
Factorial (6) = 6! = 6 * 5 * 4 * 3 * 2 * 1 = 720
Factorial (1) = 1! = 1
Factorial (0) = 0! = 1        // special definition
```

An iterative version of the function is implemented by returning 1 if n is 0 and otherwise using a loop to multiply the successive terms.

```
// iterative form of the factorial
long Factorial(long n)
{
    int prod = 1, i;

    // for n == 0 return prod = 1; otherwise
    // compute the prod = 1*2*...*n
    if (n > 0)
        for (i = 1; i <= n; i++)
            prod *= i;
    return prod;
}
```

A look at the terms in the different factorial examples provides a recursive definition for Factorial (N). In the case of 4!, the first term in 4 and the remaining terms (3 * 2 * 1) are 3!. A similar result is true for 6!, which is the product of 6 and 5!.

The recursive definition for any non-negative integer *n* involves both a stopping condition and the recursive step:

$$n! = \begin{cases} 1, & n = 0 \quad \text{// stopping condition} \\ n * (n-1)!, & n > 0 \quad \text{// recursive step} \end{cases}$$

We can think of Factorial(*n*) as an n-machine that computes *n*! by carrying out the multiplication *n* * (*n*−1)!. For the machine to function, it must be networked with a series of other machines that pass information back and forth. The 0-Machine is the exception because it can work independently and produce the result 1 without assistance from another machine. We describe the necessary networking and interaction of machines to have the 4-machine compute 4!.

The 4-Machine (4*3!) must start up the 3-Machine
The 3-Machine (3*2!) must start up the 2-Machine
The 2-Machine (2*1!) must start up the 1-Machine
The 1-Machine (1*0!) must start up the 0-Machine

The action of the individual machines is described in Figure 10.2. Once the 0-Machine is activated, we get an immediate result of 1, which is passed back to

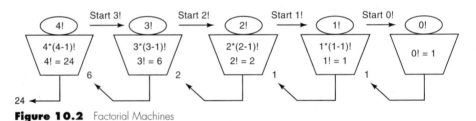

Figure 10.2 Factorial Machines

the 1-Machine. The 1-Machine then has the information to complete the multiplication and return the result to the 2-Machine.

```
1 * 0! = 1 * 1 = 1
```

Successively from the 1-Machine to the 4-Machine, the necessary return values are made available:

1-Machine uses value 1 from 0-Machine and computes 1 * 0! = 1
2-Machine uses value 1 from 1-Machine and computes 2 * 1! = 2
3-Machine uses value 2 from 2-Machine and computes 3 * 2! = 6
4-Machine uses value 6 from 3-Machine and computes 4 * 3! = 24

The evaluation of N! must carefully distinguish the 0! case that represents the stopping condition and the other cases ($N > 0$) that represent the recursive steps. This distinction is fundamental to the design of a recursive algorithm. The programmer implements the distinction with an IF ... ELSE statement. The IF block handles the stopping conditions and the ELSE block processes the recursive step. In the case of a factorial, the IF block evaluates the single stopping condition $N = 0$ and returns a result 1. The ELSE block handles the recursive step by evaluating the expression $N * (N - 1)$! and returning the result.

```
// recursive form of the factorial
long Factorial(long n)
{
    // stopping condition is n == 0
    if (n == 0)
        return 1;
    else
        // recursive step
        return n * Factorial(n - 1);
}
```

Figure 10.3 describes the sequence of function calls used to compute Factorial (4). Assume that initially the function is called from the main program. Within the function block, the ELSE statement executes with parameters 3, 2, 1, and 0. The last function call executes the IF statement with $n = 0$. Once the stopping condition is reached, the recursive chain of calls is broken and the series of computations begins in the order 1*1, 2*1, 3*2, and 4*6. The final value 24 is returned to the main program.

EXAMPLE 10.2

The IF..ELSE condition distinguishes the stopping condition and the recursive step for the power function and the sum function in Section 10.1. In the

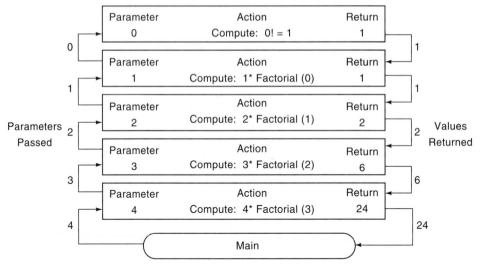

Figure 10.3 Factorial Stack

power function, the case power$(0,0) = 0^0$ is not defined and an error message is produced.

1. Power Function (Recursive Form)

```
// compute x to the power n using recursion
float power(float x, int n)
{
    // stopping condition is n == 0
    if (n == 0)
        // 0 to the power 0 is undefined
        if (x == 0)
        {
            cerr<<"power(0,0) is undefined"<< endl;
            exit(1);
        }
        else
            // x to the power 0 is 1
            return 1;
    else
        // recursive step:
        // power(x,n) = x * power(x,n-1)
        return x * power(x,n-1);
}
```

2.   Sum Function (Recursive Form)

```
// compute 1+2+ ... +n recursively
int S(int n)
{
    // stopping condition is n == 1
    if (n == 1)
        return 1;
    else
        // recurvsive step: S(n) = n + S(n-1)
        return n + S(n-1);
}
```

Program 10.1   Using Factorial

This program illustrates the recursive form of the factorial function. The user inputs four integers and prints their factorial.

```cpp
#include <iostream.h>

// compute n! = n*(n-1)*(n-2)...(2)(1), 0!=1 recursively
long Factorial(long n)
{
    // if n == 0, then 0! = 1; otherwise, n! = n*(n-1)!
    if (n == 0)
        return 1;
    else
        return n * Factorial(n - 1);
}

void main (void)
{
    int i, n;

    // enter 4 positive integers and compute n! for each
    cout << "Enter 4 positive integers: ";
    for (i = 0; i < 4; i++)
    {
        cin >> n;
        cout <<  n << "! = " << Factorial(n) << endl;
    }
}

/*
<Run of Program 10.1>
```

```
Enter 4 positive integers: 0 7 1 4
0! = 1
7! = 5040
1! = 1
4! = 24
*/
```

10.3   Recursive Code and the Runtime Stack

A function is a sequence of instructions that are executed in response to a function call. The execution process begins by having the calling block set up an **activation record** that includes the list of parameters and the location of the next instruction to execute after returning to the calling block.

Parameters	Location
<actual parameters>	<next instruction>

Activation Record

When the function is called, data from the activation record are pushed on a system-supplied stack (runtime stack). The data combine with local variables to define an activation frame that is made available to the function.

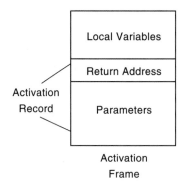

Activation Frame

The process of exiting the function code identifies the location of the next instruction (Figure 10.4) and then destroys the data on the stack that correspond to the activation record. A recursive function makes repeated calls to itself using a modified parameter list for each call. The process pushes a series of activation records on the stack until we reach a stopping condition. The subsequent popping of the records gives us our recursive solution. The factorial function illustrates the use of activation records.

THE RUNTIME STACK

With the example of factorial(4), we illustrate the use of the runtime stack and activation records during execution of the recursive function. The initial call to

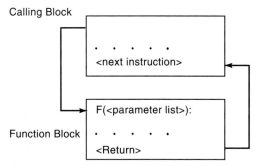

Calling Block

```
. . . . .
<next instruction>
```

```
F(<parameter list>):
. . . .
<Return>
```

Function Block

Figure 10.4 Function Call and Return

factorial is made from the main program. After executing the function, program control returns to location RetLoc1 where the value 24 (4!) is assigned to N:

```
void main (void)
{
    int N;

    // push record with call FACTORIAL(4).
    // RetLoc1 is address of the assignment
    // N == FACTORIAL(4)
    N = FACTORIAL(4);
RetLoc1
}
```

The recursive calls in the function FACTORIAL return to location RetLoc2, which computes the product n * (n−1)!. The result of the calculation is stored in the variable temp to assist the reader in tracing the code and to facilitate the illustration of the runtime stack:

```
long FACTORIAL(long n)
{
    int temp;

    if (n == 0)
        return 1;    // pop activation record
    else
    {
        // push activation record with call FACTORIAL(n-1)
        // RetLoc2 is the address of the computation
        // n * FACTORIAL(n-1)
        temp = n * FACTORIAL(n-1);
RetLoc2
        return temp;    // pop activation record
    }
}
```

Calling Block

FACTORIAL(1)	**Parameter** 0	**Return:**	RetLoc2
FACTORIAL(2)	**Parameter** 1	**Return:**	RetLoc2
FACTORIAL(3)	**Parameter** 2	**Return:**	RetLoc2
FACTORIAL(4)	**Parameter** 3	**Return:**	RetLoc2
main	**Parameter** 4	**Return:**	RetLoc1

Figure 10.5 Activation Stack

For the FACTORIAL function, the activation record has two fields.

Parameters	Location
long n	<Next Instruction>

Activation Record

The execution of FACTORIAL(4) initiates a sequence of five function calls. Figure 10.5 describes the activation record for each function call. The records enter the stack from bottom to top with the call from the main program occupying the bottom of the stack.

The stopping condition occurs in the function FACTORIAL(0) and the sequence of return statements begins to execute. The activation record at the top of the stack is popped and program control passes to the return location. The following operations describe the clearing of activation records from the stack.

Parameter Return Location   Instruction Upon Return

0	RetLoc2

RetLoc2 temp = 1 * 1; // 1 from FACTORIAL(0)
        return temp; // temp = 1;

1	RetLoc2

RetLoc2 temp = 2 * 1; // 1 from FACTORIAL(1)
        return temp; // temp = 2;

2	RetLoc2

RetLoc2 temp = 3 * 2; // 2 from FACTORIAL(2)
        return temp; // temp = 6;

3	RetLoc2

RetLoc2 temp = 4 * 6; // 6 from FACTORIAL(3)
        return temp; // temp = 24;

4	RetLoc1

RetLoc2 N = FACTORIAL(4); // back to main program

Problem-Solving with Recursion   10.4

Many computer problems have a very simple and elegant formulation that translates directly to recursive code. In Section 10.1, we give a series of examples that include the Tower of Hanoi, a maze, and combinatorics. In this section, we extend the range of examples to include a recursive definition of the binary search algorithm, the solution to a counting problem and the computing of permutations to illustrate combinatorics, a solution for the Tower of Hanoi puzzle, and design of a maze class to handle general maze problems.

BINARY SEARCH

The binary search takes a specified key and scans an ordered array with N items looking for a match with the key. The function returns the index of the match or -1 if no match occurs. The binary search algorithm can be described recursively.

Assume the sorted list A is designated with a lower bound index low and an upper bound index high. Given a key, we begin by looking for a match in the middle of the list (index mid).

```
mid = (low+high)/2     Compare A[mid] and key
```

If a match occurs, we have a stopping condition, which allows us to terminate the search and return the index mid.

If a match does not occur, we may use the fact that the list is ordered to focus our search in the "lower sublist" to the left of mid or in the "upper sublist" to the right of mid.

If key < A[mid], a match could only occur in the left half of the list in the index range low to mid−1.

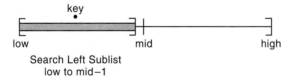

If key > A[mid], a match could only occur in the right half of the list in the index range mid+1 to high.

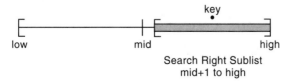

The recursive step directs the binary search to continue in a sublist. The recursive process looks at smaller and smaller sublists. Ultimately, the search fails if the sublist vanishes. This occurs when the upper limit of the list is smaller than the lower limit. The condition low > high is a second stopping condition, and the algorithm returns the index −1.

Binary Search (Recursive Form)   The template version of the binary search uses an array with elements of type T, the key value, and the lower and upper index bounds as parameters. The IF statement handles the two stopping conditions, which are (1) a match occurring or (2) failure to find the key in the list. The ELSE portion of the IF statement handles the recursive step that directs the search to continue in the lower sublist (key < A[mid]) or in the upper sublist (key > A[mid]). By means of the divide-and-conquer approach, the same algorithm is applied to successively smaller intervals until either success (match) or failure occurs.

```
// recursive version of the binary search to locate
// a key in ordered array A
template <class T>
int BinSearch(T A[], int low, int high, T key)
{
   int mid;
   T midvalue;

   // stopping condition : key not found
   if (low > high)
      return (-1);

   // compare against list midpoint and subdivide
   // if a match does not occur. apply binary
   // search to the appropriate sublist
   else
   {
      mid = (low+high)/2;
      midvalue = A[mid];
      // stopping condition : key found
      if (key == midvalue)
         return mid;      // key found at index mid

      // look left if key < midvalue; otherwise, look right
      else if (key < midvalue)
         // recursive step
         return BinSearch(A,low,mid-1,key);
      else
         // recursive step
         return BinSearch(A,mid+1,high,key);
   }
}
```

Program 10.2 Binary Search Test

The program reads a list of words from file "vocab.dat" into an array called WordList. The list of words is sorted in ASCII order. The user is prompted for a key that initiates a search in the list. If the word is found, its position in the list is printed and otherwise a message indicates that the word is not in this list. The search function is located in file "search.h".

```
#include <iostream.h>
#include <fstream.h>

#include "strclass.h"
#include "search.h"          // include BinSearch

void main(void)
{
    // we search an array of ordered strings from stream fin
    String wordlist[50];
    ifstream fin;

    String word;
    int pos, i;

    // open file "vocab.dat" containing alphabetized words
    fin.open("vocab.dat");

    // read until end of file and initialize wordlist
    i = 0;
    while(fin >> wordlist[i])
        i++;

    // prompt for a word
    cout << "Enter a word: ";
    cin >> word;

    // use the binary search to look for the word
    if ((pos = BinSearch(wordlist,0,i,word)) != -1)
        cout << word << " is in the list at index "
             << pos << endl;
    else
        cout << word << " is not in the list." <<  endl;
}

/*
<Input file "vocab.dat">
```

```
array
class
file
struct
template
vector


<Run #1 of Program 10.2>
Enter a word: template
template is in the list at index 4


<Run #2 of Program 10.2>
Enter a word: mark
mark is not in the list.
*/
```

COMBINATORICS: THE COMMITTEE PROBLEM

Combinatorics provides algorithms to count the number of ways that an event can occur. In the classical committee problem, we start with two non-negative integers N and K and determine the value C(N,K) which is the number of different ways of selecting a committee of K members out of total collection of N people.

We explore a solution for the general problem by looking at a specific example with N = 5 and K = 2. At first, the simplicity of the case might lead us to apply a little organization and quickly produce an exhaustive list of 10 different options. Assume the people in the organization are named A, B, C, D, and E. The possible committees surround the group of members.

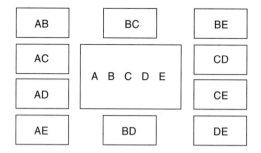

This approach would not work for larger numbers and we need to use a divide-and-conquer strategy that will split the problem into simpler subproblems. In the process, we develop a recursive solution to the committee problem.

Simplify the problem by having person A leave the group. We are left with four persons B, C, D, and E.

Subproblem 1:
Ask the four persons remaining in the group to form all possible committees with two members. There are six possible different subcommittees.
   List 1: (B,C), (B,D), (B,E), (C,D), (C,E), (D,E)

Note that each of the new committees does not contain the absent person A.

Subproblem 2:
Ask the four members of the group to form all possible committees with one member.
   (B), (C), (D), (E)
Each of these committees is one short of our desired two-member group. They become a two-member committee by adding person A. The resulting two-member committees are
   List 2: (A,B), (A,C), (A,D), (A,E)

We claim that the two-member committees from subproblem 1 and subproblem 2 describe all possible committees for the original problem. The following picture describes the two cases:

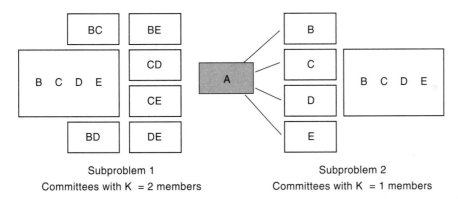

Subproblem 1
Committees with K = 2 members

Subproblem 2
Committees with K = 1 members

The six groups in list 1 represent all committees that do not contain person A. The four groups in list 2 represent all committees that contain A. Since a committee must either contain or not contain A, the 10 committees in the two lists comprise all possible committees with two people.

Algorithm Design   In the divide-and-conquer (recursive) analysis, we handle the general problem that counts the number of committees of K members selected from N people. We ask one person (person A) to leave and then consider the N−1 remaining people. The total number of committees consist of the number of committees with K members chosen from the N−1 people (person A is not included) and the number of committees with K−1 persons chosen from N−1 people (A will be added). The first group has size C(N−1,K) and the second group has size

C(N−1,K−1). A smaller K−1 member committee in the second group will expand to a K member committee once person A joins the group.

```
C(N,K) = C(N-1,K-1) + C(N-1,K)        // recursive step
```

The stopping conditions consist of several extreme cases that can be directly analyzed.

If K > N, there are not enough people to form any committee. The total possible committees with K members chosen from N people is 0.

If K = 0, a committee is formed with no members and this occurs in only one way.

If K = N, every person must be on the committee. Only by selecting a committee of the whole can this occur.

```
C(N,N) = 1      C(N,0) = 1      C(N,K) = 0    K > N
```

By combining the stopping conditions and the recursive step, we can implement the recursive function comm(n,k) = C(n,k). The function is contained in the file "comm.h".

```cpp
// determine the number of committees with k members that
// can be chosen from n persons
int comm (int n, int k)
{
   // stopping condition; too few persons
   if (k > n)
      return 0;
   // stopping condition; committee of the whole or 0 members
   else if (n == k || k == 0)
      return 1;
   else
      // recursive step: all committees without person A
      // plus all committees that include person A
         return comm(n-1,k) + comm(n-1,k-1);
}
```

Program 10.3 Building Committees

The user inputs the number of candidates n and the number of committee members k. Output gives the value C(n,k) as the number of possible committees.

```cpp
#include <iostream.h>

#include "comm.h"        // include the function comm
```

```
void main (void)
{
    int n, k;

    cout << "Enter # of candidates and # on a committee: ";
    cin >> n >> k;

    cout << "The # of possible committees is "
        << comm(n,k) << endl;
}


/*

<Run #1 of Program 10.3>

Enter # of candidates and # on a committee: 10 4
The # of possible committees is 210

<Run #2 of Program 10.3>

Enter # of candidates and # on a committee: 9 0
The # of possible committees is 1
*/
```

COMBINATORICS: PERMUTATIONS

Many interesting recursive algorithms involve arrays. In this section we look at the problem of generating all permutations of N items. The algorithm involves passing an array by value and, since C++ passes all arrays by address, array copying must be done.

A **permutation** on N items $(1, 2, \ldots, N)$ is an ordered arrangement of the items. For $N = 3$, the ordering $(1\ 3\ 2)$ is a different permutation than $(3\ 2\ 1)$, $(1\ 2\ 3)$, and so forth. A classical combinatorics problem determines that the number of permutations is $N!$, which is intuitively clear by looking at the individual positions in a permutation. For position 1 there are N choices since all N items are available. For position 2, there are $N-1$ choices since one item is used for position 1. The number of choices decreases by one as we move down the position list.

Number of Choices

The total number of permutations is the product of the number of choices in each position.

$$\text{Permutation}(N) = N * (N-1) * (N-2) * \ldots * 2 * 1 = N!$$

A more interesting recursive algorithm derives a listing of all the permutations of N items for $N \geq 1$. For demonstration purposes, we derive by hand the 24 (4!) permutations of 4 items. A listing of the different permutations begins with four separate columns whose items have the same first element. Each column is further partitioned into three pairs denoting the same second item in the list.

1	2	3	4
1 2 3 4	2 1 3 4	3 1 2 4	4 1 2 3
1 2 4 3	2 1 4 3	3 1 4 2	4 1 3 2
1 3 2 4	2 3 1 4	3 2 1 4	4 2 1 3
1 3 4 2	2 3 4 1	3 2 4 1	4 2 3 1
1 4 2 3	2 4 1 3	3 4 1 2	4 3 1 2
1 4 3 2	2 4 3 1	3 4 2 1	4 3 2 1

A hierarchy tree contains the ordered paths that correspond to the permutations and illustrates the algorithm for computing the number of permutations. Initially, there are four choices—1, 2, 3, and 4—corresponding to the four columns. Moving down the tree, the subsequent levels split into 3, 2, and 1 items, respectively. The total number of paths (permutations) is

$4 * 3 * 2 * 1 = 4!$

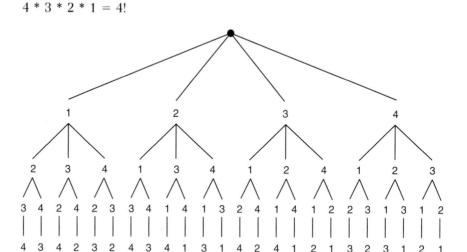

An algorithm for listing all of the permutations follows the paths of the tree. As we progress from level to level, we specify the next position in the permutation. The process constitutes the recursive step.

Index 0:

An iterative process looks at all possible first entries for index 0 in a permutation. In our example, there are $N = 4$ possible first entries.

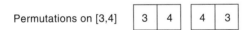

Index 1:
At the next level in the tree, each node gives rise to $N-1$ nodes consisting of the $N-1$ items other than the first item. For instance, node 1 corresponds to the permutations that begin with 1 at index 0. The path that branches to node 2 at the next level corresponds to permutations that have 1 2 in the first two positions, and so forth. We can iteratively identify the second entry in the permutation by scanning items 2, 3, and 4.

Index 2:
At the next level in the tree, each node branches into two paths that represent the permutations on 2 items. for instance, at node 2, the items are [3,4] and the orderings are

Permutations on [3,4] | 3 | 4 | | 4 | 3 |

The resulting permutations on 4 items are

| 1 | 2 | 3 | 4 | | 1 | 2 | 4 | 3 |
| 0 | 1 | 2 | | 0 | 1 | 2 |

Index 3:
Once the third item in the list is fixed, the last entry is determined since a permutation does not allow repeat values. This becomes the stopping condition. Each node completes a distinct permutation.

Algorithm Design   The C++ code to implement the algorithm stores each permutation as an array of N elements. Prior to each call, the recursive function creates a copy of the array so that values remain in the same array positions upon return from a recursive step. Remember that our implementation for $N = 4$ must ultimately create 24 different arrays. Initially, we create four arrays containing 1, 2, 3, and 4 in the first position. At the next level, each of the four existing arrays creates three arrays, which retain the first entry from the base array, and so forth.

```
void copy(int x[], int y[], int n)
{
    for (int i=0;i < n;i++)
        x[i] = y[i];
}
```

The recursive algorithm progressively places items in an array permlist at indices
0, 1, 2, . . . , $N-1$.

1. A stopping condition occurs at index $N-1$. At that point, the N element permutation is complete and the array of items is printed.

2. *Recursive step:* The recursive step progresses through the indices of the array from index 0 to $N-2$.

    At index k ($0 \le k < N-1$), the first k items are already set in the array permlist. We iteratively scan the other items and place them at position permlist[k]. This is done by exchanging each item in the remainder of the list with the number at permlist[k]. For instance, assume $N = 4$, $k = 1$, and permlist[0] $= 1$. The iterative steps place 2, 3, and 4 in index 1.

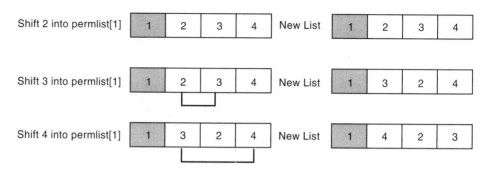

After each exchange, the resulting list is then copied to a temporary list and passed to the recursive function permute along with the next index and parameter N. Figure 10.6 illustrates calling permute with permlist[1] $== 2$.

The permutations are created in the order (1234) and (1243). Figure 10.7 illustrates calling permute when we exchange 3 into permlist[1]. The iteration then exchanges 4 into permlist[1] and the recursive process continues with the array 1423.

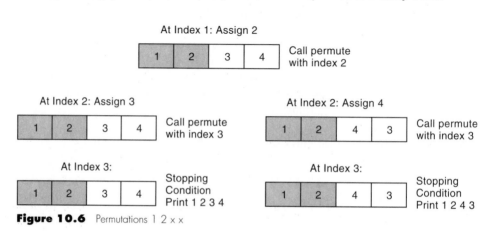

Figure 10.6 Permutations 1 2 x x

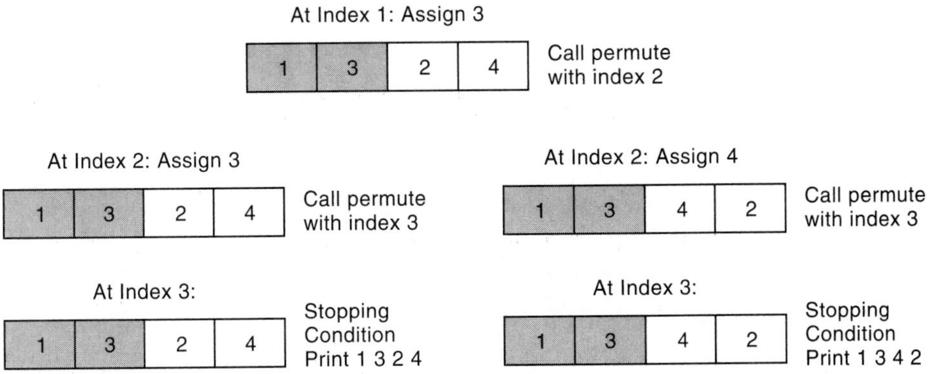

At Index 1: Assign 3

| 1 | 3 | 2 | 4 |

Call permute with index 2

At Index 2: Assign 3

| 1 | 3 | 2 | 4 |

Call permute with index 3

At Index 2: Assign 4

| 1 | 3 | 4 | 2 |

Call permute with index 3

At Index 3:

| 1 | 3 | 2 | 4 |

Stopping Condition Print 1 3 2 4

At Index 3:

| 1 | 3 | 4 | 2 |

Stopping Condition Print 1 3 4 2

Figure 10.7 Permutations 1 3 x x

Recursive Function Permute

```cpp
// UpperLimit is maximum number of elements to permute
const int UpperLimit = 5;

// copy n element array y to array x
void copy(int x[], int y[], int n)
{
    for (int i=0;i < n;i++)
        x[i] = y[i];
}

// permlist is an n element array of integers. generate
// the permutations of the elements whose indices
// are in the range start <= i <= n-1. when a permutation
// is complete, print the entire array. to permute all n
// elements, begin with start = 0
void permute(int permlist[], int start, int n)
{
    int tmparr[UpperLimit];
    int temp, i;

    // stopping condition: land at last array element
    if (start == n-1)
    {
        // print the permutation
        for (i=0;i < n;i++)
            cout << permlist[i] << "   ";
        cout << endl;
    }
    else
        // recursive step: exchange permlist[start] and
        // permlist[i], make a copy of the array in temparr,
```

```
        // and permute elements of tmparr from start+1
        // through end of array
        for (i=start;i < n;i++)
        {
            // exchange permlist[i] with permlist[start]
            temp = permlist[i];
            permlist[i] = permlist[start];
            permlist[start] = temp;

            // create a new list and call permute
            copy(tmparr,permlist,n);
            permute(tmparr,start+1,n);
        }
}
```

Program 10.4 Permutations

This permutation problem is run with N = 3. The functions copy and permute are stored in the include file "permute.h".

```
#include <iostream.h>

#include "permute.h"        // include function Permute

void main(void)
{
    // permlist contains the n numbers we permute
    int permlist[UpperLimit];
    int n,i;

    cout << "Enter a number 'n' between 1 and "
         << UpperLimit << ": ";
    cin >> n;

    // initialize permlist to {1,2,3,...,n}
    for (i=0;i < n;i++)
        permlist[i] = i+1;
    cout << endl;

    // print permutations of elements in array
    // permlist from indices 0 to n-1
    permute(permlist,0,n);
}

/*
<Run of Program 10.4>
```

```
Enter a number 'n' between 1 and 5: 3

1   2   3
1   3   2
2   1   3
2   3   1
3   1   2
3   2   1
*/
```

Tower of Hanoi   The Tower of Hanoi puzzle, discussed in Section 10.1, is an example of a recursive algorithm that simply solves the problem and hides the details. This section develops the recursive steps and the stopping conditions for the repositioning of the disks.

> *Puzzle Statement:* The puzzle board contains three pegs called the start peg, middle peg, and end peg. On the start peg are placed N disks that are stacked in increasing order of size with the largest at the bottom. The goal of the puzzle is to move all N disks from the start peg to the end peg. Disks are moved one at a time with the rule that a larger disk may never be placed on top of a smaller disk.

Figure 10.8 describes the movement of pegs for the case of $N = 3$. The pegs are labeled the start peg (S), the end peg (E), and the middle peg (M). We use this

Original three-disk tower on S.

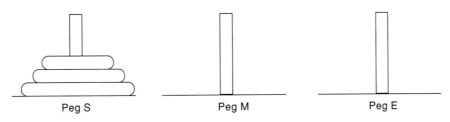

Peg S   Peg M   Peg E

Step 1: Move the small disk to E (S–> E).

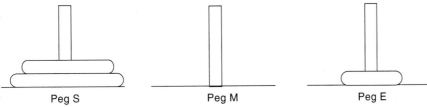

Peg S   Peg M   Peg E

Figure 10.8   Tower of Hanoi ($N = 3$)

Step 2: Move the medium disk to M (S –>M).

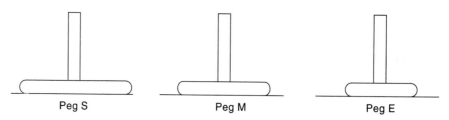

Step 3: Move the small disk to M (E –>M).

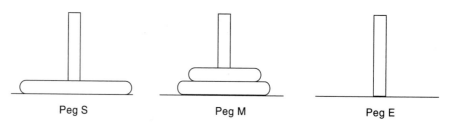

Step 4: Move the large disk to E (S –>E).

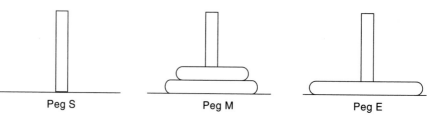

Step 5: Move the small disk to S (M –>S).

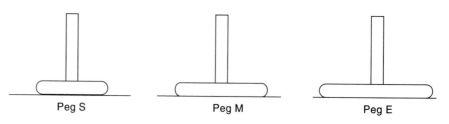

Step 6: Move the medium disk to E (M –>E).

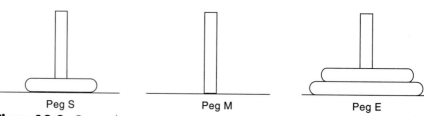

Figure 10.8 Continued

Step 7: Move the small disk (in the one-disk tower) to E. The three-disk tower is complete.

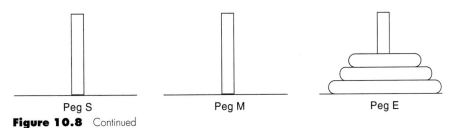

Figure 10.8 Continued

relatively simple case to identify the recursive process. The recursive algorithm is given in terms of N pegs.

Tower of Hanoi Algorithm   The example with three disks can be generalized to a three-step recursive algorithm (Figure 10.9). The function Hanoi declares the pegs as String objects. In the parameter list, the order of the variables are

startpeg $-$ middlepeg $-$ endpeg

and imply that we are moving disks from startpeg to endpeg using middlepeg to temporarily store the disks. If $N = 1$, we have a special stopping condition, which can be handled by moving the single disk from the start peg to the end peg.

```
cout << "move " << startpeg << " to " << endpeg << endl;
```

Step 1: Move N – 1 disks from S to M.

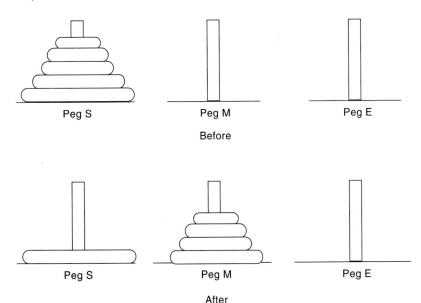

Figure 10.9 Disk Movement in the Tower of Hanoi

Step 2: Move 1 disk from S to E.

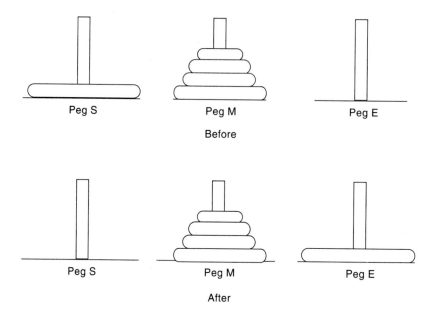

Step 3: Move N − 1 disks from M to E.

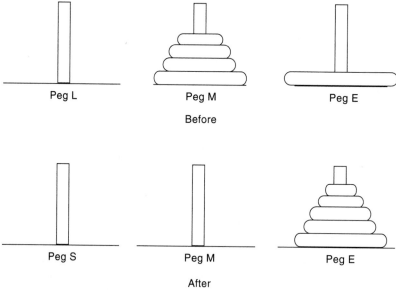

Figure 10.9 Continued

Otherwise, we have the three-step process to move the N disks from the start peg to the end peg. The first step in the algorithm moves N−1 disks from startpeg to middlepeg using endpeg. Hence, the order of parameters in the recursive function call are startpeg, endpeg, and middlepeg:

```
// use endpeg for temp storage
Hanoi(n-1,startpeg,endpeg,middlepeg);
```

The second step merely moves the largest disk from the start peg to the end peg:

```
cout << "move " << startpeg << " to " << endpeg << endl;
```

The third step in the algorithm moves N−1 disks from middlepeg to endpeg using startpeg for temporary storage. Hence, the order of parameters in the recursive function call are middlepeg, startpeg, and endpeg:

```
// use startpeg for temp storage
Hanoi(n-1,middlepeg,startpeg,endpeg);
```

Program 10.5   Tower of Hanoi

The three peg names are strings "start", "middle", and "end", which are passed as parameters to the function. The program begins by prompting the user to enter the number of disks N. We call the recursive function Hanoi to obtain a listing of the moves that will transfer the N disks from peg "start" to peg "end".

The algorithm requires $2^N - 1$ moves. For 10 disks, the puzzle requires 1023 moves. In our test case, N = 3 and the number of moves is $2^3 - 1 = 7$.

```
#include <iostream.h>

#include "strclass.h"

// move n disks from startpeg to endpeg,
// using middlepeg as the intermediate peg
void hanoi (int n, String startpeg, String middlepeg,
            String endpeg)
{
    // stopping condition: move one disk
    if (n == 1)
        cout << "move  " << startpeg << " to " << endpeg << endl;

    // move n-1 disks to middlepeg, move bottom disk
    // to endpeg, then move n-1 disks from middlepeg to endpeg
```

```
        else
        {
            hanoi(n-1,startpeg,endpeg,middlepeg);
            cout << "move   " << startpeg << " to "<< endpeg << endl;
            hanoi(n-1,middlepeg,startpeg,endpeg);
        }
    }

    void main()
    {
        // number of disks and the peg names
        int n;
        String startpeg = "start ",
               middlepeg = "middle",
               endpeg = "end   ";

        // prompt for n and solve the puzzle for n disks
        cout << "Enter the number of disks: ";
        cin >> n;
        cout << "The solution for n = " << n << endl;
        hanoi(n,startpeg, middlepeg, endpeg);
    }

    /*
    <Run of Program 10.5>

    Enter the number of disks: 3
    The solution for n = 3
    move   start  to end
    move   start  to middle
    move   end    to middle
    move   start  to end
    move   middle to start
    move   middle to end
    move   start  to end
    */
```

MAZE HANDLING

Many recursive algorithms use the principle of **backtracking.** The principle applies when we are faced with a problem that requires a number of steps and decisions. In an effort to obtain a final solution, we create a series of partial solutions step by step that appear to be consistent with the requirements of the final solution. If we take a step or make a decision that is inconsistent with a final solution, we backtrack one or more steps to the last consistent partial solution. The old addage of two steps forward and one step backward may apply. At times backtracking may entail one step forward and *n* steps backward where *n* is large. In this section, we look at backtracking in the familiar context of mazes. For our analysis, we assume

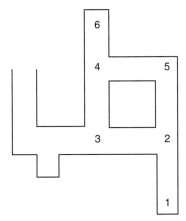

Figure 10.10 Maze with a Cycle

that our maze does not have a cycle that would allow us to wander about in circles. This is not a necessary restriction since backtracking applies to mazes with cycles as long as we maintain a map that indicates when a node is revisited along the path. Figure 10.10 features a maze with a cycle involving intersections 2, 3, 4, and 5.

Algorithm Analysis   A maze is a set of intersections. The traveler enters from one direction and departs along one of three paths: to the left, straight ahead, or to the right. A path is identified by the number of the next intersection. If there is no exit along a path, we associate a value 0 to indicate that movement is blocked in that direction. An intersection with no exits is a cul-du-sac or, more vividly, a dead end.

In the spirit of adventure and with a willingness to backtrack, the traveler enters the maze at the starting intersection and boldly begins to seek out the goal, which is the end intersection and freedom. Each intersection on the path represents a partial solution. Unfortunately, the spirit of adventure can lead to a cul-du-sac and the need to backtrack (retrace one's steps) to a previous intersection on the path.

To organize our choices, we follow a recursive strategy at each intersection. We first attempt to depart along the left-hand path (if it exists) and create a path to the end. The choice becomes inconsistent with our goal only when it leads to a dead end. At that point, we backtrack to the intersection and attempt to depart straight ahead and proceed to the end. Again a dead end makes this inconsistent and we choose the exit on the right. If that choice fails, we are at a dead end at the current intersection and we backtrack to a previous valid ("consistent") intersection. The strategy is relatively simple to describe and relatively easy to code as a recursive function. The problem of writing an iterative version of the function will be evident from a partial trace along the seven-intersection maze shown in Figure 10.11. The resulting path out of the maze follows the intersections $1 - 2 - 6 - 7$.

The maze walk strategy guarantees that once the traveler exits an intersection, there will be no return until all possible choices further along the path have been

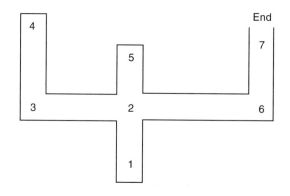

Intersection	Action	Result	
1	Exit straight	Enter 2	
2	Exit left	Enter 3	
3	Exit right	Enter 4	
4 (Dead-end)	Backtrack	Enter 3	
3 (Dead-end)	Backtrack	Enter 2	
2	Exit straight	Enter 5	
5 (Dead-end)	Backtrack	Enter 2	
2	Exit right	Enter 6	
6	Exit left	Enter 7	(end)

Figure 10.11 *Mini-Maze*

tried and result in a dead end. Furthermore, an intersection is not officially put on the path until we have an assurance that it leads out of the maze. Once the traveler arrives at the end of the maze, we can retrace the history of the walk and identify all intersections on the path.

The Maze Class   A maze is a structure that consists of data (intersections) and methods that allow us to set up the maze and traverse the intersections using our traversal strategy. We assume that each intersection is a record with fields indicating the result of exiting left, forward, or right. The integer value in a field defines the next intersection in the path if we exit in that direction. A 0 value indicates that the direction is blocked. The record is implemented as the struct Intersection.

```
// record that specifies the next intersection you
// visit when departing left, straight or right
// from the current intersection
struct Intersection
{
    int left;
    int forward;
    int right;
};
```

The maze class consists of an integer value indicating the size of the maze, the end of the maze, and the list of maze intersections that are allocated using a dynamic array. All data access is provided by the constructor that builds the maze and by a method that traverses the maze looking for a path. The maze data is read from a file. It consists of the number of intersections, the three exit values for each intersection, and the number for "EXIT", an exit intersection for the maze. The value EXIT is not considered to be an intersection. For instance, the data for the Mini-Maze in Figure 10.11 follow:

```
6          // number of intersections
0 2 0      // 1: exit forward and enter 2
3 5 6      // 2: exit left to 3; forward to 5; right to 6
0 0 4      // 3: exit right to 4
0 0 0      // 4: 4 is a dead-end
0 0 0      // 5: 5 is a dead-end
7 0 0      // 6: exit left to End
7          // number of exit intersection
```

- -
MAZE CLASS SPECIFICATION

DECLARATION

```
#include <iostream.h>
#include <fstream.h>
#include <stdlib.h>

class Maze
{
   private:
      // number of intersections in the maze and number of
      // the exit intersection
      int mazesize;
      int EXIT;

      // the array of maze intersections
      Intersection *intsec;
   public:
      // constructor; read data from file <filename>
      Maze(char *filename);

      // traverse and solve the maze
      int TraverseMaze(int intsecvalue);
};
```

DESCRIPTION

The constructor is passed the name of the file that contains the maze data. In the process, we identify the number of intersections and can allocate memory for the dynamic array intsec.

TraverseMaze is a recursive function that finds the solution to the maze. The parameter intsecValue is initially 1, indicating that the traveler enters the maze at intersection 1. During the recursive process, the variable maintains the number of the current intersection under consideration. The declaration and implementation of the maze class are found in the file "maze.h".

MAZE CLASS IMPLEMENTATION

The constructor is responsible for setting up the maze. As such, it opens the input file, reads the maze size, initializes the array of intersections, and assigns the exit intersection.

```cpp
// build maze by reading intersections and the exit
// intersection number from filename
Maze::Maze(char *filename)
{
    ifstream fin;
    int i;

    // open filename. terminate if not found
    fin.open(filename, ios::in | ios::nocreate);
    if (!fin)
    {
        cerr << "The maze data file " << filename
             << " cannot be opened!" << endl;
        exit(1);
    }

    // 1st entry of file is the number of intersections in maze
    fin >> mazesize;

    // allocate an array of maze intersections. we do not use
    // index 0, so we must allocate mazesize+1 records. a next
    // intersection number of 0 indicates a dead end
    intsec = new Intersection[mazesize+1];

    // read the intersections from the file
    for (i = 1; i <= mazesize; i++)
        fin >> intsec[i].left >> intsec[i].forward
            >> intsec[i].right

    // read the number of the exit intersection and close file
    fin >> EXIT;
    fin.close();
}
```

The recursive strategy is managed by the TraverseMaze method, which takes the current number of the intersection (intsecValue) as a parameter. The function is called from a previous intersection and returns the value 1 (TRUE) if some path can be found from the current intersection to the exit intersection. If intsecValue is 0, we have run into a wall and immediately return with 0 (FALSE).

   The heart of the method is a decision tree that allows the traveler to launch conditionally on a path that will terminate at the exit intersection.

Case 1: If intsecValue == EXIT, we have successfully arrived at our destination. We print the intersection value and broadcast TRUE back to the previous intersection in the path that is waiting to see if we were successful.

Case 2: If we are not at the EXIT, we leave our intersection on the left and await a message TRUE or FALSE that indicates if the path to the left is successful. If we get a message of TRUE, we print the current value and broadcast TRUE back to the previous intersection.

Case 3: This case is similar to case 2 except that we are not at the EXIT and were not successful in attempting to go left. We then leave forward and await a message TRUE or FALSE that indicates if the path forward is successful. If it is, we print the current intersection and broadcast TRUE back to the previous intersection.

Case 4: This is identical to cases 2 and 3 but handles an exit to the right.

If none of the cases sends back a message of TRUE, then the current intersection is a dead end. Return a message FALSE to indicate this fact. The ability to pass information back to the previous intersection (previous instance of TraverseMaze) derives from the recursive structure of the code. Ultimately, TraverseMaze(1) returns TRUE or FALSE to the main program to indicate if the maze has a free passage along some path.

```
// solve the maze using backtracking
int Maze::TraverseMaze(int intsecvalue)
{
    // if intsecvalue = 0, we are at a dead end;
    // otherwise, we attempt to find a valid direction
    // in which to move
    if (intsecvalue > 0)
    {
        // stopping condition: we have located the exit point
        if (intsecvalue == EXIT)
        {
            // print intersection number and return True
            cout << intsecvalue << "   ";
            return 1;
        }


        // attempt to go left
        else if (TraverseMaze(intsec[intsecvalue].left))
        {
            // print intersection number and return True
            cout << intsecvalue << "   ";
            return 1;
        }
```

```
        // left leads to dead end. try going straight
        else if (TraverseMaze(intsec[intsecvalue].forward))
        {
           // print intersection number and return True
           cout << intsecvalue << "   ";
           return 1;
        }

        // left and straight lead to dead end. try going right
        else if (TraverseMaze(intsec[intsecvalue].right))
        {
           // print intersection number and return True
           cout << intsecvalue << "   ";
           return 1;
        }
     }

     // we are at a dead end. return False.
     return 0;
}
```

Program 10.6   Solving a Maze

We test the maze for the Mini-Maze in Figure 10.11 (input file "maze1.dat") and then for the following maze (input file "maze2.dat"): This maze has no solution. The last run traverses the large maze in Figure 10.1 (input file "bigmaze.dat"). In each case the path is printed in reverse order.

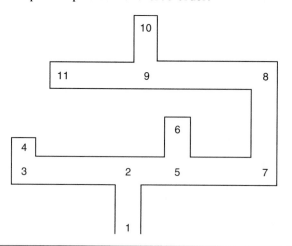

```
#include <iostream.h>

#include "maze.h"           // include the maze class
```

```
void main (void)
{
    // the file containing the maze parameters
    char filename[32];

    cout << "Enter the data file name: ";
    cin >> filename;

    // build the maze by reading the file
    Maze  M(filename);

    // solve the maze and print the result
    if (M.TraverseMaze(1))
        cout << endl << "You are free!" << endl;
    else
        cout << "No path out of the maze" << endl;
}

/*
<Run #1 of Program 10.6>

Enter the data file name: maze1.dat
7  6  2  1
You are free!

<Run #2 of Program 10.6>

Enter the data file name: maze2.dat
No path out of the maze

<Run #3 of Program 10.6>

Enter the data file name: bigmaze.dat
19  17  16  14  10  9  8  2  1
You are free!
*/
```

Evaluating Recursion   10.5

Recursion is often not an efficient method to solve a problem. Consider the factorial problem. An iterative algorithm uses a for loop rather than the repeated function calling and parameter passing in the recursive algorithm. Recursion has a cruel irony. Often it simplifies both the algorithm design and coding only to fail for lack of runtime efficiency. This conflict is illustrated with the Fibonacci sequence:

1, 1, 2, 3, 5, 8, 13, 21, 34, . . .

The terms of the sequence F(n) are defined recursively for n ≥ 1. The first two terms are explicitly defined as 1. From that point on, each term is the sum of the previous two terms.

$$F(n) = \begin{cases} 1 & \text{if } n = 1 \text{ or } 2 \\ F(n-1) + F(n-2) & \text{if } n > 2 \end{cases}$$

The definition translates immediately to a recursive function. Assume F(n) is the nth term in the Fibonacci sequence for n ≥ 1.

```
Stopping Conditions:   F(1) = 1     F(2) = 1
Recursive Step:        For N ≥ 3, F(n) = F(n-1) + F(n-2);
```

The C++ function Fib implements the recursive function F. It is passed a single integer parameter n and returns a long integer result.

```cpp
// recursive generation of the nth Fibonacci number
long Fib(int n)
{
   // stopping condition: f1 = f2 = 1
   if (n == 1 || n == 2)
      return 1;

   // recursive step: Fib(n) = Fib(n-2) + Fib(n-1)
   else
      return Fib(n-1) + Fib(n-2);
}
```

You immediately observe that the function Fib makes multiple calls to itself with the same parameter. For example, consider N = 6. The expression Fib(N−1) + Fib(N−2) sets up a hierarchy tree of calls to "Fib" for N = 5, 4, 3, 2, and 1 (Figure 10.12).

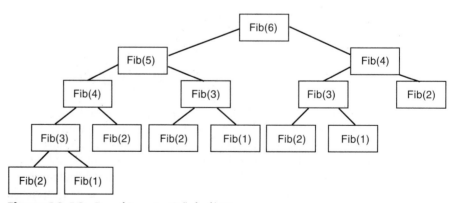

Figure 10.12 Tree of Recursive Calls for fib(6)

Note that Fib(3) is computed three times and Fib(2) is computed five times. The 15 nodes on the tree represent the number of recursive calls required to compute Fib(6) = 8.

The total number of calls, 15, is directly related to the value Fib(6). Assume NumCall(k) is the number of recursive calls to compute Fib(k)

```
NumCall(k) = 2 * Fib(k) - 1
```

For instance,

```
NumCall(6)  = 2 * Fib(6) - 1 = 2 * 8 - 1 = 15

NumCall(35) = 2 * Fib(35) - 1 = 2 * 9277465 - 1 = 18,554,929
```

The computational efficiency of the algorithm is $O(2^n)$. The running time of the recursive algorithm is exponential.

Fibonacci Numbers: Iterative Form   An iterative computation of the nth Fibonacci number uses a simple loop. The function has computational efficiency $O(n)$.

```
// compute nth Fibonacci number iteratively
long FibIter(int n)
{
   long twoback = 1, oneback = 1, current;
   int i;

   // FibIter(1) = FibIter(2) = 1
   if (n == 1 || n == 2)
      return 1;

  // current = twoback + oneback, n >= 3
   else
      for (i=3;i <= n;i++)
      {
         current = twoback + oneback;
         twoback = oneback;
         oneback = current;
      }

   return current;
}
```

For the kth Fibonacci number, $k \geq 3$ the iterative form requires $k-2$ additions and one function call. For $k = 35$, the iterative form requires 33 additions, whereas the recursive function requires more than 18.5 million function calls!

Fibonacci Numbers by Formula   The most efficient calculation of a Fibonacci number involves direct use of a formula that is derived from recurrence equations.

The derivation of the formula is beyond the scope of this book.

$$F(n) = \frac{1}{\sqrt{5}}\left[\left(\frac{1+\sqrt{5}}{2}\right)^n - \left(\frac{1-\sqrt{5}}{2}\right)^n\right]$$

Since the square root and power functions belong to the C++ <math.h> library, the nth Fibonacci number can be directly computed with efficiency O(1).

```cpp
#include <math.h>

const double sqrt5 = sqrt(5.0);

// compute nth Fibonacci number using the algebraic formula
double FibFormula(int n)
{
    double p1, p2;

    // C++ math library function
    //     double pow(double x, double y);
    // computes x to the power y
    p1 = pow((1+sqrt(5))/2.0,n);
    p2 = pow((1-sqrt(5))/2.0,n);
    return (p1 - p2)/sqrt(5);
}
```

Program 10.7   Evaluating Recursion (Fibonacci Example)

The program times the computation of the 35th Fibonacci number using the formula, the iterative function, and recursive function found in the file "fib.h". The nonrecursive functions execute in a fraction of a second, whereas the recursive function requires more than 82 seconds.

```cpp
#include <iostream.h>

#include "fib.h"

void main(void)
{
    int i;

    // print the output from FibFormula as a fixed point
    // number, no decimal places
    cout.setf(ios::fixed);
    cout.precision(0);
```

```
    // compute and print 35th Fibonacci number three ways
    cout << FibFormula(35) << endl;
    cout << FibIter(35) << endl;
    cout << Fib(35) << endl;
}


/*
<Run of Program 10.7>

  9227465      <formula takes less than 1 second>
  9227465      <iterative function takes less than 1 second>
  9227465      <recursive function takes more than 82 seconds>
*/
```

Assessing Recursion   The example of Fibonacci numbers should alert you to potential problems in the use of recursion. With the overhead of function calls, a simple recursive function could seriously deteriorate runtime performance. More seriously, a recursive call may generate layer upon layer of subsequent recursive calls that cascade out of the programmer's control and make demands that exceed the available stack space. The Fibonacci example is an extreme case. An iterative version can be easily designed and implemented.

With warnings noted, recursion remains an important design and programming tool. Many algorithms are simpler to state and design using recursion. They naturally lend themselves to a recursive implementation that distinguishes the stopping conditions and recursive step. For instance, the use of backtracking in the maze problem is facilitated by recursion.

Although recursion is not an object-oriented concept, it has some of the good characteristics of object-oriented programming design. It allows the programmer to manage the key logical components in the algorithm while hiding some of the complex implementation details. There is no hard and fast rule indicating when to use recursion. You must weigh design and runtime efficiencies. Use recursion when the algorithm design is enhanced and implementation allows for reasonable space and time efficiency during execution.

Tail Recursion   If the last action of a function is to make a recursive call, we say the function uses **tail recursion.** This recursive call requires overhead to create an activation record and to store it on the stack. When the recursive process hits a stopping condition, we must execute a series of returns that pop the activation records on the stack. We put the records on and off the stack without using them for significant computation.

Eliminating tail recursion can significantly affect the efficiency of a recursive function. A simple example illustrates the problem and suggests a typical solution. Consider the recursive function recfunc that prints the entries in an array from index n down to 0. The example is not realistic. It is chosen to provide a simple illustration of tail recursion.

```
void recfunc(int A[], int n)
{
   if (n >= 0)                // go ahead if index n is in range
   {
      cout << A[n] << "  ";
      n--;                    // decrement index n
      recfunc(A,n);
   }
}
```

Assume array A[] = {10, 20, 30}. An initial function call to recfunc(A,2) starts with n = 2 and creates the output 30 20 10.

The function recfunc illustrates a typical tail recursion situation. We can illustrate the problem with a flow control diagram that interprets $n \geq 0$ as a condition requiring a further recursive call:

```
┌→   if <recursive condition>  ←── n >= 0
│       Execute a Task         ←── output A[n]
│       Update condition       ←── decrement n (n--)
└─────── Call recfunc
```

This flow control diagram is equivalent to a WHILE loop that tests the simple condition, $n \geq 0$. In recfunc, control passes to the condition using the less efficient recursion operation.

```
┌→   while <condition>         ←── n >= 0
│       Execute a Task         ←── output A[n]
│       Update condition       ←── decrement n (n--)
└──────
```

In our example, the recursive function recfunc can be replaced by the function interfunc that employs a logically equivalent WHILE statement. The problem of removing tail recursion can be a little tricky. A good safeguard is to create a flow control diagram for the recursive function and then build the same iterative diagram using WHILE.

```
// iterative function to eliminate tail recursion
void iterfunc(int A[],int n)
{
   while (n >= 0)
   {
      cout << "While value     " << A[n] << endl;
      n--;
   }
}
```

Written Exercises

10.1 Explain why the following function may give the wrong value when executed.

```
long factorial(long n)
{
   if (n == 0 || n == 1)
      return 1;
   else
      return n * factorial(--n);
}
```

The result depends on the order in which the compiler evaluates the operands. If n=3 and the left operand is evaluated first, the result is 3*2! = 6. If the right operand is evaluated first, the result is 2*2! = 4.

10.2 What is the numerical sequence generated by the recursive function f in the following code listing?:

```
long f(int n)
{
   if (n == 0 || n == 1)
      return 1;
   else
      return 3*f(n-2) + 2*f(n-1);
}
```

10.3 What is the numerical sequence generated by the recursive function f in the following code listing?:

```
int f(int n)
{
   if (n == 0)
      return 1;
   else if(n == 1)
      return 2;
   else
      return 2*f(n-2) + f(n-1);
}
```

10.4 What is the output of the following program if the input is 5 3?

```
#include <iostream.h>

long f (int b, int n)
{
   if (n == 0)
      return 1;
```

```
        else
            return b*f(b,n-1);
    }

    void main(void)
    {
        int b, e;

        cin >> b >> e;

        cout << f(b,e) << endl;
    }
```

10.5   What is the output of the following program if the input is "This is interesting!"

```
    #include <iostream.h>

    void Q(void)
    {
        char c;

        cin.get(c);
        if ( c != '\n')
            Q();
        cout << c;
    }

    void main(void)
    {
        cout << "Enter a line of text:" << endl;
        Q();
        cout << endl;
    }
```

10.6   The maximum element in an n-element integer array can be computed recursively. Define the function

```
    int max(int x, int y);
```

that returns the maximum of two integers x and y. Define the function

```
    int arraymax(int a[], int n);
```

that uses recursion to return the maximum element of a.

Stopping Condition: n == 1
Recursive Step: arraymax = max(max(a[0], . . .a[n−2]),a[n−1])

10.7   Write a recursive function

```
    float avg(float a[], int n);
```

that returns the average of the elements in an n-element array of float values.

Stopping Condition: n == 1
Recursive Step: avg = ((n−1)/n)*(average of n−1 elements) + (n*th* element)/n

10.8 Write a recursive function

```
int rstrlen(char s[]);
```

that computes the length of a string.

Stopping Condition: s[0] == 0 (null string)
Recursive Step: length(s) = 1 + length(substring starting with 2*nd* char)

10.9 Write a recursive function that tests whether a string is a palindrome. A palindrome is a deblanked string that reads the same forward and backward. For instance, the following are palindromes:

dad   level   did   madamimadam

Use the following declaration

```
int pal(char A[], int s, int e);
```

where pal determines if the characters in A beginning with index s and ending with index e constitute a palindrome.

Stopping Condition:
  s >= e (success)
  A[s] != A[e] (failure)
Recursive Step: Is A between indices s+1 and e−1 a palindrome?

10.10 The binomial coefficients are the coefficients $C_{n,k}$ in the expansion of $(x+1)^n$,

$$(x+1)^n = C_{n,n} x^n + C_{n,n-1} x^{n-1} + C_{n,n-2} x^{n-2} + \ldots + C_{n,2} x^2 + C_{n,1} x^1 + C_{n,0} x^0$$

Note that $C_{n,n}$ and $C_{n,0}$ are both 1 for any n. The recurrence relation for the binomial coefficients is given by

$C(n,0) = 1$
$C(n,n) = 1$
$C(n,k) = C(n-1,k-1) + C(n-1,k)$

Note that each coefficient $C(n,k)$, $0 \leq k \leq n$, is the solution to the committee problem posed and solved in the text. The binomial coefficients $C(n,k)$ determine the number of ways k items can chosen from n items.

These coefficients form the famous Pascal's Triangle. In the triangle, the column 0 contains all 1's, as does the diagonal (row == column). Each of the remaining elements is the sum of the two elements in the row above in the same column and the column to the left.

```
     1
    1 1
   1 2 1
  1 3 3 1
 1 4 6 4 1
```

Write a function that creates the Pascal Triangle for a given *n*. The sample is given for *n* = 4.

10.11 Write a recursive function

```
int gcd(int a, int b);
```

to compute the greatest common divisor of strictly positive integers a and b. See the Chapter 6 software supplement for an iterative version of the function.

10.12 The following is an input file for a maze. Draw the maze and find the solution by tracing the recursive algorithm step by step.

```
11                          // number of intersections
0       2       0           // intersection 1: (left, forward, right)
4       3       6
0       0       0
0       0       5
0       0       0
7       0       0
8       11      9
0       0       0
0       0       10
0       0       0
12      0       0
12                          // exit point
```

Programming Exercises

10.1 Use function arraymax from Written Exercise 10.6 to perform the following actions:

1. Generate 10 random integers in the range 1–20,000 and store them in an array.
2. Print the array.
3. Apply arraymax and print the result. Verify that it is correct.

10.2 The sum of the first *n* integers is given by the formula

$$1+2+3+\ldots+n = n(n+1)/2$$

Initialize array A to contain the first 50 integers. The average of these array elements is then $51/2 = 25.5$. Test your solution to Written Exercise 10.7 by applying avg to A.

10.3 Test your recursive function rstrlen of Written Exercise 10.8 by reading five (5) strings from the keyboard using cin.getline and printing the string length using rstrlen and the C++ library function strlen.

10.4 Read strings until end of file, using the stream operator >> to obtain whitespace-separated "words." For each word, use the recursive function pal of Written Exercise

10.9 to determine if the word is a palindrome. If so, assign it to an element of an array of strings. At end of file, print all the palindromes found, one per line.

10.5 Printing an integer value in a specific number base is a classical arithmetic problem:

$N = 45$	Base $= 2$	Output: 101101	$[32 + 8 + 4 + 1]$
$N = 90$	Base $= 8$	Output: 132	$[1(64) + 3(8) + 2(1)]$
$N = 75$	Base $= 5$	Output: 300	$[3(5^2) + 0(5) + 0(1)]$

A general algorithm uses repeated division by base B to implement the conversion to the number base. If

$$N = d_{n-1}\, d_{n-2}\, d_{n-3} \ldots d_1\, d_0,$$

the successive remainders give the digits of N in the order d_0 to d_{n-1}.
  Define the recursive function

```
void intout(long N , int B);
```

to print N in the base B, assuming that B $\leq$ 10. Test the function in a main program that reads five pairs of numbers N,B and prints each number N in base B.

10.6 Read a positive integer n < 10. Refer to Written Exercise 10.10 and print the expansion of the polynomial $(x+1)^n$. Print each power x^i in the form x ** i.

10.7 Develop a recursive function to count the number of n-digit binary numbers that do not have two 1's in a row. (*Hint:* The number either begins with a 0 or a 1. If it begins with 0, the number of possibilities is determined by the remaining $n-1$ digits. If it begins with 1, what must the next digit be?)

10.8 The problem of finding the root of a real valued function occurs frequently in mathematics, engineering, and other sciences. If f(x) is a function, a root r of f is a real number such that f(r) = 0. In some cases, roots can be computed using an algebraic formula. For instance, all roots of the quadratic equation $f(x) = ax^2 + bx + c$ are given by the quadratic formula

$$r = \frac{-b \pm \sqrt{b^2 - 4ac}}{2a}$$

In general, there is no formula, and the roots must be found using numerical methods.
  If f(a) and f(b) are of opposite sign (f(a) * f(b) < 0) and f is well behaved, then there is a root r of f between a and b.

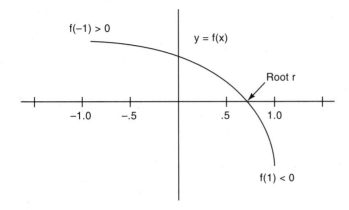

The Bisection Method is defined as follows:

Let m = (a+b)/2.0 be the midpoint of the interval a ≤ x ≤ b. If f(m) is 0.0, then r = m is a root. If not, then either f(a) and f(m) have opposite signs (f(a)*f(m)<0) or f(m) and f(b) have opposite signs (f(m)*f(b)<0).

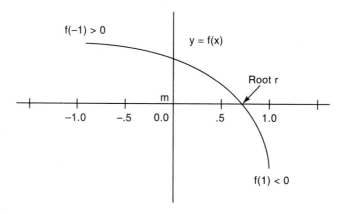

f(0) * f(−1) > 0, f(0) * f(1) < 0.
Root lies in the interval
0 < r < 1.0

If f(m)*f(b) < 0, then the root r lies in the interval m≤x≤b; otherwise, it lies in the interval a≤x≤m. Now perform the same action with the new interval whose length is half the length of the original. Continue this process until the interval has become small enough or until we have found an exact root.

Write a recursive function

```
double Bisect(double f(double x),
              double a,double b, double precision);
```

that approximates the root of a function f(x) passed as an argument. Terminate bisection if f(m) is 0.0 or the length of the subinterval is less than precision.

(a) Find the root of f(x) = $x^3 - 2x - 3$ that lies between 1 and 2.

(b) Let the function

```
double Balance(double principal, double interest,
               int nmonths, double payment);
```

compute and return the balance after paying simple interest on the given principal with monthly interest for nmonths. Use the bisection method to compute the payment on a $150,000 loan at 10% interest per year for 25 years.

10.9 Run Program 10.6 using the data from Written Exercise 10.12. Verify your solution to the exercise.

C H A P T E R   11

TREES

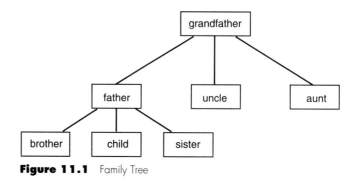

Figure 11.1 Family Tree

Arrays and linked lists define collections of objects that are sequentially accessed. The data structures are properly called **linear** lists since they have a unique first and last element and each interior item has a unique successor. A linear list is a general description for structures that include arrays, stacks, queues, and linked lists.

In many applications, objects exhibit a nonlinear order in which a member may have multiple successors. For instance, in describing a family tree, a parent may have many descendants (children). Figure 11.1 illustrates three generations of a family from the view of a child. A similar kind of ordering describes the lines of authority in a corporation that is headed by a CEO and broken down into divisional officers and managers (Figure 11.2). The ordering is referred to as a hierarchy and has its origins in the religious distribution of authority from the bishop to the pastors, deacons, and so forth.

In this chapter, we look at a nonlinear structure, called a **tree,** that consists of nodes and branches. The organization flows from a root to outer nodes, called leaves of the tree. In Chapter 13, the study of graphs that describe a nonlinear structure in which two or more nodes may flow into a same object is presented. These structures, similar to the communication grid in Figure 11.3, require separate algorithm design and provide special areas of application.

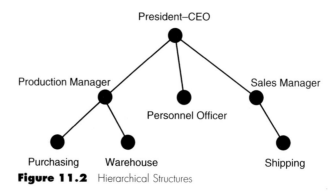

Figure 11.2 Hierarchical Structures

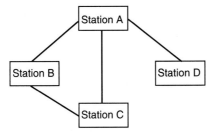

Figure 11.3   Telephone Relay Stations

TREE TERMINOLOGY

A tree structure is characterized as a set of **nodes** that originates from a unique starting node called the **root**. In Figure 11.4, node A is the root. Using the concept of a family tree, a node may be considered a **parent** and may point at 0, 1, or more nodes called its **children.** For instance, node B is the parent of children E and F. The parent of H is node D. A tree may represent several generations in the family. The children of a node and children of these children are called **descendants,** and the parent and grandparents of a node are its **ancestors.** For instance, nodes E, F, I, and J are descendants of B. Each nonroot node has a unique parent and each parent has zero or more child nodes. A node with no children, such as E, G, H, I, and J, is called a **leaf** node.

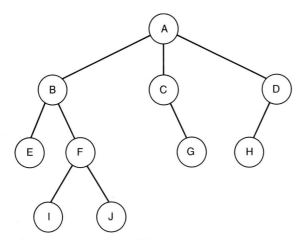

Figure 11.4   A General Tree

Each node in a tree is the root of a **subtree,** which is defined by the node and all descendants of the node. The following diagram shows three subtrees from the general tree of Figure 11.4. Node F is the root of a subtree containing nodes F, I, and J. Node G is a root of a subtree with no descendants. The definition permits us to say that node A is a root of a subtree that happens to be the tree itself.

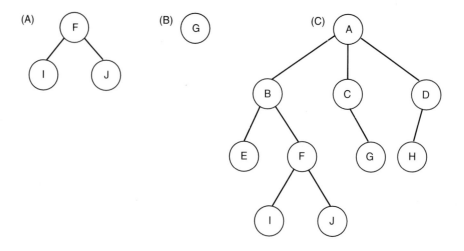

You move from a parent node to its child and other descendants along a **path.** For instance, in Figure 11.5, the path from root A to node F moves from A to C and C to F. The fact that each nonroot node has a single parent ensures that there are unique paths from any node to its descendants. The path between the root and a node provides a measure called the **level** of a node. The level of a node is the length of the path from the root to the node. The level of the root is 0. Each child of the root is a level 1 node, the next generation is level 2 nodes, and so forth. For instance, in Figure 11.5, F is a level 2 node with a path length of 2.

The **depth** of a tree is the maximum level of any node in the tree. The concept of depth can also be described in terms of a path. The depth of a tree is the length

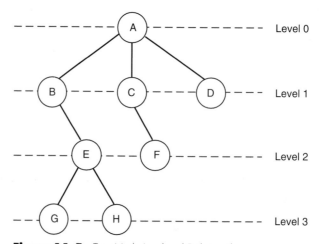

Figure 11.5   Tree Node Level and Path Length

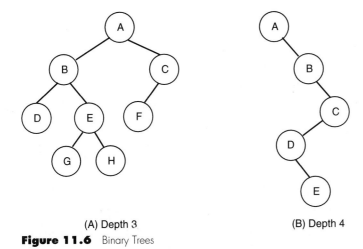

(A) Depth 3

(B) Depth 4

Figure 11.6 Binary Trees

of the longest path from the root to a node. In Figure 11.5, the depth of the tree is 3.

BINARY TREES

Although general trees find important applications, we focus on a restricted class of trees in which each parent has no more than two children (Figure 11.6). These **binary trees** have a uniform structure that allows for a variety of scanning algorithms and efficient access to elements. The study of binary trees enables you to solve most general tree problems since a general tree has an equivalent binary tree representation. This issue is studied in the exercises.

In a binary tree, each node may have 0, 1, or 2 children. We refer to the node on the left as the **left child** and the node on the right as the **right child.** The tags "left" and "right" refer to our pictorial representation of a tree. A binary tree is a recursive structure. Each node is the root of its own subtree and has children, which are roots of trees called the left and right subtrees of the node, respectively. Tree access routines are therefore naturally recursive. The following is a recursive definition of a binary tree.

A binary tree is a set of nodes B such that

(a)   B is a tree if the set of nodes is empty. (An empty tree is a tree.)

(b)   B is partitioned into three disjoint subsets:
$\{R\}$ the root node
$\{L_1, L_2, \ldots, L_m\}$ the left subtree of R
$\{R_1, R_2, \ldots, R_n\}$ the right subtree of R

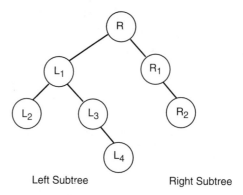

Left Subtree   Right Subtree

At any level n, a binary tree may contain from 1 to 2^n nodes. The number of nodes per level contribute to the density of the tree. Intuitively, density is a measure of the size of a tree (number of nodes) relative to the depth of the tree. In Figure 11.6, tree A contains 8 nodes in a depth of 3, while tree B contains 5 nodes with depth 4. The latter case is a special form, called a **degenerate** tree, in which there is a single leaf node (E) and each nonleaf node has only one child. A degenerate tree is equivalent to a linked list.

Trees with a higher density are important as data structures since they hold proportionately more elements near the top of the tree with a shorter path from the root. A dense tree allows us to store a large collection of data and maintain efficient access to the items. Rapid access is key to our use of trees to hold data.

Degenerate trees are one extreme measure of density. At the other extreme, a **complete binary tree** of depth N is a tree in which each level 0 to $N - 1$ has a full set of nodes and all leaf nodes at level N occupy the leftmost positions in the tree. A complete binary tree that contains 2^N nodes at level N is a **full** tree. A full tree is a binary tree in which every nonleaf node has two children. Figure 11.7 illustrates a complete and a full binary tree.

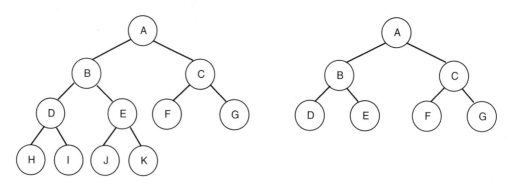

Complete Tree (Depth 3)   Full Tree (Depth 2)

Figure 11.7 Binary Tree Classification

Complete and full binary trees of depth k provide some interesting mathematical facts. In each case, there is one (2^0) node at level 0 (root), two (2^1) nodes at level 1, four (2^2) nodes at level 2, and so forth. Through the first $k - 1$ levels, there are $2^k - 1$ nodes.

$$1 + 2 + 4 + ... + 2^{k-1} = 2^k - 1$$

At level k, the number of additional nodes ranges from a minimum of 1 to a maximum of 2^k (full). With a full tree, the number of nodes is

$$1 + 2 + 4 + ... + 2^{k-1} + 2^k = 2^{k+1} - 1$$

The number of nodes N in a complete binary tree satisfies the inequality

$$2^k \leq N \leq 2^{k+1} - 1 < 2^{k+1}$$

After solving for k, we have

$$k \leq \log_2 (N) < k+1$$

For instance, a full tree of depth 3 has

$$2^4 - 1 = 15 \text{ nodes}$$

EXAMPLE 11.1
_____

1. The maximum depth in a tree with 5 nodes is 4 [Figure 11.6 (B)]. The minimum depth k of a tree with 5 nodes is

    $$k \leq \log_2(5) < k+1$$
    $$\log_2(5) = 2.32 \text{ and } k = 2$$

2. The depth of a tree is the length of the longest path from the root to a node. For a degenerate tree with N nodes, the longest path has length $N-1$.

    For a complete binary tree with N nodes, the depth of the tree is the integer value of $\log_2 N$. This is also the distance of the longest path from the root to a node. Assuming the tree has $N = 10,000$ elements, the longest path is

    $$\text{int } (\log_2 10000) = \text{int}(13.28) = 13$$

11.1 Binary Tree Structure

A binary tree structure is built with nodes. Like a linked list, these nodes contain data fields and pointer references to other nodes in the collection. In this section, we define a tree node and provide operations that enable us to build and scan a binary tree. Similar to the presentation of the Node class in Chapter 9, we declare a TreeNode class and then design a series of functions that use tree nodes to build a binary tree and scan the individual nodes.

A tree node contains a data field and two pointer fields. The pointer fields are referred to as the **left pointer (left)** and the **right pointer (right)** since they point to the left and right subtree of the node, respectively. A value NULL indicates an empty tree.

TreeNode

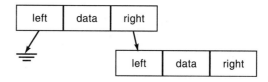

The root node defines an entry point into the binary tree, whereas a pointer field specifies a node at the next level in the tree. A leaf node has a NULL left and right pointer (Figure 11.8).

DESIGNING A TREENODE CLASS

In this section, we design a TreeNode class that declares the node objects in a binary tree. A node consists of a data field that is given as a public member so that the user may directly access its value. This allows the client to read or update the data while scanning the tree and enables a reference to the data value to be returned. This feature is used by advanced data structures such as dictionaries. The two pointer fields are private members that can be accessed with the public member functions Left () and Right (). The declaration and definition of the TreeNode class are contained in the file "treenode.h".

- -
TREENODE CLASS SPECIFICATION

DECLARATION

```
// BinSTree depends on TreeNode
template <class T>
class BinSTree;

// declares a tree node object for a binary tree
template <class T>
```

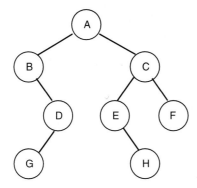

Tree

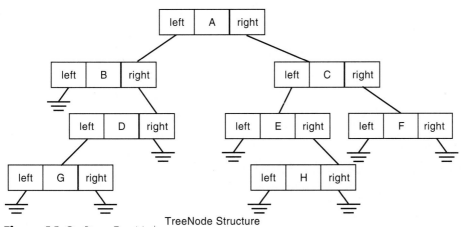

TreeNode Structure

Figure 11.8 Binary Tree Nodes

```
class TreeNode
{
    private:
        // points to the left and right children of the node
        TreeNode<T> *left;
        TreeNode<T> *right;

    public:
        // public member allowing the client to update its value
        T data;

        // constructor
        TreeNode (const T& item, TreeNode<T> *lptr = NULL,
                                 TreeNode<T> *rptr = NULL);
```

```
      // access methods for the pointer fields
      TreeNode<T>* Left(void) const;
      TreeNode<T>* Right(void) const;

      // make BinSTree a friend because it needs access to
      // left and right pointer fields of a node
      friend class BinSTree<T>;
};
```

DESCRIPTION

The constructor initializes the data and pointer fields. By using the default pointer NULL, the node is initialized as a leaf node. With a TreeNode pointer P that is passed as a parameter, the constructor connects P as the left or right child of the new node.

The access methods Left and Right return the corresponding pointer value. The BinSTree class is declared as a friend of TreeNode and can modify the pointers. Other clients must use the constructor to create the pointers and then use methods Left and Right for a tree traversal.

EXAMPLE

```
// pointers to integer tree nodes
TreeNode<int>  *root, *lchild, *rchild;
TreeNode<int>  *p;

// allocate leaf nodes with data values 20 and 30
lchild = new TreeNode<int> (20);
rchild = new TreeNode<int> (30);

// create root node with value 10 and two children
root = new TreeNode<int> (10,lchild,rchild);
```

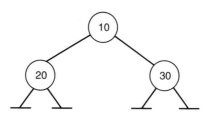

```
root->data = 50;        // assign 50 to root
```

Implementing the TreeNode Class   The TreeNode class initializes the fields of an object. The constructor has the item parameter to initialize the data field. The pointers assign a left and right child (subtree) to the node. The default value NULL applies when the node does not have a left or a right child.

```
// constructor; initialize the data and pointer fields
// The pointer value NULL assigns an empty subtree
template <class T>
TreeNode<T>::TreeNode (const T& item, TreeNode<T> *lptr,
        TreeNode<T> *rptr):data(item), left(lptr), right(rptr)
{ }
```

The methods Left and Right return the value of the left and right pointer fields. This provides a client access to the left and right child of a node.

BUILDING A BINARY TREE

A binary tree consists of a collection of TreeNode objects that are connected through their pointer fields. A TreeNode object is created dynamically with a call to the function new.

```
TreeNode<int> *p;              // declare a pointer to an integer
                               // tree node

p = new TreeNode(item);        // left and right pointer fields
                               // are NULL
```

When calling the function new, a data value must be included. If a TreeNode pointer is also passed as a parameter, the newly allocated node uses the pointer to attach a child. We define a function **GetTreeNode** that takes a data value and zero or more TreeNode pointers to allocate and initialize a binary tree node. If insufficient memory is available, the program terminates after giving an error message.

```
// create TreeNode object with pointer fields lptr and rptr.
// The pointers have default value NULL.
template <class T>
TreeNode<T> *GetTreeNode(T item,TreeNode<T> *lptr = NULL,
                         TreeNode<T> *rptr = NULL)
{
   TreeNode<T> *p;

   // call new to allocate the new node
   // pass parameters lptr and rptr to the function
   p = new TreeNode<T> (item, lptr, rptr);

   // if insufficient memory, terminate with an error message
   if (p == NULL)
   {
```

```
            cerr << "Memory allocation failure!\n";
            exit(1);
        }

        // return the pointer to the system generated memory
        return p;
    }
```

The function **FreeTreeNode** takes a TreeNode pointer and deallocates the corresponding node's memory by calling the C++ function delete.

```
    // deallocate dynamic memory associated with the node
    template <class T>
    void FreeTreeNode(TreeNode<T> *p)
    {
        delete p;
    }
```

These two functions are contained in the file "treelib.h", along with a series of binary tree functions that are introduced in Section 11.2.

Defining Sample Trees   The GetTreeNode function can be used to define explicitly each node in a tree and hence define the tree. The technique was illustrated for the three node tree with data values 10, 20, and 30. For a larger example, the process is a little tedious because you must include all of the data and pointer values.

For use in this chapter, we create the function MakeCharTree that builds three trees whose nodes contain character data. The trees are used to illustrate the TreeNode functions in the next section. Function parameters include a reference to the root of the tree and a parameter n $(0 \leq n \leq 2)$ that designates the tree. The following declarations create a TreeNode pointer called root and assign it as the roof of Tree_2.

```
    TreeNode<char> *root;           // declare a root pointer
    MakeCharTree(root,2);           // set up tree_2 based at root
```

Figure 11.9 describes the three character trees that are built by the method. A full listing of the function MakeCharTree is located in "treelib.h". The function extends the techniques from Example 11.2 to trees with 5 and 9 nodes.

11.2   Designing TreeNode Functions

A linked list is a linear structure that allows us to scan the nodes sequentially using the pointer next. Because a tree is a nonlinear structure, there is no similar scanning algorithm. We are forced to select from a variety of traversal methods of which the most commonly used are preorder, inorder, and postorder scan, Each of these methods relies on the recursive structure of a binary tree.

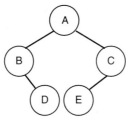

Tree_0

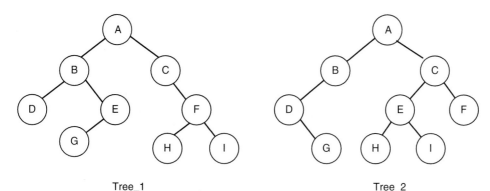

Tree_1   Tree_2

Figure 11.9 MakeCharTree Trees

Traversal algorithms are fundamental to an effective use of a tree. We first develop the recursive scanning methods and then use them to create algorithms for printing a tree, copying and deleting a tree, and determining the depth of a tree. In this section, we also develop the **breadth first** scan that uses a queue to store the nodes. This traversal method scans the tree level by level starting at the root and moving to the first generation of children, then the second generation, and so forth. The method finds important applications in organizational trees where authority flows from the head to the different organizational levels.

Our implementation of a traversal method includes a function parameter called visit that accesses the data of the node. By passing a function, we can specify an action that should occur at each node as we traverse the tree. We include a brief discussion of C++ syntax to handle a function as a parameter.

```
template <class T>
void <Traversal_Method> (TreeNode<T> *t, void visit(T& item));
```

Each time a traversal method is called, the client must pass the name of a function that performs an action on the data in the node. As the method traverses from node to node, the function is called and the action performed.

Note: The concept of a function parameter is relatively simple but requires some clarification. In general, a function can be an argument by specifying the function name, its parameter list, and its return value. For instance, function G has a function parameter f. The parameter specifies the function name (f), the parameter list (int x), and the return type (int).

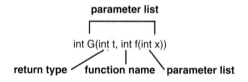

```
int G(int t, int f(int x))      // function parameter f
{
    // compute f(t) using the function f and the
    // parameter t. Return the product of this value and t
    return t * f(t);
}
```

A client, calling function G, must pass a function to f with the same structure. In our example, let the client define function XSquared that computes x^2.

```
// XSquared is a function with an integer parameter x
// and an integer return value
int xsquared(int x)
{
    return x*x;
}
```

The client calls function G with an integer parameter t and the function XSquared. The statement

```
Y = G(3, XSquared)
```

calls the function G, which in turn calls the function "XSquared" with parameter 3. The cout statement prints the output 27.

```
cout << G(3.0,xsquared) << endl;
```

RECURSIVE TREE TRAVERSALS

The recursive definition of a binary tree identifies the structure as a root along with two subtrees that are identified by the left and right pointer fields of the root. The power of recursion is manifest with the scanning methods. Each tree traversal algorithm performs three actions at a node. It visits the node (N) and recursively descends to the left subtree (L) and to the right subtree (R). Having made a descent to a subtree, the algorithm identifies that it is at a node and can perform the same three actions. The descent terminates when we reach an empty tree (pointer == NULL). The different recursive scan algorithms are distinguished by the order in which they perform their actions at a node. We develop the inorder and postorder methods in which we descend to a left subtree before descending to a right subtree. Other methods are left as exercises.

Inorder Traversal   An inorder scan begins its action at a node by first descending to its left subtree so that it can scan the nodes in that subtree. After recursively descending through the nodes in that subtree, the Inorder traversal takes the second action at the node and uses the data value. The traversal completes its action at the node by performing a recursive scan of the right subtree. In our recursive descent through subtrees, we repeat the actions of the algorithm at each new node.

The order of operations in the inorder traversal follows:

1. Traverse the left subtree.
2. Visit the node.
3. Traverse the right subtree.

We refer to this traversal as LNR (left, node, right). For Tree_0 in the function MakeCharTree, assume a "visit" means write out the value in the data field of the node.

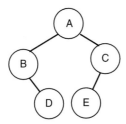

Tree_0

An Inorder scan of Tree_0 executes the following operations.

Action	Print	Observation
Descend left from A to B:		left child of B is NULL
Visit B;	B	
Descend right from B to D:		D is a leaf node
Visit D;	D	visited left subtree of A
Visit root A	A	
Descend right from A to C:		
Descend left from C to E:		E is a leaf node
Visit E;	E	
Visit C;	C	done!

The traversal order for the nodes is B D A E C. The recursive function first descends the left tree [t−>Left()] of a node and then visits the node. A second recursive step descends the right tree [t−>Right()].

```
// inorder recursive scan of the nodes in a tree.
template <class T>
void Inorder (TreeNode<T> *t, void visit(T& item))
{
        // the recursive scan terminates on a empty subtree
```

```
    if (t != NULL)
    {
        Inorder(t->Left(), visit);      // descend left
        visit(t->data);                 // visit the node
        Inorder(t->Right(), visit);     // descend right
    }
}
```

Postorder Scan   The postorder scan delays a visit to a node until after a recursive descent of the left subtree and a recursive descent of the right subtree. The order of operations produces an LRN scan (left,right,node).

1. Traverse the left subtree.

2. Traverse the right subtree.

3. Visit the node.

In the Postorder scan of Tree_0, the nodes are visited in the order D B E C A.

Action	Print	Observation
Descend left from A to B:		left child of B is NULL
Descend right from B to D:		D is a leaf node
Visit D;	D	visited children of B
Visit B;	B	visited left of A
Descend right from A to C:		
Descend left from C to E:		E is a leaf node
Visit E;	E	visited left child of C
Visit C;	C	visited right child of A
Visit root A;	A	done!

The function scans the tree from the bottom up. We descend down the left tree [t−>Left()] of a node and then the right tree [t−>Right()]. As a last operation, we finally visit the node.

```
// postorder recursive scan of the nodes in a tree.
template <class T>
void Postorder (TreeNode<T> *t, void visit(T& item))
{
    // the recursive scan terminates on a empty subtree
    if (t != NULL)
    {
        Postorder(t->Left(), visit);    // descend left
        Postorder(t->Right(), visit);   // descend right
        visit(t->data);                 // visit the node
    }
}
```

The preorder scan is defined by first visiting the node and then scanning the left and right branches (NLR).

Clearly, the prefixes *pre, in,* and *post* indicate when the "visit" occurs at a node. In each case, we descend down the left subtree before descending the right subtree. There are actually three more algorithms that select the right subtree before the left subtree. We will use the RNL scan to print a tree. The tree traversal algorithms allow us to visit all the nodes in a tree. They provide the equivalent of a sequential scan of an array or linked list. The preorder, inorder, and postorder scan functions are contained in the library "treescan.h".

EXAMPLE 11.2

1. For the character tree Tree_2, the following lists describe the order we visit nodes.

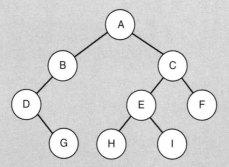

Tree_2

Preorder: A B D G C E H I F
Inorder: D G B A H E I C F
Postorder: G D B H I E F C A

2. The output for the Inorder scan of Tree_2 is produced by the following statements:

```
// visit function prints the data value
void PrintChar(char& elem)
{
    cout << elem << "   ";
}

TreeNode<char> *root;

MakeCharTree(root, 2);      // assigns Tree_2 to root

// prints a header and then scans the nodes
// using the function PrintChar to visit a node.
cout << "Inorder: ";
Inorder (root, PrintChar);
```

11.3 Using Tree Scan Algorithms

The recursive tree traversal algorithms are the basis for many tree applications. They provide an orderly access to the nodes and their data values. In this section, we illustrate the use of traversal algorithms to count the number of leaf nodes, to compute the depth of a tree, and to print a tree. In each case, we must use a scanning strategy to visit each node.

APPLICATION: VISITING TREE NODES

Many applications merely want to scan the nodes of a binary tree without concern for the order of the traversal. In these cases, the client is free to select from any of the scan algorithms. In this application, the function CountLeaf traverses the tree to count the number of leaf nodes. A reference parameter leafCount is incremented each time we identify a leaf node.

```
// the function uses the postorder scan. a visit
// tests whether the node is a leaf node
template <class T>
void CountLeaf (TreeNode<T> *t, int& count)
{
   //use postorder descent
   if (t != NULL)
   {
      CountLeaf(t->Left(), count);  // descend left
      CountLeaf(t->Right(), count); // descend right

      // check if node t is a leaf node (no descendants)
      // if so, increment the variable count
      if (t->Left() == NULL && t->Right() == NULL)
         count++;
   }
}
```

The Depth function uses a postorder scan to compute the depth of a binary tree. At each node it computes the depth of the left and right subtrees. The resulting depth of the node is 1 more than the maximum depth of its subtrees.

```
// the function uses the postorder scan. it computes the
// depth of the left and right subtrees of a node and
// returns the depth as 1 + max(depthLeft,depthRight).
// the depth of an empty tree is -1
template <class T>
void Depth (TreeNode<T> *t)
{
   int depthLeft, depthRight, depthval;

   if (t == NULL)
       depthval = -1;
```

```
    else
    {
        depthLeft = Depth(t->Left());
        depthRight = Depth(t->Right());
        depthval = 1+(depthLeft > depthRight?depthLeft:depthRight);
    }
    return depthval;
}
```

Program 11.1   Leaf Count and Depth

This program illustrates the use of the functions CountLeaf and Depth to scanning the character tree Tree_2. We print the final values of leafCount and treeDepth.

```
#include <iostream.h>

// include TreeNode class and library of functions
// include "treenode.h"
#include "treelib.h"

void main(void)
{
    TreeNode<char> *root;

    // use the character Tree_2
    MakeCharTree(root, 2);

    // variable that is updated by CountLeaf
    int leafCount = 0;

    // make call to CountLeaf function. get total leafcount
    CountLeaf(root, leafCount);
    cout << "Number of leaf nodes is " << leafCount << endl;

    // make call to Depth function and print depth of tree
    cout << "The depth of the tree is "
        << Depth(root) << endl;
}

/*
<Run of Program 11.1>

Number of leaf nodes is 4
The depth of the tree is 3

*/
```

APPLICATION: TREE PRINT

The tree print function creates a picture of the tree rotated counterclockwise 90°. Figure 11.10 illustrates the original tree, Tree_2, and the printed tree. Since the printer outputs information line by line, the algorithm uses the RNL scan and outputs nodes in a right subtree before nodes in a left subtree. For Tree_2, nodes are printed in the order F C I E H A B G D.

In the PrintTree function, the printing of a node involves both its data value and its level. The calling program passes the root with level 0. For each recursive call to PrintTree, we must indent to the level of the node. In our format, we compute the number of indented spaces as indentBlock * level where indentBlock is the constant 6 to specify the number of blank spaces per node level. To print a node, we first indent the number of blanks corresponding to the level and then output the data value. Since the function PrintTree uses the standard cout stream, the operator "<<" must be defined for type T. Figure 11.11 illustrates the levels and number of blanks that precede each node in our printing of Tree_2.

The code for PrintTree is located in the file "treeprint.h".

```
// spacing between levels
const int indentBlock = 6;

// inserts num blanks on the current line
void IndentBlanks(int num)
{
    for(int i = 0;i < num; i++)
      cout << " ";
}

// print a tree sideways using an RNL tree scan
template <class T>
```

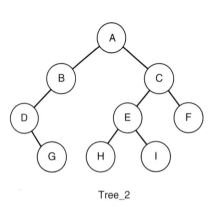

Tree_2

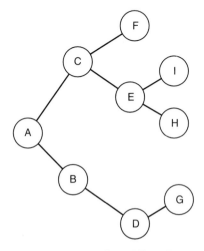

Printed Tree_2

Figure 11.10   Printed Tree_2

Levels

	0	1	2	3
12			F	
6		C		
18				I
12			E	
18				H
0	A			
6		B		
18				G
12			D	

Indent

Figure 11.11 Printing Tree_2

```
void PrintTree (TreeNode<T> *t, int level)
{
   // print tree with root t, as long as t != NULL
   if (t != NULL)
   {
      // print right branch of tree t
      PrintTree(t->Right(),level + 1);
      // indent to current level; output node data
      IndentBlanks(indentUnit*level);
      cout << t->data << endl;
      // print left branch of tree t
      PrintTree(t->Left(),level + 1);
   }
}
```

APPLICATION: COPYING AND DELETING TREES

Utility functions to copy and delete an entire tree introduce new concepts and prepare us for our development of a tree class that requires a destructor and copy constructor. A function CopyTree takes an initial tree and creates a duplicate version. The DeleteTree routine removes each node in the tree, including the root, and deallocates memory for the nodes. In this section, the functions are developed for general binary trees and included in file "treelib.h".

Copying a Tree   The function CopyTree uses a postorder scan to visit the nodes of the tree. The traversal order assures that we move to the greatest depth in the tree and then implement a visit operation, which creates a node for the new tree. The CopyTree function builds a new tree from the bottom up. It first creates the children and then links them to their parent as the parent is being created. This approach was used with the function MakeCharTree. For instance, with Tree_0, the

order of operations is

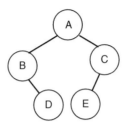

Tree_0

```
d = GetTreeNode('D');
e = GetTreeNode('E');
b = GetTreeNode('B',NULL, d);
c = GetTreeNode('C',e,NULL);
a = GetTreeNode('A',b, c);
root = a;
```

We first create the child D who is then linked to its parent B when the node is created. Similarly, E is created and then linked to its parent C during the birth or creation of C. Finally, the root node is created and linked to its children B and C.

The copy tree algorithm starts at a root and first builds the left subtree of the node and then the right subtree. Only then do we create the new node. The same recursive process is executed for each node in the tree. Corresponding to node t in the original tree, we create a new node with left and right pointers newlptr and newrptr, respectively.

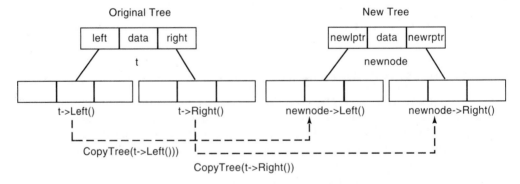

In the postorder scan, the children are visited before their parents. As a result we have created subtrees in the new tree that correspond to t−>Left() and t−>Right(). The children are linked to the parent when the parent is created.

```
newlptr == CopyTree(t->Left());
newrptr == CopyTree(t->Right());
```

```
// allocate parent and link in its children
newnode = GetTreeNode(t->data, newlptr, newrptr);
```

The process of creating the new node in the duplicate tree constitutes the visit to node t in the original tree.

The character tree, Tree_0, provides an example that illustrates the recursive CopyTree function. Assume the main program defines root1 and root2 and creates Tree_0. The function CopyTree creates a new tree based at root2. We will trace the algorithm and illustrate the events that create the five nodes in the duplicate tree.

```
TreeNode<char> *root1, *root2;      // declare two roots
MakeCharTree(root1, 0);             // root1 points at Tree_0

root2 = CopyTree(root1);            // create a copy of Tree_0
```

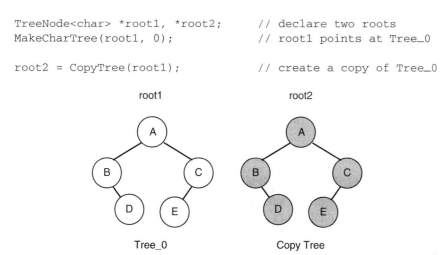

1. Scan the descendants of node A by first going to the left subtree at node B and then to node D, which is the right subtree of node B. Create a new node with data D and NULL left and right pointers [Figure 11.12(A)].

2. The children of node B have been scanned. Create a new node with data B, with a NULL left child, and with a right child that is node D from part 1 [Figure 11.12(B)]. This completes the handling of node B.

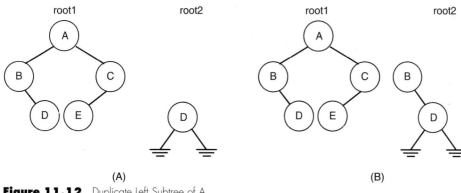

Figure 11.12   Duplicate Left Subtree of A

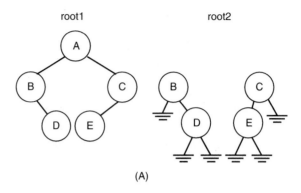

(A)

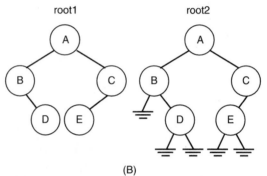

(B)

Figure 11.13 Duplicate Right Subtree of A

3. Once the left subtree of A is scanned, we begin scanning the right subtree of A and stop at node E. Create a new node with data E and NULL left and right pointers.

4. After processing E, go to its parent and create a new node with data C, with a NULL right child, and with a left child that is node E [Figure 11.13 (A)].

5. The final step occurs at node A. Create a new node with data A and with children that are node B (left) and node C (right) [Figure 11.13(B)]. This completes the copying of the tree.

CopyTree is designed as a function that returns a pointer to the newly created node. This return value is then used by the parent when it creates its own node and attaches its children. The function returns the root to the calling program.

```
// create duplicate of tree t; return the new root
template <class T>
TreeNode<T> *CopyTree(TreeNode<T> *t)
{
```

```
    // variable newnode points at each new node that is
    // created by a call to GetTreeNode and later attached to
    // the new tree. newlptr and newrptr point to the child of
    // newnode and are passed as parameters to GetTreeNode
    TreeNode<T> *newlptr, *newrptr, *newnode;

    // stop the recursive scan when we arrive at an empty tree
    if (t == NULL)
        return NULL;

    // CopyTree builds a new tree by scanning the nodes of t.
    // At each node in t, CopyTree checks for a left child. if
    // present it makes a copy of left child or returns NULL.
    // the algorithm similarly checks for a right child.
    // CopyTree builds a copy of node using GetTreeNode and
    // appends copy of left and right children to node.

    if (t->Left() != NULL)
        newlptr = CopyTree(t->Left());
    else
        newlptr = NULL;

    if (t->Right() != NULL)
        newrptr = CopyTree(t->Right());
    else
        newrptr = NULL;


    // Build new tree from the bottom up by building the two
    // children and then building the parent.
    newnode = GetTreeNode(t->data, newlptr, newrptr);

    // return a pointer to the newly created node
    return newnode;
}
```

Deleting a Tree   When an application uses a dynamic structure such as a tree, the programmer is responsible for deallocating the memory occupied by the tree. For a general binary tree, we design the DeleteTree function, which uses a postorder scan of the nodes. The ordering ensures that we first visit the children of a node before deleting the node(parent). The visit calls FreeTreeNode to delete the node.

```
    // use the postorder scanning algorithm to traverse the nodes in
    // the tree and delete each node as the visit operation.
    template <class T>
```

```
void DeleteTree(TreeNode<T> *t)
{
    if (t != NULL)
    {
        DeleteTree(t->Left());
        DeleteTree(t->Right());
        FreeTreeNode(t);
    }
}
```

A more general tree clearing routine deletes the nodes and resets the root. The function ClearTree calls DeleteTree to deallocate the nodes and then assigns the root pointer to be NULL.

```
// call the function DeleteTree to deallocate the nodes. then
// set the root pointer back to NULL
template <class T>
void ClearTree(TreeNode<T> * &t)
{
    DeleteTree(t);
    t = NULL;          // root now NULL
}
```

Program 11.2   Test: CopyTree and DeleteTree

This program uses Tree_0 and creates a copy pointed to by root2. We scan the newly created tree using a postorder traversal and convert each data value to lowercase. The PrintTree function prints the final data in tree root2.

```
#include <iostream.h>
#include <ctype.h>
#include <stdlib.h>

#include "treescan.h"
#include "treelib.h"
#include "treeprnt.h"

// used to lowercase char data values during postorder scan
void LowerCase(char &ch)
{
    ch = tolower(ch);
}

void main(void)
{
```

```
    // pointers for original and copied tree
    TreeNode<char> *root1, *root2;

    // create Tree_0 and print it
    MakeCharTree(root1, 0);
    PrintTree (root1, 0);

    // copy the tree so root is root2
    cout << endl << "Copy:" << endl;
    root2 = CopyTree(root1);

    // do postorder scan and then print tree.
    Postorder(root2,LowerCase);
    PrintTree (root2, 0);
}

/*
<Run of Program 11.2>

            C
                    E
    A
                    D
            B

Copy:
            c
                    e
    a
                    d
            b
*/
```

APPLICATION: UPRIGHT TREE PRINTING

The PrintTree function creates a sideways picture of a tree. On each line, we draw a node at its level. Although the tree is hard to view, the technique allows for the drawing of large trees. For an 80-column page of unlimited length with levels separated by indentBlock=5 spaces, a tree could hold $2^{16} - 1 = 65,535$ nodes. An upright printing of the tree is much more restricted since we need the width of the page to hold data as well as to separate levels. For relatively small trees, the picture is more realistic and attractive. In this application, we develop tools to implement a PrintVTree (upright or vertical print) function. We include a design of the algorithm and refer the reader to its implementation in "treeprint.h".

The PrintVTree function requires a new traversal algorithm that scans the tree nodes level by level starting with the root at level 0. The approach, called the

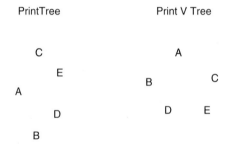

breadth first scan, or **level scan,** can no longer recursively descend into subtrees but rather must visit all nodes (siblings) on the same level and then descend to the next level. Rather than a recursive descent, we develop an iterative algorithm that uses a queue to hold the items. For each node, we insert any non-NULL left and right child in the queue. This assures us that the set of siblings will be visited in order at the next level in the tree. The character tree Tree_2 illustrates the algorithm.

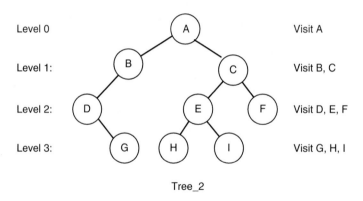

Tree_2

Level Scan Algorithm

Initialization Step:
    Insert the root node in the queue.
Iterative Steps:
    Terminate the process when the queue is empty.
    Delete the front node p from the queue and print its data value.
    Use the node to identify its children at the next level in the tree.

```
if (p->Left() != NULL)       // check for left child
    Q.QInsert(p->Left());
if (p->Right() != NULL)      // check for right child
    Q.QInsert(p->Right());
```

EXAMPLE 11.3

The following steps illustrate the level scan algorithm for Tree_0

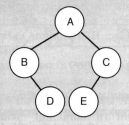

Tree_0

Initialization: Insert node A in the queue.
1: Delete node A from the queue.
    Print A.
   Insert children of A in the queue.
    Left child = B
    Right child = C
2: Delete node B from the queue.
    Print B.
   Insert children of B in the queue.
    Right child = D
3: Delete node C from the queue.
    Print C.
   Insert children of C in the queue.
    Left child = E
4: Delete node D from the queue.
    Print D.
   D has no children.
5: Delete node E from the queue.
   Algorithm terminates. Queue
   is empty.

A			

B	C		

C	D		

D	E		

E			

```
// traverse the tree level by level and visit each node
template <class T>
void LevelScan(TreeNode<T> *t, void visit(T& item))
{
    // store siblings of each node in queue so they are
    // visited in order at the next level of the tree
    Queue<TreeNode<T> *> Q;
    TreeNode<T> *p;
```

```
        // initialize the queue by inserting the root
        Q.QInsert(t);

        // continue iterative process until queue is empty
        while(!Q.QEmpty())
        {
            // delete front node and execute the visit function
            p = Q.QDelete();
            visit(p->data);

            // if a left child exists, insert it in the queue
            if(p->Left() != NULL)
                Q.QInsert(p->Left());
            // if a right child exists, insert next to sibling
            if(p->Right() != NULL)
                Q.QInsert(p->Right());
        }
    }
```

PrintVTree Algorithm   The upright printing function is passed the root of the tree, the maximum width of any data value and the width of the screen:

```
void PrintVTree (TreeNode<T> *t, int dataWidth, int screenWidth)
```

The width parameters enable us to organize the screen. To illustrate, assume the dataWidth is 2 and the screenWidth is $64 = 2^6$. The fact that the width is a power of 2 allows us to describe the level-by-level organization of data. Since we do not know the structure of the tree, we assume the room must be made for a complete binary tree. Assume a node is drawn at the coordinates (level, indentedSpaces):

Level 0:   The root is drawn at (0,32)

Level 1:   Since the root node is indented (offset) 32 spaces, the next level has an offset $32/2 = 16 = screenWidth/2^2$. The two nodes at level 1 have position (1,32−offset) and (1,32+offset), which are the points (1,16) and (1,48).

Level 2:   At level 2 the offset is $8 = screenWidth/2^3$. The four nodes at level 2 have position (2,16−offset), (2,16+offset), (2,48−offset), (2,48+offset), which are the points (2,8), (2,24), (2,40), and (2,56).

Level i: The offset is $screenWidth/2^{i+1}$. The position of each node at level i is determined during a visit to its parent at level i−1. Assume the parent has position (i−1,parentPos). If the node at level i is a left child, its position is (i,parentPos−offset). A right child has position (i,parentPos+offset).

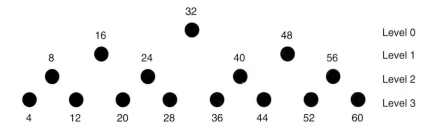

PrintVTree uses two queues and the breadth-first scan to traverse the nodes in the tree. Queue Q contains the nodes, while queue QI holds the level and print position of a node using the record type Info. When a node is added to Q, the corresponding print information is stored in QI. The items are deleted in tandem during the node visit.

```cpp
// record to hold x,y coordinates for a node in PrintVTree
struct Info
{
    int    xIndent, yLevel;
};

// queues to hold the node and the node print information
Queue<TreeNode<T> *> Q;
Queue<Info> QI;
```

Program 11.3   Upright Printing

The program prints the character tree Tree_2 assuming a 30-character page and a 60-character page. The dataWidth for the output is 1.

```cpp
#include <iostream.h>

// include PrintVTree from the tree print library
#include "treelib.h"
#include "treeprnt.h"


void main(void)
{
    // declare a character tree
    TreeNode<char> *root;

    // assign Tree_2 to root
    MakeCharTree(root, 2);
```

```
    cout << "Print tree on a 30 character screen" << endl;
    PrintVTree(root,1, 30);
    cout << endl << endl;

    cout << "Print tree on a 60 character screen" << endl;
    PrintVTree(root,1, 60);
}

/*
<Run of Program 11.3>

Print tree on a 30 character screen
                A

        B               C

      D           E     F

        G           H   I

Print tree on a 60 character screen
                        A

            B                               C

        D                       E               F

          G                   H   I

*/
```

11.4   Binary Search Trees

A general binary tree can hold a large collection of data and yet provide very fast access as we attempt to add, remove, or find an item. Building collection classes is one of the most important applications of a tree. We are familiar with the problems involved in building a general collection class from the SeqList class and its implementations with an array or with a linked list. The SeqList class features the Find method, which is implemented with a sequential search. For a linear structure, this algorithm is $O(N)$, which is inefficient for a large collection. In general, tree structures provide significantly improved searching performance, since the path to any data value is no greater than the depth of the tree. Searching performance is maximized with a complete binary tree $O(\log_2 N)$. For instance, with a list of 10,000 elements, the expected number of comparisons to find an element using the sequential search is 5,000. That same search on a complete tree would require no more than 14 comparisons. A binary tree offers great potential as an implementation structure for a list.

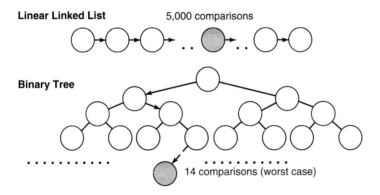

Linear Linked List 5,000 comparisons

Binary Tree

14 comparisons (worst case)

To store elements in a tree for efficient access, we must design a search structure that identifies a path to an element. The structure, called a **binary search tree,** orders the elements by means of the relational operator "<". To compare nodes in the tree, we assume all or a portion of the data field is designated as the key and that the "<" operator compares keys when placing an item in the tree. A binary search tree is constructed with the following rule:

For each node, the data values in the left subtree are less than the value of the node and the data values in the right subtree are greater than or equal to the value of the node.

Figure 11.14 shows an example of a binary search tree. The tree is called a *search* tree because we can follow a very specific path when trying to find an element (key). Starting at the root, we scan the left subtree if the key value is less than the current node. Otherwise, we scan the right subtree. The method of creating the tree allows us to search for an element along a shortest path from the root. For instance, a search for 37 starts at the root and requires four comparisons.

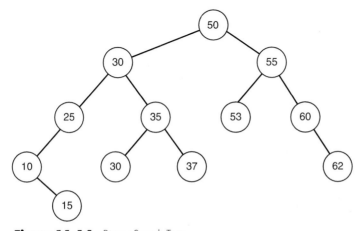

Figure 11.14 Binary Search Tree

Current Node	Action
Root = 50	Compare key = 37 and 50
	since 37 < 50, scan the left subtree
Node = 30	Compare 37 and 30
	since 37 >= 30, scan the right subtree
Node = 35	Compare key = 37 and 35
	since 37 >= 35, scan the right subtree
Node = 37	Compare key = 37 and 37. Item found.

Figure 11.15 illustrates a variety of binary search trees.

THE KEY IN A BINARY SEARCH TREE NODE

The key in a data field acts as a tag with which we can identify the node. In many applications, the data are records with separate fields. In this case, the key is one of the fields. For instance, a social security number (ssn) is a key that identifies a university student.

Social Security Number (9 character string)	Student Name (character string)	Grade Point Average (floating point number)

Key Field

```
struct Student
{
    String    ssn;
    String    name;
    float     gpa;
}
```

The key can be equated with all or a portion of the data. In Figure 11.15, the tree nodes contain a single integer data value, which is the key. In that case, node 25 has key 25 and we compare two nodes by comparing the integer values. The

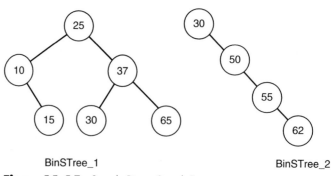

BinSTree_1   BinSTree_2

Figure 11.15 Sample Binary Search Trees

integer relational operators "<" and "==" implement the comparison. For the university student, the key is a ssn and we compare two String values. This is done by overloading operators. For instance, the following implements "<" for two Student objects:

```
int operator< (const Student& s, const Student& t)
{
    return s.ssn < t.ssn;    // compare ssn values
}
```

In our applications, we provide a variety of key/data examples. For our illustrations, we use the simple format in which the key and the data are identical.

OPERATIONS ON A BINARY SEARCH TREE

A binary search tree is a nonlinear structure for storing a list of items. Like any list structure, the tree must enable us to insert, delete, and find elements. The search tree requires an insert operation that correctly positions a new element. For instance, consider adding node 8 to BinSTree_1. Beginning at the root node 25, the location of 8 must be in the left subtree of 25 (8 < 25). At node 10, the location of 8 must be in the left subtree of 10, which is currently empty. Node 8 enters as a left child of node 10.

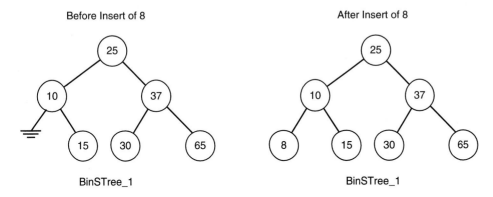

Each node enters the tree along a specific path. That same path can be used to search for the element. The find algorithm takes a key and searches in a left or right subtree of each node in the path. For instance, in BinTree_1 of Figure 11.15, the search for element 30 begins at the root node 25 and proceeds into the right subtree (30 >= 25) and then into the left subtree (30 < 37). The search terminates on the third comparison when the key matches the node value 30.

In a linked list, the delete operation unlinks a node and connects its predecessor with the next node. A similar operation is far more complex with a binary search tree since removing a node can destroy the ordering of elements in the tree. Consider the problem of deleting root 25 from BinSTree_1. The first effect is to create two disjoint subtrees that require a new root:

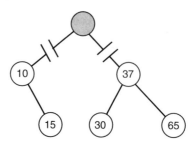

BinSTree_1

At first glance, one may be tempted to choose a child of 25, say, 37, to replace its parent. This simple solution fails since we are left with nodes on the wrong side of the root. Because the example is relatively small, we can identify that 15 or 30 would be valid replacements for the root node.

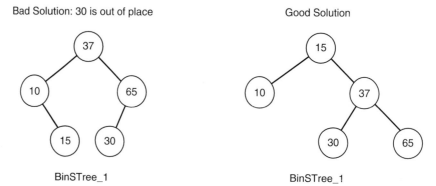

DECLARING A BINARY SEARCH TREE ADT

As a list, the abstract data type is modeled after the SeqList class. The fact that a binary search tree stores elements in a nonlinear list becomes an implementation detail that we will use when we implement its methods. You will notice that the ADT is a mirror of the SeqList ADT with the addition of the Update method, which allows us to modify a data value, and the GetRoot method, which gives us access to the root node. GetRoot provides a user with access to the root and hence to the traversal functions in "treescan.h" and the printing functions in "treeprint.h". Note that the SeqList method GetData is absent since it involves a position within a linear list.

ADT Binary Search Tree is

Data

A list of items stored in a binary tree and a data value, size, that specifies the number of items currently in the list. The

tree contains a pointer to the root of the tree and a reference
to the last location accessed in the tree. We refer to this as
the current position.

Operations

Constructor	\<same as SeqList ADT\>
ListSize	\<same as SeqList ADT\>
ListEmpty	\<same as SeqList ADT\>
ClearList	\<same as SeqList ADT\>

Find

Input:	A reference to a data value
Preconditions:	None
Process:	Search the tree by comparing the item with the data value of a node. If a match occurs, retrieve the data from the node.
Output:	Return 1 (True) if a match occurs and assign data from the matching node to the reference parameter. Otherwise assign 0 (False).
Postconditions:	Update the current position to that of the matching node.

Insert

Input:	A data item
Preconditions:	None
Process:	Search the tree using the data item to locate the position for the insertion. Add the new data item.
Output:	None
Postconditions:	Update the current position to that of the new node.

Delete

Input:	A data item
Preconditions:	None
Process:	Search the tree and locate the first occurrence of the data item. Remove the node and reattach all subtrees so that the binary search tree structure is maintained.
Output:	None
Postconditions:	Update the current position to that of the replacement node.

Update

Input:	A data item
Preconditions:	None

Process:	If the key at the current position matches the key for the data item, assign the data item to the node; otherwise, insert the data item into the tree.
Output:	None
Postconditions:	The list may have a new data value.

GetRoot

Input:	None
Preconditions:	None
Process:	Obtain the pointer to the root.
Output:	Return the root pointer.
Postconditions:	None

end ADT Binary Search Tree

Declaring the BinSTree Class   We implement the binary search tree ADT as a class with dynamic list structures. Hence the class contains the standard destructor, copy constructor, and overloaded assignment operators that allow us to initialize objects and perform assignment statements. The destructor is responsible for clearing the list when the scope of an object is closed. A similar task is performed by the function ClearList. The destructor and assignment operators along with the ClearList method call the private method DeleteTree. We also include the private method CopyTree for use by the copy constructor and overloaded assignment operator.

— —

BINSTREE CLASS SPECIFICATION

DECLARATION

```
#include <iostream.h>
#include <stdlib.h>

#include "treenode.h"

template <class T>
class BinSTree
{
    protected:        // needed with inheritance in Chapter 12
        // pointer to tree root and node most recently accessed
        TreeNode<T> *root;
        TreeNode<T> *current;

        // number of elements in the tree
        int size;
```

```
    // memory allocation/deallocation
    TreeNode<T> *GetTreeNode(const T& item,
                 TreeNode<T> *lptr,TreeNode<T> *rptr);
    void FreeTreeNode(TreeNode<T> *p);

    // used by copy constructor and assignment operator
    TreeNode<T> *CopyTree(TreeNode<T> *t);

    // used by destructor, assignment operator and ClearList
    void DeleteTree(TreeNode<T> *t);

    // locate a node with data item and its parent in tree
    // used by Find and Delete
    TreeNode<T> *FindNode(const T& item,
                     TreeNode<T>* & parent) const;
public:
    // constructor, destructor
    BinSTree(void);
    BinSTree(const BinSTree<T>& tree);
    ~BinSTree(void);

    // assignment operator
    BinSTree<T>& operator= (const BinSTree<T>& rhs);

    // standard list handling methods
    int Find(T& item);
    void Insert(const T& item);
    void Delete(const T& item);
    void ClearList(void);
    int ListEmpty(void) const;
    int ListSize(void) const;

    // tree specific methods
    void Update(const T& item);
    TreeNode<T> *GetRoot(void) const;

};
```

DESCRIPTION

The class has protected data members. This introduces an inheritance-based
construct that is discussed in Chapter 12. Protected access is functionally
equivalent to private access for this class. The variable root points to the root
node of the tree. A second pointer, called *current*, references the location of
the last list update. For instance, current points at the location of the new
item after the Insert operation, and the Find method leaves current pointing
at the node matching the data item.

The standard list handling operations use the same names and parameters as those defined in the SeqList class.

The BinSTree class contains two tree-specific operations. Update assigns a new value item at the current location in the tree or inserts a new item into the tree if it does not match the data at the current position. The method GetRoot gives us access to the tree root. With the root pointer, the user has access to functions in the libraries "treelib.h", "treescan.h", and "treeprint.h". This extends the power of the class to include a variety of tree algorithms including PrintTree.

EXAMPLE

```
BinSTree<int>  T;      // tree with integer data

T.Insert(50);          // creates a four node tree (A)
T.Insert(40);
T.Insert(70);
T.Insert(45);

T.Delete(40);          // remove the node with value 40  (B)
T.ClearList();         // deletes the nodes in the tree
```

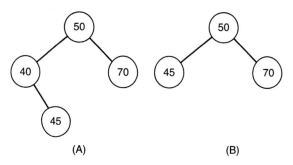

(A)   (B)

```
// tree univInfo holds student information with ssn as key
BinSTree<Student> univInfo;
Student stud;

// assign the key "986543789" and search the tree
stud.ssn = "986543789";
if (univInfo.Find(stud))
{
    // stud is in the tree. assign new gpa and update
    stud.gpa = 3.86;
    univInfo.Update(stud);
}
else
    cout << "Student is not in the data base." << endl;
```

Using Binary Search Trees   11.5

The BinSTree class is a powerful data structure that is used for dynamic list handling. A case study that develops a word concordance illustrates a typical application of a search tree. We use the structure in Chapter 14 with dictionaries. In this section we look at a series of simple programs that develop search tree applications.

Defining Sample Search Trees   In Section 11.1, the MakeCharTree function is used to create a series of binary trees with character data. A similar function, MakeSearchTree, builds binary search trees with integer data using the Insert method. For instance, the tree SearchTree_0 uses the six entries in the predefined array arr0 to construct a tree using the BinSTree object T.

```
int    arr0[6] = {30, 20, 45, 5, 10, 40},

for (i = 0; i < 6; i++)
    T.Insert(arr0[i]);              // add an element to the array
```

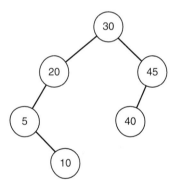

SearchTree_0

MakeSearchTree creates a second tree of eight-elements, and creates a tree with 10 random numbers in the range 10 to 99 (Figure 11.16). The function parameters include a BinSTree object and a parameter type (0 ≤ type ≤ 2) that designates the tree. The code for MakeSearchTree is located in file "makesrch.h".

Inorder Traversal   The LNR inorder traversal of a binary tree visits the left subtree of a node, then the node, and finally the right subtree. When this traversal method is applied to a binary search tree, the nodes are visited in sorted order. This fact is evident when you note the relative value of nodes in the subtrees of the current node. All nodes in the left subtree of the current node have a data value that is less than the value of the current node, and all nodes in the right subtree of the current node have a data value that is greater than or equal to the current

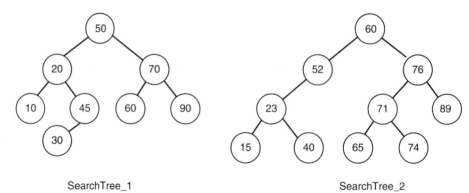

SearchTree_1   SearchTree_2

Figure 11.16 MakeSearchTree Trees

node. The inorder traversal of a binary tree ensures that for each node we first visit the smaller nodes in its left subtree and then the larger nodes in its right subtree. The collective result gives us a traversal of the nodes in ascending order.

Program 11.4   Using a Search Tree

This program uses the function MakeSearchTree to create SearchTree_1 with values

    50, 20, 45, 70, 10, 60, 90, 30

Using the method GetRoot, we gain access to the root of the tree, which allows us to call PrintVTree. GetRoot also allows us to print the items in ascending order using Inorder with the function parameter PrintInt. The program concludes by deleting data items 50 and 70 and reprinting the tree.

```
#include "makesrch.h"         // include function MakeSearch
#include "treescan.h"
#include "treeprnt.h"         // for PrintVTree
#include "bstree.h"           // use BinSTree class for Inorder

// print an integer value. used by the function Inorder
void PrintInt(int& item)
{
    cout << item << "   ";
}

void main(void)
{
```

```
    // declare a tree of integer values
    BinSTree<int> Tree;

    // create search tree #1 and print upright with 40 char width
    MakeSearchTree(Tree, 1);
    PrintVTree(Tree.GetRoot(),2,40);

    // inorder scan of the tree visits values in increasing order
    cout << endl << endl << "Sorted List: ";
    Inorder(Tree.GetRoot(),PrintInt);
    cout << endl;

    cout << endl << "Deleting data values 70 and 50." << endl;
    Tree.Delete(70);
    Tree.Delete(50);
    PrintVTree(Tree.GetRoot(),2,40);
    cout << endl;
}

/*
<Run of Program 11.4>

                   50

        20                    70

   10          45        60        90

        30

Sorted List: 10   20   30   45   50   60   70   90

Deleting data values 70 and 50.

                   45

        20                    60

   10          30        90
*/
```

DUPLICATE NODES

A binary search tree may have duplicate nodes. In the Insert operation, we continue to scan the right subtree if our new item matches the current node value. As a result, duplicate nodes occur in the right subtree of a matching node. For instance, the following tree is generated from the list 50 70 25 90 30 55 25 15 25.

List: 50, 70, 25, 90, 30, 55, 25, 15, 25

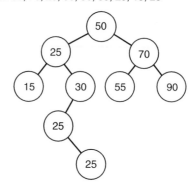

Many applications do not allow duplicate nodes but rather use a field in the data structure to count the number of occurrences of an item. This is the principle of a concordance that keeps track of line numbers on which a word occurs. Instead of placing a word in the tree several times, we handle duplicate occurrences of the word by placing multiple entries in a list of line numbers. Program 11.5 illustrates a direct approach that maintains a count of duplicates as a separate data item.

Program 11.5 Occurrence Counts

The record IntegerCount contains an integer variable number and a count field that is used to store the frequency of occurrences of the integer in a list. The number field acts as the key, with overloaded operators "<" and "==" allowing us to compare two IntegerCount records. We use these operators for the Find and Insert functions.

The program generates 100,000 random numbers in the range 0 . . . 9 and associates each with an IntegerCount record. The Find method first determines if the number is already in the tree; if so, the count field is incremented and we update the record. Otherwise, a new record is inserted in the tree. The program concludes with an inorder scan of the tree that prints the numbers and their counts. With random access, each item in the range 0 to 9 is equally likely to occur. Hence, each item should occur approximately 10,000 times. The IntegerCount record and its two operators are in the file "intcount.h".

```
#include <iostream.h>

#include "random.h"        // generate random integers
#include "bstree.h"        // include BinSTree class
#include "treescan.h"      // for function Inorder
#include "intcount.h"      // defines IntegerCount record
```

```
// called by Inorder to print an IntegerCount record
void PrintNumber(IntegerCount& N)
{
    cout << N.number << ':' << N.count << endl;
}


void main(void)
{
    // declare a tree of IntegerCount record values
    BinSTree<IntegerCount> Tree;

    long n;
    IntegerCount N;
    RandomNumber rnd;

    // generate 100000 random integers in range 0..9
    for(n=0;n < 100000L;n++)
    {
        // generate an IntegerCount record with a random key
        N.number = rnd.Random(10);

        // search for the key in the tree.
        if (Tree.Find(N))
        {
            // key found, increment count and update
            N.count++;
            Tree.Update(N);
        }
        else
        {
            // when int first appears, insert with count field 1.
            N.count = 1;
            Tree.Insert(N);
        }
    }

    // inorder scan outputs records in order by key field
    Inorder(Tree.GetRoot(),PrintNumber);
}

/*
<Run of Program 11.5>

0:10116
1:9835
2:9826
3:10028
```

```
4:10015
5:9975
6:9983
7:10112
8:10082
9:10028
*/
```

11.6   The BinSTree Implementation

The BinSTree class describes a nonlinear list with basic operations to insert, delete, and find items. Besides the list-handling methods, memory management operations have a vital role in the class implementation. The private methods CopyTree and DeleteTree are used by the constructor, destructor, and assignment operator to allocate and deallocate nodes in the list.

BinSTree Class Data Members   A binary search tree is defined by its root pointer, which is used to start the Insert, Find, and Delete operations. The BinSTree class contains a data item *root,* which is a tree node pointer that is initially set to NULL and references the tree's root node. The value of root is available to the client using GetRoot, enabling calls to traversal and print functions. A second pointer called *current* maintains a location in the tree for updates. The Find operation sets current to the matching node, and the pointer is used by Update to change data in the list. The Insert and Delete methods reposition current to the new node or its replacement. A BinSTree object is a list whose size is continually updated with the Delete and Insert methods. The current number of items in the list is maintained by the private data member size.

```
// pointer to tree root and node most recently accessed
TreeNode<T> *root;
TreeNode<T> *current;

// number of elements in the tree
int size;
```

Memory Management   The allocation and deallocation of nodes for the Insert and Delete methods and the utilities CopyTree and DeleteTree are accomplished by means of GetTreeNode and FreeTreeNode. GetTreeNode is modeled after the function in "treelib.h". It allocates memory and initializes the data and pointer fields of a node. FreeTreeNode directly calls the delete operator to deallocate memory.

Constructor, Destructor, and Assignment   The class contains a constructor that initializes the data members. A copy constructor and overloaded assignment operator use the private CopyTree method to create a new binary search tree for the current object. The algorithm for CopyTree is developed in Section 11.3 for the TreeNode class. In the same section, we developed the algorithm for deleting the nodes of a tree, which is implemented in the BinSTree class by DeleteTree and used by both the destructor and ClearList methods.

The overloaded assignment operator copies the right-hand side object to the current object. After checking that the object is not being assigned to itself, the function clears the current tree and uses CopyTree to create a duplicate of the right-hand side (rhs). The pointer current is assigned the root pointer, the list size is copied, and a reference to the current object is returned.

```
// assignment operator
template <class T>
BinSTree<T>& BinSTree<T>::operator= (const BinSTree<T>& rhs)
{
// can't copy a tree to itself
if (this == &rhs)
   return *this;

// clear current tree. copy new tree into current object
ClearList();
root = CopyTree(tree.root);

// assign current to root and set the tree size
current = root;
size = tree.size;

// return reference to current object
return *this;
}
```

LIST OPERATIONS

The Find and Insert methods start at the root and traverse a unique path through the tree. Using the definition of a binary search tree, the algorithm traverses the right subtree when the key or new item is greater than or equal to the value of the current node. Otherwise, the algorithm traverses the left subtree.

The Find Operation   The Find operation uses the private member function Find-Node that takes a key and traverses a path down the tree. The operation returns a pointer to the matching node and a pointer to its parent. If the match occurs at the root, the parent pointer is NULL.

```
// search for data item in the tree. if found, return its node
// address and a pointer to its parent; otherwise, return NULL
```

```
template <class T>
TreeNode<T> *BinSTree<T>::FindNode(const T& item,
                                   TreeNode<T>* & parent) const
{
    // cycle t through the tree starting with root
    TreeNode<T> *t = root;

    // the parent of the root is NULL
    parent = NULL;

    // terminate on empty subtree
    while(t !== NULL)
    {
        // stop on a match
        if (item == t->data)
            break;
        else
        {
            // update the parent pointer and move right or left
            parent = t;
            if (item < t->data)
                t = t->left;
            else
                t = t->right;
        }
    }

    // return pointer to node; NULL if not found
    return t;
}
```

The information about the parent is used with the Delete operation. With Find, we are only interested in assigning the current location to the matching node and assigning the data from the node to the reference parameter item. The Find method returns True (1) or False (0) to indicate if the search was successful. Find requires that relational operators "==" and "<" compare the data in the nodes. The operations must be overloaded if they are not defined for the data type.

```
    // search for item. if found, assign the node data to item
    template <class T>
    int BinSTree<T>::Find(T& item)
    {
        // we use FindNode, which requires a parent parameter
        TreeNode<T> *parent;

        // search tree for item. assign matching node to current
        current = FindNode (item, parent);
```

```
      // if item found, assign data to item and return True
      if (current != NULL)
      {
         item = current->data;
         return 1;
      }
      else
         // item not found in the tree. return False
         return 0;
   }
```

The Insert Operation   The Insert method takes a new data item and searches the tree to add the item in the correct location. The function iteratively scans the path of left and right subtrees until it locates the insertion point. For each step in the path, the algorithm maintains a record of the current node (called t) and the parent of the current node (called parent). The process terminates when we identify an empty subtree (t == NULL), which indicates that we have found the location to add the new item. At this location, the new node is inserted as a child of the parent. For instance, the following steps insert 32 in the tree depicted in Figure 11.17.

1. The method begins at the root node and compares item 32 with the root value 25 [Figure 11.17(A)]. Since 32 >= 25, we traverse the right subtree and look at node 35.

    t is node 35 and parent is node 25

2. Considering 35 to be the root of its own subtree, we compare item 32 with 35 and traverse the left subtree of 35 [Figure 11.17(B)].

    t is NULL and parent is node 35

3. Using GetTreeNode, we are able to create a leaf node with data value 32. The new node is then inserted as the left child of node 35 [Figure 11.17(C)]:

```
      // assignment to left possible because
      // BinSTree is a friend of TreeNode
      newNode = GetTreeNode(item, NULL, NULL);
      parent->left = newNode;
```

The pointers parent and t are local variables that change as we scan down the path to find the insertion point.

```
// insert item into the search tree
template <class T>
void BinSTree<T>::Insert(const T& item)
{
```

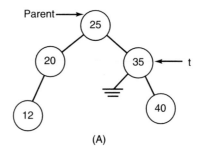

(A)

Step 1: Compare 32 and 25
Traverse the Right Subtree

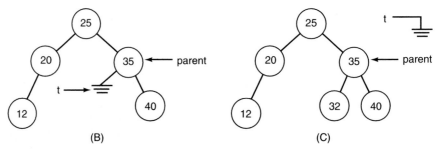

(B)

Step 2: Compare 32 and 35
Traverse the Left Subtree

(C)

Step 3: Insert 32 as
Left Child of Parent

Figure 11.17   Inserting into a Binary Search Tree

```
// t is current node in traversal, parent the previous node
TreeNode<T> *t = root, *parent = NULL, *newNode;

// terminate on empty subtree
while(t != NULL)
{
    // update the parent pointer. then go left or right
    parent = t;
    if (item < t->data)
        t = t->left;
    else
        t = t->right;
}

// create the new leaf node
newNode = GetTreeNode(item,NULL,NULL);

// if parent is NULL, insert as a root node
if (parent == NULL)
    root = newNode;
```

```
   // if item < parent->data. insert as left child
   else if (item < parent->data)
      parent->left = newNode;

   else
      // if item >= parent->data. insert as right child
      parent->right = newNode;
   // assign current as address of new node and increment size
   current = newNode;
   size++;
}
```

The Delete Operation   The Delete operation removes a node with a given key from the tree. The deletion is performed by first using the utility method FindNode, which locates the node in the tree along with a pointer to its parent. If the item is not found in the list, the Delete operation quietly returns.

Deleting a node from the tree requires a series of tests to determine how the children of the node are going to be reattached to the tree. The subtrees have to be reconnected in such a way that the binary search tree structure is preserved.

A call to the FindNode function returns a pointer DNodePtr that identifies the node D that is to be deleted. A second pointer, PNodePtr, identifies the parent P of the deleted node. The Delete method sets out to find a replacement node R that will connect to the parent and thus take the place of the deleted node. The variable RNodePtr identifies this replacement node R.

The algorithm for finding a replacement must consider four cases that depend on the number of children attached to the node. Note that when the parent is NULL, the root is being deleted. This situation is covered by our cases, with the additional factor that the root must be updated. Since BinSTree is a friend of the Tree Node class, we have access to private members left and right.

Situation A: Node D has no children. It is a leaf node.
Update the parent node to have an empty subtree.

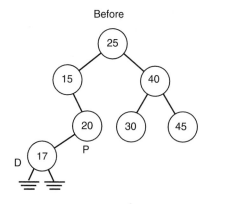

Before

Delete leaf node 17:
PNodePtr–>left is DNodePtr

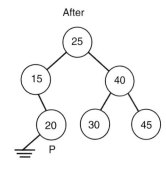

After

No replacement is necessary
PNodePtr–>left is NULL

The update can be accomplished by setting RNodePtr to NULL. When we attach the NULL replacement node, the parent points to NULL.

```
RNodePtr = NULL;
        . . .
PNodePtr-> left = RNodePtr;
```

Situation B: Node D has a left child but no right child.
Attach the left subtree of D to the parent.

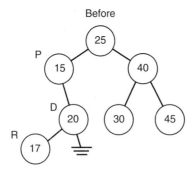
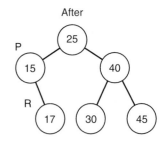

Before

After

Delete node 20 with only a left child:
Node R is the left child

Attach node R to the parent

The update is accomplished by setting RNodePtr to the left child of D and then attaching node R to the parent.

```
RNodePtr = DNodePtr->left;
        . . .
PNodePtr->right = RNodePtr;
```

Situation C: Node D has a right child but no left child.
Attach the right subtree of D to the parent.

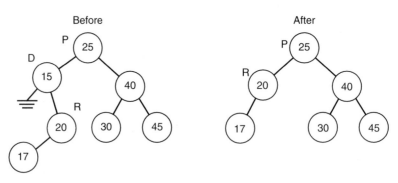

Before

After

Delete node 15 with only a right child:
Node R is the right child

Attach node R to the parent

Like C, the update is accomplished by setting RNodePtr to the right child of D and then attaching node R to the parent.

```
RNodePtr = DNodePtr->right;
         . . .
PNodePtr->left = RNodePtr;
```

Situation D: Deleting a node with two children.

A node with two children has elements in its subtrees that are less than and greater than or equal to its key value. The algorithm must select a replacement node that maintains the correct ordering among the items. Consider the following example.

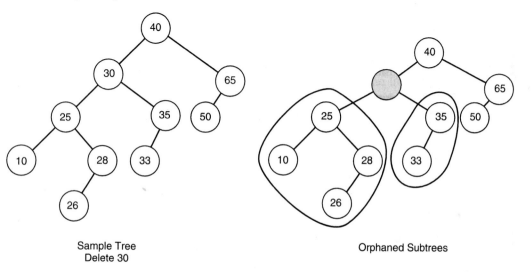

Sample Tree
Delete 30

Orphaned Subtrees

After deleting node 30, we create two orphaned subtrees that must be reattached to the tree. We need a strategy to select a replacement node from the remaining pool of nodes. The resulting tree must satisfy the binary search tree condition. We use a max-min principle.

Select as the replacement node R, the rightmost node in the left subtree. This is the largest node whose data value is less than that of the node to be deleted. Unlink this node R from the tree, connect its left subtree to its parent, and then connect R at the deleted node. In the sample tree, node 28 is the replacement node. We connect its left child, node 26, to its parent node 25. Finally, replace the deleted node 30 with replacement node 28.

A simple algorithm is used to find the rightmost node in the left subtree.

Step 1: Since the replacement node R is less than the deleted node D, descend to the left subtree of D. Descend to node 25.

Step 2: Since R is the largest of the nodes in the left subtree, locate its value by descending down the path of right subtrees. During the descent, keep track of the predecessor node, which is called PofRNodePtr (parent of the replacement node). In our example, descend to node 28. PofRNodePtr is node 25.

The descent down the path of right subtrees distinguishes two cases.

If the right subtree is empty, the current location is the replacement node R, and PofRNodePtr is the deleted node D. To update, we attach the right subtree of D as the right subtree of R and attach the parent of the deleted node P to R.

```
RNodePtr->right = DNodePtr->right;
PNodePtr->left = RNodePtr;
```

If the right subtree is not empty, the scan ends with a leaf node or a node with only a left subtree. In either case, unlink the node R from the tree and relink the children of R to the parent node PofRNodePtr. In each case, the right child of node PofRNodePtr is reset with the statement

```
(**)      PofRNodePtr->right = RNodePtr->left;
```

1. R is a leaf node. Unlink it from the tree. Since RNodePtr−>left is NULL, statement (**) sets the right child of PofRNodePtr to NULL.

2. R has a left subtree. Statement (**) attaches this subtree as the right child of PofRNodePtr.

The algorithm finishes by substituting node R for the deleted node. First, attach the children of D as the children of R. R replaces D as the root of the subtree formed by D.

```
RNodePtr->left = DNodePtr->left;
RNodePtr->right = DNodePtr->right;
```

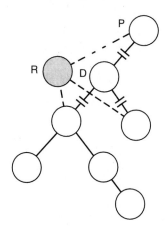

Complete the link to the parent node P.

```
// deleting the root node. assign new root
if (PNodePtr == NULL)
    root = RNodePtr;
```

```
// attach R to the correct branch of p
else if (DNodePtr->data < PNodePtr->data)
    PNodePtr->left = RNodePtr;
else
    PNodePtr->right = RNodePtr;
```

The alternative to the approach of linking R into the tree in place of D is to leave node D in place and copy the data in R to D. However, if the data consumes a large amount of memory, this is a costly operation. Our approach involves changing only two pointers.

Delete Method

```
// if item is in the tree, delete it
template <class T>
void BinSTree<T>::Delete(const T& item)
{
    // DNodePtr = pointer to node D that is deleted
    // PNodePtr = pointer to parent P of node D
    // RNodePtr = pointer to node R that replaces D
    TreeNode<T> *DNodePtr, *PNodePtr, *RNodePtr;

    // search for a node containing data value item. obtain its
    // node address and that of its parent
    if ((DNodePtr = FindNode (item, PNodePtr)) == NULL)
        return;

    // If D has a NULL pointer, the
    // replacement node is the one on the other branch
    if (DNodePtr->right == NULL)
        RNodePtr = DNodePtr->left;
    else if (DNodePtr->left == NULL)
        RNodePtr = DNodePtr->right;

    // Both pointers of DNodePtr are non-NULL.
    else
    {
        // Find and unlink replacement node for D.
        // Starting on the left branch of node D,
        // find node whose data value is the largest of all
        // nodes whose values are less than the value in D.
        // Unlink the node from the tree.

        // PofRNodePtr = pointer to parent of replacement node
        TreeNode<T> *PofRNodePtr = DNodePtr;

        // first possible replacement is left child of D
        RNodePtr = DNodePtr->left;
```

```
        // descend down right subtree of the left child of D,
        // keeping a record of current node and its parent.
        // when we stop, we have found the replacement
        while (RNodePtr->right != NULL)
        {
            PofRNodePtr = RNodePtr;
            RNodePtr = RNodePtr->right;
        }

        if (PofRNodePtr == DNodePtr)
            // left child of deleted node is the replacement.
            // assign right subtree of D to R
            RNodePtr->right = DNodePtr->right;
        else
        {
            // we moved at least one node down a right branch
            // delete replacement node from tree by assigning
            // its left branch to its parent
            PofRNodePtr->right = RNodePtr->left;

            // put replacement node in place of DNodePtr.
            RNodePtr->left = DNodePtr->left;
            RNodePtr->right = DNodePtr->right;
        }
    }

    // complete the link to the parent node.
    // deleting the root node. assign new root
    if (PNodePtr == NULL)
        root = RNodePtr;
    // attach R to the correct branch of P
    else if (DNodePtr->data < PNodePtr->data)
        PNodePtr->left = RNodePtr;
    else
        PNodePtr->right = RNodePtr;

    // delete the node from memory and decrement list size
    FirstTreeNode(DNodePtr);
    size--;
}
```

Tree Update Methods   After a Find, the user may wish to update data fields in
the current node. For this purpose, we provide an Update method that takes a data
value as a parameter. If a current node is defined, Update compares the current
node's value with the data value and, if they are equal, performs an update to the
node. If the current node is undefined or the data items do not match, the new data
value is inserted into the tree.

```
// if current node is defined and its data value matches item,
// assign node value to item; otherwise, insert item in tree
template <class T>
void BinSTree<T>::Update(const T& item)
{
    if (current !=NULL && current->data == item)
        current->data = item;
    else
        Insert(item);
}
```

11.7 Case Study: Concordance

A common problem in textual analysis is to determine the frequency and location of words in a document. The information is stored in a **concordance,** which lists the distinct words in alphabetical order and makes reference to each line on which the word is used. For instance, consider the quotation

> Peter Piper picked a peck of pickled peppers. A peck of pickled peppers Peter Piper picked. If Peter Piper picked a peck of pickled peppers, where is the peck that Peter Piper picked?

The word "piper" occurs 4 times in the text and appears on lines 1, 2, and 3. The word "pickled" occurs 3 times and appears on lines 1 and 2.

This case study creates a concordance for a text file using the following design:

Input: Open the document as a text file and input the text word by word, keeping track of the current line (line 1, line 2, etc.).

Action: Define a record that consists of a word, its frequency count, and a list that holds the line numbers for each occurrence. In a line, extract each word of text. For the first occurrence of a word in the text, create a record and insert it in the tree. If the word is already in the tree, update the frequency and line number list.

Output: After reading the file, print an alphabetized list of words, the frequency count, and the ordered list of lines on which the word occurred.

For a large document, a binary search tree is an efficient structure for storing words. The resulting tree is usually reasonably balanced and easy to update.

Data Structures

The data value in each tree node is a Word object that contains a string, the frequency count and a linked list of line numbers. The object also contains the line number on which the word last occurred. This ensures that we can handle multiple occurrences on a line and put the line number in the list only once.

wordText	count	LinkedList\<int\> LineNumbers	LastLineNo

The member functions for the Word class overload the relational operators "==" and "<" and the standard input/output stream operators.

```
class Word
{
    private:
        // wordText is word of text, count is its frequency
        String wordText;
        int count;

        // the line count is shared among all Word objects
        static int lineno;

        // last line number where the word occurred. used to know
        // when to insert a line number into lineNumbers
        int lastLineNo;
        LinkedList<int> lineNumbers;

    public:
        // constructor
        Word(void);

        // public class operations
        void CountWord (void);
        String& Key(void);

        // comparison operators used by BinSTree class
        int operator== (const Word& w) const;
        int operator< (const Word& w) const;

        // Word stream operators
        friend istream& operator>> (istream& istr, Word& w);
        friend ostream& operator<< (ostream& ostr, Word& w);
};
```

mplementing the Word Class

For each word, the constructor initializes the count (frequency) to 0 and the last line number to −1. The overloaded relational operators "<" and "==" are necessary for the tree class operations of Insert and Find and are implemented by comparing the text strings of the two objects. The code for these functions is found in the file "word.h".

This class declares the static data member lineno. This variable is private and accessible only to class members and friends. However, it is actually defined external to the class under the name "Word::lineno". As such, it is shared by all word objects. This is appropriate, since all such objects need access to the current line number of the input file. The use of static data members allows data sharing with access control and is preferable to the use of global variables.

The Input Operator ">>"   The input operator reads data from the stream one word at a time. A word must begin with a letter and be followed by an optional sequence of letters or digits. Input of a word begins by reading and discarding all nonalphabetic characters. This ensures that we skip all whitespace and punctuation marks between words. We terminate the input process if an end of file occurs. If an end of line is found, we increment the global variable lineno.

```
// skip all leading whitespace and non-alphabetic characters
while (istr.get(c) && !isalpha(c))
    // if the end of line is found, increment line number count
    if ( c == '\n')
        w.lineno++;
```

When the beginning of the word is identified, the ">>" operator gathers the characters by reading letters or digits until a nonalphanumeric character is found. The characters of the word are converted to lowercase and stored in a local C++ string variable *wd*. This allows us to make our concordance case insensitive. If the end-of-line character is found after the word, it is placed back into the stream and found when reading the next word from the document. The function terminates by assigning wd to wordText, setting count to 0 and setting lastLineNo to the value lineno.

```
// if not at end of file, read the word
if (!istr.eof())
{
    // convert the first char of word to lowercase, assign to wd
    c = tolower(c);
    wd[i++] = c;

    // read consecutive alphabetic or numeric characters and
    // convert each to lower case
    while (istr.get(c) && (isalpha(c) || isdigit(c)))
        wd[i++] = tolower(c);

    // null terminate the C++ string wd
    wd[i] = '\0';
```

```
    // if newline after current word, save for next word
    if (c == '\n')
        istr.putback(c);

    // assign wd to wordText, count to 0 and lastLineNo to lineno
    w.wordText = wd;
    w.count = 0;
    w.lastLineNo = w.lineno;
}
```

The CountWord Function   After reading a word from the text, we call the function CountWord, which updates the count value and the list of line numbers. The count is first incremented. If count is 1, the entry is new to the tree and the line number of its first occurrence is added to the list. If the word is already in the list, a check is made to see if the line number has changed since the last time the word was encountered. If it has, the current line number is placed in the list and used to update lastLineNo.

```
    // record the occurrence of a word
    void Word::CountWord (void)
    {
        // increment the word's occurrence count
        count++;

        // if this is the first time the word has occurred or
        // it has occurred on a new line, insert it into the
        // list and change lastLineNo to the current line
        if (count == 1 || lastLineNo != lineno)
        {
            lineNumbers.InsertRear(lineno);
            lastLineNo = lineno;
        }
    }
```

The Output Operator "<<"   The stream output operator prints the word and the count, followed by the ordered list of line numbers on which the word occurs.

<text>. . . . .<count>: l_1 l_2 ... l_n

This is accomplished by printing the text and writing the count right justified in a field with the fill character set to ".". The line numbers are printed by traversing the linked list.

```
    //output a Word object to a stream
    ostream& operator<< (ostream& ostr, Word& w)
    {
```

```
        // output the word
        ostr << w.wordText;

        //output count right justified with leading '.' characters
        ostr.fill('.');
        ostr << setw(25-w.wordText.Length()) << w.count << ": ";
        ostr.fill(' ');        // set fill char back to blank

        // traverse the list and print the line numbers
        for(w.lineNumbers.Reset(); !w.lineNumbers.EndOfList();
                        w.lineNumbers.Next())
            ostr << w.lineNumbers.Data() << "    ";
        ostr << endl;

        return ostr;
}
```

Program 11.6   Text Concordance

The program defines the binary search tree concordTree, which stores Word objects. After opening the text file "concord.txt", the stream input operator reads words until end of file. Each word is either inserted in the tree or used to update information if the word previously occurred. After all the words are processed, an inorder scan is executed and the words are printed in alphabetical order. The Word class is contained in file "word.h".

```
#include <iostream.h>
#include <fstream.h>
#include <stdlib.h>

#include "word.h"           // include the Word class
#include "bstree.h"         // include the BinSTree class
#include "treescan.h"       // for Inorder scan

// used by function Inorder
void PrintWord(Word& w)
{
    cout << w;
}

void main(void)
{
    // declare a tree of Word objects read from stream fin
    BinSTree<Word> concordTree;
    ifstream fin;

    Word w;
```

```
    // open the file "concord.txt"
    fin.open("concord.txt", ios::in | ios::nocreate);
    if (!fin)
    {
        cerr << "Cannot open 'concord.txt'" << endl;
        exit(1);
    }

    // read Word objects from fin until end of file
    while(fin >> w)
    {
        // search for w in the tree
        if (concordTree.Find(w) == 0)
        {
            // w not in tree. update word count and insert word
            w.CountWord();
            concordTree.Insert(w);
        }
        else
        {
            // w in tree. update word count and update word in tree
            w.CountWord();
            concordTree.Update(w);
        }
    }

    // print the tree in alphabetical order
    Inorder(concordTree.GetRoot(), PrintWord);
}

/*
<File "concord.txt">

Peter Piper picked a peck of pickled peppers. A peck of pickled
peppers Peter Piper picked. If Peter Piper picked a peck of
pickled peppers, where is the peck that Peter Piper picked?

<Run of Program 11.6>

a.....................3: 1  2
if....................1: 2
is....................1: 3
of....................3: 1  2
peck..................4: 1  2  3
peppers...............3: 1  2  3
peter.................4: 1  2  3
picked................4: 1  2  3
pickled...............3: 1  3
piper.................4: 1  2  3
```

```
that...................1: 3
the....................1: 3
where.................1: 3
*/
```

Written Exercises

11.1 Explain why a tree is a nonlinear data structure.

11.2 What is the minimum depth of a binary tree that contains

    (a)   15 nodes
    (b)   5 nodes
    (c)   91 nodes
    (d)   800 nodes

11.3 (a)   Draw a binary tree that contains 10 nodes and has depth 5.
    (b)   Draw a binary tree that contains 14 nodes and has depth 5.

11.4 A binary tree contains the data values 1 3 7 2 12.

    (a)   Draw two trees of maximal depth containing the data.
    (b)   Draw two complete binary trees in which the parent value is greater than either child value.

11.5 Draw all possible binary trees that contain 3 nodes.

11.6 Is it true that a binary tree with n nodes must have exactly n − 1 edges (non-NULL pointers)?

11.7 Consider the following binary tree:

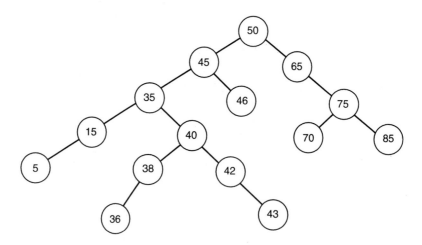

    (a)   If the value 30 is inserted into the tree, which node is its parent?
    (b)   If the value 41 is inserted into the tree, which node is its parent?
    (c)   Traverse the tree using preorder, inorder, and postorder scans.

11.8 Describe the action of function F. Assume F is a member function of the BinSTree class.

```
template <class T>
void F(TreeNode<T>* & t,T item)
{
    if (t == NULL)
        t = GetTreeNode(item);
    else if (item < t->data)
        F(t->left,item);
    else
        F(t->right,item);
}
```

Why it is critical for t to be passed by reference?

11.9 For each sequence of characters, draw the binary search tree and traverse the tree using inorder, preorder, and postorder.

(a) M, T, V, F, U, N
(b) F, L, O, R, I, D, A
(c) R, O, T, A, R, Y, C, L, U, B

11.10 For Written Exercise 11.9, traverse each tree using the traversal orders RLN, RNL, NRL, and level order.

11.11 For each sequence of integers, draw the binary search tree and traverse the tree using inorder, preorder, postorder, and level order scans.

(a) 30, 20, 10, 6, 5, 35, 56,1, 32, 40, 48
(b) 60, 25, 70, 99, 15, 3, 10, 30, 38, 59, 62, 34
(c) 30, 20, 25, 22, 24, 23

Is tree (c) a good structure for searching? Explain your answer.

11.12 For Written Exercise 11.11, traverse each tree using the RLN, RNL, and NRL scans.

11.13 Modify MakeCharTree so it builds the following trees as cases 3 and 4:

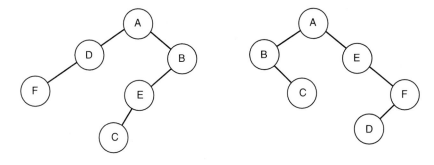

Tree (A)   Tree (B)

11.14 (a) What is the traversal order if the level-order algorithm is modified to place nodes on a stack instead of a queue? Illustrate your analysis by using Tree_2 presented in Section 11.1.

(b) Assume the nodes are inserted into a priority queue, with ordering determined by the data field. Using this algorithm, give the traversal order for Tree_2.

11.15 Use MakeCharTree as a model to define a function MakeIntTree that builds the following binary search trees. Explicitly build all nodes.

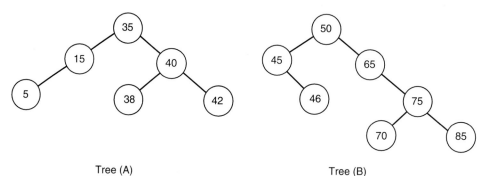

Tree (A)   Tree (B)

11.16 (a) The following integer sequence is obtained by traversing a binary search tree in preorder. Construct a tree that has such an ordering.

50   45   35   15   40   46   65   75   70

(b) Construct a binary search tree that would produce the following inorder traversal of its elements:

40   45   46   50   65   70   75

11.17 Use the following binary search tree for parts (a) through (e). The original tree is used for each part.

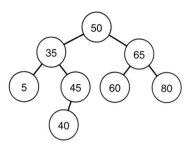

(a) Show the tree after inserting the values 1, 48, 75, 100.
(b) Delete nodes 5, 35.
(c) Delete 45.
(d) Delete 50.
(e) Delete 65, insert 65.

11.18 Modify the function CopyTree to create a new function TCopyTree that has a parameter "target." During the copy process, the function copies only the nodes whose data value is greater than target. If the value is less, the node is copied as a leaf node with no left and right subtrees. Note that in the copy process, you must delete all of the nodes in both the left and right subtrees when creating the leaf node.

```
TreeNode<T> *TCopyTree (TreeNode<T> *t, T target);
```

11.19 Write a function

```
TreeNode<T> *ReverseCopy(TreeNode<T> *tree);
```

that copies the tree by exchanging all left and right pointers.

11.20 Write a function

```
void PostOrder_Right(TreeNode<T> *t, void visit(T&
item));
```

that traverses a tree in a RLN scan.

11.21 Write a function

```
void *InsertOne(BinSTree<T>&t, T item);
```

that inserts item in t binary search tree if it is not already in the tree. Otherwise, the function quietly returns without inserting a new node.

11.22 Write a function

```
TreeNode *Max(TreeNode *t);
```

that returns a pointer to the maximum node of a binary search tree. Do this iteratively.

11.23 Write a function

```
TreeNode<T> *Min(TreeNode<T> *t);
```

that returns a pointer to the minimum node of a binary search tree. Do this recursively.

11.24 The integers from 1 to 9 are used to build a 9-node binary search tree with no duplicate data values.

(a)   Give the possible root node values if the depth of the tree is 4.
(b)   Answer (a) for depths of 5, 6, 7, and 8.

11.25 For each of the lists of letters, draw the binary search tree that results when the letters are inserted in the order specified:

(a)   D, A, E, F, B, K   (b)   G, J, L, M, P, A
(c)   D, H, P, Q, Z, L, M,   (d)   S, J, K, L, X, F, E, Z

11.26   Write an iterative function

```
template <class T>
int NodeLevel(const BinSTree<T>& T, const T& elem);
```

that determines the depth of elem in the tree. Return −1 if it is not in the tree.

11.27   (a)   Assume a string is the data value in a tree node. ASCII order compares two strings. Construct the binary search tree that results when the following C++ keywords are inserted in the order given:

for, case, while, class, protected, virtual, public, private, do, template, const, if, int

(b)   Traverse the tree using preorder, postorder, and inorder scans.

11.28   (a)   A binary tree node is sometimes modified to contain a pointer to its parent node. Create the class PTreeNode by modifying the TreeNode class to maintain this pointer.

(b)   Write the function

```
template <class T>
void PrintAncestors(PTreeNode<T> *t);
```

that prints the data for the chain of nodes leading from node t to the root.

(c)   Using the techniques in MakeCharTree, build Tree_2 using PTreeNode objects.

11.29   Some problems, such as implementing a game on a computer, involve general trees. In a general tree, a node may have more than two children. For instance, the following is a tree whose maximum child count is 3 (ternary tree).

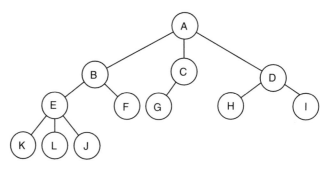

(a)   In a general tree, is an inorder traversal unambiguously defined?

(b)   Give the preorder and postorder traversal of the ternary tree.

(c)   A general tree can be converted to a binary tree using the following algorithm:

(1)   The left pointer of each node in the binary tree points to the leftmost child of the corresponding node in the general tree.

(2)   The right pointer of each node in the binary tree points to a sibling (node with the same parent) of the node in the general tree.

When drawing the binary tree, place each child directly below a node and place a sibling to the right. Arrange the tree in node columns. For instance, the following is the binary tree corresponding to the sample tree:

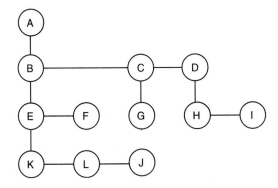

If the tree is turned 45° clockwise, a more familiar binary tree results:

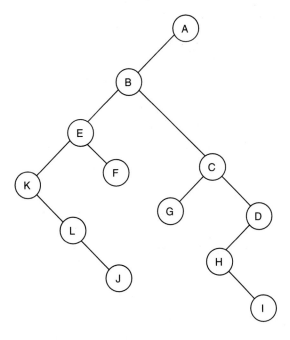

Traverse the binary tree using preorder, inorder, and postorder scans. What similarities do you find among these scans and those for the general tree?

(d) For the following general tree, do the following:

(1) Traverse it using preorder and postorder scans.
(2) Draw the corresponding binary tree.
(3) Traverse the binary tree using preorder, inorder, and postorder scans.

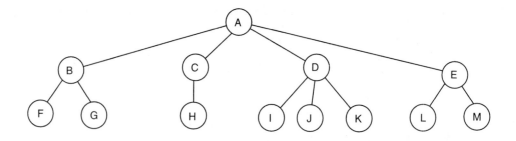

11.30 Since a binary tree with n nodes has n+1 NULL pointers, half the storage allocated for pointers is wasted. A clever algorithm makes use of this wasted space. Whenever a left pointer is NULL, make it point to the inorder predecessor of the node. Whenever the right pointer is NULL, make it point to the inorder successor of the node. This structure is known as a **threaded tree,** and the pointers are known as **threads.** A node of a threaded tree can be represented by a simple extension of the TreeNode class. Add private logical variables leftThread and rightThread, which indicate whether the corresponding pointer is a thread, and methods LeftThread, RightThread, which return their values. Assume the class is named ThreadedTreeNode. Write an iterative function

```
template <class T>
void ThreadedInorder(ThreadedTree<T> *t);
```

that traverses tree t using an inorder scan and prints the node values.

Programming Exercises

11.1 Write a function

```
int CountEdges(TreeNode<T> *tree);
```

that counts the number of edges (non-NULL pointers) in a binary tree. Test the function by using Tree_1 from "treelib.h".

11.2 Write a function

```
void RNL(TreeNode<T> *tree, void visit(T& item));
```

that visits a tree using RNL traversal. Read 10 integers and place them in a binary search tree using the BinSTree class. Traverse the tree using RNL. What ordering of the data is produced by this traversal?

11.3 Use the functions you developed in Written Exercises 11.15(a) and (b) and write a main program that prints the two trees. Print the tree from (a) using PrintTree and the tree from (b) using PrintVTree.

11.4   Use the function InsertOne from Written Exercise 11.21. In a test program, build a tree with eight nodes. The input data must have duplicates. Use PrintTree to illustrate the resulting tree.

11.5   In a main program, use the BinSTree class to create a tree with 500 randomly generated integer values in the range 1 to 10000. Use the functions Max and Min from Written Exercises 11.22 and 11.23, respectively, to compute the maximum and minimum of the numbers.

11.6   Modify the concordance problems (Program 11.6) so that the number of occurrences of each word on each line is shown in the output using the format

```
LineNumber (#occurrences)
```

For example

```
<Input>   one two one two three
<output>  one..............2: 1(2)
          three............1: 1(1)
          two..............2: 1(2)
```

11.7   (a)   Write a function

```
void LinkedSort(Array<int>& A);
```

that sorts A by inserting its elements into an ordered linked list and copying the sorted data values back into A.

(b)   Write a function

```
void TreeSort(Array<int>& A);
```

that sorts A by inserting its elements into a binary search tree, traversing the tree inorder, and copying the sorted data values back into A. (HINT: Perform the inorder traversal and array element assignment by writing a recursive function.)

```
void InorderAssign(TreeNode<int> *t,
                   Array<int>& A, int i);
```

(c)   Write a main program that creates an array of 10,000 random integers and uses a system timer to determine the effort required for each of the algorithms in (a) and (b). Each function must sort the same data.

11.8   An arithmetic expression involving the binary operators add (+), subtract (−), multiply (*), and divide (/) can be represented using a **binary expression tree.** In a binary expression tree, each operator has two children that are either operands or subexpressions. Leaf nodes contain an operand and nonleaf nodes contain a binary operator. The left and right subtrees of an operator describe a subexpression that is evaluated and used as one of the operands for the operator. For instance, the expression a+b*c/d − e corresponds to the binary expression tree.

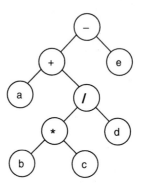

(a) Perform preorder, inorder, and postorder traversals of the binary expression tree. What relationship exists among these scans and the prefix, infix, and postfix (RPN) notation for the expression?

(b) For each arithmetic expression, build the corresponding expression tree. By scanning the tree, give the prefix, infix,and postfix form of the expression.

(1) a + b = c * d + e   (2) / a − b * c d
(3) a b c d / − *   (4) * − / + a b c d e

(c) A recursive algorithm can be developed that reads an expression in prefix form and builds the expression tree.

- If the term is an operand, use the data value to create a leaf node whose left and right pointers are NULL.

- If the term is an operator, assign it as the data value of the node and then create both its left and right children.

Write the function

```
void BuildExpTree(TreeNode<char> *t, char * & exp);
```

that builds an expression tree from the prefix expression contained in the NULL-terminated string exp. Assume the operands are single-letter identifiers in the range a to z and the operators are selected from the characters '+', '-', '*', and '/'.

(d) Write a main program that reads an expression and creates the expression tree. Print the tree vertically using PrintVTree and print the infix and postfix form of the expression.

11.9 Use the function TCopyTree from Written Exercise 11.18. In a test program, create a binary search tree with 10 nodes containing integer data. Input a target value and use TCopyTree to copy the nodes. Print the original and the copied tree using PrintVTree.

CHAPTER 12

INHERITANCE AND ABSTRACT CLASSES

Inheritance is a fundamental concept in object-oriented programming. This chapter develops the key features of inheritance that were briefly introduced in Chapter 1. We focus on the concept of inheritance and its implementation in C++, using the base class Shape and a family of derived geometric figure classes.

Polymorphism and virtual functions are discussed very simply in Section 12.3 and applied to the problem of displaying properties of geometric objects.

Section 12.4 develops the concept of an abstract base class. In addition to any functionality it provides, an abstract base class forces the implementation of its pure virtual functions in derived classes. An abstract class for the general linear or nonlinear list is developed.

An iterator is an object that traverses data structures, such as an array, linked list, or tree. As such, it is a **control abstraction.** Section 12.5 develops iterators by defining an abstract base class and using it to derive iterators for the SeqList and Array classes. The Array iterator is used to merge sorted runs, a technique used in Chapter 14 as well.

Section 12.6 applies inheritance to derive an ordered list class from the linked list version of the SeqList class developed in Chapter 9. The class is used as a filter to create sorted runs that are merged when sorting an external file.

The optional Section 12.7 shows how inheritance and polymorphism can be used to develop arrays and linked lists containing objects of different types. When it is useful and appropriate, inheritance is used in subsequent chapters to develop data structures.

A View of Inheritance   12.1

From the view of zoology, inheritance describes the common attributes and special characteristics among species of animals. For instance, let the class Animal represent animals including monkeys, cats, birds, and so forth. Although all share the attribute animal, there are different families of animals with special characteristics. Each of the animal types is further partitioned into species. For instance, the cat family is partitioned into lions, tigers, cheetahs, and so forth.

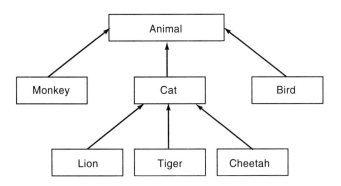

The entire range of living animals can be described with a hierarchy tree that passes from kingdom through species. "A cat is an animal," "a tiger is a cat," and so forth. A higher level indicates attributes that are derived from items on a lower level. Relationships are valid over multiple levels such as "a tiger is an animal."

Inheritance hierarchies exist in programming. You are encouraged to review Section 1.4, which develops Point, Line, and Rectangle objects and relates them using inheritance. Those classes include Draw methods, which draw the figures on the screen from a base point. In this section, we develop similar classes for closed geometric figures such as circles, rectangles, and so forth and isolate methods that are common to all the classes.

Our geometric objects share common attributes. They are all shapes that can be drawn on the screen and each figure has a base point that anchors its position. For instance, we draw a circle about its center and position a rectangle using its upper left-hand corner. In addition, each figure is drawn with a fill pattern that is identified by an integer value. In most graphics libraries, value 0 specifies an empty fill pattern inside the figure. For instance, the following graphic includes the drawing of a circle about (x_1, y_1) with the solid fill pattern. The rectangle is drawn from the corner (x_2, y_2) with a brick fill pattern.

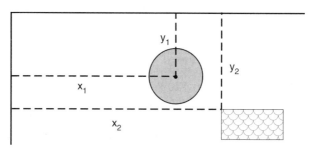

From the collection of geometric classes, we isolate the common attributes of base point and fill pattern and define the Shape class that contains these data members. The class contains methods to return the coordinates of the base point, to reposition the base point, and to retrieve or alter the fill pattern. A system-dependent Draw method initializes the graphics system so that the draw operations for the different geometric shapes will use the designated fill pattern. Draw is a **virtual function,** which means that it is designed to be redefined in a virtual class. Virtual functions are discussed in Section 12.3.

In Chapter 1, we developed a Circle class with measurement operations for the area and circumference (perimeter). These operations can apply to any closed figure and we include them in the Shape class. The methods are not defined in the Shape class but serve as a template for their definition in a derived class. They are known as **pure virtual functions,** and Shape is known as an **abstract class.** We include here an outline for the specification of the Shape class although many of the concepts are developed in Sections 12.3 and 12.4. The different elements that are included in the class specification preview the topics of this chapter.

```
class Shape
{
    protected:
        float x, y;      // horizontal and vertical positions
        int fillpat;

    public:
        // default constructor
        Shape(float h=0, float v=0, int fill=0);
            . . .
        // virtual function that is called by a Draw method
        // in a derived class. initializes the fill pattern
        virtual void Draw(void) const;

        // derived classes must define Area and Circumference
        virtual float Area(void) const = 0;
        virtual float Perimeter(void) const = 0;
};
```

We use the Shape class in an inheritance hierarchy. In each case, our derived class uses the methods from the Shape class and creates specific methods that override the generic methods in the abstract class. For instance, a Circle object is a Shape (base point at its center) along with its radius. It contains a Draw method to display a circle (with fill pattern) on a drawing surface. The class has specific Area and Perimeter methods that use the radius and the constant π. In the inheritance chain, a Circle is derived from a Shape.

Similarly, a Rectangle object is a Shape (base point at its upper left-hand corner) along with the length of its two sides (length and width). The Draw method outlines a rectangular box using length and width and places a fill pattern in the interior. The formulas

area = length * width
perimeter = 2 * (length + width)

are the basis for the Area and Perimeter methods. In the inheritance chain, a Rectangle is derived from a Shape.

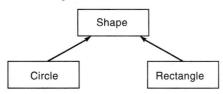

CLASS INHERITANCE TERMINOLOGY

In C++, inheritance is defined for classes. The concept implies that a **derived class** inherits data and operations from a **base class.** The derived class may itself be a base class for another layer of inheritance. The system of classes that use inheritance forms a **class hierarchy.**

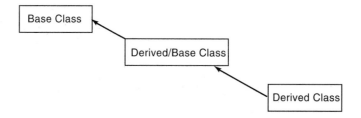

A derived class is often referred to as a **subclass** with a corresponding base class described as a **superclass.**

12.2 Inheritance in C++

The base class that starts an inheritance chain has an ordinary class declaration. The declaration for the derived class is modified to reference its relationship with the base class.

Base Class

```
// declaration of ordinary C++ class
class BaseCl
{
    <data and methods>
}
```

Derived Class

```
// declare a derived class with reference to its base class
class DerivedCL: public BaseCL
{
    <data and methods>
}
```

BaseCL is the name of the base class which DerivedCL inherits. The keyword **public** specifies that **public inheritance** is used. C++ allows a derived class to be defined with public, private, or protected inheritance. Most software development is done using public inheritance. Protected inheritance is seldom used and private inheritance is discussed in the exercises.

EXAMPLE 12.1

1. The Shape class is a base class for the derived class Circle.

    ```
    class Shape
    {<Members>}

    class Circle: public Shape // Circle inherits Shape class
    {<Members>}
    ```

2. For the Animal, Cat, and Tiger inheritance chain, the corresponding class declarations are

    ```
    class Animal
    {<Members>}

    class Cat: public Animal
    {<Members>}

    class Tiger: public Cat
    {<Members>}
    ```

With public inheritance, the private members in the base class remain private and are accessible only to member functions in the base class. Public members in the base class are accessible to all the member functions in the derived class and to any client of the derived class. In addition to private and public members, C++ defines **protected** members that have special meaning in a base class. When the base class is inherited, its protected members may be accessed by all methods in the derived class but not by any client of the class.

```
class BaseCL
{
   private:
      {<Members>}    // accessible only by members of BaseCL
   protected:
      {<Members>}    // accessible to members in DerivedCL and
                     // BaseCL
   public:
      {<Members>}    // accessible by all clients
}
```

If we have a hierarchy chain with more than one derivation, each derived class retains access to all the protected and public members of the higher base classes in the chain. Figure 12.1 illustrates class hierarchies with one and two derived classes, respectively. The arrows on the left specify the access of derived class

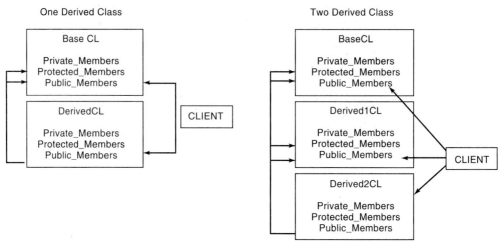

Figure 12.1 Access to Base Classes Data Assuming Public Inheritance

members to the different modes of base class data. The right side of each diagram illustrates that a client may access only the public members of the base and derived classes.

CONSTRUCTORS AND DERIVED CLASSES

In an inheritance chain, a derived object inherits the data and methods from the base class. We say that the base class is a *subtype* of the derived class. The resources of the derived object are expanded to include those of the base object.

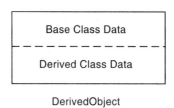

DerivedObject

When a derived object is created, its constructor is called to initialize its data. At the same time, the object inherits data from the base class that are initialized by the base class constructor. Because a constructor is called when an object is declared, interaction must occur among the constructors for the base and derived classes. When a derived object is declared, the constructor for the base class executes first, followed by the constructor for the derived class. It is intuitive that the beginning of the inheritance chain must be built first, since a derived class often uses base class data. If the chain is longer than two classes, the initialization process begins with the initial base class and progresses throughout the chain of derived classes:

```
DerivedCL   obj;    // BaseCL constructor called;
                    // then DerivedCL constructor
```

When a base class constructor requires parameters, the derived class constructor must explicitly call this base constructor and pass the necessary parameters.
This is done by placing the base class constructor name and parameters in the
parameter initialization list of the derived class constructor. If the base class has
a default constructor and its default values are assumed, the derived class does not
need to execute the default constructor explicitly. However, it is good practice to
do so.

EXAMPLE 12.2

Assume the following declaration for a base class constructor

```
BaseCL(int n, char ch);    // constructor has two parameters
```

Typically, the parameter list for the derived class constructor is a superset of
the base class constructor.

```
// constructor is a superset containing at least the two
// parameters required by the base class constructor
DerivedCL(int n, char ch, int sz);
```

The derived constructor must initialize the base class object by explicitly calling
the base class constructor in the initializer list. The following is a sample
implementation for the derived class constructor:

```
// call constructor BaseCL(n,ch) in the initializer list
// the expression data(sz) is a standard assignment of
// value sz to a data member
DerivedCL::DerivedCL(int n, char ch, int sz) :
            BaseCL(n,ch), data(sz)
{ }
```

In an inheritance chain, destructors are called in the opposite order of the
constructors. First, the destructor for the derived class is called, followed by the
destructors for member objects, followed by the destructors for base classes in the
reverse order of their appearance. Intuitively, a derived object is created after the
base object and so should be destroyed before the base object. If a derived class
does not have a destructor but the base class does, a destructor is automatically
generated for the derived class. This destructor destroys the derived class members
and executes the base class destructor.

Resolving Name Conflicts in Inheritance Classes in an inheritance chain can contain members with identical names. A member of a derived class is not in the same scope as the equivalent member (same name) in a base class. The declaration in the derived class hides the declaration in the base class rather than overloading it. The class scope operator "::" must be used to refer to a method of the same name in the base class. For example, consider the chain

```
class BaseCL                    class DerivedCL: public BaseCL
{                               {
   public:                         public:
       . . .                           . . .
       void F(void);                   void F(void);
       void G(int x);                  void G(int x);
       . . .                           . . .
};                              };
```

Assume that the implementation of the function G in the derived class must make a call to the function G in the base class. The derived class must prepend the scope operator BaseCL:: to gain access to the base class method G.

```
void DerivedCL::G(float x)
{
    . . .
    BaseCL::G(x);      // use scope operator in member function
    . . .
};
```

For a client with a derived object, a call to F is handled by the method F in the DerivedCL class. A call to F in the base class must be implemented by prepending the scope operator:

```
derived OBJ;
```

For client calls

```
OBJ.F();          // references function F in derived class
OBJ.base::F();    // references the function F in the base class
```

Application: Inheriting the Shape Class In Section 12.1 we introduced the Shape class as an example of an abstract base class. Its data and methods can be used by the geometric Circle and Rectangle classes. The Shape class is used as a base class for the derivation of classes describing geometric figures. We illustrate many of the technical details of inheritance by first declaring the Shape class as a base class and then deriving the Circle class. The derivation of the Rectangle class is given in Section 12.3 where virtual functions are discussed.

SHAPE CLASS SPECIFICATION

DECLARATION

```
// a generic class that defines a point, a fill pattern and
// methods to access and change these parameters. the class
// is inherited by geometric figure classes that implement
// specific draw, area, and perimeter calculations
class Shape
{
    protected:
        // horizontal and vertical pixel positions on the screen
        // data used by methods in a derived class
        float x, y;

        // fill pattern for the draw functions
        int fillpat;

    public:
        // constructor
        Shape(float h=0, float v=0, int fill=0);

        // methods to access x and y coordinates of base point
        float GetX(void) const;              // return x coordinate
        float GetY(void) const;              // return y coordinate
        void SetPoint(float h, float v);  // change base point

        // methods to access the fill pattern for the shape
        int GetFill(void) const;             // return fill pattern
        void SetFill(int fill);              // change fill pattern

        // pure virtual functions. a derived class must define a
        // specific Area and Perimeter method
        virtual float Area(void) const = 0;
        virtual float Perimeter(void) const = 0;

        // virtual function that is called by a Draw method in a
        // derived class initializes the fill pattern
        virtual void Draw(void) const;
};
```

DESCRIPTION

The constructor has default values that define a base point (0,0) in the upper left-hand corner of the window. The default fill pattern of 0 usually implies no fill.

GetX and GetY return the value of the x and y coordinates of the base point, and SetPoint allows the client to change the base point. Similar methods, GetFill and SetFill, provide access to the fill pattern.

The Draw method initializes the drawing system so that figures are drawn with the pattern fillpat. We assume the client is responsible for opening the graphics window and shutting down the drawing surface. The methods Area and Perimeter are pure virtual functions. They are declared in the Shape class and act like a template. Their definition must be given by each derived class that inherits the Shape class.

- -

SHAPE IMPLEMENTATION

The full declaration of the Shape class is given in the file "geometry.h". In this section we describe in detail the constructor and the Draw function.

The constructor requires the coordinates of the base point and the fill pattern. The client can change their value using SetPoint and SetFill.

```
// constructor. initialize coordinates and fill pattern
Shape::Shape(float h, float v, int fill):
        x(h), y(v), fillpat(fill)
```

Draw calls the primitive graphics system function SetFillStyle. When an actual figure is drawn by a derived class, this fill style is used.

```
void Shape::Draw(void) const
{
   SetFillStyle(fillpat);   // call graphics system function
}
```

- -

THE DERIVED CIRCLE CLASS

In Chapter 1 we declared the Circle class to have a radius and methods to compute area and circumference (perimeter). The radius was passed to the constructor when an object was created and could not be accessed. In this section, we extend the class to include drawing capabilities and methods to access the radius. The draw methods inherit a point and fill pattern from the Shape class.

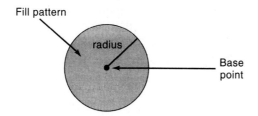

Fill pattern

radius

Base point

DECLARATION

```
// constant data used by the Area and Perimeter methods
const float PI = 3.14159;

// declaration of Circle class with base class Shape
class Circle: public Shape
{
    protected:
        // if Circle class becomes a base class, derived class
        // may have access to the radius
        float radius;

    public:
        // constructor with parameters for the center, radius,
        // and fill pattern
        Circle(float h=0, float v=0, float r=0, int fill = 0);

        // radius access methods
        float GetRadius(void) const;
        void SetRadius(float r);

        // circle Draw method; calls Draw in Shape class
        virtual void Draw(void) const;

        // measurement methods
        virtual float Area(void) const;
        virtual float Perimeter(void) const;
};
```

DESCRIPTION

Draw draws a circle at base point (x,y) with radius r.

The class declaration and implementation are contained in file "geometry.h".

CIRCLE CLASS IMPLEMENTATION

The implementation of the Circle class assumes the existence of a file "graphlib.h" that contains low-level drawing operations. The constructor for the Circle class is passed parameters to initialize the Shape base class and its own data member radius.

```
// constructor; parameters h and v initialize base point
// in Shape class. Point (h,v) represents center of circle.
// parameter fill initializes fill pattern for Shape class.
// r is only parameter used exclusively by Circle class.
// base object in Shape class is initialized by constructor
// Shape(h,v,fill) in the initializer list
Circle::Circle(float h, float v, float r, int fill):
        Shape(h,v,fill), radius(r)
{}
```

The Draw Operation   Call the Draw method from the base class (Shape::Draw) to set the fill pattern. Since the data in the base class have protected access, the Circle Draw method may access the data in the base class. However, a client of the object may not access the base point's coordinates directly.

```
// draw the circle with center (x,y) and given radius
void Circle::Draw(void) const
{
    Shape::Draw();     // sets the fill pattern
    DrawCircle(x,y, radius);
}
```

Program 12.1   Circle Draw Operations

This program illustrates the use of the Circle and Shape classes. After declaring two Circle objects, we execute a series of Shape class and Circle class methods.

```
#include <iostream.h>

#include "graphlib.h"
#include "geometry.h"

void main(void)
{
    // declare objects C, D with fill patterns 7 and no fill
    Circle C(1.0, 1.0, 0.5, 7), D(2.0, 1.0, 0.33);
    char   eol;        // used for delay before drawing figures

    cout << "Coordinates of C are " << C.GetX() << " and "
         << C.GetY() << endl;

    cout << "Circumference of C is " << C.Perimeter() << endl;
    cout << "Area of C is " << C.Area() << endl;
```

```
    cout << "Type <return> to view figures: ";
    cin.get(eol);    // wait until newline is typed

    // system dependent call to initialize the drawing surface.
    InitGraphics();

    // draw circle C with fill pattern 7 and radius 0.5
    C.Draw();
    // draw circle D with default fill pattern 0 and radius 0.33
    D.Draw();

    // relocate circle D to (1.5,1.8); radius to 0.25; fill to 11
    D.SetPoint(1.5,1.8);
    D.SetRadius(.25);
    D.SetFill(11);
    D.Draw();

    // delay for client input and shut down graphics
    ViewPause();
    ShutdownGraphics();
}

/*
<Run of Program 12.1>

Coordinates of C are  1 and 1
Circumference of C is 3.14159
Area of C is 0.785398
Type <return> to view figures:
*/
```

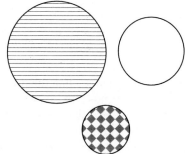

WHAT CANNOT BE INHERITED

While a derived class inherits access to the protected data members of the base class, some members and properties of a base class are not inherited. Constructors are not inherited and hence are not declared as virtual methods. If the base class constructor requires parameters, the derived class must have its own constructor, which calls the base class constructor. Friendship is not inherited. If function F is a friend of class A and class B is derived from A, then F is not automatically considered to be a friend of B.

12.3 Polymorphism and Virtual Functions

The concept of polymorphism was discussed from a nontechnical viewpoint in Section 1.3, and rereading that material is helpful. In this section, we expand our presentation of polymorphism and give some examples.

Object-oriented programming provides a property called **polymorphism.** The term is derived from ancient Greek and means "many forms." In programming, polymorphism means that the same method can be defined for objects of different class types. The specific action of the method will vary with the classes. C++ supports polymorphism using **dynamic binding** and **virtual member functions.** Dynamic binding allows different objects in a system to respond to the same message in a manner specific to each type. The receiver of the message is determined dynamically at run time.

To use polymorphism, declare a member function in the base class to be virtual by placing the keyword **virtual** in front of the declaration. For example, in the class BaseCL, the functions F and G are declared to be virtual:

```
class BaseCL
{
   private:
      ...
   public:
      ...
      virtual void F(int n);
      virtual int G(long m);
      ...
};
```

When declaring a derived class, the member functions F and G with precisely the same parameter lists and return type must be included. In the derived class, the keyword virtual does not have to be used because the virtual attribute is inherited from the base class. However, it is a good idea to include the keyword virtual in the derived class so the reader does not have to look at the base class declaration to determine that it is a virtual function.

```
class DerivedCL: public BaseCL
{
   private:
      ...
```

```
    public:
        ...
        virtual void F(int n);
        virtual int G(long m);
        ...
};
```

Once the inheritance chain and virtual member functions are defined, we can discuss new access conditions for our class members. Assume DObj is a DerivedCL object:

```
DerivedCL DObj;
```

The number function F in the derived class is accessed using the object name. The function F in the base class is accessed with the object name and the base class scoping operator:

```
DObj.F(n);              // derived class member function
DObj.BaseCL::F(n);      // base class member function
```

These calls are examples of **static binding.** The compiler realizes that the client is calling a specific version of F in either the base or derived class. However, polymorphism comes into effect when pointers or references are used. Consider the declarations

```
BaseCL      *P, *Q;
BaseCL      BObj;
DerivedCL   DObj;
```

Since the derived class is a subtype of the base class, a derived object can be assigned to a base class object. During the assignment, the portion of the derived object's data that is in the base class is copied.

```
BObj = DObj;
```

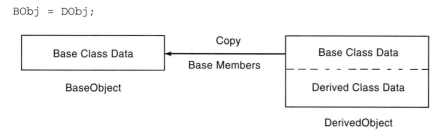

At the same time, the assignment of a base object to a derived object is not valid since some data items in the derived class may be undefined. For instance, consider the following assignment statements.

```
Bobj = DObj;     // copies base class data portion to BObj
Dobj = BObj;     // invalid. derived class data not initialized
```

In the context of pointers and references, a base class pointer can point to a derived object, so the following assignments are legal:

```
Q = &BObj;       // assigns address of a BaseCL object to a
                 // BaseCL pointer
P = &DObj;       // assigns address of a DerivedCL object to a
                 // BaseCL pointer
```

The statement

```
Q->F(n);  // call method F in the BaseCL class
```

calls the function F in the base class. A similar statement for P illustrates the essence of polymorphism since it calls the method F in the DerivedCL class even though P is a pointer to the BaseCL class.

```
P->F(n);  // call method F in the DerivedCL class
```

When access is through a pointer or a reference, C++ determines which version of the function to call based on the actual object to which the pointer or reference is directed. This process is known as **dynamic binding.**

Each object that has at least one virtual function contains a pointer to a runtime **virtual function table.** The table contains the starting addresses of all the virtual functions declared in the class. When a virtual function is called through a pointer or reference, the runtime system uses the object's address to access the pointer to the virtual function table, follows the pointer to the table, looks up the function address, and calls the function.

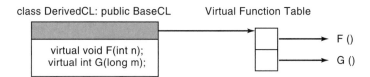

In our example, P points to an object of type DerivedCL, so the version of F in the class DerivedCL is called. This allows the creation of a variety of objects, all referenced by base class pointers. When virtual functions are executed, the version of the function appropriate to the actual object type is called. Polymorphism allows functions that take base class pointer or reference arguments to be reused with new versions of the virtual functions in derived classes.

DEMONSTRATING POLYMORPHISM

We began the chapter with a simple example of inheritance involving animal hierarchies. From the base Animal, we proceed through the Cat class and then to specific types of cats, such as the Tiger. A Tiger "is a" Cat, and a Cat "is an" Animal.

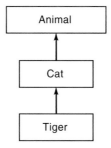

The following classes simulate the animal hierarchy by developing the classes Animal, Cat, and Tiger. Each class contains a string that is initialized by the constructor and designed to give specific information about the object. Each class has an Identify method that prints the information.

ANIMAL CLASS DECLARATION

```
class Animal
{
    private:
        char animalName[20];
    public:
        Animal(char nma[])
        {
            strcpy(animalName,nma);
        }

        virtual void Identify(void)
        {
            cout << "I am a " << animalName << " animal" << endl;
        }
};
```

CAT CLASS DECLARATION

```
class Cat: public Animal
{
    private:
        char catName[20];
    public:
        Cat(char nmc[], char nma[]): Animal(nma)
        {
            strcpy(catName,nmc);
        }
```

```
            virtual void Identify(void)
            {
               Animal::Identify();
               cout << "I am a " << catName << " cat" << endl;
            }
       };
```

TIGER CLASS DECLARATION

```
   class Tiger: public Cat
   {
      private:
         char tigerName[20];
      public:
         Tiger(char nmt[], char nmc[], char nma[]): Cat(nmc,nma)
         {
            strcpy(tigerName,nmt);
         }

         virtual void Identify(void)
         {
            Cat::Identify();
            cout << "I am a " << tigerName << " tiger" << endl;
         }
   };
```

Program 12.2   Animal Polymorphism

This program illustrates static and dynamic binding with two functions, Announce1 and Announce2, which execute the Identify method for the object that is passed as a parameter. Two different parameter passing techniques are used:

Announce1—pass an Animal object by value
```
   void Announce1(Animal a)
   {
      // example of static binding; the compiler directs the
      // execution of the Identify method of an Animal object
      cout << "In static Announce1, calling Identify:" << endl;
      a.Identify();
      cout << endl;
   }
```

Announce2–pass a pointer to an Animal object

```
// Announce2—pass a pointer to an Animal object
void Announce2(Animal *pa)
{
    // dynamic binding is used. the Identify method of
    // the object pointed to by pa is called
    cout << "In dynamic Announce2, calling Identify:" << endl;
    pa->Identify();
    cout << endl;
}
```

The main program declares an Animal object A, a Cat object C, and a Tiger object T. With the "Announce" functions, we illustrate the effect of different modes of parameter passing. Static binding is demonstrated by passing the Tiger object T to Announce1. Polymorphism is highlighted with three separate calls to Announce2 using pointers to objects A, C, and T. As another example of polymorphism, the method Identify is executed using an Animal pointer initialized to point at a Cat object. The Identify method for Cat is called. The last code sequence demonstrates the assignment of a derived object to a base object. The base class data portion of the derived object is copied to the right hand side.

The animal classes and the Announce functions are contained in the file "animal.h"

```
#include <iostream.h>
#include <string.h>

#include "animal.h"

void main(void)
{
    Animal A("reptile"), *p;
    Cat C("domestic", "warm blooded");
    Tiger T("bengal", "wild", "meat eating");

    // static binding. Announce1 has a value parameter
    // since T is a Tiger, function executes Animal Identify
    Announce1(T);        // static binding; calls Animal method

    // examples of polymorphism. since parameter is a pointer,
    // Announce2 uses dynamic binding to execute Identify method
    // of the actual object parameter
    Announce2(&A);       // dynamic binding; calls Animal method
    Announce2(&C);       // dynamic binding; calls Cat method
    Announce2(&T);       // dynamic binding; calls Tiger method

    // direct call to the Identify method in the animal class
    A.Identify();        // static binding
    cout << endl;
```

```
    // dynamic binding; call made to the Cat method
    p = &C;
    p->Identify();
    cout << endl;

    // assignment of Tiger object to Animal object
    // copy inherited animal data
    A = T;
    A.Identify();          // identify animal data from Tiger T
    cout << endl;
}


/*
<Run of Program 12.2>

In static Announce1, calling Identify:
I am a meat eating animal

In dynamic Announce2, calling Identify:
I am a reptile animal

In dynamic Announce2, calling Identify:
I am a warm blooded animal
I am a domestic cat

In dynamic Announce2, calling Identify:
I am a meat eating animal
I am a wild cat
I am a bengal tiger

I am a reptile animal

I am a warm blooded animal
I am a domestic cat

I am a meat eating animal
*/
```

APPLICATION: GEOMETRIC FIGURES AND VIRTUAL METHODS

The Shape class can be used as a base for a series of derived geometric classes including the Circle and Rectangle classes. In this application, we give the specification for the Rectangle class and use it in the same program with Circle to illustrate the use of virtual functions.

In the rectangle class, the base point is the upper left-hand corner of the object.

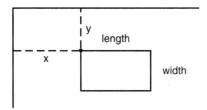

Like the Circle class, Rectangle overrides the base class Draw method with its own virtual Draw method that displays the rectangle. The class also defines Area (length *width) and Perimeter (2*(length+width)) along with methods to retrieve and change the length and width values. We present the class declaration and refer the reader to the file "geometry.h" in the program supplement for the implementation.

```
// derived Rectangle Class; inherits the Shape class
class Rectangle: public Shape
{
   protected:
      // protected data members that describe a rectangle
        float length, width;

   public:
      // constructor. has parameters for base point, length,
      // width, and fill pattern
      Rectangle(float h=0, float v=0, float l=0,
                float w=0, int fill = 0);

      // rectangle data access methods
      float GetLength(void) const;
      void SetLength(float l);
      float GetWidth(void) const;
      void SetWidth(float w);

      // override the virtual functions in the base class
      virtual void Draw(void) const;   // draw the rectangle
      virtual float Area(void) const;
      virtual float Perimeter(void) const;
};
```

Program 12.3   Geometric Classes and Virtual Functions

This program illustrates dynamic binding and polymorphism for the Shape (base) class, Circle (derived) class, and Rectangle (derived) class. Circle C is a static object, and variables one, two, and three are pointers to a Shape object.

Using static binding, the area and circumference (perimeter) of circle C are computed with the methods C.Area() and C.Circumference(). Shape pointer variables are defined to point at dynamically created Circle and Rectangle objects. Using dynamic binding, the area and perimeter of the objects are computed using the appropriate Area/Perimeter method in a derived class. Pointer three is assigned the address of Circle C and hence we dynamically bind the appropriate Circle methods when calling for the area and perimeter of C.

Dynamic binding allows us to use the three base class pointers to execute the Draw method for the three figures.

```cpp
#include <iostream.h>

#include "graphlib.h"
#include "geometry.h"

void main(void)
{
    // Circle C is centered at (3,1) with radius 0.25;
    // variable three is a shape pointer to circle C
    Circle C(3,1,.25, 11);
    Shape *one, *two, *three = &C;
    char eol;

    // Circle *one is centered at (1,1) with radius 0.5.
    // Rectangle *two based at (2,2) with length = width = 0.5.
    one = new Circle(1,1,.5,4);
    two = new Rectangle(2,2,.5,.5,6);

    cout << "Area/perimeter of C and figures one-three:" << endl;
    cout << "C: " << C.Area() << "  " << C.Perimeter() << endl;
    cout << "one: " << one->Area() << "  "
         << one->Perimeter() << endl;
    cout << "two: " << two->Area() << "  "
         << two->Perimeter() << endl;
    cout << "three: "<< three->Area() << "  "
         << three->Perimeter() << endl;

    cout << "Type <return> to view figures." << endl;
    cin.get(eol);

    // initialize the graphics system
    InitGraphics();

    one->Draw();    // draws circle
    two->Draw();    // draws rectangle
    three->Draw();  // draws circle
```

```
    ViewPause();
    // shut down the graphics system
    ShutdownGraphics();
}

/*
<Run of Program 12.3>

Area/perimeter of C and figures one-three:
C: 0.196349  1.570795
one: 0.785398  3.14159
two: 0.25  2
three: 0.196349  1.570795
Type <return> to view figures one and two and three.
*/
```

VIRTUAL METHODS AND THE DESTRUCTOR

A class destructor must be defined when a class allocates dynamic memory. If the class will be used as a base class, its destructor should be made virtual. This is a subtle but important fact that must be considered when we maintain lists of objects through base class pointers. If the destructor for the base class is not virtual, a base class that references a derived class object will not cause the derived class destructor to execute. The following situation illustrates the problem. Assume the BaseCL class constructor dynamically allocates an array of seven integers. Its destructor must be designed to deallocate the data.

```
    class BaseCL
    {
        . . .
      public:
          BaseCL (...);      // allocate 7 element array
          ~BaseCL (void);    // deallocate (not virtual)
    }
```

The class Derived inherits Base and performs the same actions.

```
class DerivedCL    : public BaseCL
{
    . . .
    public:
        DerivedCL (...);       // allocate 7 element array
        ~DerivedCL (void);     // deallocate (not virtual)
}
```

Assume p is a BaseCL pointer that is assigned to a dynamic DerivedCL object and we call the delete function:

```
Base *p = new DerivedCL();    // construct a DerivedCL object

delete p;                      // calls the base class destructor
```

The dynamic data generated by the derived class are not destroyed. If the Base destructor is declared virtual, the Derived destructor is called. In this case the base class destructor is also called, but not until after the destructor for the derived class.

In general, if a class will be used as a base class in an inheritance hierarchy, make sure it has a virtual destructor, even if you have to create a destructor that does nothing, such as

```
virtual BaseCL::~BaseCL(void)
{}
```

This ensures that if a derived class has a destructor, that destructor will be executed.

12.4 Abstract Base Classes

Our discussion of inheritance has led to the use of virtual methods in the base class, with methods of the same name appearing in derived classes. Because the base method is defined as virtual, we can use dynamic binding and be assured that the correct version will be called. For instance, the Shape class defines a virtual Draw method and gives it the primitive task of setting the fill pattern. Each of our derived geometric classes has its own overloaded Draw function that sketches the specific shape. In the same Shape class, we defined virtual area and perimeter methods. These operations are not meaningful for a Shape object that consists of a point and a fill pattern. We assume the operations are going to be meaningfully defined for the derived geometric classes. By declaring the operations as virtual methods in the base class, we are assured that dynamic binding will call the correct version for the specific geometric object. We could define functions that return 0.

```
// place holder function definitions in the base class
float Shape::Area(void) const
{
   return 0.0;          // area of a point
}

float Shape::Perimeter(void) const
{
   return 0.0;          // perimeter of a point
}
```

Rather than forcing the programmer to create such place holder implementations, C++ allows the use of **pure virtual functions** by appending "= 0" to the definition. For instance,

```
virtual float Area(void) const = 0;
virtual float Perimeter(void) const = 0;
```

The use of a pure virtual function in the base class implies that no implementation will be given. The definition also forces an implementation in each derived class. For instance, each derived geometric class must define an Area and Perimeter method. By including pure virtual functions in the Shape class, we ensure that no separate Shape objects can be created. The class can only be used as a base for another class. A class with one or more pure virtual functions is known as an **abstract class.** Any class derived from an abstract class must provide an implementation of each pure virtual function, or it is also an abstract base class and may not generate objects.

EXAMPLE 12.3

The abstract class BaseCL contains two pure virtual functions and hence is an abstract base class.

```
class BaseCL
{
    . . .
   public:
       virtual void F(void) = 0;     // pure virtual function
       virtual void G(void) = 0;     // pure virtual function
};
```

The derived class DerivedCL defines F but not G, and so DerivedCL remains an abstract class.

```
class DerivedCL: public BaseCL
{
    public:
        // since G is not defined, a DerivedCL object
        // cannot be declared
        // class remains an abstract base class for another
        // derived class that defines G.
        virtual void F(void);
};
```

The following declaration results in a compiler error:

```
DerivedCL D;
```

Error:

```
cannot create instance of abstract class 'DerivedCL'
```

ABSTRACT BASE CLASS—LIST

An abstract class acts like a template for its derived classes. It may contain data and methods that are shared by all derived classes. By using pure virtual functions, it provides a declaration of the public methods that must be implemented by a derived class. As an example, we design the abstract List class as a template for list collections. The class has a data value size that is used to define the methods ListSize and ListEmpty. These functions are available to each derived class provided the class correctly maintains size when adding or deleting an item or clearing the list. While the methods ListSize and ListEmpty are provided by the base class, they may be overridden in a derived class or may be accepted as the default. The remaining methods are declared as pure virtual functions in the base class and must be overridden in the derived class. A function such as Insert depends on the particular collection class. In one derivation, Insert may place data in a sequential list. For a binary search tree or a dictionary collection, a different insertion algorithm is required.

LIST CLASS SPECIFICATION

```
template <class T>
class List
{
    protected:
        // number of elements in list updated by derived class
        int size;
```

```
    public:
        // constructor
        List(void);

        // list access methods
        virtual int ListSize(void) const;
        virtual int ListEmpty(void) const;
        virtual int Find (T& item) = 0;

        // list modification methods
        virtual void Insert(const T& item) = 0;
        virtual void Delete(const T& item) = 0;
        virtual void ClearList(void) = 0;
};
```

LIST METHOD IMPLEMENTATION

The list modification methods in any derived class must maintain the base class data member size. The value of size is initialized to 0 by the List constructor.

```
// constructor sets size to 0
template <class T>
int List<T>::List(void): size(0)
{}
```

List class methods ListSize and ListEmpty depend only on the value of size. They are implemented in the base class and then used by any derived class.

```
// return the list size
template <class T>
int List<T>::ListSize(void) const
{
    return size;
}

// test for an empty list
template <class T>
int List<T>::ListEmpty(void) const
{
    return size == 0;
}
```

DERIVING SEQLIST FROM ABSTRACT BASE CLASS LIST

We first introduced the SeqList class in Chapter 1 and then gave array and linked list implementations in subsequent chapters. We now revisit SeqList as a class derived from the abstract List class. The methods DeleteFront and GetData do not appear in the abstract class because they apply only to a sequential list.

SEQLIST CLASS SPECIFICATION

DECLARATION

```
template <class T>
class SeqList: public List<T>
{
   protected:
       // linked list object, available to derived class
       LinkedList<T> llist;

   public:
       // constructor
       SeqList(void);

       // list access methods
       virtual int Find (T& item);
       T GetData(int pos);

       // list modification methods
       virtual void Insert(const T& item);
       virtual void Delete(const T& item);
       T DeleteFront(void);
       virtual void ClearList(void);

       // SeqListIterator needs access to llist
       friend class SeqListIterator<T>;
};
```

DESCRIPTION

By inheriting the abstract base class List, the SeqList class must follow the operations specified in List. Since SeqList implements a sequential list, the method GetData, with its position parameter, and the method DeleteFront, which deletes the first node of the list, are added to the public methods in the derived class.

The methods Insert, Delete, and ClearList maintain the protected base class data member size. As a result, the methods ListSize and ListEmpty do not need to be overridden.

A SeqList object can be traversed by a tool called an *iterator*. The tool, declared as a SeqListIterator object, must have access to llist. The access is provided by declaring SeqListIterator as a friend. The topic of iterators is covered in the next section. The derived version of SeqList is included in the file "seqlist2.h".

- -

SEQLIST IMPLEMENTATION (DERIVED CLASS VERSION)

Much of the work for the implementation was completed in Chapter 9. We must define the functions Insert, Delete, ClearList, and Find. We repeat their linked list definition with the added responsibility to maintain the data value size from the List class. For instance, the Insert method is:

```
// use method InsertRear to add item at the rear of the list
template <class T>
void SeqList<T>::Insert(const T& item)
{
    llist.InsertRear(item);
    size++;                     // update size in List
}
```

In the derived class, the constructor SeqList calls the List constructor, which sets size to 0.

```
// default constructor, initialize the base class
template <class T>
SeqList<T>::SeqList(void): List<T>()
{}
```

Iterators   12.5

Many list handling algorithms assume that we can scan the items and take some action. A class derived from List provides methods to add and delete data values. In general, it does not provide methods that are explicitly used to scan the list. Rather it assumes that some external process will traverse the list and maintain a record of the current position in the list.

For an array or a SeqList object L, we can traverse a list using a loop and a position index. For a SeqList object L, the method GetData accesses the data value.

```
for (pos = 0; pos < List Size(); pos++)
    cout << L.GetData(pos) << "  ";
```

For binary trees, hash tables, and dictionaries, list traversal is more complex. For instance, tree traversal is recursive and can be done using a recursive inorder, preorder, or postorder scan. These scanning methods can be added to a binary tree maintenance class. However, a recursive function does not allow the client to stop the traversal process, perform other tasks, and then continue the iteration. As we shall see in Chapter 13, an iterative traversal can be done by maintaining tree node pointers on a stack. The tree class will need to contain an iterative implementation for each traversal order, even though a client may not perform a tree traversal or may consistently use one traversal order. It is preferable to separate the data abstraction from the control abstraction. A solution to the problem of list traversal is to create an **iterator** class whose job is to traverse the elements of a data structure such as a linked list or tree. An iterator is initialized to point at the start of the list (head, root, etc.). The iterator provides methods Next() and EndOfList() that allow us to move through the list. The iterator object maintains a record of the state of the iterator between calls to Next.

With an iterator, the client can stop the scanning process, examine the contents of a data item, and perform other tasks as well. The client is given a tool to traverse the list without having to maintain underlying indices or pointers. By having a class include an iterator as a friend, we can associate a traversal object with the class and give the iterator access to the items in the list. Implementation of the iterator methods uses the underlying structure of the list.

In this section we include a general discussion of iterators. Using virtual functions, we declare an abstract base class that is used for the construction of all iterators. The abstract class provides a common interface for all iterator operations, although the derived iterator classes differ in implementation.

THE ITERATOR ABSTRACT BASE CLASS

We define the abstract Iterator class as a template for general list iterators. Every iterator we develop for the remainder of the text is derived from this class, which is contained in the file "iterator.h".

— —

ITERATOR CLASS SPECIFICATION

DECLARATION

```
template <class T>
class Iterator
{
    protected:
        // indicates whether iterator has reached end of list
        // must be maintained by the derived class
        int iterationComplete;

    public:
        // constructor
        Iterator(void);

        // required iterator methods
        virtual void Next(void) = 0;
        virtual void Reset(void) = 0;

        // data retrieval/modification method
        virtual T& Data(void) = 0;
```

```
        // test for end of list
        virtual int EndOfList(void) const;
};
```

DISCUSSION

An iterator is a list traversal tool. Its basic methods are Reset (set to the first data element), Next (set position at next item), and EndOfList (identify end of list). The function Data accesses the data value of the current list element.

ITERATOR CLASS IMPLEMENTATION

The abstract class has a single data value, iterationComplete, that must be maintained by Reset and Next in each derived class. Only the constructor and method EndOfList are implemented in this abstract class.

```
        // constructor. sets iterationComplete to 0 (False)
        template <class T>
        Iterator<T>::Iterator(void): iterationComplete(0)
        {}
```

The EndOfList method simply returns the value of iterationComplete. The data value is set to 1 (True) by the derived method Reset if the list is empty. The derived class method Next must set iterationComplete to True when Next would advance past the end of the list.

DERIVING LIST ITERATORS

SeqList has been used extensively in this book and served as the basis for design of the abstract List class. Because of its importance, we begin by deriving the SeqListIterator. The iterator maintains a pointer listPtr that points at the SeqList object that is currently being scanned. Since the SeqListIterator is a friend of the derived SeqList, it is allowed access to the private members of SeqList.

SEQLISTITERATOR CLASS SPECIFICATION

DECLARATION

```
        // SeqListIterator derived from the abstract class Iterator
        template <class T>
        class SeqListIterator: public Iterator<T>
        {
            private:
                // maintain local pointer to SeqList we are traversing
                SeqList<T> *listPtr;
                // we must maintain the previous and current positions as
                // we traverse the list
                Node<T> *prevPtr, *currPtr;
```

```
public:
    // constructor
    SeqListIterator(SeqList<T>& lst);

    // Traversal methods we must define
    virtual void Next(void);
    virtual void Reset(void);

    // Data retrieval/modification method we must define
    virtual T& Data(void);

    // reset iterator to traverse a new list
    void SetList(SeqList<T>& lst);
};
```

DISCUSSION

The iterator implements the virtual functions Next, Reset, and Data, which were declared pure virtual in the base Iterator class. The method SetList is specific to the SeqListIterator class and allows the client to make a runtime assignment of the iterator to another SeqList object. The iterator is included with the SeqList class in file "seqlist2.h".

EXAMPLE

```
SeqList<int> L;                    // creates a list

SeqListIterator<int> iter(L);   // create iterator; attach to list L
cout << iter.Data();             // prints current data value
iter.Next();                      // move to next position in list

// loop that scans the list and prints its data values
for (iter.Reset(); !iter.EndOfList(); iter.Next())
    cout << iter.Data() << "    ";
```

BUILDING THE SEQLIST ITERATOR

When the iterator is created by the constructor, it is bound to a specific SeqList and all of its operations apply to that list. The iterator maintains a pointer to the SeqList object.

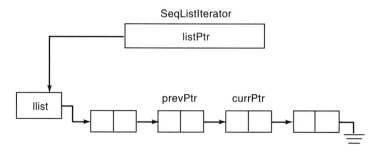

After attaching the iterator to the list, we initialize iterationComplete and set the current position to the front of the list.

```
// constructor. initialize base class and local SeqList pointer
template <class T>
SeqListIterator<T>::SeqListIterator(SeqList<T>& lst):
     Iterator<T>(), listPtr(&lst)
{
   // account for the fact that the list could be empty
   iterationComplete = listPtr->llist.ListEmpty();
   // position the iterator at the front of the list
   Reset();
}
```

Reset restores the initial state of the iterator by initializing iterationComplete and setting the pointers prevPtr and currPtr to their position at the front of the list. The SeqListIterator class is also a friend of the LinkedList class and thus has access to the data member front.

```
// move to the beginning of the list
template <class T>
void SeqListIterator<T>::Reset(void)
{
   // reassign the state of the iteration
   iterationComplete = listPtr->llist.ListEmpty();

   // if the list is empty, return
   if (listPtr->llist.front == NULL)
      return;

   // move list traversal mechanism to the first node
   prevPtr = NULL;
   currPtr = listPtr->llist.front;
}
```

The **SetList** method is the runtime equivalent of the constructor. A new SeqList object lst is passed as a parameter and the iterator now traverses lst. Reassign listPtr and call Reset.

```
// iterator must now traverses lst. reassign listPtr and call
// Reset
template <class T>
void SeqListIterator<T>::SetList(SeqList<T>& lst)
{
   listPtr = &lst;

   // position traversal mechanism at lst data value in new list
   Reset();
}
```

The iterator can gain access to the data value in the current list element with the method **Data().** The function returns the data value of the item by using currPtr to access the data value of a LinkedList node. If the list is empty or the iterator is at end of list, a call to Data terminates the program after printing an error message.

```
// return the data value in the current list element
template <class T>
T& SeqListIterator<T>::Data(void)
{
    // error if the list is empty or the traversal has completed
    if (listPtr->llist.ListEmpty() || currPtr == NULL)
    {
        cerr << "Data: invalid reference!" << endl;
        exit(1);
    }
    return currPtr->data;
}
```

The movement from item to item is provided by the method **Next.** The scanning process continues until the current position reaches the end of the list. This condition is flagged by the integer value iterationComplete, which must be maintained by Next.

```
// advance to the next list element
template <class T>
void SeqListIterator<T>::Next(void)
{
    // if currPtr is NULL, we are at end of list
    if (currPtr == NULL)
        return;

    // move prevPtr/currPtr forward one node
    prevPtr = currPtr;
    currPtr = currPtr->NextNode();

    // if we have arrived at the end of linked list, signal that
    // the iteration is complete
    if (currPtr == NULL)
        iterationComplete = 1;
}
```

Program 12.4   Using the SeqListIterator Class

Each month, a company creates a record (SalesPerson) that includes a sales-man's id number and the number of units sold. The list salesList contains the store's accumulated SalesPerson information. A second list, idList, maintains a list of only the employee id numbers. From file "sales.dat", we read several months of sales information and add each record to salesList. Since the records cover several months, we may have several records for the same salesperson. However, an employee is included only once in idList.

Once the data is entered, we assign iterators idIter and salesIter, to the corresponding lists. By scanning the idList, we identify each employee by id number and use this id as a parameter to the function PrintTotalSales. This function scans the sales list and computes the total number of units sold by the employee that matches an id parameter. The function concludes by printing the employee id number and total sales.

```cpp
#include <iostream.h>
#include <fstream.h>

#include "seqlist2.h"

// use SeqList inherited from List and SeqListIterator
// record that holds the sales person's id no and units sold
struct SalesPerson
{
    int idno;
    int units;
};

// operator == compares employees by id no
int operator == (const SalesPerson &a, const SalesPerson &b)
{
    return a.idno == b.idno;
}

// take the id as a key and scan the list. add the units sold by
// employee with id number == id. print final information
void PrintTotalSales(SeqList<SalesPerson> & L, int id)
{
    // declare a SalesPerson variable and initialize fields
    SalesPerson  salesP = {id, 0};

    // declare the sequential list iterator and use it to
    // scan the list
    SeqListIterator<SalesPerson> iter(L);

    for(iter.Reset();!iter.EndOfList();iter.Next())
        // if a match with id occurs, add the number of units
        if (iter.Data() == salesP)
            salesP.units += (iter.Data()).units;
```

```cpp
   // print the sales person's id and total units sold
   cout << "Sales person " << salesP.idno
        << "    Total Units Sold " << salesP.units << endl;
}

void main(void)
{
   // lists will contain SalesPerson records and employee id
   SeqList<SalesPerson> salesList;
   SeqList<int> idList;

   ifstream salesFile;      // file containing input data
   SalesPerson salesP;      // variable holding input
   int i;

   // open the input file
   salesFile.open("sales.dat", ios::in | ios::nocreate);
   if (!salesFile)
   {
      cerr << "File 'sale.dat' not found!";
      exit(1);
   }
   // read data in form  'idno  units' to end of file
   while (!salesFile.eof())
   {
      // read data fields and insert into SeqList salesList
      salesFile >> salesP.idno >> salesP.units;
      salesList.Insert(salesP);
      // if id not in  idlist, add it
      if (!idList.Find(salesP.idno))
          idList.Insert(salesP.idno);
   }

   // set up iterators for the two lists
   SeqListIterator<int> idIter(idList);
   SeqListIterator<SalesPerson> salesIter(salesList);

   // scan the id list and use each entry as a parameter to
   // the function PrintTotalSales to add up the total
   // number of units sold by the employee
   for(idIter.Reset();!idIter.EndOfList();idIter.Next())
       PrintTotalSales(salesList, idIter.Data());
}

/*

<File 'Sales.dat'>
300      40
100      45
```

```
200      20
200      60
100      50
300      10
400      40
200      30
300      10


<Run of Program 12.4>


Sales person 300    Total Units Sold 70
Sales person 100    Total Units Sold 95
Sales person 200    Total Units Sold 110
Sales person 400    Total Units Sold 40
*/
```

ARRAY ITERATOR

When looking to bind iterators to list classes, we may overlook the Array class because of ready access to the index operator. In fact, an Array iterator is a useful abstraction. By initializing the iterator to begin and end at a particular element, the use of indices is eliminated from the application. Furthermore, multiple iterators can simultaneously traverse the same array. We provide an example of multiple iterators by merging two sorted runs held in the same array.

ARRAYITERATOR CLASS SPECIFICATION

DECLARATION

```
#include "iterator.h"

template <class T>
class ArrayIterator: public Iterator<T>
{
    private:
      // current location, starting and ending points
      int currentIndex;
      int startIndex;
      int finishIndex;

      // address of the Array object that we must traverse
      Array<T> *arr;
    public:
      // constructor
      ArrayIterator(Array<T>& A,int start=0,int finish=-1);
```

```
                    // standard iterator operations required by base class
                    virtual void Next(void);
                    virtual void Reset(void);
                    virtual T& Data(void);
          };
```

DISCUSSION

The constructor binds an Array object to the iterator and initializes the starting and finishing indices of the array. The starting value defaults to 0, which sets the iterator at the first array element. The finishing index has a default value of -1 indicating that the client accepts the index of the last item in the array as the upper bound. At any point in the iteration, currentIndex is the index of the current array element. The index is given an initial value of startIndex. The ArrayIterator class is found in the file "arriter.h".

The Array iterator has the minimum set of public member functions that override the pure virtual functions in the base class.

EXAMPLE

```
          // array of 50 floating point numbers in the range 0 to 49
          Array<double> A(50);

          // array iterator scans A over the index range 3 to 10
          ArrayIterator<double> arriter(Arr,3,10);

          // print array elements with indices 3 .. 10.
          for (arriter.Reset();!arriter.EndOfList();arriter.Next())
             cout << arriter.Data() << " ";
```

APPLICATION: MERGING SORTED RUNS

Chapter 14 makes a formal study of sorting algorithms including an external merge sort that orders a data file on disk. This algorithm takes a list of elements and separates them into sorted sublists called **runs.**

Definition:

In a list X_0, X_1, ..., X_{n-1}, the sublist X_a, X_{a+1}, ..., X_b is a run provided

$$X_i \leq X_{i+1} \quad \text{for } a \leq i < b$$
$$X_{a-1} > X_a \quad \text{if } a > 0$$
$$X_{b+1} < X_b \quad \text{if } b < n - 1$$

Example: the sublist X_2 ... X_5 is a run in array X

X: 20 35   15 25 30 65   50 70 10

The merging process folds the runs together to create even longer ordered sublists until we finally arrive at a sorted list.

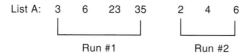

This application covers a very limited portion of the full algorithm. We assume the data are stored as two runs in an N-element array. The first run spans the range 0 to $R - 1$ and the second run spans the range R to $N - 1$. For instance, in the seven-element array A, the runs split at index $R = 4$.

An item-by-item merge of the runs produces the sorted list. We establish the current traversal location at the beginning of each run. Compare the values at the current locations and copy the smallest value to an array. When a value from a run is used, move forward to the next value in the run and continue the comparisons. Since the sublists are initially ordered, we copy elements to the output array in sorted order. When one run is exhausted, copy the remaining items from the other run to the output array.

This algorithm is elegantly implemented using three iterators, left, right, and output. The iterator left traverses the first run, right traverses the second, and output is used to assign data values to the output array. Figure 12.2 illustrates the algorithm for selected items in the sample data.

Program 12.5   Merging Sorted Runs

The function Merge takes two runs stored in an Array object A and merges them into the local Array object Out. This process uses iterators left and right that are initialized by the parameters lowIndex, endofRunIndex, and highIndex. The iterator output is used to assign the sorted data to Out. The comparison process terminates when we reach an end of a run. The function Copy appends the data from the remaining run to the array Out. After resetting the iterator for the output array, we copy the sorted list back to the A.

This program reads a list of 20 integer values from the file "rundata". During input, we store the data in array A and identify the end of run index that will be used by the Merge function. Merge is called to sort the array, and it is printed.

```
#include <iostream.h>
#include <fstream.h>

#include "array.h"
#include "arriter.h"

// copy values in one array to another by using their iterators
void Copy(ArrayIterator<int>& Source, ArrayIterator<int>& Dest)
```

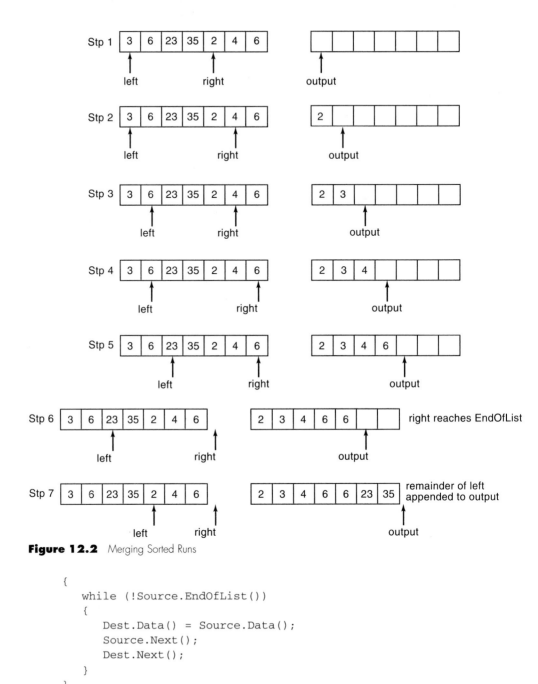

Figure 12.2 Merging Sorted Runs

```
{
    while (!Source.EndOfList())
    {
        Dest.Data() = Source.Data();
        Source.Next();
        Dest.Next();
    }
}

// merge the sorted runs in array A. the first run spans indices
// lowIndex..endOfRun-1 and the second endOfRun..highIndex
```

```
void Merge(Array<int>& A,int lowIndex, int endOfRunIndex,
           int highIndex)
{
    // array in which the runs are combined. has same size as In
    Array<int> Out(A.ListSize());

    // left traverses 1st run, right traverses 2nd
    ArrayIterator<int> left(A,lowIndex,endOfRunIndex-1);
    ArrayIterator<int> right(A,endOfRunIndex,highIndex);

    // output puts sorted data to Out.
    ArrayIterator<int> output(Out);

    // copy until we hit the end of one or both runs
    while (!left.EndOfList() && !right.EndOfList())
    {
        // if left run data value smaller or equal, assign it to
        // Out. advance to next left run element
        if(left.Data() <= right.Data())
        {
            output.Data() = left.Data();
            left.Next();
        }
        // assign data from right run and advance right
        else
        {
            output.Data() = right.Data();
            right.Next();
        }
        output.Next();              // advance output
    }

    // if one of the runs is not complete, copy it to Out
    if (!left.EndOfList())
        Copy(left,output);
    else if (!right.EndOfList())
        Copy(right,output);

    // reset the iterator for Out and copy from Out to A
    output.Reset();

    ArrayIterator<int> final(A);   // use for copying back to A.

    Copy(output, final);
}

void main(void)
```

```
{
    // array to contain the sorted runs read from stream fin
    Array<int> A(20);
    ifstream fin;
    int i;
    int endOfRun = 0;

    // open data file "rundata"
    fin.open("rundata", ios::in | ios::nocreate);
    if (!fin)
    {
        cerr << "Cannot open the file 'rundata'" << endl;
        exit(1);
    }

    // read 20 data values in two sorted runs
    fin >> A[0];

    for(i=1;i < 20;i++)
    {
        fin >> A[i];
        if (A[i] < A[i-1])
            endOfRun = i;
    }

    // merge runs A [0]..A[endOfRun-1] and A[endOfRun]..A[19]
    Merge(A,0,endOfRun,19);

    // print the sorted runs, 10 data values per line
    for(i=0;i < 20;i++)
    {
        cout << A[i] << "   ";
        if (i == 9)
            cout << endl;
    }
    cout << endl;
}

/*
<File "rundata">

1 3 6 9 12 23 33 45 55 68 88 95
2 8 12 25 33 48 55 75

<Run of Program 12.5>

1 2 3 6 8 9 12 12 23 25
33 33 45 48 55 55 68 75 88 95
*/
```

ARRAYITERATOR IMPLEMENTATION

The constructor sets up the initial state of the iterator. It binds the iterator to the array and initializes the three indices. If startIndex and finishIndex use default values (0 and −1), the iterator ranges over the entire array.

```
// constructor. initialize the base class and data members
template <class T>
ArrayIterator<T>::ArrayIterator(Array<T>& A,int start,
                                int finish): arr(&A)
{
   // last available array index
   int ilast = A.ListSize() - 1;

   // initialize index values. if finish == -1,
   // traverse whole array
   currentIndex = startIndex = start;
   finishIndex = finish != -1 ? finish : ilast;

   // indices must be in range of array
   if (!((startIndex>=0 && startIndex<=ilast) &&
        (finishIndex>=0 && finishIndex<=ilast) &&
        (startIndex <= finishIndex)))
   {
      cerr << "ArrayIterator: Index parameter incorrect!"
         << endl;
      exit(1);
   }
}
```

Reset reassigns the current index to the starting point and indicates that a new traversal is beginning by initializing iterationComplete to 0.

```
// reset to the start of the array
template <class T>
void ArrayIterator<T>::Reset(void)
{
   // set current index to starting traversal index
    currentIndex = startIndex;

   // the iteration is not complete yet
   iterationComplete = 0;
}
```

The method **Data** uses currentIndex to access the data item. If the current traversal location is past the end of list, the method generates an error message and terminates the program.

```
// return the value of the current array element
template <class T>
T& ArrayIterator<T>::Data(void)
{
    // can't call Data if we have traversed entire array
    if(iterationComplete)
    {
        cerr << "Iterator has passed the end of the list!"
            << endl;
        exit(1);
    }


    return (*arr) [currentIndex];
}
```

If the iteration is complete, Next simply returns; otherwise, it increments currentIndex and updates the logical base class variable iterationComplete.

```
// advance to the next array element
template <class T>
void ArrayIterator<T>::Next (void)
{
    // if iteration is not complete, increment currentIndex
    // if it passes finishIndex, the iteration is complete
    if (!iterationComplete)
    {
        currentIndex++;
        if(currentIndex > finishIndex)
            iterationComplete = 1;
    }
}
```

12.6 Ordered Lists

The SeqList class creates a list whose items are added at the rear of the list. The resulting list does not have any particular order. In many applications, a client wants to use a list structure with the added condition that items are stored in order. In this way, the application can efficiently determine when an item is not in a list or output the items as a sorted list.

To create an ordered list, we use SeqList as a base class and develop the derived OrderedList class that inserts items in ascending order using the "<" operator. This is a powerful example of inheritance in action. We redefine only the Insert method since all other list operations do not affect ordering and can be inherited from the base class.

ORDEREDLIST CLASS SPECIFICATION

DECLARATION

```
#include "seqlist2.h"

template <class T>
class OrderedList: public SeqList<T>
{
   public:
      // constructor
      OrderedList(void);

      // override Insert to form ordered list.
      virtual void Insert (const T& item);
};
```

DESCRIPTION

All list operations except Insert are taken directly from SeqList since they do not alter the ordering. Only Insert must be defined since it overrides the SeqList Insert method. It traverses the list and inserts an item into the list at a position that maintains the order.

The OrderedList class is contained in the file "ordlist.h".

ORDEREDLIST CLASS IMPLEMENTATION

The OrderedList class defines a constructor that simply calls the SeqList constructor. This initializes the base class and, in turn, initializes the List base class. We have an example of a three-class hierarchy chain.

```
// constructor. initialize the base class
template <class T>
OrderedList<T>::OrderedList(void): SeqList<T>()
{}
```

The class defines a new Insert function that places an item in the list at the proper location. The new Insert method uses the built-in traversal mechanism of the LinkedList class to search for the first data value that is larger than the new item. InsertAt is used to place the new value in the linked list at the current location. If the new value is larger than all existing values, the data value is appended to the list. The Insert method is responsible for incrementing the size variable in the base class List.

```
// insert item into the list in ascending order
template <class T>
```

```
void OrderedList<T>::Insert(const T& item)
{
   // use the linked list traversal mechanism to locate the
   // insertion point
   for(llist.Reset();!llist.EndOfList();llist.Next())
      if (item < llist.Data())
         break;

   // insert item at the current list location
   llist.InsertAt(item);
   size++;
}
```

Application: Long Runs   Program 12.5 described that portion of the merge sort algorithm that included merging two sorted runs into a single sorted run. The program assumed that our input data were preprocessed into two runs. In this application we discuss techniques that filter (preprocess) data to generate longer runs.

Assume that a large block of data is stored in random order in an array or on disk. In this form, the data likely consists of a series of short runs. For instance, the following 15-character data set consists of eight runs.

```
CharArray: [a k] [g] [c m t] [e n] [l] [c r s] [c] [b f]
```

An attempt to use a merge sort to order the data would be initially frustrated by the number of short runs that would have to be combined. In our example, four merges combine the short runs.

```
[a g k] [c e m n t] [c l r s] [b c f]
```

The merge sort requires us to combine four runs into two in the next pass and then finally create a sorted list when the resulting runs are merged. The algorithm would be improved if the data were initialized to have reasonably long runs. This could be accomplished by scanning the items and collecting them into sorted sublists. An external sort algorithm must contend with relatively slow disk access times and thus often includes a filter to preprocess the data. We must be careful that the time spent filtering the data improves the overall efficiency of the algorithm.

An ordered list provides a simple example of a filter. Assume an initial array or file contains N elements. We insert each group of k elements into an ordered list and copy the list back to the array. The filter guarantees that runs will be at least k elements long. For instance, assume k is 5 and we process the characters in CharArray. The resulting runs are:

```
[a c g k m]   [c e l n t]   [b c f r s]
```

An improved version of this filter is developed with heaps in Chapter 13.

Program 12.6 Long Runs

This program filters an array of 100 random integers in the range of 100 to 999 into runs of at least 25 elements using an ordered list. Each new random number is inserted in OrderedList object L. For every 25 elements, the Copy function deletes the elements from list L and inserts them back into array A. The program concludes by printing the resulting array A.

```cpp
#include <iostream.h>

#include "ordlist.h"
#include "array.h"
#include "arriter.h"
#include "random.h"


// traverse an integer Array and print each item
// 10 integers per line
void PrintList(Array<int>& A)
{
    // use the Array iterator
    ArrayIterator<int> iter(A);
    int    count;

    // traverse the list and print
    count = 1;
    for(iter.Reset();!iter.EndOfList();iter.Next(), count++)
    {
        cout << iter.Data() << "   ";
        // print the list, 10 data values per line
        if (count % 10 == 0)
            cout << endl;
    }
}

// delete items from ordered list L and insert into array A.
// update loadIndex which identifies the next index in A
void Copy(OrderedList<int> &L, Array<int> &A, int &loadIndex)
{
    while (!L.ListEmpty())
        A[loadIndex++] = L.DeleteFront();
}

void main(void)
{
    // create runs in A by using ordered list L
    Array<int>  A(100);
    OrderedList<int> L;
```

```
    // random number generator
    RandomNumber rnd;

    int i, loadIndex = 0;

    // generate 100 random numbers in range 100 to 999. filter
    // them through a 25 element ordered list. when the list
    // fills, copy the elements to array A using Copy
    for (i = 1; i <= 100; i++)
    {
        L.Insert(rnd.Random(900) + 100);
        if (i % 25 == 0)
            Copy(L,A,loadIndex);
    }
    // print the final array A containing the runs
    PrintList(A);
}


/*
<Run of Program 12.6>

110  116  149  152  162  240  345  370  422  492
500  532  578  601  715  730  732  754  815  833
850  903  929  947  958  105  132  139  139  190
205  216  221  243  287  348  350  445  466  507
513  524  604  634  641  730  784  940  969  982
296  375  412  437  457  466  507  550  594  652
725  728  771  799  803  815  859  879  909  915
940  990  991  992  994  101  118  123  155  310
343  368  372  434  443  489  515  529  557  574
641  739  774  784  829  875  883  922  967  972
*/
```

12.7 Heterogeneous Lists

A collection that stores objects of the same data type is referred to as a **homogeneous** collection. Up to this point in the book, our collections have all been homogeneous. In contrast, a collection that holds objects of different types is **heterogeneous.** Since the type of C++ data structures is determined at compilation time, we must introduce new programming techniques to implement heterogeneous collections. In this section, we implement heterogeneous arrays and linked lists by assuming that every object in the list is derived from a common base class.

HETEROGENEOUS ARRAYS

A fully general discussion of heterogeneous arrays is beyond the scope of this book. We limit our discussion to arrays of pointers to different objects. In this process, we revisit an example from Chapter 1 that illustrated polymorphism. For convenience, the example is restated:

> There is a set of basic operations that must be done when painting any house. In addition, each different type of house requires special techniques that are unique to the type of house. For instance, you may sand the siding on a wood frame house and wash the siding on a vinyl-sided house. In the context of object-oriented programming, the houses represent different classes derived from the base class House that contains common painting operations. The method, called Paint, is associated with each class.

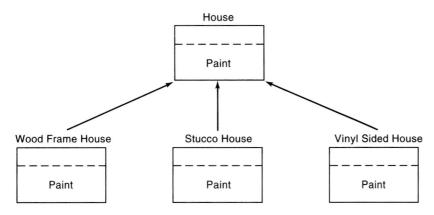

The base class House contains the identification string "House" along with a virtual Paint method that prints the string. Each derived class overrides this Paint method and indicates the type of house being painted.

```
// base class for house painting hierarchy
class House
{
    private:
        String id;         // id for House
    public:
        // constructor. initialize id to "House"
        House(void)
        {
            id = "House";
        }

        // virtual method. prints the string "House"
        virtual void Paint(void)
        {
            cout << id;
        }
};
```

Each derived class contains a string identifying the type of house. The virtual Paint method prints the string and calls the base class Paint method. The declaration of WoodFrameHouse is a model. A complete description of the house classes is contained in file "houses.h".

```
class WoodFrameHouse: public House
{
    private:
        // id for WoodFrameHouse
        String id;
    public:
        // constructor. assign id = "Wood Frame"
        WoodFrameHouse(void): House()
        {
            id = "Wood Frame";
        }

        // virtual method. print id and call Paint in base class
        virtual void Paint(void)
        {
            cout << "Painting a " << id << " ";
            House::Paint();
        }
};
```

To describe the concept of a heterogeneous array, we define an array contractorList that consists of five pointers to the base class House. The array is initialized by randomly selecting from classes WoodFrameHouse, StuccoHouse, and VinylSidedHouse and assigning a derived house object to each pointer in the array. For example, the following is a list of five houses determined by contractorList.

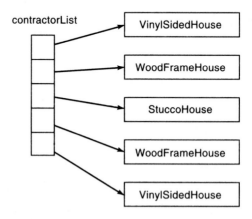

We can think of the array of pointers as being a list of five addresses that identify homes to be painted. The contractor assigns crews to do the work. In our example the contractor assigns a house address to each crew and assumes they will carry out the correct Paint operation once they arrive at the house and see its type.

Program 12.7 Heterogeneous Array

This program traverses the array contractorList of pointers and calls the Paint method for each object. Since each object is referenced by a pointer, dynamic binding ensures that the Paint method for the correct class is executed. This corresponds to the contractor assigning crews to go to the houses on the list and paint them.

```cpp
#include <iostream.h>

#include "random.h"     // include random number generator
#include "houses.h"     // including the painting hierarchy

void main(void)
{
    // dynamic list of House addresses
    House *contractorList[5];
    RandomNumber rnd;

    // construct the list of 5 houses to be painted
    for (int i=0;i < 5;i++)
        // randomly choose house type 0, 1, 2, create the object,
        // and assign its address in contractorList.
        switch(rnd.Random(3))
        {
            case 0: contractorList[i] = new WoodFrameHouse;
                    break;
            case 1: contractorList[i] = new StuccoHouse;
                    break;
            case 2: contractorList[i] = new VinylSidedHouse;
                    break;
        }

    // paint houses using method Paint. Since it is virtual,
    // dynamic binding is used and the correct method is called
    for (i=0;i < 5;i++)
        contractorList[i]->Paint();
}

/*
<Run of Program 12.7>

Painting a Wood Frame House
Painting a Stucco House
Painting a Vinyl Sided House
Painting a Stucco House
Painting a Wood Frame House
*/
```

HETEROGENEOUS LINKED LISTS

Like heterogeneous arrays, each object in the heterogeneous list structure is derived from a common base class. Each base portion of a class object contains a pointer to the next object in the list. Using polymorphism, the pointer is used to execute methods in the derived object, regardless of its type.

We illustrate these concepts by developing a linked list of geometric objects that are derived from a node type variant of the Shape class.

— —

NODESHAPE CLASS SPECIFICATION

DECLARATION

```
#include "graphlib.h"

// Base class Shape
class NodeShape
{
    protected:
      // coordinates of the base point, fill pattern and pointer
      // to the next node
      float x, y;
      int fillpat;
      NodeShape *next;

    public:
      // constructor
      NodeShape(float h = 0, float v = 0, int fill = 0);

      // virtual drawing function
      virtual void Draw(void) const;

      // list handling methods
      void InsertAfter(NodeShape *p);
      NodeShape *DeleteAfter(void);
      NodeShape *Next(void);
};
```

DESCRIPTION

The coordinates (x,y) provide the base point for a derived object that is to be drawn with the fill pattern fillpat. Shape contains a Draw method that initializes the graphic system's fill pattern and a pointer field next that points to the succeeding Shape object in the linked list. Methods InsertAfter and DeleteAfter maintain a circular list by inserting or deleting a node following the current one, and method Next returns the pointer to the following node.

The NodeShape class is contained in the file "shapelst.h".

NODESHAPE CLASS IMPLEMENTATION

The implementation of the NodeShape follows the model of the CNode class in Chapter 9. Since we assume a circular list, the constructor must initialize a node to point to itself.

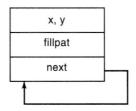

```
// constructor. initialize base point, fill pattern, and set
// node to point to itself
NodeShape::NodeShape(float h, float v, int fill):
                    x(h), y(v), fillpat(fill)
{
    next = this;
}
```

Deriving Linked Geometric Classes   The geometric classes CircleFigure and RectangleFigure can be derived from the NodeShape class. In addition to the base class methods, these classes provide a Draw method by overriding the virtual method Draw in the base class. Area and perimeter methods are not included. We use the CircleFigure class to illustrate the concepts.

```
// CircleFigure is derived from NodeShape base class
class CircleFigure: public NodeShape
{
    protected:
      // radius of the circle
      float radius;

    public:
      // constructor
      CircleFigure(float h, float v, float r, int fill);

      // virtual drawing function. draws a circle
      virtual void Draw(void) const;
};

// constructor. initialize base class and radius
CircleFigure::CircleFigure(float h, float v, float r, int fill):
            NodeShape(h,v,fill), radius(r)
{}
```

```
// set fill pattern by calling base class Draw and draw circle
void CircleFigure::Draw(void) const
{
    NodeShape::Draw();
    DrawCircle(x,y,radius);
}
```

We also include in "shapelst.h" a new geometric class RightTriangle, which describes a right triangle determined by the leftmost point of the hypotenuse, its base, and its height.

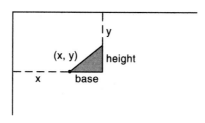

To form a linked list, declare a NodeShape header called listHeader. Beginning with the header, dynamically create nodes and append each one to the end of the list using InsertAfter. For instance, the following iteration creates a four-node list that interleaves circle and right triangle objects:

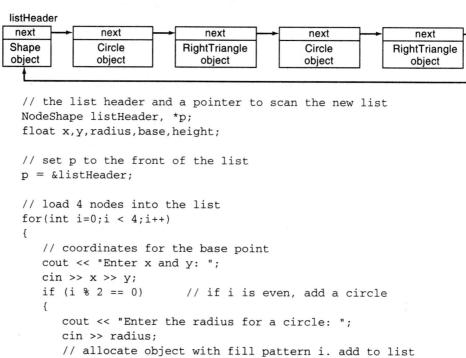

```
// the list header and a pointer to scan the new list
NodeShape listHeader, *p;
float x,y,radius,base,height;

// set p to the front of the list
p = &listHeader;

// load 4 nodes into the list
for(int i=0;i < 4;i++)
{
    // coordinates for the base point
    cout << "Enter x and y: ";
    cin >> x >> y;
    if (i % 2 == 0)        // if i is even, add a circle
    {
        cout << "Enter the radius for a circle: ";
        cin >> radius;
        // allocate object with fill pattern i. add to list
        p->InsertAfter(new Circle(x,y,radius,i));
```

```
   }
   else                     // i is odd. add a right triangle
   {
      cout << "Enter base and height for a right triangle: ";
      cin >> base >> height;
      p-InsertAfter(new RightTriangle(x,y,base,height,i));
   }
   // move p to the node that has just been created
   p = p->Next();
}
```

Dynamic binding is critical when traversing the list and drawing the objects. At each node in the following code segment, the pointer p actually references a Circle or RightTriangle object and Draw is a virtual function. The Draw method of the derived class is executed.

```
p = listHeader.Next();
while (p != &listHeader)
{
   p->Draw();
   p = p->Next();
}
```

We are now ready to present a complete problem in heterogeneous list creation and management.

Program 12.8 Heterogeneous Lists

This program extends the principles from the example and creates a linked list that includes objects of type Circle, Rectangle, and RightTriangle. The file "figures" designates the items in the list. A line has the following format:

```
<figure>  <base point x,y>  <figure parameters>
```

The figure is specified with a character c (circle), r (rectangle), or t (right triangle). The base point is a pair of floating point numbers; parameters include a radius or sides. For example, the following are sample input parameters for each of the figures:

```
c 0.5 0.5 0.25        // circle with center at (1/2,1/2)
                      // and radius 1/4
r 1.0 0.25 .5 .5      // rectangle with base at (1,1/4)
                      // and sides 1/2, 1/2
t 2.0 0.75 .25 .5     // right triangle with base at (2,3/4)
                      // and sides 1/4, 1/2
```

The program reads the file and forms a linked list of geometric objects. During traversal of the list, the figures are drawn.

```cpp
#include <iostream.h>
#include <fstream.h>
#include <stdlib.h>

#include "graphlib.h"
#include "shapelst.h"

void main(void)
{
    // listHeader is the header for the circular list of shapes
    NodeShape listHeader, *p, *nFig;

    // figures: 'c'(circle),'r'(rectangle),'t'(right triangle)
    char figType;

    // starting fill pattern is no fill
    int pat = 0;
    float x, y, radius, length, width, tb, th;

    // read figure data from stream fin
    ifstream fin;

    // open the file "figures" containing the figure data
    fin.open("figures",ios::in | ios::nocreate);
    if (!fin)
    {
        cerr << "Cannot open 'figures'" << endl;
        exit(1);
    }

    // set p to point to list header
    p = &listHeader;

    // read until end of file and build linked list of figures
    while(!fin.eof())
    {
        // read figure type and base point
        fin >> figType;
        if (fin.eof())
            break;
        fin >> x >> y;

        // build the particular figure
        switch(figType)
        {
```

```
        case 'c':
            // read radius and insert circle
            fin >> radius;
            nFig = new CircleFigure(x,y,radius,pat);
            p->InsertAfter(nFig);
            break;
        case 'r':
            // read length and width and insert rectangle
            fin >> length >> width;
            nFig = new RectangleFigure(x,y,length,width,pat);
            p->InsertAfter(nFig);
            break;
        case 't':
            // read base and height and insert right triangle
            fin >> tb >> th;
            nFig = new RightTriangleFigure(x,y,tb,th,pat);
            p->InsertAfter(nFig);
            break;
        }

        // increment fill pattern. advance pointer to list rear
        pat = (pat+1) % 12;
        p = p->Next();
    }

    // initialize the graphics system
    InitGraphics();

    // start at 1st figure, chain the list and draw each one
    p = listHeader.Next();
    while (p != &listHeader)
    {
        p->Draw();
        p = p->Next();
    }

    // pause to view figures and shut down the graphics system
    ViewPause();
    ShutdownGraphics();
}

/*

<Run of Program 12.8>
    <graphic here>


*/
```

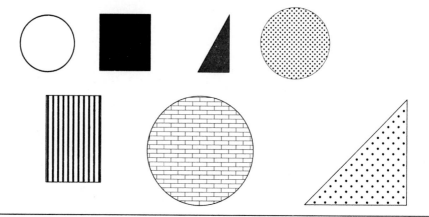

Written Exercises

12.1 (a) Using the animal hierarchy in Section 12.1 as a model, develop a hierarchy tree for the following:

Vehicle, Automobile, Diesel, Gas, Airplane, Electric, Propeller, Jet

(b) Give the base classes for Electric, for Jet.

(c) List all the classes that are both base and derived classes.

(d) What are derived classes for Vehicle?

12.2 Use the following declarations

```
class BASE
{
    private:
        Base_Priv;
    protected:
        Base_Prot;
    public:
        Base_Pub;
};

class DERIVED: public BASE
{
    private:
        Derived_Priv;
    protected:
        Derived_Prot;
    public:
        Derived_Pub;
};
```

(a) The base and derived classes each contain private, protected, and public members. Fill in the table to indicate access rights of a client or an object to members. An "X" in a row indicates that the object has access to the member. For instance, in (a), a derived object has access to a protected member of the base class and a client has access to a public member of a base class.

	Base_Priv	Base_Prot	Base_Pub	Derived_Priv	Derived_Prot	Derived_Pub
BASE						
DERIVED		X				
CLIENT			X			

(b) A class can be derived using **private** inheritance. In this case, all the public and protected members of the base class are available to the derived class. However, to a client of the derived class, the public members of the base class are considered private and are not accessible. This type of inheritance is sometimes applied when the base class is used merely as an implementation vehicle for the derived class. Complete the table for this type of inheritance.

	Base_Priv	Base_Prot	Base_Pub	Derived_Priv	Derived_Prot	Derived_Pub
BASE						
DERIVED						
CLIENT						

12.3 You are given the outline of class Base. Explain what is wrong with each derived class declaration.

```
class Base
{
    ...
  public:
     Base(int a, int b);
     ...
};
```

(a)
```
class DerivedCL1: public Base
{
  private:
     int q;
```

```
            public:
                DerivedCL1(int z): q(z)
                {}
                ...
        };
```

(b)

```
        class DerivedCL2: public Base
        {
            private:
                ...
            public:
                // DerivedCL2 has no constructor
                ...
        };
```

12.4 Consider the following outline for a base and derived class:

```
    class BaseCL
    {
        protected:
            int data1;
            int data2;
        public:
            BaseCL(int a, int b = 0): data1(a), data2(b)
            {}

            BaseCL(void): data1(0), data2(0)
            {}
                ...
    };

    class DerivedCL
    {
        private:
            int data3;
        public:
            // constructor ONE
            DerivedCL(int a,int b,int c = 0);
            // constructor TWO
            DerivedCL(int a);
                ...
    };
```

(a) Write constructor ONE so that *a* is assigned to the derived class and *b* and *c* are assigned to the base class.

(b) Write constructor TWO so that *a* is assigned to the derived class and the default constructor for the base class is used.

(c) Assuming the definition of the constructors for the DerivedCL class, give the values of data1, data2, and data3 in the following objects:

```
DerivedCL obj1(1,2), obj2(3,4,5), obj3(8);
```

12.5 The following program illustrates the order of execution of constructors and destructors in an inheritance chain. The three classes Base1, Base2, and Derived each have a constructor and a destructor. Give the output of the program.

```cpp
#include <iostream.h>

class Base1
{
   public:
      Base1(void)
      {
         cout << "Base1 constructor called." << endl;
      }

      ~Base1(void)
      {
         cout << "Base1 destructor called." << endl;
      }
};

class Base2
{
   public:
      Base2(void)
      {
         cout << "Base2 constructor called." << endl;
      }

      ~Base2(void)
      {
         cout << "Base2 destructor called." << endl;
      }
};

class Derived: public Base1, public Base2
{
   public:
      Derived(void): Base1(), Base2()
      {
          cout << "Derived class constructor called." <<
          endl;
      }
```

```
            ~Derived(void)
            {
                cout << "Derived class destructor called." <<
                endl;
            }
        };

        void main(void)
        {
            Derived objD;
            {
                Base1 objB1;
                {
                    Base2 objB2;
                }
            }
        }
```

12.6 Consider the following inheritance chain:

```
class Base
{
    ...
    public:
        void F(void);
        void G(int x);
    ...
};

class Derived: public Base
{
    ...
    public:
        void F(void);
        void G(float x);
    ...
};

void Derived::G(float x)
{
    ...
    Base::G(10);   // use scope operator in member function
    ...
};
```

For the declaration

```
Derived OBJ;
```

(a) How does the client reference the function F in the base class?
(b) How does the client reference the function F in the derived class?
(c) How does the compiler respond to the statement OBJ.G(20)?
    Note: As we stated in Section 12.5, it is not good practice to create class structures like this one where a nonvirtual function is overridden in the derived class.

12.7 Section 12.2 builds the inheritance chain consisting of the abstract base class Shape and the Circle class. The following program uses the classes. Read the program and answer the questions that follow.

```
#include <iostream.h>

#include "graphlib.h"
#include "geometry.h"

void main(void)
{
    Circle C;

    C.SetPoint(1,2);
    C.SetRadius(0.5);
    cout << C.GetX() << " " << C.GetY() << endl;

    C.SetPoint(C.GetX(),3);
    cout << C.GetX() << " " << C.GetY() << endl;
    C.SetFill(11);

    InitGraphics();
    C.Draw();
    ViewPause();
    ShutdownGraphics();
}
```

(a) Explain why GetX can be called from the derived class.
(b) Explain why x can be referenced inside the definition of the method Draw.
(c) What is the output of the program?
(d) Explain why the statement

```
    C.SetPoint(3,5);
```

is legal but the statements

```
    C.x = 3;
    C.y = 5;
```

are not.

12.8 What is the output of the program?

```cpp
#include <iostream.h>
#include <string.h>

class Base
{
    private:
        char msg[30];
    protected:
        int n;
    public:
        Base(char s[], int m = 0): n(m)
        {
            strcpy(msg,s);
        }

        void output(void)
        {
            cout << n << endl << msg << endl;
        }
};

class Derived1: public Base
{
    private:
        int n;
    public:
        Derived1(int m = 1):Base("Base",m-1),n(m)
        {}

        void output(void)
        {
            cout << n << endl;
            Base::output();
        }
};

class Derived2: public Derived1
{
    private:
        int n;
    public:
        Derived2(int m = 2):Derived1(m-1),n(m)
        {}
        void output(void)
        {
```

```
            cout << n << endl;
            Derived1::output();
        }
};

void main(void)
{
    Base B("Base Class",1);
    Derived2 D;

    B.output();
    D.output();
}
```

12.9 Explain why the Area and Circumference methods in the Shape class are pure virtual functions.

12.10 Consider the class declarations:

```
class Base
{
    private:
        int x,y;
    ...
};

class Derived: public Base
{
    private:
        int z;
    ...
};
```

For the declarations:

```
Base B;
Derived D;
```

(a) Is the assignment

```
    B = D;
```

legal? Why? Draw a picture illustrating your answer.

(b) Is the assignment

```
    D = B;
```

legal? Why? Draw a picture illustrating your answer.

12.11 Consider the following classes:

```
class BaseCL
{
    protected:
        int one;
    public:
        BaseCL(int a): one(a)
        {}

        virtual void Identify(void)
        {
            cout << one << endl;
        }
};

class DerivedCL: public BaseCL
{
    protected:
        int two;
    public:
        DerivedCL(int a, int b): BaseCL(a), two(b)
        {}

        virtual void Identify(void)
        {
            cout << one << " " << two << endl;
        }
};
```

and the functions:

```
void Announce1(BaseCL x)
{
    x.Identify();
}

void Announce2(BaseCL& x)
{
    x.Identify();
}

void Announce3(BaseCL *x)
{
    x->Identify();
}
```

Give the output from the code segment:

```
BaseCL A(7), *p, *arr[3];
DerivedCL B(3,5), C(2,4);
```

```
    Announce1(A);
    Announce1(C);
    Announce2(B);
    Announce3(&C);
    p = &C;
    p->Identify();
    for(int i=0;i < 3;i++)
        if (i == 1)
            arr[i] = new BaseCL(7);
        else
            arr[i] = new DerivedCL(i,i+1);
    for(i=0;i < 3;i++)
        arr[i]->Identify();
```

12.12 Explain why the destructor should be declared virtual in any class that may serve as a base class.

12.13 Develop an abstract base class StackBase that declares the stack operations Push, Pop, Peek, and StackEmpty. The base class must contain the protected integer variable numElements and define the method StackEmpty to return the value of this variable. A derived Stack class must increment numElements with each Push operation and decrement it for each Pop operation. Implement a derived class Stack in two different ways using an array and a linked list.

12.14 Using the model from Written Exercise 12.13, develop an abstract class QueueBase that describes a queue. The class must contain at least one method that is not pure virtual.

12.15 What is an iterator? Why does an iterator often have to be a friend of the class whose data elements it traverses? What does it mean to say an iterator is a control abstraction?

12.16 Develop the Queue class by deriving it from the abstract class QueueBase in Written Exercise 12.14 and using an SeqList object included by composition. Make the class QueueIterator a friend, and derive the class QueueIterator from SeqListIterator. All that is needed is a constructor.

12.17 Implement the function

```
    template <class T>
    T GetRear(Queue<T>& q);
```

that returns the element at the rear of the queue. If the queue is empty, print an error message and terminate the program. Use the QueueIterator developed in Written Exercise 12.16.

12.18 Assume you have an Array of String objects. Use an ArrayIterator to traverse the list and replace all tab characters by four spaces.

12.19 Write a function

```
    void RemoveDuplicates(Array<int>& A);
```

that removes all duplicate data values from the array and resizes the object accordingly. For instance, if A is initially the 20-element array

```
    A = {1,3,5,3,2,3,1,4,6,3,5,4,2,6,7,8,1,3,9,7},
```

after calling RemoveDuplicates

```
A = {1 3 5 2 4 6 7 8 9}   (A.ListSize() = 9)
```

Use at least two ArrayIterator objects, one to specify the location for a unique data value and the other to scan to the end of the array.

12.20   Implement a function

```
template <class T>
T Max(Iterator<T>& collIter);
```

that finds the maximum value of the data contained in the collection for which collIter is an iterator. Assume that the operator ">" is defined for type T. Note that this function makes use of the fact that the iterator methods are virtual.

12.21   Show how we can exploit virtual functions to form an array of pointers to Circle and Rectangle objects (heterogeneous array) and traverse the array, printing the area and perimeter of the figures.

Programming Exercises

12.1   Implement the inheritance hierarchy of Written Exercise 12.1. Each class constructor must contain an Identify method that prints information about its base classes and itself. Write a test program that declares objects of each class type.

12.2   A box can be derived from a rectangle.

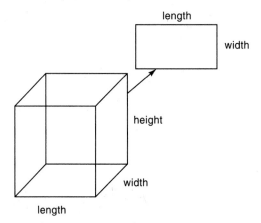

Write classes Rectangle and Box which implement the inheritance chain. The Rectangle class has an area function and a volume function that returns 0. The Box class has an area and a volume function. Test your classes by using them in a main program that prompts for the type of figure and relevant dimensions. Define an object of each type and print the area and volume of the figure.

12.3   Use the SeqList class to derive the class MidList with declaration

```
template <class T>
class MidList: public SeqList<T>
{
```

```
    public:
        <constructor>
        virtual void Insert(const T& elt);
        virtual void Delete(const T& elt);
    };
```

The method Insert places elt in the middle of the list. Delete removes an item from the middle of the list. The Delete operation assumes the user checks the list size to ensure that an element is present. Develop the implementation of MidList and use it in the following test program:

Read five integers and insert them in the list with Insert. Print the list. Delete two integers from the list and again print out the list and the list size.

12.4 This exercise develops an inheritance structure for a problem in data processing. The class Employee contains data items name and ssn, a constructor, and the operation PrintEmployeeInfo that prints the name and ssn fields. The data associated with a salaried employee includes a fixed monthly salary in addition to the base class data. The derived class SalaryEmployee contains the salary and the PrintEmployeeInfo operation that prints the employee data in both the base and derived classes. In addition to information from the base class Employee, temporary employee data includes an hourly pay rate and the hours worked in a given month. The information is stored in a TempEmployee class, which consists of the data items hourlypay and hoursworked and the operation PrintEmployeeInfo.

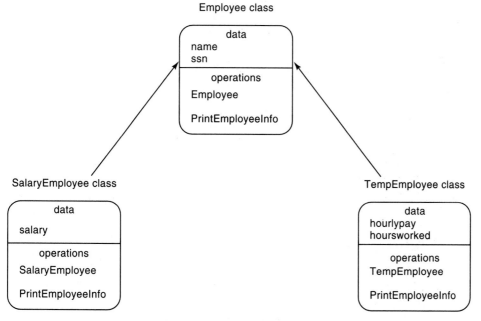

Implement this hierarchy and place it in the file "employee.h". Write a main program that declares an object for a salaried and a temporary employee and calls PrintEmployeeInfo for each object.

12.5 Create a new implementation of Array as a class derived from the abstract List class. You must deal with an important structural problem. The underlying List class has defined a series of pure virtual methods that must be overridden in the derived Array class. Some methods may not have meaning or purpose in the derived class. The following table identifies the problem methods and aids in your redefinition.

```
ListSize
    Return the number of elements in the Array object.
ListEmpty
    Returns False since we assume an array is never empty.
ClearList
    Error! operation has no meaning for an Array object.
Find
    Perform a sequential search for the data element.
Insert
    Error! An array is a direct access structure. Insert
    is ambiguous for an Array object.
Delete
    Error! The operation of removing an item is ambiguous
    for an Array object.
```

Test your implementation by running Program 12.5.

12.6 Use either implementation of the Stack class developed in Written Exercise 12.13 to read a string of characters and determine if it is a palindrome.

12.7 This exercise uses the Queue and QueueIterator classes developed in Written Exercises 12.14 and 12.16. In a test program, read a list of integers until 0 is encountered, inserting the positive numbers in one queue and the negative numbers into another. Use QueueIterator objects to traverse and print the elements of each queue.

12.8 Write a program to test the function GetRear developed in Written Exercise 12.17.

12.9 In a main program, read a series of lines from a file and insert each one into an element of an Array of String objects. Use an ArrayIterator to traverse the list and replace all tab characters by four spaces. Print the modified strings. Note that this exercise uses the result from Written Exercise 12.18.

12.10 Test your implementation of the function RemoveDuplicates in Written Exercise 12.19 by running the following main program.

```
void main(void)
{
    Array<int> A(20);
    int data[] = {1,3,5,3,2,3,1,4,6,3,5,4,2,6,7,8,1,3,9,7};
    for(int i=0;i < 20;i++)
        A[i] = data[i];

    RemoveDuplicates(A);

    for(i=0;i < A.ListSize();i++)
        cout << A[i] << " ";
```

```
       cout << endl;
    }

    /*
    <Run of Program>

    1 3 5 2 4 6 7 8 9
    */
```

12.11   Define an Array<int> object containing the integers 1..10 and an SeqList<char> object whose data values are 'a' ... 'e'. Use the function Max of Written Exercise 12.20 to print the maximum value in each list.

12.12   Add the methods Area and Perimeter to classes NodeShape, CircleFigure, RectangleFigure, and RightTriangleFigure of Section 12.7. Define the methods in base class Nodeshape to return 0. Develop a program similar to Program 12.8 that creates a heterogeneous list of derived objects. The program should cycle through the list and print the area and perimeter of each figure. A second pass through the list should print the figures.

C H A P T E R 13

ADVANCED
NONLINEAR STRUCTURES

This chapter continues the development of binary trees and introduces additional nonlinear structures. In Chapter 11, trees are implemented with dynamically generated nodes. This chapter describes array-based trees that model an array as a complete binary tree. They provide powerful applications when developing heap structures and the interesting Tournament sort. We provide an extensive study of heaps and use the concept to implement the heap sort and priority queues.

Binary search trees implement lists and provide a search structure with average search time $O(\log_2 n)$. However, the efficiency deteriorates when the tree is not well balanced. We develop a new type of tree called an AVL tree, which is height balanced and maintains the good properties of a binary search tree.

Iterators are introduced in Chapter 12 and are used to implement the SeqListIterator and ArrayIterator classes. In this chapter, the concept of an iterator is extended to trees and graphs. This powerful scanning tool allows us to traverse a nonlinear structure using simple methods that are usually available only to linear lists. An inorder tree iterator is developed and adds functionality to trees. It is used to develop the treesort.

A graph is a generalized hierarchical structure that contains nodes called vertices and edges that connect pairs of vertices. Graphs are an important topic in finite mathematics and feature a series of classical algorithms that find application in the field of operations research. We conclude this chapter by developing the basic theory of graphs and designing a class that will handle a variety of applications.

Array-Based Binary Trees   13.1

In Chapter 11, we use tree nodes to build a binary tree. Each entry has a data field and left and right pointer fields that identify the left and right subtrees of the node. An empty tree is represented by a NULL pointer. Insertions and deletions are done by dynamically allocating nodes and assigning pointer fields. This representation handles trees ranging from degenerate to complete trees. In this section, we introduce a sequential (array) representation of a tree that uses an array entry to store the data and indices to identify the nodes. We derive a very powerful relationship between an array and a complete binary tree, a relationship that finds applications with heaps and priority queues.

Recall from Chapter 11 that a complete binary tree of depth n contains all possible nodes through level $n - 1$ and nodes at level n are placed left to right with no gaps. An array A is a sequential list whose items can represent nodes on a complete binary tree with root A[0]; first-level children A[1] and A[2]; second-level children A[3], A[4], A[5], and A[6]; and so forth. The root node has index 0 and the remaining nodes are assigned indices in level order. Figure 13.1 illustrates the complete tree for an array A with 10 elements.

```
int A[10] = {5, 1, 3, 9, 6, 2, 4, 7, 0, 8};
```

Although arrays find a natural tree representation, there is no straightforward representation of a general binary tree as an array. The problem lies with possible

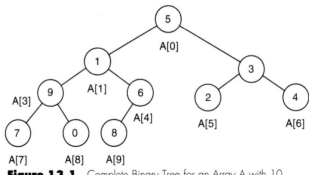

Figure 13.1   Complete Binary Tree for an Array A with 10
Elements

missing nodes that must correspond to unused array elements. In the following
example, the array includes four unused items, which is a one-third vacancy rate.
A degenerate tree with only right subtrees would be even less efficient.

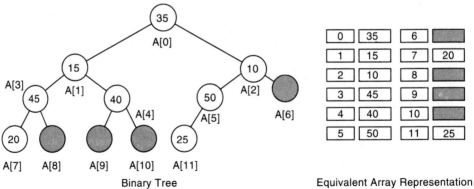

Binary Tree   Equivalent Array Representation

The power of array-based trees becomes manifest when direct access to node
data is required. There are simple index calculations that identify the children and
the parent of nodes. Table 13.1 uses the tree shown in Figure 13.1. It identifies the
nodes at each level of the tree as well as the children and parents.

For each node A[i] in an *N*-element array, the indices of the child nodes are
computed by the following formula:

Item A[i]   Left child index is $2*i + 1$
                                       undefined if $2*i + 1 \geq N$

Item A[i]   Right child index is $2*i + 2$.
                                       undefined if $2*i + 2 \geq N$

TABLE 13.1

Level	Parent	Value	Left Child	Right Child
0	0	A[0] = 5	1	2
1	1	A[1] = 1	3	4
	2	A[2] = 3	5	6
2	3	A[3] = 9	7	8
	4	A[4] = 6	9	10 = NULL
	5	A[5] = 2	11 = NULL	12 = NULL
	6	A[6] = 4	13 = NULL	14 = NULL
3	7	A[7] = 7	—	—
	8	A[8] = 0	—	—
	9	A[9] = 8	—	—

In passing from child to parent, we note that the parent for nodes A[3] and A[4] is A[1], the parent for nodes A[5] and A[6] is A[2], and so forth. In general, the formula for computing the parent of node A[i] is:

Item A[i]   Parent index is $(i - 1)/2$.
                                  undefined if $i = 0$

EXAMPLE 13.1

With array-based tree traversals, we can move down a path of children and move up a path of parents. The paths in this example traverse the following array.

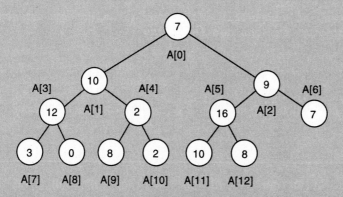

1. Start at the root and select the path of smaller children
   Path: A[0] = 7, A[2] = 9, A[6] = 7
2. Start at the root and select the path of left children
   Path: A[0] = 7, A[1] = 10, A[3] = 12, A[7] = 3

3. Start at node A[10] and select the path of parents
    Path: A[10] = 2, A[4] = 2, A[1] = 10, A[0] = 7

APPLICATION: THE TOURNAMENT SORT

Binary trees find important applications as decision trees in which each node represents a branch with two possible outcomes. One such application uses the tree to maintain a record of players competing in a single-elimination tournament. Each nonleaf node corresponds to the winner of a contest between two players. The leaf nodes give a list of the original players and their pairing in the tournament. For instance, in the tennis tournament David is the winner, beating Don in the final match. Both competitors get to the finals by winning preliminary matches. Don beats Alan and David beats Manny. The tournament pairings and outcomes are recorded as a tree.

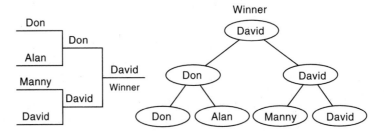

In a single-elimination tournament, we very rapidly move to a winner. For instance, with four players, the tournament involves three matches, whereas competition with $2^4 = 16$ players requires $2^4 - 1 = 15$ matches.

The tournament gives us a winner but does not clearly identify the second best player. While Don lost in the finals to the winner, he may not be the second best player. We need to give Manny a chance since he could have played a first-round match against the only player capable of beating him. To find the second best player, we must remove David and redraw the competition tree to set up a match between Don and Manny.

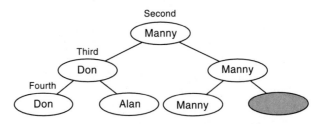

Once a winner of that match is determined, we have the correct ranking of the players.

Manny wins:	Ranking:	David Manny Don Alan
Don wins:	Ranking:	David Don Manny Alan

A tournament tree can be used to sort a list of N items. In the process we develop an efficient algorithm that makes full use of an array-based tree. Set up an array-based tree to hold the N items as leaf nodes in the bottom row of the tree. The elements are stored at level k where $2^k \geq N$. Assuming that we are sorting the list in ascending order, we compare each pair of elements and store the smaller (winner) in the parent node. The process continues until we have the smallest element (winner) in the root node. For instance, the following tree gives the initial setup for an array of $N = 8$ integers. The elements are stored at level 3 where $2^3 = 8$.

```
A[8] = {35, 25, 50, 20, 15, 45, 10, 40}
```

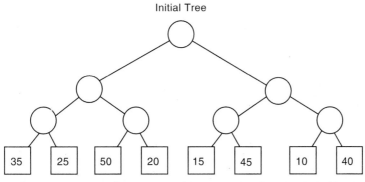

Initial Tree

At level 2, we begin to "play the matches" and locate the smaller of the pair in the parent node. For instance, Tree[7] and Tree[8] compete and the smaller value 25 is stored in Tree[3]. Comparisons are made for all pairs at level 2 and level 1. The final comparison places the smallest element in the root node at level 0.

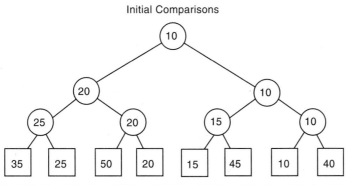

Initial Comparisons

Once the smallest element is located in the root, remove it and reassign it to the array. In the first case, reassign 10 to A[0] and then update the tree to look for the next smallest element. In the tournament model, some matches must be replayed. Since 10 was initially located in A[13], allow the first round loser A[14] = 40 to reenter in the tournament. Assign A[14] to its parent A[6], and replay matches at index 6 (15 beats 40) and at index 2 (15 beats 20). The result places 15 in the root and identifies it as the second smallest element in the list. The root can then be assigned to A[1], and the process continues.

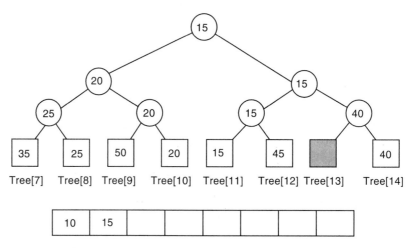

The process continues until each leaf node is eliminated. In our example, the last (largest) node plays a series of matches and wins them all by default. After inserting 50 at A[7], we have a sorted list.

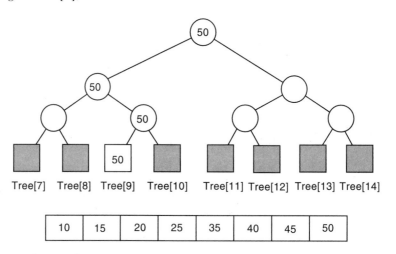

Computational Efficiency The efficiency of the tournament sort is $O(n \log_2 n)$. For an array with $n = 2^k$ elements, $n - 1$ comparisons (matches) are required to identify the smallest element. This is evident when we note that 1/2 of the contestants are eliminated at each level as we move toward the root. The total number of matches is

$$2^{k-1} + 2^{k-2} + \ldots + 2^1 + 1 = 2^k - 1 = n - 1.$$

The tree is then updated and the remaining $n - 1$ elements are processed by making $k - 1$ comparisons along the path of parents. The total number of comparisons is:

$$
\begin{aligned}
(n - 1) + (k - 1)*(n - 1) \quad &= (n - 1) + (n - 1)*(\log_2 n - 1) \\
&= (n - 1)\,(\log_2 n)
\end{aligned}
$$

Although the number of comparisons in the tournament sort is $O(n \log_2 n)$, the use of space is considerably less efficient. The tree requires $2 * n - 1$ nodes to hold the $k - 1$ levels of competition.

Tournament Sort Algorithm To implement the tournament sort, we define a DataNode class and create an array-based tree of its objects. The class has members that hold a data item, the location of the item in the bottom row of the tree, and a flag that indicates if the item is still active in the tournament. The operator "<=" is overloaded for comparison of nodes.

```
template <class T>
class DataNode
{
   public:
       // data value, index in the tree, boolean flag
       T data;
       int index;
       int active;

       friend int operator <= (const DataNode<T> &x,
                               const DataNode<T> &y);
};
```

The sort is implemented with the function TournamentSort and the utility UpdateTree that recomputes the comparisons along the path of parents. A full listing of functions and variables that provide the tournament sort are contained in the file "toursort.h".

```
// set up array-based tree, copy the elements of array a to
// new tree; sort elements and copy their value back to
// the array
template <class T>
void TournamentSort (T a[], int n)
{
```

```
// tree is the root of the array-based tree
DataNode<T> *tree;
DataNode<T> item;

// minimum power of 2 that is >= n
int bottomRowSize;

// number of nodes in the complete tree
// whose last row has bottomRowSize entries
int treesize;

// starting index of the bottom row
int loadindex;
int i, j;

// call PowerOfTwo to determine the needed size of
// the bottom row of the tree.
bottomRowSize = PowerOfTwo(n);

// compute the size of the tree and dynamically
// allocate its nodes
treesize = 2 * bottomRowSize - 1;
loadindex = bottomRowSize-1;
tree = new DataNode<T>[treesize];

// copy the array a to the tree of DataNode objects
j = 0;
for (i = loadindex; i < treesize; i++)
{
   item.index = i;
   if (j < n)
   {
      item.active = 1;
      item.data = a[j++];
   }
   else
      item.active = 0;
   tree[i] = item;
}

// make initial set of comparisons to find the smallest item
i = loadindex;
while (i > 0)
{
   j = i;
   while (j < 2*i)      // process pairs of competitors
   {
      // have a match. compare value tree[j] with its
      // competitor tree[j+1]. assign the winner to
      // the parent position
      if (!tree[j+1].active || tree[j] < tree[j+1])
         tree[(j-1)/2] = tree[j];
```

```
      else
         tree[(j-1)/2] = tree[j + 1];
      j += 2;              // go to next pair of competitors
   }
   // move up to the next level for competition among
   // the winners of the previous matches
   i = (i-1)/2;
}

// handle the other n-1 elements. copy winner from the root
// to the array. make the winner inactive. update tree
// by allowing the winner's competitor to re-enter the
// tournament
for (i = 0; i < n-1; i++)
{
   a[i] = tree[0].data;
   tree[tree[0].index].active = 0;
   UpdateTree(tree,tree[0].index);
}
// this copies the largest value to the array
a[n-1] = tree[0].data;
}
```

The **Update** function is passed the index i that represents the original location of the smallest current element in the bottom row of the tree. This is the node that is being deleted (made inactive). The value that lost the opening round competition to the ultimate winner (smallest value) is allowed to reenter the tournament.

```
// the parameter i is the starting index of the current
// smallest element in the list (tournament winner)
template <class T>
void UpdateTree(DataNode<T> *tree, int i)
{
   int j;

   // identify competitor of winner i. allow that competitor
   // to re-enter tournament by assigning it to parent node
   if (i % 2 == 0)
      tree[(i-1)/2] = tree[i-1];    // competitor is left node
   else
      tree[(i-1)/2] = tree[i + 1];  // competitor is right node

   // with the winner out of the tournament (made inactive),
   // replay those matches that involved this inactive player
   i = (i-1)/2;
   while (i > 0)
   {
      // at position i, is competitor a left or right node?
```

```
        if (i % 2 == 0)
           j = i-1;
        else
           j = i + 1;
        // see if your competitor is inactive (no match)
        if (!tree[i].active || !tree[j].active)
           if (tree[i].active)
              tree[(i-1)/2] = tree[i];
           else
              tree[(i-1)/2] = tree[j];
        // we have a competition. winner assigned to parent
        else
           if (tree[i] < tree[j])
              tree[i-1)/2] = tree[i];
           else
              tree[(i-1)/2] = tree[j];
        // move to next level of competition (parent level)
        i = (i-1)/2;
     }
     // tournament with new competitor is over. next smallest
     // value is available in the root
  }
```

13.2   Heaps

Array-based trees find an important application with **heaps,** which are complete binary trees having a level order relationship among the nodes. For a **maximum heap,** the value of a parent is greater than or equal to the value of each of its children. For a **minimum heap,** the value of the parent is less than or equal to the value of each of its children. These situations are depicted in Figure 13.2. In a maximum heap, the root contains the largest element; in a minimum heap, the root contains the smallest element. This book develops minimum heaps.

THE HEAP AS A LIST

A heap is a list with an ordering that stores a set of data in a complete binary tree. An ordering, called **heap order,** states that each node in the heap has a value that is less than or equal to the values of its children. With this ordering, the root has the smallest data value. As an abstract list structure, a heap allows us to add and delete items. The insertion process does not assume that the new item occupies a specific location but only requires that heap order is maintained. A deletion, however, removes the smallest item (root) from the list. A heap is used in those applications where the client wants direct access to the minimum element. As a list, the heap does not provide a Find operation and direct access to list elements is read-only. All heap handling algorithms are responsible to update the tree and maintain heap order.

A heap is a very efficient list management structure that takes full advantage of its complete binary tree structure. For each insertion and deletion operation, the

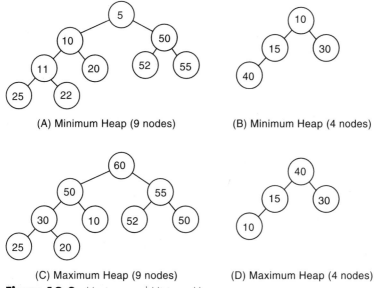

Figure 13.2 Maximum and Minimum Heaps

heap restores its order ("heapifies") by scanning only short paths from the root down to the end of the tree. A heap finds important applications in the implementation of a priority queue and in sorting a list of elements. Rather than using slower sorting algorithms, we can insert the elements into a heap and order them by repeatedly deleting the root node. This gives rise to the extremely fast heapsort.

We discuss the internal organization of a heap in our development of the heap class. The algorithms to add and remove items are presented in the implementation of the Insert and Delete methods. Example 13.2 explores a heap and illustrates some of its operations.

EXAMPLE 13.2

1. *Creating a Heap:* An array has a corresponding tree representation. In general, the tree does not satisfy the heap condition. By rearranging the elements, a "heaped" tree is created.

Original list: 40 10 30   Heaped Tree: 10 40 30

A[0]   A[0]

40   10

10   30   40   30

A[1]   A[2]   A[1]   A[2]

2. *Inserting an Element:* A new element is added to the end of the list and then the tree is updated to restore the heap condition. For instance, the following steps add 15 to the list.

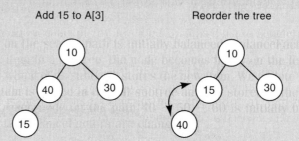

Add 15 to A[3]   Reorder the tree

3. *Deleting an Element:* Deletion always occurs at the root A[0]. The last element in the list is used to fill the vacated position, and the resulting tree is updated to restore the heap condition. For instance, the following steps delete 10.

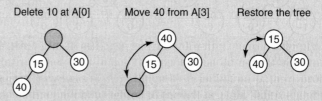

Delete 10 at A[0]   Move 40 from A[3]   Restore the tree

THE HEAP CLASS

Like any linear or nonlinear list, a heap has operations that insert and delete data items and that return status information, such as the size of the list. These methods and the array that holds the array-based binary tree are encapsulated into the class Heap.

- -
HEAP CLASS SPECIFICATION

DECLARATION

```
#include <isostream.h>
#include <stdlib.h>

template <class T>
class Heap
{
```

```
    private:
        // hlist points at the array which can be allocated by
        // the constructor (inArray == 0) or passed as a
        // parameter (inArray == 1)
        T *hlist;
        int inArray;

        // max elements allowed and current size of heap
        int maxheapsize;
        int heapsize;              // identifies end of list

        // error message utility function
        void error(char errmsg[]);

        // utility functions for Delete/Insert to restore heap
        void FilterDown(int i);
        void FilterUp(int i);
    public:
        // constructors/destructor
        Heap(int maxsize);         // create empty heap
        Heap(T arr[],int n);       // "heapify" arr
        Heap(const Heap<T>& H);    // copy constructor
        ~Heap(void);               // destructor

        // overloaded operators: "=", "[]", "T*"
        Heap<T>& operator= (const Heap<T>& rhs);
        const T& operator[] (int i);

        // list methods
        int ListSize(void) const;
        int ListEmpty(void) const;
        int ListFull(void) const;
        void Insert(const T& item);
        T Delete(void);
        void ClearList(void);
};
```

DESCRIPTION

The first constructor takes a size parameter and uses it to dynamically allocate
memory for the array. The resulting heap is initially empty and new elements
are added with the Insert method. A destructor, copy constructor, and assignment operator support the use of dynamic memory. A second constructor takes
an array as a parameter and binds the heap with the array. The constructor
orders the array as a heap. In this way, a client can impose a heap structure
on an existing array and take advantage of heap properties.

The overloaded index operator "[]" allows the client to access a heap object as an array. Since the operator returns a constant reference, access is read-only.

The methods ListEmpty, ListSize, and ListFull return information on the current size of the heap.

The Delete method always removes the first (smallest) item in the heap. Insert places an element in the list and maintains heap order.

EXAMPLE

```
Heap<int> H(4);              // a 4-element heap of integers
int A[] = {15,10,40,30};     // a 4-element array
Heap<int> K(A,4);            // bind A to heap K

H.Insert(85);                // add 85 to heap H
H.Insert(40);                // add 40 to heap H
cout << H.Delete();          // print 40, smallest element in H

//print "heapified" array A
for (int i = 0; i < 4; i++)
   cout << K[i] << "  ";     // print 10 15 40 30

K[0] = 99;                   // invalid statement
```

Program 13.1   Illustrating the Heap Class

This program starts with an initialized array A and then imposes a heap structure on its elements.

A: 50, 20, 60, 65, 15, 25, 10, 30, 4, 45

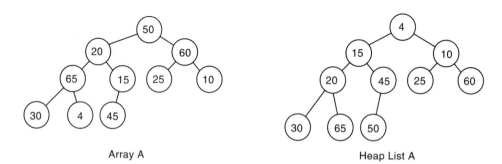

Array A   Heap List A

Elements are deleted from the heap and printed until the heap is empty. Since the heap is reorganized after each deletion, the elements are printed in ascending order.

```cpp
#include <iostream.h>

#include "heap.h"

// print the  array of n elements
template <class T>
void PrintList (T A[], int n)
{
    for(int i=0;i < n;i++)
        cout << A[i] << "  ";
    cout << endl;
}

void main(void)
{
    // initialized array of 10 elements
    int A[10] = {50, 20, 60, 65, 15, 25, 10, 30, 4, 45};


    cout << "Initial array:" << endl;
    PrintList(A,10);

    // declare a heap that binds array A as its list
    Heap<int>  H(A,10);

    // print the heapified version of array A
    cout "Heapified array:" << endl;
    PrintList(A,10);

    cout "Deleting elements from the heap:" << endl;
    // repeatedly extract smallest value
    while(!H.ListEmpty())
        cout << H.Delete() << "   ";
    cout << endl;
}

/*
<Run of Program 13.1>

Initial array:
50   20   60   65   15   25   10   30   4   45
Heapified array:
4   15   10   20   45   25   60   30   65   50
Deleting elements from the heap:
4   10   15   20   25   30   45   50   60   65
*/
```

13.3 Implementing the Heap Class

We provide a thorough discussion of the heap insertion and deletion operations and the utility methods FilterUp and FilterDown. The utility methods are responsible for updating the heap when it is created or modified.

Heap Insertion   A new item is initially added at the end of the heap. This locates the element in the list but may violate the heap condition. If the new item has a value that is less than its parent, exchange the values. The following figure represents the possibilities.

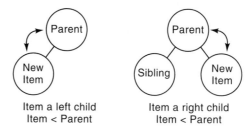

The exchange restores the heap condition at the parent location but may violate the condition at higher levels in the tree. Our process must now consider the new parent as a child and check the heap order at its parents. If the new item is relatively small, we must reposition it higher in the tree along its path of parents. Consider the following example, which assumes the existence of a nine-element heap H:

```
H.Insert(8);      // insert item=8 into the heap
```

Insert 8 into A[9]: Insert the new item at the rear of the heap. The location is identified with the index heapsize that maintains a count of the current number of items in the heap.

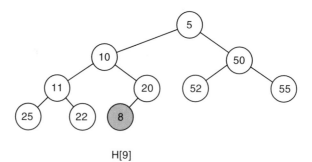

H[9]

Position value 8 on the path of parents: Compare 8 with the parent 20. Because the child is less than its parent, exchange their values (A). Continue on the path of parents. Item 8 is now less than its parent H[1]=10, and we must exchange their values (B). The process stops since the next parent satisfies the heap condition.

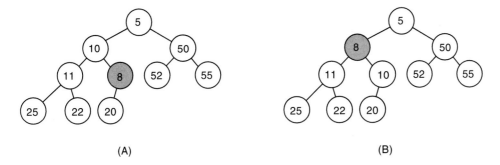

(A)   (B)

The insertion process scans the path of parents and terminates when a "small" parent is found (parent ≤ item) or when we reach the root node. Since the root node does not have a parent, the new value is located in the root.

The Insert operation uses a filter method to place a node in the path of parents. The method FilterUp places the new item in its correct position along the path of parents moving from index i to the root.

```
// utility to restore the heap; starting at index i,
// move up tree from parent to parent. exchange elements if
// the child has a value less than the parent
template <class T>
void Heap<T>::FilterUp (int i)
{
   int currentpos, parentpos;
   T target;

   // currentpos is an index that traverses path of parents.
   // target is value hlist[i] and is repositioned in path
   currentpos = i;
   parentpos = (i-1)/2;
   target = hlist[i];

   // traverse path of parents up to the root
   while (currentpos != 0)
   {
       // if parent <= target, heap condition is ok. break!
       if (hlist[parentpos}<= target)
          break;
       else
       // move child value to parent and update indices to
       // look at the next parent.
       {
```

```
        // move data from parent position to current
        // position. update current position to parent
        // position. compute next parent.
            hlist[currentpos] = hlist[parentpos];
            currentpos = parentpos;
            parentpos = (currentpos-1)/2;
        }
    }
    // the correct location has been discovered; assign target
    hlist[currentpos] = target;
}
```

The public Insert method first checks for a full heap and then begins the insert operation. After placing the item at the end of the heap, the method uses FilterUp to adjust the heap.

```
// insert a new item in the heap and update the structure
template <class T>
void Heap<T>::Insert(const T& item)
{
    // check for a full heap and terminate if True
    if (heapsize == maxheapsize)
        error("Heap full");
    // store the item at the end of the heap and increment
    // heapsize; call FilterUp to restore the heap condition
    hlist[heapsize] = item;
    FilterUp(heapsize);
    heapsize++;
}
```

Heap Deletion   Data is always deleted from the root of the tree. After removing the value, the root is vacant and we initially fill it with the last element in the heap. However, this choice of a replacement may violate the heap condition, and we must begin to traverse the path of small children and correctly locate the value in the heap. If the replacement value is greater than either of its children, it does not satisfy the heap condition and we must exchange positions with its smallest child. The scan continues until the value is correctly located as a parent or until we reach the end of the list. In that case, we have placed the value in a leaf node. For example, in the following heap, Delete removes the root node 5 from the heap.

Delete the root node 5 and replace it with the last node 22: The last item in the heap is copied to the root. The new root may not satisfy the heap condition, and we must scan a path of children to correctly locate the value.

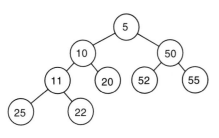

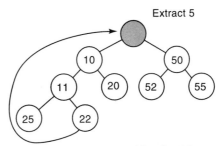

Initial Heap   Replace the root with value 22

Scan the path of smallest children and locate value 22: Compare the root 22 with its children. The smallest child at H[1] is less than 22, and the parent and child can exchange positions (A). At level 1, the new parent at H[1] is compared with its children at H[3] and H[4]. The smallest child has value 11 and must exchange positions with its parent (B). The resulting tree satisfies the heap condition.

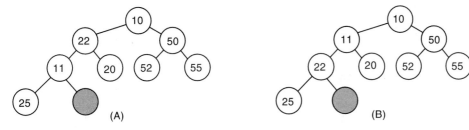

Delete Method   The Delete operation uses the FilterDown method to place a node on the path of smallest children. The function receives an initial index i from which the scan begins. For a deletion, FilterDown is called with parameter 0 since the replacement value is copied from the end of the heap to the root. The method FilterDown is also used by a constructor to build the heap.

```
// utility to restore the heap; starting at index i,
// exchange parent and child so that subtree from i is a heap
template <class T>
void Heap<T>::FilterDown (int i)
{
    int currentpos, childpos;
    T target;

    // start at i and set its value as the target
    currentpos = i;
    target = hlist[i];

    // compute the left child index and begin a scan down
    // the path of children, stopping at end of list (heapsize)
    childpos = 2 * i + 1;
```

```
        while (childpos < heapsize)              // check for end of list
        {
            // index of right child is childpos+1. Set childpos to
            // index of the smaller of the two children
            if ((childpos+1 < heapsize) &&
                    (hlist[childpos+1] <= hlist[childpos]))
                childpos = childpos + 1;

            // parent is less than children, heap ok. quit
            if (target <= hlist[childpos])
                break;
            else
            {
             // move value of smaller child to the parent;
             // position of smaller child is now vacated
             hlist[currentpos] = hlist[childpos];

             // update indices to continue the scan
             currentpos = childpos;
             childpos = 2 * currentpos + 1;
            }
        }
        // assign target to the most recently vacated position
        hlist[currentpos] = target;
}
```

The public Delete method copies the value at the root node to a temporary variable and then replaces the root with the last value in the heap. After the heap size is decremented, FilterDown updates the heap. The value in the temporary variable is then returned to the client.

```
// return the value of the first element and update the heap.
// a deletion with an empty heap creates an error message and
// terminates the program
template <class T>
T Heap<T>::Delete(void)
{
    T tempitem;

    // check for an empty heap
    if (heapsize == 0)
        error("Heap empty");

    // copy the root to tempitem; replace the root with the last
    // value in the heap and decrement the heap size
    tempitem = hlist[0];
```

```
        hlist[0] = hlist[heapsize-1];
        heapsize--;

        // call FilterDown to position the new root value in heap
        FilterDown(0);

        // return the original root value
        return tempitem;
    }
```

Heapifying an Array   The Heap class provides a constructor that uses an existing array as its list and converts it to a heap. The process is called "heapifying" the array. The algorithm successively applies the FilterDown method to all nonleaf nodes. The index of the last heap element is $n - 1$. Its parent is at index

$$\text{currentpos} = \frac{(n - 1) - 1}{2} = \frac{n - 2}{2}$$

and defines that last non-leaf node in the heap. This parent node gives the starting index for heapifying the array. If we execute FilterDown with indices in the range currentpos down to 0, we guarantee that each parent node satisfies the heap condition. As an example, consider the integer array that follows:

int A[10] = {9,12,17,30,50,20,60,65,4,19};
Leaf node indices: 5, 6, ..., 9
Parent node indices: 4, 3, ..., 0

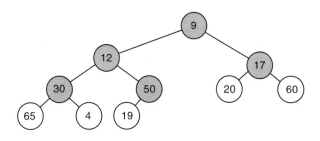

Initial List

The following sequence of pictures illustrates the "heapifying" process. For all calls to FilterDown, the affected subtree is highlighted:

FilterDown (4): The value H[4] = 50 is greater than its child H[9] = 19 and must exchange with its child (A).
FilterDown (3): The value H[3] = 30 is greater than its child H[8] = 19 and must exchange with its child (B).

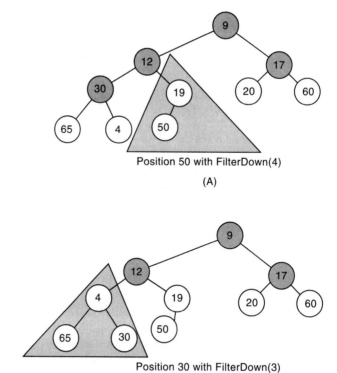

Position 50 with FilterDown(4)

(A)

Position 30 with FilterDown(3)

(B)

At level 2, the parent H[2] = 17 already satisfies the heap condition. The function FilterDown(2) makes no changes:

FilterDown (1): The value H[1] = 12 is greater than its child H[3] = 4 and must exchange with the child (C).
FilterDown (0): The process terminates at the root node. The value H[0] = 9 must exchange positions with its child H[1]. The resulting tree is a heap (D).

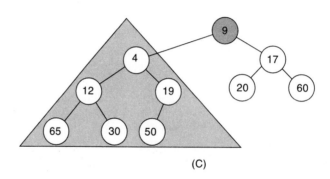

(C)

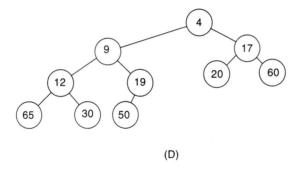

(D)

Constructor

```
// constructor to convert an array to a heap
// the array and its size are passed as parameters
template <class T>
Heap<T>::Heap(T arr[],int n)
{
    int  j, currentpos;

    // n <= 0 is an invalid array size; terminate program
    if (n <= 0)
        error("Bad list size.");

    // use n to set heap size and maximum heap size; assign
    // the array arr to the heap list
    maxheapsize = n;
    heapsize = n ;
    hlist = arr;

    // set currentpos to the last parent index; call FilterDown
    // in a loop with index in the range currentpos down to 0;
    currentpos = (heapsize - 2)/2
    while(currentpos >= 0)
    {
        // establish heap condition for subtree with root
        // hlist [currentpos]
        FilterDown(currentpos);
        currentpos--;
    }
    // set inArray to True so Heap will not deallocate array
    inArray = 1;
}
```

APPLICATION: HEAP SORT

The heap sort is a very efficient $O(n \log_2 n)$ sort. The algorithm uses the fact that the smallest element is in the root (index 0) and that Delete extracts this value.

To apply the heap sort to array A, declare a Heap object with array A as a parameter. The constructor converts A into a heap. The sort is executed by repeatedly deleting A[0] and inserting it at the rear of the list at locations A[N−1], A[N−2], ..., A[1]. Recall that when an item is deleted from the heap, the previous rear element becomes the replacement value in the root and is no longer part of the heap. We are free to copy the deleted item into that position. The heapsort deletes the smallest element in the list and stores it at the rear of the array. The next smallest element is then deleted and stored at the second last position and so forth. The array A is sorted in descending order. In the exercises, the reader is asked to build a maximum heap class, whose application orders an array in ascending order.

The following steps implement the heap sort for the five-element array A:

int A[] = {50, 20, 75, 35, 25};

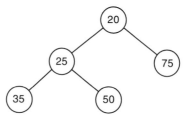

Heapified Tree

Delete 20 and store in A[4]   Delete 25 and store in A[3]

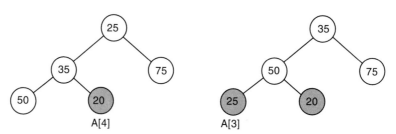

Delete 35 and store in A[2]   Delete 50 and store in A[1]

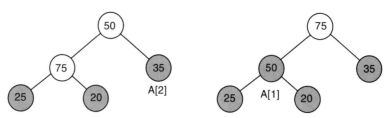

Since the only remaining element 75 is in the root, the array is sorted: A = 75 50 35 25 20.

The following is an implementation of the heap sort algorithm. The function HeapSort is contained in the file "heapsort.h".

HeapSort

```
// include the Heap class
#include "heap.h"

// sort array A in descending order
template <class T>
void HeapSort (T A[], int n)
{
    // constructor converts A to a Heap
    Heap<T> H(A,n);
    T elt;

    // iteration that loads element A[n-1] ... A[1]
    for(int i = n-1;i >= 1;i--)
    {
     // delete smallest element from heap and store in A[i]
     elt = H.HDelete();
     A[i] = elt;
    }
}
```

The Computational Efficiency of the Heap Sort   An n-element array corresponds to a complete binary tree of depth $k = \log_2 n$. The initial phase to heapify the array always requires $n/2$ FilterDown operations. Each of these requires no more than k comparisons. During the second phase of the sort, the FilterDown operation executes $n - 1$ times. In the worst case, the operation requires k comparisons. By combining the two phases, the worst case complexity of the heap sort is

$$k * \frac{n}{2} + k * (n - 1) = k * \left(\frac{3n}{2} - 1 \right)$$

$$= \log_2 n \times \left(\frac{3n}{2} - 1 \right)$$

which is of order $O(n \log_2 n)$.

The heap sort does not require any additional storage, since the sort is done in place. The tournament sort is also an $O(n \log_2 n)$ algorithm but requires the allocation of an array-based tree with $2^{k+1} - 1$ nodes, where k is the smallest integer such that $n \le 2^k$. Some $O(n \log_2 n)$ sorts have a worst case behavior of $O(n^2)$. The tree sort in Section 13.7 is an example. In contrast, the heap sort is $O(n \log_2 n)$, regardless of the initial distribution of the data.

Program 13.2 Comparing Sorts

The HeapSort function is used to sort an array A of 2000 random integers. For comparison, arrays B and C are assigned the same elements and are used with the TournamentSort and ExchangeSort functions. The ExchangeSort function is found in the file "arrsort.h". The sorts are timed with the function TickCount that returns the number of 1/60th seconds that have elapsed since system startup. The exchange sort, whose efficiency is $O(n^2)$, allows us to vividly contrast a slower algorithm with the tournament and heap sorts of order $O(n \log_2 n)$. The function PrintFirst_Last prints the first and last five elements in the array. The codes for the function are not included in the program listing but are available in the program supplement in the file "prg13_2.cpp".

```cpp
#include <iostream.h>

#include "random.h"
#include "arrsort.h"
#include "toursort.h"
#include "heapsort.h"
#include "ticks.h"                    // for TickCount

enum SortType {heap,tournament,exchange};
void TimeSort(int *A, int n, char *sortName, SortType sort)
{
    long tcount;
    // TickCount is a system dependent function. it returns
    // the number of 1/60 th secs. since system startup.

    cout << "Sorting with" << sortName << ':' << endl;
    // start the count then sort array A. assign to
    // tcount the elapsed sort time t in 1/60 th secs.
    tcount = TickCount ();
    switch(sort)
    {
        case heap:              HeapSort(A,n);
                                break;
        case tournament:        TournamentSort(A,n);
                                break;
        case exchange:          ExchangeSort(A,n);
                                break;
    }
    tcount = TickCount() - tcount;
    // print the first 5 and last 5 elements of sorted array
    for (int i=0; i < 5; i++)
        cout << A[i] << " ";
    cout << "...";
```

```
    for (i=n-5; i<n; i++)
       cout << A[i] << " ";
    cout << endl;

    cout << sortName << "time is" << tcount << "\n\n";
}

void main(void)
{
    // pointers for arrays A, B, and C
    int *A, *B, *C;
    RandomNumber rnd;

    // dynamically allocate memory and load arrays
    A = new int [2000];
    B = new int [2000];
    C = new int [2000];

    // load the arrays with 2000 identical random numbers
    for(int i=0;i < 2000;i++)
        A[i] = B[i] = C[i] = rnd.Random(10000);
    TimeSort(A,2000,"Heap sort",heap);
    delete [] A;
    // repeat process for the tournament sort
    TimeSort(B,2000,"Tournament sort",tournament);
    delete [] B;

    // repeat process for the exchange sort
    TimeSort(C,2000,"Exchange sort",exchange);
    delete [] C;
}

/*
<Run of Program 13.2>
Sorting with Heap sort:
9999  9996  9996  9995  9990  . . .  11  10  9  6  3
Heap sort time is 16

Sorting with Tournament sort:
3  6  9  10  11  . . .  9990  9995  9996  9996  9999
Tournament sort time is 36

Sorting with Exchange sort:
3  6  9  10  11  . . .  9990  9995  9996  9996  9999
Exchange sort time is 818
*/
```

Priority Queues   13.4

Priority queues were introduced in Chapter 5 and used in an event-driven simulation study. The client is given access to an insert operator and a delete operator that removes an element of highest priority from the list. In Chapter 5, we used arrays to implement the underlying list for a PQueue object.

In this section, we define the heap implementation of a priority queue. Since we are using a minimum heap, we assume that the items have an ascending order of priority. A deletion from the heap returns the smallest (highest priority) element from the priority queue. The heap implementation provides great efficiency for the PQDelete method since it requires only $O(\log_2 n)$ comparisons. This compares to the $O(n)$ comparisons in the array implementation.

We conclude the section by designing a filter that will convert an array of items into long runs. The filter, using a priority queue, significantly enhances the efficiency of the merge sort when ordering large sets of data on a file. The topic is discussed in Chapter 14.

PQUEUE CLASS SPECIFICATION (HEAP VERSION)

DECLARATION

```
#include "heap.h"

template <class T>
class PQueue
{
   private:
     // heap that stores the queue list
     Heap<T> *ptrHeap;

   public:
     // constructor
       PQueue  (int sz);

       // priority queue modification operations
       void  PQInsert(const T& item);
       T PQDelete(void);
       void ClearPQ(void);

       // priority queue test methods
       int PQEmpty(void) const;
       int PQFull(void) const;
       int PQLength(void) const;
};
```

DESCRIPTION

The constructor is passed a size parameter that is used to dynamically allocate the heap structure ptrHeap. The methods are implemented by simply calling the corresponding methods in the heap class. For instance, PQDelete uses, the heap deletion method.

```
// delete the first element in the queue by deleting the
// root of the corresponding heap. return the deleted value
template <class T>
T PQueue<T>::PQDelete(void)
{
    return ptrHeap-> Delete();
}
```

The implementation of PQueue is found in the file "pqueue.h".

APPLICATION: LONG RUNS

The merge sort is a primary algorithm for ordering large external files. The efficiency of the algorithm is improved when the data are filtered or preprocessed into long runs. In Chapter 12, we have already seen one such filter that reads the data k-elements at a time and sorts it. In this way the resulting data has runs of minimum length k. In this application, we use a k-element priority queue and create runs whose lengths are often significantly longer than k. The algorithm reads the items from the original list A and passes them through a priority queue filter. The elements are returned to the list in the form of long runs.

We illustrate the algorithm with an example that assumes array A has 12 integers and that priority queue PQ1 is a filter with k = four elements. Priority queue PQ1 holds elements that will ultimately appear in the current run. A second priority queue, PQ2, holds elements for a next run. We use two indices to scan the array. The variable loadIndex identifies the item that is currently being read. The variable currIndex identifies the last item that was released from PQ1 and returned to the array. In the example, array A initially breaks into six runs with the longest run containing three elements:

```
A = [13] [6 61 96] [26] [1 72 91] [37] [25 97] [21]
```

After filtering the elements, we will have three runs with the longest run having seven elements.

Start by loading PQ1 with elements A[0] to A[3] from the list. Since a priority queue releases elements in ascending order, we have a tool to sort at least four elements into a run. We will do even better. Delete the first item (minimum value) from PQ1 and assign it to A[currIndex] = A[0] = 6. This leaves PQ1 with an empty slot and starts the first run. Since the first four items from A have been copied to PQ1, we continue to process the element of A at loadIndex = 4. At each step in the process, compare A[loadIndex] with A[currIndex]. If the item at loadIndex is greater, it will ultimately appear in the current run and hence is stored in PQ1. Otherwise, it will appear in the next run and hence is stored in PQ2. We describe the action for each entry in the example. After processing an item, we use the following format to list the reloaded entries in A, the entries that must still be read, and the contents of both priority queues.

```
A:    <items loaded in runs>    A[loadIndex] . . . <remaining items>
PQ1:  <store for current run>   PQ2:  <store for next run>
```

Step by Step Run:
Item A[4] = 26 > A[currIndex] = 6. Store 26 in PQ1 and release 13 from PQ1 to the list at A[1].

    A: 6 13   A[5] to A[11]: 1 72 91 37 25 97 21
    PQ1: 61 96 26   PQ2: <empty>

Item A[5] = 1 < A[currIndex] = 13. Hence, value 1 is part of the next run. Store 1 in PQ2 and release 26 from PQ1 to the list at A[2].

    A: 6 13 26   A[6] to A[11]: 72 91 37 25 97 21
    PQ1: 61 96   PQ2: 1

Item A[6] = 72 is greater than entry 26 in the current run. Store it in PQ1 and release 61. Similarly, the next item 91 goes into PQ1 prior to a release of 72 into the current run at currIndex = 4.

    A: 6 13 26 61 72   A[8] to A[11]: 37 25 97 21
    PQ1: 91 96   PQ2: 1

Items A[8] = 37 and A[9] = 25 are less than 72 and will belong to the next run. They are stored in PQ2. At the same time, two entries from PQ1 are released to the array and the queue is then empty.

    A: 6 13 26 61 72 91 96   A[10] to A[11]:   97 21
    PQ1: <empty>   PQ2: 1 37 25

We have completed the current run and can begin the next run. Copy the elements from PQ2 to PQ1 and release the smallest element from the newly filled queue PQ1. In this example, release 1 from PQ1 and begin the next run.

    A: 6 13 26 61 72 91 96 1   A[10] to A[11]: 97 21
    PQ1: 25 37   PQ2: <empty>

Item A[10] = 97 > 1 and is stored in PQ1. We then release the minimum value 25 from PQ1.

    A: 6 13 26 61 72 91 96 1 25   A[11]: 21
    PQ1: 37 97   PQ2: <empty>

Item A[11] = 21 < 25 and must wait for the next run. We store it in PQ2 and release 37.

    A: 6 13 26 61 72 91 96 1 25 37   <list scan complete>
    PQ1: 97   PQ2: 21

The scan of the original list is complete. Release all elements from PQ1 into the current run and then all elements from PQ2 into the next run.

Run 1:   6 13 26 61 72 91 96
Run 2:   1 25 37 97
Run 3:   21

Runs Algorithm We implement the long runs algorithm using the LongRunFilter class. Its private members include the array and the two priority queues that hold the current and next run. The constructor binds a class object with the array and creates the associated priority queues. The algorithm is supported by the private methods LoadPQ that inserts elements from the array into PQ1 and CopyPQ that copies elements from PQ2 to PQ1.

DECLARATION

```
template <class T>
class LongRunFilter
{
   private:
       // pointers that identify the key parameters in the filter
       // A is the list, PQ1 and PQ2 are the two priority queues
       T   *A;
       PQueue<T>       *PQ1, *PQ2;

       int loadIndex;
       // gives the size of the array and the priority queue
       int arraySize;
       int filterSize;

       // copy entries from priority queue PQ2 to PQ1
       void CopyPQ (void);
       // loads items from array A to priority queue PQ1
       void LoadPQ (void);
   public:
       // constructors/destructor
       LongRunFilter(T arr[],int n, int sz);
       ~LongRunFilter(void);

       // create long runs
       void LoadRuns(void);

       // evaluating the runs
       void PrintRuns(void) const;
       int CountRuns(void) const;
};
```

DISCUSSION

The constructor initializes the data members and load elements from the array into PQ1 thus setting items for the first run. The method LongRuns is the main algorithm, filtering elements from the array into long runs.

The methods PrintRuns and CountRuns illustrate the algorithm. We use them to compare runs in an array before and after calling LoadRuns.

The full implementation of the LongRunFilter class is given in file "longrun.h".

```
// scan array A and create long runs by running the elements
// through the filter
template <class T>
void LongRunFilter<T>::LoadRuns(void)
{
    T     value;
    int currIndex; = 0;

    if (filterSize == 0)
        return;

    // start by loading the smallest element from PQ1 into A
    A[currIndex] = PQ1->PQDelete();

    // fill PQ1 with elements from A
    // now look at the remaining elements in A
    while (loadIndex < arraySize)
    {
        // look at next element from the list
        value = A[loadIndex++];
        // if element is greater or equal to A[currIndex]
        // it belongs to the current run and is put in PQ1
        // otherwise it goes in PQ2 for the next run
        if (A[currIndex] <= value)
           PQ1->PQInsert(value);
        else
           PQ2->PQInsert(value);
        // once PQ1 is empty, current run is complete, copy
        // elements from PQ2 to PQ1 and begin the next run
        if (PQ1->PQEmpty())
            CopyPQ();

        // extract element from PQ1 and put in the run
        if (!PQ1->PQEmpty())
            A[++currIndex] = PQ1->PQDelete();
    }

    // clean up elements from current run and then from
    // the next run.
```

```
    while (!PQ1->PQEmpty())
        A[++currIndex] = PQ1->PQDelete();
    while (!PQ2->PQEmpty())
        A[++currIndex] = PQ2->PQDelete();
}
```

Program 13.3   Long Runs

This program illustrates the use of the long run filter. The first example takes a small array of 15 elements and filters them with 4-element priority queues. The output includes a list of run before and after calling the filter. A more realistic example looks at a 10000-element array and filters the list using 5-, 50-, and 500-element priority queues. In each case, we print the number of resulting runs.

```
#include <iostream.h>

// include the random number generator and the filter class
#include "random.h"
#include "longrun.h"

// copy array A to array B
void CopyArray(int A[], int B[], int n)
{
    for (int i = 0; i < n; i++)
        B[i] = A[i];
}

void main()
{
    // a 15 element integer array to illustrate the filter
    int demoArray[15];

    // large 10000 element arrays to count runs
    int *A = new int[10000], *B = new int[10000];
    RandomNumber rnd;

    // filters will have sizes 5, 50 (5*10), and 500 (5 * 100)
    int  i, filterSize = 5;

    // create random list of 15 integers; set up filter
    for (i = 0; i < 15; i++)
      demoArray[i] = rnd.Random(100);
    LongRunFilter<int> F(demoArray, 15, 4);
```

```
    // print the list before and after creating long
    // runs with a 4 element filter
    cout << "Raw List" << endl;
    F.PrintRuns();
    cout << endl;
    F.LoadRuns();
    cout << "Filtered List" << endl;
    F.PrintRuns();
    cout << endl;

    // initialize an array with 10000 random integers
    for (i = 0; i < 10000; i++)
        A[i] = rnd.Random(25000);

    cout << "Runs with 3 filters" << endl;
    // set up a raw list and count the number of runs
    LongRunFilter<int> LR(A, 10000, 0);
    cout << "Number of runs in initial 10000 element array is "
        << LR.CountRuns() << endl;

    // test filter size 5, 50, and 500 and count the runs
    for (i = 0; i < 3; i++)
    {
        CopyArray(A,B,10000);
        LongRunFilter<int> LR(B, 10000, filterSize);

        // create the long runs
        LR.LoadRuns();
        cout << "  Runs with a filter of " << filterSize
            << " is " << LR.CountRuns() << endl;

        // increase the filter size ten-fold
        filterSize *= 10;
    }
}

/*
<Run of Program 13.3>

Raw List
36
22    79
26    84
44    88
44    66    81
19    86
40
2     47
```

```
Filtered List
22  26  36  44  44  66  79  81  84  86  88
2   19  40  47

Runs with 3 filters
Number of runs in initial 100000 element array is 5077
  Runs with a filter of 5 is 991
  Runs with a filter of 50 is 101
  Runs with a filter of 500 is 11


*/
```

AVL Trees   13.5

Binary search trees are designed for rapid access to data. Ideally, the tree is reasonably balanced and has height approximately $O(\log_2 n)$. With some data, however, a binary search tree can be degenerate. In that case, the height is $O(n)$ and access to the data is significantly slowed. In this section, we develop a modified tree class that gives us the power of binary search trees without worst case conditions. We develop AVL trees in which every node is height-balanced. By this we mean that for each node in an AVL tree, the difference in height of its two subtrees is at most 1.

In the AVL tree class, new versions of the insert and delete methods ensure that the nodes remain height-balanced. Figure 13.3 illustrates the equivalent AVL tree and binary search tree representations for an array. The pair in (A) represents a simple five-element array whose elements are in ascending order. The second example (B) pictures the two trees with elements from array B. The binary search tree in (A) has a height of 5, whereas the AVL tree has a height of 2. In general, the height of an AVL tree never exceeds $O(\log_2 n)$; thus, it becomes a powerful storage collection when rapid access to its elements is demanded.

```
A[5] = {1,2,3,4,5}          B[8] = {20,30,80,40,10,60,50,70}
```

In this section, we use the approach from Chapter 11 that builds a search tree out of tree nodes. We begin by defining the AVLTreeNode class and then use these objects to design an AVLTree class. Our focus is on the AVL tree methods Insert and Delete. The algorithms for these methods require careful design to ensure that each node in the new tree remains height-balanced.

AVL TREE NODES

AVL trees have a representation that is similar to binary search trees. The operations are identical except for Insert and Delete, which must constantly monitor the relative heights of the left and right subtrees of a node. To maintain this information, we extend our definition of a TreeNode object to include a balanceFactor field.

left	data	balanceFactor	right

AVLTreeNode

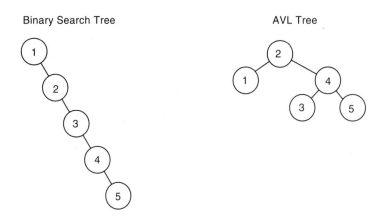

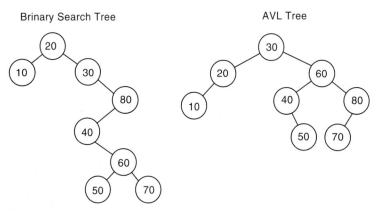

Figure 13.3   AVL and Binary Search Trees Representation of an Array

The value of the field is the difference between the height of the right and left subtrees.

```
balanceFactor = height(right subtree) - height(left subtree)
```

If the balanceFactor is negative, the node is "heavy on the left" since the height of the left subtree is greater than the height of the right subtree. With a positive balanceFactor, the node is "heavy on the right." A height-balanced node has a balanceFactor of 0. In an AVL tree, balanceFactor must fall in the range -1 to 1.

Figure 13.4 describes three AVL trees with tags -1, 0, or $+1$ on each node to indicate the relative size of the left and right subtrees.

-1: Height of the left subtree is one greater than the right subtree.
  0: Height of the left and right subtrees are equal.
$+1$: Height of the right subtree is one greater than the left subtree.

By using inheritance tools, we can derive the AVLTreeNode class from the TreeNode base class. An AVLTreeNode object inherits the fields for a TreeNode and appends

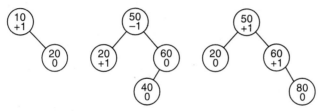

Figure 13.4 AVL Trees

the additional balanceFactor field. The two data members left and right in TreeNode are protected so that AVLTreeNode or other derived classes have direct access to them. The AVLTreeNode class is found on the program supplement in the file "avl-tree.h".

- -
AVLTREENODE CLASS SPECIFICATION

DECLARATION

```
// inherits the TreeNode class
template <class T>
class AVLTreeNode: public TreeNode<T>
{
   private:
      // additional data member needed by AVLTreeNode
      int balanceFactor;
      // used by AVLTree class methods to allow assignment
      // to a tree node pointer without casting
      AVLTreeNode<T>* & Left(void);
      AVLTreeNode<T>* & Right(void);

   public:
      // constructor
      AVLTreeNode (const T& item, AVLTreeNode<T> *lptr = NULL,
                  AVLTreeNode<T> *rptr = NULL, int balfac = 0);

      // return left/right TreeNode pointers as
      // AVLTreeNode pointers; handles casting of types
      AVLTreeNode<T> *Left(void) const;
      AVLTreeNode<T> *Right(void) const;

      // method to access new data field
      int GetBalanceFactor(void);

      // AVLTree methods needs access to Left and Right
      friend class AVLTree<T>;
};
```

DISCUSSION

The data member balanceFactor is private since only the AVL insert and delete operations should update the value.

In the constructor, the parameters include data for the underlying TreeNode structure along with the default parameter balfac = 0.

The client may access the pointer fields using Left and Right. A new definition of these methods is necessary since the return value is a pointer to the larger AVLTreeNode structure.

The general reasons for declaring virtual destructors are discussed in Section 12.3. In our development, we derive the AVLTree class from the BinSTree class and, in doing so, reuse the base class destructor and ClearList. These base class methods destroy nodes by executing the delete operator. In each case, the pointer refers to an AVLTreeNode object, not a TreeNode object. If the destructor in the node base class TreeNode is virtual, dynamic binding is used when delete is called and it deletes an AVLTreeNode object.

EXAMPLES

```
AVLTreeNode<char> *root;    // the root of an AVL tree

// the function creates the following AVLTree. Each node
// is assigned a balance factor
```

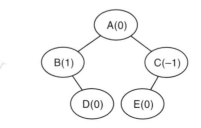

```
void MakeAVLCharTree(AVLTreeNode<char>* &root)
{
   AVLTreeNode<char> *a, *b, *c, *d, *e;

   e = new AVLTreeNode<char>('E',NULL,NULL, 0);
   d = new AVLTreeNode<char>('D',NULL,NULL, 0);
   c = new AVLTreeNode<char>('C',e,NULL,-1);
   b = new AVLTreeNode<char>('B',NULL,d,1);
   a = new AVLTreeNode<char>('A',b,c,0);
   root = a;
}
```

Implementing the AVLTreeNode Class   The constructor for the AVLTreeNode class calls the base class constructor and initializes balanceFactor.

```
// constructor; initialize balanceFactor and the base class.
// default pointer values NULL initialize node as a leaf node
template <class T>
AVLTreeNode<T>::AVLTreeNode (const T& item,
     AVLTreeNode<T> *lptr, AVLTreeNode<T> *rptr, int balfac):
  TreeNode<T>(item,lptr,rptr), balanceFactor(balfac)
{}
```

The methods of Left and Right in the AVLTreeNode class simplify client access to the fields. An attempt to access the left child with the base class method Left returns a pointer to a TreeNode. A type conversion would be needed to return a pointer to the larger node structure. The following statements illustrate the problem.

```
AVLTreeNode<T> *p, *q;

q = p->Left();                   // invalid operation

q = (AVLTreeNode<T> *)p->Left();   // type casting required
```

Rather than forcing the repeated type conversion of pointers, we define methods Left and Right for the AVLTreeNode class and return AVLTreeNode pointer values.

```
// return left after casting it to an AVLTreeNode pointer
template <class T>
AVLTreeNode<T>* AVLTreeNode<T>::Left(void)
{
   return (AVLTreeNode<T> *)left;
}
```

The AVL Tree Class   13.6

An AVL tree provides a list structure that is similar to a binary search tree with the added condition that the tree remains height balanced after each insertion and deletion operation. Since an AVL tree is an extended binary search tree, we use inheritance to derive an AVLTree class from the BinSTree class.

The Insert and Delete method must be overridden to meet the AVL conditions. In addition, we define the copy constructor and the overloaded assignment operator in the derived class since we are building trees with the larger node structure.

- -
AVLTREE CLASS SPECIFICATION

DECLARATION

```
// constants to indicate the balance factor of a node
const int leftheavy = -1;
const int balanced = 0;
const int rightheavy = 1;
```

```
// derived search tree class
template <class T>
class AVLTree: public BinSTree<T>
{
    private:

        // memory allocation
        AVLTreeNode<T> *GetAVLTreeNode(const T& item,
                AVLTreeNode<T> *lptr,AVLTreeNode<T> *rptr);

        // used by copy constructor and assignment operator
        AVLTreeNode<T> *CopyTree(AVLTreeNode<T> *t);

        // used by Insert and Delete method to re-establish
        // the AVL conditions after a node is added or deleted
        // from a subtree
        void SingleRotateLeft (AVLTreeNode<T>* &p);
        void SingleRotateRight (AVLTreeNode<T>* &p);
        void DoubleRotateLeft (AVLTreeNode<T>* &p);
        void DoubleRotateRight (AVLTreeNode<T>* &p);
        void UpdateLeftTree (AVLTreeNode<T>* &tree,
                        int &reviseBalanceFactor);
        void UpdateRightTree (AVLTreeNode<T>* &tree,
                        int &reviseBalanceFactor);

        // class specific versions of the general Insert and
        // Delete methods
        void AVLInsert(AVLTreeNode<T>* &tree,
            AVLTreeNode<T>* newNode, int &reviseBalanceFactor);
        void AVLDelete(AVLTreeNode<T>* &tree,
            AVLTreeNode<T>* newNode, int &reviseBalanceFactor);

    public:
        // constructors, destructor
        AVLTree(void);
        AVLTree(const AVLTree<T>& tree);

        // assignment operator
        AVLTree<T>& operator= (const AVLTree<T>& tree);

        // standard list handling methods
        virtual void Insert(const T& item);
        virtual void Delete(const T& item);
};
```

DESCRIPTION

The constants leftheavy, balanced, and rightheavy are used by the insertion and deletion algorithms to describe the balance factor of a node.

The method GetAVLTreeNode handles node allocation for the class. By default, the balanceFactor of the new node is set to 0.

This class defines a new CopyTree function for use with the copy constructor and overloaded assignment operator. Although the algorithm is identical to CopyTree in BinSTree, the function correctly creates the larger AVLTreeNodes as it builds the new tree.

The functions AVLInsert and AVLDelete implement the Insert and Delete methods, respectively. The private methods such as SingleRotateLeft are used in the implementation of AVLInsert and AVLDelete. We declare the public Insert and Delete methods as virtual functions that override those in the BinSTree base class. Except for these tree modification methods, we inherit all of the other search tree operations from BinSTree.

EXAMPLE

```
AVLTree<int>    avltree;        // AVLTree list of integers
BinSTree<int>   bintree;        // BinSTree list of integers

for (int i = 1; i <= 5; i++)
{
    bintree.Insert(i);          // Creates trees (A) and (B)
    avltree.Insert(i);
}
```

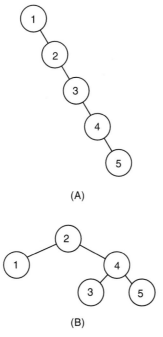

(A)

(B)

```
avltree.Delete(3);                // remove 3 from the AVL tree

// The function AVLPrintVTree is equivalent to the upright
// print function in Chapter 11. It enhances output by
// including both the data value and the balance factor.
// tree (C) is AVLTree (B) with 3 deleted
// AVLPrintVTree is located in file "avltree.h"

AVLPrintTree((AVLTreeNode<int> *)avltree.GetRoot(),0);
```

```
          2: 1
         /    \
      1: 0    4: 1
                  \
                  5: 0
```

(C)

MEMORY ALLOCATION FOR THE AVLTREE

The AVLTree class is derived from BinSTree and inherits most of its operations. We develop separate memory allocation and copy methods when we need to create the larger AVLTreeNode objects, as illustrated by GetAVLTreeNode.

```
// allocate an AVLTreeNode; terminate the program on a memory
// allocation error;
template <class T>
AVLTreeNode<T> *AVLTree<T>::GetAVLTreeNode(const T& item,
                    AVLTreeNode<T> *lptr, AVLTreeNode<T> *rptr)
{
    AVLTreeNode<T> *p;

    p = new AVLTreeNode<T> (item, lptr, rptr);
    if (p == NULL)
    {
        cerr << "Memory allocation failure!" << endl;
        exit(1);
    }
    return p;
}
```

Base class methods are sufficient to remove the larger AVLTreeNodes. The DeleteTree method from the BinSTree class makes use of the virtual destructor in the TreeNode class.

AVLTree Insert Methods   The power of an AVL tree is its ability to create and maintain height-balanced trees. This power is made possible by the AVL insertion and deletion algorithms. In our AVLTree class, we describe an Insert method that overrides the same operation in the BinSTree base class. The actual implementation of Insert uses the recursive method AVLInsert to store the new element. We first give the C++ code for Insert and then focus on the recursive method AVLInsert that implements the algorithm by the AVL tree authors Adelson-Velskii and Landis.

```
template <class T>
void AVLTree<T>::Insert(const T& item)
{
    // declare AVL tree node pointer; using base class method
    // GetRoot. cast to larger node and assign root pointer
    AVLTreeNode<T> *treeRoot = (AVLTreeNode<T> *)GetRoot(),
                   *newNode;

    // flag used by AVLInsert to rebalance nodes
    int reviseBalanceFactor = 0;

    // get a new AVL tree node with empty pointer fields
    newNode = GetAVLTreeNode(item,NULL,NULL);

    // call recursive routine to actually insert the element
    AVLInsert(treeRoot, newNode, revise BalanceFactor);

    // assign new values to data members in the base class
    root = treeRoot;
    current = newNode;
    size++;
}
```

The heart of the insertion algorithm is the recursive method AVLInsert. Like its counterpart in BinSTree, it traverses the left subtree if item < node value and the right subtree if item $\geq$ node value. This private function has a parameter called tree, which maintains a record of the current node in the scan, the new node to insert in the tree, and a flag called revisebalanceFactor. As we scan the left or right subtree of a node, the flag notifies us if any balanceFactors in the subtree have been changed. If so, we must check that AVL height balance is preserved. If the insertion of the new node disrupts the equilibrium of the tree and distorts a balance factor, we must reestablish the AVL equilibrium. We develop the algorithm using a series of examples.

AVL Insert Algorithm   The insert process resembles that used by the binary search tree. We recursively scan down a path of left and right children until an empty subtree is identified and then tentatively insert the new node at that location. During the process, we visit each node in the search path from the root to the new entry.

Since the process is recursive, we have access to the nodes in reverse order and can update the balance factor in a parent node after learning of the effect of adding the new item in one of its subtrees. At each node in the search path, we determine if an update is necessary. We are confronted with three possible situations. In two cases, the node maintains AVL balance and no restructuring of subtrees is necessary. Only the balanceFactor of the node must be updated. The third case unbalances the tree and requires us to perform a single or double rotation of nodes to rebalance the tree.

Case 1: A node on the search path is initially balanced (balanceFactor = 0). After adding a new item in a subtree, the node becomes heavy on the left or the right, depending on which of its subtrees stores the new item. We update balanceFactor to −1 if the item is stored in the left subtree and 1 if stored in the right subtree. For instance, each node on the path 40 − 50 − 60 is initially balanced. After inserting 55, the balanceFactors are changed.

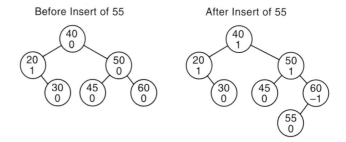

Case 2: A node on the path is weighted to the left or right subtree and the new item is stored in the other (lighter) subtree. The node then becomes balanced. For instance, compare the status of the tree before and after inserting 55.

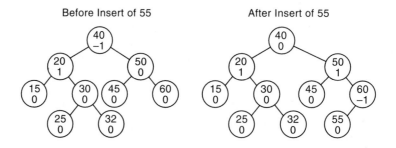

Case 3: A node on the path is weighted to the left or right subtree and the new item is positioned in the same (heavier) subtree. The resulting node violates the AVL condition since balanceFactor is out of AVL range −1 . . . 1. The algorithm directs us to rotate nodes to restore height balance.

We illustrate the cases with pictures and an example. We assume the tree becomes unbalanced to the left, and we adjust by calling rotate right functions. The cases are symmetric when the tree becomes unbalanced to the right.

The following illustrates the action. We include additional details when developing the rotation algorithms.

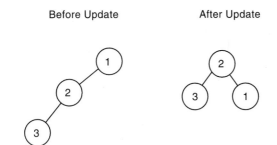

Before Update   After Update

Single Rotation

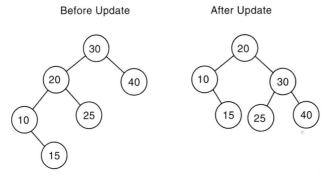

Before Update   After Update

Double Rotation

The AVLInsert Method   While traversing down the search path to insert a node, this recursive method identifies the three node update cases. When Case 3 occurs, the AVL condition is violated and we are forced to rebalance nodes. The operations are implemented by the functions UpdateLeftTree and UpdateRightTree.

```
template <class T>
void AVLTree<T>:: AVLInsert(AVLTreeNode<T>* &tree,
               AVLTreeNode<T>* newNode, int& reviseBalance Factor)
{
    // flag indicates change node's balanceFactor will occur
    int rebalanceCurrNode;

    // scan reaches an empty tree; time to insert the new node
    if (tree == NULL)
    {
        // update the parent to point at newNode
        tree = newNode;

        // assign balanceFactor = 0 to new node
        tree->balanceFactor = balanced;
```

```
      // broadcast message;  balanceFactor value is modified
      reviseBalanceFactor = 1;
}
// recursively move left if new data < current data
else if (newNode->data < tree->data)
{
   AVLInsert(tree->Left(),newNode,rebalanceCurrNode);
   // check if balanceFactor must be updated.
   if (rebalanceCurrNode)
   {
      // went left from node that is left heavy. will
      // violate AVL condition; use rotation (case 3)
      if (tree->balanceFactor == leftheavy)
         UpdateLeftTree(tree,reviseBalanceFactor);

      // went left from balanced node. will create
      // node left on the left. AVL condition OK (case 1)
      else if (tree->balanceFactor == balanced)
      {
         tree->balanceFactor = leftheavy;
         reviseBalanceFactor = 1;
      }
      // went left from node that is right heavy. will
      // balance the node. AVL condition OK (case 2)
      else
      {
         tree->balanceFactor = balanced;
         reviseBalanceFactor = 0;
      }
   }
   else
      // no balancing occurs; do not ask previous nodes
      reviseBalanceFactor = 0;
}

// otherwise recursively move right
else
{
   AVLInsert(tree->Right(), newNode, rebalanceCurrNode);
   // check if balanceFactor must be updated.
   if (rebalanceCurrNode)
   {
      // went right from node that is left heavy. will
      // balance the node. AVL condition OK (case 2)
      if (tree->balanceFactor == leftheavy)
      {
         // scanning right subtree. node heavy on left.
         // the node will become balanced
         tree->balanceFactor = balanced;
```

```
            reviseBalanceFactor = 0;
        }
        // went right from balanced node. will create
        // node heavy on the right. AVL condition OK (case 1)
        else if (tree->balanceFactor == balanced)
        {
            // node is balanced; will become heavy on right
            tree->balanceFactor = rightheavy;
            reviseBalanceFactor = 1;
        }
        // went right from node that is right heavy. will
        // violate AVL condition; use rotation (case 3)
        else
            UpdateRightTree(tree, reviseBalanceFactor);
    }
    else
        reviseBalanceFactor = 0;
    }
}
```

AVLInsert identifies situations for case 3 that cause a node to violate the AVL condition. The insert uses the methods UpdateLeftTree and UpdateRightTree to carry out the rebalancing. These private functions select the appropriate single or double rotation to balance a node and then set the flag reviseBalanceFactor to 0 (FALSE) to notify the parent that the subtree is balanced. We give the code before describing specific details for the rotations.

```
template <class T>
void AVLTree<T>::UpdateLeftTree (AVLTreeNode<T>* &p,
                        int &reviseBalanceFactor)
{
    AVLTreeNode<T> *lc;

    lc = p->Left();            // left subtree is also heavy
    if (lc->balanceFactor == leftheavy)
    {
        SingleRotateRight(p);    // need a single rotation
        reviseBalanceFactor = 0;
    }
    // is right subtree heavy?
    else if (lc->balanceFactor == rightheavy)
    {
        // make a double rotation
        DoubleRotateRight(p);
        // root is now balanced
        revisedBalanceFactor = 0;
    }
}
```

Rotations   Rotations are necessary when the parent node P becomes unbalanced. A **single right rotation** occurs when both the parent node (P) and the left child (LC) become heavy on the left after inserting the node at position X. We rotate the nodes so that LC replaces the parent, which becomes a right child. In the process, we take the nodes in the right subtree of LC (ST) and attach them as a left subtree of P. This maintains the ordering since nodes in ST are greater than or equal to LC but less than P. The rotation balances both the parent and left child.

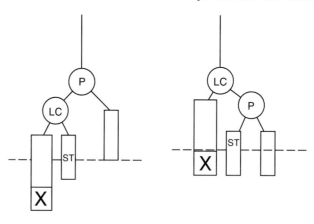

```
// rotate clockwise about node p;   make lc the new pivot
template <class T>
void AVLTree<T>::SingleRotateRight (AVLTreeNode<T>* &p)
{
    // the left subtree of p is heavy
    AVLTreeNode<T> *lc;

    // assign the left subtree to lc
    lc = p->Left();

    // update the balance factor for parent and left child
    p->balanceFactor = balanced;
    lc->balanceFactor = balanced;

    // any right subtree st of lc must continue as right
    // subtree of lc.  do by making it a left subtree of p
    p->Left() = lc->Right();

    // rotate p (larger node) into right subtree of lc
    // make lc the pivot node
    lc->Right() = p;
    p = lc;
}
```

In the following AVL tree, an attempt to insert 5 causes node 30 to violate the AVL condition. At the same time, the left subtree of node 15 (LC) becomes heavy and we call the SingleRotateRight routine to reorder the nodes. In the process, the parent node (node 30) becomes balanced and node 10 becomes heavy on the left.

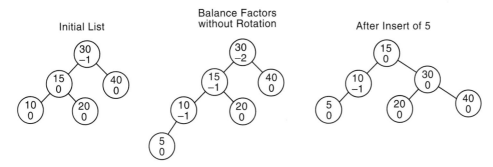

A **double right rotation** occurs when the parent node (P) becomes heavy on the left and the left child (LC) become heavy on the right. NP is the root of the heavy right subtree of LC. We rotate the nodes so that NP replaces the parent node. In the following diagrams, we describe two cases where the new node is inserted as a child of NP. In each case, NP becomes the parent node and the original parent P rotates to the right subtree of NP.

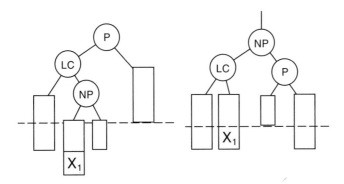

In the first diagram, we see the shift of node X_1 after it is inserted in the left subtree of NP. The second diagram illustrates the repositioning of X_2 after its insertion in the right subtree of NP.

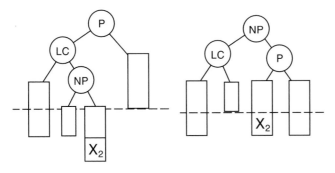

```
// double rotation right about node p
template <class T>
void AVLTree<T>::DoubleRotateRight (AVLTreeNode<T>* &p)
{
    // two subtrees that are rotated
    AVLTreeNode<T> *lc, *np;

    // in the tree, node(lc) <= node(np) < node(p)
    lc = p->Left();      // lc is left child of parent
    np = lc->Right();    // np is right child of lc

    // update balance factors for p, lc, and np
    if (np->balanceFactor == rightheavy)
    {
        p->balanceFactor = balanced;
        lc->balanceFactor = rightheavy;
    }
    else if (np->balanceFactor == balanced)
    {
        p->balanceFactor = balanced;
        lc->balanceFactor = balanced;
    }
    else
    {
        p->balanceFactor = rightheavy;
        lc->balanceFactor = balanced;
    }
    np->balanceFactor = balanced;

    // before np replaces the parent p, take care of subtrees
    // detach old children and attach new children
    lc->Right() = np->Left();
    np->Left() = lc;
    p->Left() = np->Right();
    np->Right() = p;
    p = np;
}
```

The following trees illustrate double rotation. An attempt to insert 25 unbalances the root node 50. In this case, node 20 (LC) has a heavy right subtree and a double rotation is required. The new parent node (NP) becomes node 40. The original parent rotates to the right subtree and attaches node 45, which also rotates from the left side of the tree.

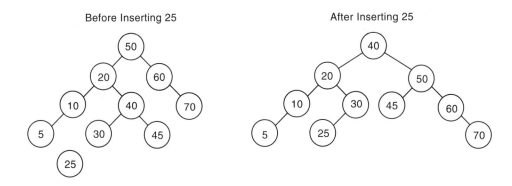

Before Inserting 25

After Inserting 25

EVALUATING AVL TREES

The value of AVL trees depends on the application, since you have the additional overhead of maintaining height balance as you insert and delete nodes. If the tree repeatedly adds or removes items, the operations can require a significant amount of time. On the other hand, if you have data that turns a binary search tree into a degenerate tree, you lose the efficiency of a tree in searching for elements and can effectively use an AVL tree.

There is no worst case AVL tree since the structure approximates a complete binary tree. A Find operation executes in $O(\log_2 n)$ time. Empirical evidence indicates that rotations are required on approximately 50% of the insertions and deletions. The complexity of the balancing operations indicates that AVL trees should be used only when data searches are the dominant operations.

Program 13.4   Evaluating AVL Trees

This program compares AVL and binary search trees on *N* random entries. The items are stored in a single array and are inserted into the two trees. We scan the array and search for each item in each tree, maintaining the accumulated length of each search. This is the depth of the node from the root. For output, we compute the average depth of an element in the binary search tree and the AVL tree.

The program is run on 1000 and 10,000 elements. For random data, note that the AVL tree depths are somewhat better. In a worst case scenario, a degenerate search tree with 1000 elements has an average depth of 500 items, whereas the AVL tree maintains a steady average depth of 9.

```
#include <iostream.h>
#include "bstree.h"
#include "avltree.h"
#include "random.h"
```

```cpp
// loads array, binary search tree and AVL tree with same n
// random numbers in the range 0 - 999
void SetupLists( BinSTree<int> &Tree1, AVLTree<int> &Tree2,
                 int A[], int n)
{
   int i;
   RandomNumber rnd;

   // store random number in array A and use value to
   // inserts a new node in binary search and avl trees
   for (i = 0; i < n; i++)
   {
      A[i] = rnd.Random(1000);
      Tree1.Insert(A[i]);
      Tree2.Insert(A[i]);
   }
}


// searching for item in tree t.  add to accumulated total,
// the length of path from root to the value
template <class T>
void PathLength(TreeNode<T> *t, long &totallength, int item)
{
   // once item is found or if item is not in the list, return
   // the length of the path has been determined
   if (t == NULL || t->data == item)
      return;
   else
   {
      // moving to the next level;  increment total length
      totallength++;
      if (item < t->data)
         PathLength(t->Left(), totallength, item);
      else
         PathLength(t->Right(), totallength, item);
   }
}


void main(void)
{
   // variables for trees and array
   BinSTree<int>    binTree;
   AVLTree<int>     avlTree;
   int    *A;

   // total length of searches to find items from array A in
   // BinSTree and AVLTree
   long totalLengthBintree = 0, totalLengthAVLTree = 0;
   int n,i;
```

```
      cout << "How many nodes do you want in the trees? ";
      cin >> n;

      // setup the lists for the array and the trees
      A = new int[n];
      SetupLists(binTree,avlTree,A,n);

      for (i = 0; i < n; i++)
      {
         PathLength(binTree.GetRoot(), totalLengthBintree, A[i]);
         PathLength((TreeNode<int> *)avlTree.GetRoot(),
                    totalLengthAVLTree, A[i]);
      }

      cout  << "Average search length for BinSTree is "
            << float(totalLengthBintree)/n << endl;
      cout  << "Average search length for AVLTree is "
            << float(totalLengthAVLTree)/n << endl;
   }

/*

<Run #1 of Program 13.4>

How many nodes to test? 1000
Average search length for BinSTree is 10.256
Average search length for AVLTree is 7.901

<Run #2 of Program 13.4>

How many nodes to test? 10000
Average search length for BinSTree is 12.2822
Average search length for AVLTree is 8.5632

*/
```

Tree Iterators   13.7

We have observed the power of iterators for the traversal of linear structures that include arrays and sequential lists. The scanning of nodes in a tree is more difficult since a tree is a nonlinear structure and there is no one traversal order. The TreeNode utilities of Chapter 11 provide preorder, inorder, and postorder algorithms, which allow us to scan a tree recursively and execute a function at each node. The problem with each of these traversal methods is that there is no escape from the recursive process until it completes. We cannot stop the scan, examine the contents of a node, perform various operations on the data, and then continue the scan at another node of the tree. By using an iterator, a client has a tool to scan the nodes of a tree as if they form a linear list without the burdensome details of the underlying scanning algorithm.

THE INORDER ITERATOR

In Chapter 12, we developed the abstract Iterator class to establish a set of basic list traversal methods. The Iterator class gives a common format for traversal methods independent of the implementation details in a derived class. In this section, we use this base class to derive an inorder binary tree iterator. The inorder scan, when applied to a binary search tree, visits the data in increasing order and is a useful tool. The construction of preorder, level order, and postorder iterators are left as an exercise.

DECLARATION

```
// Inorder iterator for a binary tree; uses Iterator base class
template <class T>
class InorderIterator: public Iterator<T>
{
    private:
        // maintain a stack of TreeNode addresses
        Stack< TreeNode<T> * > S;
        // tree root and current node
        TreeNode<T> *root, *current;

        // traverse a left path. used by Next
        TreeNode<T> *GoFarLeft(TreeNode<T> *t);
    public:
        // constructor
        InorderIterator(TreeNode<T> *tree);

        // implementations of basic traversal operations
        virtual void Next(void);
        virtual void Reset(void);
        virtual T& Data(void);

        // assign new tree list to iterator
        void SetTree(TreeNode<T> *tree);
};
```

DESCRIPTION

InorderIterator follows the general iterator pattern. The method EndOfList is implemented in the base class Iterator. The constructor initializes the base class and locates the first inorder node using GoFarLeft. The class is found in the file "treeiter.h".

EXAMPLE

```
TreeNode<int> *root;                // a binary tree
InorderIterator treeiter(root);     // attach an iterator
```

```
// print first node in scan; for inorder traversal
// node is the leftmost node in the tree
cout << treeiter.Data();

// scan the nodes and print their value
for (treeiter.Reset(); !treeiter.EndOfList(); treeiter.Next())
    cout << treeiter.Data() << " ";
```

INORDERITERATOR CLASS IMPLEMENTATION

An iterative inorder traversal emulates the recursive scan by using a stack to hold node addresses. Start at the root node and traverse the chain of left subtrees placing on a stack the pointers to each of the nodes in the chain. The process stops at a node with a NULL left pointer. This becomes the first node that is visited in the inorder scan.

The method GoFarLeft starts at node address t and stacks the addresses of all nodes in the path until a NULL pointer is found. Calling GoFarLeft with t=root locates the first node to be visited.

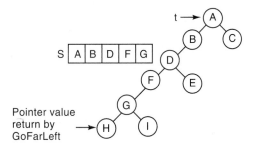

```
// return address of last node on the left branch from t,
// stacking node addresses as we go
template <class T>
TreeNode<T> *InorderIterator<T>::GoFarLeft(TreeNode<T> *t)
{
    // if t is NULL, return NULL
    if (t == NULL)
        return NULL;

    // go as far left in the tree t as possible, stacking each
    // node address on S until a node is found with a NULL
    // left pointer. return a pointer to that node
    while (t->Left() != NULL)
    {
        S.Push(t);
        t = t->Left();
    }
    return t;
}
```

After initializing the base class, the **constructor** sets the data member root to the root of the binary search tree. The first node in the inorder traversal is obtained by calling GoFarLeft with root as its parameter. The return value is assigned to the TreeNode pointer current.

```
// initialize iterationComplete. base class sets it to 0, but
// tree may be empty. first node in traversal is farthest
// node left.
template <class T>
InorderIterator<T>::InorderIterator(TreeNode<T> *tree):
        Iterator<T>(), root(tree)
{
    iterationComplete = (root == NULL);
    current = GoFarLeft(root);
}
```

The Reset method is essentially the same as the constructor, except that it clears the stack.

Before the first call to **Next,** current already points to the first node in an inorder scan. Next implements the inorder traversal from node to node. It implements steps 1 and 2 of the following algorithm.

1. If the right branch of the node is not empty, move to the right and traverse the chain of left branches, placing pointers to each node on a stack, until a node with a NULL left pointer is found.

2. If the right branch of the node is empty, we have completed the scan of the node's left branch, the node itself, and its right branch. The address of the next node to visit is on the stack. If the stack is not empty, pop it to determine the next node in the scan. If the stack is empty, all nodes have been visited and we have completed the scan.

The following picture depicts the execution of an iterative scan for a five node tree.

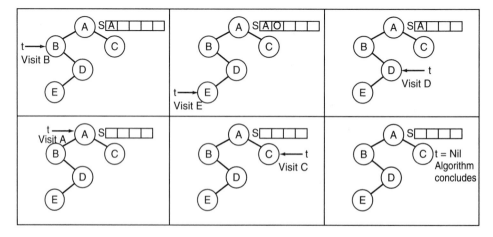

```
template <class T>
void InorderIterator<T>::Next(void)
{
    // error if we have already visited all the nodes
    if (iterationComplete)
    {
        cerr << "Next: iterator has passed the end of the list!"
            << endl;
        exit(1);
    }

    // we have visited node current
    // if have a right subtree, move right and go far left,
    // stacking up nodes on the left subtree
    if (current->Right() != NULL)
        current = GoFarLeft(current->Right());

    // no right subtree but there are other nodes we have
    // stacked that we must process. pop stack into current
    else if (!S.StackEmpty())        // move up the tree
        current = S.Pop();

    // no right branch of current node and no stacked nodes.
    // the traversal is complete
    else
        iterationComplete = 1;
}
```

APPLICATION: TREESORT

When an InorderIterator object traverses a search tree, the resulting items are traversed in sorted order and we can generate another sort algorithm called the TreeSort. The algorithm assumes the items are initially stored as an n element array. The search tree acts like a filter with the elements copied from the array to the tree using the search tree insert algorithm. By traversing the tree inorder and inserting the elements back into the array, the resulting list is sorted. Figure 13.5 illustrates sorting an 8-element integer array. The tree sort algorithm is implemented by the function TreeSort that is contained in file "treesort.h."

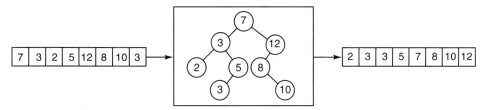

Figure 13.5   The TreeSort

```
#include "bstree.h"
#include "treeiter.h"

// use a binary search tree to sort an array
template <class T>
void TreeSort(T arr[], int n)
{
    // binary search tree in which array data is placed
    BinSTree<T> sortTree;
    int i;

    // insert each array element into the search tree
    for (i=0;i < n;i++)
        sortTree.Insert(arr[i]);

    // declare an inorder iterator for sortTree
    InorderIterator<T> treeSortIter(sortTree.GetRoot());

    // traverse tree inorder. assign each element back to arr
    i = 0;
    while(!treeSortIter.EndOfList())
    {
        arr[i++] = treeSortIter.Data();
        treeSortIter.Next();
    }
}
```

Efficiency of the Tree Sort   The expected number of comparisons needed to locate a data value in a binary search tree is $O(\log_2 n)$. Since the tree sort places n values in the tree, we intuitively find the average computational efficiency to be $O(n \log_2 n)$. However, the worst case is $O(n^2)$, which occurs when the list is already sorted or is in reverse order. The corresponding search tree is a degenerate tree in the form of a linked list. A more analytical look at the worst case indicates that $O(n^2)$ comparisons are required. The first insertion requires 0 comparisons. The second insertion requires two comparisons (1 with the root node and 1 to determine in which subtree to insert the value). The third insertion requires three comparisons, the 4*th* insertion requires four comparisons, . . . , the n*th* insertion requires n comparisons. The total number of comparisons is:

```
0+2+3+4+ ... +n
= (1+2+3+4+ ... +n) - 1
= n(n+1)/2 - 1 = O(n²)
```

Storage must be allocated for each node of the tree, and the worst case is no better than the exchange sort.

When n random data values are repeatedly inserted into a binary search tree, we expect the tree to be relatively balanced. The best case occurs when the tree is complete. We can evaluate an upper bound for this best case by looking at a full tree of depth d. At each level i, $1 \le i \le d$, there are 2^i nodes. Since it requires i+1 comparisons to place a node at level i, the tree sort for the full tree takes (i+1) * 2^i comparisons to locate all of the elements at level i. If we recall that $n = 2^{d+1} - 1$, the following inequality leads to the Big-O measure of efficiency.

$$\sum_{i=1}^{d} (i + 1)2^i \le (d + 1) \sum_{i=1}^{d} 2^i = (d + 1)(2^{d+1} - 2)$$

$$= (d + 1)(2^{d+1} - 1 - 1) = (d + 1)(n - 1)$$
$$= (n - 1) \log_2(n + 1)$$
$$= O(n \log_2 n)$$

The calculation shows that the best case for the tree sort is $O(n \log_2 n)$.

Graphs   13.8

A tree is a hierarchical structure that consists of nodes emanating from a root. The nodes are connected by pointers that link a parent to its children. In this section we introduce a graph, which is a generalized hierarchical structure. A graph is composed of a set of data items called **vertices** and a set of **edges** that connect pairs of vertices. The edge $E = (V_i, V_j)$ connects vertex V_i to V_j:

Vertices = $\{V_0, V_1, V_2, V_3, \ldots, V_{m-1}\}$
Edges = $\{E_0, E_1, E_2, E_3, \ldots, E_{n-1}\}$

If the vertices represent cities and the edges represent a highway system, movement can occur in both directions between the cities. The edges do not have an associated direction and G is called an **undirected graph.**

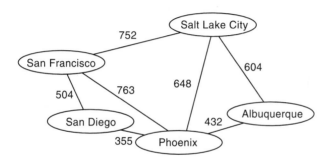

Directed Graph   Undirected Graph

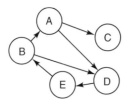   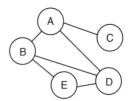

Vertices V = {A,B,C,D,E}   Vertices V = {A,B,C,D,E}
Edges E = {(A,C),(A,D),(B,A),(B,D), (D,E),(E,B)}   Edges E = {(A,B),(A,C),(A,D),(B,A),(B,D),
                                                            (B,E),(C,A),(D,A),(D,B),(D,E)
                                                            (E,B),(E,D)}

Figure 13.6   Directed and Undirected Graph

If the edges represent a communication system, there may be a flow of information from one node to another but not in the reverse direction. In this case, G becomes a **directed graph** or **digraph.** Figure 13.6 describes graph G as both a directed and undirected graph. Our development focuses on directed graphs.

For a digraph, an edge is given by the pair (V_i, V_j) where V_i is the starting vertex and V_j is the ending vertex. A **path,** $P(V_S, V_E)$, is sequence of vertices $V_S = V_R$, $V_{R+1}, \ldots, V_{R+T} = V_E$, where V_S is the starting vertex, V_E is the ending vertex, and each successive pair is an edge. In a digraph, we refer to a directed path from V_B and V_E. In the case of the digraph, there may not be a path from V_E to V_B. For instance, in the digraph G of Figure 13.6,

Path(A,B) = {A, D, E, B}   Path(E,C) = {E,B,A,C)
Path(B,A) = {B,A}   Path(C,E) = {}   // no path

CONNECTED COMPONENTS

The concept of path also defines connectivity in a digraph. Two vertices V_i and V_j are **connected** if there is a path from V_i to V_j. A digraph is **strongly connected** if there is a directed path from any vertex to any other vertex. The digraph is **weakly connected** if for each pair of vertices V_i and V_j, there is a directed path $P(V_i, V_j)$ or $P(V_i, V_j)$. Figure 13.7 illustrates the connectedness of a digraph.

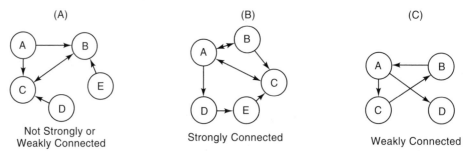

(A)	(B)	(C)
Not Strongly or Weakly Connected	Strongly Connected	Weakly Connected

Figure 13.7   Strong and Weak Connected Components in a Digraph

We extend the concept of strongly connected vertices to form a **strongly connected component,** which is a maximal set of vertices $\{V_i\}$ such that for each pair V_i and V_j there is a path from V_i to V_j and a path from V_j to V_i. A **cycle** is a path with three or more vertices that connect a vertex to itself with no repeated edges. In the directed graph (C) of Figure 13.7, there are cycles for vertices A (A->C->B->A), B, and C. A graph that contains no cycles is called an **acyclic** graph.

In a **weighted digraph,** there is an associated value or weight for each edge. In a transportation digraph, the weights could represent distances between cities. In a job scheduling graph, the value of an edge could define the length of time to finish a task.

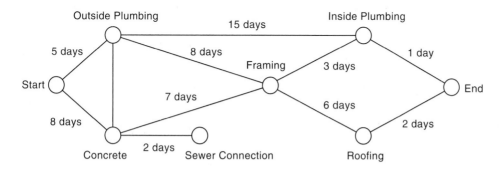

The Graph Class 13.9

In this section we describe a data structure for a weighted digraph. We start with the mathematical definition of a graph as the foundation for the Graph ADT. The vertices are given as a list of elements, while the edges are defined as a list of ordered pairs that connect the vertices.

DECLARING A GRAPH ADT

A weighted digraph consists of vertices and weighted edges. The ADT is designed around operations that will add or delete these data items. For each vertex V_i, the ADT identifies all adjacent vertices V_j that are connected to V_i by an edge $E(V_i, V_j)$.

ADT Graph **is**

    Data

        A set of vertices $\{V_i\}$ and edges $\{E_i\}$. An edge is a pair (V_i, V_j) that indicates there is a link from vertex V_i to vertex V_j. Associated with each edge is a weight that defines a cost to travel along edge (V_i, V_j).

    Operations

      Constructor

        Input: None

Process:	Creates the graph as a set of vertices and edges.

InsertVertex

Input:	A new vertex.
Preconditions:	None
Process:	Insert the vertex in the set of vertices.
Output:	None
Postconditions:	The vertex list is increased.

InsertEdge

Input:	A pair of vertices V_i and V_j and a weight W.
Preconditions:	V_i and V_j must be in the set of vertices and the edge (V_i, V_j) must not be in the set of edges.
Process:	Insert the edge (V_i, V_j) with value W in the set of edges.
Output:	None
Postconditions:	The set of edges is increased.

DeleteVertex

Input:	A reference to the vertex V_D.
Preconditions:	The input value must be in the set of vertices.
Process:	Delete the vertex from the list of vertices and delete all edges of the form (V, V_D) or (V_D, V) that establish a link to vertex V_D.
Output:	None
Postconditions:	The set of vertices and the set of edges are modified.

DeleteEdge

Input:	A pair of vertices V_i and V_j.
Preconditions:	The input values must be in the set of vertices.
Process:	If the edge (V_i, V_j) exists, delete it from the edge list.
Output:	None
Postconditions:	The set of edges is modified.

GetNeighbors

Input:	A vertex V.
Preconditions:	None
Process:	Identify all vertices V_E such that (V, V_E) is an edge.
Output:	Return the list of all such vertices.
Postconditions:	None

```
GetWeight
    Input:              A pair of vertices Vᵢ and Vⱼ.
    Preconditions:      The input values must belong to the
                        set of vertices.
    Process:            Retrieve the weight of the edge (Vᵢ,
                        Vⱼ) if it exists.
    Output:             Return the weight of the edge or 0 if
                        the edge does not exist.
    Postconditions:     None

end ADT Graph
```

Representing Graphs   There are a variety of representations for the vertices V and edges E in a digraph. A simple technique stores the members of V as a sequential list $V_0, V_1, \ldots, V_{m-1}$. The edges of a graph are identified by an $m \times m$ square matrix, called an **adjacency matrix,** in which row i and column j correspond to vertices V_i and V_j, respectively. Each entry (i, j) in the matrix gives the weight of the edge $E_{ij} = (V_i, V_j)$ or 0 if the edge does not exist. For an unweighted digraph, an entry in the adjacency matrix has boolean values 0 and 1 to indicate whether the pair corresponds to an edge in the graph. For instance, the following are digraphs with their respective adjacency matrices:

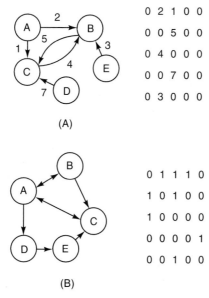

```
0 2 1 0 0
0 0 5 0 0
0 4 0 0 0
0 0 7 0 0
0 3 0 0 0
```

(A)

```
0 1 1 1 0
1 0 1 0 0
1 0 0 0 0
0 0 0 0 1
0 0 1 0 0
```

(B)

Another representation of a graph associates with each vertex a linked list of its adjacent vertices. The list identifies the neighbors of the vertex. This dynamic model stores information on precisely the edges that actually belong to the graph. For a weighted digraph, each node in the linked list contains a weight field. The following lists provide a representation of digraph (A) and (B).

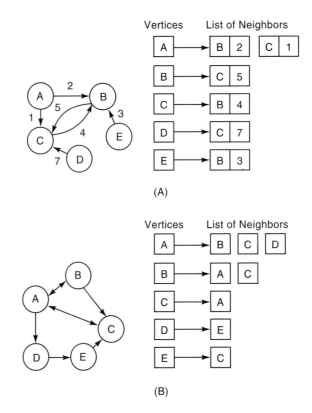

(A)

(B)

In this section, use develop a Graph class that assumes the adjacency matrix representation of edges. We use a static model of a graph that assumes an upper bound on the number of vertices. The use of matrices simplifies the class implementation and allows us to focus on a variety of graph algorithms. An implementation using the linked list representation is given in the exercises. The main features of the Graph class are a representation of the Graph ADT, an input method ReadGraph, and a series of search algorithms that produce a depth first and breadth first traversal of the vertices. The class also includes a vertex list iterator for use with applications.

GRAPH CLASS SPECIFICATION

DECLARATION

```
const int MaxGraphSize = 25;

template <class T>
class Graph
{
```

```
    private:
        // key data including list of vertices, adjacency matrix
        // and current size (number of vertices) of the graph
        SeqList<T> vertexList;
        int edge [MaxGraphSize][MaxGraphSize];
        int graphsize;

        // methods to find vertex and identify position in list
        int FindVertex(SeqList<T> &L, const T& vertex);
        int GetVertexPos(const T& vertex);

    public:
        // constructor
        Graph(void);

        // graph test methods
        int GraphEmpty(void) const;
        int GraphFull(void) const;

        // data access methods
        int NumberOfVertices(void) const;
        int NumberOfEdges(void) const;
        int GetWeight(const T& vertex1, const T& vertex2);
        SeqList<T>& GetNeighbors(const T& vertex);

        // graph modification methods
        void InsertVertex(const T& vertex);
        void InsertEdge(const T& vertex1, const T& vertex2,
                        int weight);
        void DeleteVertex(const T& vertex);
        void DeleteEdge(const T& vertex1, const T& vertex2);

        // utility methods
        void ReadGraph(char *filename);
        int MinimumPath(const T& sVertex, const T& eVertex);
        SeqList<T>& DepthFirstSearch(const T& beginVertex);
        SeqList<T>& BreadthFirstSearch(const T& beginVertex);

        // iterator used to scan the vertices
        friend class VertexIterator<T>;
};
```

DESCRIPTION

The data members for the class include the vertices that are stored in a sequential list, the edges that are represented by a two-dimensional integer matrix, and data value graphsize, which counts the number of vertices. The value graphsize is returned by the method NumberofVertices.

The utility method FindVertex checks whether a vertex already exists in list L. This is used by the search methods. The method GetVertexPos translates a vertex to a position in vertexList. The position corresponds to a row or column index in the adjacency matrix.

The ReadGraph method is given the name of the file that is used to input the vertices and edges of a graph.

A VertexIterator is derived from the SeqListIterator class and enables the user to scan the vertices. The iterator simplifies applications.

EXAMPLE

```
Graph<char>  G;                    // graph with char vertices
G.ReadGraph("graph.dat");          // read data from "graph.dat"
```

```
            // Sample input for the graph
    <Number of Vertices>   4
    Vertex₀                A
    Vertex₁                B
    Vertex₂                C
    Vertex₃                D
    <Number of Edges>      5
    Edge₀     Weight₀      A C 1
    Edge₁     Weight₁      A D 1
    Edge₂     Weight₂      B A 1
    Edge₃     Weight₃      C B 1
    Edge₄     Weight₄      D A 1
```

```
VertexIterator<char> Viter(G);   // iterator for vertices
SeqList<char>L;

for (viter.Reset(); !viter.EndOfList(); viter.Next())
{

    cout << "For vertex " << viter.Data() << ": Neighbors are ";

    L = G.GetNeighbors(viter.Data());

    // print the neighbors
    SeqListIterator<char>  liter(L);      // list of neighbors
    for (liter.Reset(); !liter.EndOfList(); liter.Next())
        cout << liter.Data() << "   ";
}
```

GRAPH CLASS IMPLEMENTATION

The constructor for the Graph class is responsible for initializing the Max-GraphSize × MaxGraphSize adjacency matrix and setting the graph size to 0. The constructor sets each entry in the matrix to 0 to indicate that there are no edges.

```
// constructor initializes entries in the adjacency matrix
// to 0 and sets the graphsize to 0
```

```
template <class T>
Graph<T>::Graph(void)
{
    for (int i = 0; i < MaxGraphSize; i++)
        for (int j = 0; j < MaxGraphSize; j++)
            edge[i][j] = 0;
    graphsize = 0;
}
```

Counting Graph Components   The private data member graphsize maintains the size of the vertex list. Its value can be accessed with the method NumberOfVertices. The class operator GraphEmpty indicates whether the graphsize is 0.

Accessing Graph Components   The components of a graph are contained in the vertex list and the adjacency matrix. For the vertices, a **vertex iterator** allows us to scan the items in the vertex list. The iterator is a friend in the Graph class so that it has access to vertexList. The graph iterator is inherited from the SeqListIterator class.

```
template <class T>
class VertexIterator: public SeqListIterator<T>
{
    public:
        VertexIterator(Graph<T>& G);
};
```

The constructor simply initializes the base class to traverse the private data member vertexList. The following code gives the implementation of this constructor:

```
template <class T>
VertexIterator<T>::VertexIterator(Graph<T>& G):
    SeqListIterator<T> (G.vertexList)
{}
```

The iterator scans items in the vertexList and is used to implement the function **GetVertexPos** that scans the vertex list and returns the position of the vertex in the list. The following iterator code searches for the vertex:

```
template <class T>
int Graph<T>::GetVertexPos(const T& vertex)
{
    SeqListIterator<T> liter(vertexList);
    int pos = 0;

    while(!liter.EndOfList() && liter.Data() != vertex)
    {
        pos++;
        liter.Next();
```

```
        }
        return pos;
    }
```

For each edge, the method **GetWeight** returns the weight of the edge connecting vertex1 and vertex2. The method uses GetVertexPos to get the position of the two vertices in the list and hence the row-and-column entry in the adjacency matrix. If either vertex is not in the list, the method returns -1.

For a vertex parameter, the method **GetNeighbors** creates a list of all adjacent vertices. The method scans the adjacency matrix and identifies a list of nodes V_E such that (V, V_E) is an edge. The list is returned as a parameter and can be scanned using a SeqList iterator. If the vertex has no neighbors, the method returns an empty list.

```
// return the list of all adjacent vertices
template <class T>
SeqList<T>& Graph<T>::GetNeighbors(const T& vertex)
{
    SeqList<T> *L;
    SeqListIterator<T> viter(vertexList);

    // allocate an SeqList
    L = new SeqList<T>;

    // look up pos in list to identify row in adjacency matrix
    int pos = GetVertexPos(vertex);
    // if vertex not in list of vertices, terminate
    if (pos == -1)
    {
        cerr << "GetNeighbors: vertex not in graph." << endl;
        return *L;   // return empty list
    }
    // scan row of adjacency matrix and include all vertices
    // having a non-zero weighted edge from vertex
    for  (int i = 0; i < graphsize; i++)
    {
        if (edge[pos][i] > 0)
            L->Insert(viter.Data());
        viter.Next();
    }
    return *L;
}
```

Updating Vertices and Edges   To insert an edge, we use GetVertexPos to check that both vertex1 and vertex2 are in the vertex list. If either item is not found, an error message occurs and the method returns. Once the positions pos1 and pos2 of the vertices are established, InsertEdge places the weight of the edge in (pos1,pos2) of the adjacency matrix. This operation has computing time $O(n)$ since each execution of GetVertexPos is $O(n)$.

The Graph class provides the method DeleteVertex to remove a vertex from the graph. If the vertex is not in the list, an error message is printed and the method returns. If it is present, however, we must delete all edges that create a link with the deleted vertex. There are three regions in the adjacency matrix that must be adjusted. Hence, the operation has computing time $O(n^2)$ since each region is a portion of the $n \times n$ adjacency matrix.

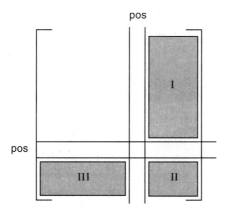

Region I: Shift the column index to the left.
Region II: Shift the row index up and the column index to the left.
Region III: Shift the row index up.

```
// delete a vertex from vertex list and update the adjacency
// matrix to remove all edges linked to the vertex.
template <class T>
void Graph<T>::DeleteVertex(const T& vertex)
{
    // get the position in the vertex list
    int pos = GetVertexPos(vertex);
    int row, col;

    // if vertex is not present, notify and return
    if (pos == -1)
    {
        cerr << "DeleteVertex: vertex is not in the graph."
            << endl;
        return;
    }

    // delete the vertex and decrement graphsize
    vertexList.Delete(vertex);
    graphsize--;

    // the adjacency matrix is partitioned into three regions
    for (row = 0; row < pos; row++)            // region I
        for (col = pos + 1;col < graphsize;col++)
            edge[row][col-1] = edge[row][col];
```

```
    for (row = pos+1;row < graphsize;row++)      // regionII
        for (col = pos + 1; col < graphsize; col++)
            edge[row-1][col-1] = edge[row][col];

    for (row = pos+1;row < graphsize;row++)      // region III
        for (col = 0; col < pos; col++)
            edge[row-1][col] = edge[row][col];
}
```

To delete an edge, we simply remove the link between the two vertices. After testing that the vertices are in vertexList, the method DeleteEdge assigns a 0 weight to the edge and leaves the other edges unchanged. If the edge is not in the graph, the program prints an error message and returns.

GRAPH TRAVERSALS

When scanning a nonlinear structure, we must develop a strategy to access the nodes and to mark them once they are visited. Binary trees define a series of searching methods that have a counterpart with graphs. The preorder binary tree scan uses the strategy of visiting a node and then driving down the subtrees. For graphs, the **depth-first** search is a generalization of the preorder traversal. The starting vertex is passed as a parameter and becomes the first vertex that is visited. As we move down a path until we reach a "dead end", we store adjacent vertices on a stack so that we can return and search down other paths if unvisited vertices remain. The visited vertices is the set of all vertices that are reachable from the starting vertex.

Trees feature a level order scan that starts at the root and visits the nodes by level down to the depth of the tree. With a graph, the **breadth-first** search uses a similar strategy by starting at an initial vertex and visiting each of its adjacent vertices. The scan continues to the next level of adjacent vertices, and so forth, until we reach the end of a path. The algorithm uses a queue to store the adjacent vertices as we scan from level to level in the graph. We illustrate both searching algorithms with the following graph. In each case, the initial vertex is A.

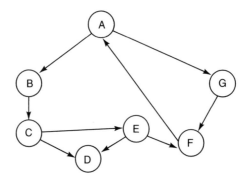

Depth-First Search   The search algorithm uses a list L to maintain a record of visited vertices and a stack S to store adjacent vertices. After placing the initial vertex on the stack, we begin an iterative process that pops a vertex from the stack and then visits the vertex. We terminate when the stack is empty and return the list of visited vertices. For each step, use the following strategy.

> Pop a vertex V from the stack and check with list L to see if V has been visited. If not, we are visiting a new vertex and use the opportunity to get a list of its adjacent vertices. We insert V in list L so that it is not revisited. We conclude by pushing the adjacent vertices of V that are not already in L on the stack.

For our sample graph, assume A is the starting vertex. The search begins by popping A from the stack and processing the vertex. Insert A in the list of visited nodes and push the adjacent vertices B and G on the stack. After handling A, the storage structures for S and L have the following data:

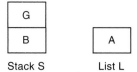

The iteration continues by popping G from the stack. Since this vertex is not yet in L, we add it to L and add its single adjacent vertex F to the stack:

After popping F from the stack and placing the vertex in L, we reach a dead-end since the neighbor A of F is already in list L. In the stack, this leaves vertex B, which was originally identified as a neighbor of A during the first phase of the search:

The search continues by visiting nodes B and C in that order. The stack then contains nodes D and E, which are the neighbors of C:

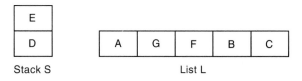

Both D and F are adjacent to E and eligible to enter the stack. However, F was visited along the path A–G–F and is not used again. Node D is pushed on the stack for a second time because our algorithm does not recognize that D was also available from C:

Stack S   List L

The search completes by visiting node D. The second occurrence of D is discarded because the vertex is already in the list:

List L

```cpp
// from a starting vertex, return depth first scanning list
template <class T>
SeqList<T> & Graph<T>::DepthFirstSearch(const T& beginVertex)
{
    // stack to temporarily hold waiting vertices
    Stack<T> S;

    // L is list of nodes on the scan; adjL holds the
    // neighbors of the current vertex. L is created
    // in dynamic memory so a reference to it can be
    // returned
    SeqList<T> *L, adjL;
    // iteradjL used to traverse neighbor lists
    SeqListIterator<T> iteradjL(adjL);
    T vertex;

    // initialize return list; push starting vertex on stack
    L = new SeqList<T>;
    S.Push(beginVertex);

    // scan continues until the stack is empty
    while (!S.StackEmpty())
    {
        // pop next vertex
        vertex = S.Pop();
        // check if it is already in L
        if (!FindVertex(*L,vertex))
        {
            // if not, put it in L and get all adjacent vertices
            (*L).Insert(vertex);
            adjL = GetNeighbors(vertex);
```

```
            // set iterator to current adjL
            iteradjL.SetList(adjL);

            // scan list of neighbors; put on stack if not in L
            for(iteradjL.Reset();!iteradjL.EndOfList();iteradjL.Next())
                if (!FindVertex(*L,iteradjL.Data()))
                    S.Push(iteradjL.Data());
        }
    }
    // return depth first scan list.
    return *L;  // return list
}
```

Breadth-First Search   The breadth-first search uses a queue as does the level order scan of a binary tree. The algorithm uses the techniques developed for the depth-first search. Vertices are placed in a queue instead of a stack. An iterative process removes vertices from the queue until it is empty.

Delete a vertex V from the queue and check to see if V is in the list of visited nodes. If V is not in L, we have a new vertex, which must be added to L. At the same time, we get all neighbors of V and insert them in the queue provided they are not in the list of visited nodes.

If the algorithm were executed for the same graph used to illustrate the depth-first search, the vertices are visited in the order

A B G C F D E

Complexity Analysis   In the search algorithms, we visit each vertex, which requires computing time $O(n)$. Once a vertex is added to the list of visited nodes, we check a row of the adjacency matrix to identify all of its adjacent nodes. Each row is $O(n)$ and hence the total computing time of each search algorithm is $n*O(n) = O(n^2)$. The number of comparisons required by the adjacency matrix representation of a graph is independent of the number of edges in the graph. Even if the graph has relatively few edges ("sparse graph"), we still must make n comparisons for each vertex in the graph. With a list representation of a graph, the computing time of the search algorithms depends on density of the edges in the graph. In the best case, there are no edges and the length of each adjaceny list is 1. The computing time for each search would be $O(n + n) = O(n)$. In the worst case, each vertex is connected to every other vertex and the length of each adjacency list is n. A search algorithm in this case has order $O(n^2)$.

APPLICATIONS

We recall that a digraph is strongly connected if there is a direct path from any vertex to any other vertex. A **strong component** is a subset of vertices that are strongly connected to each other. A strongly connected graph has one strong compo-

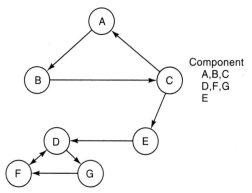

Figure 13.8 Strong Components

nent, but any graph can be partitioned into a series of strong components. For instance, in Figure 13.8, the graph is partitioned into three strong components.

In the theory of graphs, classical algorithms are used to determine the strong components. In the following application, we use depth-first search to design a nonoptimized method for finding the strong components of a graph. The depth-first search is used by function PathConnect that tests whether there are direct paths from vertex v to w and returns a boolean value of TRUE or FALSE:

```
template <class T>
int PathConnect (Graph<T> &G, T v, T w)
{
   SeqList<T> L;

   // find vertices connected to v
   L = G.DepthFirstSearch(v);
   // if w is in the list, return TRUE
   if (L.Find(w))
      return 1;
   else
      return 0;
}
```

The function ConnectedComponent begins with an empty list of vertices named markedList. Throughout the algorithm, the list contains the collection of vertices that have been located in a strong component. Using an iterator, a loop traverses each vertex of the graph. For each vertex V, check to see if it is in markedList. If not, a new strong component containing V must be built. Clear the list scList that will contain the new strong component and use the depth-first search to locate the list L of all vertices reachable from V. For each element of L, use PathConnect to determine if there is a path back to V. Whenever such a path exists, put the vertex in scList and markedList. Note that V is added to both scList and markedList. Since there is a path from V to each vertex in scList and a path from each vertex in scList back to V, it follows that there is a path between any two vertices in scList. The vertices are the next strong component. Since each vertex in scList is also in markedList, it will not be considered again.

```cpp
template <class T>
void ConnectedComponent (Graph<T> &G)
{
    VertexIterator<T> viter(G);
    SeqList<T> markedList, scList, L, K;

    for (viter.Reset(); !viter.EndOfList(); viter.Next())
    {
        // loop checks each vertex viter.Data()
        if (!markedList.Find(viter.Data()))

        // if not marked, put in a strong component
        {
            scList.ClearList();

            // Get vertices connected to viter.Data()
            L = G.DepthFirstSearch(viter.Data());

            // Scan list to see if the node is connected
            // back to viter.Data()
            SeqListIterator<T> liter(L);
            for (liter.Reset();!liter.EndOfList();liter.Next())
                if (PathConnect(G,liter.Data(),viter.Data()))
                {
                    // insert vertices in the current strong
                    // component and in markedList
                    scList.Insert(liter.Data());
                    markedList.Insert(liter.Data());
                }
            PrintList(scList);    // Print the strong component
            cout << endl;
        }
    }
}
```

Program 13.5   **Strong Components**

This program finds the strong components for the graph in Figure 13.8. The graph is entered from file "sctest.dat" using ReadGraph. The functions PathConnect, ConnectedComponent, and PrintList are found in the file "conncomp.h".

```cpp
#include <iostream.h>
#include <fstream.h>
```

```
#include "graph.h"

#include "conncomp.h"

void main(void)
{
    Graph<char> G;

    G.ReadGraph("sctest.dat");

    cout << "Strong Components:" << endl;
    ConnectedComponent(G);
}

<Run of Program 13.5>

Strong Components:
A   B   C
D   G   F
E
```

Minimum Path   The depth-first and breadth-first search identify vertices that are on a path from the intial node. The algorithms do not attempt to optimize the movement from vertex to vertex and identify a minimum path, a problem that we now address. Many applications want to select a path that requires a minimum "cost" as measured by the accumulated weights on a path between vertices. To find a minimum path between two nodes, we introduce a new class, called PathInfo, whose objects specify paths connecting two vertices and a data value that measures the cumulative cost of traveling on a path between the vertices. The PathInfo objects are stored in a priority queue that provides us with access to the object in the queue having minimum cost.

```
template <class T>
struct PathInfo
{
    T startV, endV;
    int cost;
};

template <class T>
int operator <= (const PathInfo<T>& a, const PathInfo<T>& b)
{
    return a.cost <= b.cost;
}
```

Since a graph may allow for different paths between vertices, two PathInfo objects can connect the same vertices but have different cost functions. For instance, there are three paths connecting vertex A to vertex D. Each has a different cost.

Path	Cost
A – C – D	13
A – B – D	14
A – B – C – D	11

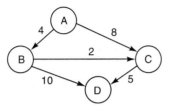

The PathInfo class defines the "<=" operator by comparing the cost value. The algorithm looks at PathInfo objects that are stored in a priority queue and selects the one with the minimum path. The following graph illustrates the algorithm used to identify a minimum path algorithm that connects a starting vertex, sVertex, with an ending vertex, eVertex. If there is no path connecting the vertices, the algorithm terminates and prints the message. In the example, the starting vertex is A and the ending vertex is D.

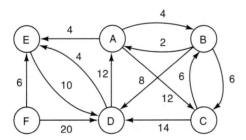

Start by creating the first PathInfo object that connects sVertex to itself with initial cost 0. Insert the object in the Priority Queue.

A to A	0

Priority Queue

To find a minimum path, we follow an iterative process that deletes objects from the priority queue. If the ending vertex in the object is eVertex, we have a minimum path whose cost is the data value cost. Otherwise, we look at all neighbors of the current vertex endV and look to extending our path from sVertex along one more edge.

In our example, we wish to find the minimum path from A to D. We delete the single PathInfo object, which has A as endV. If A is the designated eVertex, the process is finished and the minimum cost is 0. If A is not the end vertex, we store it in list L, which contains all vertices whose minimum path from A is known. We identify vertices B, C, and E as the neighbors of A. Create PathInfo objects corresponding to each vertex and place them in the priority queue. The cost from

A to each of these nodes is

```
cost A to <neighbor> = cost(A,endV) + weight(endV,<neighbor>)
```

PathInfo Object	**startV**	**endV**	**cost**
$O_{A,B}$	A	B	4
$O_{A,C}$	A	C	12
$O_{A,E}$	A	E	4

The objects enter the priority queue in the following order:

A to B	4		A to E	4		A to C	12

Priority Queue

For the next step, delete object $O_{A,B}$ from the priority queue. Vertex B is endV with a minimum cost of 4. Since B is not in L, we enter it into the list. Clearly no subsequent path can have a cost A to B of less than 4 since if one existed we would have a subpath

$$A - X - \ldots - B$$

and X would be a neighbor of A with distance of less than 4. Then X would have been deleted from the priority queue prior to B.

We identify the neighbors of B, which are A, C, and D. Since A is already in L, we focus on C and D and create PathInfo objects to enter the priority queue.

PathInfo Object	**startV**	**endV**	**cost**
$O_{B,C}$	B	C	$10 = 4 + 6$
$O_{B,D}$	B	D	$12 = 4 + 8$

The resulting priority queue has four members. Note that two different objects terminate at vertex C. The minimum value 10 just entered the priority queue and represents the path A–B–C. The direct path A–C, which was identified in step 1, has a cost of 12.

A to E	4		A to C	12		B to C	10		B to D	12

Priority Queue

After deleting object $O_{A,E}$ and identifying the minimum cost from A to E as 4, we create object $O_{E,D}$ with cost 14.

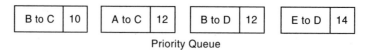

B to C	10		A to C	12		B to D	12		E to D	14

Priority Queue

In the next deletion from the priority queue, object $O_{B,C}$ is the minimum value and we can add C to list L since we identify 10 as the minimum cost from A to C.

Assume endVertex is D and we are waiting to delete an object with D as the end vertex. After handling node C, we identify its neighbors as B and D. Since B is already handled, only object $O_{C,D}$ enters the priority queue with

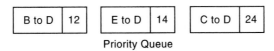

Object	startV	endV	distance
$O_{C,D}$	C	D	24 = 10 + 14

When object $O_{A,C}$ is deleted from the priority queue, it is discarded because C is already in the list. The priority queue now has three elements.

| B to D | 12 | | E to D | 14 | | C to D | 24 |

Priority Queue

With the removal of $O_{B,D}$ from the priority queue, we identify the minimum cost of A to D as 12.

```
template <class T>
int Graph<T>::MinimumPath(const T& sVertex, const T& eVertex)
{
    // priority queue into which info about path cost
    // from sVertex is placed
    PQueue< PathInfo<T> > PQ(MaxGraphSize);
    // used when inserting PathInfo entries
    // into the priority queue or deleting entries
    PathInfo<T> pathData;
    // L holds list of all vertices reachable from sVertex
    // whose cost we have considered. adjL is neighbor
    // list of vertices we are visiting. adjLiter is used
    // to traverse adjL.
    SeqList<T> L, adjL;
    SeqListIterator<T> adjLiter(adjL);
    T sv, ev;
    int mincost;


    // formulate initial priority queue entry
    pathData.startV = sVertex;
    pathData.endV = sVertex;
    // cost from sVertex to sVertex is 0
    pathData.cost = 0;
    PQ.PQInsert(pathData);

    // process vertices until we find a minimum path to
    // eVertex or the priority queue is empty
    while (!PQ.PQEmpty())
    {
```

```
    // delete a priority queue entry and record its
    // ending vertex and cost from sVertex.
    pathData = PQ.PQDelete();
    ev = pathData.endV;
    mincost = pathData.cost;

    // if we are at eVertex, we have found the minimum
    // path from sVertex to eVertex
    if (ev == eVertex)
        break;

    // if ending vertex is already in L, do not consider
    // it again
    if (!FindVertex(L,ev))
    {
        // insert ev into L
        L.Insert(ev);
        // find all neighbors of the current vertex ev. for
        // each neighbor that is not in L, generate an entry
        // and insert it into priority queue with starting
        // vertex ev
        sv = ev;
        adjL = GetNeighbors(sv);
        // adjLiter traverses new list adjL
        adjLiter.SetList(adjL);
        for(adjLiter.Reset();!adjLiter.EndOfList();
                              adjLiter.Next())
        {
            ev = adjLiter.Data();
            if (!FindVertex(L,ev))
            {
                // create new entry for the priority queue
                pathData.startV = sv;
                pathData.endV = ev;
                // cost is current minimum cost plus the cost
                // of going from sv to ev
                pathData.cost = mincost+GetWeight(sv,ev);
                PQ.PQInsert(pathData);
            }
        }
    }
}

// return success or failure
if (ev == eVertex)
    return mincost;
```

```
    else
        return -1;
}
```

___

___

Program 13.6   Airline Transportation System
___

An airline transportation system lists the cities on a route. The user enters a source city and the minimum path method determines the shortest travel distance between the source and all possible destinations. The airline travels to major cities in the West.

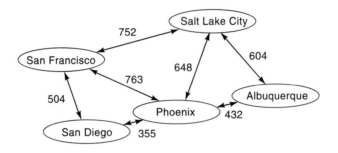

___

```
#include <iostream.h>
#include <fstream.h>

#include "strclass.h"
// include the graph class with the MinimumPath method
#include "graph.h"

void main(void)
{
    // vertices are strings (airline cities)
    Graph<String>   G;
    String  S;

    // input the vertices for transportation graph
    G.ReadGraph("airline.dat");

    // prompt for the departure city
    cout << "Give the minimum distance when departing from ";
    cin >> S;
```

```
        // using a graph iterator, scan the list of cities and
        // determine the minumum distance from the departure city
        VertexIterator<String>  viter(G);
        for (viter.Reset(); !viter.EndOfList(); viter.Next())
            cout << "Minimum distance from " << S << " to "
                    << viter.Data() << " is "
                    << G.MinimumPath(S,viter.Data()) << endl;
}
/*

<Run #1 of Program 13.6>

Give the minimum distance when departing from SaltLakeCity
Minimum distance from SaltLakeCity to SaltLakeCity is 0
Minimum distance from SaltLakeCity to Albuquerque is 604
Minimum distance from SaltLakeCity to Phoenix is 648
Minimum distance from SaltLakeCity to SanFrancisco is 752
Minimum distance from SaltLakeCity to SanDiego is 1003

<Run #2 of Program 13.6>

Give the minimum distance when departing from SanFrancisco
Minimum distance from SanFrancisco to SaltLakeCity is 752
Minimum distance from SanFrancisco to Albuquerque is 1195
Minimum distance from SanFrancisco to Phoenix is 763
Minimum distance from SanFrancisco to SanFrancisco is 0
Minimum distance from SanFrancisco to SanDiego is 504
*/
```

REACHABILITY AND WARSHALL'S ALGORITHM

For each pair of vertices in a graph, we say that V_j is reachable from V_i if and only if there is a directed path from V_i to V_j. This defines the **reachability relation R.** For each vertex V_i, the depth-first search identifies the list of all vertices that are reachable from V_i. If we use the depth-first search for each vertex of the graph, we get a series of reachability lists that identify the relation R:

V_1:   \<Reachability List for V₁\>
V_2:   \<Reachability List for V₂\>
. . .
V_n: \<Reachability List for Vₙ\>

The same relation can also be described with an $n \times n$ **reachability matrix** that has a 1 in location (i, j) provided $V_i \ R \ V_j$. The following define the reachability lists and reachability matrix for the graph:

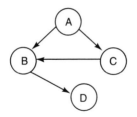

Reachability Lists   **Reachability Matrix**

A: A B C D   1 1 1 1
B: B D   0 1 0 1
C: C B   0 1 1 0
D: 0 0 0 1

The reachability matrix can be used to determine whether a path exists between two vertices. If the element at (i,j) is 1, there is a minimum path between V_i and V_j. We can use the vertices in the reachability list to augment the edges in the original graph. If there is a path from vertex v to w (w is reachable from v), we add the edge $E(v,w)$ that connects the two vertices. The extended graph G' consists of the vertices V from G and edges linking vertices that are connected by a directed path. The extended graph is called the **transitive closure.** For instance, the transitive closure of G is shown here:

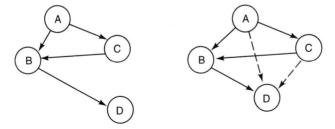

The problem of finding the reachability list with the depth-first search is left as an exercise. A more elegant approach uses a famous algorithm by Stephan Warshall who observed the following. The reachability matrix of a graph can be constructed by a process that assigns a 1 in the matrix for each pair of vertices linked by a common vertex. Assume we are building reachability matrix R and vertices a, b, c correspond to indices i, k, j. If R[i][k] = 1 and R[k][j] = 1, set R[i][j] = 1.

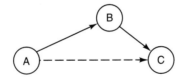

The Warshall algorithm looks at all possible triples by creating three nested loops with indices *i*, *j*, and *k*. For each pair *(i,j)*, we add an edge $E(v_i, v_j)$ if there is a vertex v_k such that $E(v_i, v_k)$ and $E(v_k, v_j)$ are in the extended graph. By repeating this process, we add edges that connect any pair of reachable nodes. This builds the reachability matrix.

An intuitive argument illustrates the Warshall algorithm. Assume that vertices *v* and *w* are reachable with a directed path of five vertices that connect *v* to *w*. There is a sequence of vertices that form the path

$$V = X_1, X_2, X_3, X_4, X_5 = W$$

In the reachability matrix, if we have a path from *v* to *w*, we must show that the Warshall algorithm would ultimately identify the same path. With the triple nesting of loops, we look at all possible vertex triples. Assume that vertices x_1 to x_5 occur in that order. As we look at the different triples, x_2 is identified as a common node linking x_1 and x_3. Hence, by Warshall, we introduce a new edge $E(x_1, x_3)$. With the pair x_1 and x_4, we have x_3 as a common vertex since the path connecting x_1 and x_3 was found in a previous stage of the iteration and so we create the edge $E(x_1, x_4)$. Continuing this analysis, x_4 is a common vertex linking x_1 and x_5 and hence we add the edge $E(x_1, x_5)$ and assign R[1][5] = 1.

We illustrate Warshall's algorithm on the following graph. The edges in dotted lines are added to form the transitive closure.

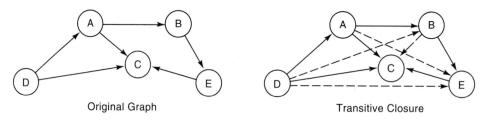

Original Graph   Transitive Closure

Reachability Matrix
1 1 1 0 1
0 1 1 0 1
0 0 1 0 0
1 1 1 1 1
0 0 1 0 1

Warshall's algorithm has computing time $O(n^3)$. In scanning the adjacency matrix, we have three nested loops. Even the list representation of a graph results in the $O(n^3)$ complexity.

Program 13.7 Using Warshall's Algorithm

The Warshall Algorithm is used to create and print the reachability matrix.

```cpp
#include <iostream.h>
#include <fstream.h>

#include "graph.h"

template <class T>
void Warshall(Graph<T>& G)
{
    VertexIterator<T> vi(G), vj(G);

    int i, j, k;
    int WSM[MaxGraphSize][MaxGraphSize];   // Warshall matrix
    int n = G.NumberOfVertices();

    // create the initial matrix
    for(vi.Reset(),i=0;!vi.EndOfList();vi.Next(),i++)
        for(vj.Reset(),j= 0;!vj.EndOfList();vj.Next(), j++)
            if (i == j)
                WSM[i][i] = 1;
            else
                WSM[i][j] = G.GetWeight(vi.Data(),vj.Data());

    // look at all triples. assign 1 to WSM when an edge from
    // vi to vj exists or there is a triple vi - vk - vj
    // connecting vi and vj.
    for (i = 0; i < n; i++)
        for (j = 0; j < n; j++)
            for (k = 0; k < n; k++)
                WSM[i][j] |= WSM[i][k] & WSM[k][j];

    // print each vertex and its row of the reachability
    // matrix
    for (vi.Reset(), i=0;!vi.EndOfList();vi.Next(), i++)
    {
        cout << vi.Data() << ":   ";
        for (j = 0; j < n; j++)
            cout << WSM[i][j] << "   ";
        cout << endl;
    }
}

void main(void)
{
    Graph<char> G;

    G.ReadGraph("warshall.dat");

    cout << "The reachability matrix is:" << endl;
    Warshall(G);
}
```

```
/*
<Run of Program 13.7>

The reachability matrix is:
A:  1  1  1  0  1
B:  0  1  1  0  1
C:  0  0  1  0  0
D:  1  1  1  1  1
E:  0  0  1  0  1
*/
```

Written Exercises

13.1   Draw the complete tree corresponding to each of the following arrays:

(a)   int A[8] = {5, 9, 3, 6, 2, 1, 4, 7};

(b)   char *B = "array-based tree";

13.2   For each of the following trees, give the corresponding array:

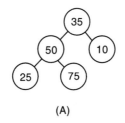

(A)

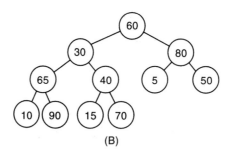

(B)

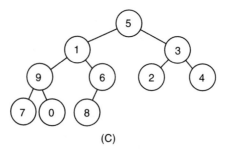

(C)

13.3 Write (a) preorder and (b) inorder recursive scan functions for array-based trees. Use the code developed for linked tree nodes as a model.

13.4 Assume A is an array-based tree with 70 members.

    (a) Is A[45] a leaf node?
    (b) What is the index of the first leaf node?
    (c) Who is the parent of A[50]?
    (d) Who are the children of A[10]?
    (e) Does any item have exactly one child?
    (f) What is the depth of the tree?
    (g) How many leaf nodes does the tree have?

13.5 (a) Write a function that takes an array of N elements of type T and performs a level order scan of the corresponding array-based tree. Your routine should use a queue to store the elements. Output the elements with a newline inserted at each change of level.

    (b) Can you design a simpler version of the level order scan that takes advantage of the fact that we have an array representation of the tree?

13.6 In a complete binary tree, show that the number of leaf nodes is greater than or equal to the number of nonleaf nodes. In a full binary tree, show there are more leaf nodes than nonleaf nodes.

13.7 A complete binary tree B, containing 50 nodes, represents an array.

    (a) What is the level of the tree?
    (b) How many nodes are leaf nodes? Nonleaf nodes?
    (c) What is the index of the parent of B[35]?
    (d) What is the index of the children of node B[20]?
    (e) What is the index of the first node with no children? With one child?
    (f) What are the indices for all nodes at level 4 in the tree?

13.8 Hand code the steps of the Tournament sort while sorting the array A = {7, 10, 3, 9, 4, 12, 15, 5, 1, 8}.

13.9 Modify the tournament sort so that both the leaf and nonleaf nodes contain the actual data from the array. Include the modified code in a function ModTournamentSort.

13.10 For each tree indicate whether it is a heap (maximum or minimum).

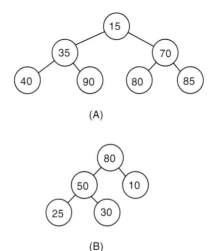

(A)

(B)

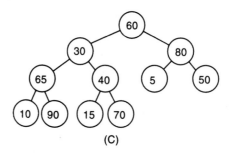

(C)

13.11 Take each nonheap tree from Written Exercise 13.10 and create both a maximum heap tree and a minimum heap tree. For each minimum (maximum) heap tree, create the corresponding maximum (minimum) heap.tree.

13.12 Use the FilterDown and constructor algorithms to "heapify" the following tree and create a minimum heap:

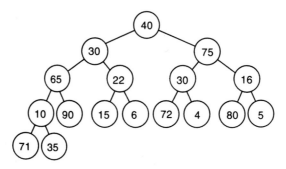

13.13 The exercise inserts and deletes elements in heaps (A) and (B). Corresponding to each heap, there is a sequence of operations that are to be executed sequentially. Use the result of the previous operation as you execute each part of the exercise.

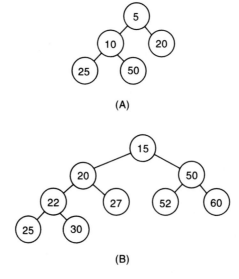

Heap (A)		**Heap (B)**	
(a)	insert 15	(a)	delete 22
(b)	insert 35	(b)	insert 35
(c)	delete 10	(c)	insert 65
(d)	insert 40	(d)	delete 15
(e)	insert 10	(e)	delete 27
		(f)	insert 5

13.14 (a) What is the largest number of nodes that can exist in a tree that is both a minimum heap tree and a binary search tree? Do not allow duplicate values.

(b) What is the largest number of nodes that can exist in a tree that is both a maximum heap tree and a binary search tree? Do not allow duplicate values.

13.15 For the following heap, list the value of the nodes along the designated path:

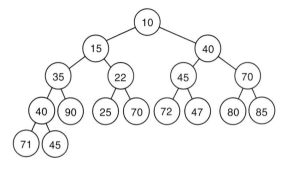

(a) the path of parents beginning with node 47
(b) the path of parents beginning with node 71
(c) the path of minimal children beginning with node 35
(d) the path of minimal children beginning with node 10
(e) the path of minimal children beginning with node 40 (level 1)

13.16 Begin with the array and build the corresponding minimum heap.

(a) `int A[10] = {40, 20, 70, 30, 90, 10, 50, 100, 60, 80};`
(b) `int A[8] = {3, 90, 45, 6, 16, 45, 33, 88};`
(c) `char *B = "heapify";`
(d) `char *B = "minimal heap";`

13.17 Implement the priority queue class PQueue using BinSTree class. (*Hint:* Modify the PQDelete method to search for the minimal element and delete it from the tree.)

13.18 For each of the following, construct the AVL tree that results from inserting the items:

(a) <int> 30, 50, 25, 70, 60, 40, 55, 45, 20
(b) <int> 44, 22, 66, 11, 0, 33, 77, 55, 88
(c) <int> 1, 2, 3, 4, 5, 6, 7, 8, 9, 10
(d) <String> tree, AVL, insert, delete, find, root, search
(e) <String> class, object, public, private, derived, base, inherit, method, constructor, abstract

13.19   Develop an iterative preorder scan function Preorder_I. The function should emulate the following recursive function Preorder. We include hints to help you design the algorithm.

```
template <class T>
void Preorder (TreeNode<T> *t, void visit(T& item))
{
    while (t != NULL)
    {
        visit(t->data);
        Preorder(t->Left(), visit);
        t = t->Right();
    }
}
```

Each node is visited, followed by a visit of the left subtree and then the right subtree. An iterative preorder scan must emulate the recursive scan by using a stack to hold node addresses. Suppose we are at node A of a binary tree and execute the visit. We must next visit the left subtree of A and come back at a later point to visit the right subtree of A. In order to remember that the right subtree visit must still be executed, we store (push) the right pointer of A on a stack. After visiting all of the nodes on the left subtree of A, the stack is popped and we return to scan the right subtree. These two situations are shown in the following picture.

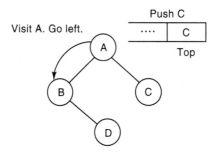

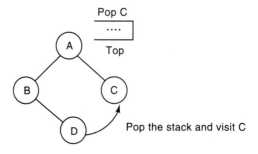

The iterative scan algorithm uses the following steps. Starting with the root node, a loop traverses the tree in preorder.

1. Visit a node.
2. Save the address of the right child of the node on a stack of node addresses.
3. Move to the left child.

Whenever a NULL node is encountered in the loop, a new right child is processed by popping the stack. The loop terminates when a NULL pointer is encountered and there are no more right children on the stack.

13.20 The function Postorder_I traverses a tree in postorder. The problem is more difficult than an inorder or preorder traversal since we must distinguish between moving down the left branch (state 0) or returning to a parent node (state 1). When moving up the tree, there are two possible actions—visit the right branch of a node or visit the node. The state is maintained in the integer variable state. If state == 0, motion is down the tree. If state == 1, motion is up. When coming up the tree, the parent of the current node is on the top of the stack. To determine if we are coming from the left, compare the node pointer to the parent's left pointer. If they agree and the parent has a right subtree, go down the subtree; otherwise, visit the node and continue up the tree.

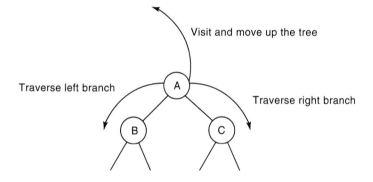

Draw a series of diagrams such as those in Figures 13.5 and 13.6 to illustrate how the algorithm works in the following program.

```
#include <iostream.h>

#include "treenode.h"
#include "treelib.h"
#include "stack.h"

void printchar(char& item)
{
    cout << item << "   ";
}

template <class T>
void Postorder_I(TreeNode<T> *t, void visit(T& item))
{
```

```
    Stack<TreeNode<T> *> S;
    TreeNode<T> *child;
    int state = 0, scanOver = 0;

    while (!scanOver)
    {
      if (state == 0)
      {
        if (t != NULL)
        {
          S.Push(t);
          t = t->Left();
        }
        else
          state = 1;
      }
      else
      {
        if (S.StackEmpty())
          scanOver = 1;
        else
        {
          child = t;
          t = S.Peek();
          if (child == t->Left() && t->Right() != NULL)
          {
            t = t->Right();
            state = 0;
          }
          else
          {
            visit(t->data);
            S.Pop();
          }
        }
      }
    }
}

void main(void)
{
    TreeNode<char> *root;

    MakeCharTree(root, 0);
    PrintTree(root,0);
    cout << endl;
    Postorder_I(root,printchar);
    cout << endl;
}
```

```
<Run>

        C
                E
A
                D
        B
D   B   E   C   A
```

13.21   For each of the following digraphs, give the adjacency matrix and the adjacency lists:

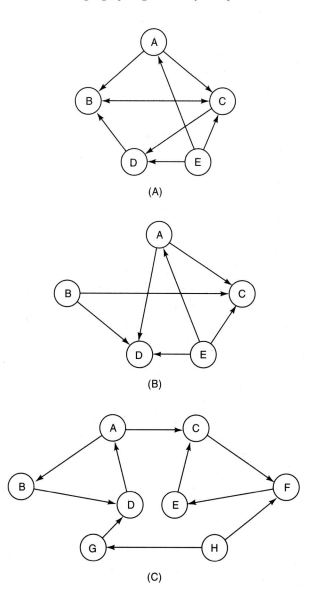

(A)

(B)

(C)

13.22 Use the graphs from Written Exercise 13.21 to answer the following questions on paths. If no path exists, respond No Path.

(a) In (A), find a directed path from E to B.
(b) In (B), find a directed path from A to E.
(c) In (C), find directed paths from B to E and E to B.
(d) In (B), find all nodes that are connected to A, to E.
(e) In (C), find all nodes X for which there is a path P(A,X) and P(X,A).
(f) List the connected components in each of the graphs.
(g) Which of the graphs are strongly connected? Weakly connected?

13.23 Use the graphs from Written Exercise 13.21 to answer the following questions. List the nodes in the order of their traversal for both the depth-first search and the breadth-first search.

(a) In (A), start at vertex A.
(b) In (B), start at vertex A.
(c) In (C), start at vertex A.
(d) In (B), start at vertex B.

13.24 Create a partial implementation of the Graph Class that uses the adjacency list representation. Define a class VertexInfo that contains the name of the vertex and a linked list that will hold information on the adjacent nodes. The information on adjacent nodes can be stored in a struct that includes the name of the ending vertex and the weight of the edge connecting the starting and ending vertices. You must add the overloaded comparison operator "==" to the class VertexInfo. The operator compares vertex names.

(a) Implement the constructor.
(b) Implement the methods GraphEmpty, NumberOfVertices, GetNeighbors, InsertVertex, InsertEdge, and DepthFirstSearch.

13.25 (a) Modify the function MinimumPath to create a function MinimumLength, which identifies the minimum number of nodes on a path from the starting vertex to the ending vertex. If a path does not exist, return -1.
(b) Create a function VertexLength that takes a graph G and a starting vertex V as parameters and prints the vertices in G and their length from V. Use the function MinimumLength from (a).

13.26 Describe the action of the following function:

```
template <class T>
SeqList<T> RV(Graph<T> &G)
{
    SeqList<T> L;
    VertexIterator<T> viter(G);
    ListIterator<T> liter(L);

    for (viter.Reset(); !viter.EndOfList(); viter.Next())
    {
```

```
        cout << viter.Data() << ":        ";
        L = G.BreadthFirstSearch(viter.Data());
        liter.SetList(L);
        PrintList(L);
        cout << endl;
    }
}
```

13.27 For each of the following adjacency matrices, draw the corresponding graph. Assume the vertices are characters A, B, and so forth.

(a)
```
0 1 1 1
1 0 1 1
1 1 0 1
1 1 1 0
```

(b)
```
0 1 1 0 0
0 0 0 1 0
1 0 0 0 1
1 0 0 1 0
0 1 0 1 0
```

13.28 For each of the following graphs, give the reachability matrix.

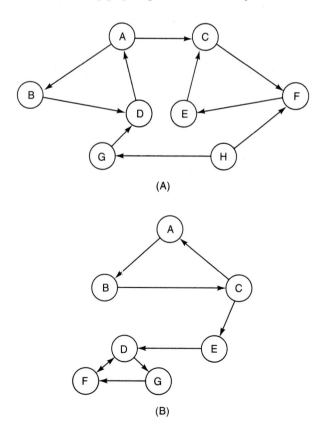

(A)

(B)

Programming Exercises

13.1 Consider the preorder scan for array-based trees from Written Exercise 13.3. Use the function to determine the number of leaf nodes, the number of nodes with one child, and the number of nodes with two children. Use global variables nochild, onechild, and twochildren to store your information in a program that tests and prints the values of the global data:

```
int A[50];      // store data 0, 1, 2, . . . , 49
int A[100];     // store data 0, 1, 2, . . . , 99
```

13.2 (a) In a test program, use the Tournament sort to order the following strings. Create an array of String objects and pass them to the TournamentSort function.

class, object, public, private, derived, base,
inherit, method, constructor, abstract

(b) In Written Exercise 13.9, you wrote a modified tournament sort called ModTournamentSort. Using this implementation of the sort, create an array of 100 random integers in the range 0 to 999 and sort them in ascending order. Print the resulting array.

13.3 Modify the Heap class to implement maximum heaps. Call the new class MaxHeap and test its operations using a variation of Program 13.3, which sorts an array of elements.

13.4 In the Heap class, implement the FilterUp and FilterDown routines recursively. Test your work by initializing a heap with an array of 15 random integers in the range 0 to 99. Use the HDelete routine to remove the N elements from the heap and print their values.

13.5 A computer system runs programs (processes) by assigning a priority to each process. Priority 0 is the highest priority and 39 the lowest. When a process is to be executed, a process request record is inserted into a priority queue. When the CPU is available, a process request record is deleted, and the process is run. The process request record has the following declaration:

```
struct ProcessRequestRecord
{
    int priority;
    String name;
};
```

The name field identifies the process. Randomly generate 10 process request records whose names are "Process A", "Process B", . . . , "Process J" and whose priority value is in the range 0 to 39. Print each record and then insert it into a priority queue. Then delete each record from the queue and print it.

13.6 Define a struct that contains a data value and a priority level.

```
template <class T>
struct PriorityData
{
   T data;
   int priority;
}
```

Use the struct and a priority queue to implement the Queue class. (Hint: Declare a queue as a list of PriorityData records. The items are stored in a priority queue ordered by the priority level of each record. Define an integer PL that is incremented when an item is inserted into the list. The value PL is assigned as the priority level of the record.)

Test your queue by reading five integers. Let QInsert store each item in the queue. Then, until the queue is empty, delete the items and print their value.

13.7 Use the model from Programming Exercise 13.6 and the MaxHeap class from Programming Exercise 13.3 to implement a stack using a priority queue.

Test the new stack class by reading five integers. Let Push store the values in a stack. Until the stack is empty, delete the items using Pop and print their value.

13.8 Develop an iterator class ArrPreorderIterator that traverses an array-based tree in preorder. Its declaration is as follows:

```
template <class T>
class ArrPreorderIterator: public Iterator<T>
{
   private:
      Stack<int> S;
      T *A;
      int arraySize;
      int current;
   public:
      ArrPreorderIterator(T *Arr, int n);
      virtual void Next(void);
      virtual void Reset(void);
      virtual T& Data(void);
};
```

Test the class by traversing the tree determined by the array

```
int A[15] = {1,4,6,2,8,9,12,25,23,55,18,78,58,14,45};
```

and printing it in level order and preorder.

13.9 The unary operator "++" can be overloaded only as a member function. The tree iterator member function Next is naturally implemented using this operator. The following is the declaration of the operator and an example of its use.

```
void operator++ (void);
```

Traverse a binary search tree.

```
BinSTree<Type> *tree;


    . . .

InorderIterator<T> inorderIter(tree.GetRoot());
while(!inorderIter.EndOfList()
{

    . . .

    inorderIter++;
}
```

Implement Next for the InorderIterator class using "++" and test the new implementation by running a program that enters 25 random integers into a binary search tree and then sorts them using the tree sort function.

13.10 Develop an iterator class LevelorderIterator that traverses a binary search tree in level order. The class declaration is

```
template <class T>: public Iterator<T>
class LevelorderIterator
{
    private:
        Queue<TreeNode<T> *> S;
        TreeNode<T> *root, *current;
    public:
        LevelorderIterator(TreeNode<T>* lst);
        virtual void Next(void);
        virtual void Reset(void);
        virtual T& Data(void);
};
```

In a main program, create the binary search tree with data

```
int data[] =
{100,55,135,145,25,106,88,90,5,26,67,45,99,33};
```

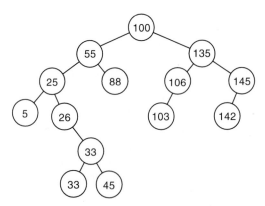

Print the tree with PrintTree and then use LevelOrderIterator to traverse the tree.

13.11 Develop a class PostOrderIterator by executing the following algorithm:

Initialize the iterator by pushing all node addresses on the stack during an NRL traversal. During traversal, the current node is always on the top of the stack and the next node is obtained by popping the stack.

Test the iterator by traversing and printing the data in the tree used for Programming Exercise 13.10.

13.12 Develop a class PostorderIterator by adapting the postorder traversal algorithm presented in Written Exercise 13.20. Test the iterator by scanning the tree given in Programming Exercise 13.10.

13.13 Using ReadGraph, create a data file for graphs A and B. Write a main program that inputs the data and then uses function VertexLength from Written Exercise 13.25 to print the length of each vertex from A. Test your program by making runs with each graph.

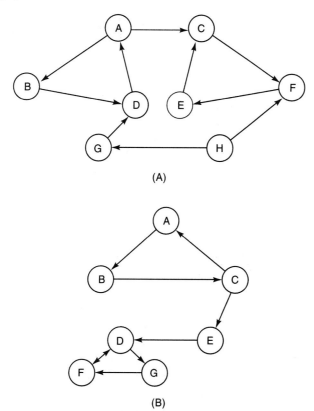

(A)

(B)

13.14 Use the graphs from Programming Exercise 13.13 and Warshall's algorithm to print the reachability matrix for each graph.

C H A P T E R   1 4

ORGANIZING
COLLECTIONS

We conclude this book with a general chapter on data organization. In the process we develop a series of classical algorithms to sort data. In previous chapters, we introduced sorting to illustrate general list structures. For instance, we introduced the radix sort as an application of queues. We now focus on sorting arrays and introduce the classical selection sort, the bubble sort, and the insertion sort, which require $O(n^2)$ comparisons. Although the algorithms are not efficient for practical use for a large number of data items, they illustrate the main approaches for sorting of an array. We conclude with the famous QuickSort.

Chapter 4 presents the sequential and binary search algorithms that represent the basic list search algorithms. In this chapter we extend our study of searching to hashing, which uses a key to provide very rapid access to elements and provides $O(1)$ complexity. We develop a generalized hash table class that allows arbitrary data types.

In this book, we have emphasized data that are stored in memory. For larger data sets, the data may be stored on disk and require external methods for access. We develop the BinFile class to handle binary files and use its methods to illustrate both the external indexed sequential search and the external merge sort algorithm.

A section on associative arrays or dictionaries generalizes the concept of an array index. This concept allows us to organize data using noninteger indices. We use associative arrays to build a small word dictionary.

Basic Array Sorting Algorithms   14.1

We begin with three algorithms that cover the main techniques of in-place sorting in ascending order. In each case, we develop the computational efficiency of the algorithm.

THE SELECTION SORT

The selection sort uses a process that is modeled on our experience. A kindergarten teacher often uses a selection technique to line up the children by height. Given a group in random order, the teacher repeatedly selects the smallest child from the group and moves him or her to a line that is forming in ascending order. This process, which is described by the following series of pictures, continues until all of the children have been moved to the ordered line.

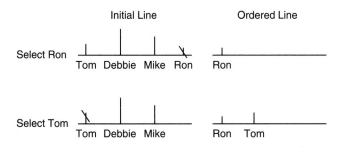

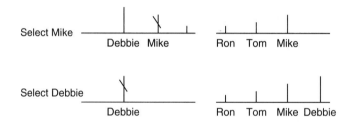

For a computer algorithm, we assume that the n data items are stored in an array A and make n − 1 passes over the list. On pass 0 (the first pass), we select the smallest element in the list and exchange it with A[0], the first element in the list. After completing pass 0, the front of the list (A[0]) is ordered and the tail (A[1] to A[n − 1]) remains unordered. Pass 1 looks at the unordered tail of the list and selects the smallest element, which is then stored in A[1]. Pass 2 locates the smallest element in the sublist A[2] to A[n − 1] and exchanges it with A[2]. The process continues through N − 1 passes at which point the tail of the list is reduced to a single element (the largest in the list) and the entire array is sorted.

Consider the selection sort algorithm for array A with five integer values 50, 20, 40, 75, and 35:

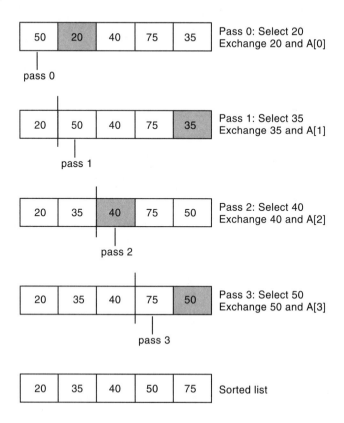

For pass I, the selection process scans sublist A[I] to A[n − 1] and sets smallIndex as the index of the smallest element. After completing the scan, the elements A[I] and A[smallIndex] exchange positions. The SelectionSort function and supporting Swap utility are stored in the file "arrsort.h".

```
// sort an array of n elements of type T using the
// selection sort algorithm
template <class T>
void SelectionSort(T A[], int n)
{
    // index of smallest item in each pass
    int smallIndex;
    int i, j;

    // sort A[0]..A[n-2], and A[n-1] is in place
    for (i = 0; i < n-1; i++)
    {
        // start the scan at index i; set smallIndex to i
        smallIndex = i;
        // j scans the sublist A[i+1]..A[n-1]
        for (j = i+1; j < n; j++)
            // update smallIndex if smaller element is found
            if (A[j] < A[smallIndex])
                smallIndex = j;
        // when finished, place smallest item in A[i]
        swap(A[i], A[smallIndex]);
    }
}
```

Computational Complexity of the Selection Sort   The selection sort re-quires a fixed number of comparisons that depend only on the size of the array and not on the initial distribution of the data. In pass i, the number of comparisons with sublist $A[i + 1]$ to $A[n − 1]$ is

$$(n − 1) − (i + 1) + 1 = n − i − 1$$

The total number of comparisons is

$$\sum_{0}^{n-2} (n − 1) − i = (n − 1)^2 − \sum_{0}^{n-2} i$$
$$= (n − 1)^2 − (n − 1)(n − 2)/2$$
$$= \frac{1}{2} n(n − 1)$$

The complexity of the algorithm as measured by the number of comparisons is $O(n^2)$ and the number of exchanges is $O(n)$. There is no best or worst case since the algorithm makes a fixed number of passes and scans a specified number of elements in each pass. The $O(n \log, n)$ heapsort is a generalization of the selection sort.

THE BUBBLE SORT

In Chapter 2, we introduced the exchange sort. This sort makes $n - 1$ passes and requires a fixed number of comparisons for each pass. In this section, we discuss the bubbble sort, which also performs a series of interchanges on each pass.

For an array A with n elements, the bubble sort requires up to n − 1 passes. For each pass, we compare adjacent elements and exchange their values when the first element is greater than the second element. At the end of the each pass, the largest element has "bubbled up" to the top of the current sublist. For instance, after pass 0 is complete, the tail of the list (A[n − 1]) is sorted and the front of the list remains unordered.

Let's look at the details of the passes. In the process, we maintain a record of the last index that is involved in an exchange. The variable lastExchangeIndex is used for this purpose and is set to 0 at the start of each pass. Pass 0 compares adjacent elements (A[0], A[1]), (A[1], A[2], . . ., A[n − 2], A[n − 1]). For each pair (A[i], A[i + 1]), exchange the values if A[i + 1] < A[i] and update lastExchangeIndex to i. At the end of the pass, the largest element is in A[n − 1] and the value lastExchangeIndex indicates that all elements in the tail of the list from A[lastExchangeIndex+1] to A[n − 1] are in sorted order. For subsequent passes, we compare adjacent elements in the sublist A[0] to A[lastExchangeIndex]. The process terminates when lastExchangeIndex = 0. The algorithm makes a maximum of n − 1 passes.

We illustrate the bubble sort algorithm with the five-element array A = 50, 20, 40, 75, 35.

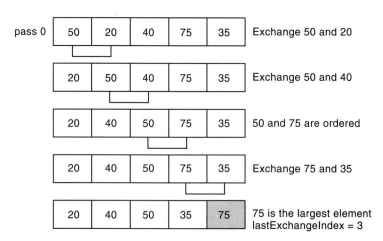

Since lastExchangeIndex is not 0, the process continues. In pass 1, we scan the sublist of elements A[0] to A[3] = A[lastExchangeIndex]. The new value of lastExchangeIndex becomes 2.

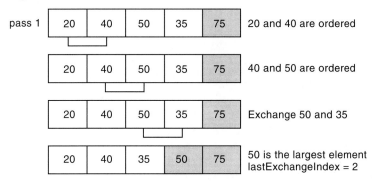

For pass 2, scan the sublist A[0] to A[2] and exchange 40 and 35. The resulting value of lastExchangeIndex is 1.

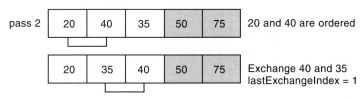

For pass 3, make the single comparison of 20 and 35. There are no exchanges, lastExchangeIndex is 0, and the process terminates.

```
// BubbleSort is passed an array A and the list count n. it
// sorts the data by making a series of passes as long as
// lastExchangeIndex > 0.
template <class T>
void BubbleSort (T A[], int n)
{
    int i,j;
    // Index of last exchange
    int lastExchangeIndex;

    // i is the index of last element in the sublist
    i = n-1;
```

```
// continue the process until no exchanges are made
while (i > 0)
{
    // start lastExchangeIndex at 0
    lastExchangeIndex = 0;

    // scan the sublist A[0] to A[i]
    for (j = 0; j < i; j++)
        // exchange a pair and update lastExchangeIndex
        if (A[j+1] < A[j])
        {
            swap(A[j],A[j+1]);
            lastExchangeIndex = j;
        }

    // set i to index of the last exchange. continue sorting
    // the sublist A[0] to A[i]
    i = lastExchangeIndex;
}
}
```

Computational Complexity of the Bubble Sort   The bubble sort maintains a record of the last exchange so that redundant scanning is not required. This gives marked efficiency to the algorithm for special cases. Most notably, the bubble sort makes a single pass over a list of elements that is already sorted in ascending order. Its best case is therefore $O(n)$. The worst case efficiency for the bubble sort occurs when the list is in descending order. The process requires all $n - 1$ passes. On pass i, there are $(n - i - 1)$ comparisons and $(n - i - 1)$ interchanges. The complete sort requires $n(n - 1)/2$ comparisons and a like number of exchanges. The complexity for this worst case is $O(n^2)$ comparisons and $O(n^2)$ exchanges. The analysis for the general case is more complicated since some of the passes may be skipped. It can be shown that the average number of passes k is still $O(n)$ and, hence, the total number of comparisons is $O(n^2)$. Even though the bubble sort may terminate in less than $n - 1$ passes, it normally requires many more interchanges than the selection sort and its average performance is slower. The exchange sort generally outperforms the bubble sort since it requires fewer interchanges.

THE INSERTION SORT

The insertion sort is similar to a familiar paper-shuffling process that orders a list of names. The registrar puts each person on a 3×5 card and then rearranges the cards in alphabetical order by sliding a card forward in the stack until it finds its correct location. As the process goes on, the cards at the front of the stack are sorted and those at the rear of the stack are waiting to be processed. We describe the process with our list of five integer values: A = 50, 20, 40, 75, 35.

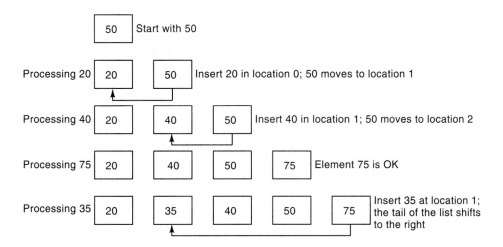

The function InsertionSort is passed an array A and the size of the list n. Let's look at pass i ($1 \le i \le n - 1$). The sublist $A[0]$ to $A[i - 1]$ is already sorted in ascending order. The pass assigns $A[i]$ to the list. Let $A[i]$ be the TARGET and move down the list, comparing the target with items $A[i - 1]$, $A[i - 2]$, and so forth. Stop the scan at the first element $A[j]$ that is less than or equal to TARGET or at the beginning of the list ($j = 0$). As we move down the list, slide each element to the right ($A[j] = A[j - 1]$). When we have found the correct location for $A[i]$, insert it at location j.

```
// insertion sort orders sublists A[0] ... A[i], 1 <= i <= n-1.
// for each i, insert A[i] in the correct position A[j]
template <class T>
void InsertionSort(T A[], int n)
{
    int i, j;
    T    temp;

    // i identifies the sublist A[0] to A[i].
    for (i = 1; i < n; i++)
    {
        // index j scans down the list from A[i] looking for
        // correct position to locate target. assigns it to A[j]
        j = i;
        temp = A[i];
        // locate insertion point by scanning downward as long
        // as temp < A[j-1] and we have not encountered the
        // beginning of the list
        while (j > 0 && temp < A[j-1])
        {
            // shift elements up list to make room for insertion
```

```
            A[j] = A[j-1];
            j--;
        }
        // the location is found; insert the temp
        A[j] = temp;
    }
}
```

Computational Complexity of the Insertion Sort   The insertion sort requires a fixed number of passes. The $n - 1$ passes insert elements $A[1]$ to $A[n - 1]$. For a general pass i, the insertion occurs in the sublist $A[0]$ to $A[i]$ and requires on the average $i/2$ comparisons. The total number of comparisons is

$$1/2 + 2/2 + 3/2 + \cdots + (N - 2)/2 + (N - 1)/2 = N(N - 1)/4$$

Unlike the other methods, the insertion sort does not use exchanges. The complexity of the algorithm is $O(n^2)$, which measures the number of comparisons. The best case occurs when the original list is already sorted. In pass i, the insertion occurs at $A[i]$ and the total number of comparisons is $n - 1$ with complexity $O(n)$. The worst case occurs when the list is sorted in descending order. Each insertion is at $A[0]$ and requires i comparisons. The total number of comparisons is $n(n - 1)/2$ with complexity $O(n^2)$.

14.2   QuickSort

Up to this point in the chapter, we have developed a series of algorithms that provide in-place sorting of array elements with $O(n^2)$ computational efficiency. In contrast, the tree-based algorithms (tournament, tree) provide significantly better $O(n \log_2 n)$ performance. Despite that fact that their use with arrays requires copying the elements to and from the tree structure, the improved sort efficiency warrants the extra overhead. The heap sort is an in-place $O(n \log_2 n)$ array sorting method that is widely used. However, the QuickSort, developed by C.J.A. Hoare, actually outperforms the heap sort for most sorting applications. It is the fastest known sorting algorithm.

QUICKSORT DESCRIPTION

Like most array sorting algorithms, the QuickSort technique is derived from familiar experiences. To sort a large stack of papers by name, we can split the papers into two piles with some pivot character such as K separating the list. All names less than or equal to K go in one pile and the rest go into the second pile. We then take each pile and split it into two parts. For instance, in Figure 14.1, the partition points are 'F' and 'R'. We continue to subdivide the piles into smaller and smaller stacks.

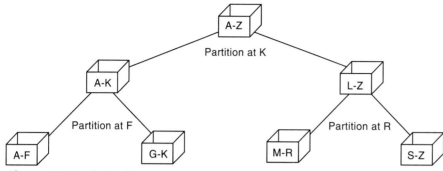

Figure 14.1   The QuickSort Partition

The QuickSort algorithm uses the partition approach to sort a list. The algorithm determines a pivot value to split the list into two parts. Unlike the sorting of papers, we do not have the luxury of a floor on which to spread the different piles. QuickSort separates the elements into parts within the array. We introduce the algorithm with an example and then add the technical details. Assume that array A contains 10 integer values:

A = 800, 150, 300, 600, 550, 650, 400, 350, 450, 700

Scanning Phase   We scan the entire range of elements in the list A[0] to A[9]. The range extends from low = 0 to high = 9 with a middle index at mid = 4. The first pivot value is A[mid] = 550 and the algorithm separates the elements of A into two sublists S_l and S_h. Sublist S_l is the lower sublist and will contain the elements that are less than or equal to the pivot. The higher sublist S_h will contain the elements that are greater than the pivot. Since we know that the pivot will ultimately end up in S_l, we temporarily move it to the low end of the range and exchange its value with A[0] (A[low]). This allows us to scan the sublist A[1] to A[9] using two indices scanUp and scanDown. The variable scanUp is initially set at index 1 (low + 1) and is responsible for locating elements in sublist S_l. Variable scanDown is set at index 9 (high) and locates elements for sublist S_h. The goal of the pass is to identify the elements in each of the sublists.

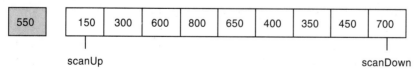

The creativity of QuickSort derives from the interaction between the two indices as they scan the list. scanUp moves up the list, whereas the index scanDown moves down the list. We move scanUp forward looking for an element A[scanUp] that is greater than the pivot. At that point the scan stops and we prepare to relocate the element to the upper sublist. Before the relocation can occur, we move the index scanDown downward in the list and wait for it to identify an element that is less than or equal to the pivot. We then have two elements that are in the wrong sublists and can exchange them.

```
Swap(A[scanUp],A[scanDown])    // swap misplaced partners
```

The process continues until scanUp and scanDown pass each other with scan-Down = 5, scanUp = 6. At this point, scanDown has first entered into the lower list, which contains the elements less than or equal to pivot. We hit the separation point between the two lists and have identified the final location for pivot. In the example, swap 600 and 450, 800 and 350, 650 and 400.

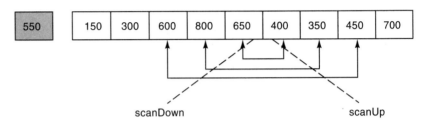

We then exchange the pivot A[0] with A[scanDown].

```
Swap(A[0],A[scanDown])
```

The result creates sublist A[0]–A[4] whose elements are less than those in sublist A[6]–A[9]. The pivot (550) at A[5] creates two sublists that are approximately one half the size of the original list. These two sublists are processed using the same algorithm in what we call the recursive phase.

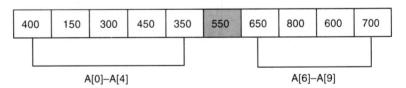

Recursive Phase   Process the two sublists S_l (A[0]–A[4]) and S_u (A[6]–A[9]) using the same methods.

Sublist S_l: The range of the sublist is 0 to 4 with low = 0, high = 4, mid = 2, and pivot is A[mid] = 300. Exchange pivot and A[low] and assign initial value to scanUp and scanDown:

```
scanUp = 1 = low+1
scanDown = 4 = high

scanUp stops at index 2 (A[2] > pivot)
scanDown stops at index 1 (A[1] < pivot)
```

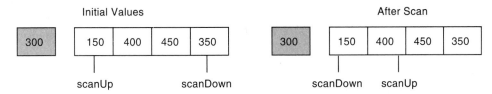

Since scanDown < scanUp, the process halts and scanDown is the separation point between two smaller sublists A[0] and A[2]–A[4]. Complete the process by exchanging A[scanDown] = 150 and A[low] = 300. Note that the location of pivot leaves us with a one-element sublist and a three-element sublist. The recursive process terminates on an empty or single-element sublist.

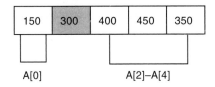

Sublist S_u: The range of the sublist is 6 to 9 with low = 6, high = 9, mid = 7, and pivot is A[mid] = 800. Exchange pivot and A[low] and assign initial values to scanUp and scanDown:

```
scanUp = 7 = low+1
scanDown = 9 = high

scanUp stops when it passes the end of the list (value = 10)
scanDown remains at its initial position
```

Since scanDown < scanUp, the process halts and scanDown locates the insertion point for pivot. Complete the process by exchanging A[scanDown] = 700 and A[low] = 800. Note that the location of pivot leaves us with a three-element sublist and an empty sublist. The recursive process terminates on an empty or single-element sublist.

700	650	600	800

Completing the Sort

```
Process sublist 400, 450, 350 (A[2]-A[4])
    pivot = 450
```

The scanning process arranges the elements in order 350, 400, 450. One more recursive call is need with the two-element sublist 350, 400.

```
Process sublist 700, 650, 600 (A[6]-A[8])
     pivot = 650
```

After scanning, the elements are arranged in the order 600, 650, 700. The values 600 and 700 constitute two one-element sublists.

The QuickSort is complete and the resulting list is sorted.

150	300	350	400	450	550	600	650	700	800

QUICKSORT ALGORITHM

The recursive algorithm partitions a list A[low] to A[high] about a pivot, which is selected from the middle of the list:

```
pivot = A[mid];     // mid = (high+low)/2
```

After exchanging the pivot value with A[low], set the indices scanUp = low+1 and scanDown = high to point at the beginning and end of the list. The algorithm manages the two indices. scanUp first moves up the list as long as it does not exceed scanDown and points at elements that are less than or equal to pivot.

```
// index scanUp traverses the elements that
// are less than or equal to pivot
while (scanUp <= scanDown && A[scanUp] <= pivot)
    scanUp++;          // go to the next element
```

After scanUp is positioned, scanDown moves down the list as long as it refers to elements that are greater than pivot.

```
// scan down upper sublist; stopping when scanDown identifies
// an element <= pivot. the scan must stop at A[low] = pivot
while (pivot < A[scanDown])
scanDown--;
```

On conclusion of this loop, if scanUp < scanDown, the vertices identify two elements that are in the wrong sublists. The values are exchanged.

```
// exchange a large element in the lower sublist
// with a small element from the higher sublist
Swap (A[scanUp],A[scanDown])
```

The swapping of elements terminates when scanDown is less than scanUp. At this point, scanDown identifies the top of the left sublist that contains the elements less than or equal to pivot. The index scanDown is the pivot location in the list. Retrieve the pivot value from A[low]:

```
Swap(A[low],A[scanDown]);
```

QuickSort uses recursion to process the sublists. After locating the pivot to split the list, we recursively call QuickSort with parameters low to mid−1 and mid+1 to high. The stopping condition occurs when a sublist has fewer than two elements since a one-element or empty list is ordered. QuickSort is located in file "arrsort.h".

```
// QuickSort accepts an array and two range parameters
template <class T>
void QuickSort(T A[], int low, int high)
{
    // local variables holding the mid index of the range and
    // its value A[mid] and the scanning indices
    T   pivot;
    int scanUp, scanDown;
    int mid;

    // if the range is not at least two elements, return
    if (high - low <= 0)
        return;
    else
        // if sublist has two elements, compare them and
        // exchange their values if necessary
        if (high - low == 1)
        {
        if (A[high] < A[low])
            Swap(A[low], A[high]);
        return;
        }

    // get the mid index and assign its value to pivot
    mid = (low + high)/2;
    pivot = A[mid];

    // exchange the pivot and the low end of the range
    // and initialize the indices scanUp and scanDown.
    Swap(A[mid], A[low]);
    scanUp = low + 1;
    scanDown = high;

    // manage the indices to locate elements that are in
    // the wrong sublist; stop when scanDown < scanUp
```

```
            do
            {
                // move up lower sublist; stop when scanUp enters
                // upper sublist or identifies an element > pivot
                while (scanUp <= scanDown && A[scanUp] <= pivot)
                    scanUp++;

                // scan down upper sublist; stop when scanDown locates
                // an element <= pivot; we guarantee a stop at A[low]
                while (pivot < A[scanDown])
                    scanDown--;

                // if indices are still in their sublists, then they
                // identify two elements in wrong sublists.
                // exchange them
                if (scanUp < scanDown)
                {
                    Swap(A[scanUp], A[scanDown]);
                }
            }
            while (scanUp < scanDown);

            // copy pivot to index (scanDown) that partitions sublists
            A[low] = A[scanDown];
            A[scanDown] = pivot;

            // if the lower sublist (low to scanDown-1) has 2 or more
            // elements, make the recursive call
            if (low < scanDown−1)
                QuickSort(A, low, scanDown-1);

            // if higher sublist (scanDown+1 to high) has 2 or more
            // elements, make the recursive call
            if (scanDown+1 < high)
                QuickSort(A, scanDown+1, high);
        }
    }
```

Computational Complexity of the QuickSort   A general analysis of QuickSort efficiency is difficult. We can better illustrate its complexity and get a handle on the number of comparisons by considering rather ideal circumstances. Assume that n is a power of 2, $n = 2^k$ ($k = \log_2 n$). In addition, assume that the pivot lies in the middle of each list so that QuickSort partitions the sublist into two approximately equal-sized sublists.

In the first scan, there are $n-1$ comparisons. The result of the pass creates two sublists of approximate size $n/2$. In the next phase, processing each sublist requires approximately $n/2$ comparisons. The total comparisons in this phase is $2(n/2) = n$. The next phase processes four sublists that require a total of $4(n/4)$ comparisons, and so forth. Eventually, the splitting process terminates after k passes with the resulting sublists having size 1. The total number of comparisons is approximately

$$n + 2(n/2) + 4(n/4) + \ldots + n(n/n) = n + n + \ldots + n$$
$$= n * k = n * \log_2 n$$

For a general list, the computational complexity of the QuickSort is $O(n \log_2 n)$. The ideal case we have discussed is actually realized when the array is already sorted in ascending order. In this case, the pivot is precisely in the middle of each sublist.

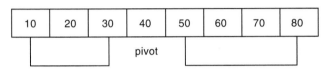

Sorted List (Ascending Order)

If the array is in descending order, the first scan finds the pivot in the middle of the list and exchanges each element in both the lower and higher sublists. The resulting list is almost sorted, and the algorithm has the order $O(n \log_2 n)$.

Sorted List (Descending Order)

80	70	60	50	40	30	20	10

Exchange A[low] and A[mid]. Perform scan.

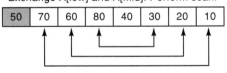

After first scan

40	10	20	30	50	80	60	70

The worst case scenario for QuickSort occurs when the pivot consistently falls in a one-element sublist and leaves the rest of the elements in the second sublist. This occurs when the pivot is always the smallest element in its sublist. For example, the data 3, 8, 1, 5, 9 exhibits this behavior. In the initial scan, there are n comparisons and the large sublist contains $n-1$ elements. In the next scan, the large sublist requires $n-1$ comparisons and yields an $n-2$ element sublist, and so forth. The total number of comparisons is

$$n + n-1 + n-2 + \ldots + 2 = n(n+1)/2 - 1$$

The complexity is $O(n^2)$, a case that is no better than the selection or insertion sort. However, this case is pathological and is unlikely to occur in practice. In general, the average performance of the QuickSort is the most competitive of the sorts we have discussed.

QuickSort is the algorithm of choice for most generic sort utilities. If you cannot tolerate its worst case performance, you may want to select the heapsort that is a more robust $O(n \log_2 n)$ algorithm that depends only on the size of the list.

COMPARISON OF ARRAY SORT ALGORITHMS

We compare a collection of sorting algorithms by executing each with 4000, 8000, 10000, 15000, and 20000 integer values. Each sort is applied with the same set of random data. Units of ticks ($1/60^{th}$ of a second) were used to time the execution of each algorithm. Among the $O(n^2)$ sorts, the insertion sort timing reflects the fact that only $i/2$ comparisons are required in pass i. It clearly outperforms the other $O(n^2)$ sorts. Note that the bubble sort exhibits the poorest overall performance. The results with a graph are displayed in Figure 14.2.

Special runs using 20000 integers in ascending and descending order illustrate the efficiency of the sorts for these extreme cases. The bubble and insertion sorts

	Exchange Sort	Selection Sort	Bubble Sort	Insertion Sort
n = 4000	12.23	17.30	15.78	5.67
n = 8000	49.95	29.43	64.03	23.15
n = 10000	77.47	46.02	99.10	35.43
n = 15000	173.97	103.00	223.28	80.23
n = 20000	313.33	185.05	399.47	143.67

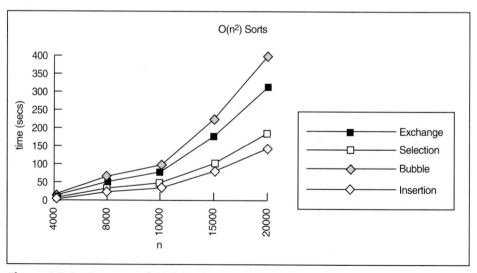

Figure 14.2   Comparison of $O(n^2)$ Sort Times

perform only one pass over the data in ascending order, whereas the selection sort depends only on the list size and performs 19999 passes. When the data is in descending order, the exchange, bubble, and insertion sorts exhibit their worst case behavior, whereas the selection sort performs as usual.

$O(n^2)$ Sorts for Ordered Lists

	Exchange Sort	Selection Sort	Bubble Sort	Insertion Sort
n = 8000 (Ascending Order)	185.27	185.78	.03	.05
n = 8000 (Descending Order)	526.17	199.00	584.67	286.92

In general, the QuickSort is the fastest sorting algorithm. With its $O(n \log_2 n)$ efficiency, it clearly dominates any $O(n^2)$ algorithm. In fact, note in Figure 14.3 that it is faster than any of the other $O(n \log_2 n)$ sorts that were developed in Chapter 13. Note that the QuickSort handles the extreme cases in $O(n \log_2 n)$ time. The tree sort becomes $O(n^2)$ in both these cases, since the tree formed is degenerate.

$O(n \log_2 n)$ Sorts

	Tournament Sort	Treesort	Heapsort	Quicksort Sort
n = 4000	0.28	0.32	0.13	0.07
n = 8000	0.63	0.68	0.28	0.17
n = 10000	0.90	0.92	0.35	0.22
n = 15000	1.30	1.40	0.58	0.33
n = 20000	1.95	1.88	0.77	0.47
n = 8000 (Ascending Order)	1.77	262.27	0.75	0.23
n = 8000 (Descending Order)	1.65	275.70	0.80	0.28

Figure 14.3 Comparison of $O(n \log_2 n)$ Sort Times

Program 14.1 Comparing Sorts

This program implements a comparison of sort algorithms that provides data for Figures 14.2 and 14.3. Only the basic structure of the program is provided; however, a complete listing is given in the program supplement file "prg14_1.cpp". Timing is provided by the function TickCount, which returns the number of sixtieths of a second that have elapsed since the start of the program. The function is found in the file "ticks.h".

```
#include <iostream.h>

// include files containing the sort algorithm
#include "arrsort.h"
. . . . .

// enum type that describes initial state of the array data
enum Ordering {randomorder, ascending, descending};

// enum type to identify the sort algorithm
enum SortType {exchange, selection, bubble, insertion,
               tournament, tree, heap, quick};

// copy n element array y to array x
void Copy(int *x, int *y, int n)
{
    for(int i=0;i<n;i++)
        *x++ = *y++;
}


// general sort function that takes an array with the
// given ordering and implements the specified sort
void Sort(int a[], int n, SortType type, Ordering order)
{
    long time;

    cout << "Sorting " << n;
    // describe the ordering of the data
    switch(order)
    {
        case random:     cout << " items. ";
                         break;
        case ascending:  cout << " items in ascending order. ";
                         break;
        case descending: cout << " items in descending order. ";
                         break;
    }
    // check the clock to get the starting time of the sort
    time = TickCount();

    // describe the type of sort and then execute it
    switch(type)
    {
        case exchange:   ExchangeSort(a,n);
                         cout << "Exchange sort: ";
                         break;
        case selection:  SelectionSort(a,n);
                         cout << "Selection sort: ";
                         break;
```

```
        case bubble:      . . . .
        case insertion:   . . . .
        case tournament:  . . . .
        case tree:        . . . .
        case heap:        . . . .
        case quick:       . . . .
    }

    // compute the time by measuring the difference between the
    // starting time and current time. convert to seconds
    time = TickCount () - time;
    cout << time/60.0 << endl;
}

// run the sorts for n data values and the given ordering
void RunTest(int n, Ordering order)
{
    int i;
    in    *a, *b;

    SortType stype;
    RandomNumber rnd;

    // allocate memory for the two n element arrays a and b
    a = new int [n];
    b = new int [n];

    // determine which data ordering to use
    if (order == randomorder)
        // initialize array b with random integers
        for (i = 0; i < n; i++)
        {
            b[i] = rnd.Random(n);
        }
    else if(order == ascending)
        // sort data 0,1,2,3, . . . ,n−1
        for (i = 0; i < n; i++)
        {
            b[i] = i;
        }
    else
        // sort data n−1,n−2, . . . ,1,0
        for (i = 0; i < n; i++)
        {
            b[i] = n−1−i;
        }

    // copy data to a. execute each sort with specified order
    for(stype=exchange;stype <= quick;stype = SortType(stype+1))
    {
```

```
        Copy(a,b,n);
        Sort(a, n, stype, order);
    }

    // delete the two dynamic arrays
    delete [] a;
    delete [] b;
}


// sort 4000,8000,10000,15000 and 20000 random data
// items. then sort an ordered and unordered list with
// 20000 data items.
void main(void)
{
    int nelts[5] = {4000,8000,10000,15000,20000},i;

    cout.precision(3);
    cout.setf(ios::fixed | ios::showpoint);

    for (i=0; i < 5;i++)
        RunTest(nelts[i],randomorder);

    RunTest(20000,ascending);
    RunTest(20000,descending);
}
```

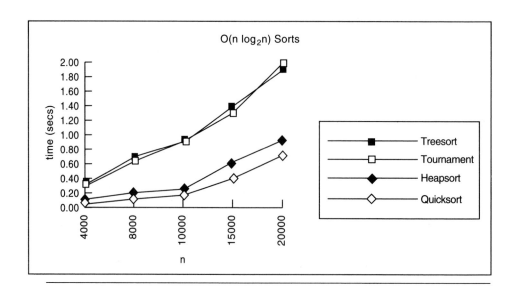

14.3 Hashing

In this book, we have derived a series of list structures that allow the client to search for and retrieve data. In each structure, a Find method takes a key and traverses the list looking for a matching data item. The efficiency of the process depends on the list structure. For a sequential list, Find relies on an $O(n)$ scan of the items, whereas a binary search tree and the binary search provide more efficient $O(\log_2 n)$ search time. Ideally, we would like to retrieve data in $O(1)$ time. In this case, the number of comparisons needed is independent of the number of data elements. When a key is used as an index into an array, an element is retrieved in $O(1)$ time. For example, a sandwich shop identifies its menu by number to simplify bookkeeping. A delicious "pastrami on rye" is just #2 in the data base. The shop owner is left with a very simple search method that associates key 2 with a record in the list.

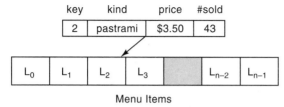

Menu Items

We are familiar with other examples. Customer records at a video store contain a seven-digit phone number. The phone number is the key that is used to obtain a customer's record.

phone number	Customer name, movies rented, etc.

Keys do not need to be integers. For instance, a compiler forms a table termed the **symbol table** that contains all the identifiers used in the program along with pertinent information about each identifier. The key for each symbol table record is the string representing the identifier.

KEYS AND A HASH FUNCTION

In general, few keys are as simple as those used by the sandwich shop. While they provide access to the data, most would not serve as an index to an array of records. For instance, a phone number may identify a customer, but the video store could not maintain a 10 million-element array.

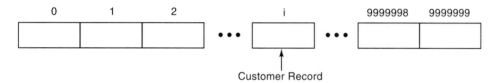

In most applications, a key is used to provide an indirect reference to the data. A function, called a **hash function,** maps the key into a range of integers and then uses the integer value to access the data. Let's explore these ideas.

Assume we have a set of data records with an integer key. A hash function HF maps the key to an integer value in the index range 0 to $n-1$. Associated with the hash function is a table with indices in the same 0 to $n-1$ range. The table, called a **hash table,** holds the data or a reference to the data.

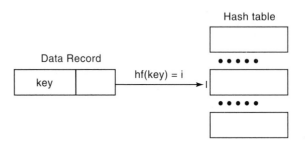

EXAMPLE 14.1
_____

Assume Key is a positive integer and HF(Key) is the value of the ones digit of the key. The index range is 0–9. For instance, if Key is 49, HF(Key) = HF(49) = 9. The hash function uses the modulo-10 operator to return the value.

```
// hash function returning the ones digit of the key
int HF(int key)
{
    return key % 10;
}
```

A hash function is frequently "many to one," resulting in **collisions.** With the hash function in Example 14.1, HF(49) and HF(29) both have the result 9. In general, all numbers with the same ones digit hash to the same value. When a collision occurs, we have two or more data values associated with the same entry in the hash table. Since the two items cannot occupy the same position in the table, we must develop a strategy to handle the collisions. Collision resolution schemes are discussed after an introduction to several types of hashing functions.

HASHING FUNCTIONS

A hash function must map a key to a integer value in the range 0 to $n-1$. Its design should limit collisions and guarantee efficient execution. Several methods satisfy these conditions.

The **division method** is the most commonly used hashing technique, requiring two steps. First the key must be transformed into an integer and then the value must be telescoped into the range 0 to $n-1$ using the remainder operator. In practice, the division method is used in most hashing applications.

EXAMPLE 14.2

1. The key is a five-digit number, and the hash function extracts the low-order two digits. For instance, if the number is 56389, then HF(56389) = 89. The low-order two digits are the remainder on division by 100.

    ```
    int HF(int key)
    {
        return key % 100;      // division by 100 method
    }
    ```

    The effectiveness of the hash function depends on whether it produces a uniform distribution throughout the range $0 \ldots n-1$. If the last two digits correspond to a year of birth, the hash function would produce too many collisions if used to identify the youngsters playing in a community's Little League program.

2. The key is a C++ string. The hash function maps the string to an integer by forming the sum of its first and last characters and then dividing by a hash table size of 101.

    ```
    // hash function for a string; return value
    // in the range 0 to 100.
    int HF(char *key)
    {
        int len = strlen(key), hashf = 0;

        // if length is 0 or 1, return key [0]; otherwise,
        // compute the sum of the first and last characters
        if (len <= 1)
           hasf = key[0];
        else
           hashf = key[0] + key[len-1];

        return hasf % 101;    // divide by 101
    }
    ```

    This hash function causes a collision when the first and last characters of the string are the same. For example, the strings "start" and "slant" both hash to the index 29. This same type of behavior is exhibited by the hash function that forms the sum of the characters of the string.

```
    int HF(char *key)
    {
        int hashf = 0;

        // sum of characters of key and divide by 101
        while(*key)
            hashf += *key++;

        return hashf % 101;
    }
```

The strings "bad" and "dab" hash to the same index. A better hashing function is produced if the bits in the characters are shuffled about in computing hashf. A better hash function for strings is presented in conjunction with Program 14.2

In general, making n large spreads the hash indices throughout a larger range. Furthermore, mathematical theory tells us that the distribution will be more uniform if n is a prime number.

OTHER HASH METHODS

The **midsquare technique** converts the key to an integer, squares this value, and returns a succession of bits extracted from the middle of the square. Assuming that the key is an integer and an integer is implemented using 32 bits, the following hash function extracts the middle 10 bits of the squared key.

```
// return the middle 10 bits of key*key
int HF(int key)
{
    key *= key;             // square key
    key >>= 11;             // discard the low order 11 bits
    return key % 1024;      // return the low order 10 bits
}
```

The **multiplicative method** uses a random real number f in the range $0 \le f < 1$. The fractional part of the product $f *$ key yields a number in the range 0 to 1. When this number is multiplied by n (hash table size), the integer portion of the product gives a hash value in the range 0 to $n-1$.

```
// hash function using multiplicative method; returns
// a hash value in the range 0..700
int HF(int key)
{
    static RandomNumber rnd;
    float f;
```

```
    // multiply key and a random number in range 0 to 1
    f = key * rnd.fRandom();
    // take the fractional part of f
    f = f - int(f);
    // return a number in range 0 to n
    return 701*f;
}
```

COLLISION RESOLUTION

When two or more data items have the same hash value, they cannot occupy the same position in the hash table. We are left with the option of locating the new item at another position in the table or of creating separate lists for each hash value. A list contains all data values that have the same hash value. These options represent two classical strategies for collision resolution called **linear probe open addressing** and **chaining with separate lists.** We illustrate open probe addressing with an example but focus on separate lists because it represents the dominant strategy.

Linear Probe Open Addressing   This technique assumes that each entry in the hash table is marked as vacant. As a result, we can determine if the entry is occupied before we try to add a new item. If the location is full, the algorithm implements circular "probing" around the table to find the first open table slot; hence its name. If the size of the table is large relative to the number of items to store, the process works well since a good hashing function will uniformly distribute table indices over the range and collisions will be minimal. As the ratio of table size to the number of data records approaches 1, the inefficiencies of the process are apparent. We use an example with seven data records to illustrate linear probe addressing.

EXAMPLE 14.3

Assume the items have type DataRecord and are stored in an 11-element hash table.

```
struct DataRecord
{
    int key;
    int data;
};
```

The hash function HF uses division with the modulo-11 operator to create a value in the range 0 to 10.

```
HF(item) = item.key % 11
```

The following data are stored in the hash table. Each entry is annotated with the number of probes required to place the element in the table.

```
List: {54,1},{77,3},{94,5},{89,7},{14,8},{45,2},{76,9}
```

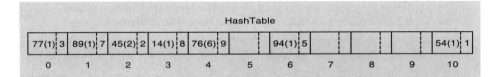

The first five items hash to different values and can be stored directly in the table. For instance, HF({54,1}) = 10 and the item is placed in Table [10]. The first collision occurs between keys 89 and 45 since they both hash to 1. The item {89,7} occurs first in the list and occupies hash Table [1]. That location is occupied when we attempt to load {45,2}. Probe open addressing begins a sequential scan (probe) of the table looking for an empty slot. In this case hash Table [2] is open and the item is added to the table. Key 76 illustrates an inefficiency in the algorithm. It hashes to 10, which is an occupied location. The probe must implement a sequential scan of five additional locations before finding the first open slot at hash Table [4]. The total number of probes to store all the items in the list is 13, or an average of 1.9 probes per item.

An algorithm to implement open probe addressing is given in the exercises.

Chaining with Separate Lists   A second approach to hashing defines the hash table as an array of collections such as linked lists or trees. Each collection is called a **bucket** and holds a set of data records that hash to the same table location. This new collision resolution strategy is referred to as **chaining with separate lists.**

Hash table

Bucket 0	Key	data					

| Bucket 1 | | | | | | | |

• • •

| Bucket n − 1 | | | | | | key | data |

If the table is an array of linked lists, a data item is simply inserted as another node in the list. To locate an item, apply the hash function to determine the linked list and execute a sequential search.

EXAMPLE 14.4
_____

The list of seven DataRecords and the hash function HF from Example 14.3 illustrate separate chaining:

```
List: {54,1},{77,3},{94,5},{89,7},{14,8},{45,2},{76,9}
HF = item.key % 11
```

Each new item is inserted at the rear of its linked list. In the following table, each data value is annotated by the number of probes required to store it in the table.

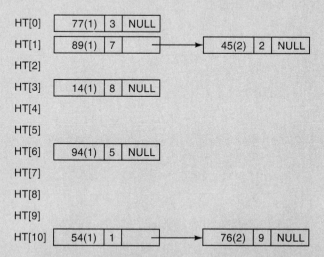

Note that if we count a node insertion as a probe, the total number of probes to insert the 7 data items is 9, or an average of 1.3 probes per item.

Chaining with separate lists is generally faster than open probe addressing because only keys that hash to the same table location are searched. Furthermore, open probe addressing assumes a fixed-length table, whereas in chaining with separate lists, entries in the hash table are dynamically allocated. The list size is limited only by the amount of memory. The primary disadvantage of chaining is the space required to allocate the additional node pointer field. In general, the dynamic structure of separate chaining makes it the preferred choice for hashing.

Hash Table Class   14.4

This section defines a very general HashTable class that implements hashing using chaining with separate lists. The class is derived from the abstract List class and provides a storage mechanism with very efficient access methods. The class allows data of any type, with the restriction that the comparison operator "==" must be defined for the data type. The client must overload "==" to compare the key fields of two data items.

We also develop a HashTableIterator to facilitate the collection of data from the hash table. A HashTableIterator object finds important application when we need to sort and print the data set.

The declaration and implementation of these classes is contained in the file "hash.h".

HASHTABLE CLASS SPECIFICATION

DECLARATION

```
#include "array.h"
#include "list.h"
#include "link.h"
#include "iterator.h"

template <class T>
class HashTableIterator;


template <class T>
class HashTable: public List<T>
{
   protected:
       // number of buckets; represents size of the hash table
       int numBuckets;

       // the hash table is an array of linked lists
       Array< LinkedList<T> > buckets;

       // the hash function and addr of last data item accessed
       unsigned long (*hf)(T key);
       T *current;

   public:
       // constructor with parameters including size of hash
       // table and the hash function
       HashTable(int nbuckets, unsigned long hashf(T key));

       // list handling methods
       virtual void Insert(const T& key);
       virtual int Find(T& key);
       virtual void Delete(const T& key);
       virtual void ClearList(void);
       void Update(const T& key);

       // the associated iterator has access to the data members
       friend class HashTableIterator<T>;
};
```

DESCRIPTION

A HashTable object is a list of elements of type T. It implements all the methods required by the abstract base class List. The client must supply the hash table size and a hash function that converts an element of type T to an unsigned long integer. This return type allows hash functions with a wide data range. The division by the hash table size is done internally.

Insert, Find, Delete, and ClearList provide the basic list handling methods. A separate Update method is included to allow the update of a hash table element that is already in the table.

The methods ListSize and ListEmpty are supplied by the base class. The data member current always points the last data value accessed. It is used by the Update method and derived classes that must return data references. An example of such a class is discussed in Section 14.7.

EXAMPLE

Assume NameRecord is a record containing a name field and a count field

```
struct NameRecord
{
    String  name;
    int  count;
}
```

```
// a 101-element hash table whose data type is NameRecord
// and whose hash function is hash
HashTable<NameRecord> HF(101,hash);
```

```
// insert the record {"Betsy",1} into the table
NameRecord rec;         // a NameRecord variable
rec.name = "Betsy";     // assign name = "Betsy" and count = 1
rec.count = 1;
HF.Insert(rec);         // insert the record
cout << HF.ListSize();  // print the table size of 1
```

```
// Retrieve the data value corresponding to the key "Betsy",
// increment its count field by 1 and then update the record
rec.name = "Betsy";
if (HF.Find(rec)        // look for "Betsy"
{
    rec.count += 1;     // update data field
    HF.Update(rec);     // update the data record in the table
}
else
    cerr << "Error: \"Betsy should be in the table.\"\n";
```

The HashTableIterator class is derived from the abstract Iterator class and contains methods to traverse the data values in the table.

- -

HASHTABLEITERATOR CLASS SPECIFICATION

DECLARATION

```
template <class T>
class HashTableIterator: public Iterator<T>
{
    private:
        // points to the hash table that must be traversed
        HashTable<T> *hashTable;

        // index of the current bucket being traversed and a
        // pointer to the linked list
        int currentBucket;
        LinkedList<T> *currBucketPtr;

        // utility to implement Next()
        void SearchNextNode(int cb);
    public:
        // constructor
        HashTableIterator(HashTable<T>& ht);

        // basic iterator methods
        virtual void Next(void);
        virtual void Reset(void);
        virtual T& Data(void);

        // arrange for the iterator to traverse another table
        void SetList(HashTable<T>& lst);
};
```

- -

DESCRIPTION

Next traverses the hash table by moving from list (bucket) to list and traversing the nodes of each list. The data values produced by the iterator are not in any order. The method uses the function SearchNextNode, which locates the next list that must be traversed.

- -

EXAMPLE

```
// declares an iterator for the HashTable object HF
HashTableIterator<NameRecord> hiter(HF);

// scan all of the elements in the data base
for(hiter.Reset();!hiter.EndOfList();hiter.Next())
```

```
{
    rec = hiter.Data();
    cout << rec.name << ": " << rec.count << endl;
}
```

APPLICATION: STRING FREQUENCY

The HashTable class is used to store a set of strings and determine their frequency in a file. Each string is stored in a NameRecord object that contains the string name and a count of its frequency.

```
struct NameRecord
{
    String name;
    int count;
};
```

The hash function mixes the bits of the string characters by shifting the current hash value three bits to the left (multiplying by 8) before adding the next character. In the n character string $= c_0 c_1 \ldots c_{n-2} c_{n-1}$,

$$\text{hash}(s) = \sum_{i=0}^{n-1} c_i 8^{n-i-1}$$

This calculation prevents the problems with string hashing functions discussed in Example 14.2.

```
// function for use by the Hash class
unsigned long hash(NameRecord elem)
{
    unsigned long hashval = 0;

    // shift hashval left three bits and add in next character
    for (int i=0; i < elem.Length(); i++)
       hashval = (hashval << 3) + elem.name[i]
    return hashval;
}
```

Program 14.2 Computing String Frequency

The program reads strings from the file "strings.dat" and stores them in a 101-element hash table. Each string is read from the file and, if it has not been encountered, is stored in the table. For duplicate strings, the record is retrieved from the hash table and its count field is incremented. The program terminates by defining an iterator that is used to step through the hash table and print the entries. The NameRecord definition, the hash function and the "==" operator defined for NameRecord data are contained in the file "strfreq.h".

```cpp
#include <iostream.h>
#include <fstream.h>
#include <stdlib.h>

#include "hash.h"
#include "strclass.h"
#include "strfreq.h"

void main(void)
{
    // read the strings from stream fin
    ifstream fin;
    NameRecord rec;
    String token;
    HashTable<NameRecord> HF(101,hash);

    fin.open("strings.dat", ios::in | ios::nocreate);
    if (!fin)
    {
        cerr << "Could not open \"strings.dat\"!" << endl;
        exit(1);
    }

    while(fin >> rec.name)
    {
        // look for string in table; if present, update count
        if (HF.Find(rec))
        {
            rec.count += 1;
            HF.Update(rec);
        }
        else
        {
            rec.count = 1;
            HF.Insert(rec);
        }
    }

    // print the strings and their frequency
    HashTableIterator<NameRecord> hiter(HF);

    for(hiter.Reset();!hiter.EndOfList();hiter.Next())
    {
```

```
            rec = hiter.Data();
            cout << rec.name << ": " << rec.count << endl;
        }
}

/*
<File "strings.dat">

Columbus Washington Napoleon Washington Lee Grant
Washington Lincoln Grant Columbus Washington

<Run of Program 14.2>

Lee: 1
Washington: 4
Lincoln: 1
Napoleon: 1
Grant: 2
Columbus: 2
*/
```

HASHTABLE CLASS IMPLEMENTATION

The class is derived from the abstract List class, which provides the methods ListSize and ListEmpty. We discuss the HashTable class data members and the operations that implement the pure virtual functions Insert, Find, Delete, and ClearList.

The key data member in the class is the Array object buckets, which defines an array of linked list objects that constitute the hash table. The function pointer hf defines the hash function, and numBuckets is the hash table size. The pointer current identifies the last data item that was accessed by a hash table method. Its value is set by the Find and Insert methods and used by the Update method to change the value of a data item in the table.

List Handling Methods   Insert computes the hash value (bucket index) and searches the LinkedList object to verify whether the data item is already in the table. If a match is found, Insert replaces the data item, updates current to point at the data value, and returns. If no match occurs, Insert adds the data item to the end of the list, sets current to point at the new data value, and increments the list size.

```
template <class T>
void HashTable<T>::Insert(const T& key)
{
    // hashval is the bucket number (index of the linked list)
    int hashval = int(hf(key) % numBuckets);

    // lst is an alias for buckets[hashval]. avoids indexing.
    LinkedList<T>& lst = buckets[hashval];
```

```
        for(lst.Reset();!lst.EndOfList();lst.Next())
            // if match key, update data and return
            if (lst.Data() == key)
            {
                lst.Data() = key;
                current = &lst.Data();
                return;
            }
        // data corresponding to key is not found. Add item to list
        lst.InsertRear(key);
        current = &lst.Data();
        size++;
    }
```

Find applies the hash function and traverses the resulting list looking for a match. If one is found, it copies the data to key, assigns current to the address of the matching node and returns True. Otherwise, the method returns False.

```
    template <class T>
    int HashTable<T>::Find(T& key)
    {
        // compute the hash value and set lst to point at its
        // corresponding  LinkedList
        int hashval = int(hf(key) % numBuckets);
        LinkedList<T>& lst = buckets[hashval];

        // scan the nodes in the linked list looking for a match
        // with the key
        for(lst.Reset();!lst.EndOfList();lst.Next())
            // if a match occurs, get the data value, set current and
            // return
            if (lst.Data() == key)
            {
                key = lst.Data();
                current = &lst.Data();
                return 1;                     // return True
            }
        return 0;                             // otherwise, return False
    }
```

The method Delete traverses the resulting list and deletes the node if a match occurs. This method, along with ClearList and Update, are located in the file "hash.h".

HASHTABLEITERATOR CLASS IMPLEMENTATION

This class must step through the data scattered about in the hash table. As a result, it is more interesting and more difficult to implement than the HashTable class. The

hashTableIterator

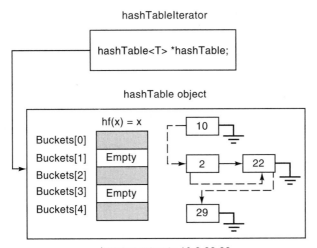

Iterator extracts 10 2 22 29

Figure 14.4 HashTableIterator

traversal of the data items in the table begins with a search for a nonempty bucket in the array of lists. When a nonempty bucket is found, we traverse all of the nodes in that list and then continue the process by looking for another nonempty bucket. The iterator reaches the end of the list when a bucket containing elements has been traversed and there are no remaining buckets to search.

An iterator must be bound to a list. In this case, the member variable hashTable is assigned the address of the hash table. Since HashTableIterator is a friend of HashTable, it has access to all of its private variables, including the Array object buckets and its size numBuckets. The variable currentBucket is the index of the linked list that is currently being traversed, and currBucketPtr is a pointer to the list. Each bucket is traversed by using the built-in iterator in the LinkedList class. Figure 14.4 illustrates the iterator traversing a hash table with four entries.

The method SearchNextNode is called to locate the next list that must be traversed. Search all buckets beginning with bucket cb until a nonempty list is found. Assign currentBucket the index of this list and currBucketPtr the address of the list. If there are no nonempty lists, return with currentBucket = −1.

```
// beginning at index cb, look for the next
// non-empty list to scan
template <class T>
void HashTableIterator<T>::SearchNextNode(int cb)
{
    currentBucket = -1;

    // if index cb > table size, terminate search; scan is over
    if (cb > hashTable->numBuckets)
        return;
```

```
// otherwise search from current list to end of table
// for a non-empty bucket and update private data members
for(int i=cb;i < hashTable->numBuckets;i++)
    if (!hashTable->buckets[i].ListEmpty())
    {
        // before return, set currentBucket index to i and
        // set currBucketPtr to the new non-empty list.
        currBucketPtr = &hashTable->buckets[i];
        currBucketPtr ->Reset();
        currentBucket = i;
        return;
    }
}
```

The constructor initializes the Iterator base class and sets the private pointer variable hashTable to the address of the hash table. Call SearchNextNode with parameter 0 to locate a nonempty list.

```
// constructor;  initialize both the base class
// and HashTable.  SearchNextNode identifies
// the first non-empty bucket in the table
template <class T>
HashTableIterator<T>::HashTableIterator(HashTable<T>& hf):
    Iterator<T>(hf), hashTable(&hf)
{
    SearchNextNode(0);
}
```

Next advances one element forward in the current list. If we reach the end of the list, the function SearchNextNode updates the iterator so it traverses the next nonempty bucket.

```
// move to the next data item in the table
template <class T>
void HashTableIterator<T>::Next(void)
{
    // using current list, move to next node or end of list
    currBucketPtr->Next();

    // at end of list, call SearchNextNode to identify the next
    // non-empty bucket in the table
    if (currBucketPtr->EndOfList())
        SearchNextNode(++currentBucket);

    // set the iterationComplete flag to check if the cur-
       rentBucket
    // index is at end of list,
    iterationComplete = currentBucket == -1;
}
```

The Performance of Searching Methods   14.5

In this book we have introduced four searching methods, the sequential search, the binary search, binary tree searching, and hashing. The running time of search methods is normally determined by deriving the average number of comparisons needed to locate an item in the list. We have seen that the sequential search is $O(n)$, whereas the binary search and the binary tree search are $O(\log_2 n)$.

An analysis of hashing performance is more involved. Its performance depends on the quality of the hashing function and the size of the hash table. A good hashing function provides a uniform distribution of hash values. When combined with a relatively large table, the number of collisions is reduced. The size of the table gives rise to the **load factor** for the hash table. If a hash table has m entries and n are currently in use, the load factor λ for the table is defined by

$$\lambda = n/m$$

When the table is empty, λ is 0. As more items are added to the table, λ increases as does the chance of collisions. For open probe, λ attains its maximum value of 1 when the table is full ($m = n$). When chaining with separate lists is used, the individual linked lists can grow as large as needed, so λ can be larger than 1.

We can give an intuitive argument for the complexity of hashing using chaining. The worst case occurs when all data items hash to the same table location. If a linked list contains n data elements, the search time for the list is $O(n)$, so the worst case performance for chaining is $O(n)$.

For the average case with a relatively uniform hash distribution, we expect $\lambda = n/m$ elements in each linked list. Thus, the search time for each linked list is $O(\lambda) = O(n/m)$. If we assume that the number of elements placed in the table is bounded by some amount, say, $R*m$, then the search time for each list is $O(R*m/m) = O(R) = O(1)$, and chaining is an $O(1)$ method. Data access in a hash table that implements chaining with separate lists is performed in constant time, independent of the number of data items.

A formal mathematical analysis of hashing is beyond the scope of this book. Table 14.1 lists formulas for the approximate number of probes needed for successful and unsuccessful searches with each hashing method when the number of hash table entries m is large. Each formula is a function of the load factor λ. See Knuth, 1973 for a discussion of these and related results. When $\lambda = 1$, a successful search requires an average m/2 probes, whereas an unsuccessful search requires m probes.

	Probes for Successful Search	Probes for Unsuccessful Search
Open Probe	$\dfrac{1}{2(1-\lambda)} + \dfrac{1}{2}, \lambda \neq 1$	$\dfrac{1}{2(1-\lambda)^2} + \dfrac{1}{2}, \lambda \neq 1$
Chaining	$1 + \dfrac{\lambda}{2}$	$e^{-\lambda} + \lambda$

TABLE 14.1
Formulas for the Complexity of Hash Methods

The table shows us that the open probe method is reasonably good as long as the load factor λ remains small. In general, chaining is a better method. For instance, when $m = n$ ($\lambda = 1$), chaining requires only 1.5 probes for a successful search but open probe is searching a full table and requires an average of $m/2$ probes. When the table is half full ($\lambda = \frac{1}{2}$), chaining requires 1.25 probes for a successful search, whereas open probe requires 1.5.

Clearly, hashing is an extremely fast searching method. However, each of the four search methods has its uses. The sequential search [$O(n)$] is effective when the number of elements n is small, and the data do not have to be sorted. The binary search [$O(\log_2 n)$] is very fast but requires that the data be sorted in an array. The binary search is not suited to situations where the data values are determined at runtime (e.g., compiler symbol table), since an ordered array is an ineffective vehicle for list insertion and deletion. For these problems, the binary tree search [$O(\log_2 n)$] and hashing [$O(1)$] are competitive. The binary tree search is not as fast but has the nice side effect of generating ordered data when an inorder scan is performed. Hashing is the best method when quick access to unordered data is required.

14.6   Binary Files and External Data Operations

Many applications need to access data on disk files. In this section we give an overview of binary file I/O using the class **fstream,** which is contained in the file "fstream.h". In the process we develop the BinFile class, which contains methods to open and close a binary file, to access individual records in the file, and to execute block reads and writes of data to the file. Large data sets may contain several million records that cannot all reside in memory. We need to manage the data while it resides externally and extend searching and sorting algorithms to files. We give a brief introduction to the topic since a detailed discussion of files and external searching and sorting lies beyond the scope of this book.

BINARY FILES

A text file contains ASCII characters with a newline sequence separating lines. A binary file consists of data records that vary from a single character (byte) to more complex structures that include integers, floating point values, and arrays. At the hardware level, file data records are stored on a disk in fixed-length data blocks. The disk blocks are normally not contiguous. However, the logical view of a file pictures file data as a sequence of records. File systems allow direct access to the individual data records, allowing us to treat a file as an external array of records. As data records are read or written, the system maintains the **file pointer,** which is the current position in the file.

File as a Direct access structure

A file is also a sequential structure that maintains a file pointer at the current position within the data. The I/O read and write operations access data at this current position and then shift the current position to the next data record.

File as sequential access structure

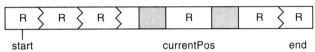

The C++ fstream class describes file objects that can be used for both input and output. When creating an object, we use the open method to attach a physical file name and access mode. The possible modes are defined in the base class ios.

Mode	Action
in	open file for reading
out	open file for writing
trunc	erase file records before reading or writing
nocreate	if the file does not exist, do not create an empty file. return a stream error condition
binary	open file in binary mode (not a text file)

EXAMPLE 14.5

```
1.  #include <fstream.h>
    fstream  f;                              // declare a file
    // open text file "Phone" for input. if the file does
    // not already exist, indicate an error condition
    f.open("Phone", ios::in | ios::nocreate);
2.  fstream  f;                              // declare a file
    // open a binary file for input and output
    f.open("DataBase", ios::in | ios::out | ios::binary);
```

Each file object has a file pointer associated with it that identifies the current record for input or output. For an input file, the function tellg() returns in bytes the location of the current file pointer as an offset from the beginning of the file. For an output file, the function tellp() returns in bytes the location of the current file pointer. The functions seekg() and seekp() allow the user to reposition the current file pointers. The seek functions take an offset parameter that measures the number of bytes from the beginning (beg), ending (end), or current position (cur) in the file. If a file is used for both input and output, use the seek functions tellg and seekg.

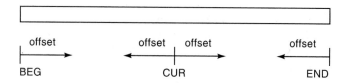

For instance, the following functions illustrate the action of the functions seekg and tellg:

```
// binary file of integer values
fstream f;

f.open("datafile",ios::in | ios::nocreate | ios::binary);
        . . .
// reset current position to start of file
f.seekg(0, ios::beg);
// set current position at last data value
f.seekg(-sizeof(int), ios::end);
        . . .
// move current position to next record
f.seekg(sizeof(int), ios::cur);


        . . .
// move to the end of the file
f.seekg(0,ios::end);
// print number of bytes in the file
cout << f.tellg() << endl;
// print number of data values in the file
cout << f.tellg()/sizeof(int);
```

The fstream class has primitive read and write methods that perform I/O with a byte stream. Each method takes the address of a buffer and a count that indicates the number of bytes to transfer. The buffer is an array of characters that stores the data as they are sent or received from disk. I/O operations with non-character data types require a (char *) cast. For instance, the following operations transfer a block of integer data to and from a file:

```
fstream f;                      // declare an fstream object
int data = 30, A[20];           // initialize data value and array

// write integer 30 as a 'sizeof(int)' block of characters
f.write(char*) &data, sizeof(int));

// reads 20 integers from file f to array A
f.read(char*)A, 20*sizeof(int));
```

THE BINFILE CLASS

Many applications include a file to handle input and output of data. In this section, we abstract the file from any application and define a class that provides generic file handling operations for binary files. This is an example of a class that quietly hides low-level system details from the user. As a template-based class, the client may use files to hold a variety of different data types.

- -

BINFILE CLASS SPECIFICATION

DECLARATION

```
// system files containing hierarchy of file handling methods.
#include <iostream.h>
#include <fstream.h>
#include <stdlib.h>

#include "strclass.h"

// file access types
enum Access  {IN, OUT, INOUT};
// type of seeks that can be performed
enum SeekType {BEG,CUR,END};

template <class T>
class BinFile
{
   private:
      // C++ file stream object with its name and access type
      fstream  f;
      Access accessType;     // file access type
      String fname;          // physical file name
      int fileOpen;          // is the file open?

      // parameters measuring file as a direct access structure
      int Tsize;             // size of a data record
      int fileSize;          // number of file records

      // prints an error message and terminates the program
      void Error(char *msg);

   public:
      // constructors and destructor
      BinFile(const String& fileName, Access atype = OUT);
      ~BinFile(void);
```

```
                    // copy constructor. an object must be passed by
                    // reference. terminates the program
                    BinFile(BinFile<T>& bf);


                    // file utility methods
                    void Clear(void);    // truncate records in the file
                    void Delete(void);   // close file and remove it
                    void Close(void);    // close the file
                    int  EndFile();      // tests EOF condition
                    long Size();         // returns number of file records
                    void Reset(void);    // reset the file to first record
                    // locate file pointer pos records from beginning,
                    // current location or end of the file
                    void Seek(long pos, SeekType mode);

                    // block read of n data values into address A
                    int  Read(T *A, int n);
                    // block write of n data values from address A
                    void Write(T *A, int n);
                    // value of record at current location
                    T Peek(void);
                    // copy data to record at index pos
                    void Write (const T& data, long pos);
                    // read record from index pos
                    T Read (long pos);
                    // write a record at end of the file
                    void Append(T item);
               };
```

DISCUSSION

The constructor is responsible for opening the file and initializing the class parameters. When creating a BinFile object, the client must designate the file access mode (IN, OUT, or INOUT). Files that have mode OUT are truncated when they are opened. An IN file must exist when it is created or an error message terminates the program. If a file is declared INOUT, file records can be read or written. After opening the file, the constructor sets the data member fileOpen to 1 (True), indicating that file operations such as Read are valid.

The class contains a copy constructor that writes an error message if it is called. File objects are attached to a physical file when they are created. Allowing a file to be copied would require that the new object must open the same file. On some systems, this is not possible and, if allowed, can lead to a dangerous situation. A BinFile object must be passed by reference.

A file can be handled as a direct access array. The methods Write and Read take a record index pos and read or write a data item at that position in the file. The block Read and Write methods are used to perform multiple record I/O.

The block Read method returns the number of records read or 0 if end of file is encountered. It is possible that fewer than n records remain in the file. Hence the return value may be less than n. The address of the data and the number of records are passed as parameters. The transfer begins at the current file location. The method Peek allows the client to retrieve the current value in the file without advancing the file pointer.

The method EndFile returns a logical value indicating whether the end of file has been reached. Use this method with IN files only. For the other file types, use a for loop that stops when the loop variable exceeds the last record index in the file.

The method Close shuts down the stream to the file but does not remove the physical file. Use Close if the file is to be opened by another object, perhaps with a different mode.

The method Clear truncates the file so it has zero size and leaves the file open. Delete closes the file and removes it from the file system. These methods set fileOpen to 0 (False). Subsequent attempts to access the file terminate the program. Seek allows repositioning of the file pointer. The parameter mode specifies whether the file pointer is repositioned pos records from the beginning, current position or end of the file.

EXAMPLE

```
// file of integers for I/O; physical name is "demofile"
BinFile<int> BF("demofile", INOUT);

BinFile<int> BG("outfile", OUT); // file of integers for output

int i, m = 5, n = 10, A[10];      // integer variables

// will write this data to "demofile"
int vals[] = {30,40,50,60,70,80,90,100};

for (i=0;i < 5;i++)
    BF.Write(&i,1);

BF.Append(m);                    // put 5 at end of file
BF.Reset();                      // set to beginning of file
BF.Write(n,0);                   // put 10 at front of file
cout << BF.Size() << endl;       // print file size of 6
cout << BF.Read(3) << endl;      // print 3 (value of record 3)
BF.Read(A,2);                    // read two values into A
cout << A[0] << "  " << A[1];    // print values
BF.Reset();                      // reset to front of list
cout << BF.Peek() << endl;       // print 10
BF.Read(A,4);                    // read 4 integers into A
BG.Write(A,4);                   // write A[0]-A[3] to BG
```

```
A[0] *= 2;                      // double value of A[0]
BG.Write(A[0],0);              // write new value to 1st record
BF.Seek(2,beg);                // seek to record 2 of BF
BF.Write(vals,8);              // write 30..100 to the file (begin
                               // at record 2)
BF.Reset();                    // reset to start of "demofile"
// read and print "demofile" using Size
for(i=0;i < BF.Size();i++)
{
    BF.Read(&m,1);
    cout << m << "   ";
}
cout << endl;
BF.Delete();                           // remove file BF
BG.Close();                            // close "outfile"

BinFile<int> BH("outfile", IN); // reopen "outfile" for input

while(!BH.EndFile())                   // read and print "outfile"
{                                      // use EndFile
    BH.Read(&m, 1);
    cout << m << "   ";
}
cout << endl;
BH.Close();                            // close "outfile"
<Output>
6
3
4  5
10
10  1  30  40  50  60  70  80  90  100
20  1  2  3
```

BINFILE IMPLEMENTATION

The full implementation of the class is contained in file "binfile.h". In this section, we discuss the constructor, the direct access read method, a block write of n records, and the utility method Clear.

The constructor is responsible for opening the file and initializing the class parameters. When creating an object, we pass the file name and the access type to the constructor.

```
// constructor; opens file with given file name and access
template <class T>
```

```
BinFile<T>::BinFile(const String& fileName, Access atype)
{

    // stream open operation includes access type; for IN, a
    // file is not created if does not exist; for OUT, any
    // existing data are thrown away (truncated); for INOUT,
    // the file has input and output capability
    if (atype == IN)
        f.open(fileName, ios::in | ios::nocreate | ios::binary);
    else if (atype == OUT)
        f.open(fileName, ios::out | ios::trunc | ios::binary);
    else
        f.open(fileName, ios::in | ios::out | ios::binary);
    if(!f)
        Error("BinFile constructor: file cannot be opened");
    else
        fileOpen = 1;

    accessType = atype;


    // compute the number of records in the file


    // Tsize is the number of bytes in the data type
    Tsize = sizeof(T);
    if (accessType == IN || accessType == INOUT)
    {
        // compute number of records in an input file by seeking
        // to the end of the file, calling tellg to obtain the
        // file size in bytes, and then dividing by the data
        // size. reset to the beginning of the file
        f.seekg(0,ios::end);
        fileSize = f.tellg()/Tsize;
        f.seekg(0,ios::beg);
    }
    else
        fileSize = 0;      // size is 0 for OUT files

    // record physical file name in fname
    fname = fileName;
}
```

File Access   Using the seekg method, we can treat a file like a direct access
array. Read takes the position parameter pos. By combining the data size and the
pos parameter, seekg locates the current file pointer at the record and extracts the
data value.

```
// Read returns the data at record pos in the file
template <class T>
T BinFile<T>::Read (long pos)
{
    // variable to hold the data item
    T data;

    if (!fileOpen)
        Error("BinFile Read(int pos): file closed");

    // the Read method is invalid with an 'OUT' only file
    if (accessType == OUT)
        Error("Invalid file access operation");
    // test for valid pos in range 0 to fileSize-1
    else if (pos < 0 || pos >= fileSize)
        Error("Invalid file access operation");

    // position the current file pointer and extract data
    // using the fstream read method
    f.seekg(pos*Tsize, ios::beg);
    f.read((char *)&data,Tsize);

    // if the access mode is IN and we have read all records,
    // set the stream eof bit
    if (accessType == IN)
        if (f.tellg()/Tsize >= fileSize)
            f.clear(ios::eofbit);   // sets eof bit
    return data;
}
```

When using a file as a sequential access device, the Write method can be defined to copy multiple records to the file. The address of the data and the number of records are passed as parameters. The fstream write method copies the stream of bytes to the output file. Since the write may begin inside the file, care must be taken to assure that fileSize is correctly maintained.

```
// writes an n-element list from array A to the file
template <class T>
void BinFile<T>::Write(T *A, int n)
{

    long previousRecords;

    // Write is an invalid operation with an 'IN' only file
    if (accessType == IN)
        Error("Invalid file access operation");
```

```
    if(!fileOpen)
        Error("BinFile Write(T *A, int n): file closed");

    // compute the new file size. call tellg to compute number
    // of file records prior to output point. determine if
    // file size will expand. if so, increment fileSize by
    // the number of records that will be added
    previousRecords = f.tellp()/Tsize;
    if (previousRecords + n > fileSize)
        fileSize += previousRecords + n - fileSize;

    // the number of bytes to write is n * Tsize;
    f.write((char *)A,Tsize*n);
}
```

Utility Methods   The class features a series of utility methods to manage the file. The Clear method removes the current records from the file by first closing the file and then reopening it with truncation, using the initial set of file parameters that are stored as private data members.

```
// Clear deletes file records by closing and then opening file
template <class T>
void BinFile<T>::Clear(void)
{
    // an 'IN' file cannot be cleared
    if (accessType == IN)
        Error("Invalid file access operation");

    // close and then open the file
    f.close();
    if (accessType == OUT)
        f.open(fname, ios::out|ios::trunc|ios::binary);
    else
        f.open(fname, ios::in|ios::out|ios::trunc|ios::binary);
    if (!f)
        Error("BinFile Clear: cannot reopen the file");

    fileSize = 0;
}
```

EXTERNAL FILE SEARCHING

We have developed a series of internal list structures to store data. A similar set of structures can be defined for data in a file. The efficiency of external searching and sorting techniques depends on our method of organizing the file records. We extend the concept of hashing to include file structures and use BinFile methods to access the data.

Hashing techniques provide efficient search algorithms that can be extended to external structures. A hash function associates with a data record an integer in the range 0 to $n - 1$. This value can be used as an index into an array of records, where the data are stored with open probe addressing. In the more efficient method of chaining with separate lists, the value can be used as an index into an array of lists. Both storage methods can be used with files. In this section, we use separate lists, where the file holds the linked lists. We create the hash table in memory and use it to make repeated access to the slower disk device.

A file node contains both the data and a file index.

FileDataRecord

The records are stored on the disk in a linked list with the field nextIndex identifying the position of the next record in the file. To set up the linked lists, we create a hash table in memory that references the linked lists in the file. A hash function associates each data record with an index in the table.

```
int hashtable[n];    // array of file index values
```

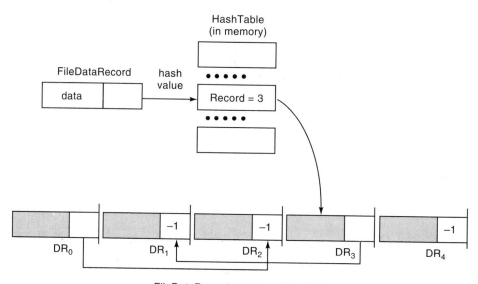

FileDataRecord structures (on disk)

The hash table is implemented as an n-element array. Initially the table is empty (each entry set to -1) to indicate that no records have been stored in the file. As we enter a record from the data base, the hash function defines an index in the table. If the table entry is empty, we store the record on disk and assign its file position in the table. Thus, a table entry gives the position on disk of the first record that hashes to that value. Once there is a table entry, we can use its value to access the corresponding linked list and insert the new record. The insert process writes the record to disk and updates pointers in the nextIndex field.

We illustrate the process with a simple example that highlights the main features. Our data type is an integer and is stored in a file as a FileDataRecord node.

```
// a node that stores a data record in a file
struct FileDataRecord
{
    // data is an integer in this example; in general
    // the data field is often a complex record
    int data;
    int nextIndex;    // location of the next record on disk
};
```

The hash function maps the data value (integer) to its ones digit.

```
h(data) = data % 10;    // h(456) = 6    h(891) = 1    h(26) = 6
```

Our example stores the following data records in a file:

```
456    64    84    101    144
```

The first two entries hash to empty table values and hence can be directly inserted as nodes in the file. The first node is stored at disk position 0 and the second node at 1. After adding the nodes, the corresponding table values are assigned the positions.

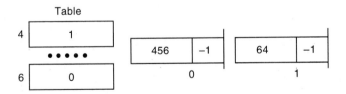

For data value 84, the table entry has value 1, which identifies a linked list. The new record is inserted at the front of the list.

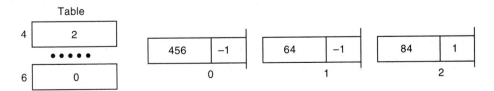

After loading 101 and 144, the file contains five FileDataRecord nodes that are logically stored as three linked lists. The table entries contain the starting nodes for the lists.

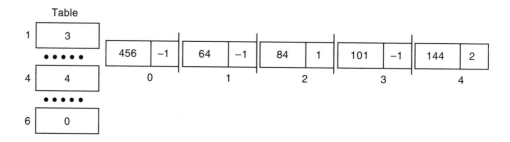

This storage method effectively uses the direct access structure of a file. We create storage space for the data by appending the record to the file and then updating the table entry. The hash table is often stored in a separate file and then loaded into memory when we need to access the data base.

Program 14.3 External Hashing

This program illustrates the external hashing algorithm discussed in this section. The function LoadRecord adds a new record to the file and the function PrintList takes a hash value and prints the linked list of records. LoadRecord inserts each record at the front of the linked list. No attempt is made to avoid duplicates. The main program inserts 50 random integers whose values are in the range 0 to 999. To illustrate a search, the user is asked to enter a hash value and the items in the corresponding linked list are printed.

```cpp
#include <iostream.h>

#include "random.h"
#include "binfile.h"

const long Empty = -1;

// a node that stores a data record in a file
struct FileDataRecord
{
    // data is an integer in this example; in general,
    // the data field is often a complex record
    int data;
    long nextIndex;   // location of the next record on disk
};
```

```
// startindex is an index in the table. to handle case where
// we need to update the first entry, it is passed by reference
void LoadRecord(BinFile<FileDataRecord> &bf, long &startindex,
                FileDataRecord &dr)
{

    // if the table is not empty, startindex points to the head
    // of the list; otherwise startindex is -1
    // bf.Size() locates the next node in the file
    dr.nextIndex = startindex;
    startindex = bf.Size();

    // append new record in file
    bf.Append(dr);
}

// scan a list of nodes in the file and print their data value
void PrintList(BinFile<FileDataRecord> &bf, long startindex)
{
    // index is the first position in the list
    long index = startindex;
    FileDataRecord rec;

    // index moves to end of list (index = -1)
    while (index != Empty)
    {
        // get record; output its value and go to next record
        rec = bf.Read(index);
        cout << rec.data << "   ";
        index = rec.nextIndex;
    }
    cout << endl;
}

void main(void)
{
    // table of file node indices; hash range is 0 to 9
    long hashTable[10];

    // random number generator and a data record
    RandomNumber rnd;
    FileDataRecord dr;
    int i, item, request;

    // open file "DRfile" with I/O access
    BinFile<FileDataRecord> dataFile("DRfile", INOUT);

    // initialize the table to have empty entries
    for(i = 0; i < 10; i++)
        hashTable[i] = Empty;
```

```
        // enter 50 random integers in the range 0 to 999
        for (i = 0; i < 50; i++)
        {
            item = rnd.Random(1000);
            // initialize and then install the data record
            dr.data = item;
            LoadRecord(dataFile, hashTable[item % 10],  dr);
        }

        // prompt for a hash table index and print the list
        cout << "Enter a hash table index: ";
        cin >> request;
        cout << "Printing entries that hash to " << request << endl;
        PrintList(dataFile, hashTable[request]);

        // remove the data file
        dataFile.Delete();
    }

/*
<Run of Program 14.3>

Enter a hash table index: 5
Printing entries that hash to 5
835   385   205   185   455   5
*/
```

EXTERNAL FILE SORT

The sorting of external data poses a special problem when the file is too large to fit into internal memory. Since all of the data cannot be made resident in one array, we must use temporary files to store items. In this section, we develop external merge sorts that use three files. We discuss algorithms for both a straight merge and a natural merge that uses runs. The algorithms can be extended to n-way merges that use $n > 3$ files.

In Chapter 12 we introduce a simple merge that combines two ordered lists into a single list. The **straight merge sort** uses this process by merging fixed-length sublists. Assuming the elements are initially stored in file fC and that files fA and fB are temporary external files that split the data, the algorithm uses the following steps:

1. Split fC into two halves by alternately writing an element from fC to fA and then from fC to fB. This creates a sequence of one-element sublists in each new file.

2. Pair off the sublists and select one element from fA and one element from fB. Merge them into a two-element ordered sublist in fC. Continue until all the elements from the two files have been copied back to fC.

3. Repeat step 1 by alternately writing the ordered two-element sublists from fC to files fA and fB.

4. Merge each pair of two-element sublists from fA and fB into a four-element sublist in fC. Continue until all the elements are copied back to fC.

5. Repeat the step that alternatively splits fC into four-element, eight-element, . . . sublists in files fA and fB. Then merge each pair of sublists into eight-element, sixteen-element, and so on ordered sublists in fC. The process terminates when files fA and fB consist of a single ordered sublist, which merges to form a complete sorted file in fC.

We illustrate the straight merge sort for a file fC with the following 20 integers.

5   15   35   30   20   45   35   5   65   75   40   50   60   70   30   40   25
10   45   55

In step 1, fC splits into two temporary files containing 10 one-element sublists. The merge in step 2 creates ordered two-element sublists.

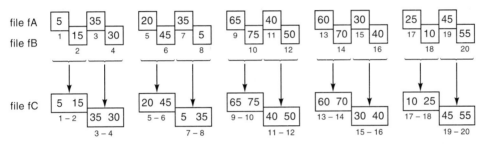

With step 3, files fA and fB hold two-element sublists that merge into four-element sublists in fC.

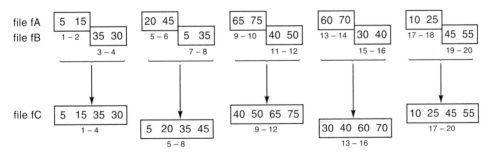

The process of splitting sublists in the temporary files and then merging them back to fC requires three more passes that create ordered eight-element, sixteen-element and finally twenty-element sublists in fC. After the final pass, fC is an ordered file. When creating the eight- and sixteen-element sublists, there is an "odd-size" sublist at the tail of fA that is simply copied back to fC. On the final pass, a sixteen-element sublist in fA and four-element sublist in fB are merged and the process terminates.

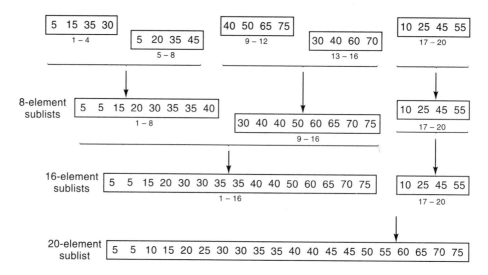

Analysis of the Straight MergeSort   The straight MergeSort consists of a series of passes that begin with one-element sublists. Each pass doubles the size of the sublists until their size $s \geq n$. This requires $\log_2 n$ separate passes during which all n elements are copied to the temporary files and then copied back to file fC. The straight MergeSort requires a total of $2 * n * \log_2 n$ data accesses with order $O(n \log_2 n)$.

LONG RUN MERGESORT

The straight MergeSort uses ordered sublists that start with length 1 and then progress to lengths 2, 4, 8, and so forth. Eventually ordered sublists comprise the entire file and the external sort is completed. The MergeSort algorithm occupies a disproportionate amount of time with the small sublists, splitting them between the two temporary files and merging them back to the original file. The algorithm is far more efficient with longer sublists since there are fewer runs and the file operations do not have to be done as frequently. In this section, we modify the straight MergeSort to allow us to begin with relatively long sublists and more efficiently complete the sort. The algorithm takes a file fC and an internal memory buffer to create ordered sublists. We take the original file and read the data in blocks into the buffer. Each block is then sorted using a fast internal sort (QuickSort). The blocks are alternatively copied to temporary files fA and fB. The merge begins with sublists that initially have greater length.

To illustrate the effect of using longer sublists, Table 14.2 compares times to sort 30,000 random integers using a one-element block (straight MergeSort) and blocks of size 10, 100, and 1000.

File Merge Implementation   The function MergeSort creates two temporary files and then implements a series of passes that split successive runs into the

Block Size	Time to Sort a File of 30,000 Integers (secs.)
1	205
10	75
100	49
1000	31

TABLE 14.2
Effects of
External Sorting
Using Long
Runs

temporary files fA and fB and then merges them back to the original file fC. It repeats the split/merge process until the file fC consists of a single run.

```
// function to sort file fC using runs which are multiples of
// blockSize. initially blocks of data are read, sorted using
// QuickSort and then written as runs to separate temporary
// files fA and fB
template <class T>
void MergeSort(BinFile<T>& fC, int blockSize)
{
    // temporary file to split the runs from fC
    BinFile<T> fA("fileA", INOUT);
    BinFile<T> fB("fileB", INOUT);

    // the total size of the file and the blockSize
    int size = int (fC.Size()), n = blockSize;
    int k = 1, useA = 1, readCount;
    T *A;

    // reset file pointer for fC to the front of the file
    fC.Reset();

    // for small file, read data from fC, sort, and copy back
        if (size <= blockSize)
        {
            // allocate a buffer to hold the data and do a block
            // read of the data
            A = new T[size];
            if (A == NULL)
            {
                cerr << "MergeSort: memory allocation failure." << endl;
                exit(1);
            }
            fC.Read(A,size);

            // sort it using a fast internal sort method
            QuickSort(A,0,(int)size-1);
```

```
                  // clear the file and rewrite the sorted data
                  fC.Clear();
                  fC.Write(A,size);

        // deallocate the buffer and return
        delete [] A;
        return;
           }
           else
           {
              // allocate the buffer and read blocks to end of file
              A = new T[blockSize];
              if(A == NULL)
              {
                 cerr << "MergeSort: memory allocation failure." << endl;
                 exit(1);
              }
              while (!fC.EndFile())
              {
                 readCount = fC.Read(A,blockSize);
                 if (readCount == 0)
                    break;

                 // sort the block and then alternate writing the run
                 // to fA and fB
                 QuickSort(A,0,readCount-1);
                 if (useA)
                    fA.Write(A,readCount);
                 else
                    fB.Write(A,readCount);
                 useA = !useA;
              }
              delete [] A;
           }

        // merge split files back to fC with runs of size blockSize

        Merge(fA, fB, fC, blockSize);

        // double the size of the current sorted runs
        k *= 2;
        n = k * blockSize;

        // when n is >= the size of the file, fC has one run
        // and is sorted
        while (n < size)
        {
           // on each pass, split the runs; remerge into runs of
           // double the length
```

```
        Split(fA, fB, fC, k, blockSize);
        Merge(fA, fB, fC, n);
        k *= 2;
        n = k * blockSize;
    }

    // remove the temporary files
    fA.Delete();
    fB.Delete();
}
```

For each pass, the function Split scans the runs in file fC and alternately copies them to files fA and fB. For each call to the function, the size of the sublists have doubled to length k*blockSize. Since the block size represents the buffer size that is used, a sublist is copied in k blocks to a file. The process terminates when all the runs in file fC have been copied to the temporary files.

```
// scan runs in file fC and alternate their distribution to
// files fA and fB. for the current split, the runs have
// size k*blockSize
template <class T>
void Split(BinFile<T> &fA, BinFile<T> &fB, BinFile<T> &fC,
           int k, int blockSize)
{
    int useA = 1;
    int i = 0;
    int readCount;

    // copies to files using block reads and writes
    // of size blockSize
    T *A = new T[blockSize];
    if(A == NULL)
    {
        cerr << "MergeSort: memory allocation failure." << endl;
        exit(1);
    }

    // initialize the files before splitting the files
    fA.Clear();
    fB.Clear();
    fC.Reset();

    // distribute runs from file fC until end of file
    while (!fC.EndFile())
    {
        // read a block of data into a dynamic array;
```

```
        // readCount is the number of items read
        readCount = fC.Read(A,blockSize);

        // if readCount is 0, we have an end of file
        if (readCount == 0)
            break;

        // write block to file fA (if useA is True) or to fB
        if (useA)
            fA.Write(A,readCount);
        else
            fB.Write(A,readCount);

        // alternate the file after writing k blocks to the file
        if (++i == k)
        {
            i = 0;
            useA = !useA;
        }
    }

    // deallocate the dynamic memory
    delete [] A;
}
```

Once the runs have been copied to the temporary files fA and fB, the merging of data back to the original file can begin. The process is handled by the function Merge that joins pairs of runs from the two temporary files and creates a single ordered run. If file fA has an extra run, this is copied to file fC using a call to CopyTail.

```
// merge runs of length n from files fA and fB to file fC
template <class T>
void Merge (BinFile<T> &fA, BinFile<T> & fB,
            BinFile<T> &fC, int n)
{
    // currA and currB represent the current position in the
    // run in each file
    int currA = 1, currB = 1;

    // data items read from fA and fB respectively. haveA/haveB
    // are 1/0 (True or False) to indicate if an item was read
    // from the respective file.
    T dataA, dataB;
    int haveA, haveB;

    // initialize the files before the merge begins
    fA.Reset();
```

```
fB.Reset();
fC.Clear();

// get an item from each file
fA.Read(&dataA,1);
fB.Read(&dataB,1);

for (;;)
{
    // if (dataA <= dataB) then copy dataA to fC and update
    // current position in the current run in fA
    if (dataA <= dataB)
    {
        fC.Write(&dataA,1);
        // get next item from fA;  if item not found we have
        // end of file and must copy tail of fB to fC; if
        // current position is > n, then we have completed
        // the run in fA and should copy tail of fB
        if ((haveA = fA.Read(&dataA,1)) == 0 || ++currA > n)
        {
            // copy element from fB that has been read from
            // the stream and update current position in fB
            fC.Write(&dataB,1);
            currB++;
            CopyTail(fB,fC,currB,n);

            // size of fA >= size of fB; if at end of fA, done
            if (!haveA)
                break;
            // otherwise in a new run; reset current position
            currA = 1;

            // get next item in B. if none present, we have
            // only one run in A remaining which we must copy
            // to fC. copy the currently available element from
            // fA before breaking to print tail of fA
            if ((haveB = fB.Read(&dataB,1)) == 0)
            {
                fC.Write(&dataA,1);
                currA = 2;
                break;
            }
            // otherwise set current position in run in fB
            currB = 1;
        }
    }
    else
    {
```

```
                // copy dataB to fC and update the current position in fB
                fC.Write(&dataB,1);


                // check for end of run or end of file in fB
                if ((haveB = fB.Read(&dataB,1)) == 0 || ++currB > n)
                {
                    // if end occurs, write item that is already read
                    // from fA, update its position and then write the
                    // tail of the run
                    fC.Write(&dataA,1);
                    currA++;
                    CopyTail(fA,fC,currA,n);
                    // if no more items in fB, set current position in
                    // fA and prepare to copy the last run in fA
                    if (!haveB)
                    {
                        currA = 1;
                        break;
                    }


                    // otherwise, set current position in fB and get
                    // an item from fA
                    currB = 1;
                    if ((haveA = fA.Read(&dataA,1)) == 0)
                        break;
                    currA = 1;
                }
            }
        }


        // this copies the tail of the last run in fA if it exists
        if(haveA && !haveB)
            CopyTail(fA,fC,currA,n);
    }
```

When merging two runs, we reach the end of one run first. The function CopyTail copies the tail of the other run to the output file.

```
// n is current size of a run; copy tail of a run from file fX
// to fY; variable currRunPos is the current index in the run.
template <class T>
void CopyTail (BinFile<T> &fX, BinFile<T> &fY,
               int &currRunPos, int n)
{
    T data;
```

```
    // copy each item from current position to end of the run
    while (currRunPos <= n)
    {
        // if no item is read, we have an end of file
        // and hence an end of run
        if (fX.Read(&data, 1) == 0)
            return;
        currRunPos++;
        // update the current position and write item to file fY
        fY.Write(&data,1);
    }
}
```

Program 14.4   MergeSort Comparisons

This program uses the natural mergesort to order a file with 1000 random
integers using runs of 100 elements. The file is initially created with the function
LoadFile. The first 45 elements of the original file and the sorted file are printed
using PrintFile.

```
#include <iostream.h>
#include <iomanip.h>

#include "binfile.h"
#include "merge.h"
#include "random.h"

// print the elements from BinFile f in rows of 9 items each
void PrintFile (BinFile<int> &f, long n)
{
    // initialize n to the size of the file
    int data;
    long i;

    n = (f.Size() < n) ? f.Size() : n;

    // reset the file pointer to front of the file
    f.Reset();

    // use a sequential scan of the file, read each element and
    // print its value.  separate each 9 elements with a newline
    for (i = 0; i < n; i++)
    {
```

```
            if (i % 9 == 0)
                cout << endl;
            f.Read(&data, 1);
            cout << setw(5) << data << "   ";
        }
        cout << endl;
}

// create a file with n random integers in the range 0 to 32767
void  LoadFile(BinFile<int> &f, int n)
{
    int i, item;
    RandomNumber rnd;

    // reset file
    f.Reset();

    // load the file with n random numbers
    for (i = 0; i < n; i++)
    {
        item = rnd.Random(32768L);
        f.Write(&item,1);
    }
}

void main(void)
{
    // fC is initialized with random data and sorted
    BinFile<int> fC("fileC", INOUT);

    // create a file with 1000 random integer values
    LoadFile(fC,1000);

    // print the first 45 elements of the initial list
    cout << "First 45 elements of the data file:" << endl;
    PrintFile(fC,45);
    cout << endl;

    // execute the merge sort
    MergeSort(fC, 100);

    // print the first 45 elements of the sorted list
    cout << "First 45 elements of the sorted data file:"
         << endl;
    PrintFile(fC,45);

    // remove the file
    fC.Delete();
}
```

```
/*
<Run of Program 14.4>

First 45 elements of the data file:

14879   26060   28442   20710   19366   10959   17112    7880   22963
16103   22910    6789    4976   19024    1470   25654   31721   28709
  997   23378   14186   14986   21650    7351   25237   28059    5942
 9593   20294   27928    8267    9837   17191    8398   18261   21620
 5139     964   10393   16777   15915   18986   22175    2697   20409

First 45 elements of the sorted data file:

   19      76      94      98     106     119     188     192     236
  259     308     344     346     371     383     424     463     558
  570     605     614     714     741     756     794     861     864
  891     910     923     964     979     997    1000    1007    1029
 1051    1079    1112    1223    1232    1347    1470    1515    1558
*/
```

Dictionaries   14.7

A data element stored in an array is accessed by an index that specifies its position in the array. For example, if A is an array, then A[n] is at position n in the array. The index is not stored as part of the data. A **dictionary (table, associative array)** is an indexed data structure similar to an array. However, the index values as well as the data values can be of any type. For instance, if CommonWords is a dictionary, then CommonWords ["decide"] might be the definition of the word "decide". Unlike arrays, a dictionary index is related to the data rather than just specifying the location in which it is stored. Also, there is no limit to the number of elements a dictionary can hold.

A dictionary is termed an **association structure** because it maintains a list of keys and associated data values. For instance, a language dictionary is a table of words (the keys) and their definitions (values). Dictionaries differ from arrays because the actual position of their elements is hidden. Access is never performed by directly specifying a position in a list but is accomplished only through the use of a key as an index.

A dictionary takes a key related to a data value in the dictionary and uses the key as an index to access the data. The underlying data are internally maintained as a set of key-value pairs, also termed **associations.** Those key-value pairs can be stored in a linked list, a tree, or a hash table. If the data are stored in order by key, we say that the table is **ordered.** Figure 14.5 illustrates the dictionary concept.

To implement a working dictionary, we first develop a method of storing key-value pairs by developing the class KeyValue. Each key-value pair is a KeyValue object with a constant key, and any two objects can be compared using "==" and

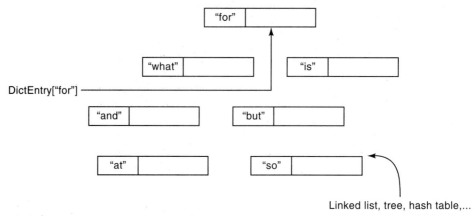

DictEntry["for"]

Linked list, tree, hash table,...

Figure 14.5   Dictionary (Associative Array)

"<". The comparisons are based on the key. This is our first example of a template class having two template parameters, where K is the type of the keys, and T is the type of the value associated with the key.

KEYVALUE CLASS SPECIFICATION

DECLARATION

```
template <class K, class T>
class KeyValue
{
   protected:
      // key cannot be changed once it is initialized
      const K key;

   public:
      // data is publicly accessible
      T value;

      KeyValue(K KeyValue, T datavalue);

      // assignment operators. do not alter the key member
      KeyValue<K,T>& operator= (const KeyValue<K,T>& rhs);

      // comparison operators. based on the two keys
      int operator== (const KeyValue<K,T>& value) const;
      int operator== (const K& keyval) const;
      int operator< (const KeyValue<K,T>& value) const;
      int operator< (const K& keyval) const;
```

```
// only public means of accessing the key
K Key(void) const;
```

DESCRIPTION

The constructor creates a key-value pair. There is no default constructor, and once an object is created the key cannot be changed. The assignment operator alters the value member only, and the relational operators compare keys. The method Key is available for reading the key.

EXAMPLE

The following declares a key-value pair containing a social security number as the key (String) and a data record as the value.

```
struct Data
{
    char name[30];
    int yearsThisCompany;
    int jobclass;
    float salary;
};

Data empData = {"George Williams",10,5,45000.00};
KeyValue<String,Data> Employee("345789553",empData);
```

The implementation of the class is very simple and is found in the file "keyval.h".

The implementation of the quite sophisticated dictionary concept is actually relatively easy. Choose a collection class to store KeyValue objects. The classes OrderedList, BinSTree, and AVLTree can be used to store ordered key-value pairs. To store key-value pairs without ordering, use the collection classes SeqList or HashTable. Each of these classes has the methods Insert, Delete, Find, etc. What we must do to create a dictionary is to extend such a collection so that it has an indexing operator "[]". The operator creates an association between a key used as an index and the value field of the corresponding KeyValue object stored in the collection. We have used inheritance in this book to express the "is a" relationship. Another application is to extend the functionality of a base class. We will use inheritance to extend a collection of KeyValue pairs to have the "[]" operator and other dictionary-related operations. Figure 14.6 illustrates this idea by showing how a Dictionary class can be derived from several base classes.

We develop a class Dictionary that is derived from the BinSTree class, so it maintains an ordered dictionary. The creation of other ordered and unordered dictionary implementations is given in the exercises.

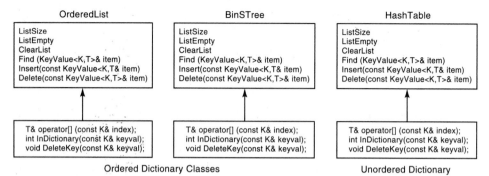

Figure 14.6 Extending a Collection of KeyValue Objects to a Dictionary

DICTIONARY CLASS SPECIFICATION

DECLARATION

```
#include "keyval.h"
#include "bstree.h"
#include "treeiter.h"

template <class K, class T>
class Dictionary: public BinSTree< KeyValue<K,T> >
{
    // default value for creation of a dictionary entry.
    // used by index operator, InDictionary, and DeleteKey
    private:
        T defaultValue;

    public:
        // constructor
        Dictionary(const T& defval);

        // index operator.
        T& operator[] (const K& index);

        // additional dictionary methods
        int InDictionary(const K& keyval);
        void DeleteKey(const K& keyval);
};
```

DESCRIPTION

The indexing operator does most of the work. When called, the dictionary is checked for the presence of the key. If an entry with that key is present, a reference to the data element is returned. If not, a new dictionary entry is created and a reference to the new value is returned. In this way, all dictionary entry creation and data updates are done by using the indexing operator. There is no default constructor for the KeyValue class, so both the key and the data value must be specified. As a result, when "[]" creates an object, it must have a default value. This default data value is provided as a parameter to the constructor. The value must be chosen carefully so the new dictionary entry is ready for participation in expressions.

For instance, a dictionary might contain a String key specifying a word and a String value that contains the definition of the word. Declare the Dictionary object BasicDict as

```
// defaultValue is NULL string
Dictionary<String,String> BasicDict(");
```

Assume in the statement that follows, BasicDict["sextet"] is referenced for the first time. The operator "[]" creates a dictionary entry for "sextet" having the NULL String as its value. The String "+=" operator concatenates "A group of six" onto the NULL string to create an initial definition for the word.

```
BasicDict["sextet"] += "A group of six";
```

The method InDictionary checks whether the collection contains a key-value pair whose key field is keyval, and DeleteKey removes the dictionary entry whose key is keyval. The methods ListEmpty, ListSize, and ClearList are available from the base class. The base class methods Insert, Find, and Delete are also available for dealing directly with KeyValue objects, but they are not ordinarily used in dictionary operations.

Most applications require a dictionary iterator to collect the data for output. Since a Dictionary object is derived from BinSTree, the class InorderIterator can be used to declare a simple class DictionaryIterator as follows:

```
template <class K, class T>
class DictionaryIterator:
                          public InorderIterator<KeyValue<K,T>>
{
   public:
      // constructor
      DictionaryIterator(Dictionary<K,T>& dict);

      // begin iteration of a new dictionary
      void SetList(Dictionary<K,T>& dict);
};

// constructor. dict "extends a" BinSTree object. just use
// its public method GetRoot to initialize the
```

```
// InorderIterator base class
template <class K, class T>
DictionaryIterator<K,T>::DictionaryIterator
                          (Dictionary<K,T> & dict):
              InorderIterator< KeyValue<K,T> >(dict.GetRoot())
{}


// use the base class method SetTree
template <class K, class T>
void DictionaryIterator<K,T>::SetList(Dictionary<K,T> & dict)
{
    SetTree(dict.GetRoot());
}
```

The implementation of Dictionary and DictionaryIterator are found in the file "dict.h".

Program 14.5   Constructing a Word Dictionary

This program declares a Dictionary object wordDictionary with a String key and String data. The default value for a dictionary data entry is the NULL string. The file "defs.dat" contains lists of words and their definitions. The word is placed at the beginning of the line and is followed by one blank. The remainder of the line contains the definition. A loop reads each word and uses it as a key to append its definition to the dictionary.

The dictionary iterator object dictIter is created and used to traverse the dictionary. As each KeyValue pair is obtained, the function PrintEntry is called to print the dictionary entry. This function prints the word followed by a hyphen and then prints the definitions organized in 65-character lines. A word is never split between lines.

```
#include <fstream.h>
#include <stdlib.h>

#include "keyval.h"      // iterator returns KeyValue objects
#include "dict.h"        // include the Dictionary class
#include "strclass.h"    // both key and value fields are Strings

// take a KeyValue object containing a word and
// its definition(s). print it
void PrintEntry(const KeyValue<String,String>& word)
{
    KeyValue<String,String> w = word;
    // word is followed by " - ", so word starts at print
```

```
    // position word length + 3
    int linepos = w.Key().Length() + 3;
    int i;

    // print the word followed by " - "
    cout << w.Key() << " - ";
    // print definition(s) on a sequence of 65 character lines
    while(!w.value.IsEmpty())
    {
        // determine if unprinted portion will fit within 65 char
        // line. compute index of the last character on the line
        if(w.value.Length() > 65-linepos)
        {
            // the string will not fit. move backward and find
            // first blank character. we will not split a word
            // between lines
            i = 64-linepos;
            while(w.value[i] != ' ')
                i--;
        }
        else
            // string fits on the line.
            i = w.value.Length()-1;
        // output the substring that fits on the line
        cout << w.value.Substr(0,i+1) << endl;
        // remove substring we just printed. prepare for new line
        w.value.Remove(0,i+1);
        linepos = 0;
    }
}


void main(void)
{
    // stream from which we read the data
    ifstream fin;
    String word, definition;
    // the dictionary
    Dictionary<String,String> wordDictionary("");

    // open the file "defs.dat" of words and their definitions
    fin.open("defs.dat",ios::in | ios::nocreate);
    if (!fin)
    {
        cerr << "The file 'defs.dat' is not found." << endl;
        exit(1);
     }

    // read a word and then a definition. using index operator,
    // insert the word and the definition or update the existing
```

```
        // definition by concatenating the current one
        while(fin >> word)
        {
            if (fin.eof())
                break;
            // read blank following word
            definition.ReadString(fin);
            wordDictionary[word] += definition;
        }

        // declare an iterator to traverse the dictionary in order
        DictionaryIterator<String,String> dictIter(wordDictionary);

        // traverse dictionary. print each word and its definition(s)
        cout << "The dictionary is:" << endl << endl;
        for(dictIter.Reset();!dictIter.EndOfList();dictIter.Next())
        {
            PrintEntry(dictIter.Data());
            cout << endl;
        }

    wordDictionary.ClearList();
}

/*
<File "defs.dat">

program A list of the acts, speeches, pieces.
finish To bring to an end.
cause Anything producing an effect or result.
sextet A group of six performers.
program A sequence of operations executed by a computer.
velocity Quickness of motion; swiftness.
cook To prepare by boiling, baking, frying, etc.
muff A cylindrical covering of fur to keep the hands warm.
banner A headline running across a newspaper page.
sextet A composition for six instruments.

<Run of Program 14.5>

The dictionary is:

banner - A headline running across a newspaper page.

cause - Anything producing an effect or result.

cook - To prepare by boiling, baking, frying, etc.

finish - To bring to an end.
```

```
muff - A cylindrical covering of fur to keep the hands warm.

program - A list of acts, speeches, pieces. A sequence of
operations executed by a computer.

sextet - A group of six performers. A composition for six
instruments.

velocity - Quickness of motion; swiftness.
*/
```

_____

DICTIONARY CLASS IMPLEMENTATION

The constructor initializes the base class and the default value:

```
//constructor. initialize base class and default value
template <class K, class T>
Dictionary<K,T>::Dictionary(const T& defaultval):
     BinSTree< KeyValue<K,T> >(), defaultValue(defaultval)
{}
```

The "[]" operator creates a KeyValue object targetKey with the given key and the default value and searches for the key in the tree. If the key is not found, it inserts targetKey into the tree. The base class member current points to the node just found or inserted. Return a reference to the data value in the node.

```
// index operator. here is where most of the work is done
template <class K, class T>
T& Dictionary<K,T>::operator[] (const K& index)
{
   // define a target KeyValue object with the default value
   KeyValue<K,T> targetKey(index,defaultValue);

   // search for key. if not found, insert targetKey
   if(!Find(targetKey))
      Insert(targetKey);

   // return reference to data value found or inserted.
  return current->data.value;
}
```

To implement InDictionary create a KeyValue object tmp with the given key and the default value. Search for the key in the tree and return the result.

```
// see if KeyValue object exists with given key
template <class K, class T>
int Dictionary<K,T>::InDictionary(const K& keyval)
{
    // define a target KeyValue object with the default value
    KeyValue<K,T> tmp(keyval,defaultValue);
    int retval = 1;

    // search for tmp in the tree and return the result
    if(!Find(tmp))
        retval = 0;
    return retval;
}
```

DeleteKey creates a KeyValue object tmp with the given key and the default value
and deletes the entry from the tree.

```
// delete the KeyValue object with given key from dictionary
template <class K, class T>
void Dictionary<K,T>::DeleteKey(const K& keyval)
{
    KeyValue<K,T> tmp(keyval,defaultValue);

    Delete(tmp);
}
```

Written Exercises

14.1 (a) Sort the sequence 8, 4, 1, 9, 2, 1, 7, 4 using the selection sort. You should
describe the list at the end of each pass.
(b) Repeat (a) for the following list of characters:

V, B, L, A, Z, Y, C, H, S, B, H

14.2 Repeat Written Exercise 14.1 for the insertion sort.

14.3 Sort the sequence of characters C, A, M, T, B, B, A, L using the insertion sort. Trace
each step of the sort.

14.4 (a) What is the run time efficiency for the selection sort when it sorts an array of
n identical elements?
(b) Answer (a) for the insertion and bubble sorts.

14.5 Sort the array A using the bubble sort. After each pass, define the list and indicate
the sublist that must still be sorted.

A = 85, 40, 10, 95, 20, 15, 70, 45, 40, 90, 80, 10

14.6 Use the quick sort algorithm to sort array A. Select the pivot from the midpoint in
the list. During each pass, list all exchanges that will move a corresponding pair of

elements in the lower and upper sublist. List the ordering of elements after each pass.

A: 790   175   284   581   374   799   852   685   486   347

14.7 Another version of the quick sort chooses the pivot to be A[low] instead of A[mid]. The algorithm is still $O(n \log_2 n)$, but the worst case behavior changes. How?

14.8 Array A is to be sorted by inserting its elements into a doubly linked list. By maintaining a current location in the linked list, insert an item by moving forward if the new element is larger or backward if it is smaller than the current value. Write a function DoubleSort that implements this sorting method.

```
template <class T>
void DoubleSort (T a[], int n);
```

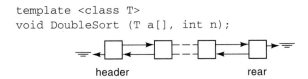

header   rear

14.9 Develop the algorithmic complexity of creating a sorted list using the technique of Written Exercise 14.8. The complexity should discuss the best, worst, and average case.

14.10 Which of the basic sorting algorithms (selection, insertion, or bubble) most efficiently handles a presorted list? Do you change your response if the initial list is sorted in reverse order?

14.11 We have considered the following sorts in this book:

Binary tree, Bubble, Exchange, Heap, Insertion, Radix, Selection, Tournament

For each sort, give the complexity, the space requirements, and make some additional comments about its efficiency. The additional comments may include whether early exit is possible when the list is already sorted, how probable the worst case is, the number of interchanges performed by the algorithm, and the size of the Big-O constant of proportionality.

14.12 A sorting method is said to be **stable** if two data items having the same value are not rearranged with respect to each other at any stage of the algorithm. For instance, in the five-element array

5_1 55   12 5_2 33

a stable sorting method guarantees that the final ordering is

5_1 5_2 12   33   55

Classify each of the sorts of Written Exercise 14.11 as to their stability.

14.13 Show that the hash function

```
hashf(x) = x % m
```

is unacceptable if m is even. Is the situation changed if m is odd? (Hint: Look at the distribution of even and odd random numbers.)

14.14   Assume that a hash function has the following characteristics:

> Keys 257 and 567 hash to 3,
> Keys 987 and 313 hash to 6,
> Keys 734, 189 and 575 hash to 5,
> Keys 122, 391 hash to 8

Assume that insertions are done in order 257, 987, 122, 575, 189, 734, 567, 313, 391.

(a)   Indicate the position of the data if open probe addressing is used to resolve collisions.

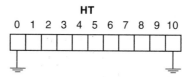

(b)   Indicate the position of the data if chaining with separate lists is used to resolve collisions.

HT

0 1 2 3 4 5 6 7 8 9 10

14.15   Repeat Written Exercise 14.14 if the order of the insertions is reversed.

14.16   Use the hash function hashf(x) = x % 11 to map an integer value to a hash table index. The data 1, 13, 12, 34, 38, 33, 27, 22 are to be inserted into the hash table.

(a)   Construct the hash table using open probe addressing.
(b)   Construct the hash table using chaining with separate lists.
(c)   For both techniques, determine the load factor, the average number of probes needed to locate one of the values in the table, and the average number of probes needed to determine that a value is not in the table.

14.17   Show that a function that maps a string to an integer by summing the characters in the string is not a good hash function. Discuss how shifting can be used to correct the situation.

14.18   The technique of **folding** is sometimes used to develop hash functions. The key is partitioned into several parts and the parts combine to produce a smaller integer value, which is then used as the hash value or is further reduced by division. Suppose a program must deal with a Social Security number as a key. Break the key into three groups of three digits, and add them. This produces an integer in the range 0 .. 2997. For instance, the Social Security number 523456795 produces the hash index 523 + 456 + 795 = 1774. Write the hash function

```
int hashf(char *ssn);
```

that implements this method. (Hint: You will need to extract the substrings and convert each to an integer.)

14.19 Consider the hash function

```
unsigned short hashf(unsigned short key)
{
    return (key >> 4) % 256;
}
```

(a) What is the size of the hash table?
(b) What are hashf(16) and hashf(257)?
(c) In general, what is the action of the hash function?

14.20 Consider the hash function

```
unsigned long hashf(unsigned long key)
{
    return (key*key >> 8) % 65536;
}
```

(a) What is the size of the hash table?
(b) What are hashf(16) and hashf(10000)?
(c) In general, what is the action of the hash function?

14.21 A problem with open probe is that it produces table **clustering.** Entries tend to "bunch together" in areas of the table as collisions occur.

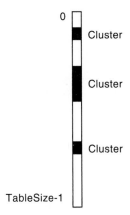

Suppose there are N table entries. If the hashing function is good, what is the probability of hashing to location p? Once data occupies table location p, location p+1 can be occupied by data hashing to location p or location p+1. What is the probability of filling location p+1? What is the probability of filling slot p+2? In general, explain why clustering occurs.

14.22   If the data is not located at the initial hashed index, the open probe method presented executes the function

```
index = (index+1) % m;     // look at next index
```

This is called a **rehash function,** and open probe is a method that resolves collisions by **rehashing.** This approach fosters clustering. A different rehash function can better distribute entries. Two integers p and q are said to be relatively prime if they have no common divisors other than 1. For instance, 3 and 10 are relatively prime as are 18 and 35. For open probe, use a rehash function of the form

```
index = (index + d) % m;
```

where d and m are relatively prime. As the relation is successively applied, the successive indices cover the range $0 \ldots m-1$. The traditional open probe method uses $d = 1$.

(a)   If d and m are not relatively prime, table entries are omitted. Show that if $d = 3$ and $m = 93$, the rehash function

```
index = (index+3) % 93
```

covers only every third table entry.

(b)   Show that if m is prime and $d < m$, then the entire table is covered by the rehash function.

(c)   Do Written Exercise 14.16(a) using the rehash function

```
index = (index + 5) % 11
```

14.23   Hash tables are suited to applications where the primary operation is retrieval. A data record is inserted and then "looked up" many times. The open probe hashing method is poorly suited to an application that requires that data elements be deleted from the hash table.

Consider the following hash table of 101 entries with hash function hashf(key) = key % 101:

0	202
1	304
2	508
3	707

100	

(a) Delete 304 by placing -1 in table location 1. What happens when a search is executed for 707? Explain in general why just marking a slot as empty is not a correct solution to the problem of deletions.

(b) A solution to the problem involves placing a key value DeletedData in the location of the deletion. When searching for a key, table locations marked with DeletedData are skipped. Use the key value -2 in the table to indicate that a deletion occurred at the particular table location. Show that this approach to deleting 304 allows a correct search for 707.

The insertion and retrieval operations in the open probe algorithm must be modified to accommodate deletions.

(c) Describe the algorithm to delete a table element.

(d) Describe an algorithm to locate an element in the table.

(e) Describe an algorithm to insert an element in the table.

14.24 Another collision resolution method that is sometimes used is **chaining with coalescing lists.** This method is similar to open probe, except that colliding data values that must be circularly located further down the table are chained together in linked list. Each chain may contain data whose keys hashed to different table locations. These lists have coalesced. For example, if hashf(x) = x % 7 and the integers 12, 3, 5, 20, and 7 are entered into the table, we have the following picture:

-1 designates empty entry and NULL pointer

0	20	1
1	7	-1
2	-1	-1
3	3	-1
4	-1	-1
5	12	6
6	5	0

(a) Do Written Exercise 14.16(a) using chaining with coalescing lists.

(b) How do you think the run time efficiency of this method compares with both open probe and chaining? Rank them for overall speed.

(c) Is the problem of performing deletions simpler than for open probe? Explain.

14.25 Given a set of keys $k_0, k_1, \ldots, k_{n-1}$, a **perfect hashing function** H is a hash function that produces no collisions.

It is not practical to find a perfect hashing function unless the set of keys is static. A situation for which a perfect hash function is desirable is a table of reserved words (such as "while", "template", "class" in C++) that a compiler searches. When an identifier is read, only one probe is necessary to determine whether the identifier is a reserved word.

It is very difficult to find a perfect hash function for a particular set of keys, and a general discussion of the subject is beyond the scope of this book. Furthermore, if a new set of keys is added to the set, the hash function normally is no longer perfect.

(a) Consider the set of integer keys 81, 129, 301, 38, 434, 216, 412, 487, 234, and the hashing function

```
H(x) = (x+18)/63
```

Is H a perfect hashing function?

(b) Consider the set of keys consisting of the strings

Bret, Jane, Shirley, Bryce, Michelle, Heather

Devise a perfect hash function for a table containing 7 elements.

14.26 The following declaration creates a text file class. The operations use the Pascal programming language as a model. Use the C++ fstream operations to implement the class.

```
enum Access {IN, OUT};   // defines the data flow of the file

class PascalTextFile
{
    private:
        fstream f;                     // C++ file stream
        char fname[64];                // file name
        Access accesstype;             // data flow is IN or OUT
        int isOpen;                    // used for Reset
        void Error(char *msg);         // used to print errors

    public:
        PascalTextFile(void);          // constructor
        void Assign(char *filename);   // sets file name
        void Reset(void);              // open for input
        void Rewrite(void);            // open for output
        int EndFile(void);             // read eof flag
        void Close(void);              // close file
        int PRead(T A[], int n);       // read n chars into A
        void PWrite(T A[], int n);     // write n chars from A
};
```

Programming Exercises

14.1 Write a program that uses the doubly linked list insertion algorithm from Written Exercise 14.8 to create an ordered list of N random integers in the range 0–1000. After creating the list, print the elements.

14.2 Implement the following sorting algorithm:

Split an n element list into halves. Sort each half using the selection sort and then merge the two halves.

(a) Perform a complexity analysis for the sort.

(b) Use the algorithm to sort an array of 20000 random integers, and time the program.

(c) Run the same program using the ordinary selection sort. Which version runs faster?

14.3 In Section 14.6, the text discusses the straight merge sort for files. Implement an internal version of the algorithm that sorts an array of n elements. Use your result to sort a list of 1000 random double values. Print the first 20 and the last 20 items.

14.4 Consider the record

```
struct TwoKey
{
    int primary;
    int secondary;
};
```

Create an array of 100 records. The primary field is to contain a random integer in the range 0 . . 9, and the secondary field must contain a random integer in the range 0 . . 100. Revise the insertion sort algorithm to maintain primary and secondary key ordering. The new algorithm identifies ties in the primary key and uses the secondary key for ordering. Use this algorithm to sort the array. Print the array with each record in the following format:

primary(secondary)

14.5 The Shell sort, named after its inventor Donald Shell, provides a simple and fairly efficient sorting algorithm. The sort begins by subdividing an n element list into k sublists, which have members

a[0], a[k+0], a[2k+0], . . .
a[1], a[k+1], a[2k+1], . . .

. . .

a[k−1], a[k+(k−1)], a[2k+(k−1)], . . .

A sublist starts with a first element a[i] in the range a[0] . . . a[k−1] and includes every successive k*th* element. For instance, with k = 4 the following array splits into three sublists:

7   5   8   6   2   4   9   1   3   0

Sublist$_0$ 7   2   3
Sublist$_1$ 5   4   0
Sublist$_2$ 8   9
Sublist$_3$ 6   1

Sort each sublist using the insertion sort algorithm. In our example, we obtain the following sublists:

Sublist₀   2   3   7
Sublist₁   0   4   5
Sublist₂   8   9
Sublist₃   1   6

and the partially sorted array

   2   0   8   1   3   4   9   6   7   5

Repeat the process with k = k/3. Continue through k = 1, at which point the list is sorted. The optimal choice for a starting value of k is left to a course on the theory of algorithms. The algorithm is successful because the data swapping occurs in noncontiguous segments of the array, which move an element a greater distance toward its final location than a swap of adjacent entries in the ordinary insertion sort.

In a main program, create an array containing 100 random integers in the range from 0 to 999. Use an initial value of k = 40 with the shell-sort to order the array. Print the original and final lists with 10 integers per line.

14.6 This exercise develops a simple spelling checker. The file "words" in the program supplement contains 500 frequently used words, separated by whitespace characters. Read the file and insert the words into a hash table. Read a document and separate it into a sequence of words, where a word is defined by the simple function

```cpp
// extract a word beginning with a letter and possibly
// other letters/digits
int GetWord (ifstream& fin, char w[])
{
    char c;
    int i = 0;

    // skip non-alphabetic input
    while ( fin.get(c) && !isalpha(c));

    // return 0 on end of file
    if (fin.eof())
        return 0;

    // record 1st letter of the word
    w[i++] = c;

    // collect letters and digits. NULL terminate
    while (fin.get(c) && (isalpha(c) || isdigit(c)))
        w[i++] = c;
    w[i] = '\0';

    return 1;
}
```

Using the hash table, print a list of words that appear to be misspelled.

14.7 Develop classes OpenProbe and OpenProbeIterator that maintain a hash table using open probe addressing. The following is the specification of an OpenProbe class. Use Written Exercise 14.23 for the implementation of the class.

```
// records in the open probe table
template <class T>
struct TableRecord
{
    // entry available (True or False)
    int available;
    T data;
};

template <class T>
class OpenProbeIterator;

template <class T>
class OpenProbe: public List<T>
{
    protected:
        // dynamically created open probe table
        // and its size
        TableRecord<T> *table;
        int tableSize;

        // hash function
        unsigned long (*hf) (T key);

        // index of last table element accessed
        int lastIndex;
    public:
        // constructor, destructor
        OpenProbe(int tabsize,unsigned long hashf(T key));
        ~OPenProbe(void);

        // standard list handling methods
        virtual void Insert(const T& key);
        virtual void Delete (const T& key);
        virtual int Find(T& key);
        virtual void ClearList(void);

        // update last table entry accessed
        void Update(const T& key);

        friend class OpenProbeIterator<T>;
};
```

Use your classes to run Program 14.2.

14.8 Place the declaration of the PascalTextFile class from Written Exercise 14.27 in file "ptf.h". Write a program that uses the class to read the file "ptf.h", translate each lowercase letter to uppercase, and write it to the file "ptf.uc". Use your operating system print command to list the contents of "ptf.uc".

14.9 Use the BinFile class for the following sequence of programs. The output from one part can be used as input for a subsequence application.

(a) The Person record defines a sequence of fields in a data base.

```
struct Person
{
    char first[20]; // first name
    char last[20];  // last name
    char id[4];     // four digit id
};
```

Define a function DelimRec that takes a Person record and a buffer.

```
void DelimRec (const Person &p, char *buffer);
```

The function converts each field of the record into a variable length string terminated by the delimiter "|". The three fields are concatenated in the buffer. For instance:

Person	First	Tom
	Last	Davis
	ID	6192
Buffer	Tom|Davis|6192|	

Write a program that inputs five Person records, one field per line, and creates a file of characters "rec1.out". For each record, create a compact buffer of length n and then write to the file the size of the buffer as a two byte short int, followed by the n characters in the buffer. If available, use a system hex dump utility to list the contents of "rec1.out".

(b) Write a program that will read successive records from file "rec1.out", expanding each delimited field into the fixed length fields of the Person record. If necessary, pad a field with blanks on the right. A Person record is now a 44-byte structure. Write your records to the file "rec2.out".

(c) Write a program that inputs a 4-digit ID and searches file "rec2.out" for a match. If found, print the first and last name of the person.

14.10 Consider the following record type

```
struct CharRec
{
    char key;
    int count;
};
```

Use the BinFile class to create a file "letcount" of 26 such records containing key values 'A', . . . , 'Z' and a count of 0. Read a text file, converting each alphabetic character to upper case. Update the count field of the corresponding record in the binary file "letcount". Print the frequency count for each character. Use the natural merge sort discussed in Section 14.6 with a block size of 4 to order "letcount" using the count field as the key. Print the resulting file.

14.11 Derive an ordered dictionary class from the OrderedList class. Use it and an associated iterator to run Program 14.5.

14.12 Derive a dictionary class from the Hash class. Use it and an associated iterator to run Program 14.5. Print the dictionary object in the order extracted by the iterator. Sort the results of the traversal and print the dictionary object in alphabetical order.

ANSWERS TO
SELECTED
WRITTEN EXERCISES

Chapter 1

1.2 (a) **ADT** *Cylinder* **is**

Data
>   The radius and height of the cylinder. The numbers
>   are floating point values > 0.

Operations
>   *Constructor*
>>   Initial Values: The radius and height of the
>>   cylinder
>>   Process: Use the initial values to
>>   specify the ADT data.
>
>   *Area*
>>   Input: None
>>   Preconditions: None
>>   Process: Compute the area using the
>>   radius and height.
>>   Output: Return the area.
>>   Postconditions: None
>
>   *Volume*
>>   Input: None
>>   Preconditions: None
>>   Process: Compute the volume using the
>>   radius and height.
>>   Output: Return the volume.
>>   Postconditions: None

end ADT *Cylinder*

1.3 Let Cyl and Hole be cylinders of radius R and Rh, respectively, and let C be a Circle of radius Rh.

(a) The volume of the resulting solid is Cyl.Volume() − Hole.Volume().

(b) The area of the solid is Cyl.Area() + Hole.Area() − 4*C.Area().

1.5
```
const float PI = 3.14159;
class Cylinder
{
    private:
       float radius, height;
    public:
       Cylinder(float r, float h): radius(r),height(h) {}
       float Area(void)
       {return 2.0*PI*radius(radius+height);}
       float Volume(void)
       {return PI*radius*radius*height;}
};
```

1.11 (a) Two or more objects in a class inheritance hierarchy have methods of the same name that perform distinct tasks. This property allows objects from a variety of classes to respond to the same message. The receiver of the message is determined dynamically at runtime.

Chapter 2

2.1 (a) 5   (b) 14   (c) 55   (d) 127

2.3 (a) 26   (b) 1055   (c) 4332   (d) 255   (e) 65536
    (f) 17   (g) 57   (h) 73   (i) FF

2.4 (a) C   (b) A6   (c) F2   (d) BDE3   (e) 11000010000
    (f) 1010111100100000

2.5 (a) 32 50 32   (b) 32 32 40

2.8 (a) 'N'   (b) 'K'   (c) '*':42_{10}, 101010_2 'q':113_{10}, 1110001_2 <cr>:13_{10}, 1101_2

2.9 V 113 8

2.11 (a) 6.75

     (d) $.111\ldots111\ldots = \frac{1}{2} + \frac{1}{4} + \frac{1}{8} + \ldots + \frac{1}{2^n} + \ldots = 1 - \left(\frac{1}{2}\right)^n$

     As n -> ∞, the fractional portion converges to 1. The decimal equivalent is thus
     $3 + 1 = 4$.

2.12 (b) 1.001

2.14 (a) 40f00000   (d) 29.125

2.17 X = 55, Y = 10, A = {5.3 6.8 8.9 1 5.5 3.3}

2.18 (a) (1) 10 bytes allocated for A
         (2) &A[3] = 6000 + 2*3 = 6006, &A[1] = 6000 + 2*1 = 6002
    (b) (1) 33 (2) A = {60,50000,-10000,10,33} (3) &A[3] =
         2050 + 4*3 = 2062

2.20 (a) 30 * 2 = 60 bytes
    (b) &A[3][2] = 1000 + 3*12 + 2*2 = 1040, &A[1][4] = 1000 + 1*12 +
        4*2 = 1020
    (c) &A[1][4] = 1020, &A[2][5] = 1034

2.22 (a) 't', 't', NULL   (b) Stockton, CA, March 5, 1994   (c) 1   (d) 1

2.23
```
void strinsert(char *s, char *t, int i)
{   char tmp[128];    // stores the tail of s
    if (i > strlen(s))    // exit if index i exceeds that of
                               the NULL character in s
            return;
    strcpy(tmp,&s[i]);    // copy tail of s to tmp
    strcpy(&s[i],t);      // copy t in place of the tail
    strcat(s,tmp);        // concatenate the tail in tmp
}
```

2.25 (b)
```
void PtoCStr(char *s)
{   int n = *s++;  // get byte count
    while(n--)            // move each char left one pos
        *(s-1) = *s++;
    *s = 0;              // NULL terminate the string
}
```

2.27
```
Complex cadd(Complex& x, Complex& y)
{
    Complex sum = {x.real+y.real,x.imag+y.imag};
    return sum;
}
Complex cmul(Complex& x, Complex& y)
{   Complex product = {x.real*y.real-x.imag*y.imag,
                       x.real*y.imag+x.imag*y.real};
    return product;
}
```

Chapter 3

3.2 (b)
```
class Box
{
        private:
            float length, width, height;
        public:
            Box(float l, float w, float h);
            float GetLength(void) const;
            float GetWidth(void) const;
            float GetHeight(void) const;
            float Area(void) const;
            float Volume(void) const;
};
Box::Box(float l, float w, float h): length(l), width(w),
height(h) {}
float Box::Area(void)
{ return 2.0*(l*w + l*h + w*h);}
```

    (c) Write a function int Qualify(Box B) that returns 1 if the box qualifies and 0 if not, e.g.,

          if ((2*(B.GetLength()+B.GetWidth()) + B.GetHeight()) < 100)
          return 1; // etc.

3.3 (a) private and public must be followed by ":". The final "}" must be followed by ";".

    (b) Y(int n, int m): p(n), q(m) {}

3.4 (a)
```
class X
{
        private:
            int a, b, c;
        public:
            X(int x = 1, int y = 1, int z = 1);
            int f(void);
};
```

    (b) X::X(int x, int y, int z):a(x), b(y), c(z) {}

3.5
```
class Student
{   ...
    public:
        Student(int id, int studgradepts, int studunits):
            studentid(id), gradepts(studgradepts),
            units(studunits)
```

```
                    {ComputeGPA();}
                        ...
            };
            void Student::UpdateGradeInfo(int newunits, int newgradepts)
            {
                    units += newunits;
                    gradepts += newgradepts;
                    ComputeGPA();
            }
```

3.8 (a)
```
            CardDeck::CardDeck(void)
            {
                    for(int i=0;i < 52;i++)
                        cards[i] = i;
                    currentCard = 0;
            }
            void CardDeck::Shuffle(void)
            {
                    static RandomNumber rnd;
                    int randIndex, tmp;

                    for(int i=0;i < 52;i++)
                    {
                        randIndex = i + rnd.Random(52-i);
                        tmp = cards[i];
                        cards[i] = cards[randIndex];
                        cards[randIndex] = tmp;
                    }
                    currentCard = 0;
            }
```

(b) The following describes the algorithm. Declare a local 52 integer array in DealHand. Use GetCard to assign n card values to the array. Use a sorting algorithm such as the exchange sort discussed in Chapter 2 to sort the n integers. Cycle through the array and use the method PrintCard to print face values of the cards.

3.9
```
            Temperature Average(Temperature& a[], int n)
            {
                    float avgLow = 0.0, avgHigh = 0.0;

                    for(int i=0;i < n;i++)
                    {
                        avgLow += a[i].GetLowTemp();
                        avgHigh += a[i].GetHighTemp();
                    }
                    avgLow /= n;
                    avgHigh /= n;
                    return Temperature(avgLow,avgHigh);
            }
```

3.11 RandomNumber rnd;

    (a) `if (rnd.fRandom() <= 0.2) ...`

    (b) `int weight;`

           `weight = 140 + rnd.Random(91);`

3.12 (a) Note: A static class member is defined outside the class but can only be accessed by member functions. All objects share the value of a static data member.

```
#include "random.h"
class Event
{
    private:
        int lowTime, highTime;
        static RandomNumber rnd;
    public:
        Event(int low = 0, int high = 1): lowTime
            (low),highTime(high)
        { if (lowTime > highTime)
          { cerr << "Lower bound exceeds upper bound."
                << endl;
            exit(1);
          }
        }
        int GetEvent(void)
        {return lowTime + rnd.Random (highTime-
        lowTime+1);}
};
// rnd is a static data member in the Event class
RandomNumber Event::rnd;
```

    (c) Event A[5] = {Event(10,20),Event(10,20),Event(10,20),Event(10,20), Event(10,20)};

        // use the default constructor for each array element

        Event B[5]; // lowTime = 0; highTime = 1

3.14 (a)
$$\begin{bmatrix} 1 & 2 & 3 \\ 0 & -7 & -8 \\ 0 & 0 & -4 \end{bmatrix} * \begin{bmatrix} X_0 \\ X_1 \\ X_2 \end{bmatrix} = \begin{bmatrix} 5 \\ -14 \\ 0 \end{bmatrix}$$

    (b) Determinate = $(1)(-7)(-4) = 28$

Chapter 4

4.2 (a) Array   (c) Stack   (e) Set   (g) File   (i) Heap

    (k) Dictionary

4.4 (b) $n^2 + 6n + 7 \le n^2 + n^2 + n^2 = 3n^2, n \ge 6$

    (d) $\dfrac{n^3 + n^2 - 1}{n + 1} \le \dfrac{n^3 + n^2 - 1}{n} = n^2 + n - \dfrac{1}{n} \le n^2 + n \le 2n^2, n \ge 1$

4.5 (a)   n = 10

(b) $2^n + n^3 \leq 2^n + 2^n = 2 (2^n)$, n $\geq$ 10

4.7   K $\log_2 n < $ Kn, n $\geq$ 1, so the algorithm is also O(n).

4.8 (b)   O(n)   (c) $O(n^2)$

4.11 (a)   (3) n/2 or O(n)   (b)   (1) 1

4.14   Deletes an element of maximum value from the list. L must be passed by reference so the runtime list is updated.

Chapter 5

5.3   <line 1> 22 <line 2> 9 <line 3> 8 <line 4> 18

5.4
```
void StackClear(Stack& S)
{   while(!S.StackEmpty())
        S.Pop();
}
```

5.6   Copies stack S1 to S2 using the intermediate stack tmp.

5.7
```
int StackSize(Stack S)
{   int size = 0;
    // S is passed by value, runtime stack is not altered
    while(!S.StackEmpty())
    {   size++;
        S.Pop();
    }
    return size;
}
```

5.9
```
void SelectItem(Stack& S, int n)
{   Stack Q;
    int i, foundn = 0;
    while(!S.StackEmpty())
    {
        i = S.Pop();
        if (i == n)
        {   foundn++;
            break;
        }
        Q.Push(i);
    }
    while(!Q.StackEmpty())
        S.Push(Q.Pop());
    if (foundn)
        S.Push(n);
}
```

5.10 (b)   a b + d e − /

5.11 (b)   a*(b + c)

5.14   <line 1> 3 <line 2> 18 <line 3> 22 <line 4> 9

5.15 Reverses a queue. Q must be passed by reference in order to modify the runtime parameter.

5.18
```
DataType PQueue::PQDelete(void)
{    DataType min;
     int i, minindex = 0;
     if (count > 0)
     {    min = pqlist[0];  // assume pqlist[0] is the
                                minimum
          // visit remaining elements, updating minimum and index
          for (i = 1; i < count; i++)
             if (pqlist[i] < min)
             // new minimum is pqlist[i]. new minindex is i
             {    min = pqlist[i];
                  minindex = i;
             }
          // shift pqlist [minindex+1]..pqlist[count-1] to the left
          i = minindex;
          while (i < count-1)
          {    pqlist[i] = pqlist[i+1];
               i++;
          }
          count--;                        // decrement count
     }
     // qlist is empty, terminate the program
     else
     {
        cerr << "Deleting from an empty priority queue!"
             << endl;
        exit(1);
     }
     return min;                          // return minimum value
}
```

Chapter 6

6.1 (a) Rule #1. The parameter lists are not distinct. Functions 1 and 2 have identical lists, and the default parameters in function 3 are not considered for overloading.

(b) Rule #1. The parameter lists are distinct. The overloading is done correctly.

(c) Rule #2. Functions 1 and 2 are acceptable, since an enum type is considered distinct from other types. However, the typedef in function 3 has no effect. The compiler considers the parameter list to be "int& x", the same as for function 1.

6.3 Maximum of a and b is 99.   Maximum of a, b, and c is 153.
1.0 + max(h1,h2) = 1.05   Maximum of t, u, and v is 70000.

6.5 Swap for C++ Strings only.
```
void Swap(char *s, char *t)
// assume that s,t contain no more than 79 characters
{   char tmp[80];
    strcpy(tmp,s);
    strcpy(s,t);
    strcpy(t,tmp);
}
```

6.7 (a)
```
ModClass::ModClass(int v): dataval(v % 7) {}
ModClass ModClass::operator+ (const ModClass& x)
{   return ModClass(dataval+x.dataval);
}
```
   (b)
```
ModClass operator* (const ModClass& x, const ModClass& y)
{   return ModClass(x.dataval * y.dataval);
}
```
   (c)
```
ModClass Inverse(const ModClass& x)
{   ModClass prod, value;
    for(int i=0;i < 7;i++)
    {   value = ModClass(i);
        prod = x * ModClass(i);
        if(prod.GetValue() == 1)
            break;
    }
    return value;
}
```

6.9
```
Complex::Complex(double x, double y):real(x), imag(y) {}
Complex Complex::operator+ (Complex x) const
{   return Complex(real+x.real, imag+x.imag);
}
Complex Complex::operator/ (Complex x) const
{   double denom = x.real*x.real+x.imag*x.imag;
    return Complex((real*x.real+imag*x.imag)/denom,
                   (imag*x.real-real*x.imag)/denom);
}
// output in format (real,imag)
ostream& operator<< (ostream& ostr,const Complex& x)
{
    ostr << '(' << x.real << ',' << x.imag << ')';
    return ostr;
}
```

6.11 (a) return ModClass(num/den);   (b) return Rational(dataval);

6.13 (a)
```
Set::Set(int a[], int n)
{    for (int i = 0; i < SETSIZE; i++)
         member[i] = FALSE;
     for(i=0;i < n;i++)
         member[a[i]] = TRUE;
}
```

(b)
```
int operator ^ (int n, Set x)
{    if (n < 0||n >= SETSIZE)
     {     cerr << " ^operator: Invalid member reference
                    " << n << endl;
           exit(1);
     }
     return (x.member[n]);
}
```

(c) (i) {1, 4, 8, 17, 25, 33, 53, 63}
     (ii) {1, 25}   (iii) 0   (iv) 1   (v) 1

(d) <output> <line 1> {1, 2, 3, 5, 7, 9, 25} <line 2> {2, 3} <line 3> 55
     <line 4> 55 is in A

(e)
```
Set Set::operator+ (Set x) const
{    int i;
     Set tmp;
     for (i = 0; i < SETSIZE; i++)
         tmp.member[i] = member[i] || x.member[i];
     return tmp;
}

void Set::Insert(int n)
{    if (n < 0||n >= SETSIZE)
     {     cerr << "Insert: Invalid parameter "
                  << n << endl;
           exit(1);
     }
     member[n] = TRUE;
}
```

Chapter 7

7.1 (a) template <class T>
          T Max(const T &x, const T &y)
          {return (x < y) ? y : x;}

     (b) char *Max(char* x, char* y)
          {return (strcmp(x,y) < 0) ? y : x;}

7.3
```
template <class T>
int Max(T Arr[], int n)
{    T currMax = Arr[0];   // assume n > 0
     int currMaxIndex = 0;
     for (int i = 1; i < n; i++)
          if (currMax < Arr[i])
          {    currMax = Arr[i];
               currMaxIndex = i;
          }
     return currMaxIndex;
}
```

7.5
```
template <class T>
void InsertOrder(T A[], int n, T elem)
{    int i = 0; // assume n > 0
```

```
            while (i < n && A[i] < elem) // locate insertion point
                i++;
            if (i < n)
                for (int j = n; j > i; j--) // move tail to right
                    A[j] = A[j-1];
            A[i] = elem;      // insert the element
    }
```

Chapter 8

8.1 (a) 0 1 2 3 4 1 2 3 4 5

(b) No. p is assigned two distinct addresses in the calls to the new function. To have p-10 be set to the start of the first list of 10 integers, the new function would have to allocate memory in consecutive blocks.

8.2 (a) `int *px = new int(5);`

(b) `a = new long[n];`

(c) `p = new DemoC;`
`p->one = 1; p->two = 500000; p->three = 3.14;`

(d) `p = new DemoD;`
`p->one = 3; p->two = 35; p->three = 1.78; strcpy(p->name,`
`"Bob C++");`

(e) `delete px;  delete [] a;   delete p;   delete p;`

8.3 (a) `DynamicInt::DynamicInt(int n)`
`{pn = new int(n);}`

(b) `DynamicInt::DynamicInt(const DynamicInt &x)`
`{pn = new int(*x.pn);}`

(c) `DynamicInt::operator int(void) // return integer value`
`{return *pn;}`

(d) `istream& operator>> (istream& istr,DynamicInt& x)`
`{    istr >> *(x.pn);`
`     return istr;`
`}`

8.4 (a) `p = new DynamicInt(50);`

(b) `r = new DynamicInt[3]; // value of each element is 0`

(c) `for(int i=0;i < 10;i++)`
`        a[i].SetVal(100);   // or a[i] = DynamicInt(100);`

(d) `delete p; delete [] q;`

8.8 (a) `DynamicType<int> *p = new DynamicType<int> (5);`

(b) `cout << *p;              // uses overloaded << operator`
`cout << p->GetValue();// use member function`
`cout << int(p);          // use int conversion operator`

(c) Allocates an array with 65 objects of type DynamicType<char>. The char value for each array element is 0 (NULL character).
Allocates a single object of type DynamicType<char>. The char value is 'A'.

(d) 35   (e) 35   (f) D D 68   (g) delete p; delete c;
                                          delete Q; // error Q is not
                                                          dynamically
                                                          allocated

8.9 (a) The parameter x is passed by value and hence would call the copy constructor. The copy constructor would repeatedly call the copy constructor, with the program executing an infinite loop.

(b) You could not have a chain of assignment operators C = B = A;

8.11 The operator '+=' adds a right-hand side r to the current Rational object and then assigns the result to the same current object. The current object given by *this. The value "*this + r" assigned to the current object (*this) and the value is returned.

8.12 (a) ArrCL<int> A(20); ArrCL<char> B; ArrCL<float> C(25);

(b) The ArrCL class does array bounds checking. A[30] is out of bounds.

(c) The 20-element array arr has values 2, 4, 6, 8, . . . , 40 whose sum is (20 * 42)/2 = 10 * 42 = 420. Both functions compute the same value.

8.13 (a) "Have a"   (b) "nice day!"   (c) "Have a nice day!"

(d) "Have a nice day!"

8.14 (a) 10   (b) y   (c) 1   (d) Index 24 is out of range.   (e) xya52c

(f) abc12ABCxya52cba

8.16 (a) 15   (b) 10   (c) 65520   (d) 1   (e) 8

8.17 (1) matches function three   (4) matches function one

8.19
```
template <class T> Set<T> Set<T>::operator~ (void) const
{ Set<T> tmp(setrange);
    for (int i = 0; i < arraysize; i++)  // form the universal set
        tmp.member[i] = ~tmp.member[i]; // set each element of
                                              tmp to  0 = 111...111
    return tmp-*this; // return the difference between the
                            universal set and the current set
}
```

8.20 (a) Set<T> UniversalSet(n);
           UniversalSet = ~UniversalSet;

(b) template <class T>
     Set<T> Difference(const Set<T>& S, const Set<T>& T) {return S * ~T;}

Chapter 9

9.1 (a) 2 3   (b) 5 3   (c) 7 7   (d) 15 15   (e) 17 17

9.3
```
Node<int> *head = NULL, *p;
for (int i = 20; i > 0; i--)
{    p = new Node<int>(i, head);
     head = p;
}
p = head;
while (p != NULL)
```

```
{      cout << p->data << "   ";
       p = p->NextNode();
}
```

9.6 (b) The next node points back to p.   (c) The next node points to itself.

9.7 (a)
```
template <class T> void InsertFront(Node<T> header,
                                            T item)
{    Node<T> *p = new Node<T>(item);
     header.InsertAfter(p);
}
```

9.9 From the current node, scan the tail of the list and add 7 to the value of each node.

9.10 Removes the first node from the list and replaces it at the end of the list.

9.11
```
template <class T>
int CountKey(Node<T> *head, T key)
{    Node<T> *p = head;
     int count = 0;
     while (p != NULL)
     {    if (p->data == key)
               count++;
          p = p->NextNode();
     }
     return count;
}
```

9.14 (a) 10 8 6 4 2   (b) 2 4 6 8 10   (c) 10 8 6 4 2
(d) 10 8 6 4 2

9.15 (a) 60 70 80 90 100   (b) 20 40 60 80 100   (c) 20 10 30 40 50 60 70 80
90 100

9.17
```
void OddEven(LinkedList<int>& L,LinkedList<int>& L1,
LinkedList<int>& L2)
{    L.Reset();
     while (!L.EndOfList())
     {    if (L.Data() % 2 == 1)
               L1.InsertAfter(L.Data());
          else
               L2.InsertAfter(L.Data());
          L.Next();
     }
}
```

9.19
```
template <class T> void DeleteRear(LinkedList<T>& L)
{    L.Reset();
     for (int i = 0; i < L.ListSize() - 1; i++)
          L.Next();
     L.DeleteAt();
}
```

9.23 Reverses the items in the linked list by copying them to an intermediate stack list and then copying them back to the linked lists.

9.27 Each queue has a LinkedList object included by composition. When the queue objects are assigned to each other, the overloaded assignment operator from the LinkedList class is called and the two lists are copied to one another.

9.29
```
template <class T> void InsertOrder(CNode<T> *header,
                                    CNode<T> *newNode)
{   CNode<T> *curr = header->NextNode(), *prev = header;
    while (curr != header && curr->data < newNode->data)
    {   prev = curr;
        curr = curr->NextNode();
    }
    prev->InsertAfter(newNode);
}
```

9.32
```
template <class T> DNode<T> *DNode<T>::DeleteNodeRight(void)
{   DNode<T> *tempPtr = next; // save address of node
    if (next == this)
        return NULL;    // we point to ourselves. quit!
    // current node points to successor of tempPtr.
    right = tempPtr->right;
    // successor of tempPtr points back to curr node.
    tempPtr->right->left = this;
}
```

Chapter 10

10.1 The result depends on the order in which the compiler evaluates the operands. If n=3 and the left operand is evaluated first, the result is 3*2! = 6. If the right operand is evaluated first, the result is 2*2! = 4.

10.2 1 1 5 13 41 121 365 1093 3281 9841 . . .

10.4 125

10.5 !gnitseretni si sihT

10.7
```
float avg(float a[], int n)
{   if (n == 1)
            return a[0];
    else
            return float(n-1)/n*avg(a,n-1) + a[n-1]/n;
}
```

10.8
```
int rstrlen(char *s)
{    if (*s == 0)
            return 0;
    else
            return 1+rstrlen(s+1);
}
```

10.12   Solution: 1 2 6 7 11 12

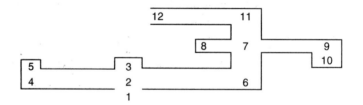

Chapter 11

11.2   (a)   3   (b)   2

11.6   Yes

11.7   (a)   15   (b)   42
      (c)   Preorder: 50 45 35 15 5 40 38 36 42 43 46 65 75 70 85

11.8   Inserts nodes into a binary search tree. Passing the pointer by reference allows the root and TreeNode pointer fields to be changed.

11.9   (a)   Preorder: M F T N V U
      (b)   Postorder: A D I R O L F

11.10 (a)   RNL: V U T N M F   (b)   RLN: R O I L A D F
      (c)   Level Order: R O T A R Y C U B L

11.14 (a)   A C F E I H B D G

11.20
```cpp
template <class T>
void PostOrder_Right (TreeNode<T> *t, void visit(T& item))
{   if (t != NULL)
    {
    // the recursive scan terminates on an empty subtree
    PostOrder_Right(t->Right(), visit); // descend right
    PostOrder_Right(t->Left(), visit);  // descend left
        visit(t->data);                 // visit the node
    }
}
```

11.22
```cpp
template <class T> TreeNode<T> *Max(TreeNode<T> *t)
{   while (t->Right() != NULL)
        t = t->Right();
    return t;
}
```

11.26
```
template <class T> int NodeLevel(TreeNode<T>*t, const T&
                                        elem)
{   int level = -1;
    while (t != NULL)
    {
        level++;
        if (t->data == elem)
            break;
        else if (elem < t->data)
            t = t->Left();
        else
            t = t->Right();
    }
    if (t == NULL)
        level = -1;
    return level;
}
```

Chapter 12

12.2

	Base_Priv	Base_Prot	Base_Pub	Derived_Priv	Derived_Prot	Derived_Pub
BASE	x	x	x			
DERIVED		x	x	x	x	x
CLIENT						x

12.3 (a) The derived class constructor does not call the base class constructor.

12.4 (a) DerivedCL::DerivedCL(int a, int b, int c): data3(a),BaseCL(b,c) {}
(b) DerivedCL::DerivedCL(int a): data3(a),BaseCL() {}
(c)

	data1	data2	data3
obj1	2	0	1
obj2	4	5	3
obj3	0	0	8

12.5 <line 1> Base1 constructor called. <line 2> Base2 constructor called.
<line 3> Derived class constructor called. <line 4> Base1 constructor called.
<line 5> Base2 constructor called. <line 6> Base2 destructor called.
<line 7> Base1 destructor called. <line 8> Derived class destructor called.
<line 9> Base2 destructor called. <line 10> Base1 destructor called.

12.7 (a) GetX is a public method in the Shape class.
(b) x is protected in the base class Shape and so can be referenced by a derived class. However, it cannot be referenced from a client.

12.8 <line 1> 1 <line 2> Base Class <line 3> 2 <line 4> 1 <line 5> 0 <line 6> Base

12.11   <line 1> 7 <line 2> 2 <line 3> 3 5 <line 4> 2 4 <line 5> 2 4 <line 6> 0 1
<line 7> 7 <line 8> 2 3

12.13
```
template <class T> class StackBase
{   protected:
        int numElements;
    public:
        StackBase(void): numElements(0) {}
        virtual void Push(const T& item) = 0;
        virtual T Pop(void) = 0;
        virtual T Peek(void) = 0;
        virtual int StackEmpty(void) { return numElements ==
                                              0 }
};
```
Implement a derived class Stack using an array (Chapter 5) or a linked list (Chapter 9).

12.19
```
int LookForMatch(Array<int>& A, int end, int elem)
{   ArrayIterator<int> aiter(A,0,end-1);
    while(!aiter.EndOfList())
    {   if (aiter.Data() == elem)  return 1;
        aiter.Next();
    }
    return 0;
}
void RemoveDuplicates(Array<int>& A)
{   ArrayIterator<int> assign(A), march(A);
    int assignIndex;
    if (A.ListSize() <= 1) return;
    assign.Next();
    march.Next();
    assignIndex = 1;
    while(!march.EndOfList())
    {   if (!LookForMatch(A,assignIndex,march.Data()))
        {   assign.Data() = march.Data();
            assign.Next();
            assignIndex++;
        }
        march.Next();
    }
    A.Resize(assignIndex);
}
```

12.20
```
template <class T> int Max(Iterator<T>& collIter, T& maxval)
// move to 1st element in the iteration
{   collIter.Reset();
    // if we are at end of list, the list is empty
    if (collIter.EndOfList())
        return 0;
    // record 1st list value and begin comparisons
    maxval = collIter.Data();
```

```
for(collIter.Next();!collIter.EndOfList();collIter.Next())
    if (collIter.Data() > maxval)
        maxval = collIter.Data();
return 1;                         // success
}
```

Chapter 13

13.2 Tree (B):60 30 80 65 40 5 50 10 90 15 70

13.3
```
template <class T> void Preorder (T A[], int currindex, int n,
                                  void visit(T& item))
{   if (currindex < n)
    {   visit(A[currindex]);                    // visit the node
        Preorder(A,2*currindex+1, n, visit);  // descend left
        Preorder(A,2*currindex+2, n, visit);  // descend right
    }
}
```

13.4 (a) YES   (c) A[24]   (e) YES A[34]

13.6 The last level has 2^n elements. The number of non-leaf nodes is $1+2+4+\ldots +2^{n-1} = 2^n - 1$.

13.7 (a) 5   (d) 41 and 42   (f) $15 - 30$

13.10 (b) is Full, Complete, MinH (d) is Complete MaxH

13.13
Initial Heap Array (A):	5	10	20	25	50			
Insert 15:	5	10	15	25	50	20		
Insert 35:	10	25	15	35	50	20	35	
Delete 5:	10	25	15	35	50	20		
Insert 40:	10	25	15	35	50	20	40	
Insert 10:	10	10	15	25	50	20	40	35

13.15 (a) 47 45 40 10   (c) 35 40 45

13.16 (b) 3, 6, 33, 88, 16, 45, 45, 90   (c) "aehpify"

13.21 For graph (B);

Matrix						Adjacency List Represenation
	A	B	C	D	E	A: C D
A	0	0	1	1	0	B: C D
B	0	0	1	1	0	C:
C	0	0	0	0	0	D:
D	0	0	0	0	0	E: A C D
E	1	0	1	1	0	

13.22 (b) No Path   (d) From A, there are paths to C and D.

13.23 (b) Depth-first: A E D C   Breadth-first: A C D E

13.26 Prints the Breadth-first search for each vertex in the graph.

Chapter 14

14.1 (a) Pass 0: 1 4 8 9 2 1 7 4   Pass 1: 1 1 8 9 2 4 7 4
Pass 2: 1 1 2 9 8 4 7 4   Pass 3: 1 1 2 4 8 9 7 4
Pass 4: 1 1 2 4 4 9 7 8   Pass 5: 1 1 2 4 4 7 9 8
Pass 6: 1 1 2 4 4 7 8 9

14.2 Pass 0: 4 8 1 9 2 1 7 4   Pass 1: 1 4 8 9 2 1 7 4
Pass 2: 1 4 8 9 2 1 7 4   Pass 3: 1 2 4 8 9 1 7 4
Pass 4: 1 1 2 4 8 9 7 4   Pass 5: 1 1 2 4 7 8 9 4
Pass 6: 1 1 2 4 4 7 8 9

14.7 When the list is already sorted in ascending or descending order, the algorithm is $O(n^2)$.

14.13. If r = x%m and q is the quotient x/m, we must have x = mq + r, and so r = x − mq. Since m is even, whenever x is even, the value of the hash function is even. All even keys hash to an even table index. The hash values are not spread about enough in the table.

14.14

	0	1	2	3	4	5	6	7	8	9	10
(a) HT	391	Empty	Empty	257	567	575	987	189	122	734	313

(b)

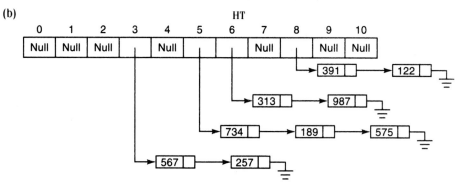

14.19 (b)   hashf(16) = 1   hashf(257) = 16

14.21 If the hashing function is good, the probability of hashing to location i is 1/N. Once data occupies table location i, the probability of filling location i+1 is 2/N. The probability of filling slot i+2 is 3/N. Clustering occurs since the probability of filling slots anywhere in a group of consecutive slots becomes greater than that of filling a single slot elsewhere in the table.

14.22 (a)   If we hash to index i, we show that the rehash function eventually cycles back to i. For this to be so, i = (i+3k) % 93 for some k. This implies that i+3k = 93q + i for some q, and so 3k = 93q. The minimum solution to this equation is k = 31, q = 1. After 31 iterations, the rehash function cycles back to i, and thus covers only 1/3 of the table.

(b)   If d is less than m, d and m are relatively prime and the table is covered by the rehash function.

14.24 (a)

0	1	2	3	4	5	6	7	8	9	10
33 8 1 3 13	−1	12 4 34 6 38	7 3	−1	27	−1	22	−1	Empty	−1	Empty	−1

14.25 (a) Yes

(b) int H(char *s)

{return (s[2] − 'a') % 7;}

14.26 void PascalTextFile::Assign(char *filename)

{strcpy(fname, filename);}

```
void PascalTextFile::Reset(void)
{    if (isOpen)
            f.seekg(0,ios::beg);
     else
     {          accesstype = IN;
                f.open(fname, ios::in | ios::nocreate);
                if (f!= NULL)
                        isOpen++;
     else
                        Error("Pascal file cannot be open");

     }
}
void PascalTextFile::PWrite(char A[], int n)
{    if (accesstype == IN)
            Error("Invalid file access operation");
     if(!isOpen)
            Error("file closed");
     f.write(A,n);
}
```

BIBLIOGRAPHY

Adel'son-Vel'skii, G. M., & Landis, E. M. (1962). An algorithm for the organization of information. *Soviet Mathematics Doklady*, 3:1259–1263.

Aho, A. V., Hopcroft, J. E., & Ullman, J. D. (1983). *Data structures and algorithms*. Reading, MA: Addison-Wesley.

Baase, S. (1988). *Computer algorithms* (2nd ed.). Reading, MA: Addison-Wesley.

Bar-David, T. (1993). *Object oriented design for C++*. Englewood Cliffs, NJ: Prentice Hall.

Booch, G. (1991). *Object oriented design*. Redwood City, CA: Benjamin/Cummings.

Budd, T. A. (1994). *Classical data structures in C++*. Reading, MA: Addison-Wesley.

Carrano, F. M. (1995). *Data abstraction and problem solving with C++, walls and mirrors*. Redwood City, CA: Benjamin/Cummings.

Collins, W. J. (1992). *Data structures, an object-oriented approach*. Reading, MA: Addison-Wesley.

Dale, N., & Lilly, S. C. (1991). *Pascal plus data structure, algorithms and advanced programming* (3rd ed.). Lexington, MA: D.C. Heath.

Decker, R., & Hirshfield, S. (1996). *Working classes, data structures and algorithms using C++*. Boston, MA: PWS.

Ellis, M. A., & Stroustrup, B. (1992). *The annotated C++ reference manual*. Reading, MA: Addison-Wesley.

Flamig, B. (1993). *Practical data structures in C++*. New York: Wiley.

Flamig, B. (1993). *Turbo C++: Step-by-step*. New York: Wiley.

Headington, M. R., & Riley, D. D. (1994). *Data abstraction and structures using C++*. Lexington, MA: D.C. Heath.

Horowitz, E., Sahni, S., & Mehta, D. (1995). *Fundamentals of data structures in C++*. New York: W. H. Freeman.

Horstmann, C. S. (1995). *Mastering object-oriented design in C++*. New York: Wiley.

Knuth, D. E. (1973). *The art of computer programming, vol. 1: Fundamental algorithms* (2nd ed.). Reading, MA: Addison-Wesley.

Knuth, D. E. (1973). *The art of computer programming, vol. 2: Seminumerical algorithms* (2nd ed.). Reading, MA: Addison-Wesley.

Knuth, D. E. (1973). *The art of computer programming, vol. 3: Sorting and searching* (2nd ed.). Reading, MA: Addison-Wesley.

Kruse, R. L. (1994). *Data structures and program design*. Englewood Cliffs, NJ: Prentice Hall.

Lewis, T. G., & Smith, M. Z. (1982). *Applying data structures* (2nd ed.). Boston: Houghton-Mifflin.

Martin, R. (1995). *Designing object-oriented C++ applications using the Booch method*. Englewood Cliffs, NJ: Prentice Hall.

Model, M. (1994). *Data structures, data abstraction*. Englewood Cliffs, NJ: Prentice Hall.

Murray, R. B. (1993). *C++ strategies and tactics*. Reading, MA: Addison-Wesley.

Naps, T. L. (1992). *Introduction to data structures and algorithm analysis*. St. Paul, MN: West.

Pohl, I. (1993). *Object-oriented programming in C++*. Redwood City, CA: Benjamin/Cummings.

Pothering, G. J., & Naps, T. L. (1995). *Introduction to data structures and algorithm analysis with C++.* St. Paul, MN: West.

Schildt, H. (1991). *C++: The complete reference.* Berkeley, CA: Osborne McGraw-Hill.

Sedgewich, R. (1992). *Algorithms in C++.* Reading, MA: Addison-Wesley.

Standish, T. A. (1994). *Data structures, algorithms, and software principles.* Reading, MA: Addison-Wesley.

Stroustrup, B. (1991). *The C++ programming language* (2nd ed.). Reading, MA: Addison-Wesley.

Stubbs, D. F., & Webre, N. W. (1989). *Data structures with abstract data types and C.* Pacific Grove, CA: Brooks/Cole.

Tenenbaum, A. M., Langsam, Y., & Augenstein, M. J. (1990). *Data structures using C.* Englewood Cliffs, NJ: Prentice Hall.

Weiss, M. A. (1994). *Data structures and algorithms analysis in C++.* Redwood City, CA: Benjamin/ Cummings.

Winder, R. (1991). *Developing C++ software.* New York: Wiley.

Wirth, N. (1976). *Algorithms + data structures = programs.* Englewood Cliffs, NJ: Prentice Hall.

Wirth, N. (1986). *Algorithms and data structures.* Englewood Cliffs, NJ: Prentice Hall.

INDEX